Brilliantly Illuminating Lamp of the Five Stages

(*rim lnga rab tu gsal ba'i sgron me*)

Practical Instruction in the King of Tantras,
The Glorious Esoteric Community

Treasury of the Buddhist Sciences series

The *Treasury of the Buddhist Sciences* series is copublished by the American Institute of Buddhist Studies and Wisdom Publications in association with the Columbia University Center for Buddhist Studies and Tibet House US.

The American Institute of Buddhist Studies (AIBS) established the *Treasury of the Buddhist Sciences* series to provide authoritative translations, studies, and editions of the texts of the Tibetan Tengyur (*bstan 'gyur*) and its associated literature. The Tibetan Tengyur is a vast collection of over 4,000 classical Indian Buddhist scientific treatises (*śāstra*) written in Sanskrit by over 700 authors from the first millennium CE, now preserved mainly in systematic 7th–12th century Tibetan translation. Its topics span all of India's "outer" arts and sciences, including linguistics, medicine, astronomy, socio-political theory, ethics, art, and so on, as well as all of her "inner" arts and sciences such as philosophy, psychology ("mind science"), meditation, and yoga.

The present work is contained in a related series comprising the collected works of Tsong Khapa Losang Drakpa (1357–1419) and his spiritual sons, Gyaltsap Darma Rinchen (1364–1432) and Khedrup Gelek Pelsang (1385–1438), a collection known in Tibetan as rJey Yab Sras gSung 'Bum. This collection also could be described as a voluminous set of independent treatises and supercommentaries, all based on the thousands of works contained in the Kangyur and Tengyur collections.

THE DALAI LAMA

Message

The foremost scholars of the holy land of India were based for many centuries at Nālandā Monastic University. Their deep and vast study and practice explored the creative potential of the human mind with the aim of eliminating suffering and making life truly joyful and worthwhile. They composed numerous excellent and meaningful texts. I regularly recollect the kindness of these immaculate scholars and aspire to follow them with unflinching faith. At the present time, when there is great emphasis on scientific and technological progress, it is extremely important that those of us who follow the Buddha should rely on a sound understanding of his teaching, for which the great works of the renowned Nālandā scholars provide an indispensable basis.

In their outward conduct the great scholars of Nālandā observed ethical discipline that followed the Pāli tradition, in their internal practice they emphasized the awakening mind of *bodhichitta*, enlightened altruism, and in secret they practised tantra. The Buddhist culture that flourished in Tibet can rightly be seen to derive from the pure tradition of Nālandā, which comprises the most complete presentation of the Buddhist teachings. As for me personally, I consider myself a practitioner of the Nālandā tradition of wisdom. Masters of Nālandā such as Nāgārjuna, Āryadeva, Āryāsaṅga, Dharmakīrti, Candrakīrti, and Śāntideva wrote the scriptures that we Tibetan Buddhists study and practice. They are all my gurus. When I read their books and reflect upon their names, I feel a connection with them.

The works of these Nālandā masters are presently preserved in the collection of their writings that in Tibetan translation we call the Tengyur (*bstan 'gyur*). It took teams of Indian masters and great Tibetan translators over four centuries to accomplish the historic task of translating them into Tibetan. Most of these books were later lost in their Sanskrit originals, and relatively few were translated into Chinese. Therefore, the Tengyur is truly one of Tibet's most precious treasures, a mine of understanding that we have preserved in Tibet for the benefit of the whole world.

Keeping all this in mind I am very happy to encourage a long-term project of the American Institute of Buddhist Studies, originally established by the late Venerable Mongolian Geshe Wangyal and now at the Columbia University Center for Buddhist Studies, and Tibet House US, in collaboration with Wisdom Publications, to translate the Tengyur into English and other modern languages, and to publish the many works in a collection called *The Treasury of the Buddhist Sciences*. When I recently visited Columbia University, I joked that it would take those currently working at the Institute at least three "reincarnations" to complete the task; it surely will require the intelligent and creative efforts of generations of translators from every tradition of Tibetan Buddhism, in the spirit of the scholars of Nālandā, although we may hope that using computers may help complete the work more quickly. As it grows, the *Treasury* series will serve as an invaluable reference library of the Buddhist Sciences and Arts. This collection of literature has been of immeasurable benefit to us Tibetans over the centuries, so we are very happy to share it with all the people of the world. As someone who has been personally inspired by the works it contains, I firmly believe that the methods for cultivating wisdom and compassion originally developed in India and described in these books preserved in Tibetan translation will be of great benefit to many scholars, philosophers, and scientists, as well as ordinary people.

I wish the American Institute of Buddhist Studies at the Columbia Center for Buddhist Studies, Tibet House US, and Wisdom Publications every success and pray that this ambitious and far-reaching project to create *The Treasury of the Buddhist Sciences* will be accomplished according to plan. I also request others, who may be interested, to extend whatever assistance they can, financial or otherwise, to help ensure the success of this historic project.

May 15, 2007

• TREASURY OF THE BUDDHIST SCIENCES •

Brilliantly Illuminating Lamp of the Five Stages

(*rim lnga rab tu gsal ba'i sgron me*)

Practical Instruction in the King of Tantras, *The Glorious Esoteric Community*

by Tsong Khapa Losang Drakpa

Introduction and Translation
by Robert A.F. Thurman

Edited by Thomas F. Yarnall

TREASURY OF THE BUDDHIST SCIENCES SERIES
TENGYUR TRANSLATION INITIATIVE
COMPLETE WORKS OF JEY TSONG KHAPA AND SONS COLLECTION

COPUBLISHED BY
THE AMERICAN INSTITUTE OF BUDDHIST STUDIES AND WISDOM PUBLICATIONS
IN ASSOCIATION WITH THE COLUMBIA UNIVERSITY CENTER
FOR BUDDHIST STUDIES AND TIBET HOUSE US

Wisdom

Treasury of the Buddhist Sciences series
Tengyur Translation Initiative
Complete Works of Jey Tsong Khapa and Sons collection
A refereed series published by:

American Institute of Buddhist Studies
Columbia University
80 Claremont Avenue, Room 303
New York, NY 10027
www.aibs.columbia.edu

Wisdom Publications
199 Elm Street
Somerville, MA 02144
www.wisdompubs.org

In association with Columbia University's Center for Buddhist Studies and Tibet House US.
Distributed by Wisdom Publications.

Library of Congress Cataloging-in-Publication Data

Names: Tsong-kha-pa Blo-bzang-grags-pa, 1357–1419, author. | Thurman, Robert A. F., translator. | Yarnall, Thomas F., editor.

Title: Brilliantly illuminating lamp of the five stages: (rim lnga rab tu gsal ba'i sgron me): practical instruction in the king of tantras, the glorious esoteric community / by Tsong Khapa Losang Drakpa; introduction and translation by Robert A.F. Thurman; edited by Thomas F. Yarnall.

Other titles: Rim lnga rab tu gsal ba'i sgron me. English

Description: Second edition. | New York: American Institute of Buddhist Studies; Somerville, MA: Wisdom Publications, 2019. | Series: Treasury of the Buddhist sciences series | "Tengyur Translation Initiative. Complete works of Jey Tsong Khapa and sons collection." | Revision of: Brilliant illumination of the lamp of the five stages. New York: American Institute of Buddhist Studies, 2010. | Includes bibliographical references and index.

Identifiers: LCCN 2018050086 (print) | LCCN 2018053673 (ebook) | ISBN 9781949163094 (ebook) | ISBN 9781949163087 (hardcover: alk. paper)

Subjects: LCSH: Tripiṭaka. Sūtrapiṭaka. Tantra. Guhyasamājatantra—Commentaries—Early works to 1800.

Classification: LCC BQ2155 (ebook) | LCC BQ2155 .T7613 2019 (print) | DDC 294.3/823—dc23

LC record available at https://lccn.loc.gov/2018050086

ISBN 978-1-949163-08-7 (cloth) ebook ISBN 978-1-949163-09-4

23 22 21 20 19 1 2 3 4 5

Cover and interior design by Gopa &Ted2, Inc. Set in Diacritical Garamond Pro 11/13.9.

Printed on acid-free paper and meets the guidelines for permanence and durability of the Production Guidelines for Book Longevity of the Council on Library Resources.

♻ This book was produced with environmental mindfulness. For more information, please visit wisdompubs.org/wisdom-environment.

Printed in the United States of America.

This work is gratefully dedicated to
His Holiness the XIVth Dalai Lama of Tibet,
and to all the Esoteric Community Yogī/nī Psychonauts
back to Vajradhara, Shākyamuni, Nāgaḍākinī, and
Nāgārjuna, and all the members of his Noble Tradition,
and the Tradition of Buddhashrījñānapada

Contents

Appendix

Glossaries

Bibliographies

Indexes

Preface to the Second Edition

I now have become Emeritus Jey Tsong Khapa Professor, formally retiring from the active teaching faculty of Columbia University, but continuing to work on the research, translation, and publication of the works in the Treasury of the Buddhist Sciences. I am delighted to see this second edition of Jey Tsong Khapa's master treatise on the practice of the perfection stages of the unexcelled yoga tantras be enhanced, brought out, and copublished by the American Institute of Buddhist Studies and Wisdom Publications. I am also happy that, for the Tibetan scholars interested, the critically edited version of the Tibetan original will now be available in the online reading room at wisdomexperience.org.

I have slightly tweaked the English title for this edition, changing it from *Brilliant Illumination of the Lamp* to *Brilliantly Illuminating Lamp*. The reason underlying the original title was my speculation that "the Lamp" referred to the diamond (*vajra*) word of the Buddha himself, as revealed in the *Esoteric Community Tantra*. Chandrakīrti's great commentary, literally the *Lamp-Illuminating* (*Pradīpoddyotana*), was given as title an odd compound with the modifying gerund following the noun, instead of preceding it as normal in Sanskrit, which hinted to me that master Chandrakīrti was honoring the *Root Tantra* as "the Lamp," by considering his word to be further illuminating the already brilliant lamp of the tantra. So I was following that hint out of respect for all the teachers of the lineage. But then I noticed again in Tsong Khapa's *Annotations* (which we will bring out in subsequent volumes of this series) a gloss on Chandrakīrti's title, explaining that Chandra's work was a brilliant lamp for illuminating any obscurities the practitioner might encounter in the *Root Tantra*. So I decided that if Jey Tsong Khapa didn't think Chandrakīrti's title expressed a special subtle praise for the *Tantra*, I need not make such a jump. Jey Tsong Khapa himself was at the very height of his insightful acuteness in the last years of his career when he wrote the present work, and so was rightfully emboldened to make his short title a kind of intensification of Chandrakīrti's *Illuminating Lamp*, calling it *Brilliantly* (Tib. *rab tu*, lit. "extremely") *Illuminating Lamp of the Five Stages*.

As before, I am extremely grateful to all those who helped me get this done as mentioned in the original preface below. To this list, I am delighted to add all those who are working with us at AIBS from Wisdom Publications—Daniel Aitken, Ben Gleason, David Kittelstrom, Lindsay D'Andrea, Brianna Quick, and Laura Cunningham—to make this volume better than before, correcting things and adorning them in a beautiful redesign. Finally I am pleased to see this emerge again in this year, the 600th anniversary of Jey Rinpoche Tsong Khapa's attainment of "communion" (*yuganaddha, zung 'jug*), tantric buddhahood with the whole body in the immediacy of the death-moment pre-between, for which he had waited for twenty-one years from his 1398 mental enlightenment until just after the winter solstice of 1419, in order to keep intact his vow of monastic celibacy for the whole of his human lifetime. May limitless beings find inspiration in every aspect of such an example of great self-restraint, vast compassion, and total generosity!

Robert A.F. Thurman (Ari Genyen Tenzin Chotrag)
Editor-in-Chief, Treasury of the Buddhist Sciences
Jey Tsong Khapa Professor Emeritus of Indo-Tibetan Buddhist Studies, Columbia University
President, American Institute of Buddhist Studies
Director Emeritus, Columbia Center for Buddhist Studies
President, Tibet House US

Ganden Dekyi Ling
Woodstock, New York
February 19, 2019 CE, Tibetan Great Miracle Celebration Day
Tibetan Royal Year 2146, Year of the Earth Sow

Series Editor's/Author's Preface

Homage to Vajrasattva!
Homage to Jey Lama, Tsong Khapa Losang Drakpa!
Homage to Venerable Geshe Ngawang Wangyal!
Homage to Tenzin Gyatso, His Holiness the Dalai Lama!

SINCE, IN THE CASE of this work, I am both the series editor and author, as well as the introducer and translator of the English version of Tsong Khapa's masterwork, this preface will be a bit longer than usual.

In 1970–1971, I spent a year in India with the American Institute of Indian Studies, working on a translation and study of Tsong Khapa's *Essence of True Eloquence: Differentiating the Interpretable and Definitive Meanings of the Buddha's Discourses.* During that year I had the privilege and pleasure of working closely on the Tibetan edition of that text in frequent meetings with His Holiness the Dalai Lama. I was given excellent instruction in the difficult points and deeper meanings of Buddhist Central Way hermeneutical thought. After his experience instructing a Westerner such as me in those ideas, His Holiness wrote his own book on the topic (with me working on the first draft of the English version), published eventually as *The Key to the Middle Way.* When I had to leave India, His Holiness charged me to take up the responsibility to see to the translation of the *Complete Works of Jey Tsong Khapa and Sons.* I most enthusiastically committed myself to undertake the task. I returned to America and received the hearty approval of this project by my root teacher, the Venerable Geshe Ngawang Wangyal. He further urged that, in order for contemporary philosophers and practitioners to appreciate the work of Tsong Khapa and his followers, they would need to have access to the Tengyur, the vast collection of Tibetan translations from the Sanskrit of the thousands of treatises of the great masters of Indian Buddhism. When I wryly said "Thanks a lot!"

to that huge expansion of the burden, he said, "Of course, not just by yourself all alone . . . in your lifetime you just set up a system and get it started." His Holiness joined up with the Venerable Geshe to back that request in due course.

The next step that led to the present work happened during my completion of the *Essence of True Eloquence.* I was getting a lot of help from an excellent commentary written by a certain Losang Puntsok (bLo bZang Phun tshogs). While studying that commentary, I came upon a statement by that lama scholar saying that he also was going to write a commentary on Tsong Khapa's *Brilliantly Illuminating Lamp of the Five Stages*, the tantric equivalent of the *Essence of True Eloquence.* It analyzed the five stages of the perfection stage of the unexcelled yoga tantra, focusing on the *Esoteric Community* noble tradition descending from Nāgārjuna. The moment I read that, I formed the resolve to translate this tantric master-treatise of Jey Lama Tsong Khapa.

In 1978, I applied again to the American Institute of Indian Studies to spend a year in India to study the unexcelled yoga tantras through this text. I thought that, in order to understand this great treatise, I would have to complete the *Esoteric Community* studies I had begun long before, back when I was a Buddhist monk. During that year in India, I began the study and translation of the work, producing also drafts of a number of associated works. Consultations with His Holiness the Dalai Lama on this second big text were extremely rewarding, as to be expected. However, toward the conclusion of that year of studies, I decided not to rush to publish it, due to the esoteric nature of its teachings. His Holiness's senior teacher, the Ganden Throneholder Kyabjey Lingtsang Rinpochey, transmitter to him (and me) of various *Esoteric Community* teachings, was strongly opposed to the general publication of such works.

Clearly, I have not rushed to publish this work, begun thirty years ago. I do so now, since almost all the main practices of unexcelled yoga tantras have been described and published—with varying degrees of clarity and explicitness—though the huge variety and immensely rich and sophisticated detail of their millennial sciences are like an ocean still largely unexplored. His Holiness the Dalai Lama has reasoned that misunderstanding of tantra already abounds, and so it is desirable and even necessary to be fully transparent about the authentic teachings. Also, in a project to make available the *Complete Works of Jey Tsong Khapa and Sons,* a large percentage of them do concern the tantras, so one cannot avoid them. Some esoteric secrets keep themselves: they are incredible to some, incomprehensible to others, and often are approached as the romantic fantasy or science fiction of a far-away ancient culture. Further, determined researchers will find almost anything nowadays, if they look hard enough. Thus, it is my hope, and my intention in publishing this book now, that they should find authentic and accurately clarified information about the amazing "mental" or "inner" science of the Indian and Tibetan masters, scientists, and yogi/nīs of the unexcelled yoga tantras of universal vehicle (*mahāyāna*) Buddhism!

In regard to the various subseries to be included in our *Treasury of the Buddhist Sciences* list, we are hereby delighted at long last to add another: the *Complete Works of Jey Tsong Khapa and Sons*, each of which builds upon the Indian works in the Tengyur. As mentioned above, it was planned at the very beginning of the idea for the Tengyur translation project. As it is decades behind schedule, it is a great relief to launch it with this book. The *Essence of True Eloquence* was my first translation of one of Tsong Khapa's key books. The publication still remains with the Princeton University Press, and they licensed an Indian edition to Motilal Banarsidass publishers in Delhi. Eventually, I hope to improve that work further and bring it back into this series.

I have many people to thank. First of all I thank the Tibetan and Mongolian scholar lamas who opened to me the treasury of the *Esoteric Community*: the late Venerable Geshe Ngawang Wangyal, who read to me the Panchen Rinpochey's summary of the path and its scope during early morning sessions in 1964; the late His Holiness Kyabjey Lingtsang Rinpochey, who admitted me first into the *Community* mandala universe; His Holiness the Dalai Lama, who has so generously given of his kind friendship, and transmitted more than I yet know, especially the special tradition of this text at Thegchen Choling in Dharamsala in 1984; the late Venerable Tara Tulku Rinpochey, for his learning, insight, patience, and humorous brilliance; the late His Eminence Serkhong Tsenshab Rinpochey, for his generosity and kindness; His Eminence Jampel Shanpen, who renewed the initiation in Amherst years later; and my cheerful friend and brilliant lama, the late Ngawang Gelek Rinpochey, for his elegant teachings of the practices. Among academic benefactors, I thank the late Professor Masatoshi Nagatomi, with whom I first read parts of the *Shrī Guhya Samāja* in Sanskrit; the late Professor Alex Wayman, my predecessor in Buddhist Studies at Columbia, who was the first American scholar to go deeply into the *Esoteric Community* literature; Dr. Lozang Jamspal, whose tireless, careful work contributes so much to the Tengyur Translation Initiative, and who went through the translation, checking line by line; Dr. Thomas Yarnall, my esteemed colleague, for his indispensable expert and meticulous assistance on all levels, from the scholarly insight and editorial revision, to the design expertise, to the publishing technicalities; Dr. Paul Hackett, another younger colleague, for his careful and laborious finding of the sources in the Tengyur that verified Tsong Khapa's many quotes, bringing their variants and Sanskrit where available into the annotations to the critically edited Tibetan text, to be published as a companion volume in a limited edition and in an e-book,[1] as well as for flagging remaining errors in the translation; Ms. Annie Bien who helped enormously with editing and polishing; Mr. Jason Dunbar of the Asian Classics Input Project, who worked originally with the Asian Classics Input Project on the digitization of Tsong Khapa's works, and later significantly improved the Tibetan edition of the text; and finally my fellow translator, Dr. Geshe Thupten Jinpa, whose interest in this text gave me the impetus to get it finalized at long last. With all of this excellent assistance and support, all delays, errors, and remaining imperfections remaining are entirely my fault.

Finally, among financial benefactors and supporters, I thank the American Institute of Indian Studies, for the senior grant thirty years ago that enabled me to live in India during 1979–1980 to study with the authentic lamas of the noble tradition and begin this work; Mr. Joel McCleary for his generous help and steady encouragement; Ms. Lavinia Currier of the Sacharuna Foundation, whose generous grants enabled the work at a crucial time to advance to the penultimate stage; Mr. Marc Benioff and Mrs. Lynne Benioff for their generous, world-changing support down the home stretch; and Mr. William T. Kistler, Mrs. Eileen Kistler, and Mr. Brian Kistler of the Kistler Foundation for their visionary recognition that amid the many crises and catastrophes afflicting the multitudes of suffering beings around the world, the recovery and translation needed to open the door for the modern mind to the inner or spiritual science of the Buddhist tradition

1. The companion volume of the critically edited Tibetan text, annotated with the found quotes from Tengyur and Kangyur texts in Tibetan and Sanskrit where available, will soon be made more widely available to specialists at wisdomexperience.org.

remains a high priority for the awakening of humanity—perhaps essential to empower us to rise to the challenges we all face together at this critical planetary moment.

Finally, my ever immeasurably increasing gratitude goes to my best friend and wonderful wife, Nena von Schlebrugge Thurman, who has given her unstinting support and inspiration over these many years.

Robert A.F. Thurman (Ari Genyen Tenzin Chotrag)
Jey Tsong Khapa Professor of Indo-Tibetan Buddhist Studies,
Columbia University;
President, American Institute of Buddhist Studies
Director, Columbia Center for Buddhist Studies
President, Tibet House US

Ganden Dekyi Ling
Woodstock, New York
February 25, 2010 CE
Tibetan Royal Year 2137, Year of the Iron Tiger

Sources, Conventions, and Abbreviations

Primary Textual Sources

The study and translation of Tsong Khapa's *Brilliantly Illuminating Lamp of the Five Stages* (*rim lnga rab tu gsal ba'i sgron me*) contained herein was produced with reference to a combination of several different sources. The primary sources were the following:

D, Derge	The Derge (*sde dge*) recension of the root text (Delhi, 1982)
Zh	The Lhasa Zhöl Parkhang printing of Tsong Khapa's *Collected Works* (*gsung 'bum*). Gray citations in square brackets embedded throughout the translation are references to this edition.
TL	A reproduction of the Tashilhunpo (*bkra shis lhun po*) printing and the Kumbum Jampaling (*sku 'bum byams pa gling*) printing: Tsong-kha-pa Blo-bzang-grags-pa, *The Collected Works (gsuṅ 'bum) of Rje Tsoṅ-kha-pa Blo-bzaṅ-grags-pa*. vol. 11. New Delhi: Ngawang Gelek Demo, 1978
TKSB	Tsong-kha-pa Blo-bzang-grags-pa, *The Collected Works (gsung 'bum) of the Incomparable Lord Tsong kha pa Blo bzang grags pa*. vol. JA. Sku-'bum: Sku-'bum-byams-pa-gling, 2000
ACIP	Electronic files from the Asian Classics Input Project (ACIP), based upon the Derge and Zh

Also consulted were the two published editions of the Tibetan translations of the root text of Nāgārjuna's *Five Stages*, as well as the excellent Sanskrit edition in the former work:

MIMAKI	MIMAKI Katsumi and TOMABECHI Tōru, *Pañcakrama*. Tokyō: Center for East Asian Cultural Studies for UNESCO (1994)
Chengdu	*Bstan 'gyur dpe bsdur ma*. Chengdu: Chengdu Peoples' Publishing House (1998–2005), vol. 18

The large number of canonical citations herein were located and checked against the Derge recension of the Kangyur and Tengyur; and often the Narthang, Lhasa, Peking, and/or Chone recensions were consulted as well. Both the index and bibliography herein list the Derge sources, with English translations of the titles and with the corresponding Tōhoku numbers. In addition, the bibliography, sorted by English title, gives the full citation information (Sanskrit and Tibetan titles, author names, location, and so on) for these Derge sources. Similar citations for noncanonical sources will likewise be found herein.

The precise locations of quoted passages, as well as text critical annotations regarding significant variants, and so on, are given in our critical edition of the Tibetan text, available in electronic format at wisdomexperience.org.

Typographical Conventions

To facilitate pronunciation for the nonspecialist, we have strived to present Sanskrit and Tibetan names (and some terms) in a phonetic form. Toward this end, while we generally have kept conventional diacritics for Sanskrit names, we have added an *h* to convey certain sounds (so *ś*, *ṣ*, and *c* are often rendered as *sh*, *ṣh* [or *sh*], and *ch* respectively), and have occasionally omitted retroflex underdots. For Sanskrit terms that have entered the English lexicon (such as "nirvana" or "mandala"), we use no diacritical marks. For Tibetan names, transliterated (Wylie) equivalents may be found in the index of Cited Personal Names (Sanskrit and Tibetan) after the phonetic rendition of the Tibetan name.

In more technical contexts—italic Sanskrit or Tibetan terms in parentheses; the longer names of Sanskrit texts (which are treated as if technical terms); Sanskrit or Tibetan passages cited in footnotes; bibliographical citations; and so on—we use standard diacritical conventions for Sanskrit, and Wylie transliterations for Tibetan. Standard Sanskrit diacritics and Wylie Tibetan transliterations will also be found for all terms in the three glossaries.

Abbreviations

THE FOLLOWING abbreviations have been used in various places throughout the present work:

[237a] Small gray citations in square brackets embedded throughout the translation are references to the folio number and side of the Zh edition. These same citations are embedded in our forthcoming Tibetan edition. Zh citations are also used in the Topical Outline (*sa bcad*) included herein as an appendix.

* An asterisk before a Sanskrit word or phrase indicates a hypothetical reconstruction from the Tibetan.

Skt. Sanskrit

Tib. Tibetan

Tōh. Tōhoku catalog (1934, Sendai, Japan) of the Derge canon.

CW Christian Wedemeyer, ed. and trans. *Āryadeva's Lamp That Integrates the Practices (Caryāmelāpakapradīpa)*. New York: American Institute of Buddhist Studies, 2007. Tsong Khapa herein frequently cites this text by Āryadeva; hence we herein frequently cite the Skt. or Tib. editions (or the English translation) of this text contained in CW.

Part One

Introduction

Introduction

1. What Is a "Buddha Vajradhara," the Goal of This Tradition?

Ablaze in the glory of wondrous signs and marks,
Forever playing in the taste of the bliss-void kiss,
Recklessly compassionate, free of extremist calm—
I bow to the Victor with the seven super-factors![2]

To study this work fruitfully, we need first of all to understand what the author thinks is the goal of the practices described within it. That is to say, we need to imagine what Tsong Khapa imagines is the kind of being called a "buddha vajradhara"—what a buddha really is—whether viewed from the tantric perspective or not. What he thinks a buddha-being is, is so utterly fantastic, even preposterous, from the perspective of our philosophically materialist modern culture, it takes a real effort of imagination, a nearly sci-fi exercise in openness of mind. We don't have to agree that in reality there is such a thing, but to understand the work at hand, it is fruitful to place ourselves in the position of Tsong Khapa's audience. To catch a glimpse of where he is coming from, we have to review the parameters he sets up for our imagining. This is an effort required to understand any form of Buddhism, but it is particularly important in the tantric or mantric context, since a lot of the work of mantric practice involves contemplative deployment of the structured imagination.

2. Tib. *rGyal ba yan lag bdun ldan*. These are the components of a buddha vajradhara's material body: (1) it has the auspicious signs and marks; (2) it is in embrace of a wisdom-intuition consort (being both the male and the female); (3) its mind is always super-bliss; (4) such bliss is ever aware of voidness; (5) its compassion avoids extremist calm; (6) its bodily continuum is uninterrupted; and (7) its enlightened deeds are unceasing.

It is also quite probable that Tsong Khapa feels he should salute Vajradhara Buddha in this technical way because even his own Tibetan Buddhist contemporaries and successors might not so easily imagine what a buddha is, in its inconceivable reality. Tsong Khapa himself said—after what he referred to as his coming to complete clarity about the uttermost subtleties of the realistic view, and what others refer to as his perfect enlightenment—that it was the opposite of what he had expected it to be, indicating that even a great scholar such as he had not fully been able to imagine what the buddha-awareness was really like. When even a Buddhist thinks of enlightenment, she thinks of a kind of awareness far greater than her habitual own, but still it is difficult to imagine a being whose consciousness is at once infinitely expanded and minutely detailed, who feels him- / her- / it-self a timeless eternity of utter freedom ecstatically blissful, and whose multi-sourced presence can manifest in relation to countless individual beings as countless different relational beings at once.

To try to express the inexpressible, from the three-buddha-body theory perspective, a buddha is a being who is not restricted to having to be enclosed in a single separate embodiment that faces an "other" universe and yet who does not neglect the countless beings who persist in feeling that they are separate, and are facing him, her, or it as an "other." When a buddha completes its, her, or his wisdom store in the buddha-truth-body (Skt. *dharmakāya*), it viscerally experiences itself as indivisibly one with all realities, and other beings and things and the spaces and energies within and around them are felt to be part of its body. This feeling feels those beings, things, and energies as configurations of a limitless bliss, as the truth body is simultaneously a bliss body, the buddha-beatific-body (Skt. *saṁbhogakāya*). This bliss feeling does not anaesthetize the buddha-being from also feeling what the beings feel of suffering; in a way the bliss energizes the ability to remain aware of the others' feelings of dissatisfaction and pain. Indeed, the awareness of others' dissatisfaction and pain in turn stimulates the spacious cloudlike truth-beatitude-indivisible buddha-body to manifest or emanate limitless forms of embodiment (Skt. *nirmāṇakāya*) as beings or things that can be perceived by the suffering beings and that perfectly mirror to them, according to their perceptual capacities, their potential freedom from suffering and their potential awareness of their own natural bliss.

Although this description of the inconceivable, amazing cognitive-dissonance-tolerant, dichotomy-reconciling nature of buddhahood is ultimately ungraspable in linear binary terms, we can imagine it with the help of limiting concepts such as voidness, freedom, nonduality, and the elaborated theory of the three bodies of buddhahood. Imagining it, we can aspire consciously to evolve toward achieving it for ourselves and those with whom we want to share it, in case it is really possible and not just a Buddhist fantasy. At any rate, the mantric or tantric path is presented as the science and art of accelerating such conscious evolution by employing a supremely subtle technology of spiritual genetic engineering of a buddha-mind and buddha-bodies.

A point that should be clarified here is that the buddha-mind is referred to in the theory as a "body of truth," and the buddha-bodies of beatitude and emanation are referred to as a "material body" (Skt. *rūpakāya*, often wrongly translated as "form body"). This may be a hint in the exoteric universal vehicle of the esoteric doctrine of the nonduality of body and mind at the ultimate or supremely subtle level.

To such an end of stimulating imagination and inspiration, Tsong Khapa embeds in his opening salutatory verse a standard formulation of the seven super-components of the material body of a buddha vajradhara (inconceivably indivisible from his and all buddhas' infinite truth body, itself completely interpenetrating all other embodied beings and discrete things).

There are seven super-components of a buddha vajradhara's material body.

1. It has the auspicious signs and marks

There are traditionally thirty-two auspicious signs and eighty auspicious marks that a buddha vajradhara's material body has in common with other buddhas such as Shakyamuni. Nāgārjuna in his *Jewel Rosary* details these 112 signs and marks, explaining in brief how each one is the evolutionary (karmic) result of specific deeds in the many lives leading up to buddhahood (see below).

The final body of a buddha is the truth or reality body, which is infinite and timeless and indivisible. The individual expands always embodied awareness to encompass the ultimate reality of infinite worlds and beings, both enlightened and unenlightened, mental and physical. At the same time, the individual momentum of positive engagement with others—the love and compassion that drives a being to evolve into the ability of providing happiness to countless others—persists in the physical omnipresence of a buddha in an equally infinite beatific body that infinitely enjoys having all reality as its body, and simultaneously encompasses the awarenesses of the infinite others who suffer due to their failure to realize their oneness with such a universe. This awareness automatically and effortlessly then manifests as infinite seemingly discrete embodiments, called "emanations." For their own evolutionary benefit, self-alienated migrating beings can interact with these emanations. Therefore, a buddha vajradhara is not just one individual, beautiful, divine embodiment, a separate superbeing in a desire realm heaven—that manifestation is just one of countless manifestations, but it is the one that best expresses to the evolutionary psychonaut, or adept, the ideal and goal he or she is aiming for.

Regarding the emanation bodies, there are said to be three kinds: artistic, incarnational, and supreme. The artistic emanation body consists of all representations of buddhas and their deeds by artists whose aim is to help beings imagine the supreme evolutionary state all beings can achieve. The incarnational emanation body is all the manifestations a buddha can create to interact with alienated beings in order to help their development, including inanimate objects such as buildings, continents, even planets, in addition to plants and animate beings. The supreme emanation body is a buddha like Shakyamuni Buddha, who manifests descent from heaven, conception, birth, and so on (the twelve deeds with which we are familiar). It is such a supreme emanation that manifests a body that carries on it the graphic demonstrations (the signs and marks) of all his or her evolutionary achievements. In this way all emanation bodies are themselves teachings for specific beings in specific evolutionary times and places.

In his *Jewel Rosary*,[3] Nāgārjuna gives a summary of the marks and their causes in a buddha's evolutionary past:

> Through proper honoring of stupas, venerables, noble ones, and the elderly, you will become a universal monarch, your glorious hands and feet marked with wheels.

3. Here I quote a number of verses to give a taste of the specifics of the biological theory of karmic evolution (*Jewel Rosary*, v. 177–97).

O King, always maintain firmly your vows about your practices; you will then become a bodhisattva, with very level feet.

By giving gifts, speaking pleasantly, fulfilling beings' wishes, and practicing what you teach, you will have hands with glorious fingers joined by luminous webs.

By always generously giving the finest food and drink, your glorious hands and feet will be soft, and along with your shoulder blades and the nape of your neck, seven areas will be broad, and your body will be large.

By never doing harm and freeing condemned persons, your body will be beautiful, straight, and tall, your fingers will be long, and the backs of your heels will be broad.

By spreading spiritual disciplines, you will have a good complexion, a good repute, your ankles will not protrude, and your body hairs will stand upward.

Due to your enthusiasm in propagating the arts and sciences, and so on, you will have the calves of an antelope, a sharp intelligence, and great wisdom.

When others desire your wealth and possessions, by disciplining yourself to give them immediately, you will have broad arms, an attractive appearance, and will become a world leader.

By reconciling friends who are in conflict, you will become supreme, and your glorious private organ will retract within [like a stallion].

By bestowing upon others excellent dwellings, your complexion will be soft, like stainless refined gold.

By granting to others superior powers and dutifully following your teachers, your each and every hair will be your ornament, including a special tuft of hair between the eyebrows.

By speaking pleasantly and meaningfully, and by acting upon the good speech [of others], you will have curving shoulders and a lionlike upper body.

> By nursing and healing the sick, the area between your shoulders will be broad, you will live in a state of ease, and all your tastes will be excellent.
>
> By conducting your affairs in accord with the Dharma, your skull dome will be beautifully elevated, and [your body] will be symmetrical like a banana tree.
>
> By speaking true and gentle words over a long time, O lord of men, your tongue will be long, and your voice like that of Brahma the creator.
>
> By always speaking truth continuously, your cheeks will be lion-like, glorious, and you will be hard to overcome.
>
> By being carefully respectful, serving others, and doing what is proper, your teeth will be shining, white, and even.
>
> By always speaking true and nondivisive words, you will have forty glorious teeth, set evenly and wondrous to behold.
>
> By gazing at beings with altruistic love without desire, hatred, or delusion, your eyes will be bright and blue, with lashes like a bull's.
>
> Thus, in brief know well these thirty-two signs of a great lion of beings, together with their [evolutionary] causes.

Nāgārjuna then goes on to mention the eighty auspicious signs, not listing them, saying it would take too long; but the lists are common in the sutras. This list gives us the feel of the Buddhist worldview. Life is evolutionary. The acts we perform of body, speech, and mind in any given life produce their result in the future of this life or in a future life. The patterns cited in this specific case of attaining the thirty-two auspicious marks of a superbeing (*mahāpurusha*) connect moral actions with biological results.

A point to be emphasized is that this counts in the Buddhist culture as a "scientific" explanation of the physical characteristics of a "supreme emanation buddha-body," such as that of Shākyamuni. Therefore, less evolved beings who have some physical marks resembling these thirty-two have been committing acts of the same type. Thus, if you are tall, with long fingers, and the backs of your heels are broad, you have been relatively less harmful to other beings in many previous lives; in numerous life-forms, and in previous human lives you have saved lives and pardoned condemned beings.

Anything in these directions—height and breadth and beauty of body, nature of hands and feet and limbs, shape of eyes, length of tongue, beauty of cheeks, and so on—all these physical traits come from past evolutionary actions of body and speech and mind. The Darwinian theory of "survival of the fittest"—meaning increase of the survival-enhancing qualities of a species (not individuals) due to the physical propagation of the offspring of better equipped individuals, generation after generation, producing mutations that cope better with the environment, that are transmitted by physical genes, and so forth—is somewhat parallel to the Buddhist theory. But added here to that picture (of the mutations of species over countless generations in coordination with environmental changes) is the individual's own personal evolution. That individual carries the results of his or her own evolutionary actions encoded in a mental gene (Skt. *gotra*) that goes from one coarse flesh and blood embodiment to another, meeting the physical genes of fathers and mothers in human or other animal forms born in mammalian womb, reptilian or avian egg, insect moisture, or magical environment.

Once persons encounter such a "karmic" biological worldview and come to think of it as realistic, either through cultural conditioning in a Buddhist culture or through historical and internal scientific investigation, they adapt their lifestyles to consciously cultivate that mental gene through skillful evolutionary actions, considering that cultivation to be the prime priority of their lives, since its results will determine the qualities of their inevitable lives far into the future. The ultimate change of lifestyle is precisely the tantric one, where individuals decide that they cannot wait for countless rebirths of gradual progress to reach the summit of positive life experience for self and other that is defined as buddhahood. And so they enter the tantric path of self-creation and self-perfection, compressing all those deaths and rebirths into a single intense lifetime or a few lifetimes in order to get to the highest goal as soon as possible.

Tantric art and contemplative technology are thus a form of genetic engineering. The main tool is the highly concentrated and stabilized creative imagination, which uses the patterns of the mandala environments and the divine embodiments (themselves derived from meritorious actions and scientific insights) to shape the spiritual gene of the practitioner. This shaped gene then simulates, in the virtual reality of the lucid-dream-like contemplative performance (Skt. *sādhana*), the death, between, and rebirth processes; first as a rehearsal of out-of-coarse- or subtle-body performances; and then as actual mind- and shape-shifting transformations in the evolutionary direction of buddhahood.

2. It is in embrace of a wisdom-intuition consort (as both the male and the female)

The highest pleasure in ordinary life is generally conceded to be the release experienced in sexual orgasm, wherein an individual melts his or her normal bodily rigidities and feels intense rapture through a blissful inner flooding of pleasurable energy. In Buddhist neuro-biology, this is explained as the bodily energies (or vital energies) dissolving away from their normal functions in the limbs and muscles and nerves (including the brain) and concentrating in the central channel of the nervous system, said to run through the body from mid-brow up to crown of head and down in front of the spine to the tip of the genital organ. These energies take with them endocrine drops that anchor blissful feelings and concentrate them into a powerful force that carries the mind with it into release from all mental and physical preoccupations. The most powerful bliss experience of this kind occurs in a "normal," egocentrically-wired being only at death, as the mental energy is released from preoccupation within the coarse body. That experience dissipates as that mental-subtle-energy continuum arises as a subtle dreamlike body in a "between state." This fairylike "between being" (Skt. *gandharva*) migrates in its state of separateness throughout all the optional forms of existence in the vast universe other than it. When eventually the gandharva being itself is attracted to the coupling of a male and a female of some species, it melts into their state of self-expanding passion and is drawn into its next coarse embodiment in a womb etc.

Therefore, that a vajradhara buddha is always in embrace with a wisdom-intuition consort indicates that this embodiment is not a coarse, non-blissful, ordinary one. It is perpetually indivisible from the bliss of orgasmic freedom, experiencing the male and female complementarity of orgasmic wholeness and contentment at all times. This gives a hint that such a being is nothing but a manifestation of the infinite bliss-void-indivisible of the infinite truth and beatific bodies, where every atom and subatomic energy is experienced as orgasmic release in creative magical emanation.

A very key point to note here—to clear up a general scholarly misapprehension about tantra, namely that it is essentially a male chauvinist tradition—is that a vajradhara buddha is both the female and the male in the embrace, not just the male exploitatively wrapping himself in some sort of subservient female as a mindless accessory. On simpler levels, the male is universal compassion and the female transcendent wisdom; the male is superbliss art and the female is profound voidness wisdom; or the male is the magic illusion body and the female the clear light transparence of the total voidness.

3. Its mind is always super-bliss

This emphasizes the transcendent nature of buddhahood: a vajradhara buddha body-mind represents the ultimate nondual awareness of enlightenment that experiences its own/everything's reality as unobstructed bliss of orgasmic freedom, nirvana. This is the reality that Shākyamuni and all buddhas proclaim as the very substance of even samsaric reality, not enjoyed by beings who misknow it as otherwise, even while their bodies and minds are essentially constituted of bliss and their whole beings are primally interpenetrated by uncreated nirvana. In the exoteric universal vehicle this is taught by the Buddha in the *Lotus Sutra* and other cataphatic sutras, wherein the Buddha shocks his dualistic elder disciples, monastic vehicle arhat saints, by proclaiming the world's purity, blissfulness, eternal selfhood, and transcendent freedom.

4. Such bliss is ever aware of voidness

This blissful wisdom that enjoys the inconceivable exquisiteness of the relative world never loses sight of its essential freedom, its ultimate peacefulness, its brilliant infinite energy that therefore has no need to do anything, and so has done all that needs to be done. So the nirvanic bliss-awareness is not contradictory to the ultimate calmness and oneness of the immanent beyond; it neither troubles the ocean of bliss with elaborations nor constrains it by clinging to non-elaboration. Being "aware of voidness" simply means that the blissed-out subjectivity remains in a limitlessly melting, nongrasping flow, in unity with an infinite horizon of openness pervading all objectivities.

5. Its compassion avoids extremist calm

The previous two super-components of a vajradhara indicate the buddha-mind's nature as the ultimate tolerance of cognitive dissonance, the reconciliation of all dichotomies, the unity of simplicity and complexity, and not simply as a collapsed state of total extinct oblivion or resigned relational bondage. Particularly, this fifth super-component indicates that a vajradhara buddha is not tempted to escape into sheer infinity without any differentiated objects; his/her/its transcendent wisdom is absolutely self-transforming into the infinite compassion that cannot abandon beings trapped by ignorance in the suffering of egocentric separateness and alienation from the multi-dimensional, inconceivable universe of freedom.

6. Its bodily continuum is uninterrupted

Being an infinite awareness beyond unity and plurality, one indivisible—with every detail—with all buddhas of the past, present, and future, along with all unenlightened beings of all those three times also, and being also indivisible with the infinite clear light transparency energy of absolute void freedom, a vajradhara buddha effortlessly responds to the needs of infinite numbers of suffering beings. A vajradhara buddha manifests from this inexhaustibly energetic nirvanic reality whatever medicine will relieve that suffering, whether it be the magical emanation of a vajradhara, a buddha, a bodhisattva, a person, a companion, an enemy, a substance, a continent, a planet, a star, a deity, a demon, a death, a rebirth, and so forth.

The fact that some sensitive humans who seek freedom and enlightenment carry subconsciously the notion that they are somehow going to escape from embodiment, going to have a rest, going to get out of entanglements, and so forth is nowhere more powerfully responded to in the Buddhist sutras than by the iconic event of the supreme emanation body Buddha's *parinirvana*, ultimate freedom understood by dualistic Buddhists as "no more rebirth." However, the proposition that a buddha simply disappears from existence upon final enlightenment is definitively refuted by the many universal vehicle presentations of nonduality.

7. Its enlightened deeds are unceasing

Seeing nirvana as here and now, as nondually and blissfully immanent within all details of differentiation and manifestation, means that there is no need at all for any interruption of embodiment. Ironically, this presents buddhahood not as the permanent extinction attractive to escapist dualists, but rather as a glorious explosion into infinite life, driven by infinite compassion into hyperdrive to manifest whatever is needed to tame whomsoever.

This last super-component of vajradharahood adds to the tantric dimension an encouraging transhistorical dimension where the aspirant needs no longer feel lost in a decadent historical era when buddhas are gone, enlightened institutions have been crushed, beings are deluded and self-destructive, and so on—just how the world looks to us when we read the news or get bogged down in confronting political confusion, venality, and incompetence. The investigator and adventurer who seeks the real meaning and purpose of life wants to live it by taking up the priceless and rare human opportunity to become truly consciously awake. This involves mastering the evolutionary process to accelerate her or his development toward the ideal evolutionary condition of bliss-freedom indivisible and wisdom-compassion irresistible, infinitely alive because firmly rooted in the transcendent rootlessness of death. This scientist-explorer can always and without fail discover the past present and future vajradhara buddhas to help her or him find knowledge, consecration, instruction, wisdom, and artfulness. As far away as they may seem at times, their enlightened deeds are unceasing, they are never retired or unavailable.

I am fully aware that this unpacking of Tsong Khapa's opening salutation reveals a worldview profoundly at odds with that of "modern" scientific materialism. I do not expect academic colleagues—committed to the institutions founded on spiritual absolutism and now devoted to scientific materialism—to be convinced that such things can be realistic: such things as real former and future life continua, mental genetic evolution, a teleology not based on an omnipotent creator god but on individual choice of purpose made by rational persons who scientifically investigate reality in systematic ways and discover the void nature of things as being in nondual harmonious equivalence with a causal coherence of lifestyle leading to buddhahood as the logical summit of evolutionary potential. However, there is no way to understand the works of the Indian and Tibetan great adepts (*mahāsiddhas*)—great yogi/nīs, scientist-explorers, astronaut-like psychonauts—unless one at least makes the effort to imagine the world they discovered, considered, and then persuasively argued is the more real world. After all, if modern or postmodern scientific materialists wish to be truly scientific, and not dogmatic and fundamentalist, they must admit that the cutting edge of science has reached the uncertainty principle, the mutual transformability of matter and energy, the inconceivability of the macro- and micro- universes, and the openness to the principle that all "laws of the universe" are hypotheses awaiting falsification by new data and new theories. Thus, the examination, evaluation, and imaginative experimental appreciation of realistic worldviews and paradigms that at first seem completely strange and outlandish is part of the advancing of the frontiers of knowledge and the deepening of scientific and humanistic wisdom.

2. Who Are the Beings Who Maintain This Tradition?

To the Lord of Secrets, collector of all secrets combined,
And to the ancestral mentors who achieved supremacy
Through the path of the Community, King of Tantras—
Indrabhūti, Nāgaḍākinī, Visukalpa, glorious Saraha,
Vajrin Nāgārjuna, Āryadeva, Nāgabodhi, Shākyamitra,
Matangi, Chandra[kīrti]pāda and the others—
I bow with the mind of ferocious faith!

Lord of Secrets

The "Lord of Secrets" (*Guhyapati, gsang ba'i bdag po*) is considered an emanation of Vajradhara Buddha, incarnating the powerful energy of all buddhas as a bodhisattva who asks Vajradhara to explain the esoteric teachings and then records what he is taught. He is usually represented as dark blue in color, often one-headed and two-armed, holding a vajra five-pronged double scepter that symbolizes the buddhas' wielding of the supreme power of the relative universe—this power being fierce love and compassion—basically the indomitable bliss of deathless freedom that seeks to go beyond being contained within any individual's experience and to share itself with all sensitive beings.

Tsong Khapa had a personal mentor and colleague named Hlodrak Khenchen Namkha Gyaltsen, who, when teaching Tsong Khapa, would be perceived as transformed into the iconic form of Vajrapaṇi. When he learned from Tsong Khapa, he would perceive Tsong Khapa as transformed into Mañjushrī. The Khenchen was gratefully credited by the late lama, Kyabjey Lingtsang Rinpochey—the Dalai Lama's senior tutor and the ninetieth Ganden Throne-holder of the Gelukpa order—with having dissuaded Tsong Khapa and his eight close followers from going on pious pilgrimage to the Buddhist holy places in India in 1399. For had they gone, they might not have returned very easily, if at all in that era, and Tibet would not have benefited from the twenty-one years of writing, teaching, and building Tsong Khapa gave to it from that time until his passing in 1419.

And what are these "secrets" of which Vajradhara/Vajrapāṇi is the "Lord"? These are the esoteric teachings of the tantras, which are the "continua" of person, reality, and teaching, that are the highest technologies of transforming the meaningless, purposeless, and miserable world of cyclic living—wherein misknowing egocentric beings struggle futilely and endlessly against an overwhelming infinite universe—into a buddhaverse of mutual love, compassion, and blissful pleasure energizing the inconceivable positive evolution of interconnected self and other.

Why are they "secret"? They are not secret from anyone who needs them, just as the formulas and procedures of subatomic quantum physics are not intrinsically secret from anyone, but are as good as secret for anyone who is unprepared by a complex and sustained education. For such persons, they are incomprehensible and useless. Moreover, there is an additional element in the need for secrecy in the context of tantra; the need to protect such unprepared persons, as they can hurt themselves in profound evolutionary ways if they misuse the powerful technologies of tantra.

A cardinal tantric technique is the art of purifying perception: to visualize and gradually learn to perceive the universe as a buddhaverse or mandalic paradise, with all beings as divine "buddhine" beings and all environments as perfected divine abodes. If this were to be employed with sustained concentration by persons who have not first had some level of experiential realization of voidness and its inevitably entailed awareness of the relativity and constructedness of all things, it would lead such practitioners into the trap of psychosis, getting them stuck in an alternate reality far more pleasant and seemingly secure than the jarring and dangerous ordinary reality. A second cardinal art of tantra is purifying self-conception: cultivating a divine buddha-identity to replace the ordinary, habitual self-identity of the ignorant person. If that were to be practiced by someone without at least some level of the realization of selflessness and its entailed insight into the constructedness of relational self, it would lead to megalomania. Thirdly, if a practitioner does not have at least some degree of detachment from primal subconscious drives of *eros* and *thanatos*, and some degree of universal compassion toward others, the powerful energies of the deeper mind and body, when aroused within the tantric atmosphere, are likely to carry the person still perceiving those energies as lust and hostility into dangerous areas of manipulative exploitation of others, which would prove enormously destructive to both self and others.

Therefore, the guardian of the secrets of the tantras is the fierce Vajrapāṇi, who appears occasionally in the exoteric sutras as a yaksha-like fierce protector of the Buddha, who dwells under his teaching throne. I recall the *Sutra of the Wise and the Fool* account where several vajrapāṇis come out from under Shākyamuni's throne to ward off the six false teachers.

Ancestral Mentors

This term "ancestral mentor" (Tib. *brgyud pa'i bla ma*), usually translated "lineage lama," is translated this way to reveal the feeling of a practicing great adept, who is not identified in her or his mind with his blood lineage and does not look back to great grandparents and so on as the most important ancestors. We can see in the case of Tibetan culture that the common institution of ancestor worship or preoccupation with bone (father) and blood (mother) lineage is almost completely neglected, having been thoroughly eroded by the commonsensically accepted, culturally embedded, biological theory of karmic evolution. That is, persons so acculturated consider their own past existences to have been in other families, nations, genders, races, even species, and so there is not a very strong connection with the blood or bone of the parents of this life and their forebears. Further, a dead parent or great grandparent is considered more likely to be reincarnated as one's neighbor than to be in some ancestral happy hunting ground awaiting veneration and the offerings of tea and cookies from successive generations.

However, in past generations, those who provided and preserved precious Dharma teachings and practices are the spiritual ancestors who engendered the good qualities and liberating realizations in oneself that really enhance one's "spiritual gene" (*gotra*, *rigs*); so they are considered the real ancestors. Spiritual adepts—and, by their conscious and subliminal example, all Tibetans—are acculturated to view their Dharma ancestors as more important than their clan forebears. The rituals of offering drops of elixir to them in one's daily prayers and performances are in effect substitutes for the more usual ancestor rituals we find in other Asian societies. Every ritual performance (*sādhana*) written by lamas such as Tsong Khapa and his successors, and performed by hundreds of thousands of monks and nuns over the centuries, includes an invocation of these ancestral mentors at the beginning and makes offerings to them during a later section of the performance.

The path of the Esoteric Community Tantra

From among the unexcelled yoga tantras, the *Esoteric Community Tantra* (*Guhyasamāja*) is considered by Tsong Khapa the paradigmatic "father tantra." I say "paradigmatic" rather than "supreme," as is often said, since every tantra proclaims itself to be "supreme." Indeed, each of them can assist the practitioner to the supreme achievement of buddhahood if properly implemented. The special virtue of the *Esoteric Community* is said to be that it has five explanatory tantras taught by Vajradhara Buddha which complement the originally revealed root tantra. It therefore provides all the materials needed for a student and practitioner to understand all tantras, many of which are less complete in their teachings.

The "father" category of tantras is critically defined by Tsong Khapa as characterizing those tantras that emphasize the methodology for attaining the magic body (*māyadeha*, *sgyu lus*), a subtle body like a dream body. The practitioner learns to release this subtle body from within his or her meditatively entranced coarse body, which subtle body can then act in the universe to accelerate the accumulation of the stores of merit and wisdom that are required for buddhahood, gathering lifetimes of merit and wisdom in a single lifetime dedicated to such meditation.

The "mother" category of unexcelled yoga tantras emphasizes the arts of deepening the wisdom of either a coarsely or a subtly embodied practitioner by plunging her or him again and again into the clear light transparence realms within the infinite event horizon of deep voidness. With all due respect, Tsong Khapa critiqued those venerated mentor scholars, such as Butön Rinpochey, who argued for a third category of "nondual" unexcelled yoga tantras, on the principle that all of them are nondual; the "mother" and "father" categories simply describe their dominant emphasis, not an exclusive focus. These most advanced tantras are all called "unexcelled" (*anuttara*), rather than "highest" (*parama*), because they reveal and make accessible the innermost core of nondual reality, and nothing can go beyond them since they contain everything within their matrix; "highest" implies a hierarchy in which the goal is somehow above and away from the "lower" things, which would carry a trace of dualism. unexcelled yoga tantra teaching is not "higher" than the four noble truths, the eightfold path, the ten transcendences, and so forth. It is the matrix in which all of those teachings are nested, and where they are fulfilled to the subtlest and most complete degree.

Although Tsong Khapa was an adept practitioner of a number of tantras other than the *Esoteric Community*—he quotes from many of them—he usually based his analytic commentaries such as this one on the *Esoteric Community* literature and its commentaries developed in the noble (Skt. *ārya*) tradition of Indian Buddhist tantrism.

Tsong Khapa goes on to mention outstanding examples of the spiritual ancestors he reveres as having brought the *Esoteric Community Tantra* teaching forward in history from the initial revelation of the Buddha to Tsong Khapa's day.

Indrabhūti

Indrabhūti was a great adept said to have been a high king of Uddiyāna. Contemporary scholars identify this land with the Swat valley presently in Pakistan, but in ancient times it possibly represented the entire country now known as Afghanistan and northern Pakistan. It is said that he was fortunate enough to have received the original revelation of the *Esoteric Community Tantra* directly from Shākyamuni as Vajradhara. It is said that the reason the *Esoteric Community* mandala universe has no charnel grounds (*shmashāna*) around it (representing samsaric existence), as do other unexcelled yoga tantras, is that since Indrabhūti was a king, he liked things clean and orderly. He would have been repelled by any graphic dis-

some saw a dead dog, and one prostitute saw a foot of the Lord Avalokiteshvara, whereby she instantly attained numerous siddhi powers. It is highly interesting that a story so similar to the legend of Asaṅga should be attached to this paragon of the deep wisdom lineage.

Chandrakīrti's greatest works were his Stages of the Enlightenment Path work, *Introduction to the Middle Way*, his commentary on Nāgārjuna's *Wisdom*, the *Lucid Exposition*, and his commentary on the *Esoteric Community Tantra*, the *Illuminating Lamp*. These latter two are known as the sun and moon, lighting up the earth of sutra and tantra, respectively. Finally, the Tibetans consider him also to be one of the "eighty-four great adepts."

About These Legendary Accounts

The attitude and hardened opinion among modern Buddhist studies scholars is that the Indian and Tibetan Buddhist scholars (and perhaps some members of the Shingon Buddhist tradition of Japan) could not manage to notice the difference between Nāgārjuna, Āryadeva, and Chandrakīrti—the philosopher sages of early and middle first millennium Buddhism—and the adepts by the same names listed here in the ancestral lineage of the *Esoteric Community Tantra* teachings. This disrespectful opinion about the naïveté, or fundamentalism, or whatever else, on the part of the many great intellects to whom it is applied will simply no longer do. It goes along with the long-established, and now perhaps subliminal, "Westerners'" chauvinist idea and racial prejudice that "Eastern" people are to be lumped together with "primitive" people (not to mention that the so-called "primitives" don't fit the caricature either). The idea is that since "Eastern" people have no sense of linear time, no interest in history, and so live in the eternal now of endless cycles, this explains their lack of progress in the sciences and their general social backwardness and economic underdevelopment. Therefore, quite naturally, modern scholars would think that such "backward" people would be so unrealistic, unscientific, and unhistorical as to think that the two Nāgārjunas, Āryadevas, and Chandrakīrtis could be the same persons. And they think the same about the many other Indian master authors who also wrote both philosophical and exoteric works of solid repute as well as works on the esoteric tantras (actually most of the great ones did).

The evidence for this truism of contemporary scholars is exclusively the presumed existence and nonexistence of texts. There is absolutely no "hard" evidence at all. The only dating used by modern scholars for these individuals comes from the recorded timing of Chinese or Tibetan translations of texts attributed to them, built upon by a certain amount of intertextual referencing. Texts in India were handwritten on palm-leaf pages and never printed until recent times. They would not last too long and would be recopied over and over, usually every few generations. Root texts and commentaries were often intermingled, so intertextual reference is sometimes an unreliable guide. Spiritual texts in particular were considered more importantly memorized than written, a tradition that came from Vedic practices. Additionally, esoteric texts were kept strictly secret, if committed at all to some handwritten pages. The tradition says that the tantric traditions were kept hidden without being written down in the human realm for over seven hundred years.

This is the place to put this contentious issue into a new light (as I will do more in detail below), in the context of this work on the perfection stage of unexcelled yoga tantra, considered by the Indo-Tibetan universal vehicle Buddhists to be the most advanced possible scientific and spiritual teaching. Since there is no hard evidence either way as to the dating, lifespans, and historical activities of these eminent personalities, it is more respectful and logical to accept the critical scholarship of the traditional analysts than it is to presume to know better and dogmatically follow our various modern, "Western," and "scientific" prejudices.

The basic presumption is that, since there are no such (we are certainly not) extraordinary, miracle-producing, highly enlightened beings with far-beyond-though-not-dissimilar-to-Einstein genius, no one ever could have been such a person, especially not a "premodern," Asian, spiritual person. Indeed, the very concept of the enlightenment of buddhahood as the complete and accurate knowledge of the exact nature of reality is preposterous to us on its face. However, we must here confront the fact that the only evidence we have for the rigid opinion that there are no other extraordinary persons up to the inconceivably extraordinary person of a buddha is our own failure to be enlightened in that way. We cannot even say we have the evidence of never having met any such person, since they have the tradition of most often hiding their enlightenment, perhaps to avoid arrest, intrusive dissection, and lethal examination such as the E.T. in the film was about to undergo when he escaped. So we might have met one or two, but were unfortunately unable to recognize them. I do not say I am so enlightened, or that I know I have met any who are, but I am open to the fact that I wouldn't have recognized one if I saw her or him. So at least I maintain an open mind.

To summarize this argument so far:

1. The presence or absence of texts in the climate of India cannot provide ironclad dating evidence. All the claims of contemporary scholars that there must be two of everybody are just speculation grounded in preconceived ideas.

2. The Tibetan scholars who accept that the two Nāgārjunas, two Āryadevas, etc. are the same persons in different eras and contexts are presenting a perfectly good hypothesis until something nonspeculative arises to disprove it. A "modernist" presumption of superior perspective is no better than a racist, nationalist, religious, or culturalist one.

3. The whole program of disproving everything "traditional" people think and believe, based on the assumed superiority of our modernist knowledge and culture, is itself obsolete in the postmodern era. A key part of our critical scholarship's quest of objective truth has to be to question the rigidity of our conditioned subjectivities and their biases and blindnesses. Through global warming (overheating), pollution, population explosion, etc., we are driving the world into extinction with our diseased, ignorance-driven, objectivist science and technology-magnified egocentrist culture. *This cannot rationally be considered superiority in knowledge and culture.* It will not do to proclaim like the late Richard Rorty that we are ethnocentric, and then just honor that fact by refusing to learn anything about any other culture or look at the world through other eyes and languages and worldviews.

4. The essence of the noble tradition of the *Esoteric Community* and other unexcelled yoga tantras, as opposed to the Jñānapāda tradition and perhaps others, is that the dialecticist centrist worldview goes along with the unexcelled yoga lifestyle. It is inner scientific and technological and not merely nonrational and mystical.

Tsong Khapa bows with powerful faith not because he is a fundamentalist—not at all—but because he has met these ancestral adepts personally, he has talked with them. They are immortal on the magic body (*māyadeha*) plane, like George Lucas's jedi masters, who can walk back and forth through time. So therefore, we need not be overobsessed with ancillary issues of historicism. My only purpose in even bringing it up myself—in the face of the sharp teeth of all my colleagues' and even students' modernist presuppositions—is only as part of helping the reader break through for a moment their habitual intellectual and even unconscious entrapment in a horizon of preconceptions wherein everything explored in this work of Tsong Khapa and other Tibetan master scholar-adepts is some sort of quaint pseudomagical thinking, primitive superstitious twaddle, perhaps of some interest historically that people were ever so crazy.

This means that Tsong Khapa himself, if he were engaged with us, would be delighted if someone were to find a brass plate engraved with a note from Vajrin Nāgārjuna that he is not the Āchārya Nāgārjuna, but his successor in philosophy and institution, his reincarnation, his namesake, his inspired descendant, or whatever.

Once in a taped interview, the present Dalai Lama of Tibet, himself a scholar and adept of this type (though he would certainly disclaim the latter honorific), once was asked the following hypothetical question by the late Carl Sagan: "Your Holiness, what would you do if we set up a careful experiment and conclusively disproved the possibility of personal reincarnation?" After a moment of thought, the Dalai Lama said, "Why I would cease to believe in it! We no longer consider the earth to be a flat continent projecting outward from an axial mountain." Sagan caught his breath from the surprise and cognitive dissonance he was experiencing from this response. After another moment, the Dalai Lama asked enthusiastically, "Now how would we go about setting up such an experiment?" Needless to say, Sagan was speechless, and looked quite relieved as both broke into hearty laughter.

So we should certainly continue to look for evidence to support, refine, or disprove the current set of scholarly historicist theories about the dating and meaning of the Buddhist tantras. But until we do find something as concrete as the brass plaque disclaimer by Vajrin Nāgārjuna, we should not avoid looking into the tantras on the terms of those who looked into them before, over centuries, scholastically as well as yogically. These masters were highly intelligent, rational, scientific-minded people. After much study and practice they came to accept the human possibility of the full enlightenment of body as well as mind via the esoteric evolutionary acceleration that uses a virtual reality subtle body-mind to develop the three bodies of buddhahood in one lifetime or two. Therefore, whether or not they had attained such a fulfillment personally, they came to accept as scientific fact that their great adept ancestors had broken the biological imperatives of our era's maximum hundred-year lifespan and could have continued their studies and teachings over centuries. Even after physical death, such spiritual ancestors could appear concretely and enduringly to disciples of later times who required their direct instruction.

I personally, as myself a product of our modernist culture, would be immensely astonished were Nāgārjuna or Tsong Khapa etc. to appear to me to resolve my doubts or give me encouragement, as my cultural conditioning and perceptual habit is still bound in materialism due to my own lack of attainment. But intellectually, I have to admit that I have seen no convincing disproof of the possibility, just prejudiced and dogmatic dismissals asserted without evidence. So I have to remain open-minded, even though skeptically so.

If anyone has concrete evidence of the impossibility of the supernormal attainments proposed in the great adept tradition, they should bring it forth. If they cannot, yet still assert the "massive facticity" of the materialist canons of possibility, they are not a scholar, a true seeker of knowledge, but a dogmatic defender of some unexamined preconception about the innate superiority of the scientific materialist worldview, the modern academic institution, and the postmodern industrial lifestyle of the crumbling, late great Euro-American empire.

3. Who Is the Inspiration of This Author?

My mentor Mañjughosha elucidates precisely
The path of the Community, which grants to one who understands
The supreme fearless eloquence concerning all sutras—
I bow with constant devotion to his lotus foot!

I need not elaborate the history of Tsong Khapa's special devotion to and mentor relationship with Mañjushrī, which I have already done in detail in my *Central Philosophy of Tibet.* Suffice it to say that, as hard-headed a logician and critical philosopher as he was, he did experience himself as in direct dialogue with the divine bodhisattva, day in and day out, discussing where to go, what to do, how to develop insight into the nature of reality, and how to practice accordingly. That is to say, his primary mentor in exoteric centrist philosophical studies, and simultaneously his root guru in the esoteric practice sense, was thought by him to be the divine bodhisattva himself—in short, his main teacher was what might be called an angelic being.

What is interesting here is that the salutation to the bodhisattva of wisdom in this context indicates the Tibetan tradition that the study of dialecticist centrism and unexcelled yoga tantra are two sides of the same coin. That is, the philosophical view of tantrism is dialecticist relativism—the view that all things are purely conventional, illusory, and dreamlike in their reality. Therefore, their nature and structure are powerfully controlled by language, relatively ultimately in the form of mantra. This view entails that the relational, conventional self is a work in progress, and that it can be shaped and accelerated in its evolution through subtle and extremely subtle mental and physical creativity as well as by coarse-reality mental, verbal, and physical activities.

This full entanglement of sutra and tantra is further indicated by Tsong Khapa's statement above that it is through mastery of the *Esoteric Community* unexcelled yoga tantra that one attains the enlightenment that bestows full explanatory eloquence about the exoteric sutra teachings. Why does he refer to the goal of enlightenment as "supreme eloquence" about Buddha's sutras? It must be because the first thing an enlightened being feels like doing is to share her or his happiness by expressing it in ways that will be effective in enlightening others. Tsong Khapa himself wrote in his enlightenment poem, "Of all a buddha's deeds, his speech is supreme. Therefore, the wise praise buddhas for their speech."

4. Who Are His Honored Tibetan Predecessors and Mentors?

Those who, driven by great waves of their store of virtues,
Such as their vows to uphold the Victor's Holy Dharma,
Endured so many hardships to visit the noble Country
And spread this path all over this snowy mountain land—
Rinchen Zangpo, who was the eye of our world,

Marpa of Hlodrak, keeper of the treasury of secrets,
And 'Gös of rTa Nag, the best translator,
Expert in amazing texts—to their feet I bow!

Although the lineage of Tibetan generation masters of the *Esoteric Community* literature and practice instruction is long, Tsong Khapa singles out for special recognition three famous translators. Rinchen Zangpo (958–1055) was a Nyingmapa when it was all of Tibetan Buddhism, before it was organized into a more formal "order" to distinguish itself from the Kadam, Kagyu, Sakya orders, etc. Marpa Lotsawa (1012–1097) was the teacher of Milarepa, and Tibetan founder of the Kagyu order. Gö Lotsawa (eleventh century) was a very important translator among the early Kadampa lamas.

The Indo-Tibetan lineage as seen by the *Esoteric Community* practitioners after Tsong Khapa runs as follows: Lord Vajradhara himself, of course; Lodrö Rinchen (*Ratnamati), a tenth-stage bodhisattva on the exoteric level who attained communion on the esoteric; the savior Nāgārjuna (ca. 100 BCE to 500 CE), who is praised for his exoteric achievement, as having "gained the supreme exaltation of the eight masteries and having made openly visible extreme-free relativity, the sole eye for seeing the ocean of sutras"; ". . . Matangipa, who gained supreme powers with ritual deeds in the great burning ground of Begara, heart-son sustained by the supreme noble one; . . . Tilopa, Shrī Jñāna (ca. 988–1069), who, attaining powers, went to the pure land of bliss and, blessed by the Holy Dākinī, performed more deeds than a thousand buddhas; . . . Nārotapa (ca. 956–1041), in whose heart was born the magical samadhi, as the Dākinī prophesied; . . . Marpa, the skilled yogi who attained powers, . . . and touched the feet of hundreds of Indian masters; . . . Wangi Dorjey (aka. 'Tshur, eleventh–twelfth century); . . . Sonam Rinchen (Jakhangpa, twelfth century), a full vessel of wondrous virtues, with distinctive marks such as crown ushnīsha, and secret vajra ensheathed, stallion-like; . . . Tsultrim Kyab (disciple of Sonam Rinchen, twelfth–thirteenth century); . . . Zhönu Ö of Serding (Serdingpa, twelfth–thirteenth century), the treasury of the two tantras, identifying the bardos, the three illusion tantra, and the messenger's swift transference to the pure land; Özer of Deding (Chöku Özer, thirteenth century), holder of the treasure of limitless virtues, who at once beheld the wisdom mandala, just entering the mandala of Shrī Kālachakra; . . . Pakpa Ö of Lake Jo, omniscient one who conquered the darkness of ignorance with the light rays of wisdom knowing reality, surpassing all ordinary perceptions and conceptions; Butön Chöje Rinchen Drub (1290–1364), who understood the words and meanings of all sutras and tantras, the second Victor of the dark age, who upheld the victory banner of the nondecline of the Buddha's teachings"; and finally ". . . Khyungpo Lhaspa (fourteenth century), supreme master, principal of mantra holders, with immeasurable strength of merit and wisdom, whose youthful body was unstained by flaws of lust."[4]

5. Who Most Needs the *Esoteric Community*?

For those whose eye is biased among sutra and tantra texts,
For whom the teachings have not dawned supreme as practices,
Who do not know exactly the subtle paths of the philosophies
Of the world ornaments, which are the only doorway
To seek the meaning of the profound buddha-statements,
And who thus take refuge in mere literal expressions,
And sit content with random personal instructions in the subtle,
Cannot, even with great effort, find the good path of the
Community—
I am going to explain it for their sake.

To be "biased" about exoteric or esoteric texts is to take one aspect or session of Buddha's teaching (Tsong Khapa considers Shākyamuni, as Vajradhara, to be the author of the tantras) and become attached to it. Then, since there are inconsistencies between sutras, and since each was taught for a specific set of disciples, if one is literalistic about the meanings and holds that the others do not measure up, are not correct, are for inferior students, and so forth, one is considered prejudiced. When all the teachings "dawn as practices" (this line drawn from the famous four-square path elaborated by Atīsha), then this kind of partiality will not prevail, and the practitioner can fulfill the aim of any teaching. Still, there are those whose studies and practice of the subtleties of logic, ethics, and critical philosophy have not prepared them to enter the tantric path. There needs to be a basis of at

4. This lineage comes from the *Community* performance (*sādhana*) script originally written by Tsong Khapa and embellished by his successors.

least a solid inferential understanding of voidness, a firm vow of the spirit of enlightenment, and a degree of transcendence of being dominated by instinctual drives for power and fame.

Students not properly prepared tend to take some simplistic version of initiation or teaching and think "Ah, I am perfect! I have the perfect teaching! My teacher gave me the inner secret precept! I'm all set, and don't need all that other stuff!" Such types of aspirants for the profound and subtle path of the *Community* will fail to find their way. Their plight motivates Tsong Khapa to write this treatise.

6. Who Are the Lucky Students of This Text?

But those who are ambitious for the personal instruction,
That comes from the path of reason and reference
That well combines all root and explanatory tantras
By means of the personal precept of the second great Vajradhara,
Should think to themselves
"How lucky am I to enter here!"
Into this path of great secrets,
Traveled by millions of heroes and heroines,
Such as Indrabhūti, Sukhanātha [Padmavajra],
Saraha, Nāgārjuna, and Nāgayoginī!

On the positive side, there are those who don't get stuck in prejudice and sectarianism, have the right preparation and do not think that access to the esoteric obviates the need to understand the profound transcendent wisdom and cultivate the magnificent spirit of enlightenment. These easily recognize that the esoteric teachings also need extensive and penetrating study as well as powerful motivation to practice, and so confidently and wholeheartedly enter the miraculous path of unexcelled yoga.

Though in a previous verse Tsong Khapa has already mentioned the ancestral mentors, in this verse he selects the mentors who are more revered for their heroic deeds than for their profound writings. He additionally mentions Mahāsukhanātha, who is usually recognized as Padmavajra, a great adept identified with Avalokiteshvara (in the eighty-four adepts' histories he is the mentor of the adept Shavari, the hunter).

7. How to Study This Text

Think it over well, your faces aglow with joy,
Allowing yourself the feelings of the brightest smile,
And, abandoning all distractions
And the three faults of vessels—
Listen [carefully to me now]!

Finally, Tsong Khapa encourages us to be happy and proud, now that we have been fortunate enough to encounter this teaching. We should approach it with proper preparation and suitable respect. His own delight in being able to share this quintessential clarification of the deepest points of the most advanced practices is infectious, and he urges the reader, student, or disciple to allow herself or himself the luxury of a great big smile. He then gets down to business, admonishing us to avoid covering the vessel of our minds with arrogance, the false idea that we already know everything there is to know about this and so seal off our receptivity and the possibility of us coming up with new insight and experience (the fault of the covered vessel); to avoid poisoning the elixir of the teaching poured into the vessel by nursing within our attitudes the distorting motivations of greed for power or fame or wealth, hateful competitiveness with rivals thinking how our new knowledge will enable us to dominate them, or delusions about how we can possess and manipulate these treasure teachings of the heart and use them to bolster our egotism and status (the fault of the poisoned vessel); and to avoid losing the teachings by being forgetful and distracted, rushing on to other things, looking for shortcuts and easy ways out, being taken in by seductive but superficial "easy" approaches and so missing the essence, the value of these supreme instructions (the fault of the vessel with holes in it that loses its contents immediately, however bountifully they are poured into it).

Part Two

English Translation of Tsong Khapa's *Brilliantly Illuminating Lamp of the Five Stages*

1. Introductory

[2b.5–34b.3]

I bow reverently to the lotus foot of Lord Mañjughosha, the mentor of all the lords of bliss!

Ablaze in the glory of wondrous signs and marks,
Forever playing in the taste of the bliss-void kiss,
Recklessly compassionate, free of extremist calm—
I bow to the Victor with the seven super-factors.

To the Lord of Secrets, collector of all secrets combined,
And to the ancestral mentors who achieved supremacy
Through the path of the *Community, King of Tantras*—
Indrabhūti, Nāgaḍākinī, Visukalpa, glorious Saraha,
Vajrin Nāgārjuna, Āryadeva, Nāgabodhi, Shākyamitra,
Matangi, Chandra[kīrti]pāda and the others—
I bow with the mind of ferocious faith!

My mentor Mañjughosha elucidates precisely
The path of the *Community*, which grants to one who
understands
The supreme fearless eloquence concerning all sutras—
I bow with constant devotion to his lotus foot!

Those who, driven by great waves of their store of virtues,
Such as their vows to uphold the Victor's Holy Dharma,
Endured so many hardships to visit the noble Country
And spread this path tall over this snowy mountain land—
Rinchen Zangpo, who was the eye of our world,

Marpa of Hlodrak, keeper of the treasury of secrets,
And 'Gös of rTa Nag, the best translator,
Expert in amazing texts—to their feet I bow!

For those whose eye is biased among sutra and tantra texts,
For whom the teachings have not dawned supreme as practices,
Who do not know exactly the subtle paths of the philosophies
Of the world ornaments, which are the only doorway
To seek the meaning of the profound buddha-statements,
And who thus take refuge in mere literal expressions,
And sit content with random personal instructions in the subtle,
And cannot, even with great effort, find the good path of the *Community*—
I am going to explain it for their sake.

But those who are ambitious for the personal instruction,
That comes from the path of reason and reference [2b]
That well combines all root and explanatory tantras
By means of the personal precept of the second great Vajradhara,
Should think to themselves
"How lucky am I to enter here!"
Into this path of great secrets,
Traveled by millions of heroes and heroines,
Such as Indrabhūti, Sukhanātha [Padmavajra],
Saraha, Nāgārjuna, and Nāgayoginī!

Think it over well, your faces aglow with joy,
Allowing yourself the feelings of the brightest smile,
And, abandoning all distractions
And the three faults of vessels—
Listen [carefully to me now]!

Here the sole lamp of the three worlds, the best leader of humans and gods, and the source of all true eloquence is the divine lord Buddha. The supreme, the consummation, and the chief principle of whatever he taught of true eloquence in accordance with the needs of the disciples, is this *Glorious Esoteric Community* (*Shrī Guhyasamāja*), the precious jewel of the three worlds. Based on that, the subject to be explained here is the stages of the path on which the fortunate person may progress to supreme enlightenment.

[* * * * * * *]

To explain this there are six parts: [I.] Arrangement of the two [kinds of] tantras; [II.] Expression of the greatness of the *Community*; [III.] The process of elucidating its inner intention; [IV.] Enumeration of the treatises in the noble (*ārya*) literature; [V.] The way its personal instructions were transmitted in Tibet; [VI.] The import of the actual precious jewel of personal instruction.

[**I.** – Arrangement of the two (kinds of) tantras]

The first has three parts: [A.] History of the origin of the various names of the unexcelled yoga tantras; [B.] Showing the difference of the two tantras according to the meaning of their names; [C.] Explaining in particular the art tantras.

[**I.A.** – History of the origin of the various names of the unexcelled yoga tantras]

There are many ways of naming the two [3a] divisions of the unexcelled tantras. The *Vow Arisal* calls them "yoga tantra" and "yoginī tantra," as in:

> Six million is ascertained
> As the number of the yoga tantras,
> And sixteen million are counted
> Of those known as yoginī tantras.

The *Buddha Skull-bowl* and the *Vajra Pavilion* also employ similar expressions. Here, for example, while "child" is the basis of differentiating into "boy" and "girl," a boy [alone] can be generally called a "child"; so while "yoga tantra" as a general name can be used for both "art" and "wisdom tantras," "yoga tantra" is [also] given to "art tantras" [alone]. Many sources also use "ḍākinī tantra" for "yoginī tantra." Such sources as the *Stainless Light* use the expressions "art tantra" and "wisdom tantra," while Nāgabodhi and Chandrakīrti use "wisdom sutra" for mother tantra. The mentors of Tibet, when citing terms paired with "yoginī tantra," use the expressions "father tantra" and "mother tantra," in agreement with the *Vajra Essence Ornament Tantra*:

> The *Vajra Essence Ornament Tantra*
> Is the grandmother of all tantras,
> Of mother ḍākinīs and father ḍākas.

[**I.B.** – Showing the difference of the two tantras according to the meaning of their names]

The second has two: [1.] Setting forth the points of doubt; and [2.] Explaining the individual positions concerx
ning them.

[**I.B.1.** – Setting forth the points of doubt]

One may doubt as follows: If the unexcelled tantras are divided into "art" and "wisdom" tantras, then is it or is it not the case that they are tantras of the nonduality of art and wisdom? If the former, [3b] it is incorrect, as the meaning of the given names "wisdom" and "art" is that they are tantras partial to wisdom or to art, and nondual tantras should be tantras equally applied to wisdom and art. If the latter, it is incorrect, since the meaning of "yoga" in "unexcelled yoga" corresponds to what is stated in the *Community Further Tantra*:

> The union of art and wisdom
> Is called "yoga."

This means that art and wisdom are evenly integrated, and not favored separately. Therefore, the unexcelled tantras of evenly integrated art and wisdom are rightly called "nondual tantras." Therefore, you should declare whether you think that the expressions "art tantra" and "wisdom tantra" are or are not contradictory to "nondual tantra."

[**I.B.2.** – Explaining the individual positions concerning them]

The second has two: [**a.**] Others' systems; and [**b.**] Our own system.

[**I.B.2.a.** – Others' systems]

Some Tibetan mentors divide the unexcelled tantras into three separate categories: art, wisdom, and nondual tantras; [they] use the criterion that the two former are partial toward art or wisdom and the latter teaches both. They take the *Hevajra* as nondual, since it calls itself

> A tantra whose nature is art and wisdom,

which [supposedly] does not contradict the fact that that tantra also calls itself a "yoginī" tantra, since they say that a nondual tantra must contain a wisdom tantra. But according to that, the definitive position is that unexcelled art and wisdom tantras are both ultimately nondual tantras. Hence, they must say how their own position, that the unexcelled tantras [4a] have three kinds—which are differentiated by the criterion of whether they teach the two separately or both together—is not contradictory to that.

Some Tibetan mentors say Kṛshnāchārya stated that a tantra beginning with "Thus did I hear . . ." is an art tantra, and a tantra beginning with "Delighted by the supreme esoteric . . ." is a mother tantra. They allow that the *Hevajra* is set up according to its own expressions: the *[Hevajra] Root Tantra* using the former [beginning], the *[Vajra] Pavilion Explanatory Tantra* [of the *Hevajra*] using the latter [beginning], and the *Sampuṭa [Tantra]* using both kinds, therefore being nondual. The *Root Tantra* of the *Supreme Bliss Tantra* has the latter [beginning], while its explanatory tantras such as the *Unexcelled Clear Articulation* begin with "Thus did I hear. . . ." Still, considering that both types of expressions are used elsewhere in the *[Unexcelled Clear] Articulation*, they posit the *Supreme Bliss Tantra* also as a nondual tantra. When one criticizes them by saying, "In that case what will ever be a mother tantra?"—they say their system is that although each tantra teaches both magnificent art and profound wisdom, the category is determined by which is less emphasized. These [mentors] consider that the two other kinds of tantras and the nondual tantras are mutually contradictory, and thus seem never to have examined the natures of the art and wisdom involved in the two kinds of tantras and the art and wisdom involved in the nondual tantras.

Other learned Tibetans say that the typology of three tantras in the unexcelled class, into art, wisdom, and [4b] nondual, is interpretable in meaning, and that in definitive meaning all unexcelled tantras are nondual. The criterion for establishing a tantra in a category of separate art or wisdom is whether or not both are taught therein; they therefore assert that these are ultimately nondual tantras. According to that, since they assert that the definitive meaning is that both art and wisdom unexcelled tantras are nondual tantras, there is a contradiction between the three incompatible criteria of establishing the three types of tantras with the example of the nondual tantra being the particular tantra of which they are especially fond. They do not accept father and mother tantras as [having] their own systems, which [stance] is refuted by their own [previous] assertion and by scriptural reference. If they were to accept them [as being distinct systems], those two would not be nondual tantras; and this last fact would preclude there being three separate criteria for the three different types of tantras.

Most of these [scholars] consider that the nondual tantras are superior to the two kinds, father and mother tantras, and insistently prove that whichever tantra they are especially fond of is itself a nondual tantra, setting up any tantras that are different from it as one or the other type of tantra.

[**I.B.2.b.** – Our own system]

The second has two parts: [i.] How to establish tantras of nondual art and wisdom; and [ii.] Showing the meaning of tantras of separate art and wisdom.

[**I.B.2.b.i.** – How to establish tantras of nondual art and wisdom]

The first has two parts: [A′] The actual meaning; and [B′] Refuting objections.

[**I.B.2.b.i.A′** – The actual meaning]

It appears that these scholars who divide the unexcelled tantras into three separate types of tantras [5a] make the basic mistake of considering the "art" and "wisdom" of "art, wisdom, nondual tantra" and the "art" and "wisdom" of "distinct art and wisdom tantras," as being objectively the same, [due to their] having the same names. Therefore, they think that "integrated wisdom and art tantra" and "distinct wisdom [tantra]" and "[distinct] art tantra," using the same "wisdom" and "art" terms, must be contradictory. Therefore, one must distinguish the two [meanings of "art" and "wisdom"].

With regard to the "yoga" involved in both yogi and yoginī unexcelled tantras, the "art" of the nonpartial, equally integrated "art and wisdom nondual" tantra refers to the spontaneous great bliss, and the "wisdom" is the famous frequently-mentioned genius that realizes the suchness of selfless voidness. All unexcelled tantras are the same in terms of their indivisible union of actual art and wisdom as such bliss and voidness, in taking this as their supreme subject of concern, and thus the condition of the nature of all unexcelled tantras is that they are actual nondual tantras. Therefore, in terms of such kinds of art and wisdom, none are established as partial to either. Thus, the father tantras and the mother tantras are said to be divisions of the basic [category of] nondual tantras, and are not to be understood as exclusive categories.

Thus, the *Stainless Light* states that really, all are just yoga tantras [5b] of the nature of art and wisdom. Likewise, the *Hevajra* states:

> The HEY syllable is great compassion,
> The VAJRA is called "wisdom."
> Listen, and I will explain
> That tantra whose nature is art and wisdom!

And so, [according to others' systems,] the *Hevajra* would not be a "wisdom tantra," because it does not say, "Listen to this 'wisdom tantra!'" Likewise, the *Community* states:

> The union of art and wisdom
> Is declared to be "yoga."
> The *Community* is declared to be "yoga,"
> The means of expression of all buddhas!

And so the *Community* would not be an art tantra. Likewise, the *Primal Buddha [Time Machine Tantra]* declares:

Yoga is not by the body of art,
Nor will it be by wisdom alone.
The Transcendent Lord declared that "yoga"
Is the union of art and wisdom.

The *Vajra Essence Commentary [on Hevajra]*[5] also explains it in that way.

Now to say that the *Community* is not an art tantra and the *Hevajra* is not a wisdom tantra is [tantamount to] rejecting that those two are partial in terms of the "art" and "wisdom" that are bliss and voidness. In our own system, it does not amount to asserting that those two are not father tantra and mother tantra [respectively]. These two are mentioned as especially famous examples of father and mother tantras, which is not to say that other tantras are not either art tantras or wisdom tantras.

[**I.B.2.b.i.B′** – Refuting objections]

One should not succumb to the notion that, based on the fact that the yoginī tantras such as *Hevajra* often mention "bliss" [6a] and the *Community* does not use the word "bliss" often—usually explaining in terms of the four voids—that great bliss is distinctive of the mother tantras and the father tantras do not employ the actual path of great bliss. The Great Adept Kṛshnāchārya explained [in the *Clarification of the Esoteric Reality*]:

The statements "Thus [did I hear . . .]"
[Expressing the bliss-void setting] of the yoga tantras,
Are like fire to the straw of other [beginnings],
[Often used] in the mother tantras;
But this is not an essential distinction,
According to the Mind Vajra.

Thus, the indivisible union of [great] bliss and voidness that is explained to be the actual meaning of the initial expression "Thus have I [heard] . . ." that is used in the art tantras is also the [essential] import of the yoginī

5. *rdo rje snying po'i 'grel pa*. This is a common alternate title for the canonical *Hevajra-piṇḍārtha-ṭīkā (kye'i rdo rje bsdus pa'i don gyi rgya cher 'grel pa)*(Tōh. 1180). See, e.g., Roerich, *Blue Annals*, p. 838.

tantras. Therefore, he explains that the Victor declared there is no distinction between the two tantras concerning their essence, which is the union of bliss and void. Particularly, in regard to determining the meaning of the beginning, "Thus have I heard . . ." of the *Community*, [Mahāsukhanātha[6]] explains more than once in the *Esoteric Accomplishment* that the reality praised as "where present, [enlightenment is] present: where absent, absent" is the indissoluble union of great bliss and voidness:

> The adept aiming at such reality
> Will attain it even without disciplines.
> If he lacks that reality, he will not attain it,
> Even performing hundreds of disciplines.

And:

> Such reality abiding as tantra
> Is clearly the glorious *Esoteric Community.*

And:

> The author of the tantra is Mind Vajra,
> [Being] both the speaker and his expression;
> As there is none other than that,
> He said nothing other than great bliss.
> From "Thus did I hear . . ."
> Up to ". . . the Lord was dwelling," **[6b]**
> The Mind Vajra himself
> Was indicated to all the buddhas
> As the glorious Great-Bliss Savior
> Described as "was dwelling."
> Thus I will explain a bit the aptness
> Of what was taught.
> "At one time" ultimately teaches, in brief,
> That the Lord spoke the truth,
> That the import of the buddhas' tantras
> Is the nature of great bliss.

6. Apparently an honorific pseudonym of the adept Padmavajra. See below.

This master Mahāsukha[nātha] is also called "Padmavajra," and [Āryadeva] frequently cites him as a source in the *Integrated Practices*; thus he is very much in agreement with the noble tradition. He explains again and again that the union of bliss and void is the actuality of the path and the meaning of the *Community*, so it must surely be acknowledged by those who uphold the noble system.

Thus, this demonstration that there is no difference among all the unexcelled tantras in taking the actuality of the path as the real indivisible union of the art of bliss and the wisdom of voidness requires that, whatever path of the two kinds of [unexcelled] tantra one enters, the generation within one's own process of the indissoluble union of bliss and void, art and wisdom be understood as indispensable. Thus, you should realize that you must discover, not merely an approximate idea of bliss and voidness, but the subtle vital points of the extraordinary bliss and voidness. [7a]

[**I.B.2.b.ii.** – Showing the meaning of tantras of separate art and wisdom]

The second has two parts: [A′] Explanation from such [texts] as the *Stainless Light*; and [B′] Explanation from such [texts] as the *Vajra Pavilion*.

[**I.B.2.b.ii.A′** – Explanation from such (texts) as the *Stainless Light*]

If the "art" and "wisdom" of "art, wisdom, nondual" tantras are as explained above, then what are the "art" and "wisdom" mentioned in tantras of separate "art" and "wisdom?"

The way of establishing them is somewhat explained in the *Stainless Light*, stating:

> In regard to certain tantras, using such mundane superficial distinctions as the mirror-intuition to symbolically purify[7] the aggregates and elements, the Transcendent Lord stated [classifi-

7. Tib. *rnam par dag pa*. In this context, "purify" means to give the underlying symbolic meaning of visual elements in mandalas and archetype deity forms. Thus the thirty-four arms of Vajrabhairava symbolize thirty-four of the thirty-seven accessories of enlightenment, thus "purifying" the arms, in the sense of stopping someone from thinking that they are intrinsically real things in themselves.

> cations such as] art and wisdom, to accord with the inclinations of less intelligent living beings.

Thus, separate "art" and "wisdom" tantras were set up according to male deities established as art from the symbolically purified aggregates and female deities established as wisdom from the purified elements. Such "art" and "wisdom" are superficial realities compared to the above ultimate reality art and wisdom, and are also said to be established in terms of the inclinations of dull-minded beings.

In regard to the way of accepting art and wisdom tantras in terms of male and female deities, the same source states:

> Superficially, when the lord does not move and the yoginīs engage in action, it is a yoginī tantra. And when the art engages in action and the wisdom does not move, it is an art tantra.

When the deity functions—as in compelling the wisdom hero [to merge] into the devotee hero and so on—and the goddesses act [7b] and the gods do not, it is a wisdom tantra; when the reverse is the case, it is an art tantra. So states [the *Stainless Light*], and the *Vajra Essence Commentary [on Hevajra]* also explains in similar fashion.

Here you may object that if, according to this, the *Time Machine* itself must be accepted as an art tantra, does that not contradict the *Stainless Light*'s statement that "by the distinction of three years, it is definitely a yoginī tantra"?

[This] explains it to be a yoginī tantra in the context of showing the number of the deities of the yoginī tantra by means of the [number of the] days of the central [channel] of three years.[8]

The way of establishing the two tantras through male and female deities is intended as a matter for changing emphasis and not as a fixed [classification]. For example, the *Esoteric Community* in the noble system is an art tantra, and yet the [creation-stage] summoning and inducting of the

8. Three lunar years of days adds up to the number of 1080, which is more than the number of deities of the usual Time Machine mandala (722), which itself is two years of central channel days plus two. Other than this hunch, I have not yet been able to solve the meaning of this cryptic aside.

wisdom hero are still accomplished without the activity of the male deities. Likewise, there are valid mother tantra texts where the female deities do not accomplish the summoning and inducting, and there is no precluding some tantras that manifest an arrangement common to both types of tantras showing both kinds [of actions, by male and female deities]. Therefore, although the *Vajra Rosary* is an explanatory tantra common to both kinds of tantras, its own actuality is said to be an art tantra. Likewise, although the *Time Machine* explains both methods, its own actuality is considered to be a yoginī tantra.

Confronted by this reasoning, some may suggest that therefore [the *Time Machine*] should be classified as a nondual tantra. Although they may wish to establish it as a nondual tantra, they cannot find a [coherent] way to establish it as a nondual tantra if they follow the intention of the *Stainless Light*. The *Stainless Light* established it as a nondual tantra according to the above-explained ultimate reality "art" [8a] and "wisdom," but the "art" and "wisdom" concerning whether the art or the wisdom acts or does not act are explained in terms of superficial reality and the inclinations of dull-minded beings.

This [commentary] teaches that the "art" and "wisdom" establishing the father and mother tantras are according to whether the male or female meditative deities' activities are set up in terms of the inclinations of dull-minded beings, but does not teach that all kinds of "art" and "wisdom" establishing tantras as "father" or "mother" are just the same. The *Stainless Light* also provides other means of establishing the two [kinds of] tantras, stating that in art tantras, the father and mother deities are equal in faces and arms due to the symbolism of equality of day and night; and in wisdom tantras, the father and mother deities are unequal in faces and arms due to the symbolism of early and late between-watches. On the strength of this, some call [the *Time Machine*] a nondual tantra in that the principal father and mother are unequal in number of faces and arms and the attendant deities have equality. But this does not seem worthwhile since that statement was made merely to show a reason as to why, in both tantras, faces and arms are said to be equal or unequal, and not to establish the meaning of art and wisdom tantras; since in those [statements] there seems to be no reference whatsoever to the meaning of "male" and "female" or "art" and "wisdom."

Furthermore, it seems they consider that being established as a nondual tantra is [a sign of being] superior to other tantras; but even though it is established as a nondual tantra by that [kind of] reason, such does not amount to any superior quality. For even though it happens that the chief deity's male and female forms have unequal numbers of faces and arms and their attendant deities have equal numbers, that aspect appears not to have any profound meaning. And one should understand this reasoning as applicable to [8b] other similar expressions of fallacious ways of establishment [of father and mother tantras].

[**I.B.2.b.ii.B′** – Explanation from such (texts) as the *Vajra Pavilion*]

The second has two parts: [1′] Refutation of others' extreme notions; and [2′] Establishing the most worthwhile position.

[**I.B.2.b.ii.B′1′** – Refutation of others' extreme notions]

The first has two parts: [a′] Others' interpretations; and [b′] Their refutation.

[**I.B.2.b.ii.B′1′a′** – Others' interpretations]

Some Tibetans consider that in [the following passages from] the fourth chapter of the *[Vajra] Pavilion*:

> This dākinī tantra is taught
> In order to establish all five dākas,
> [And] the host of the dākinīs of all the buddhas.

And:

> In order to include those who try to kill beings,
> Who turn away from realistic worldviews,
> And [others] who are spiritual women,
> And because its arts of bliss are not elaborate,
> Its short texts are vast in meaning,
> And its mantras are distinctive
> In illuminating those of lesser intellect—
> It is the essence of all tantras,
> And is taught to be a dākinī tantra.

The first four lines show that where the transcendent buddhas show bodies of dākinīs and become the principal deities as females, or where the majority of the host is female, it is a mother tantra; and where the transcendent buddhas show the bodies of the five families, or where the majority of the host is male, it is a father tantra—the former meaning being directly conveyed by that quote, and the latter being indirectly implied. Similarly, they consider that the latter quote shows that the mother tantras are taught to tame those who like to kill outsiders and who err in views and paths; by [this] key point they consider the father tantras are taught to tame [9a] those insiders who have unerring views and wish to achieve enlightenment. Thus, they assert that these two are the criteria for establishing the two [types of] tantra.

They also assert that there are another two criteria to establish the two [types of] tantras for the [following] two purposes, as [stated] in the thirteenth chapter of the *[Vajra] Pavilion*:

> Yoga tantras are taught
> In order to educate men and
> Yoginī tantras are taught
> In order to attract women.

They also believe the father tantras teach the facts of the creation stage and the mother tantras the facts of the perfection stage, based on the statement of the *Elucidation of the Esoteric Reality*:[9]

> Concerning the stages of creation and perfection,
> It is asserted that
> The yoga [tantras] teach the creation [stage]
> And the yoginī [tantras teach] the perfection [stage].

[**I.B.2.b.ii.B′1′b′** – Their refutation]

The meaning of the former quote is extremely clear from the preceding context since the *Dākinī Vajra Pavilion Tantra* was explained in order to

9. This section primarily quotes the *Vajra Pavilion* (Tōh. 419), a *Hevajra* literature text. However, the text cited here, the *Elucidation of the [Esoteric] Reality (de kho na nyid gsal ba)*, is Tōh. 1450, a commentary from the *Chakrasaṁvara* literature.

establish the mandala of the five kinds of dākas surrounded by the hosts of dākinīs of all five enlightenment clans. Thus, this is not an identification of the mother tantras. As for the five types of dākas mentioned earlier [in that text]—

> Five kinds of mandalas are declared:
> The vajrin, the permanent,
> The vajra energy,
> The god of the lotus dance, and
> The king of horses.

—they refer to the five transcendent clans; it is not that the lord of the mandala is a goddess. Thus, [9b] the [Tibetan scholars'] explanation of the first quote is incorrect.

Their explanation of the second quote is also not according to its [real] meaning. Just before that, the transcendent buddhas such as Akshobhya asked the bodhisattvas:

> How are the dākinīs and yoginīs gathered together in this vajra pavilion?

And the answer was given by the bodhisattvas such as Maitreya:

> First the Vajra-holder
> Pronounces the will for enlightenment:
> "I will liberate all living beings,
> Such as those born from eggs!"
> So why should women be neglected?
> Striving to kill living beings . . .

and so forth up to:

> . . . [is] explained as a [mother] tantra

as mentioned above. Therefore, the tantra taught as the essence of dākinī tantras in order to attract women is the *Vajra Pavilion* itself, since the context of the question is asking about the *[Vajra] Pavilion*. And as for calling it the essence of all tantras, just before that it is stated:

This essence is completely included
In the *Hevajra 500,000*

and therefore, no criterion for all mother tantras is intended; which can also be recognized in the expression "even in a slight text."

Well, then, one wonders what is the meaning of the exchange in the *Vajra Pavilion* asking, "How are women attracted?" In other treatises it is taught that in a woman's lifetime one cannot directly attain buddhahood; and thus this question concerns the statement in the unexcelled tantras that it is better to achieve buddhahood in the embodiment of a woman. Thus, the answer states that, since at the time of first conceiving the spirit [of enlightenment] one vows to establish all sentient beings [10a] on the stage of buddhahood, it is not right to neglect women. Especially since such an embodiment through its tendency to wrong views and heavy sinfulness exemplified by killing[10] reaches a superior attainment depending on this path, the *Vajra Pavilion* is said to have been taught in order to tame beings and attract women. Thus, how can it be teaching the criterion for establishing a tantra as a mother tantra?

In regard to the statement that:

Yoga tantras are taught
In order to educate men, and
Yoginī tantras are taught
In order to attract women.

—it indicates here in this *Vajra Pavilion Tantra*, in general, even while being a mother tantra, it is called "yoga tantra," as well as being called a "yoginī tantra" intending that it was taught to attract women; as quoted above:

The *Hevajra*, as a yoga tantra,
Is first explained by the victors;

10. It may be that in agricultural societies the women had to provide the food and so often had to slaughter animals to make dinner for the men and children. Otherwise, it seems weird that women are thought to be more into killing, as men are the hunters and warriors in most societies.

> Then the same thing is said to be a yoginī tantra
> To attract those of female embodiment.

First the *[Hevajra] Extensive Tantra 500,000* [is taught] and then later it is abridged as the *[Vajra] Pavilion Yoginī Tantra* in order to include women. Further, in both sections of the *[Vajra] Pavilion*, the *Hevajra* is said to be a mother tantra. Thus the appellation "yoga tantra" means the category of "yoga tantra" that is the basis of differentiation into yogi and yoginī tantras, and does not indicate the "yoga tantra" that is the opposite of the category "yoginī tantra."

Having already explained the way in which the *[Vajra] Pavilion* was taught to include women, this latter quote can be explained in that fashion, or otherwise it can be explained in terms of both father and mother tantras. [**10b**] In the unexcelled tantras there are both male and female jewel-like persons, the principal human embodiments for the supreme achievement. However, usually in the tantras and treatises, the practitioner is male, and [one of] the four kinds of women is often mentioned as his consort. In those contexts, not only the male but also the consort should be understood as a practitioner of the path; because it is repeatedly stated that just as the art is liberated conditioned by the wisdom, so the wisdom is liberated depending on the art.[11] Although that process exists in both types of tantras, the father tantras are not as extensive as the mother tantras about the nature and categories of criteria for the way of reliance on the consorts. Still, from that point of view, both tantras are said to be taught in order to train both [males and females]. Furthermore, this is only an explanation of the purpose of the two tantras, and not an establishment of the criteria for [distinguishing] father and mother tantras. For example, the *Esoteric Community* is chiefly taught for the sake of the jewel-like person, and yet that fact is not a criterion for it being a father tantra. Otherwise, as it is said in some ḍākinī tantras that they are taught for the sake of illuminating those of inferior intelligence, that too should become a criterion for their being mother tantras!

11. This is a very significant statement to support rejecting the contemporary anti-tantra scholars who insist that tantric practitioners were male chauvinists who just used women as mindless tools for their own supposed spiritual advancement.

Furthermore, these [Tibetan scholars'] way of explanation of the meaning of the quote from the *Elucidation of the Esoteric Reality* is also not according to its meaning. As said in that text:

> There are two kinds of [tantras]:
> The four of the encounter of two
> And the [one] of the union of two.
> By their creation and perfection stages,
> The yogi [tantras] are shown to be creative, and
> The perfective are called yoginī [tantras].
> The interpenetration of the two organs [11a]
> Is called "union."

Thus, with regard to the fourth of the four tantras of looking, touching and smiling, holding hands, and uniting, there are both yoga and yoginī tantras among those tantras involving the union of two organs. The first explains the stage arisen from creation and the second explains the stage arisen from perfection, and does not explain that one teaches the creation stage and the other teaches the perfection stage. Just before that quote, it states:

> By the path of the glorious *[Esoteric] Community*,
> In regard to the actuality of the two stages,
> The glorious *Community* is extremely pleasing,
> And is principal among all tantras.

This contradicts the notion that yoga tantras, such as the *Community,* chiefly teach the creation stage and do not chiefly teach the perfection stage.

As for [these Tibetan scholars'] saying that Kṛshnāchārya believed that father tantras begin with "Thus did I hear . . ." and mother tantras begin with "Delighted by the supreme secret . . ." and so forth; this is not his belief. He did not mention those two—"Thus did I hear" for father tantras, and "Delighted by the supreme secret" for the mother tantras—as criteria for [distinguishing] the two tantras, but only [to show] their non-difference in [both] being the actuality of the union of bliss and voidness. The quote supporting this has already been cited above.

Other than these, some Indians and Tibetans have promoted various methods of establishing the two tantras, but in most cases it appears that the "male-female" or "art-wisdom" [11b] used as criteria for art and wisdom tantras have no relevance whatsoever. They do not seem to explain the distinctions about being taught chiefly and not taught chiefly, or about what sort of "art" and "wisdom" are involved when they say that "[such and such] chiefly teaches art and wisdom." Their explanations of criteria are easily understood as invalid, coming from just noticing what corresponds to the two tantras. Therefore, I do not discuss them.

[**I.B.2.b.ii.B′2′** – Establishing the most worthwhile position]

Well, then, what do we take as the method for establishing father tantras and mother tantras?

Although there are some ordinary distinctions acceptable for differentiating them from the point of view of the creation stage, it is more importantly necessary to differentiate them from the point of view of [their respective] perfection stages. The establishment of all of them as nondual tantras is based on the art and wisdom of bliss and voidness, which [bliss-void art-wisdom] does not differentiate them as art and wisdom tantras, as explained above. It is also not proper to establish them [as different] according to their emphasis with regard to [superficial art and wisdom], since this would incur the fault that one would have to put *Hevajra* as a father tantra and the *Community* as a mother tantra; for "bliss" is emphasized in mother tantras such as *Hevajra* and not mentioned emphatically in the *Community*.

Thus, as for the "art" and "wisdom" mentioned in differentiating the tantras from the point of view of their perfection stages, "wisdom" is the ultimate great bliss intuition, and "art" is the superficial magic body. In regard to that, the *Vajra Pavilion*, chapter 13, sets up the mother tantras from the point of view of the former:

> "Divine Lord, how does one apply the name 'yoginī tantra'?"
> Vajradhara replied:
>
> > The art of transcendent wisdom [12a]
> > Is expressed as the yoginī.
> > By uniting with the great seal,
> > One enters into that reality,
> > And it is called the "yoginī tantra."

Here, it clearly states the designative criterion [for its being a mother tantra] in general terms. This means that, due to the connection of those two, because the tantra teaches the way of entering the voidness of ultimate suchness through union with the great seal, the *[Vajra] Pavilion* and so forth are called yoginī tantras. This is the reason [the *Vajra Pavilion*] is established as a "mother tantra," and that is the meaning of the two [lines] beginning "art of transcendent wisdom."

To explain this in detail: [a tantra] is called a "mother tantra" when it does not mainly teach how to achieve the superficial magic body from the energy of five-colored light rays that carries the great bliss intuition, and does mainly teach the process of exponential increase of realization that penetrates the ultimate voidness of suchness through the yoga of the indivisible bliss-void of the orgasmic great seal. [This is] the art of generating the four joys both in falling order, where the lily-white spirit of enlightenment falls from the crown to the penis, and in rising order, where it reverses back up into the crown. For this art of achieving the truth body of the innate transcendent wisdom is also the yoga of the indivisible union of bliss and void, and since its main component for achieving the truth body is the wisdom of the void side, it is called "mother."[12]

From the perspective of the second, as for setting up the yogi tantras, the *Angel Ocean* clearly states:

> In the royal tantras for the yogi/nīs,
> The various [12b] methods are distinctly known.[13]
> I explain to the world the magic [body]
> For [attaining] clear light magic body [union].

As for the meaning of this, "explain" means "cite." "Where?" In the kings of the yoga tantras. "What?" The magic body. "To whom?" "To the world," to such disciples. "By whom?" "By myself" says the Teacher. "How?" Through the clear light with its three preceding voids, there is the

12. This paragraph stands as Tsong Khapa's most complete definition of the "mother" type of unexcelled yoga tantra.

13. My translation follows the quote in Tsong Khapa's text, as preferable to the variant in the Derge edition; see footnote to the Tibetan ebook edition.

art of achieving the magic body by the process of the four voids. "How is it achieved?" The analyses of the various methods stated in that tantra can be especially well known.

To expand on that meaning: [a tantra] is called a "yogi" [father] tantra when it mainly teaches the way of achieving the superficial magic body from the five-colored light-ray energy of clear light and the way of generating the intuition of voidness through the four voids in the emergent order through the process of the energy's gradual collecting in the heart—the place where the clear light arises—and the four voids in the reverse order through the process of [that energy] resurrecting back out from there. This is also the yoga of the indivisible actual union of the void intuition and the energy-constituted body, and its main component is the art of the vision side for achieving the material body; thus it is called "father."[14]

As for the meaning of the quote from the *Elucidation of the [Esoteric] Reality,* it is similar to the above two [quotes], since it indicates that the two types of tantra mainly teach [respectively] the process where the magic body arises from the four voids and the process where the entry into thatness achieved as perfect from the beginning increases exponentially. As for the meaning of "mainly teach or not [13a] teach," it concerns whether or not a particular tantra teaches by putting the main emphasis on the one [or the other] method, and not merely whether or not it teaches [whichever art at all].

As it seems that authoritative authors have a way of explaining those two distinctions as the principal ones of the father and mother tantras respectively, other art and wisdom tantras being members included in those categories. And since even those not immediately obvious in regard to [whichever] process must be explained by interpretation in the light of those two poles, it is not the case that this system of interpretation does not apply to all tantras of both types.

[**I.C.** – Explaining in particular the art tantras]

The third has two parts: [1.] Threefold divisions of the art tantras; and [2.] Explanations of the *Esoteric Community* in particular.

14. This paragraph stands as Tsong Khapa's prime definition of "father" tantra.

[I.C.1. – Threefold divisions of the art tantras]

The *Vajra Essence Ornament Tantra* mentions three art tantras: "lust," "hate," and "delusion" art tantras. Concerning the first, that text states:

> Then, furthermore, to explain:
> The person who properly understands
> The tantra of the great art of lust
> Is granted accomplishment in this life.
>
> The *Esoteric Community 1,000*;
> The *Vajra Rosary 300,000*;
> The *Revelation of the Hidden Intention 4,000*;
> The *Four Goddess Dialogue 170*;
>
> The *Urad Tantra 208*;[15]
> The *Extra Explanation Tantra* for that [*Urad Tantra*];
> The *Great Commitment 55*;
> The *Five Vajra Community 1,000*;
>
> The *Compendium 1,000*;
> The *Equality Triumph 210*;
> The *Moon Esoteric Drop 1,700*;
> The *Vajra Underground 120*;
>
> The *Headdress Vajra 705*;
> The *Fierce Moon Drop 500,000*;
> The *Vajra Triumph* [13b] *90,000*;[16]
> The *Equality Esoteric 5,000*;
>
> The *Vajra Secret Ornament 5,000*;
> The *Vajra Secret Treasury 7,000*;
> The *Wishing Jewel Secret Drop 100,000*;
> The *Vairochana Magic 1,100*;

15. "Au rad" is a misspelling of *Uttara*?

16. Tib. *brgya dgu brgya*, literally nine hundred one hundreds.

The *Vajra Secret Ornament 1,000*;
The *Vajra Skull 208*;
The *Reality 70,000,000,000*;
The *Clear Ornament of Vows 100,000,000*;

The *Mañjushrī Hero 100,000*;
The *Great Secret Compendium 150*;
The *Jewel Tree 907*;
The *Time Drop 180*; and
The *Goddess Treatise 507*.

Through the specific intentions of these,
I truly teach.
Thus, by the union of both [male and female]
The categories of the tantra are taught.

And also:

All the tantras of hate and delusion
Should be likewise understood.

Here, twenty-seven[17] of the lust art tantras are mentioned by name, it being said that there are a total of 507. Hate art tantras are tantras such as the *Yamāntaka*, and delusion art tantras are such as the *Vajra Ārali*, according to the sages of Tibet. The general type of each of these two tantras is explained in the *Vow Arisal*, and should be understood from previous mention.

[**I.C.2.** – Explanations of the *Esoteric Community* in particular]

The second has two parts: [**a.**] Showing the meaning of "root tantra" and "further tantra," and showing the number of [their] explanatory tantras; and [**b.**] Showing the way in which the explanatory tantras explain.

17. Actually twenty-nine in the above list.

[**I.C.2.a.** – Showing the meaning of "root tantra" and "further tantra," and showing the number of (their) explanatory tantras]

The *Vajra Rosary Commentary* [by Alamkakalasha] explains that the *Esoteric Community* has an extensive [14a] 25,000 verse version, and a condensed 1,800 verse, eighteen-chapter, version; [so in the quote above,] the "thousand" refers to number of verses, and thus, the *Esoteric Community 1,000* mentioned above intends a rough count of the condensed version.

What are the "root," "further," and "explanatory" tantras here? Among root tantras, there are the extensive (*rgyas pa*), and the light (*nyung ngu*) or condensed (*bsdus pa*) tantras. This shows that first [Buddha] proclaimed the extremely extensive tantra and that later, since the disciples were relatively inferior in terms of lifespan and wisdom, he taught in a more condensed fashion, as they were not able to understand too easily. These two tantras, except for the mere difference of their words being more or less, are both root tantras, the former not being a root tantra for the latter.

As for the meaning of "root" in "root tantra," there appear to be three contexts: [1] one relative to the branches of the tantra, as the root of a tree is designated relative to the branches; [2] one in terms of time, as the first owner of something is called the root owner, relative to the further tantra; and [3] one in terms of the explanatory tantra, as in the usages "root" and "explanatory."

As for the first of these contexts, Chandrakīrti indicates it in the *Illuminating Lamp* statement that the *Community* is the root of all [14b] the other tantras; just how it becomes their root being explained below. Since it is both a "root" and a "tantra," the meaning of "root tantra" is complete in it; it is not self-evident that the name "root tantra" should be a literally exact name.

As for the second [context], it is illustrated in the case of the previously stated seventeen-chapter *Community* relative to the later-stated *Eighteenth Chapter*, which is the *Further Tantra*. Nāropa states that the *Reality Compendium* is a root tantra, the *Community Root Tantra* is its further tantra, and the *Eighteenth Chapter* is again the latter's further tantra. "Further" (Sanskrit *uttara*), literally "unexcelled" or "highest," can be translated either "superior" (*mchog*) or "further" (*phyi ma*); some do translate it as "superior," but the great translators seem correct in translating it as "further," as that is how commentaries also explain it.

It also seems that the intention of the *Integrated Practices* is that the *Reality Compendium* is a root tantra relative to the *Esoteric Community*. What is the reason for assigning the *Reality Compendium* as a root tantra for the *Community*, since it is not merely due to temporal priority? Granted that the *Community* is not a yoga tantra from among the four tantra classes, still in general many statements are made there in the context of the yoga tantra, and thus it has been said that it [the *Community*] and the *Reality Compendium* constitute the entire yoga tantra class. Further, the *Reality Compendium*, tending toward the "father" side, taking art and wisdom as father and mother, is also a father tantra according to the *One Hundred Fifty Ways Commentary*. [15a] Also, in the sixteenth chapter of the *Illuminating Lamp*, it is said concerning some topics of the consecrations that they should be understood from the *Reality Compendium*. Such are explained or designated intending the fact that the primary basis is contained there.

Here one might object that, if a further tantra is said to be a later explanation of an original subject, then there are fallacies such as: the concise teaching of the meaning of the tantra in the first chapter of the *Community* itself stands in relation to the next sixteen chapters, which elucidate it as a root tantra to a further tantra, and even that each succeeding chapter is a further tantra to the last one; if you do not say that such is the criterion of a further tantra, then you must say what is [the criterion]!

[As for the third context, concerning the meaning of "root tantra," in terms of the explanatory tantra, as in the usages "root" and "explanatory"]: there are many methods of setting up a further tantra in general; here let us explain the criterion for setting up the *Community Further Tantra*. The *Eighteenth Chapter* is both part of the *Community Tantra* and also was spoken later than the *Community Root Tantra*, and it elucidates the general meaning of the whole seventeen-chapter root tantra as well as the hidden difficulties of each chapter. Hence it is called the *Community Further Tantra*. Therefore, there is no fallacy of each succeeding chapter becoming the "further tantra" of its preceding chapter.

Regarding the explanatory tantras of the *Community*, the noble father and sons have explicitly mentioned five: the *Five Stages* states that the *Four Goddess Dialogue*, the *Revelation of the Hidden Intention*, and the *Vajra Rosary* are explanatory tantras; the *Lamp of Integrated Practices* states that the *Wisdom Vajra Compendium* is an explanatory tantra; and the *Illuminating Lamp* explicitly mentions the *King of the Gods Dialogue* as the source of the explanation of the first two syllables of the prologue [E VAṀ . . .]. But, since there appears in just that latter [text, the *Illuminating Lamp*], the statement that "the explanation [15b] of the remaining syllables [can be learned] from the explanatory tantras . . . ," it is not the case that the *King of the Gods Dialogue* is explicitly identified as an explanatory tantra. Further, it does not seem that the father and sons explicitly mentioned the *[Community] Eighteenth Chapter* as an explanatory tantra, although they did mention it as a further tantra. However, it must be accepted as an explanatory tantra, as Thagana [Siddha] and Jinadatta [Pandita] so accepted it.

There are some who believe the *Vajra Essence Ornament Tantra* and the *Magic Net* to be explanatory tantras, but they are not, though they do correspond with the *Community*. The *Four Goddess Dialogue Commentary* mentions a further tantra within the *Supreme of All Secrets 1,000*. The *Vajra Rosary Commentary* explains that there are two *Vajra Rosary* tantras, a 12,000 and a smaller one, and that the *Wisdom Vajra Compendium* also has a greater and a smaller, explaining that the previously quoted *Vajra Rosary* has 300,000 verses. As for the *Revelation of the Hidden Intention*, it was not translated as more than an explanatory tantra of the first twelve chapters of the *Root Tantra*.

[**I.C.2.b.** – Showing the way in which the explanatory tantras explain]

The second has two parts: [i.] How the *Further Tantra* and the *Revelation of the Hidden Intention* explain; and [ii.] How the [other] three, such as the *Vajra Rosary*, explain.

[**I.C.2.b.i.** – How the *Further Tantra* and the *Revelation of the Hidden Intention* Explain]

The other *Community* explanatory tantras explain it but are not themselves the *Community Tantra*, whereas the *Further Tantra* is both. As for how it explains the *Root Tantra*, its explanation of the [16a] common meanings of the tantra lies in its dialogues about: the meaning of the name of the tantra, *Glorious Esoteric Community Yoga Tantra*, its classification as an art tantra, and the general scheme of the tantra. Its other sections explain particular points from each of the seventeen chapters.

This commentary, inquiring into the [very practice of] elucidating the tantra, is the most perfect elucidation, arranging ingeniously all the meanings of the tantra. It was admired by Nāropa, since it is so splendid. In response to the inquiry, it is explained that, of the four groups of four chapters from the second to the seventeenth, each teaches one of the branches of service and practice. Nāropa explained also that the first chapter gives the tantra's import in brief and the other sixteen chapters explain the four branches of service and practice, and the eighteenth teaches the esoteric instruction for all of them. These chapters do not distinguish the two stages, but teach the four branches of service and practice in common for the two stages. However, [the *Further Tantra*] teaches the four branches of service and practice distinguishing between the two stages in the context of [explaining] the category of "art tantra." Each explanatory tantra has its own way of explaining the *Root Tantra* due to its [author's] particular orientation toward a special emphasis. But this *Further Tantra* explains the *Root Tantra* according to the four branches of service and practice set forth in the twelfth chapter. It is said in the *Dialogue on the Glorious Meaning of the Commentary* that the sixteen chapters explain the four branches, and the inquiries into the individual chapters are included in that. [16b]

The inquiry into the classification as art tantra is the very same as the inquiry into the meaning of the name. Thus, as the general import is included in the inquiry into the meaning of the name, it can be implied that the *Root Tantra* text can be explained mainly as explaining the name of the tantra; which is a cause of extreme wonderment! Here, since it is difficult to discern how the four-chapter sections explain the four branches of practice and service, one must know how to explain the *Root Tantra* through a good understanding of how to elucidate this, how to discern the boundaries of the four branches in each of the two stages, and especially how to explain the six branches of service of the perfection stage. And it appears that understanding how the noble system explains the *Further Tantra* depends on the same commentary of Nāropa.

The *Revelation of the Hidden Intention [Tantra]* orders its chapters in the same way as in the *Root Tantra*, and mentions almost everything mentioned in the *Root Tantra*'s chapters, so that it serves as a commentary elucidating the difficult points of each chapter. It concisely states that "such and such is the import taught by each of the seventeen chapters of this *Root Tantra*." It indicates how it is improper to explain the *Community* always literally, and elucidates the hidden definitive meanings of the interpretable meaning statements. It explains thoroughly the intentional interpretations given to one import by other [apparently] contradictory statements.

It clearly teaches most often the vajra-recitation practice hidden in the *Root Tantra* in almost every chapter. Therefore, emphasizing this [17a] recitation practice it explains the *Root Tantra* according to those procedures. In the *Illuminating Lamp* most quotes "from the *Explanatory Tantra*" are from this source, quoted as emphasizing the definitive-meaning explanations.

[I.C.2.b.ii. – How the (other) three, such as the *Vajra Rosary,* explain]

The *Vajra Rosary Short Tantra* [translations] have three different ways of dividing its chapters 19 and 20. The *Commentary* explains that, at the beginning of chapter 19 [of the *Vajra Rosary*], from [the lines]:

> Then still more should be explained,
> The self-instantaneous in variety, and so on . . .

up to [the lines]:

> . . . Various aspects are eagerly accepted

except for nine quarter-verses, the text of the end of the nineteenth chapter did not extend further, and "was left here." After that, from [the line]:

> Then yet another should be explained . . .

up to [the line]:

> . . . This should be understood from the succession of
> mentors . . .

is taken as the twentieth chapter. In general, the *Commentary* takes it to have sixty-eight chapters.[18]

The translation of the Lha Lama Zhiwa Öd is the same as above, up to "various aspects are eagerly desired," but after that it takes out the verses from "Gazing, attracting, and also signaling, know the experience of kiss-

18. Though the commentary as we have it in the Tengyur today only includes explanations of forty-four chapters, and the commentary quotes often diverge from the verses in the translation of the root text. See D. Kittay, *The Vajra Rosary Tantra*, forthcoming.

ing and its delight" up to "experiencing the orgasmic joy, an instant free from identity" and makes them the nineteenth chapter, the analysis of instantaneity. Then it takes the verses from "Then yet another should be explained, the character of the four joys . . ." up to "naturally born in the circle of emanations, let one experience joy" [17b] as the twentieth chapter, the analysis of the character of joy. In general, it has sixty-eight chapters.

As for the Zhiwa Öd translation revised by Darma Tsöndru, it is the same up to "various aspects are accepted," and afterward it repeats the verses from "Then yet another should be explained, the character of the four joys" up to "naturally born in the circle of emanations, let one experience joy." After that it repeats from "Gaze, attract, and also signal" up to "the experience of natural joy, an instant free of identity." And after that, from "The great space of all the channels" up to "the experience of natural joy, an instant free of identity," and from "The great space of all the channels" up to "it should be known from the mentor succession"—it takes all these as the nineteenth chapter, the nature of the universal joy, and generally takes it to have sixty-seven chapters.

Thus, though there appear to be many such variations, the chapter divisions of the translation by Sujana Shrījñāna and Zhiwa Öd and the Indian book of Pandita Mantrakalasha seem to be correct; because there is evident in the text both one passage explaining the four instants in forward and reverse order and another passage explaining the four joys in forward and reverse order; because the "Gaze, prod, [18a] and also signal," and so forth, is obviously an addition to "various forms are eagerly accepted"; and because the words "Yet another now should be explained" are said to be the chapter's opening words in many other chapters.

In this tantra, Vajrapāni wishes—while referring to the *Vajra Rosary*—to inquire into the two stages, which are unclearly stated only by symbols in the *Esoteric Community,* and precedes his speech by the expression "Please teach mainly from the point of view of the perfection stage." He then asks his questions concerning topics from the meaning of the name of the *Vajra Rosary* up to the nature and the way of destruction of the energies. The answers to those questions explain most of the meanings of the *Community* and also many meanings of the yoginī tantras, such as the *[Unexcelled] Clear Articulation 100,000*, although those explanations are given mostly as a factor of decisively determining the import of the *Community.* The number of the questions and answers is said by the *Commentary* to be eighty-two.

What does this tantra explain of the *Community* text in plain terms?

While it explains much of the *Root Tantra*'s third chapter and sixth chapter statements about the meditation of the mustard-seed-size jewels at the nose tips, chiefly this tantra explains the meaning of each syllable of the prologue "E VAṀ MA YA," and so on, the forty syllables that the *Illuminating Lamp* says contain all the meanings of the tantra, each by a verse such as "E is the holy wisdom. . . ."

Those texts [18b] teach mainly body isolation, speech isolation, mind isolation, and the magic body, also teaching repeatedly in other contexts the clear light and communion; thus teaching the complete perfection stage. The scheme of that path is taken as the five stages because that same text [the *Vajra Rosary*] declares:

> Through application to the vajra recitation,
> Knowing the nature of the energies,
> Cut off the energies of mental constructions,
> You will attain the mind objective.
> And by the stage of blessing the self,
> The eight accomplishments will be achieved.
> Know the divisions of luminance and so on,
> And you will attain clear realization.
> Abiding on the stage of communion,
> The yogi/nī should have no doubt
> S/he will achieve in this very life
> The gathering of all attainments.

The savior Nāgārjuna, in condensing the perfection stage into the five stages, follows this tantra, and also follows this tantra in the three samadhis, the four yogas, the thirty-two deities, and so forth on the creation stage. Therefore, when His Holiness [Nāgārjuna] in the *Condensed [Sādhana]* becomes an [alchemical] churner, he "churns the ocean of hidden waters of the *Esoteric Community* with the churning stick of the *Vajra Rosary*."[19] Thus his statement about finding the art of the practice of the *Community* was not just referring to the creation stage. It explains the many stages

19. This is a paraphrase from Nāgārjuna's *Condensed Sādhana* (Tōh. 1796; Derge rGyud 'Grel, NGI: 10b.7).

of creation and dissolution of the body in terms of the channel structure, energy-movement, and enlightenment-spirit substance as a factor in the decisive ascertainment [19a] of the internal and external vitalizing energy controls for bringing forth the four voids and the magic body, depending on the vitalizing energy controls of the outer seal of the hidden discipline of desire and of the vajra recitation, and so on. Beyond those two techniques, it further explains the limitless ways for the dawning of realization and so forth. It also declares many things such as the scheme of consecrations for attaining receptivity for the path condensed into twenty rites, the schemes for condensing the creation stage, and the determinations of the sequence of the two stages. Especially, the sixth chapter explains the keys for the vitalizing energy-control vajra recitation to open up the knot of the heart channels, and the twenty-second chapter section that collects the definitive meaning mantras of the three syllables explains how the unraveling of the heart-channel knot is the supreme unraveling of a channel knot of all the wheels [of channels]. It seems that such excellent elucidation is rarely seen.

This tantra's dominant emphasis in elucidating the *Community* lies in its clear extraction of the hidden meaning of the *Community* by explaining the meaning of each of the syllables of the prologue. Now, the way in which the other texts of the explanatory tantras become factors in deciding that very same thing must be known from the perspective of the interpretation of the schemes of the two stages. Therefore, I must somewhat explain that below. The statement from the translator's colophon of this text that "among explanatory tantras a better one than this has not previously appeared" still seems to be just how it is.

The *Four Goddess Dialogue* chiefly explains in detail the keys of the vitalizing energy-control yogas. The *Wisdom Vajra Compendium* [19b] teaches the seven ornaments, the ultimate in private instruction explaining the unexcelled yoga tantras, taking the *Community* as chief. And here, clearer than in any other explanatory tantra, is explained the attainment of the three voids and the magic body from there. The details of how these two tantras explain the *Community* will not be mentioned here, as I have already explained them in the extensive commentaries of those two texts.[20]

20. These commentaries as we have them do not seem that "extensive." One wonders whether the full transcription of the lectures Tsong Khapa gave on them is no longer extant.

Thus, inquiring thoroughly into the texts containing the private instructions of the holy father and son, with the key for easily extracting the pith of the meaning, discerning accurately with the help of the explanatory tantras the meanings sealed behind the door of the *Root Tantra* by the six parameters and four procedures, one should be able to open the door of the *Root Tantra*. One then becomes one who has the personal precept granting confidence in personal tantric instruction. And knowing how to apply the reasoning to other tantras in that way, as well, one becomes an expert in all tantras.

[**II.** – Expression of the greatness of the *Community*]

The *Root Tantra*, when mentioning the name, declares that this tantra unites all the secrets of body, speech, and mind of all the transcendent buddhas; [it] shows that all the essentials of the secrets of the vajra vehicle are united here. The *Further Tantra* also declares:

> Emaho! Extremely hard to find,
> This is the art of attaining enlightenment.
> It is the furthest of the further tantras;
> It is called the *Esoteric Community*.

It declares that, because of its rarity and importance, when performing the [intensive] four-session yoga, in studying, investigating, and worshipping, one should regard Bodhicittavajra as just like Vajradhara [20a] and salute him. Moreover, one who is the prince of practitioners of that tantra, who sees, hears, remembers, touches, and has faith in it, up to one who holds even the merest portion of the tantra, should be regarded as like Vajradhara and saluted. Thus, the *Further Tantra* states:

> Those who practice the vajras of four sessions—
> Attaining the superior and inferior varieties [of powers] such
> as invisibility,
> Realizing this unerring path by the grace of the
> buddha-mentor—
> Seeing them as like Bodhivajra, we worship them always!

Those who learn this very *Esoteric Community Tantra*—
Who recite it, read it, contemplate it,
Worship it, write it, and have it written—
Seeing them like Bodhivajra, we worship them always!

And it also declares:

Those who are master practitioners—seeing, contacting,
Remembering well, learning, indeed, even the name,
Generating faith, and living in even a part—
Seeing them like Bodhivajra, we worship them always!

The *Personal Instruction of Mañjushrī* praises the tantra as:

The tantra that unites all buddhas,
The great secret, the secret of great secrets,
Unexcelled great teaching . . .

and states that the measure of the duration of the essence of the [buddha] teaching is whether or not this very tantra exists:

This import, when it goes into the ear,
And for however long it endures there,
The jewel teaching of the Buddha
Is proclaimed to be enduring.
When the sequence of this succession is broken,
All will know it is the decline
Of the [20b] Buddha's teaching.

Not only has such emerged in those treatises concerned with this tantra, it has also been praised in other tantras as well. Both the *Red [Yamāri]* and the *Black [Yamāri] Tantra* declared:

The ultimate in tantras is the *Community*—
Nothing like it in the past, nor in the future.

The *Esoteric Accomplishment* also states:

> There is nothing superior to the *Glorious Community*,
> Which is the jewel of the three worlds.
> The supreme essence of the essence,
> The unexcelled of the unexcelled of all the tantras.
>
> Abiding in the teaching and the explanation
> Is the very stage of the yoga of perfection.
> Who do not know this *Community*,
> How can such as they attain accomplishment?
>
> Cutting off all doubts,
> Dispelling all fogs of unknowing,
> This is the treasure-case for the jewel of the Buddha.
> Abandoning utterly this *Glorious Community*,
>
> Fantasizing with many mental constructs,
> Deluded, yet desiring accomplishments,
> Is like punching one's fist at the sky
> Or like drinking the water of a mirage!

The *Illuminating Lamp* also declares:

> Up to *Ya Ra La Ha*,
> Those [tantras] ending *Ka Kha Gha*, those ending *Na Ja*,
> Those ending *Tra Dhra* and *Ma*,
> Their root is the three syllables.[21]
>
> This *Glorious Community* is the jewel case
> Of all eighty-four thousand of the heaps

21. The Sanskrit version includes more final letters; ya, ra, la, ha, ka, kha, gha, ṇa, jha, da, dha, ma. The "three syllables" seem to be the names of the tantra, *sa ma ja* (*Community*), though Tsong Khapa mentions below that Nāropa interpreted them here as being the three buddha seeds, OṀ ĀḤ HŪṀ.

Of the teachings of the great sage.
Therefore, it is the summit of the tantras.

Thus, Chandrakīrti declares that this tantra is the summit of all the tantras, being the root of all the other tantras and the treasure-case of all the sutras.

The *Wisdom Vajra Compendium* explains that tantras ending with each letter such as KA are numbered each [21a] 1,000, stating that in terms of all four of the tantra divisions. This statement of being the root of the tantras whose names end in the consonant letters is a mere example, and the masters Bhavyakīrti and Kumāra explain that it means that it is also the root of all tantras whose names end in vowels as well. The "three syllables" mentioned in "their root is the three syllables" are explained by Nāropa to be the three [buddha] seeds. The former of these is explained in the *Further Tantra* as the three secrets of body, speech, and mind, which are united in the *Esoteric Community*; thus, the *Community Tantra* is identified from the perspective of what it is uniting. Not taking this [instrument of uniting] as referring to the *Community Tantra*, but explaining it as coming down to the three vajras, the three syllables that are the import of all tantras, would be to ignore the context, since that statement teaches that the *Community Tantra* is the root of all the tantras.

As for the meaning of "root," just as a tree has many leaves and branches but comes down to the place of the root, so the tantras have many various meanings, but the ultimate essentials of all of them finally come down to the path of the *Community*—this is the meaning. And the meaning of "jewel case of all the sutras" is just the same. This teaches that if one knows how to explain this path completely, there is nothing better than that.

Kṛshnāchārya praised the intensive path of the *Community* with regard to both stages, from the perspective of its being the chief of all the tantras, as has been previously quoted. [21b] There are no degrees of superior and inferior among the unexcelled yoga tantras, as among the three lower tantra divisions, from the point of view of the stages [of practice]. Yet it is not that there are no degrees of superiority with regard to certain other distinctions. For example, a certain tantra can be superior or inferior [in clarity, specificity, and so on] within a grouping of texts that explain the two stages, and yet have no degree of superiority or inferiority with regard to the stages [of practice] of that tantra.

[**III.** – The process of elucidating the inner intention of that (*Esoteric Community*)]

The treatises composed by Indrabhūti the Greater,[22] Nāgaḍākinī, and the Earth-Lord Visukalpa have not appeared here [in Tibet], but the glorious savior Mahāsukhanātha [Padmavajra] composed the *Esoteric Accomplishment* to determine the meaning of the *Community*. Among the passages of the *Community*, this treatise mainly determines the meaning of the opening. It teaches the four meditations with their [appropriate] actions as the following stages of the path: first, the creation stage that sets up the syllables; second, characterizing your own nature as thatness while depending on the action seal; third, meditating depending on the intuition-seal in order to stabilize [that designation of your nature]; and fourth, meditation on the realization of the great seal. This text counts the deities of the mandala contained within this [fourfold process] to be seventeen. The text itself [of the *Esoteric Accomplishment*] states:

> The [mandala] definitely becomes perfect by the sequence of seventeen bodhisattvas . . .

—that is, it seems that he merely thought about "completion through seventeen [bodhisattva deities]." However, in the context of the assembly, the *Illuminating Lamp* states at the opening:

> There it is taught by just that many, the circle of deities is complete.

22. According to Paul Hackett, there are possibly as many as three Indrabhūtis in the canon: (1) Mahendrabhūti (*indra bhū ti chen po*), identified by Bhattacharyya (*Two Vajrayana Works*, p. xi) as the (step-)father of Padmasambhava and student of Anaṅgavajra (p. vii), who authored at least one text on Vajrayoginī (Tōh. 1546), (2) Madhyamendrabhūti (*indra bhū ti 'bring po*), who authored the *Śrī-sahajaśambara-svādhiṣṭhāna* (*dpal lhan skyes pa bde ba'i mchog bdag byin gyis brlabs pa*; Tōh. 1459), a Chakrasaṁvara-related text, and (3) an otherwise undistinguished "Indrabhūti" who authored several texts on the *Vajrapañjara-tantra*, *Cakrasaṁvara*, *Vajrayoginī*, *Sarvabuddhasamāyoga*, *Vajrasattva*, *Guhyagarbha*, and others.

This indicates that the mandala of thirty-two deities [22a] is not asserted [by Mahāsukhanātha]. Therefore, that refers just to the circle of buddhas, buddhesses, heroes, and heroines that completes the mandala of deities—just that much is taught in the prologue. The previous meaning is that he took everyone directly mentioned in the opening except the five families' [lords], and his point is that those [seventeen] complete the directly mentioned bodhisattva circle. This *Esoteric Accomplishment* is renowned as the "paradigm of all the other six of the accomplishment divisions," called the "Essence of Accomplishment." It also appears to be the paradigm of the *Enlightenment Song* of the Great Brahmin [Saraha] concerning essence. These are extremely important in understanding the essence of all the unexcelled tantras as the orgasmic intuitive wisdom uniting bliss and void. It does not appear that master Saraha made a special commentary on the *Esoteric Community*.

The great soul Nāgārjuna composed an elucidation of the meaning of the *Community*. We will explain his system's way of elucidation.

Master Lalitavajra composed an explanation of the tantra's prologue only, and does not appear to have treated separately the style of the path of the two stages.

Then the disciple of Lalitavajra, the great master Jñānapada, received the explanation of the meaning of the *Community* from the noble Mañjushrī [in person], and the stages [as given in his work] are renowned as the system of Jñānapada. There are two stages in his path: his creation stage having a mandala of nineteen deities headed by Mañjuvajra, according to the explanations in the *Samantabhadra Sādhana*, and in [22b] the *Four Hundred Fifty*. His perfection stage is given in the *Personal Instruction* taught by His Holiness [Mañjushrī], and in the *Liberation Drop* composed by the master himself.

From the *Personal Instruction*, at the beginning of meditating the perfection stage he explains the meditation of the indestructible drop in the heart; the branch of "vitalizing energy control" called the "branch of stopping the breath" in the meditation of the secret drop on the gem; how meditating that produces the branch of restraint called the "endurance" branch; then the branch of "mindfulness" meditating the sixteen mindfulnesses; then the vajra recitation called the emanation drop; and finally the repeated meditation of the indestructible drop in the heart center, meditated exclusively in terms of the intuitive orgasmic wisdom. It seems that this [master] explains only the last four of the six branches, leaving out the two branches "retraction" and "contemplation" that are in the *Further Tantra*. The implication of such a method of explanation is that he seems to consider that those two should be included in the creation stage, just as in the Jñānapada system's texts on the six-branched yoga, where retraction and contemplation are taught in the creation stage.

In the context of this [system], as the import of the statements in the *Further Tantra* that the ordinary service is the "four vajras" and the superior service is the "six branches," it is not that [master Jñānagarbha] considers the superior service and the creation stage to be mutually exclusive. Here in the context of the perfection stage, he seems to take the *Further Tantra* as his basis to compose [his commentary] condensing [the import of] the *Four Goddess Dialogue* and the *Vajra Essence Ornament [Tantra]*. Those [23a] in this tradition who wrote commentaries of the *Root Tantra* do not seem often[23] to [use the] explanations of the *Further Tantra*, but neither do they seem to use the ways of explanation of the other explanatory tantras. Especially, the practical instruction texts based on the *Personal Instruction* and the *Liberation Drop* have a way of teaching the perfection stage with many texts of the *Root Tantra*, and should explain the last four of the six branches of the *Further Tantra* in agreement with the *Personal Instruction* and the *Liberation Drop*; yet they seem not to explain in such a way.

The [idea that] the master Ānandagarbha composed a *Great Commentary* on the *Community*, changing its [standard] way of explanation in coarse and subtle ways, is said without examining that very commentary, and is incorrect. The *Commentary* translated by the Great Translator [Rinchen Zangpo] was [said to be] written by Ānandagarbha, [but] its explanation of the fifth chapter was included in the commentary of master Vimalagupta, and so that [work of Ānandagarbha's] cannot be the source [of the translation].[24]

23. The text literally says, "*rgyud phyi mar ma bshad pa cher mi snang na 'ang . . .*" adding a confusing extra negative where a single negative better fits the sense, apparently duplicating the second syllable of "further" (*phyi ma*).

24. Tsong Khapa here rejects the *Great Commentary* attributed to Ānandagarbha, since its interpretations are very different from Ānandagarbha's usual. He discounts the fact that Rinchen Zangpo translated a commentary by Ānandagarbha (or also falsely attributed to him), giving evidence that its fifth chapter is quoted in Vimalagupta's Commentary

All this [master's] explanations about the use of the physical consort are just made to attract some followers of the Vishṇu tantras who cannot give up attachment to the objects of sense. All statements about keeping the pledge to eat feces and urine are just made for the benefit of those involved in fake tantras and goblin tantras. Neither are made for the more gifted disciples, as is explained. He does not teach the science explained in others' explanation of the perfection [23b] stage: the yogas of the channels, energies, and drops. Thinking of these facts, the Tibetan master scholars said that Ānandagarbha elucidated the *Esoteric Community* as "yoga." Here it appears that his style of explanation of unexcelled tantra was in disagreement with the explanations of the other great Indians.

Master Shāntipa holds that the first chapter of the *Root Tantra* teaches the tantra of art-generated fruition, and the other four arts of the tantra that are the means of attaining that are taught in the other sixteen chapters. The four "triple" chapters teach service; the four "double" chapters teach practice; the four "perfected" chapters teach "performance"; the four "ecstatic" chapters teach "great realization";[25] and the *Further Tantra* illuminates all of them. This master explains the seventh chapter's meaning by relying on the *Further Tantra*, giving the nineteen deity [mandala] presided over by Akshobhya on the first stage, and the method of six-branch perfection stage practiced after achieving a stable creation stage in a way quite different from the Jñānapada, noble [Ārya], and *Time Machine* systems. His other explanations seem to be given following Jñānapada, even though they do not seem to do so explicitly in specific cases. However, I do not enlarge on this, as it seems incidental to the purpose of my elucidation.

Thus, one should understand the champions' systems of elucidating the *Glorious Community* to be the two famous systems of the noble [Ārya] and of Jñānapada.

(who lived earlier than Ānandagarbha). According to the Dharma Index, the colophons of Butön, Narthang, Peking, and Derge all agree with Tsong Khapa that this was not by Ānandagarbha. They attribute it to a Prabhāva/Āryagarbha.

25. *Seva, anusādhana, sādhana,* and *mahāsādhana* as service, practice, performance, and great realization. Describing the four sets of four chapters each as *gsum ldan, gnyis ldan, rdzogs ldan, dga ba can* is of a meaning I do not know. One theory of Gen Jamspal is that the first three refer to cosmic time periods.

[**IV.** – Enumeration of the treatises in the noble (Ārya) literature]

The fourth has three parts: [A.] How the treatises of the noble father [24a] and son were composed; [B.] How the treatises of the other three sons were composed; and [C.] How the treatises of their followers were composed.

[**IV.A.** – How the treatises of the noble father and son were composed]

Concerning how treatises were authored by the noble [Nāgārjuna] on the subject of the *Community*, the *Illuminating Lamp [Intention] Elucidation* mentions that he wrote the *Condensed [Sādhana]*, the *[Performance] Incorporating the [Community] Sutras*,[26] the *Performance of Hūṁkāra*, the *Five Stages*, the *Tantra Commentary*, and so forth. Now as for the currently existing *Community Commentary* said to be authored by the noble [Nāgārjuna], Tibetan scholars say it was made in Tibet by a certain [Indian] pandit. It cites the *Mirror of Poetry*, the *Reason in Elucidation*, the *Treasury of Clear Science*, and so on. In its conclusion, it is written:

> Awakening through meditation on the Bliss Lord state of
> the supreme Victor,
> I stay in the place of my self, the savior Jñānapada, and so on.

Further, many of the elucidations of the tantra appear to disagree with the treatises of the noble father and son. Therefore, the claim of authorship by the noble [Nāgārjuna] is just spurious.

So while he wrote the *Condensed [Sādhana]* and the *[Performance] Incorporating the [Community] Sutras* to teach the creation stage, former Tibetan masters thought the *Mandala Rite 20* was also his, and [Bhāvyakīrti, in] his *Illuminating Lamp Intention Elucidation*, also asserts that there is a *Mandala Rite* by the noble master [Nāgārjuna], and it seems [Bhāvyakīrti] was thinking mainly of this text. Later Tibetan authors considered this a spuri-

26. The *Sūtramelāpaka* is actually a tantric performance text (*sādhana*) that incorporates quotations (*sūtras*) from the *Community Tantra* to ground this sādhana in that tantra. Wedemeyer (CW, p. 50) and others have noted this and given the text a new English name, which I have followed here in modified form.

ous attribution, since the text often disagreed with Nāgabodhi's *[Mandala] Rite 20*, which was taken as authoritative by so many Indian pandits, and it even disagrees with the master's [24b] own treatises, which seem to be correct.

Concerning the perfection stage, the *Vajra Recitation Stage [of the Five Stages]* is extremely famous, and he composed the *Disclosure of the Spirit of Enlightenment* to elucidate the spirit of enlightenment proclaimed by Vairochana in the second chapter of the *Root Tantra*. There is also a commentary on this by Smṛti, and many pandits such as Abhaya cite it as an authority. In the Great Translator's translations of the *Five Stages* texts, including the *Vajra Recitation Stage* and so on, all five chapters of the single text called *Five Stages* were recorded as composed by the noble [master]. However, there is also a tradition that the *Second Stage* [*Vajra Recitation Stage* text] was composed by Shākyamitra, it being so recorded in the commentaries of Lakshmī as well as in the commentary *Jewel Rosary* [attributed to Nāgabodhi]. The translator Chag translated the five sections as separate texts.[27]

Concerning this, in the text itself it is certain that the noble master himself composed five stages, because the dedications concerning authorship of the *Five Stages* found at the ends of the [texts on the] third stage, "Self-consecration," the fourth, "Manifest Enlightenment," and the fifth, "Communion" [mention each as one of "the *Five Stages*"]. Yet, since Abhaya and Samayavajra explain in their commentaries that the noble master's disciple Shākyamitra composed the *Second Stage*, we must accept the "condensed [sādhana]" as one stage of the five, as they attest. Munishrībhadra also asserts this. In Lakshmī's commentary, he gives two explanations: his own, in which the master himself wrote the *Second Stage*, his adept's name being Nāgārjuna and his monk's name being Shākyamitra; and someone else's, in which, while the master [25a] himself wrote it, he attached his disciple's name to it as a sign of being greatly pleased with him. In the commentary

27. For these reasons, and for the reasons further articulated below, at some times Tsong Khapa will refer to and cite the *Five Stages* as a single, unified text comprised of five chapters (including, e.g., the "second stage chapter"), while at other times he will refer to and cite the individual "chapters" (particularly the second) as independent texts (e.g., "the *Second Stage* states . . ."). Our formatting and indexing herein reflects this ambiguity (within the index of cited texts we have created cross-references between the relevant related textual citations, viz. the *Five Stages*, the *Second Stage*, the *Third Stage*, and the *Fourth Stage*). Cited passages from all such chapters/texts are identified in the extant unified canonical version—the Sanskrit *Pañcakrama*, and the Tibetan *rim pa lnga pa* (Tōh. 1802).

Jewel Rosary [attributed to Nāgabodhi], it is said to be optional, according either to the former or the latter explanation.

In this regard, in the other three [perfection] stage [texts], there are offering verses and author's commitments, but no final dedications, since [Nāgārjuna] composed a common dedication for all of them at the end of the last stage [text]. And since he made a separate dedication at the end of the *Condensed [Sādhana]*, and [since it] corresponds with the summary of all five stages occurring in the context of the summary in the *Vajra Recitation Stage*, all five texts teaching the perfection stage are similar insofar as being composed by the noble [master].

Well then, why is it explained that the *Second Stage* was written by Shākyamitra?

It does not seem that this was entirely composed by the noble master, since [if so] its alternative explanations of "By the noble vajra's kindness, many tantras were heard" would seem incorrect; since it is supplied with a separate dedication in the end; and since, if the noble master had composed all of this second stage, his apparent explaining in that context of many things to be explained in the context of the "Clear Light"[28] [fourth] and "Communion" [fifth chapters] would seem improper. On the other hand, if the entire chapter was composed by the noble [master]'s disciple, Shākyamitra, statements such as "The noble master condensed the perfection stage into five stages" would seem incorrect, and it is obvious that the reference of Āryadeva's [25b] two citations [from the *Second Stage* text] as "according to the *guru's intention*" would be inaccurate. [Therefore,] since some have suggested that the beginning was written by the noble [Nāgārjuna] and the remainder he allowed Shākyamitra to compose with his authorization, those of both great and subtle intellects should reflect upon it.

If we accept it that way, the single text called the "*Five Stages*" is taken to have five chapters, including the first portion of the second stage [chapter], and we can infer that, of the two names of the second stage [chapter], the name given by the noble master is the "*Unexcelled Intention*." If we do not interpret in that way, then the *Five Stages* cannot be taken as a single text, since the *Condensed [Sādhana]* is a separate text, and because the *Second*

28. The fourth stage is sometimes called "manifest enlightenment" and sometimes "clear light."

Stage [text] has a different author. Furthermore, if it is according to that, the statement in the colophon of the first chapter, "This is the first, the stage of vajra recitation," would become improper to leave alone.

In any case, one knows from the "Vajra Recitation Stage" [chapter] that the noble master condensed [the perfection stage] into five, making the "Mind Objective" the second stage; and that also appears to be the intention of the *Stage of Arrangement*.

Again, the sages of Tibet assert the falsity of the position that the noble master composed the *Determination of the Meaning of the Four Initiations*, as the claim that "The noble one composed the stages of the four seals" is refuted in the *Sheaf of Instructions* and the *Commentary Boat*. Nevertheless, Vimalamitra and his followers accept [those texts] as being by the noble [Nāgārjuna].

In regard to the works of Āryadeva, [26a] his *Lamp of Integrated Practices* is greatly famous as the import commentary of the *Five Stages*, and master Abhaya cites his *Self-Consecration Stage* as an authoritative source. Though claimed to be a discussion of the mind isolation, his *Purification of the Mind's Obstructions* is a tantric text teaching mainly about the mind, but is not specifically an *Esoteric Community* text. This [text] is also taken to be authoritative by Abhayākara.

In regard to the claim that this master [Āryadeva] composed the *Manifest Enlightenment Stage*, the Tibetan sages allowed that it seems somewhat controversial. But since it seems to disagree greatly with the *Integrated Practices*, [it is definitely] a false attribution. Again, the Tibetan sages considered there to be some ground for investigation in the claims that this master composed a so-called *Four Procedures of Explanation*, *Ya Ra La Wa, And So On*, and a *Rite of Burning Corpses*. The first of these [texts] comments on the two verses of the *Illuminating Lamp* [beginning] "Up to *Ya Ra La Ha* . . . ,"[29] cites the *Integrated Practices* [itself] as a source, states that the *Vajra Summit*, the *Vajra Rosary*, and the *Revelation of the Hidden Intention* are root tantras, [which Āryadeva would not have done]; also it seems to have singled out the explanation of the four procedures of explanation

29. See above, p. 68 (Tib. 20b). There does not seem to be such a work in the Tengyur, and Tsong Khapa here, though he refers to a text accessible to him, indicates it to be a later work perhaps written in Tibet, referring to a very late Indian commentary on the *Illuminating Lamp*.

concerning *ya ra la wa* and so on in master Kuladhara's commentary on the *Illuminating Lamp*,[30] which means it cannot be a work of Āryadeva. As for the latter [text], it also is obviously false.

[**IV.B.** – How the treatises of the other three sons were composed]

Second, in regard to the works of Nāgabodhi or Nāgabuddhi, his *Stage of Arrangement* is very famous, emphasizing the creation stage, though teaching also the perfection stage. His *Mandala Rite 20* was taken as authoritative by many pandits such as Rāhulashrīmitra, Abhayākara, Karunashrīpāda, and [26b] Munishrībhadra. The *Terminal Action Investigation*—which determines the four voids—is taken as authoritative [by Chandrakīrti] in the *Illuminating Lamp*. However, in the translation we have nowadays, there are 160 instinctual imaginations explained in the summary; in the detailed explanation, the eighty instincts are not completely listed, and it seems to abbreviate them into fifty-four instincts; so it seems to have the faults of an incorrect Tibetan book or of a translation of a faulty Indian text.

There are many texts falsely attributed to this master; there are three commentaries on the *Five Stages* claimed to be his: the *Jewel Rosary*, the *Clear Meaning*, and the *Concise Source on the Stages*. The first of these was accepted as authority by many Tibetan mentors, but [then] more contemporary sages considered it and the *Clear Meaning* false. In the first one, there are many things in its way of elucidating the *Community* that disagree with the noble father and son: it seems to claim that the text of Buddhajñānapāda, a disciple of the master Haribhadra who accepted Chandrakīrti's text as authority, was the text of Nāgabodhi, itself accepted as authority by Chandrakīrti; and it seems to be unable to determine decisively whether Nāgārjuna or his disciple Shākyamitra wrote the *Second Stage*. So it seems merely falsely attributed to Nāgabodhi. Also the claim that the commentary, *Clear Meaning*, was composed by him is merely a false attribution.

30. Tsong Khapa here refers to a text that we no longer have. Kuladhara is not in the *Dharma Index*, Tōh. cat., or the *Blue Annals*. *Krama Tantricism of Kashmir* (vol. 1, p. 156) by Navjivan Rastogi (a book on Kashmiri Shaivism) has this entry: "*Kuladhara* (950–1000 A.D.). We know nothing about him except that he directly came into the line of the Stotrakāra after Bhāskara. He, therefore, appears to be a contemporary of Abhinavagupta." TL 28b says he is a Kashmiri, and 29b names this commentary he wrote on the *Illuminating Lamp*.

The *Concise Source on the Stages* was accepted as Nāgabodhi's by Tibetan sages, though the translator Chag asserted it was written by another scholar of the same name "Nāgabodhi." [27a] This text claims that the six stages from creation stage up to communion stage each has six [recapitulative] stages within itself, just as in the *Ornament of Realizations* each of the six transcendences has six [transcendences] within itself. When the pattern of such containment is explained, though, it seems that each stage has five meditative stages within it; it is not made definite. For example, in the context of mind isolation, there is stated the creation stage of creating the deity from moon and vajra etc., and this is asserted to be the "mind-isolation creation stage." Thus there is no distinction between explaining it in the context of that stage and practicing it as contained in the practice of that stage. Since there seem to be many such [garbled] explanations, they could only be made by a text falsely attributed to Nāgabodhi. It seems this text and the *Jewel Rosary* were composed by some other Indian [scholar].

As for the works of master Shākyamitra, we have already explained the way he wrote the *Second Stage*.[31] The *Integrated Practices Commentary* said to be by Shākyamitra might just possibly be by some author of a similar name, but if it is supposed to be the Shākyamitra disciple of the noble [Nāgārjuna] it is definitely not his work.[32]

As for the works of master Chandrakīrti, his *Illuminating Lamp* is extremely famous. The *Six-Branched Yoga* attributed to him seems to diverge from the content of the twelfth chapter of the *Lamp*. His *Vajrasattva Performance [Sādhana]* was commented on by Tathāgatarakshita and Lalitavajra, and was also accepted as a Chandrakīrti text by the [27b] Magadha Pandit Munishrībhadra. As for a root text and autocommentary called *Ornament of Realization of the Community* attributed to him, the Tibetan sages thought it worthy of investigation. These might possibly be written by someone with a similar name, but they seem only false

31. See above, p. 75 ff.

32. It is interesting that Tsong Khapa and colleagues are quite ready to consider that different Indian scholars with the same name could cause confusion as their works could be attributed to each other. The fact that they think thus critically about questions of authorship and false attribution requires us to take more seriously their insistence that Nāgārjuna, Āryadeva, Chandrakīrti, and many others who wrote important tantric treatises were the same persons who also wrote well-known philosophical treatises.

attributions if we suppose the Chandrakīrti in question to be the author of the *Illuminating Lamp*.

Now, Āryadeva, Nāgabodhi, and Shākyamitra were the most famous disciples of the noble one; still, the Marpa *Esoteric Community* tradition accepts Matangi as the noble one's disciple. Chandrakīrti was accepted as the noble [Nāgārjuna]'s [direct] disciple by former mentors such as master Gö [the translator]. Some Tibetan Mādhyamikas claim that Chandrakīrti did not meet the noble [Nāgārjuna], since [Chandrakīrti] stated at the end of the *Lucid Exposition*:

> Due to the fact that there has been a decline [in the tradition] over such a long time since the [writing of the] treatises of the noble one and his disciple, nowadays their interpretive tradition is not clear.[33]

That reason is uncertain; Chandrakīrti attained the state of scientist-adept and lived a long time, according to the report relayed by the translator Patsab transmitting what the adept Vajrāsanaguru had said. Therefore, it is not contradictory that by the end of his lifespan the treatises and disciples of Nāgārjuna had declined and yet that he had himself already met Nāgārjuna.[34] Therefore, the Tibetan sages accept the statement that "Chandrakīrti was the disciple of the noble one!" according to the assertion of the glorious Atīsha that he was the [direct] disciple of Nāgārjuna. [28a]

As the *Illuminating Lamp* declares:

> Having discovered, through the grace of Nāgārjuna,
> [the meaning of the *Esoteric Community*], sealed by all the buddhas, standing with the two stages,

33. This passage in the Derge redaction (see note to Tibetan text) gives more detail than in Tsong Khapa's paraphrase: "There has been a decline for a long time in the treatises written by the bodhisattva Nāgārjuna, who went to the Sukhāvatī buddhaverse, and in the society of his disciples; since his sun has set, the interpretive tradition is not at all clear."

34. There is also the point that the *Lucid Exposition* is an exoteric philosophical text, and so Chandra was referring to the long time since the writing of Nāgārjuna's exoteric works such as the *Wisdom*. Or perhaps Chandra wrote those words in that colophon early in his own career, before he attained the stage of scientist-adept.

> [I], Chandrakīrti, bow to the Glorious Lord Vajrasattva, and
> will explain it systematically.

Chandrakīrti discovered the imports of the *Community* from Nāgārjuna. In this regard, Bhavyakīrti stated [in his commentary on Chandrakīrti's *Illuminating Lamp*, entitled the *Illuminating Lamp Intention Elucidation*]:

> He says he discovered [the profound import] by the grace of glorious Nāgārjuna; and this indicates he was a personal disciple in the presence of the illustrious Nāgārjuna, and not an indirect one.

And [the tradition] that the Brahmin Rāhulabhadra-Saraha instructed Nāgārjuna and [also] instructed Chandrakīrti was recounted along with their virtues, by [Bhavyakīrti's] *Illuminating Lamp [Intention] Elucidation*:

> In the city of Konkana,
> On the peak of Shrī Parvata,
> The man first had lived there
> In the place of solitude.
>
> He was like the lord of humans and gods.
> He taught the supreme Dharma
> Received from the mouth of Rāhula[bhadra-Saraha].
> May he triumph here on this earth!
>
> Having propitiated that very [master Rāhulabhadra]
> That yogi obtained the universal vehicle,
> He achieved the [eighth] stage, working to help others—
> May the illustrious Nāgārjuna triumph!
>
> Winning the very same jewel from [Nāgārjuna],
> And becoming famous in the three worlds,
> He crossed the ocean of the *Community*—
> May that illuminator, Chandrakīrti, triumph!

So it is said. Also, masters such as the pandit Kumāra, disciple of Lakshmīmkara, said [in his *Illuminating Lamp Concise Commentary "Heart Mirror"*]:

> These [statements] demonstrate that [Chandrakīrti] was the real disciple in the presence of Nāgārjuna [28b] and so was really in possession of the personal instructions.

Thus, all those who elucidate the *Community* following the noble father and sons, such as Nāropa, Abhayākara, Karunashrīpāda, the Kashmiri Lakshmī, Munishrībhadra, Bhavyakīrti, Kumāra, Kuladhara, Tathāgatarakshita, and Līlāvajra, all accept Chandra[kīrti]pāda as being worthy of trust just like the noble ones.

[**IV.C.** – How the treatises of their followers were composed]

As for treatises written by other Indians about the *Community*, following the noble father and son, there is the commentary on the *Further Tantra* called *Esoteric Lamp*, which some editions claim to be authored by Lord Nāropa and some claim to be authored by Yashobhadra, the colophon to the translation of Smṛti stating:

> This is a form of annotating commentary on root and explanatory [tantras by] Samantabhadra, *Akāshagarbha, Yashobhadra, Nāropa, and Jñānasiddhi.

Smṛti was the disciple of both Nāropa and Jñānagarbha.

There seem to be two texts supposedly composed by Nāropa and translated by Marpa, a large text called the *Five Stages, Personal Instruction in the Community*, and a smaller one called *Concise Five Stages Elucidation*. The first of these expresses many gross errors contradicting the *Five Stages* and the *Integrated Practices*, such as the claim that the path of the dull and the mediocre disciples was gradual like the rungs on a ladder while the path of the sharp disciple was instantaneous; therefore it seems only falsely attributed to Nāropa [29a] by some Tibetans. The *Concise Five Stages Elucidation* is taken as authoritative by both traditions of Marpa's personal instruction in the *Community*, apparently descending through the teacher, Tsur. In regard to most of the personal instructions of mentor Marpa, they are present in various short Indian texts, but there do not appear to be any extra short texts on the personal instruction in the five stages, and so this one seems to be taken as the authoritative treatise. And this seems to have the combined import of all the great treatises of the noble tradition; hence it should be accepted as the authoritative root treatise of the Marpa tradition's personal instruction in the five stages. [Nevertheless,] in its colophon it states:

> The noble father and son explained the process
> Of the *Glorious Esoteric Community Tantra*,
> And Nāropa found that very inner intention.
> [But] with a commentator who does not know
> How to explain the tantra on his own, concisely,
> This blessed path is not in common.

Such a statement deprecating the *Illuminating Lamp* was made, interpolated there by one who was intending to praise Nāropa but did not know how to praise him. For, in his commentary on the *Further Tantra*, Nāropa [himself] states:[35]

> This elucidation of the import of the *Further Tantra*
> Follows according to the *Illuminating Lamp*,
> And explains the secret instruction of Nāgārjuna.

And:

> Depending in order upon the personal instruction
> Of masters Nāgārjuna, Āryadeva,
> Nāgabodhi, Shākyamitra,
> And Chandrakīrti, and so forth,
> I compose . . . [etc.]

By this you should know how to refute the multitude who uphold the superiority of the commentary on the *Tantra* alone composed by the Khapa Ronyam Dorjey, disciple of Tsur, who explains the *Tantra* itself in disagreement with the *Illuminating Lamp*, [29b] claiming the supremacy of the tradition of Nāropa.

The *Commentary* up to the middle of the forty-fourth chapter made by

35. This and the following verses do not appear to be the work of Nāropa, but rather occur in Smṛtijñānakīrti's colophon to Yashobhadra's *Esoteric Lamp*.

the pandit Alaṁkadeva or Alaṁkakalasha on the explanatory tantra *Vajra Rosary* does accord with the noble father and sons.

The commentary on the *Condensed [Sādhana]* called *Precious Rosary*, said to be by Shāntipa, is considered by Tibetan scholars to be falsely attributed, not even the work of a man of the same name. There is the difficult-point commentary by Vibhūti on the *Condensed [Sādhana]*; and in comment on the *Five Stages* along with the *Condensed [Sādhana]*, there are three: the *Moonlight*, written by Abhaya; the difficult-point commentary by Kṛshṇa Samayavajra; and the difficult-point commentary by Bhavyakīrti.

Munishrībhadra wrote the *Captivator of Yogi/nīs* on four [of the five] stages and on the *Condensed [Sādhana]*, leaving out the second stage. And there is the *Five Stages Difficult Point Commentary* by Vīryabhadra, and the commentary on the five stages by the Kashmiri scholar Lakshmī [the *Clear Meaning of the Five Stages*]. Including all the above-mentioned falsely attributed texts, these are the texts of the noble tradition.

I have already explained about the *Integrated Practices Commentary* and the commentary on the *Vajrasattva Sādhana*.[36]

There is the *Illuminating Lamp* extensive commentary, the *Illuminating Lamp [Intention] Elucidation* [by Bhavyakīrti]; the *Illuminating Lamp Concise Commentary "Heart Mirror"* [by Kumāra]; and the *Illuminating Lamp Extensive Commentary* by Karuṇashrīpāda. There is the *Illuminating Lamp Explanation Verses* by Kuladhara; [30a] the *Illuminating Lamp Concise Difficult Point Elucidation* by a Bhāvaviveka, someone with a similar name as the Bhāvaviveka who is the author of the *Wisdom Lamp*;[37] and the *Illuminating Lamp Subcommentary* said to be by an Āryadeva, apparently having the same name, but not being the well-known Āryadeva. This text and that falsely attributed to Nāgabodhi, the commentary *Clear Meaning [of the Five Stages]*, seem to be [Indian], not Tibetan [misattributed texts].

There is also Shraddhā's *Explanation of Vajra Recitation,* which discusses the *Revelation of the Hidden Intention [Tantra]*, and his *Elucidation of the Seven Ornaments*; Ekādashanirghosha's *Stages of the Path of Vajradhara*;

36. See p. 79 ff. above.

37. Again, Tsong Khapa here critically rejects an attribution, supporting the argument that he could have done so with the supposed "doubles" of Nāgārjuna etc. if he had a reason to do so.

Rāhulashrīmitra's *Mandala Rite*; and Samayavajra's *Mandala Rite* and his *Vajrasattva Pūjā Art*. These constitute the texts of the noble tradition.

Here, I give a contextual verse:

> When this earth upholds the great burden
> Of the jewels of hundreds of thousands of sage adepts,
> With great effort one partakes of the eloquence
> From the presence of each of them.
> When they decline by the power of time,
> The heart's essence of them all,
> Put into writing in the many treatises,
> Should be well studied and practiced,
> Relying on the mentor's personal instruction.
> The wise know this replaces [their living presence],
> And thus you can discern the paths [of practice],
> Distinguishing authentic from spurious.

[**V.** – The way the private instructions [of the *Community*] were transmitted in Tibet]

The illustrious Atīsha taught the *Illuminating Lamp* in Ngari, and the lineage of the *Five Stages* gradually descends from there. [30b] The great being Rinchen Zangpo made the basic translation and the polished determination of many treatises of the five masters, the noble father and sons, and of the *Root Tantra* and the *Revelation of the Hidden Intention* and other [explanatory] tantras. But that tradition of explanation did not survive long. Mentor Marpa was renowned as having seven styles of explaining the *Esoteric Community*. Although he seems to have studied the *Illuminating Lamp* under Nāropa, along with the Kashmiri Ākarasiddhi, he did not begin its explanation in Tibet. However, he spread very widely the private instruction in the *Five Stages*.

The master Gö visited India twelve times, relying in general upon seventy pandit mentors and upon two ḍākinī mentors. He investigated the noble tradition of the *Community* in particular, and he relied upon the Bengali sage Abhijña, the Zahor sage Tsunmojen, the Koṅkana sage Meghavegin, the Kashmir throne-holding Chandahari, Jñānākara who was blessed by Mañjushrī, the Nepali Tilgyi Tsahangu, the Nepali Dzongi Nagakoti, the pandit Saraha, the sage of Bodhgaya Kṛshṇa Samayavajra, the sage of Vikramashila Dīpaṁkarashrījñāna [Atīsha]—and these last two he heard in Tibet. From them he learned the explanations of the texts based on the treatises of the five members of the noble tradition. He also determined well the initiations and the secret instructions. He took Abhijña, Tsunmo-jen, and Kānhapa [Kṛshṇa Samayavajra] as his supreme mentors, taking the traditions of those three [31a] as chief both in explanation of texts and also in personal instructions. Since the miraculous activities of the *Community* entered the life of this mentor, he had many disciples upholding his pioneering style of teaching, producing four sages in each phase of his life, early, middle, and late, and the continuum of his teaching still survives until today.

There is also a personal instruction in the *Five Stages* descending from Jñānākara to Nagtso [the translator]. Further, the translator Patsab also studied the noble tradition of the *Community* and translated many treatises. As above explained, these translators who translated the extensive commentaries of the *Illuminating Lamp* first gave a measure of teachings, but their styles did not last long. The translator Shudpu and the translator Chag studied Gö's style of teaching in Tibet, and then met [other] pandit mentors and developed their own method of explaining the noble tradition.

Thus, although there are many other styles of teaching the tantra in the noble tradition of the *Esoteric Community* spread in Tibet from India, the very style of teaching of the precious master Gö is seen as the supreme of all these.

[VI. – The import of the actual precious jewel of personal instruction]

The sixth has two parts: [A.] The way of learning the general path or that common to the two universal vehicles; and [B.] The way of learning the special, uncommon *Community* path.

[**VI.A.** – The way of learning the general path or that common to the two universal vehicles]

First, as for the basis for first entering into the vajra vehicle, it is stated in the *Vajra Rosary Tantra*:

> Which excellences does a disciple need
> To be the vessel of the yoga tantra?

In response to this question:

> Faithful and reverent to the mentor,
> Always [**31b**] persisting in virtuous actions,
> Abandoning all bad thoughts;
> Having widely learned the discourses,
> Abandoning killing and harming,
> With the total effort arising
> From the messianic resolve to save beings;
> The one who has such excellences
> Is the fine disciple of great faith.

If one teaches a disciple without those good qualities of fitness, the disciple will be ruined in this and future lives, and the master will be far distanced from the gaining of accomplishment in terms of the swift arisal of the path in his experience. From the same [*Vajra Rosary Tantra*]:

> Just as you don't keep lion's milk
> In an earthen vessel,
> Do not bestow upon unfit disciples
> This tantra of great yoga.
>
> That disciple will die in that instant
> And will be ruined in this and future lives.
> If he teaches private instructions to the unfit,
> The master's accomplishments also will decline.

Further, granted that the characteristics of the physical foundation of the disciple need not be newly achieved, the characteristics of the excellences of the mental foundation—such as faith in the Dharma, reverence for the mentor, constant perseverance in the tenfold path of virtuous action, wide learning in the textual teaching, and effort motivated by the intense aspiration of resolve to save living beings—these are not spontaneous in beginning disciples and so must be newly created. They are not to be generated after having been [mistakenly] recognized as originally fit and already having been introduced into the vehicle of mantra. Thus, those qualities of the fit vessel are produced by cultivating the mind in the path common to both [exoteric and esoteric] universal vehicles.

As the *Vajrapāṇi Initiation Tantra* [32a] also states:

> "O great bodhisattva! This extremely magnificent mandala of great mantric spells, this extreme profundity, this unfathomable immeasurable, this much more secret than secret, this which is not properly taught to sinful beings—you, O Vajrapāṇi, proclaim it very rarely! If one has not previously learned it, how can one explain it to beings?"
>
> Vajrapāṇi replied, "Mañjushrī! Whoever engages in the meditation of the spirit of enlightenment, whenever they achieve the spirit of enlightenment, then, Mañjushrī, those bodhisattvas who practice the bodhisattva deeds through the door of the secret mantra vehicle should be introduced to the mandala of great mantric spells where they are consecrated in great wisdom; but those who have not finished their attainment of the spirit of enlightenment, they should not be introduced. One should not let them even look at the mandala. One should not show them either gestures or mantras."

Thus, he states that those who have not completed their cultivation of the spirit of enlightenment are not fit to be initiated. The *Mentor Fifty* also states:

> The disciple of pure aspiration,
> Who takes refuge in the three jewels

And who follows the mentor
Should be given daily recitations,[38]
Then blessed by mantras etc.
And made a vessel of the noble Dharma . . .

Here "pure aspiration" [32b] refers to the cultivation of the spirit of enlightenment. The ["refuge"] taken is the uncommon refuge, and, according to the *Mentor Fifty*, after having received the blessing of the method of relying by thought and deed on the tantric mentor, one should be made a fit vessel by initiation.

Also from the *Integrated Practices*:

> The process is like this: at the very beginning one becomes educated in the aspiration of the buddha vehicle. When one has become educated in the aspiration of the buddha vehicle, one becomes educated in the samadhi of single-mindedness on the new vehicle.

Thus in entering the *Community* path, you must learn gradually and not suddenly. After having established this necessity of the method of gradual learning, he declares that you must cultivate the spirit of enlightenment, the aspiration of the universal vehicle, the buddha vehicle.

As for the way to cultivate completely the willing and acting spirits of enlightenment, this is how it comes from the private instruction of the great Lord Atīsha. First, he teaches that you should practice properly the method of reliance in thought and deed on a universal vehicle spiritual mentor with the necessary qualifications. He then teaches the great import and the difficulty of finding evolutionary leisure; you educate yourself in that attitude and generate the great ambition to extract the essence of this life of evolutionary leisure. The best way to take this essence is to enter the

38. Tsong Khapa's commentary on this (*bla ma lnga bcu pa'i rnam bshad*) indicates that the "given daily repetitions" refers to the *Mentor Fifty* text itself. Cf. Sparham, *Fulfillment of All Hopes* (78–79, 122): ***sbyin par bya*** *zhes bshad gzhir bya'o, ,gang sbyin na rang dbang dor nas bla ma'i rjes su 'jug pa'i bsten tshul gyi gzhung 'di'o, ,ci zhig gi don du sbyin zhe na,* ***kha bton bya bar sbyin pa*** *ste.* . . . "'Give!' means make it a basis for explanation. What is to be given? It is this text on how to be devoted to a mentor by giving up one's independence and following. For what purpose is it given? It is given as a daily recitation."

universal vehicle; of which the door is the spirit of enlightenment itself. If this authentically emerges in your personal experience, you become a non-artificial universalist. If it is just lip service, you become merely a verbal universalist. Thus, the wise person [33a] dispels gradually the resistance to that spirit, and conceives it in complete form.

Prior to that, if you have not reversed your ambition for this life, it will be an obstacle either to the individual or universal vehicle; so you should be mindful of death. This life will not last long. Then, you should reflect on the wandering in the bad states after death, which will reverse the interest in this life. After that, you can reverse the interest that craves successes in the future life by thinking over thoroughly the drawbacks of all states of the life cycle. In this way, you should orient the mind to transcendent liberation.

After that, in order to reverse the interest in your own peace and happiness, you should persist in cultivating love, compassion, and the spirit of enlightenment rooted in them; in this way, you cultivate the non-artificial spirit of enlightenment. Then, having recognized the deeds of the bodhisattvas, you generate the desire to learn them. When you can take up the burden of the deeds of the buddha-children, you can uphold the bodhisattva vow and practice its precepts. When you can take up the burden of the vow and commitments of the vajra vehicle, studying the *Mentor Fifty*, and perfecting the ways of relying on the mentor, you should enter into the mantra [vehicle].

Intending such a procedure, Rāhulashrīmitra, the eminent member of the noble tradition of the *Esoteric Community*, said, [in his *Illumination of the Communion*]:

> At such a stage,
> At a time of favorable date and stars,
> The disciple should join palms together and bow,
> Confess all sins,
> And renew the threefold refuge.
> Relying well on the spirit of [33b] enlightenment,
> Undertake the layperson's vow
> And the bodhisattva's vow,
> And the vow of monthly purification.
> The following procedures
> Are to rely in the best way on the vajra master,

And here I do not write
Out of fear of prolixity.
Having thus served, one requests the mentor,
"Please grant me initiation!"

Thus before initiation, one should uphold the individual liberation [vows], the conception and vow of the spirit of enlightenment, and then one should request the mentor to confer initiation. The vows of the upasaka layman and its purification, the monk-for-a-day vow, are in terms of the householders. The monastics who enter the tantras must totally purify their vows of renunciation and so on. This is also stated in the *Vajra Summit*:

Abandoning killing, stealing, sex,
Lying, and intoxicants,
Abiding in the lay vows,
Attain the king of science state.
If one is a monastic,
Persist in all three vows,
Individual liberation, spirit of enlightenment,
And supreme scientist-adept vows.

If you do not practice well the above stages of the path of the common vehicle, not having cut off ambition for this life, your aspiration for the Dharma will not be stable. Not having produced a faith that is not just verbal profession, you will not take refuge with a deeply committed mind. Without attaining firm certainty in the effects of evolution, you will become filled with ambivalence, without [34a] any specific determination to uphold whatever vow. Without generating a core aversion to the life cycle, your aspiration for liberation will be no more than a superficial idea. Without generating the non-artificial, aspiring spirit of enlightenment footed in love and compassion, you become merely a nominal universalist. Without feeling an intense desire to practice the messianic deeds in general, a heartfelt vow of the activated spirit of enlightenment will not arise. Without gaining a precise general understanding of quiescence and insight, even the subtle samadhi will become erroneous. Until you have gained certitude about the view of selflessness, which precludes all such [errors], you should practice the general path of the two universal vehicles.

This is the precept emerging from the confluence of three streams, one descending from His Holiness Maitreya through Asaṅga, one from His Holiness Mañjushrī through Nāgārjuna, and the last [also from Mañjushrī] through Shāntideva. The great Lord Atīsha maintained that this teaching must be employed whether you enter the door of the vajra vehicle or that of the transcendence vehicle.

Well, one may wonder if this is the position of the Tibetan mentors of the *Esoteric Community*.

The master Gö also taught that the meaning of the above quote from the *Integrated Practices* was that the prerequisite of both creation and perfection stages is the cultivation of the view that realizes voidness and the spirit of enlightenment rooted in compassion. The *Four Point Treatise*[39] [by Serdingpa]—the instruction in the five stages of the Marpa tradition—explains that the yogi/nī with complete initiation must practice by establishing the basis for achieving the path. One must take refuge in the three jewels, have confidence in the ripening of the fruits of evolution, habituate oneself to the ten virtues, take the vow of individual liberation preceded by the common refuge, and develop the aspiring and acting spirit [of enlightenment], [34b] preceded by the uncommon refuge. This teaching, which shows in detail how to guide the mind in that way, is called the "stages of the path." So it is not that such is not the system of the former Tibetan mentors who learned the *Community* path.

Having developed a rather thorough understanding of the complete body of the path, you should actually begin to practice such a teaching distinctive from others by its provision of a complete basis for progressing on the path. This is the program for practicing the ordinary path, which I have already explained elsewhere [in the *Great Treatise on the Stages of the Enlightenment Path*].

39. See note to the text under the Tibetan folio 68b below.

2. General Learning of the Tantric Path

[34b.3–66a.3]

[**VI.B.** – The way of learning the special, uncommon *Community* path]

The second has four parts: [1.] How to become a fit vessel for the path of the two stages; [2.] Having become fit, how to purify vows and commitments; [3.] Having purified vows and commitments, how to meditate; and [4.] How the fruition will be attained at meditation's end.

[**VI.B.1** – How to become a fit vessel for the path of the two stages]

When a qualified master has initiated a fit disciple with the initiation rites proclaimed in the tantras, with their import having been elucidated by the authorities, the door of the mantra [vehicle] teaching is opened, setting in place the infallible relativity for the path to be developed in personal experience and the fruition to be attained. Hence, having first become a fit vessel for entrance into mantra, one should achieve the second fitness authorizing one's study of the path of mantra by means of the pure initiation. I have already explained that process elsewhere [in my *Great Treatise on the Stages of Mantra*].

[**VI.B.2.** – Having become fit, how to purify vows and commitments]

During the time of initiation, one calls to witness all the mentors, buddhas, and bodhisattvas [35a] and undertakes to uphold the vows and pledges taken in their presence. So it is indispensable to know how to [uphold them] and to have the experience of maintaining [them], before one can contemplate the path. The procedure of doing that should be learned from the previous extensive explanations in the *Mentor Fifty*, the *Vow Upholding*, the *Famous Treatise*, and the *Elucidation of the Root Downfalls and Gross Infractions.*

When one finds certitude in the fact that the practices concerning the pure initiations and the vows must begin to lead one into the two stages, one's preliminary practices such as mentor yoga, the hundred syllable [mantra-recitation], and the mandala [offering] come in the wake of that [initiation, as is proper. Otherwise,] if one finds that certitude only afterward, it seems that the realization possible through the previous practices does not develop; so strive to understand this [importance of initiations and vows] beforehand.

[**VI.B.3.** – Having purified vows and commitments, how to meditate]

The third has three parts: [a.] Verifying the order of the two stages; [b.] How to meditate the two stages in order; and [c.] The conduct that is the method of heightening the impact on the two stages.

[**VI.B.3.a.** – Verifying the order of the two stages]

The person who aspires to the ultimate does not fail to meditate the creation stage. One follows the order of meditation by first thoroughly cultivating the creation stage and later entering the perfection stage. [Nāgārjuna,] in the *Five Stages*, makes the order definite:

> To those well situated on the creation stage
> And yet aspiring to the perfection stage,
> The perfect buddhas taught this method
> Just like the rungs of a ladder.

[Āryadeva adds] in the *Integrated Practices*, which extensively elucidates the intention of the *Five Stages*:

> "Alienated individuals such as us, through our beginningless habitual investment in the variety of outer [35b] things, are involved in the habitual investment in conceptual thinking by the cause of the [reificatory] instincts for intrinsic realities in such [things] as existence and non-existence, one and many,

> duality and nonduality, neither existence nor non-existence, permanence and impermanence. Thus if they learn the samadhi of the perfection stages, must they practice according to the usual stages? Or may they spiritually realize those instantaneously through the personal precept of the mentor?"
>
> The vajra master replies, "Practice entering by stages, and not suddenly."

Thus, when asked: if those who are engaged with objects under the influence of instincts beginninglessly invested in the four extremes should practice the perfection [stages] beginning gradually from the first stages, or should practice suddenly by means of a profound precept of a mentor, without needing such [a gradual procedure]; [Āryadeva] answers that, other than gradual practice, there is no door of sudden entrance. And he establishes that by quoting the authority of the *Mission to Laṅka [Sutra]* and the *Heroes' March Samadhi Sutra*. Thus, even if it were thought that the finest, jewel-like disciple to enter this path would never [need to] have a beginner's stage, there would result the absurdity that one should be liberated from the beginning without requiring any path [at all]. It is essential that one accept [the inevitability of having] a beginner's stage. One must accept [Āryadeva's] statement in the *Integrated Practices*:

> In order for beginner [36a] beings
> To enter into the ultimate reality,
> The perfect buddhas created this artful system,
> Just like rungs of a ladder.

Here some protest that the sudden practice is taught thinking of some powerful persons who practiced the lower paths in many former lives, and so [in this life] do not need to be led through lower paths but are properly led through the higher paths.[40]

This is like saying that when one investigates whether or not one needs first to go through the paths of accumulation and application to generate the

40. Here we encounter a definitive position taken in regard to the nowadays still controversial debate between sudden enlightenment and gradual enlightenment.

insight path, one does not need any preliminary accumulation or application paths, giving the reason that one has already attained the insight path. It is a ridiculous [because so obvious] objection. Thus, just as, although one can put one's boat aside when one gets across a river, one must still depend on it while crossing; so, although one can abandon the creation stage once one has attained the non-artificial, core realization of the perfection stage, the artificial creation stage is necessary in the process of attaining that. Thus for the beginner, the creation stage is very highly recommended and very important. As the *Vajra Angel* states:

> In order to realize the core yoga
> One should practice the artificial
> Meditation and recitation.
> Once one realizes the core yoga,
> Since it is realized by going out
> Beyond the artificial yoga,
> One should not practice any artifice.
> For example, one takes a boat
> And goes across the water,
> And then leaves it, once beyond.
> Artifices are like that:
> Such rites as mandalas and so on,
> Which are made with the [36b] artificial mind,
> Since they clear up one's [habitual] outer actions,
> Are recommended for beginners.
> All those accomplishments are present here [in the creation stage],
> But not in the knowledge reality of the Victor.

The same points are made in the *Liberation Drop* and the *Spring Drop*. Also, as for the meaning of some statements in them that not liberation but only painful hardships will be attained by striving in the artificial practices, they mean that such will be the result if one only strives in such paths and does not [go on to] meditate the perfection stage [at all]. They do not mean that one who aspires to enlightenment should not employ those [artificial practices]. One can understand this by applying the meaning of the example of the boat. So do not make the statement about abandoning the boat on the other side of the water your grounds for abandoning the boat on this side of the water!

Here one might object that it is all right to establish the definiteness in the order of the two stages by references from the tantras, but how can references from sutras establish anything?

[Sutra references were also used here] to help us understand that, although there are differences of speed between sutra and tantra, they are similar in that beginners need to enter gradually. As for the statements about the order of the two stages in the tantras, the *Vajra Rosary* states:

> Then, at the beginning, the yogi/nī who knows
> The six yogas achieves the supreme;
> Then one should recite very extensively
> The letter *H* without any vowel.

Here, as for the six yogas: in the first application there are yoga, continuing yoga, and so on to make four; and then the mandala triumph and the evolution triumph to make six. Reciting the letters without vowels is explained as referring to the vajra recitation.

As the *Esoteric Accomplishment* states:

> In the glorious [37a] *Community*,
> The savior of beings taught very clearly
> Four things to be meditated,
> On the higher than highest path.
>
> First, one should establish the letter,
> And abide on the stage of creation.
> Second, the lords of yoga should meditate
> The very reality of the self.
>
> Third, one meditates the wisdom seal
> The supreme divine substance.
> Fourth, proclaimed the highest,
> One meditates the universal seal.

Misunderstanding the many texts such as the *Enlightenment Songs* (*Dohas*), which explain that, relying on a progression through such stages of the path in the context of meditating primarily the innate [orgasmic] wisdom, one ceases the elaborated meditations of the creation stage; it seems that [some] have [mistakenly] thought that the system of the Great Brahmin was sudden and the system of Nāgārjuna was gradual. Nevertheless, the interpretation that asserts two paths, a gradual one for dull and mediocre intellects in the stage of first entering in this path, and a sudden one for the extremely sharp intellects, is contradictory to the tantra and to all authoritative treatises. But I have already extensively explained these interpretations in the *Great Treatise on the Stages of Mantra*.

[**VI.B.3.b.** – How to meditate the two stages in order]

The second has two parts: [i.] The way to meditate the creation stage; and [ii.] The way to meditate the perfection stage.

[**VI.B.3.b.i.** – The way to meditate the creation stage]

First, if one must first meditate the creation stage, since it is the prior of the two stages, how does one learn the stages of what sort of creation stage?

To this there are two: [A′] The need to meditate what sort of creation stage; and [B′] How to learn that creation stage. [37b]

[**VI.B.3.b.i.A′** – The need to meditate what sort of creation stage]

In the twelfth chapter of the *Root Tantra*, the creation stage is explained in terms of the four branches of service and performance. And the meaning of this is explained by the *Illuminating Lamp*, [including all stages of the path] from the meditation on the stage of wisdom to the end of the evolution triumph. The phrase from that very chapter:

> Again, one should perform service
> With firm discipline, by means of the four vajras . . .

indicates the creation stage; the *Illuminating Lamp* explains that it refers to the summary creation stage. That is also explained as the meaning of the passage from the *Further Tantra*:

> First, voidness and enlightenment;
> Second, the concentration of the seed;

Third, the completion of matter itself;
Fourth, the establishment of the letter.

When Nāropa explains this as referring [to the path] from the meditation on the stage of wisdom up to the mandala triumph, he intends the extensive creation [stage] by means of the four vajras. Stating it in brief, it indicates [the process] from the wisdom stage up to the establishment of the letters in the vajra and the lotus. Again, it is merely stated directly. After that, one must supply the subtle [yoga] and recitation, and so on.

[Chandrakīrti] explains in the eleventh chapter of the *Illuminating Lamp* the single-minded [focus] on the six clans, from meditating the wisdom stage up to the triply nested heroes. He states that one's mental process develops when practicing that in four sessions; this has the same meaning as the concise performance. The treatises of the noble father and sons teach no division of contemplative performance into extended and concise other than this.

Therefore, in this system, without beginning from a solitary hero form such as Vajradhara [38a] and stabilizing his clear vision and then proceeding to practice the rest of the performance—other than such a way of practice, just by meditating the deity as father-mother in union one cannot develop the root of virtue that produces the complete realization of the perfection stage. Therefore, as for what some advocates of the Marpa system say—that the meditation on the wheel of the mandala is [only] necessary to accomplish the variety of ritual deeds; that, as the prerequisite of the perfection stage, it is sufficient to meditate on the wisdom body made by a mere instantaneous creation of the father-mother deity from within the realm of voidness; and that just that is what is indicated by "abiding well on the creation stage"[41]—this does not agree with any of the genuine treatises of the noble tradition, and even contradicts their own [Marpa] system. As the *Concise Five Stages Elucidation* states:

Who vividly realizes the forms
Of this creation stage, the deity body
And the supreme mandala of perfect buddhas,
And learns it thoroughly, that one will be fulfilled.

41. PK, vs. I.2a.

To assert that one must create a wisdom body preliminary to meditating the perfection stage disagrees with the *Integrated Practices* statement that the wisdom body is created from the magic body and there is no [actual] deity body from the creation stage up to the mind isolation. And especially the division into the mantra body and the wisdom body on the creation stage is a notion that has no place in this system. In short, by knowing just what sort of meditation on the creation stage serves to develop one's spiritual process to produce a complete realization of the perfection stage, it is crucial to meditate something more than the minimal creation stage. [38b] Further, the *Root* and *Commentary [Tantra]* thirteenth chapters state that, in order to guard the mind of the beginner against distraction, one must meditate the protection wheel in four sessions.

[**VI.B.3.b.i.B′** – How to learn that creation stage]

The stage of learning in the creation stage is stated in the *Integrated Practices*:

> When learning the aspiration for the buddha vehicle, one learns the samadhi of single-mindedness [of the new vehicle]. When learning that, one learns the yoga of imagination. When learning that, one abides in the beginner's samadhi.

Here, the *Integrated Practices Commentary*'s interpretation, that the single-mindedness [yoga] is the instantaneous learning of the creation stage and the imagination yoga is the learning through many moments, is incorrect; for the *Illuminating Lamp* explains that the single-mindedness [samadhi] is the creation of Vairochana, and so on, from the five enlightenments.

Again, some people, basing themselves on the *Illuminating Lamp*'s eleventh-chapter explanation that the single-mindedness [samadhi] is the creation one by one of Vairochana and so forth, interpret first the single-mindedness as learning a single deity; then, once one has learned that, [interpret] the learning of the yoga of imagination as learning the entire sadhana performance. This also is invalid, because in that explanation of the single-mindedness [samadhi] on Vairochana and so on, [Chandrakīrti] mentions the meditating on the mandala with holistic visualization.

Therefore, the "single" in single-mindedness does not indicate either that the mindfulness of the deity is [achieved] all in one move, or that one is mindful of only one deity, but rather that either one is singly mindful of deities or one is mindful of oneself as one with the deity. In general that can apply to meditation of the deities both at subtle and coarse levels, but [39a] here it refers to the deity yoga of the coarse habitat and inhabitant mandala.

Again, it is stated that one learns this path according to the procedure declared in the *Integrated Practices*: when learning archery, one learns first with a big target and only after having developed [skill] does one learn with a small one. So when one learns the creation stage first, up to the mandala triumph, one produces the vivid vision of the coarse [deities]. Only having learned those does one then learn the yoga of imagination, such as meditating on the mandala within a subtle drop, and so on. "Imagination" or "conceptualization yoga" is the general name of the creation stage, but here it is used as the general name of the yoga of the subtle, just as [in] the sixth chapter of the *Illuminating Lamp*, [Chandrakīrti] refers to the meditation on the yoga of the subtle as the learning of the yoga of imagination.

The samadhi of the beginner is the yoga of the first stage: "to abide in that" is to stabilize it or to perfect it. In the creation stage, there are profound anticipatory relationalities [contributing to] the production of each realization of the perfection stage. It also has a great store of excellences, such as having one's spiritual continuum blessed by the victors and their offspring; being looked after through all one's lives by one's patron deity; never being apart from remembrance of the Buddha; being able to complete the stores easily through the [contemplative] practices of offering, praising, and so forth; not being affected by injuries from demons; and such as being able to achieve many ritual accomplishments such as peace and so forth in this very life. Therefore, it is extremely important to practice until it regularly happens that, whatever one's invited visualization of the habitat [39b] and inhabitant mandala on the coarse and subtle levels, it dawns as one wishes and does not dawn as one does not wish, and until one can abide one-pointedly upon it for a long time. And here I do not enlarge on other things [here] unexplained, as I have already explained them elsewhere.[42]

42. Especially in the creation-stage section of the *Great Treatise on the Stages of Mantra*. See Yarnall 2013.

[**VI.B.3.b.ii.** – The way to meditate the perfection stage]

The second has three parts: [A′] Summary meaning of the two [syllables] E VAṀ, the main subject of the perfection stage in general; [B′] Detailed explanation of the meaning of the two [syllables] E VAṀ; and [C′] Explaining the perfection stage of this tantra in particular.

[**VI.B.3.b.ii.A′** – Summary meaning of the two (syllables) E VAṀ, the main subject of the perfection stage in general]

In general, all the keys of the import of unexcelled yoga tantra are condensed into the meaning of the preliminary forty syllables such as E VAṀ. And further, the chief of those imports is condensed in the import of the first two syllables.

In that regard, the *Vajra Rosary Tantra* states:

> Why is the first phrase of the tantra
> "Thus did I," and so on?
> What is the detailed meaning
> Of the first words, "Thus [EVAṀ]," and so on?

Here the first two lines ask how the meaning of the prefatory expression in tantras, such as the *Community* becomes the meaning of the two syllables E VAṀ. The last two lines ask what is the detailed meaning of each one, E, VAṀ, and so on. Of these two questions, in answer to the latter, a verse is put forth explaining each syllable. And in answer to the former, three meanings of EVAṀ are stated:

[1] The EVAṀ of the goal, fruition;

[2] The EVAṀ of the path, the means of attainment; and

[3] The EVAṀ that is the sign (*linga*) which brings about that [attainment].

[1] Of the first, the *E* means the support where the Teacher stays and performs the teaching of the Dharma, [40a] called in some tantras the "secret," in some the "realm of space," or likewise the "vagina" (*bhaga*), the "source-triangle," the "lotus," the "lion's throne," and so on. The meaning of VAṀ consists of the names given the Teacher in the various tantras such as "Vajri," "Vajrasattva," "Vajrabhairava," "Vajreshvara," "Heruka," "Kālachakra," "Ādibuddha," and so on. As [the *Vajra Rosary*] states:

In *E*, the secret, space-realm,
Vagina, source, or lotus,
The yogi/nī sits in the lion's seat,
Teaching the supreme miracle:

Called Vajrasattva, VAṀ Vajra,
Vajrabhairava, Īshvara,
Heruka, Kālachakra,
And Ādibuddha.

Here, further, the definitive meaning of "secret" and so on is voidness, and the definitive meaning of "Vajrasattva" and so on is great compassion; thus, this [EVAṀ] indicates the indivisibility of voidness and compassion. As [the *Vajra Rosary*] states:

EVAṀ is the seal of the transcendent buddhas,
The indicator of nonduality,
The indivisibility of void and compassion,
Wherefore it expresses that reality.

There, the seal of the transcendent buddhas,
Showing nondual intuitive wisdom,
Is stated in the opening of all tantras.

[2] Now the second *E* [of the path] means wisdom voidness, VA means liberative art of great compassion, and the drop [*anusvāra* = *Ṁ* sound] means the indivisible union of that art and wisdom. That very thing is declared to be the seal stamping the great king of Dharma, abbreviated into its chief [40b] meaning pervading the 84,000 forms of Dharma. As is stated in the *Vajra Rosary*:

E is declared to be voidness,
Likewise, VA to be compassion,
The *Ṁ*-drop the product of their union:
The supreme miracle of their union.

Pervading the eighty-four thousand Dharma groups,
It is summarized as the Dharma seal;

The very seal of the great king,
Stated first in the tantras.

That intuitive wisdom of such nonduality, expressed in whatever tantra, that very thing is supreme, and its teaching is indispensable. As [the *Vajra Rosary*] states:

Condensed meaning of all tantras,
Voidness and compassion indivisible,
Wherein that same is proclaimed,
That is the seal of the transcendent buddhas.

E VAṀ, the two syllables—
Where those two are not,
There is no thatness.

Also the *Esoteric Accomplishment* praises the actual meaning of the two syllables as the essence of the path of enlightenment:

Abiding in the beginning of the tantra,
Supreme quintessence of the essence,
That very thing the Great Bliss Savior
Called the "Secret Thatness."
Source of the happiness of buddhas,
Bodhisattvas, and all beings,
King of tantras of secret imagination,
It abides in the *Glorious Community*.
To the pure syllables E VAṀ
All three realms reverently pay homage.

And:

In that so-called "realm of space,"
Appearing like a full sesame pod,
Transcendent buddhas are everywhere
As numerous as grains of Ganga's sands.

> Having served the reality of those syllables,
> By that artful performance,
> The buddhas and bodhisattvas
> Attain the [41a] unexcelled state.

Therefore, from that same text [the *Esoteric Accomplishment*]:

> Here, if the two syllables,
> Are not at the start of a tantra,
> It is unacceptable.

It states that the two syllables are definitely necessary at the starting preface of all unexcelled tantras. [Yet] here the intention is that even though the syllables E VAṀ are not explicitly present, their definitive meaning must be present.

[3] Of the third, the *E* [of the sign] means the support, the vagina (*bhaga*) of the mother, the VA means the father's phallus that depends on it, and the Ṁ-drop that abides in that dependent phallus is the ground of all the bliss such as the great bliss of Vajrasattva, which manifests the various emanations [as the *Vajra Rosary* states]:

> *E* has the character of the vagina,
> Know it as the supporting lotus.
> VA is the supported phallus,
> And the form of drop abides there
> Held by the supported phallus,
> Causing the various emanations,
> Abode of ground of all bliss,
> The universal bliss of Vajrasattva.

That [passage] indicates the liberative art that develops the EVAṀ of the path from the union of the E and the VAṀ, the signs of father and mother. Further, this EVAṀ of the signs, which are the vital points of the body, [along with] the liberative art that develops the path—EVAṀ through penetrating those vital points within one's own body is also proclaimed in the *Sampuṭa [Tantra]*:

The *E* syllable truly abides
In the wheels at the crown and navel;
Likewise, one wants the VAṀ syllable
Truly staying at heart and throat.

The meaning of EVAṀ here is explained as the abiding of the *E* as the triangular shape in the crown and navel channel-wheels [41b] and the VAṀ syllable as the round shape in the heart and throat channel-wheels. Here "sign" refers to the sign that is the mark of shape.

Thus, if one desires to attain the goal-EVAṀ by understanding it thoroughly, one understands its art: the process of the union of both E and VAṀ of the path according to the teachings in both [father and mother] tantras. Then, as the art of developing that [path-EVAṀ], one becomes expert in the external sign-EVAṀ—the union with the consort—and in the internal sign-EVAṀ—the process of penetrating the vital points of the channel-wheels. There, in the use of the art of developing that path, all the vital keys of both [father and mother] tantras are condensed, and thus one can understand thoroughly how all tantras become the meaning of the two syllables E VAṀ and its components. Then, one can well understand the many praises in the tantras of the import of the two syllables as being the [most] vital import of all.

[VI.B.3.b.ii.B′ – Detailed explanation of the meaning of the two (syllables) E VAṀ]

The second has two parts: [1′] Detailed explanation of the definitive meaning of both E and VAṀ; and [2′] Showing how, to produce that, one must penetrate the vital points in the body through the entry of the sign EVAṀ.

[VI.B.3.b.ii.B′1′ – Detailed explanation of the definitive meaning of both E and VAṀ]

One may think, "If the chief import of all tantras is the import of EVAṀ, and its definitive import is voidness and compassion, the meanings of those two must be explained."

This has two parts: [a′] Explaining the meanings of the voidness and compassion involved in bliss-void-indivisibility; and [b′] Explaining the meaning of the voidness and compassion involved in the two reality indivisibility.

[**VI.B.3.b.ii.B′1′a′** – Explaining the meanings of the voidness and compassion involved in bliss-void-indivisibility]

As the letter *E* and the shape of the reality-source [42a] are triangular, they symbolize the suchness of selflessness. At the same time, the triangle also symbolizes the three doors of liberation. Thus, the symbolic meaning of the syllable *E* is voidness, signlessness, and wishlessness; [those three] being the voidness of intrinsic reality of things as entities, causes, and effects, [respectively]. Therefore, if one's view of voidness is not perfect, the meaning of the syllable *E* will not be complete[ly understood]. Even though one has that [perfect view], if one lacks the great bliss arisen from penetrating the vital points of the external and internal body, the meaning of the syllable VA will not be complete[ly understood]. And even if one has both of those, if one does not know how to conceive the view of voidness in that melted state and how to unite bliss and voidness by having turned voidness into objectivity and great bliss into subjectivity, realizing the former unerringly with the latter; then, the meaning of the Ṁ-drop will be incomplete[ly understood]. Therefore, if one wants to understand the meaning of the EVAṀ as the indivisibility of bliss and voidness, one must understand [all] those things.

This has three parts: [i′] Explaining the import of voidness; [ii′] Explaining the import of bliss; and [iii′] Explaining the process of union of bliss-void-indivisible.

[**VI.B.3.b.ii.B′1′a′i′** – Explaining the import of voidness]

The first has three parts: [A′′] Identifying the root of the life cycle; [B′′] Teaching the corresponding system of investigating the view of selflessness, which terminates that [life cycle]; and [C′′] Refuting positions that differ [from that].

[**VI.B.3.b.ii.B′1′a′i′A′′** – Identifying the root of the life cycle]

[Āryadeva] states in the *Integrated Practices*:

> Thus, persons without a spiritual teacher, not understanding the full insight into the reality of their own minds, constructing their vain and hollow "I"-habit and "mine"-habit and so deeming things to be good and evil, and so on, experience suffering [42b] in the beginningless life cycle.

Thus, by the power of confusion due to the truth-habit that does not know the reality of the mind, relying on the habits of personal self and its property, they wander in the life cycle. This is supported by references from sutras, such as the *Eight Thousand* and the *Purification of Evolutionary Obstructions [Sutra].* [In the *Integrated Practices*, Āryadeva] states that its meaning was taught by the savior Nāgārjuna:

> If in actuality all this is
> Voidness and nonproduction,
> How does evolution move one through this life cycle
> Of engagement in pleasure and suffering?
> As soon as the childish begin to claim a self,
> Because of taints such as desire,
> They become dependent through imagination;
> [And they are afflicted by suffering.]
> But all these are but merely mind.
> Really emergent in the form of illusions,
> And thus through virtuous and nonvirtuous acts,
> One is born in happy and wretched migrations.

Further, Anaṅgavajra, the disciple of the savior Mahāsukhanātha [Padmavajra], declared [in his *Accomplishment Ascertaining Wisdom and Art*] that one wanders in the life cycle by the power of the truth-habit that invests the truthless with truth [status]; and that one will not be liberated from the life cycle as long as one maintains the materialism of the truth-insistence:

> From them there is the great increase
> Of such as birth and death,
> For those whose minds insist on the untrue,
> The life cycle of extreme suffering happens.

As long as they keep the great materialism,
So long do those of such feeble intelligence
Reside in the prison of existence.

This [point] is similar to that [made by the master Nāgārjuna] in the *Precious Rosary*, that if one does not cease the truth-habit regarding the aggregates then one will not terminate birth driven by the power of evolutionary action and affliction:

As long as there is the aggregate-habit
There will be the "I"-habit concerning it.
As long as there is the "I"-habit, there will be evolution;
And from that there will be rebirth. [43a]

[**VI.B.3.b.ii.B′1′a′i′B″** – Teaching the corresponding system of investigating the view of selflessness, which terminates that (samsaric life cycle)]

Therefore, not only must one realize voidness, realizing the nonreality of the aggregates, in order to purge completely the instinct for the truth-habit, the root of the life cycle, but the wisdom realizing nonreality is indispensable for cutting the bonds of wandering in the life cycle under the influence of evolution and addictions. And that import has already been contemplated by those disciples and hermit buddhas who have cut the bonds of the life cycle. These [points] have been extensively explained elsewhere. As [Nāgārjuna] stated in the *Disclosure of the Spirit of Enlightenment*:

Those who do not know voidness,
Have no basis for liberation,
And they will wander in confusion
Imprisoned in life in the six migrations.

And as Anaṅgavajra states [in his *Accomplishment Ascertaining Wisdom and Art*]:

Thus, [some]one with a spiritual teacher
Wishing to eliminate the habitual error

Of wanting to enjoy the three migrations,
Should abandon the habit of materialism.

Therefore, not only when entering the philosophical vehicle, but also on the vajra vehicle, one must seek the understanding of the view that realizes selfless voidness and meditate upon its import in order to eliminate the materialism at the root of the life cycle. Likewise, the *Vajra Essence Ornament Tantra* says:

A certain yogi/nī understands one thing,
Goes into solitude and strives there,
Purifies sins, achieves buddhahood in this life.
Meditating on objective selflessness, [43b]
S/he realizes omniscience.

Thus here, when a yogi/nī understands and meditates in solitude, s/he will attain buddhahood in this life. Such a yogi/nī is explained as meditating on objective selflessness. There are a great many [passages] like that.

Thus to abandon truth-habits and realize selflessness, one must refute the object [seemingly] held by the self-habits and realize its non-existence; it is not sufficient to merely withdraw the mind, not allowing it to move out toward the object of the truth-habits. As the Lord of Reasoning [Dharmakīrti] declared:

Without refuting its object [the presumed self], one cannot eliminate [the self-habit].

And Āryadeva says:

When you see all objects as selfless,
You will destroy the seed of [samsaric] existence.

And in the *Introduction to the Central Way*, [Chandrakīrti] also declares:

Seeing intellectually that all faults of addictions
Arise from the futile views [of self and property],
And having realized that it is the self that is its object,
The yogi/nī effects the negation of the self.

The method of first generating a precise understanding of the view of selflessness is explained in the tantric and centrist treatises without any difference. As [Nāgārjuna] explains in the *Disclosure of the Spirit of Enlightenment*:

> Those bodhisattvas who engage in practice through the door of secret mantra, having thus conceived the superficial spirit of enlightenment, whose nature is willing, then should generate the ultimate spirit of enlightenment by the power of meditation. Therefore, one must describe its nature.

After having said that, [Nāgārjuna] determines selflessness: by negating the personal self advocated by the outsider schools; [44a] [by negating] the objective self advocated by the Buddhist monastic schools as truly existent subject and object; and [by negating] the [more subtle objective self] advocated by the experientialists as the true mind devoid of substantial subject-object dichotomy. For he states that, before the tantric practitioner [can] generate the ultimate spirit of enlightenment by the force of meditation, [s/he must learn] the method of investigating the view of selflessness according to the treatises of the central way. While the two realist schools of the individual [vehicle] advocate true subject and object, none of the noble disciples and hermit buddhas [still] hold such a position. It should be understood that these two patterns [of philosophical realism only] express the view of the [still] alienated individuals who are embarked on their [individual vehicle] path.

[**VI.B.3.b.ii.B'1'a'i'C''** – Refuting positions that differ (from that)]

Concerning this, a certain someone advocates his own view, quoting the *Summary Teaching*—[43]

> The voidness come from analysis of the aggregates
> Is essencelessness, like a plantain tree,
> But that does not serve as the voidness
> Endowed with supremacy in all aspects.

43. The rather generic title *Summary Teaching* (*mdor bstan pa*) is used for a number of texts. In this case this passage is from the anonymously written text *Śrīman-vimalaprabhā-tantrāvatāraṇī-vādācala-hṛdayāloka* (*dpal ldan dri ma dang bral ba'i 'od kyi rgyud la 'jug pa'i bshad sbyar mi gyo ba'i snying po snang ba*) (Tōh. 1349).

—arguing that the meditation on the voidness determined by analysis with discriminating wisdom of the object of the self-habit is not the [voidness used in the] system of tantra.[44]

[We reply:] "You are very discerning. You assert that the meditation on the meaning of selflessness, having been well ascertained and determined by references and reasons, is a meditation on essencelessness!" As for the meaning of the reference [from the *Summary Teaching*], the fifth chapter of the *Great Commentary Stainless Light* states:

> The voidness resulting from the analytic [dissolution] of things having the nature of masses of atoms is far different than an annihilative voidness.

According to this, [44b] if one has not well identified the parameters of the centrist's rational negandum, one might come to understand that "The meaning of realitylessness, reached through rational analysis of aggregates and so on, is the disestablishment of everything such as birth and cessation, and so on." [But this] is the thought behind the cessation [presumed to be a] nihilistic voidness, and is not the universal cessation achieved by the analysis of discriminating wisdom. If that were not so, then the quote from the second chapter of the *Stainless Light* [would be wrong:]

44. The phrase "voidness endowed with supremacy in all aspects" (*rnam pa thams cad mchog ldan pa'i stong nyid*) in this verse seems to be a rendition of the technical term *rnam pa kun [gyi] mchog ldan pa'i stong pa nyid*, which is a Tibetan translation of the term *sarva-ākāravara-upeta-śūnyatā*. This expresses the idea that various absolutists (such as Dolpopa) seized upon. As D.S. Ruegg explains: "[This] expression was used earlier as an epithet of the Sambuddha, e.g. at the end of the *Mahāparinirvāṇasūtra*. . . . In the *Ratnagotravibhāga* . . . and elsewhere . . . [this expression] occupies a prominent place in the theory of absolute reality" (*Literature of the Madhyamaka*: 84n). However, elsewhere (*Buddha-nature, Mind and the Problem of Gradualism in a Comparative Perspective*: 184, 190) Ruegg also explains Kamalashīla's and Shāntarakshita's centrist understanding of this term. In brief, they consider that just as *vipaśyanā* must be conjoined with *śamatha* (as *prajñā* must be with *caryā*), so *śūnyatā* must be conjoined with liberative art (*upāya*). They then maintain that—in opposition to a "one [-sided] method" (*ekanaya*) which views emptiness alone as a self-sufficient method (*śūnyatānaya*)—it is this emptiness conjoined with liberative art that is "emptiness endowed with all excellent qualities" (*sarva-ākāravara-upeta-śūnyatā*). (Thanks to T. Yarnall for this note.)

> That consciousness ultimately exists
> Is not asserted by the wise;
> It is like a lotus of the sky,
> Free from the natures of unity and plurality.

The nonreality of the consciousness aggregate is discerned by the reason of freedom from unity and plurality and the example of the sky flower. It is stated:

> That very fact is realized by the centrist

and:

> It is established as selfless and so on. This is declared summarily, you should realize it in detail from the expansive sutras.

Thus, selflessness is briefly stated in that text, and it is said one must look extensively in the texts of the centrists. And this would be contradicted [by your position above]. Furthermore, from the *Great Commentary [Stainless Light]*:

> The "vajra" is the great unbreakable and uncuttable; and that same thing being a vehicle, it is the vajra vehicle; and the tantric way and the transcendence way become mixed in one as nature of effect and cause.

Here the view of voidness of the transcendent wisdom, the causal vehicle, and the great bliss of the tantric vehicle, the fruitional vehicle, are said to be mingled in union. And therefore, it is a great philosophical mistake to assert that the *Time Machine* system has a way of determining [45a] the view that is different from the view determined in the transcendent wisdom vehicle.

Thus, although there are many contexts in the *Root Tantra* where the view of voidness is determined, when Vairochana states in the second chapter:

> Being free from all things;
> Abandoning aggregates, elements, media,

And the object and subject [dichotomy];
Through the equality of objective selflessness,
One's own mind primally unproduced—
That is the reality of voidness.

Thus, in the *Disclosure of the Spirit of Enlightenment*, [Nāgārjuna] accomplishes the determination of the void aspect [of what is] taught to be the spirit of enlightenment. Therein, the first phrase refutes the self that is imagined by the fundamentalists. The next two lines refute the true subject-object dichotomy imagined by the realist schools. The remainder refutes the truth of the mind imagined by the idealists.

After that, [the *Disclosure* continues]:

"Something" is a construct;
Constructlessness is voidness.
Wherein constructs become apparent,
How can voidness be [realized] there?

The mind with the aspects of construct and construction
Is not beheld by the transcendent buddhas.
Wherein there are construct and construction,
Therein there is no enlightenment spirit.

Herein "construct" refers to the three constructs such as the construct of the personal self, and it does not refer to all kinds of constructs. The same text states:

The buddhas always assert the spirit of enlightenment
As of the nature of voidness,
Unobscured by the constructs of the ideas
Of self, aggregate, and so forth. **[45b]**

To elucidate the import of the statement that all things are like a dream in the fifteenth chapter of the *Root Tantra*, [Nāgārjuna] declared the stage of self-consecration. Regarding the process of analysis by individuating wisdom, in comment on the ninth chapter of the *Root Tantra*, the *Revelation of the Hidden Intention Explanatory Tantra* states that an effect coming from a cause is to be individually analyzed by the following procedure: though it occurs when unanalyzed, it abides nowhere at all when analyzed. And the *Vajra Rosary* states in its sixteenth chapter that one should analyze the three times by differentiating three times in each of them. The *Vajra Essence Ornament Tantra*, a corresponding art tantra, states that voidness is determined by analyzing the directional facets in atoms of material things and by analyzing mind instants each into three [periods]. Thus, they [all] explain the method of seeking the understanding of the [realistic] view as in the transcendence vehicle.

It is stated in the *Esoteric Accomplishment*:

> One analytically discerns the actuality of this three-realm
> world
> As free of intrinsic reality in terms of unity and multiplicity.

And:

> If one analytically investigates through the path
> All these three realms
> Up to the peak of existence,
> The aggregates do not exist in truth.
> Who is it who analytically investigates?
> Here, what is to be investigated?
> Thatness, just that alone, by striving,
> As long as one investigates,
> So long all is clear light.

[46a] This does not refer to the occasion of merely seeking preliminary understanding but rather to the subsequent occasion of meditation. However, this should not be taken as a repeated investigation by discriminating wisdom at the time of joining bliss and void after orgasmic joy—the fourth joy—and clear light—the fourth void—have dawned. [Rather, it] should be taken as [such an investigation] in the occasion of the aftermath, having emerged from equipoise. [And both of] these two are different from the practice of repeated analysis with discriminating wisdom taught in the transcendence vehicle when the practitioner on the stage of practice cultivates the equipoise of insight through faith.

In summary, concerning the position on the view of voidness, the great treatises write about four levels of superiority: all universal vehicle philosophers except the dialecticist centrists accept the personal selflessness in agreement with its determination by the scripturalists; the experientialists accept voidness as [things being] devoid of substantial subject-object dichotomy and as things being devoid of the intrinsically identifiable imaginative construction that is intrinsically ascriptive and descriptive designation; the dogmaticist centrists [accept the view of] voidness as the negation of the truth-status of all things without negating the conventionally intrinsically identifiable status [of things]; and the dialecticists [accept] the view of realitylessness that negates all things' intrinsic identifiability in terms of both realities.

Concerning these, the fourth is the view of voidness mentioned in the joining of bliss and void in terms of the jewel-like [46b] person who is the disciple of the unexcelled mantra vehicle. And the voidness involved in the bliss-void-union of other disciples can occur as either the idealist or the dogmaticist view, depending on the disciple. Thus, in terms of the view of selflessness, there are worst, mediocre, excellent, and extremely excellent. Although among the elucidators of the mantric treatises there seem to be some who advocate the union of bliss and void in terms of the idealist view, there do not seem to be any who [do so] in terms of just the above-explained view of personal selflessness. Therefore, it is necessary to discover surely a certitude in at least the voidness that is the idealists' voidness of subject-object dichotomy. However, the interpretations of these have been extensively explained elsewhere.[45]

[**VI.B.3.b.ii.B′1′a′ii′** – Explaining the import of bliss]

If one should wonder, "Well then, what is the 'bliss' of 'bliss-void-union'?"

Here, when mental fluency arises through the cultivation of only the samadhi of mental one-pointedness, and the physical neural energies have become serviceable by the power of that, the body fluency, having the form of inner benefit, arises. Based on that, according to the *Stages of Yoga Practice*, physical bliss and great mental joy arise. This [state] commonly occurs for all those who cultivate the sustained focus on thoughtlessness, whether they are outsider or insider, individualist or universalist, sutra or tantra

45. Especially in Tsong Khapa's *Essence of True Eloquence.*

practitioner. I have already explained its pattern in [47a] the *Great Treatise on the Stages of the Enlightenment Path*, giving supportive references. Therefore, such bliss is not the bliss of this [context].

Further, relying on the meditation on the in-breath and out-breath taught in the philosophical vehicle, or on the meditation "breath-control in deity yoga meditation," which is stopping the out-breath and holding the breath within, taught in the action tantra *Ultimate Contemplation* and in the performance tantra *Vairochana Enlightenment*, samadhis generating great bliss in body and mind arise. Nevertheless, such are not the breath-yoga that penetrates the vital points of the neural wheels of the inner body, and therefore such bliss is not the bliss mentioned in the bliss-void-union of the unexcelled vehicle. Thus, [such blisses] are not the same as [those of] the neural energy vajra recitation and the vaselike breath control [of the perfection stage].

Master Buddhaguhya explained that the deity yoga of blocking the out-breath and holding the neural energy within is used in the yoga tantras as well. Beyond those [above mentioned], the explanation of vaselike [energy-] meditation in a *Heart Sutra Commentary*,[46] and some peoples' occasional explanation of the [presence of the] higher tantras' body vital-point penetration in some contexts in the lower tantras—these are not to be relied upon as they are fabricated by those who make up things themselves, not understanding thoroughly the specifics of the paths of sutra and tantra and of lower and higher tantras.

In short, in the three tantra classes from the yoga tantras down and in the philosophy vehicle, many transcendent, immaculate blisses [arising from] the unerring meditation [47b] on the import of voidness are taught, but there is no teaching of the bliss of the melting of the enlightenment spirit in the blaze of furor by the power of penetrating the vital-points of the physical channel system and forcing the neural energies into the central channel. Thus, their "bliss" does not refer to the bliss of bliss-void-union. As it is stated in the *Sheaf of Instructions*:

> If one were to argue: "Well, even those who have attained the first contemplation experience bliss like [that of] the chakravarti kings, what need to mention the [persons who attain the]

46. The commentary with this statement has not yet been identified.

> realization of both selflessnesses? Therefore, since it exceeds even extreme joy, the first stage is called 'Intense Joy.'"
>
> [Then, one answers:] "True, [but] this is not the orgasmic bliss. And therefore, as it is not the "great bliss" [of unexcelled yoga tantra,] [that great bliss] is not a technique accessible at the stage of beginners; though the hole of a needle is called 'a space-hole,' it does not become equal to space."

Here is an answer to the argument that considers that "since it is declared that extensive bliss arises in one who attains the first contemplation even without understanding selflessness at all, there is no question about extensive bliss of contemplating voidness arising in one on the transcendence vehicle who meditates frequently having realized the two selflessnesses precisely; also the first stage, 'intense joy,' is so called because the bliss arising there is very much greater; thus the unexcelled [yoga tantra] vehicle is not any more excellent than the transcendence vehicle from the point of view of bliss." While it is true that a great bliss arises from meditating voidness, [48a] it is not the orgasmic bliss, and so it is not the great bliss declared in the unexcelled [vehicle]. And since in the context of the beginner on the transcendence vehicle there is no technique mentioned to actually develop the orgasmic bliss, [the text] states that it is not that [the unexcelled vehicle] is not superior from the point of view of great bliss.

Again, from that same text [*Sheaf of Instructions*]:

> If one should protest: "Well then, in the *Transcendent Wisdom [Sutra]*, is there no mention of 'the bliss of the unexcelled, truly perfect enlightenment?'"
>
> [The answer is:] "It is so mentioned; but this is not a teaching of the art of this [orgasmic bliss]; because this does not indicate the orgasmic great bliss that serves as [the essence of] art. Therefore, that [orgasmic bliss] is to be realized only by this process."

Thus, in the transcendence vehicle, the path orgasmic great bliss, which is the art that causes the fruitional bliss of enlightenment, is not taught. So even though it is permitted to mention "great bliss" in the context of fruition, there is a great difference in the two vehicles.

It is also stated in a hidden manner in the *Esoteric Accomplishment* that that very orgasmic joy is not taught in the sutras and the lower tantra classes:

> Again, that very thing abiding in the tantra [continuum]
> Is clear in the glorious *Esoteric Community*.
> Where many elaborations become increased,
> Elsewhere it is taught in a hidden manner.
> In the divisions of action and performance,
> And in the collections of sutras and so forth,
> The unique supreme joy abides in many forms.
> In the very jewel vessel of the aggregates
> Due to the different inclinations of beings,
> By striving for that, having hidden it,
> The Buddha Savior makes [such] arrangements.

Therefore, [48b] the statement that "the unique supreme joy itself abides in many forms in them" means that [the Buddha] taught in many diverse ways wishing to lead [beings] gradually to that same supreme joy, and does not mean that that very same [bliss] is taught in those texts. Otherwise, he would have to teach the higher consecrations in those [texts]; since it is prohibited to teach the principle of great bliss without conferring the secret consecration and so forth. Thus, this demonstration that this orgasmic bliss is the noble distinction not shared with the other vehicles and other tantras is explained in all unexcelled tantras and their authoritative elucidations. I do not cite them here in fear of prolixity.

Thus, although there are many immaculate blisses, other than the orgasmic bliss, from meditating after unerringly ascertaining voidness, if one is a practitioner of this process, such blisses are understood as caused by achieving a rough insight on the transcendence vehicle. And in a similar way, even though one enters [a bliss] connected with the very stable deity yogas, it is not [the bliss that is] the import of the unexcelled [yoga's] perfection stage. Even though this can be understood from [getting] just a rough idea of the treatises of the lower tantras, as this is the occasion of still having a rather feeble power of intellect, a great many people seem to hold even the first bliss mentioned above as being the great bliss of the bliss-void-union of the unexcelled [yoga tantra].

Thus, the bliss mentioned in "bliss-void-union" [49a] is the orgasmic joy, which first arises when the furor blazing by force of the [right] *rasanā* and [left] *lalanā* [channel] neural energies entering the [central] *avadhūti* channel melts the enlightenment spirit. Though such bliss resembles the other blisses mentioned in the mere fact of being bliss, it has an extremely distinctive import, so they should be precisely distinguished without confusion.

In that regard, on this vehicle the "unconditional compassion" is also mentioned, declared often as in the declaration of the *Sheaf of Instructions*:

> Liberative art is the objective-free great compassion that accomplishes the aims of beings, which has the nature of orgasmic universal bliss.

[VI.B.3.b.ii.B′1′a′iii′ – Explaining the process of union of bliss-void-indivisible]

The third has two parts: [A′′] The actual meaning; and [B′′] Rebutting objections.

[VI.B.3.b.ii.B′1′a′iii′A′′ – The actual meaning]

"Well then," one may wonder, "what is the method of indivisibly uniting voidness and the bliss of unconditional compassion?"

It is stated in the *Glorious Sampuṭa [Tantra]*:

> The actuality of non-elaboration
> Is renowned as "wisdom."
> And actual compassion fulfills
> Beings' aims like a wish-granting gem.
> Wisdom abiding in the non-objective,
> And real nonperceiving great compassion
> Become one, organic with the mind,
> Like space [immersed] in space.

As for the meaning of that, [Anaṅgavajra's] *Accomplishment Ascertaining Wisdom and Art* explains:

> Knowing and known are distinguished,
> Joined they are analyzed thoroughly,
> And the realitylessness of things [discovered];
> That very thing is pronounced "wisdom."
> The compassion that extracts beings
> From the ocean of suffering and its causes [49b]
> Is passionately attached to beings,
> And so is called a "[loving] passion."

Thus, wisdom ascertains realitylessness, investigating while distinguishing bodies and minds, and the universal passion, the art through which beings' aims are fulfilled, is the orgasmic bliss explained as compassion [as the same text goes on to state]:

> Mixed like milk and water
> United nondualistically,
> The union of these two
> Is called "wisdom art."

Thus one should understand them according to this statement of their union as like the mixing of milk and water.

Furthermore, as for the actual indivisibility of bliss and its [void] reality, since the very establishment of [bliss's] substance establishes already its actuality as indivisible from its voidness, it is not necessary for the yogi/nī to make them experientially indivisible. Likewise, it is not necessary for [one] bliss-[cognition] to seal another cognition realizing voidness, nor for [a cognition] previously having developed bliss to be sealed by another [cognition] with the view of voidness. This is because it is not the case that voidness-realization and bliss [as initially separate entities] mutually [then] become one anothers' actualities. For example, although [virtues such as] generosity etc. are combined with the view of selflessness, generosity etc. do not arise as the actuality of such a view of thatness.

If one wonders: "Well then, how are they to be understood?"

[Here, when] that conscious subjectivity produced as the actuality of orgasmic bliss unerringly realizes the import of its objective voidness, its subject-object-union itself [already] is the union of bliss-void-indivisible. Further, at the time of the objective [clear light's] orgasmic [bliss-void-indivisibility], subject and object become experientially uniform, like water merging in milk, and even the subtlest [trace of] dualism [50a] is terminated. Whereas before the arising of the objective orgasmic [bliss-void-indivisibility] experiential uniformity is only imagined, since one has not [yet] directly experienced thatness and must [gradually] enter [the experience of] thatness by means of a conceptually imaginative conscious attitude. As such is the process of [the subjectivity] uniting nondually with the objective voidness, the process of uniting in indivisible actuality [both the] bliss [mind] and the mind realizing voidness is the integrated creation of the undifferentiable actuality of the two minds.

Since there is nothing [here] that exceeds the centrist method of decisive realization of voidness, there are no grades of superiority between the voidness view of this vehicle and [that of] the transcendence vehicle. Though the object to be ascertained is the same, no other subjectivity has the same power to realize voidness as the orgasmic bliss subjectivity; so though the voidness is not different, the bliss art [that realizes it in the Vajrayana] is declared to be distinctively superior. If one does not determine selfless voidness with decisive insight, one is not liberated from the life cycle; and if one does not generate the orgasmic bliss as the means of ascertainment, one lacks the vitalizing energy of the supreme path of mantra: thus, since either one by itself is not enough, it is declared that both are necessary. As Saraha says:

> Entering voidness lacking compassion,
> That one will not find the supreme path.
> Or if one meditates only compassion,
> One will stay here in the life cycle
> And will not attain liberation.
> Who can unite both of them
> Will not settle down
> In either life cycle or liberation.

In this *Enlightenment Song*, [50b] he explains orgasmic wisdom itself as the essence of the path, referring to orgasmic bliss as "compassion." When one generates orgasmic bliss as explained above, and coarse thoughts are eliminated and the mind naturally abides unmoving, one [might misunderstand] the mere nondiscursive meditation of bliss itself—free of expansion toward any object at all—as the meditation on voidness; but then the explanation that meditation on bliss alone will not liberate from the life cycle would be incorrect. Thus, it is necessary to cultivate the certitude [about the void side] from the thorough determination of the import of selflessness.

[**VI.B.3.b.ii.B′1′a′iii′B″** – Rebutting objections]

One might object: If meditating voidness is cultivation of the certitude of orgasmic bliss's ascertainment of the import of selflessness, then it contradicts the *Sampuṭa [Tantra]*'s statement not to meditate holding either voidness or nonvoidness:

> Don't meditate the void,
> And don't meditate the nonvoid!
> The yogi/nī who does not abandon the void
> Cannot abandon the nonvoid.
> Holding to both void and nonvoid,
> Concepts proliferate without diminish,
> Full abandoning [is another] construct—
> Therefore, abandon both [holding and abandoning]!

[To this we answer:] The meaning of this reference is explained in the *Sheaf of Instructions* as follows: In order to abandon absolutism about material things etc. by [knowing] the voidness of ultimate existence and abandon nihilism by [knowing] nonvoidness due to superficial existence, you stop meditating by holding on to [either] voidness of superficial existence [or] nonvoidness of ultimate existence. Since the ultimate identitylessness of material things etc. is itself [none other than] the superficial actuality of material things etc., it is [also] incorrect to abandon the [51a] actuality of the ultimately void and the superficially non-void. Thus, all extremist constructs develop from holding things ultimately nonvoid and conventionally void as if non-existent. Thus, the [above] treatise means that abandoning ultimate void produces absolutistic constructs and abandoning conventional nonvoid produces constructs nihilistic about evolutionary effects; and so it does not mean what you say. For just prior to that quote [the *Sampuṭa Tantra*] states the holding of inessentiality:

> The truth realm is extreme equality,
> To be realized as like a plantain tree.

And it also states that the ascertainment of identitylessness through strenuous analysis is the cause of ending all suffering and attaining supreme happiness:

> Wishing to end all suffering
> And to attain the supreme bliss of perfect buddhahood,
> Stabilize the mind and strenuously investigate,
> And negate the reality of such identity!

Furthermore, "holding to the nonvoid" means holding things as truths, and "holding to the void" means holding as truth, in spite of the fact that things lack truth, the voidness that is [itself, also,] devoid of any truth substance. The *Accomplishment [Ascertaining] Wisdom and Art* states:

> A wise person who wants to eliminate error
> Should abandon materialism.
> Since even nominally different [things]
> Are not conceptually discernable,
> The wise wholly give up materialism,
> And do not construct insubstantiality either. **[51b]**
> Just as a burning lamp can be extinguished,
> But once extinguished you can't affect it,
> You can [extinguish] materialism itself,
> But not the holding of insubstantiality.

Thus it states that, just as one should abandon the truth-habit about substances, called "materialism" for short, the truth-habit about voidness void of such true substance may be nominally different but is actually indistinguishable as a truth-holding construct and so should also be abandoned. As for the meaning of "like a lamp" and so on, though it is easy to reverse the truth-habit when you show the truthlessness of something held as truth, when you hold as truth the means of reversing the truth-habit about that something, namely the voidness of truth of that thing, it is like not being able to digest the medicine used to cure indigestion of food, with the same meaning as the statement from *The Centrist Treatise* about having the incurable view.[47] This same master [Nāgārjuna] should be understood as negating meditation with a truth-habit toward birthlessness and selflessness in his *Disclosure of the Spirit of Enlightenment* statement:

Whoever meditates voidness
—Whether called "birthlessness," "voidness," or "selflessness"—
As having the inferior nature,
That is not [the proper] means of meditating that.

As he also says in the *World-Transcending Praise*:

You have taught the elixir of voidness
In order to eliminate all imaginations;
Whoever becomes invested in that,
You find utterly absurd.

Thus, as such reasonings are often stated in the sutras and interpretative commentaries, this is the way you should understand them; and not as to contradict the other frequent statements about meditating with the view toward voidness, selflessness, and [52a] birthlessness, and so on. You should not let [such statements critiquing the truth-habit about voidness] obstruct your developing the certitude of selflessness, the means of cutting the root of the life cycle. Although for the alienated individual such certitude is not nonconceptual, [that is,] free of subtle conceptuality, it closely corresponds with nonconceptual wisdom. From the *Esoteric Community* commentaries, the *Flower Bouquet*, the *Sheaf of Instructions*, and the *Introduction to the Art of Self-Accomplishment*, it is clearly stated that meditating on it develops

47. Famous verse in Nāgārjuna's *Wisdom* (ch. XIII, v. 8): "The Victors proclaimed voidness as the transcendence of all views. Hence, who adopts voidness as an [absolutist] view is thereby pronounced incurable."

the nonconceptual. I have already explained this fully elsewhere[48] and do not continue here fearing prolixity.

In short, making certain that not even an atom is a fit object for the orientation of the sign-habit—which is the truth-habit toward any thing of life or liberation—and seeing that all the causal activities of relativity are perfectly compatible with that fact, finally, as for the realization of voidness wherein by the power of reason one finds certainty free of the two extremes about that object, the sutras and their elucidative commentaries repeatedly state its limitless benefits, such as that even mere doubt tending toward the fact shatters ordinary existence. Furthermore, the unexcelled vajra vehicle thoroughly ascertains that same thing in the same way by mobilizing the distinctive subjectivity of the orgasmic joy, and explains the measureless immediate and ultimate advantages of the bestowal of the supreme in this very life through the great bliss subjectivity. [52b] Therefore, the discerning one should engage in the personal instruction that integrates the view profoundly certain of the impact of selflessness and the art that develops the extraordinary great bliss, and should feel reverence for the quest of the orgasmic wisdom that combines bliss and void indivisibly.

The *Community Further Tantra* states that when one asks the meaning of "spirit of enlightenment" in the *Root Tantra*, the spirit of enlightenment is said to be the inseparability of voidness and compassion. And in regard to the statements of the spirit of enlightenment in the second chapter of the *Root Tantra*, the *Illuminating Lamp* mentions two spirits of enlightenment, which are those of the ultimate clear light and of ultimate communion. Of these two, the former is the objective orgasmic [intuition]; so it is not that [such orgasmic spirit of enlightenment] is not explained in the system that combines the bliss-void-indivisible voidness and the compassionate spirit of enlightenment. The *Five Stages* also states:

> Out of all eighty-four thousand teachings,
> The Great Sage declared that [clear light]
> [To be] the quintessence of the essence,
> Defining manifest enlightenment.[49]

48. I.e., in both the *Great Treatise on the Stages of the Enlightenment Path* and the *Great Treatise on the Stages of Mantra*.

49. PK, III, v. 69 (Tomabechi 2006, ch. 2, v. 69, p. 145).

Here [Nāgārjuna] states that the quintessence of the essence of manifest enlightenment is the objective clear light, and that refers to the objective orgasmic spirit of enlightenment of bliss-void-indivisible. Among the unexcelled tantras and their authoritative elucidations, in some of them the bliss side is clear and the way of realizing voidness not as clear, and in some of them the way of realizing voidness is clear and the bliss side is not so clear. So one should understand them as meaning the union of both bliss and void, and not mistakenly take them to be separable.

Although the message of [53a] bliss-void-indivisible is as widely renowned as the wind, the understanding of the way of uniting the great bliss—specially distinctive among blisses—and the ultimate reality of voidness—specially distinctive among voidnesses—is extremely rare. With this in mind, Saraha said [in an *Enlightenment Song*]:

> Though the story is told from house to house,
> The locale of great bliss is not well understood.

So one should not be easily satisfied with just a bit of it, but should strive persistently to realize this import, which is more greatly secret than secret.

[**VI.B.3.b.ii.B′1′b′** – Explaining the meanings of the voidness and compassion involved in bliss-void-indivisibility]

This has two parts: [i′] The actual meaning; and [ii′] The reason for the need for such explanation.

[**VI.B.3.b.ii.B′1′b′i′** – The actual meaning]

If the way in which bliss-void-indivisible voidness and compassion are the meaning of EVAṀ is as above explained, how is the spirit of enlightenment that is voidness and compassion as the two-realities-indivisible explained as the meaning of EVAṀ?

In regard to that very bliss-void-indivisible above explained, many commentators on the yoginī tantras teach a bliss-void communion and a two-reality communion. There also are such teachings in terms of the import of communion in the noble system. But the system of savior Nāgārjuna does not interpret communion to be just that bliss-void-indivisible that is the objective orgasmic [intuition]. The spirit of enlightenment is also declared in the *Community Further Tantra*:

> Peace, beginningless and endless,
> Inexhaustible principle not substantial, not insubstantial.
> Voidness and compassion inseparable—
> That is called "enlightenment spirit."

Here I should explain the enlightenment spirits of the above-explained two [53b] communions. Here "insubstantial" refers to voidness and "substantial" refers to compassion, and those two are referred to as wisdom and art. As the text continues:

> The insubstantial is wisdom,
> And art has the nature of the substantial.

This is the context of explaining the import of the yoga of art and wisdom in equilibrium. And this is according to the *Illuminating Lamp*'s declaring the meaning of the statement of the equilibrium of art and wisdom in the sixth section of [Chandrakīrti's] *Six-Branched Yoga*, that it is the communion uniting superficial reality art and ultimate reality wisdom.

In general, there are many arts and wisdoms, but here the art and wisdom of communion is identified. Although [usually] actual ultimate reality is the uncompounded reality of things, here "ultimate reality" refers to the clear light wisdom that enters the single taste of that reality and great bliss, often stated to be [the ultimate reality] where subject and object cannot be distinguished. Thus, in this context, objective orgasmic wisdom has two types; one on the occasion of the objective clear light alone and another on the occasion of the clear light of communion. The first of these is the stage of clear light or the stage of clear enlightenment explained in the *Five Stages* as the fourth stage, and the second is one half of the fifth stage communion stage. [54a] Thus, as for the mere objective orgasmic [intuition] of bliss-void-indivisible explained in other treatises, from among the two kinds of the ultimate explanation included in the four procedures [of explanation], it is the clear light ultimate—above that there is the communion ultimate, to which it still has not arrived.

If such is the ultimate reality [clear light void] side, which is one part of communion, what is the other part, the superficial reality side?

This [noble] system differs from other treatises' explanations of superficial reality. Here the superficial reality is repeatedly explained to be the totally pure magic body, adorned with the [112] signs and marks, developed from the material cause of the wisdom energy of the five light rays, which serves as mount for, and functions as one reality with, the wisdom-intuition of voidness. At the end of the three voids of mind isolation there arises a superficial magic body made of the energy of five light rays; and that is the [type of] magic body that is called the stage of self-consecration, the third of the five stages. These will be extensively explained [below].

Therefore, the import of the E and VA syllables is the indivisible unification of the objective clear light and the purified magic body, according to the above explanations. And the import of the *Ṁ*-drop is the mode of union in a single actuality; as mind in the first type [of bliss-void communion] and as body in the second type [of ultimate-superficial communion]. This second import of EVAṀ is the ultimate communion. Further, in the statement in the *Community Explanatory Tantra*, the *King of the Gods Dialogue*:[50]

> When the Omniscient Lord dwells here
> In the magic [of] the two syllables E VAṀ—
> At the start of teaching the holy Dharma,
> He elucidates for the sake of that EVAṀ. [54b]

"The magic" is communion, thus indicating the second import of EVAṀ. There are two communions, those of learner and master. They are also mentioned by the noble [Nāgārjuna] with the terms "wisdom" and "compassion," as in the *Five Stages*:

> When one proceeds in the knowledge
> Of the oneness of wisdom and compassion,
> That is called "communion"—
> This stage is the sphere of Buddha.

50. According to Alex Wayman (1991, 85) the *Devendraparipṛcchā* was never translated into Tibetan. It only exists in cited passages, mainly in the *Illuminating Lamp*, where it is cited as a *Community* explanatory tantra; but see above, Tib. 15a–b.

The import of EVAṀ, which is the union of magic body and voidness wisdom from the third stage self-consecration on, is the hidden meaning EVAṀ. In these [noble] systems, the import explained as the four voids is the same as that explained in the yoginī tantras and their elucidative commentaries as the four joys. [But], while in this system the magic body is taught as made of neural energy and mind between the third and fourth voids, in the yoginī tantra literature such is not explained as occurring between the third and fourth joys. While in this system the magic body is taught as made of mere neural energy and mind after the objective clear light, in those other tantras it is not taught as occurring after the objective orgasmic joy. Thus, this explicit teaching of the method of making from neural energy the learner's magic body, the immediate cause of the fruitional material [buddha-] body, and the third stage magic body that is in turn the immediate cause [of that learner's magic body]—this is the unexcelled distinctive excellence of this supreme system.[51]

[**VI.B.3.b.ii.B′1′b′ii′** – The reason for the need for such explanation]

Here one could wonder that even if it might be that in this unexcelled yoga tantra such a way of achieving the magic body is doubtless necessarily taught, [55a] how do we know that it is necessary definitely to teach such a way to achieve the magic body?

You[52] with discerning intelligence—listen! I am going to determine this extremely hard-to-understand point with authentic proofs. There are four: [A′′] The proof through the perspective of its being the extraordinary cause of the [buddhas'] material body; [B′′] the proof through the perspective of its being the extraordinary key of the base of purification; [C′′] the proof relying on the key of the way to create the deity; and [D′′]

51. Since Tsong Khapa argues that the defining criterion of a father tantra is its emphasis on the creation of the magic body, this insight about the sequence of production of the various stages of the magic body is highly significant in revealing the source of his insight.

52. Tsong Khapa rarely uses the second person direct pronoun, but his use of it here to call his students to attention supports our more frequent use of it, especially when he is exhorting the reader to practice or understand this or that key element of the teachings. In fact, as the colophon reveals, he is lecturing to present students in composing this treatise, and scribes are writing down what he says, so his mode of address is directly personal.

the proof relying on the key of [its being] the actuality of the indivisibility of art and wisdom.

[**VI.B.3.b.ii.B′1′b′ii′A″** – The proof through the perspective of its being the extraordinary cause of the (buddhas') material body]

The *Ornament of Realizations* states:

> The spiritual conception is for the sake of others,
> Desiring the utterly perfect enlightenment.

Thus, as for example one suffering from thirst mainly aims at getting [something to] drink but may [also] aim at [obtaining] a vessel as a means of getting it, so the [messianic] universalists, while they mainly aim to fulfill the interests of others, forced by their minds being moved by universal compassion that cannot tolerate beings tormented by sufferings and bereft of happiness, they further see that if they do not attain [the vessel of] buddhahood, there is no other method for them to achieve that fulfillment of [others' needs]. So for one with such an ambition for perfect enlightenment as a method of that [fulfillment of others' needs], the two universal vehicles, of mantra and of transcendence, are similar; since they do not differ in their spiritual conceptions.

Thus, since among the two buddha-bodies, that which accomplishes beings' needs through direct manifestation is the material body [**55b**] and not the truth body, the material body is the main objective. Thus, a distinctive cause homogeneous with that art which is the means of attaining the material body—an unexcelled distinctive specialty lacking in other vehicles, other tantras, and the first stage [of unexcelled yoga]—is necessary in the context of the perfection stage. In that light, if there is no wisdom realizing voidness, one cannot attain freedom of liberation from the bonds of the life cycle. Such wisdom also exists for the individual vehicle; but if the aspect of the art that causes the [buddhas'] material body is lacking, however much you meditate on voidness, you only attain freedom liberated from identity-bound existence, and do not attain omniscience. Therefore, among the arts that produce the material body, while realization of voidness is indispensable, the system of both universal vehicles requires meditation [additionally] certain of the complete art aspect, even though still carrying this distinctive realization of voidness all the way up to the truth body. However, in the transcendence universal vehicle, though there is meditation on a path conducive to the truth body, there is no meditation on the deity body, which is conducive to the material body. Here, as for the detailed explanations of such [topics] as the two vehicles' ranking in terms of their arts of [creating] the material body, the way in which the two paths conducive to the two bodies are the same in terms of requiring meditation, and the necessity to accept this in the path of all four tantras, and so on, I will not elaborate them here, as I have already done so in the *Great Treatise on the Stages of Mantra*.

Further, as for the deity yogas of the three lower tantras, compared to the unexcelled yoga tantra, they are extremely remote [in their serving] as causes of the [buddhas'] material body. [56a] And the deity yogas of the first stage of unexcelled yoga tantra are merely the means of developing the roots of virtue that prepare for the realizations of the perfection stage. But the perfection-stage deity yoga, so extremely distinctive from those, must serve in general as the [main] cause of the material body, and particularly must be a cause homogeneous with the [32] signs and [80] marks that serve as the immediate cause of the material body, which is the fruition at the end of the learning path of the perfection stage.

In this context, as for the transcendence vehicle cause of the material buddha-body, in general there are the many stores of merit, and in particular, through the causes of the physical signs—such as the escorting of mentors [being the evolutionary cause of the light-webbed fingers], and so on—one attains the stages in [the process of] accumulating these stores over many lifetimes. One [thus gradually] attains a body conducive to the fruitional signs and marks, further getting better and better on higher and higher stages, and at the time of the final existence, one will attain the ultimate signs and marks of the learning path of that [transcendence] path. Thereupon, at the time of buddhahood, the homogeneous preceding [causes] of the signs and marks of that body are taught to serve as the homogeneous causes of the fruitional signs and marks; and it is not claimed that there is any sudden transformation without attaining the prior body with signs and marks. Likewise, on the attainment of buddhahood in a single lifetime through the path of the unexcelled yoga tantra, it is not stated that one must achieve the body adorned with signs and marks just by achieving a body; if one does not attain a certain type of body adorned with signs and marks on the learning path, there will be no homogeneous cause, and there cannot be any sudden transformation.

Therefore, from the occasion of the perfection-stage learner's path, [56b] one must attain the body adorned with the signs and marks. One cannot create the body adorned with the signs and marks by meditating deity yoga with this gross evolutionary body. It is insufficient to use only the body meditated in the mind as the deity body, as in the occasion of the creation stage. One needs a distinctive deity yoga that attains the body adorned with signs and marks other than those [above meditational bodies]. And since no material cause of that other than the neural energies is appropriate, the process of achieving the magic body from the energies is definitely necessary. Furthermore, as I will later prove, relying on the explanatory tantras *Vajra Rosary* and *Revelation of the Hidden Intention*, there are two types of bodies among basic reality sentient beings; the temporary gross body and the neural-energy-mind-created subtle body. Then I will explain how, just as the subtle orgasmic mind is accepted as the material cause of the intuitive wisdom truth buddha-body, the same applies in all respects as necessary in the achieving of the material buddha-body from the material cause of the subtle body made only of neural-energy-mind.

[VI.B.3.b.ii.B′1′b′ii′B″ – The proof through the perspective of its being the extraordinary key of the base of purification]

The unexcelled tantras teach a stage of the new creation of both the distinctive habitat of the environment of the measureless mansion and the distinctive inhabitants of the living deities. The tantra intends that the process of creating the environment should be accepted as corresponding to the creation and destruction of the universe which is the basic reality environment. By the key of that reasoning, the process of the creation of the living deities and so on [57a] must be structured according to the basic reality of sentient beings' birth, death, and between stages. And this must be done not only on the creation stage but also on the perfection stage. At that time, it is understood that, at the end of the realization of clear light, taken as the process of death, one must create a magic body from mere neural-energy-mind at the end of the clear light, in keeping with the process of creating the between state from mere neural-energy-mind, separate from the old body of the gross aggregates. I am not going to expand on this here, as I have extensively already explained it in my *Stage of Arrangement Commentary* [on] the treatise of the Glorious Nāgabodhi. But I will explain the *Vajra Rosary* statements of how the arrangements of the perfection stage should be made in the same way.

[**VI.B.3.b.ii.B′1′b′ii′C″** – The proof relying on the key of the way to create the deity]

Beginning from the action tantra, when the yogi/nī practices the methods of deity creation, it is taught in some way that one rises in a deity body after each immersion in the void. Finally in the context of the perfection stage, the yogi/nī does not just do that as merely a focused imagination, but must actually arise in the deity body after entering the void. The key here is that if one knows how to create the magic body one can do that, and not otherwise; thus after entering into clear light as in the process of death one must create a deity body made from neural energy-mind as in the [basic reality] between.

On this point, in the *Integrated Practices*,[53] [Āryadeva] answers the question "How is the wisdom body created, since the deity body does not appear from the creation stage to body isolation, nor in speech or mind isolation?" [57b] His answer gives the import of the statement of the way to create the magic body from neural-energy. Further, as for the teachings—beginning from the creation stage—of arising in a deity body after entering the void, they do not include the way to create the deity body, which is not just creating it through an imaginative visualization. Thus, to answer the question about the way to create the deity body, [Āryadeva] teaches the magic body.

[**VI.B.3.b.ii.B′1′b′ii′D″** – The proof relying on the key of (its being) the actuality of the indivisibility of art and wisdom]

Having completed the creation stage, learning thoroughly the perfection stage, at the time of activity when ready for the [tantric] conduct, with the exception of the conceptual duties explained in the elaborated conducts, such as salutations and response to salutations and so on, and in the investigation of realitylessness of things in the aftermath periods,

53. This refers to chapter VI of the *Integrated Practices* (CW, pp. 243–52; 427–37; 581–89).

and so on, one is prohibited from the merit-accumulating activities taught for the aftermath periods in the transcendence vehicle and in the lower tantras, such as making stupas, reading sutras, offering mandalas, and so forth. Many other tantras make this kind of statement, along with the *Esoteric Accomplishment*:

> Do not salute deities
> Made of wood, stone, or clay;
> Worship the body itself!
> Venerate it as a mentor and bow to it!
>
> Don't make stupas etc. from earth and stone,
> Do not delight in books,[54]
> And don't make hand gestures in mandalas and so on,
> Even in your dreams!
>
> And don't prostrate yourself
> To those engaged in the three vehicles!

Especially in the context of the extremely non-elaborated conduct, it is taught that one should abandon all elaborations [58a] other than during eating, urinating, and defecating, and one should meditate on clear light alone by the process of immersion in the clear light.

In the *Ten Stages Sutra* [the Buddha stated]:

> At the time of terminating addictions with their seeds, when one meditates exclusively on the tolerance of the ultimate that is equipoised on the import of thatness, you will not have my measureless body, wisdom, and land and so on; so you must make efforts to create them, without abandoning this door of tolerance!

Here he does not just urge meditation on equipoised nonconceptual wisdom alone, but exhorts [the bodhisattvas] in the aftermath state to accumulate the store of merit, the cause of the material buddha-body. If a

54. From the Skt. *ratim*. It would be hard to make a sutra in earth or stone!

discerning person examines those two procedures [of the sutras and of the perfection stage], it is clear that there are distinctive homogeneous causes of the two bodies within the orgasmic joy and fourth void clear light meditations taught in unexcelled yoga tantra. Though according to the transcendence vehicle, the eighth stage equipoised nonconceptual wisdom provides a coordinating condition for the matter body, it is clear that the material cause is incomplete. And as for how it is complete in the former [tantric] case, while it is easy to understand how that orgasmic joy clear light wisdom is the material cause of the wisdom truth body, as for what serves as the material cause of the [compassion] matter body, it is clear that it is the magic body made of the five light ray neural-energies engaged with as being [nondually] the same in actuality as the void wisdom. Taking it that way, [58b] [the magic body] serves as the indivisible actuality of art and wisdom in terms of its being [nondually] the material cause of both bodies; and otherwise it is very difficult.

Now, it is taught in the context of performing the conduct that develops the impact of the perfection stage, after, as already explained, one has purified one's spiritual process through the ordinary path, has well maintained one's initiation and vows, and has completed the creation stage. It is not taught elsewhere. Thus, if you obstruct the [bodhisattva] deeds that accumulate extensive stores, saying "there is a quick path through nonattachment to any of those arrangements," you will ruin both yourself and others. The *Enlightenment Songs* and so on of the Great Brahmin teach the way that must practice the essential concerning orgasmic wisdom, abandoning other elaborated deeds in those contexts of the advanced path as already explained. It is an error to think that "he is teaching here the path of sudden attainment that the most intelligent practitioner must implement from the first entering of the path." So the essential adept literature requires investigation with a fine intelligence.

Relying on those key points just explained, as for the bliss-void-indivisible art and wisdom explained in other treatises, if you understand this explanation of the import of the *Communion* interpreted by the system of the noble father and sons as part of the pair of the two-reality-indivisible communion as the import of EVAṀ, it is very crucial for complete understanding of the systems of other tantras. The essence of the hidden meaning explanation—among the four [explanatory] procedures—taught as the meaning of the *Esoteric Community of All Realized Lords* [59a] is the third stage magic body.

And the essence of the ultimate explanation [explanatory procedure] is the communion body. And this point, which is the most greatly secret among the most extremely esoterically secret, is not taught clearly anywhere other than in this system. And it seems that even if you doggedly inquire into this system, it is hard to discover correctly even the rough general meaning. Therefore, those of intelligence should make intense efforts to realize it through the kindness of long propitiated, expert, spiritual friends.

[**VI.B.3.b.ii.B′2′** – Showing how, to produce that, one must penetrate the vital points in the body through the entry of the sign EVAṀ]

The second has two parts: [a′] The way one must penetrate the vital points in the body to generate the orgasmic [intuition] of bliss-void-indivisible; and [b′] The way one must penetrate the vital points in the body to generate the two-reality-indivisible communion.

[**VI.B.3.b.ii.B′2′a′** – The way one must penetrate the vital points in the body to generate the orgasmic (intuition) of bliss-void-indivisible]

The first has two parts: [i′] Teaching the two arts in general; and [ii′] Explaining them separately.

[**VI.B.3.b.ii.B′2′a′i′** – Teaching the two arts in general]

As already explained, tantra has no system of seeking the ultimate understanding of the import of the thatness of selflessness beyond that of the transcendence vehicle. For, if you just withdraw the mind within, without destroying the truth-habit orientation via precise rational negation of the conceptual object held by the truth-habit, your [meditation] will not constitute a [new] habit pattern counter to the truth-habit, and will not dislodge the truth-habit in the slightest. And, if you seek selflessness as the negatee negated to discover the import of selflessness at a level coarser than that taught by the dialecticist centrists, you will not negate the truth-habit orientation [**59b**] on the subtle level, and so the truth-habit will remain. And finally, even if you negate it at a more subtle level, since you will not have a footing on which to develop by force of reason the certitude of relativity within that import, your negation will become a nihilistic void. Therefore, although there is no difference [between vehicles] in their ways to determine the import of thatness, when you meditate on it, no other subjectivity than the great bliss of enlightenment spirit melted by the blazing furor kindled by the left and right channel energies entering and dissolving into the *dhūti* [central channel] has an equal power to swiftly purify the obscurational instincts with the orgasmic [wisdom] of its meditation on its ascertainment of the import of voidness. Therefore, that bliss must certainly be generated.

Further, thinking that it could not be generated without piercing the vital points in the body, [the Buddha] taught two arts of penetrating the vital points in the body, one art relying on the science consort and one art of meditating on the inner channels, energies, and drops. As for the first of these, he did not mention in the lower tantras [the need] to work with the mind of lust from arousal and gazing and so on, having openly looked at the evolutionary consort, but taught arousal, gazing, and hand-holding toward the goddess meditated as not being in sexual union with one. And so those tantras are called "arousal tantras." The unexcelled yoga tantras teach the art of uniting with both the evolutionary consort and the wisdom consort; so they are called "union tantras." Those tantras that do not teach the art of developing great bliss by uniting with the consort [60a] also do not teach the union with the wisdom consort, nor do they teach the art of developing bliss from melting enlightenment spirit through the meditation of inner channels, energies, and drops. Tantras wherein the former is taught teach the latter two as well; [that is,] tantras that teach the art of piercing the vital points in the inner body also teach the union with the two consorts. Those arts are all similar in their development of great bliss by the force of gathering and dissolving [right] *rasanā* and [left] *lalanā* [channel] energies into the *dhūti* [central channel]. That they are all necessary means that they generate the previously ungenerated orgasmic joy that is the distinctively excellent subjectivity for ascertaining voidness, they maintain the continuity of the already generated [joy], and they cause its increase from full to full.

[VI.B.3.b.ii.B′2′a′ii′ – Explaining them separately]

The second has two parts: [A′′] The art of the science consort; and [B′′] The art of meditating the inner channels, energies, and so forth.

[**VI.B.3.b.ii.B'2'a'ii'A''** – The art of the science consort]

Here one might protest that "if those arts of piercing the vital points in the body are arts for injecting the *rasanā* and *lalanā* energies into the *dhūti* [channel], the arts of meditating the inner channels, energies, and drops can allow them to be so; but [just] by uniting with the two [kinds of] consort, they cannot [function] like that; therefore it is incorrect that all those arts should function in that way."

In regard to being able [to function] in that way [just by] depending on the evolutionary consort, you must have both an objective [evolutionary consort] and a support [wisdom consort] with full qualifications as explained in the tantras. Since that is very extremely rare, it is not stated for persons [other than the jewel-like disciple].

In regard to the full qualifications [for such a consort], the *Sheaf of Instructions* states:

> Art [beings] possessing wisdom [consorts], [60b] by sexually uniting, inject the energies of *lalanā* and *rasanā* channels into the central *dhūti* and make the furor blaze. Further, they burn up the aggregates and so on, and cause the melting of the moon.

Thus it explains that, by uniting with the consort, the left and right energies enter the *dhūti* channel, furor blazes, and the spirit of enlightenment melts. Tathāgatavajra explains that at that time the energies moving in the nostrils cease, [signifying that] the energies have entered the *dhūti* channel. That art is the external vitalizing energy control. It is not that this path of vitalizing energy control is not explained in the unexcelled yoga tantras—the explanations are many. Though the key of the reason that this art compresses the energies into the *dhūti* channel seems very hard to understand, if you get a rough idea of it, it seems to be very excellent for understanding the many imports of the tantras. The usual reflection of what happens when you depend on the evolutionary consort is just what happens when you depend on the wisdom consort; and when you depend on the wisdom consort, there is also an occasion when the left and right energies penetrate the channel. This depends on knowing the personal instruction of the vitalizing energy control of the lower door explained in the *Further Tantra* among the three types of vitalizing energy control.

[**VI.B.3.b.ii.B′2′a′ii′B″** – The art of meditating the inner channels, energies, and so forth]

As for the art of meditating the inner channels, neural-energies, drops, and so on in the center—there in whichever vital point of the body, of the channel wheel of the *avadhūti* central channel wound up with the *rasanā* and *lalanā*—there are some doors for injecting the *rasanā* and *lalanā* energies into the *dhūti*. As for the way of injecting, there are many approaches; such as vajra recitation and the energy yogas such [61a] as vase-breathing in the two *Community* systems, the many drop yogas such as occur in the treatise of Ghaṇṭapāda,[55] and the furor meditations such as those in the treatises of Ḍombi Heruka and Kṛshṇāchārya and others. Further, in the *Time Machine* literature one injects the two energies into the central channel by meditating the vaselike energy-union in the place of the navel wheel, and Ḍombi Heruka and Kṛshṇāchārya accomplish it by meditating the furor visualization in the navel. Hence, first you penetrate the vital point in the navel wheel. The Jnānapāda system prefers to penetrate the vital point first in the heart center, then in the secret place, and again in the heart center. The noble system accomplishes the vital point penetration first in the place of the secret wheel and then in the place of the heart-center wheel.

In this context, it is incorrect to claim, as some definitely do, that the yoginī tantras' system accomplishes it from the navel: since Ghaṇṭapāda first meditates on the drop in the heart center; Kukuripa, [in his *Heruka Sādhana*] following the *Mahāmāyā Tantra*, first practices vitalizing energy control and vajra recitation in the heart center; and Saroruha in the *Hevajra Sādhana* explains that you enter the clear light by withdrawing all elaborations into the heart center. Therefore, the authoritative masters state their individual approaches, and the tantras themselves also speak accordingly, and each of them have their own distinctive specialties.

In regard to them again, although such and such a treatise sometimes explains clearly "that is the art of injecting the *rasanā* and *lalanā* energies into the central channel," [61b] most of the explanations are usually unclear. So at the time of meditation, by means of the explanations of the meditation and so forth on the visualization of the three channels and so forth, having,

55. Presumably his *Supreme Bliss Five Stages* text, *Śrī-cakrasaṁvara-pañcakrama* (Tōh. 1433).

by a few keys, set drops and letters and so forth in the center of whichever channel wheel, it is hard to understand the art of injecting the *rasanā* and *lalanā* energies into the *dhūti*. Therefore, it is necessary to know this from detailed investigation of the clear explanations, and [also from] comparative evaluation of the many treatises of the tantras and the authorities.

Thus, though there are many different doors for injecting the two energies into the *dhūti*, those arts cause the furor to burn, melt the enlightenment spirit, and give the fruition of the wisdom of the four joys or the four voids. And, having identified the wisdom of orgasmic joy, or of clear light, both [father and mother] tantras are similar on the topic of the art of cultivating its continuum. However, by reason of the fact that among them there are many different causal specifics, there are many different inner specifics even among the fruitional orgasmic [bliss intuitions] and clear lights.[56]

By meditating through knowing the extraordinary meditation systems that [teach you to] meditate by focusing visualization of letters, drops, and so on at the major vital points of the body such as the center of the body's channel wheels or the lower aperture of the *dhūti*, when the mind is held in those spots, by the key of energy and mind being functionally coordinated, though one is not overtly practicing energy meditation, it serves as an art of injecting the two energies into the *dhūti*. If you know this reason well, [62a] you will understand the key of many authentically reliable perfection-stage treatises, and you will obtain certainty about them.

In such a way, if you understand individually without confusion the tendencies to emphasize distinctive potencies of those individual doors of injecting the two energies into the *dhūti*, though those treatises are by no means synonymous, their signatures emerge in their holding in unison as the essence of the path the cultivation of the continuum of the union of the bliss-void of the orgasmic [intuition] and the clear light through ascertaining the pattern of the arisal of the wisdom of the four joys and the four voids as the fruition of the injection of the two energies into the *dhūti*. And, since this unerringly nails down the final summation of the personal instruction, you will attain full confidence about the definitive meaning of the tantras. Thinking of that pattern, Saraha said [in an *Enlightenment Song*]:

56. Even at the fruitional level, there are many fine distinctions to be made, and so the complexity of the causal processes relates to the inner differences of fruitional experiences.

Eating and drinking, enjoying sexual union,
Again and again fill the circle!
By such teaching as this,
You will achieve transcendence of the world;
Here we have triumphed,
Hitting the world of ignorance on the head!

Where energy and mind no longer move,
And sun and moon no longer function,
Ignorant ones, in that place the mind will be relieved!
The arrow maker has herein taught all personal
instructions.

Thus, he says that, by relying on the art of penetrating the vital points in the outer and inner body, injecting the sun and moon energies into the *dhūti* channel and dissolving them, burning the furor and melting the enlightenment spirit, and filling the body and uniting bliss and void, you eradicate ignorance and encompass all personal instructions. **[62b]** If you do not understand according to the above explanations, you might think that "since the individual doors of generating the orgasmic [intuition] do not emerge as synonymous, they must be mutually contradictory"; or some might meditate on the praise of their own instructions and think that all other synonymous explanations are incorrect in the context of that one instruction; and others, having great attachment only to their own instructions, make invidious comparisons with any others.

[**VI.B.3.b.ii.B′2′b′** – The way one must penetrate the vital points in the body to generate the two-reality-indivisible communion]

The second has two parts: [i′] Explaining how the perfection-stage paths must be generated according to the processes of birth, death, and between; and [ii′] explaining the art of penetrating the vital points in the body relying on that.

[**VI.B.3.b.ii.B′2′b′i′** – Explaining how the perfection-stage paths must be generated according to the processes of birth, death, and between]

Due to the intention of all the unexcelled yoga tantras, the creation of the habitat and inhabitant mandalas on the first stage is effected in correspondence with the processes of creation and destruction of the inanimate and animate worlds. And this does not happen in the lower tantras. Creating [these worlds] in such a way is in order to create the paths through such stages. And further, the creation stage, being meditated to correspond to the aspects of the perfection-stage path, is just the means of developing the root of virtue that generates the perfection stage. Thus, the main thing is that [the creation stage] has the purpose of developing the paths of the perfection stage in correspondence to the processes of beings' birth and death. This procedure is clearly explained in the *Community* literature. As the *Vajra Rosary Tantra* states:

> Just as there is no thing left after being burned by fire,
> So one proceeds [to death] by dissolving into the immobile.
> Again, when the energy of life arises,
> The various energies of the body,
> Consciousness together [63a] with them,
> Again abide in the triple world;
> From that there is action, and from that birth;
> And from that the instincts of lust and so on;
> And from that again death and birth.
> Thus, it is like the turning of a wheel.
> As above, it is to be manifested [and mastered]
> By the stages of vajra recitation and so on.

This quote is the answer to the question about the destruction of the neural-energy at the time of death. And it says that, just as there is no substance of the wood left after being burned by fire, so at the time of death the energies gradually dissolve into the vital energy and one dies. Again from the death clear light the energy of evolution arises, and it and consciousness together take birth and abide in the three worlds. From that evolutionary energy again the instinctual notions such as lust are produced, thereby accumulating good and bad evolutionary momentum, dying, being born again, and so going on like the turning of a wheel. And as for the above-explained five stages such as the vajra recitation, they serve as parallel to the divisions of the processes of birth and death in natural [basic] time.

As for the way they so serve: the continuous action of the energy inhaling and exhaling is the natural vajra recitation, as the same [text, the *Vajra Rosary Tantra,*] says:

> The beings of the three realms
> Depend on vitalizing energy and control,
> As the king of secret mantra recitations
> Abandons unknowing, meditation, and reading.

Thus at the end of the energies having repeated [their movements] all day and night, the energies' movement out and in stops, and the elements gradually dissolve. The experiences of luminance, radiance, and imminence arise, [63b] and it is the mind isolation stage. After imminence, the death clear light arises at the stage of clear light, which is called the "natural truth body." At the end of the death clear light, the between body is developed separate from the old body from just the neural-energy and mind abiding in the complex of the old aggregates; this being the magic body stage, it is called the "natural beatific body." In the natural time, there are not two separate stages of the magic body, the impure and the pure; and yet I will explain below how this [natural sequence] can represent the two types of magic body of the path-time. Now the natural between beatific body is not perceived as the object of the ordinary fleshly eye, but when it takes birth in the birth state it becomes the object of that eye, as the natural emanation body.

In regard to this pattern, the *Five Stages* states:

> That very magic is superficial reality,
> And also the body of full beatitude,
> Its very self becomes the fairy being,
> And itself indeed the vajra body.

Thus it explains the third stage magic body as the fairy being in the between, whereby you can understand both tendencies, to call the path magic body "the between" and to call the natural between the "path magic body." Such expressions arise by reason of the fact that the very same energy-mind that goes into the between for one who lacks the personal instruction in skill in liberative art arises as the magic body of full beatitude for one who has the personal instruction in liberative artistry. As the *Integrated Practices* states:

> So doing, the alienated individual enters the existence between that causes the life cycle. And the same thing, for those who have obtained the personal instruction of all transcendent buddhas through the process of the mentor's transmission, is called the "self-consecration." Thus, [64a] just as walls and paintings appear in a mirror, so the reality of the vajra body emanates the being itself as the body endowed with all supreme aspects, which one can never get enough of seeing, a body adorned with the thirty-two signs of a great being.

By the key of both father and sons explaining thus about the between, you will attain understanding about how—since death and birth are the spinning on the wheel of the life cycle as the impulsive birth and death of the person who lacks the personal instruction, and yet for one who has the personal instruction, what becomes death arises as the truth body and what becomes impulsive birth-taking arises as the emanation body—[authors] might indicate the natural processes with the names of the two path-time bodies, and indicate the two path-time bodies with the names of the two natural processes. In the *Stage of Arrangement*, it is clearly taught that, having understood both stages of the mind objective through abiding in the vajra recitation—as it is explained that one realizes the clear light in the processes of death by means of the two [holistic and dissolving] contemplations—one must generate in one's process the perfection-stage paths according to the processes of death. Those following the system of the translator Gö, though they explain the processes of existential birth and death as the basis of purification of both stages, do not employ the schemes of the three bodies and the five stages in the context of basic time. But those who follow the Marpa system—depending on the *Concise Five Stages* quote:

> The experience of becoming, [death,] and birth
> Is taught to be combined in a single session in a day

—very excellently employ the terms of the three bodies for birth, death, and between, and the terms of the five stages for the basic time vajra recitation and so on. [64b] Such usage is necessary since it is for the purpose of generating the path in one's process according to the processes of birth and death in natural existence.

Even though you use such terms, it will not be good if you do not know the purpose, and explain that the instructions about death as the truth body and so forth are to be practiced only at the time of death and the between, or if you use the terms of the ground-time five stages in some way other than the above-explained. As for the meaning of implementing the five stages in a single day, a certain Marpa system follower says that one day's inhalation and exhalation is vajra recitation, the instinctual notions dissolving in the heart center is the mind objective, sleep is clear light, dream arisal is magic body, and waking is communion. As for his interpretation of the general sleep and dream instruction as the personal instruction of the noble system, except for knowing how to explain depending on the *Integrated Practices*, a clear explanation is not explicit anywhere in the noble system texts. Although the *Illuminating Lamp* quotes one reference from that context in the *Integrated Practices*, it is merely quoted [and not explained]. If we interpret according to the intention there, one can call the vajra recitation as above, the first three of the four voids that arise between the start of sleep and the arisal of dream are called the mind objective, and this basic clear light is called the sleep truth body. Here not the mere arisal of dream but the existence of a specific body in the dream is the stage of magic body, called the dream beatific body. And this can represent the third stage and fifth stage magic bodies. Then, waking is the [65a] emanation body, this not being just mere waking but a specific kind of awakening. As for Indian [masters] other than the above-mentioned followers of the five noble father and sons, they don't explain the five stages of becoming, birth, and death, the ground three bodies, and the single-day five stages. Still, as for what emerges from the personal instructions of Nāropa, it is definitely necessary, as being the intention of the above-explained texts. And I have explained them here since, if you know well such a way of determining the five stages in the natural, basic context, then you can discover a great certainty about the keys of the personal instruction of the [nine] mergers.

[**VI.B.3.b.ii.B′2′b′ii′** – Explaining the art of penetrating the vital points in the body relying on that]

Such attainment of the two magic bodies from mere neural-energy-mind, as it is attained in correspondence with the [basic natural] between, the four voids preceding it must be achieved according to the four voids of the death time. In that regard, the tantric *Vajra Rosary* states:

> As for the energies' supreme decline,
> Who truly understands it,
> Knows the nature in an instant of death,
> And mutually truly condenses them,
> Dissolving [them] as in the process of birth.

Thus, according to the stages of emergence in the time of birth, at the time of death one dissolves through the ascending process.[57] Again the text [the *Vajra Rosary*] continues:

> The addictive mind, the vitalizing energy itself,
> Will always truly proceed.
> First, at the time of transit,
> It becomes like the form of a fish.

Thus, at the time of first transition, the vitalizing energy is created, and from it, gradually, there develop the nine [other] energies, such as the evacuative energy and so forth. "The vitalizing energy abides in the heart center," it is said. [65b] Thus, as the vitalizing energy is said to abide in the heart center, at the time of death the neural-energy-mind dissolves into the heart center. This tantra agrees with Ārya Asaṅga also, in explaining that the heart center is the first place of entrance of the consciousness in the center of the father's and mother's semen and ovum, that the body develops from there up and down, and that finally at the time of death the consciousness

57. Tib. *mas rim*, i.e., "stages from below," i.e., ascending, though one thinks of the dissolution at death as being a process of descending energies down from the brain and sense doors located in the head.

exits from the heart center. This does not contradict the statements from the *Sampuṭa [Tantra]* and so forth that at the time of death the consciousness transits from the nine doors such as eye and ear. For, since the heart center is the chief support of the mind, consciousness cannot transit from any other door until it has emerged from the abode of the heart center indestructible [drop]; and the personal instructions for the death-transition in those sections of those tantras are stated in the *Sheaf of Instructions* to require training in the yoga of ejecting consciousness from the heart center.

Therefore, you should proceed according to the basic [natural] five stages. By meditating the indestructible in the heart center and by doing vajra recitation by inhaling, holding, and exhaling the energy while visualizing the heart center, finally you can stop the in and out of the energy and gradually dissolve it into the heart center and experience the dawn of the four voids, after which you will achieve the extremely subtle magic body from just the energy and mind abiding within the gross body. Then, you will achieve the magic body after the metaphoric clear light, and the communion body after the objective clear light. Since that beatific body cannot be seen by the ordinary eye, but can be seen by the flesh eye [only] when it upholds the body of gross aggregates, it then [can make itself into] an emanation body.

Thus, in the noble system the best spot [66a] for penetrating the vital points in the body is the center of the channel wheel at the heart center; and so you should hold this as the import of "vital point." And this ultimate personal instruction of expert liberative artistry for transforming this turning the wheel of the life cycle by the rosary of birth, death, and between of the natural basic time into the death truth body, between beatific body, and birth emanation body—its liberative arts being such as this king of vitalizing energy controls sufficiently [practiced by remembering to] identify the personal instruction within the very inhalation and exhalation of the energy through which each living being abides automatically. This is the personal instruction identifying the three bodies of the great Vajradhara, the noble Nāgārjuna. I will explain below the way of penetrating the vital points in the body by practicing according to the single-day five bodies.

3. *Explanation of the Perfection Stage of This Tantra in Particular*

[66a.3–83b.6]

[**VI.B.3.b.ii.c′** – Explaining the perfection stage of this tantra in particular]

The third, explaining the perfection stage of this tantra in particular, has three parts: [1′] Explanation of the way of thorough evaluation of the ultimate private instruction; [2′] The need to reconcile the other private instructions of the ancient mentors with this [ultimate private instruction]; and [3′] The actual explanation of the stages of the path of the perfection stage.

[**VI.B.3.b.ii.c′1′** – Explanation of the way of thorough evaluation of the ultimate private instruction]

The ultimate location of the private instruction of the five stages is the *Esoteric Community Root Tantra*, so that is the ultimate treatise of that instruction. However, within that tantra the five perfection stages are sealed, or [kept] inexplicit and concealed, and the explanatory tantras make statements that release those seals and explicate that hidden import. That being the case, it is declared that, if you do not [receive] personal explanation from a qualified mentor who knows how to fully explain the meaning of the tantra by connecting the *Root* and its explanatory tantras, even the jewel-like person will not fully [66b] understand the import of the tantra. Therefore, it must depend on the private instruction of the mentor. As the *Five Stages* states:

That truth stands well sealed
In the glorious *Community Tantra*;
Following the *Explanatory Tantras*,
Realize it from the mentor's speech.

Such is the import of the statement that one must understand from the mentor's speech the import sealed or concealed in the *Root Tantra*, which should not be interpreted as [condoning] the accepting of any oral tradition of the mentors that, by their avoiding writing, is not established in the tantra. If you do interpret it in that way, it becomes an obstacle to generating the unexcelled reverence for the *Root* and its explanatory tantras. You will not discover the import of the tantra and you will persist in the same tendency during future lives as well.

Such a type of concealment is one in which the import concealed is taught in the tantra where it is hidden, but concealed by not being explicit. As the *Vajra Rosary Tantra* states:

The very clear truth of mantra,
That truth is supremely secret;
I do not explain it wheresoever,
Considering those who lack the destiny;
But what I have hidden in all the tantras,
Listen and that will I explain.

Thus, such a topic as the vajra recitation is concealed in the lower tantras by not being taught at all, which is the type of concealment of not being taught [at all] in such a tantra. In such a case, as the private instruction cannot be found therein at all, one must seek it elsewhere. One must understand the difference between these two ways of concealment.

So the *Vajra Rosary* declares:

Some people who do not know [the way],
And who very much want to go
To the far shore of the four oceans,
Yet who do not inquire into the path—[67a]
How are they going to get there?
In the same way, the practitioner
Who lacks the private instruction

> Gotten with great difficulty
> Will remain without fruition.
> Again, even the wise practitioner
> Can get angry; that moment of anger
> Destroys fruition and sends him to the Raurava hell.
> Therefore, with all efforts, and with respect,
> One should learn the private instructions
> From the lineage of mentors.

Here one might imagine that "this declares the drawbacks of lacking the mentor's private instructions, even though one might be skilled in the *Root* and its explanatory tantras, and so it is not correct to accept the *Root* and its explanatory tantras as the ultimate private instruction." But the "wise" [person] mentioned here is a person learned in the other sciences and lacking in the mentor's private instruction, and is not a person skilled in the *Root* and its explanatory tantras. This is because lacking that private instruction precludes being skilled in the two [kinds of] tantras; because the statement occurs in a context in that tantra where, in response to Vajrapāṇi's question about what is the private instruction, the Buddha clearly states that private instruction; and because there is no contradiction at all between the necessity of the instruction of the mentor who teaches connecting root and explanatory tantras and the *Root* and its explanatory tantras [themselves] being the supreme instruction.

In regard to those tantric texts, it is shown that, after having sought the understanding that is thorough knowledge of the paths to be traveled from the beginner's stage up to buddhahood, if one then does not put into practice the instructions, but travels the path by sitting in stolid confusion, it is like the person who wants to cross over the ocean without learning the way from one who knows the way, but proceeding in total confusion. [67b] Thus, you should understand this reference as a source [for the fact] that, before practicing the private instruction, you must develop a full insight about it. And the noble father and sons, seeing that the above-explained mentor's knowledge of teaching by connecting root and explanatory tantras would be hard to find in the future, and that writing down the mentor's precept discovered by such mentors' connecting the *Root* and its explanatory tantras would [cause it to] remain even for a long time, wrote many treatises on the instruction in the two stages such as the *Five Stages* and the *Lamp of Integrated Practices*. And those contain the ultimate keys of the precept that must be known from the mouth of the mentor who has discovered the import of the tantra.

As for their not being able to take much effect in contemporary persons even though in actuality they are the ultimate instructions, it is because of the key point that the powers of the mind in later times have been gradually diminished from [their level] in previous times, and is not because the ultimate keys of the precepts are not clear in those texts. In those texts, it is not only just that the import is not concealed and unclear, as it is in the *Root Tantra*, but also—[out of awareness that] even though they explained the concealed meaning clearly, their treatises would become unclear as the passage of time would make the persons' minds unclear—as a method of generating such realization [in the minds of future disciples], they made commentaries that elucidated the verbal meaning extremely clearly. Also, as a way of providing realization of the import of that, even if they did not directly [write a commentary] they wrote extra notes on the precept as well.

[**VI.B.3.b.ii.c′2′** – The need to reconcile the other private instructions of the ancient mentors with this (ultimate private instruction)]

If you thoroughly evaluate the stages of the manuals composed by the Tibetan saints in the light of the instructions of this [noble tradition], you must do it by long study of the way properly to connect [68a] *Root* and its explanatory tantras, of the treatises of the five father and sons along with their accessory [texts], and also by thorough study of all the additional private instruction [texts]. The master Gö wrote a work known as the *Great Voidness Session*, which extensively elucidated the instructions in these two stages, and nowadays we see sixteen oral traditions of Nāropa's instructions, descended through master Marpa. Among these, there is the manual of the five stages [falsely] attributed to the mentor Marpa called *Lama's Speech Light Rays Teaching*, which takes as authority the apparitional *Nondual Triumph Tantra*, and agrees with the interpretations of that tantra alone. Since it seems to disagree with the verifiable instructions of the Marpa tradition, it would not seem to have been authored by that mentor. Of the manuals written by Serdingpa, who witnessed the two traditions in the succession from Tsurton to Geypawa, the contents are in agreement with the explanations of the *Concise Five Stages Elucidation* of other lineages.

Now the root word on this precept of the Marpa tradition is the *Concise*

Five Stages Elucidation, as above explained, and it appears that Serdingpa also relied on that. In the writings of Serdingpa on the personal instruction of the *Community*, there are things from the yoginī tantra, such as the meditations of body-invasion, soul-ejection, and furor, that seem to have been put forth on some sort of a basis in the *Concise Five Stages Elucidation*. And the reason why that treatise teaches those things will be explained below.

Although there seem to be many other gross and subtle [68b] precepts of the *Community*, the principal ones are the four [by Serdingpa (twelfth century)],[58] the *Five Point Treatise on the Five Stages*,[59] the *Four Point Treatise*,[60] the *Five Stages Single Session*, and the *Wheel Endowed*. These are manuals teaching completely the imports of the five stages of this tradition. Thus it is not the case that the ancient mentors did not write complete manuals [of the private instructions] and only transmitted them orally.

Now, the first four subjects of the *Five Point* exist in the written annotation of the precepts, and so are not explained in that treatise except in subject outline. Thus the *Five Point* teaches just that instruction of meditating the two stages in a single session, in connection with the signs of the path. Therefore, it is the precept of meditating the five stages in a single session.

The *Four Point* teaches four subjects, the practitioner, the place, the companion, and the actual instruction, the content of which actual instruction is the same as in the above work.

The *Five Stages Single Session* is renowned [also] as the *Father Tantra Quintessence*.[61] As it says:

58. According to the TBRC online database, Serdingpa (gser sdings pa gzhon nu 'od; twelfth century) wrote the following five texts: (1) *gsang 'dus don lnga ma*; (2) *gsang 'dus rim lnga 'khor lo'i can*; (3) *gsang 'dus rim lnga gdan rdzogs*; (4) *gsang 'dus rim lnga'i khrid skor*; (5) *gsangs 'dus 'khor lo med pa don bzhi ma*. Presumably our *Five Point Treatise on the Five Stages* (*rim lnga don lnga ma*) = (1) *gsang 'dus don lnga ma*; our *Four Point Treatise* (*don bzhi ma*) = (5) *gsangs 'dus 'khor lo med pa don bzhi ma*; our *Five Stages Single Session* (*rim lnga gdan rdzogs*) = (3) *gsang 'dus rim lnga gdan rdzogs*; and our *Wheel Endowed* (*'khor lo can*) = (2) *gsang 'dus rim lnga 'khor lo'i can*. These remain to be investigated in more detail.

59. *rim lnga don lnga ma.*

60. *don bzhi ma.*

61. Tsong Khapa refers to the *Five Stages Single Session* by this alternate title again below, Tib. 83a.

There are six points in the instruction;
Meditation of creation and perfection in one sitting,
Investigating forward and reverse ignorance,
Channeling bliss into the path,
Furor, soul-ejection, and invasion [yogas].

Though this six-point teaching is the complete way of teaching the imports of the Marpa tradition literature on the *Community* precept, the main thing is the meditation of creation and perfection at one sitting.

The *Wheel Endowed*, though it teaches the five stages, gets its name [by concentrating] on the meditation of the mantra wheel in the heart center; in it also occurs the precept of the [way of] completion of the five stages within the [mantra] wheel-possessing [heart center] in a single sitting. That instruction of meditating the mantra wheel in the heart [69a] occurs in all four of the texts, from which point of view they can all be called "wheel endowed." Since the complete meditation in the *Wheel Endowed* of the five stages in a single session is called "complete sitting of the five stages," all four of the texts are the "instruction in the five stages single session."

In the *Four Point*, when expressing the number of instructions transmitted by Geypawa to Jakhangpa, while his head was aching, the above four texts are not mentioned, but the mentioned *Five Stages Single Session Vital Manual* refers to all those teachings. The reason why such a name is used is that they are interpreted as relying on the teaching of the meditation of five stages in a single session; as the *Concise Five Stages* states:

Various vehicles, transcendences,
Existence, birth, living, and so on,
As differentiated by differences of time,
Unite them in a single session and meditate on them.

The master Nāropa bestowed upon mentor Marpa four distinctive instructions relying on four superb tantras. Among them, he was said to have bestowed the "Instruction on meditating the five stages completely in a single session relying on the *Glorious Esoteric Community*"; and the above explained should be understood as just this.

The more recent sages of Tibet say that the transmission concerning the instructions of the Marpa tradition of the *Community* is committed to writing. Of those who uphold the instructions of this tradition, except for just a few of them, some of them write miscellaneously about the *Community* precept, some of them seem to arrange them in one section in the context of the six yogas of Nāropa. And even if they do not set them forth in one section in writing by such an arrangement, [69b] it is not that they do not write them down. And also, it is not that they were not written down before those authoritative manuals of the Marpa tradition.

The above-mentioned four [texts on] the precept of the complete sitting are from one author, but they either represent the different statements of different or earlier and later mentors or are [different] because of the various changes of the mind of the one author. For there seem to be many inconsistencies and many writing mistakes that are continued for some time. Therefore, their explanations of the import of the *Concise Five Stages* organize and combine the instructions transmitted from Nāropa's disciple Jñānākara to Nagtso and the other instructions transmitted by Marpa, and some become and some do not become the import of the *Concise Five Stages*. All of them ground themselves on the *Root* and its explanatory tantras and on the undisputable treatises of the five father and sons. From among them, some are openly upheld [as valid], some not, and even those correct ones not upheld in a way are [preserved] there in that their meaning is attained [indirectly]. And if one explains that such are by reason of the errors of those somewhat not fulfilling the intention of the first instruction, due to the length of the transmission, [nevertheless], it seems that the potency of the Marpa tradition *Community* instructions came to be completely extracted; and that is how it is to be explained.

[**VI.B.3.b.ii.c′3′** – The actual explanation of the stages of the path of the perfection stage]

The third has four parts: [**a′**] Categories of the perfection stage; [**b′**] Certification of their order; [**c′**] Certification of their number; and [**d′**] The import of the individual divisions (of the perfection stage).

[**VI.B.3.b.ii.c′3′a′** – Categories of the perfection stage]

The first has two parts: [**i′**] The actual categories; and [**ii′**] The way to reconcile the five stages and the six branches.

[**VI.B.3.b.ii.c′3′a′i′** – The actual categories]

Here one wonders, "how many stages are included within the perfection stage?" [70a] The *Root Tantra*—Patsab translation, sixth chapter—states that:

> In mantra [practice], by the visualized body,
> And by speech that urges [Vajrasattva] in the mind,
> You attain the extreme and supreme accomplishment,
> The mind's delight, and [perfect] beatitude.

As for the meaning of this, "in mantra [practice], visualized" refers to speech isolation. "By body" refers to the body emanated as the means of attaining vajra recitation; that is, the body isolation. The "speech" isolation is thereby attained, and "that urges" the Vajrasattva who abides "in the mind," in the heart center. By precisely taking him as object, one should attain the four "extreme" and "supreme" [accomplishments, i.e., the voids and joys of the mind objective] in the yogi tantras. The "extreme and supreme" is the mind isolation developed from the vajra recitation. "Accomplishment" refers to the self-consecration, [i.e., the creation of the magic body]. "The mind's delight" refers to the ultimate reality clear light that is the means of purifying the magic body. "Beatitude" is declared when one is liberated in the communion body of great Vajradhara. Thus, here there are said to be six stages such as body isolation and so forth.

As for the translations of both *[Root] Tantra* and commentaries in this context, the new translations are better. This verse is quoted in the *Integrated Practices* in the context of the single-clan body isolation, and [our explanation above] does not contradict the explanation of its meaning there, as being that, having developed the body vajra, one engages with the speech vajra by connecting tongue, palate, and lips, while the mind vajra is the means of urging [Vajrasattva] therein; and by the union of these three [vajras], the mind is delighted and satisfied and one attains accomplishment. Some vajra words can be given many different explanations. [70b] For example, when the *[Root Tantra]* seventh chapter proclaims that one will attain the supreme accomplishment when one kills the host of transcendent lords, the savior Nāgārjuna interprets this as referring to the retraction of one's visualization into clear light, while Āryadeva explains it as referring to entrance into the perfection-stage clear light.

In the *Illuminating Lamp* on the first chapter, [Chandrakīrti] makes the creation stage one stage and the perfection stage four stages from mind objective. In regard to that, from that same text, it states:

> It is the condensed meaning of all tantras . . .

—so this is an interpretation that condenses all the main meanings, without putting into five stages a single element of the subjects of the tantra. Though master Bhavyakīrti and company explain that "The mantra body is very much attained" refers to the vajra recitation, it is better to follow the Tibetan scholars who include body isolation and speech isolation within the mind objective, since that accords with the reference to the first two isolations in the context of the hiddenness of the mind in the *Vajra Rosary*, the tantra of the hidden meaning explanation of the setting of the [main] tantra.

In the *Summary Teaching of the Five Stages*, the noble [Nāgārjuna] makes the perfection stage into five stages, taking the vajra recitation as the first, which follows the system in the final chapter of the *Vajra Rosary Explanatory Tantra*. In the *Integrated Practices*, "That same thing is five!" is similar to those, while in its detailed explanation, it makes a whole chapter out of the body isolation and states six stages. In the *Stage of Arrangement*, [71a] the vajra recitation is interpreted as the first stage and the mind objective as the second, showing its preference of a system of five stages like the *Summary Teaching*.

That the noble master does not explain body isolation clearly—except for a brief mention in the *Third Stage* [chapter of the *Five Stages*]—is extensively explained in the *Integrated Practices*. Here one might wonder about the reason why the noble master does not speak of it in the way [Āryadeva] does in the *Integrated Practices*, putting it before the speech isolation. Concerning this, the Kashmiri Lakshmī and Bhavyakīrti explain that the expression "well abiding on the creation stage" refers to both the triple-samadhi creation stage and to the body isolation, thereby claiming that the noble master also indicates body isolation as preliminary to speech isolation. As for "creation stage" referring to body isolation, it must be accepted because of the explanations of body isolation as the creation stage in the *Moonlight Commentary* and so forth. As for the *Five Point* statement:

> The noble master did not interpret the creation stage as completing the magic body . . .

and the *Four Point* statement:

> the creation stage preliminarily includes the magic body . . .

they consider the mode of deity creation of the body isolation and that of the creation of Vajradhara as the magic body to be the same; but as for saying that it seems that both are considered creation stage—including the magic body in the creation stage—it only refers to the body-isolation magic body as included in creation stage, and does not refer to any body isolation apart from the creation stage. This does not accord with any of the treatises of the noble literature [71b] and seems to be an explanation coming from not understanding the meaning of the *Concise Five Stages Elucidation*.

As for my own interpretation, the noble master did not mention the second stage body isolation, taken as the second part of a twofold body isolation, prior to the speech isolation, considering it contained within the vajra recitation stage. Thus, the first two isolations can be contained within the mind objective stage and the perfection stage considered to have four stages overall. Or the vajra recitation can be taken separately, subsuming the body isolation, and there are five stages. Or the body isolation can be taken separately and there can be six stages. All this is not contradictory, since it is [simply] a matter of separating or including.

Again, in the *Community Further Tantra* the perfection stage as the supreme service is proclaimed as the six branches of yoga such as retraction:

> Taking it as the six branches of service,
> It is to be supremely achieved;
> The practice of others will not bring forth
> The supreme accomplishment.

> Retraction, contemplation,
> Vitalizing energy control, and endurance,
> Mindfulness, and samadhi—
> These are called the six branches of yoga.

This first verse states that if you do not attain the supreme by way of the six branches, you will not attain it; and so all unexcelled yoga tantra accomplishments of the supreme must complete the six branches—but it is not necessary that one must do it exactly according to every system's interpretation of the six yogas. Otherwise, all perfection stages must become the same. And since [72a] the reasoning must equally apply to all creation stages, [the Buddha's] teaching of infinite tantras for the sake of different disciples would have been pointless, since the teaching of one tantra would have sufficed. Therefore, though most creation-stage visualization practices are similar in being contained within the three samadhis such as the primary application, there are many differing methods that must be interpreted as carrying the meaning of those three. Likewise, although all perfection stages are similar in having to be interpreted as arrangements of the six yoga branches, they have many things of dissimilar meaning. Sometimes even [yoga branches] such as "retraction" and so on may have the same names [in different tantras' perfection stages] and not need to be interpreted as synonymous. For there seem to be innumerable cases in both sutras and tantras where the name is the same and the referents different, and where the same referent has different names.

[**VI.B.3.b.ii.c′3′a′ii′** – The way to reconcile the five stages and the six branches]

The second has two parts: [A′′] Setting forth the various systems; and [B′′] Analyzing their correctness and incorrectness.

[**VI.B.3.b.ii.c′3′a′ii′A′′** – Setting forth the various systems]

The first has two parts: [1′′] Setting forth the systems of the [Indian] commentators; and [2′′] Setting forth the systems of the Tibetan mentors.

[**VI.B.3.b.ii.c′3′a′ii′A″1″** – Setting forth the systems of the (Indian) commentators]

Here the means of inclusion are the six stages including body isolation, and those to be included are the six branches of yoga. Now there are many systems of these, similar in names but divergent in meaning; such as the six branch systems of the three Bodhisattva Commentaries,[62] of the *Personal Instruction of Mañjushrī* and its commentaries, of the *Flower Bouquet*, of the *Sheaf of Instructions*, and of the Tathāgatavajra explanation based on the Lūyipa *Supreme Bliss* tradition, and so forth. [72b] Here I am not going to describe all the ways of their being reconciled, but am going to show the way to reconcile the six branches as explained in the *Illuminating Lamp* in elucidating the textual meaning of the *Further Tantra*.

Here, the "retraction," which the *Moonlight Commentary* has included with "contemplation" in the abbreviated creation stage, is the deity meditation. With it go the fivefold contemplation branch, with the judgment and discrimination that analyze in terms of superficial and ultimate, the joy and bliss from the confrontation with the immersion in thatness, and the one-pointedness of mind from aiming the mind exclusively at voidness. Here, the compressing of the energies in the indomitable [central channel] is explained as "vitalizing energy control," not included in these five stages [of "contemplation"]; and yet this reconciles with the vajra recitation. "Endurance" is explained as the magical vajradhara body, of the nature of clear light; so the "endurance" [branch] is reconciled with the magic body and the clear light. The instantaneous perfection of the vajradhara body after the clear light is reconciled with the "mindfulness" [branch], and the same thing meditated as the nature of communion is the "samadhi" branch; the last two branches being reconciled with the communion stage. This is said by the followers of the *Illuminating Lamp* to be the explanation of the concise essence.

The *Illuminating Lamp [Intention] Elucidation* [by Bhavyakīrti] explains that retraction and contemplation are included in mind isolation,

62. Namely, the famous Kālachakra commentary, *Vimalaprabhā* (*Stainless Light*; Tōh. 1347) by Pundarīka (Avalokiteshvara); Vajrapāṇi's *Lakṣābhidhānād uddhṛta-laghutantra-piṇḍārtha-vivaraṇa-nāma* (*Supreme Bliss Eulogy Commentary*; Tōh. 1402); and Vajragarbha's *Hevajrapiṇḍārthaṭīkā* (*Commentary on the Concise Meaning of the Hevajra*; Tōh. 1180).

vitalizing energy control in vajra recitation, endurance in clear light, and mindfulness and samadhi in communion; and the *Heart Mirror* is similar. But those two [texts] follow the *Illuminating Lamp* system of reconciling the six yogas with the five stages. [73a]

The master Ekādashanirghosha[63] explains that the [*Further Tantra*] verse "ten faculties" and so on mentions retraction as the foundation of body isolation, and the four verses "five desires" and so forth mention contemplation as body isolation [itself]. In this treatise the two lines "secret tantra" and so on appear to be missing. Further, the two verses "of five wisdoms" and so forth are claimed to refer to vitalizing energy control as speech isolation, and the two lines "then independence" and so forth to refer to the endurance branch as mind isolation. The magic body is mentioned by the line "produced from that interior illumination," and the explanation concludes that it is an arrangement hiding the fifth branch, in order to break the pride of the intelligent. As for the holistic meditation, the method of realizing clear light, "art and wisdom united" proclaims the union of art and wisdom as the joining of the vajra and lotus of father and mother. And as for the dissolvent meditation, it is shown by two lines "all things in summary are compressed in the way of a lump" and three and a half verses "then as the way of creating the five signs, the mind becomes the vajra of cessation" and so forth. And clear light, he says, as it is a great secret, is explained by confusing the fifth and sixth stages. That means that he is claiming that the "mind is cessation vajra" refers to the fifth branch and the three lines "art and" and so on are the text for the sixth branch. [73b] He claims that communion is referred to by the five lines "becoming firm" and so on. He claims that magic body, clear light, and communion are all three apart from the mindfulness branch. And the three lines "from in the center" indicates the samadhi branch, explained as the path of spontaneous accomplishment. The three lines referring to the sixth branch were previously explained as referring to clear light, so he must believe one part of clear light to be in the sixth branch. Though this author does not directly quote the *Illuminating Lamp* as source, he seems to be explaining the six branches depending on the *Illuminating Lamp*'s explanation of the *Further Tantra*, and so that is his way of reconciling [the branches and stages].

63. Tōh. 1823, cited above, Tib. 30a, is the *only* text by this author in the entire Tengyur.

[VI.B.3.b.ii.C′3′a′ii′A″2″ – Setting forth the systems of the Tibetan mentors]

The scholar Lan of the Gö tradition divided the six branches into two sections, the thatness samadhi and the deeds that conform to it, then saying that retraction corresponds to the deeds at the time of the magic body and the other five branches correspond to samadhi. He claims that the contemplation branch with its judgment and discrimination becomes body isolation, joy becomes the benefit of body isolation, vitalizing energy control becomes speech isolation, bliss its benefit, one-pointedness becomes mind isolation, the benefit of contemplation "actuality of all buddhas" becomes magic body, endurance becomes clear light, and mindfulness and samadhi become communion; [he claims that] this also is the way the *Illuminating Lamp* explains the division of the six yoga branches.

A certain scholar of the Marpa tradition claims that retraction corresponds to body isolation, contemplation to mind isolation, [74a] vitalizing energy control to vajra recitation, endurance to mind objective, mindfulness to magic body, and samadhi corresponds to clear light and communion, seeming to say that the latter is included in the former two. He also believes this to be the way to reconcile [this system with] the six branches of the *Time Machine*.

A certain recent Tibetan scholar argued that Abhayākara's explanation of retraction and contemplation as creation stage [in his *Moonlight* commentary on Nāgārjuna's *Five Stages*] is incorrect, since the *Further Tantra* explains that the four vajras of service connected with the creation stage are the means of achieving common accomplishments, stating that:

> practicing by means other than the six branches, the supreme accomplishment will not be attained,

and so [Abhaya's interpretation] contradicts that the six branches must be the uncommon service, the means of achieving the supreme, and the creation stage is not the means of achieving the supreme. Also the [above scholar] Lan's statement that retraction corresponds to the conduct and contemplation to body isolation is very incorrect, since sequence is contradicted when the beginning of achieving the supreme involves the conduct, and since body isolation will not have the slightest benefits of knowledge and knowable. Therefore, since the *Stainless Light* states:

> The pure self-consecration is the sign
> Of beholding the three realms in the void . . .

and the *Vajrapāni Praise Commentary* states:

> Here "self-consecration" means that retraction beholds the superficial reality such as smoke and so on, . . .

retraction and contemplation are included in magic body, vitalizing energy control in vajra recitation, endurance in clear light, and mindfulness, like the previous vision in the occasion of retraction and contemplation, in the magic body in its aspect of beholding purified reflections and at the same time in mind isolation in its aspect of the path of the experience of the bliss of melting. [74b] For mind isolation becomes the path of luminance, radiance, and imminence, and they are analogues of the three joys. And finally, he claims that samadhi is communion. Thereby, he explains the method of reconciling the *Time Machine* six branches with the five stages.

[**VI.B.3.b.ii.c′3′a′ii′b″** – Analyzing their correctness and incorrectness]

The second has two parts: [1″] Analyzing the accuracy of the [Indian] commentators; and [2″] Analyzing the accuracy of the Tibetan explanations.

[**VI.B.3.b.ii.c′3′a′ii′b″1″** – Analyzing the accuracy of the (Indian) commentators]

In regard to the *Moonlight* refutation of including retraction and contemplation in the creation stage, it is not contradicted by the statement that the creation stage is the means of achieving common accomplishments and the six branches are the means of achieving the supreme accomplishment. If it were, it would contradict the achievement of both accomplishments by a single path, in which case the perfection-stage path could not lead to achievement of common accomplishments. The statement that

> practicing by other than the six branches practice, the supreme [accomplishment] will not be achieved

indicates that the supreme accomplishment will not be achieved by other practices than those of the six branches, and definitely does not indicate that paths other than the six branches are never a means of achieving the supreme accomplishment. Though the supreme accomplishment is not achieved by the creation stage alone, how can that preclude the creation stage from being a cause of the supreme accomplishment? Otherwise, it would be the same for the perfection stage, and also, as each of the perfection stage's six branches do not [alone] lead to the achievement, they would not become the path of achieving the supreme. If the creation stage were definitely unfit as means of achieving the supreme, how would this not contradict his own explanation about the meaning of "common" in the context of mentioning common and supreme types of service, that a common cause is cause of both accomplishments? [75a] The import of teaching the visualization practices of the Divine Lord Akshobhya and the [Buddha] Supreme Bliss Wheel and so on would become uncertain, and all statements that they are arts for attaining buddhahood in the context of the benefits of their meditations would become contradicted.

Here you may wonder that, if both paths are arts for both accomplishments, why were they mentioned separately as means of achieving common and supreme [accomplishments, respectively]? Since without regard to the perfection stage it leads to achievement of common accomplishments, the creation stage is a means of achieving common accomplishments, at the same time it is the means of developing the root of virtue needed to realize the perfection stage. The perfection stage is the chief path for achieving the supreme, and so is mentioned as the means for achieving the supreme. Thus, as means of achievement, the two are not mutually exclusive.

While retraction and contemplation are explained in terms of the perfection stage by other authoritative scholars, because that is the intention of the *Personal Instruction*, it seems necessary to explain them also in terms of the creation stage; thus in general we should not interpret retraction and contemplation as wholly in either creation or perfection stages, but should accept both parts [of each of them]. In particular, we should interpret them according to the explanation in the context of whichever stage of the text is at hand. Thus, as according to the noble tradition they are explained in their perfection-stage context, I think it is good [so to interpret them in that context].

It does not seem proper that endurance should refer to the magic body, as I will explain below.

As for the correctness or incorrectness of the *Illuminating Lamp [Intention] Elucidation*'s way of reconciling [the branches and stages], it will be easy to understand if I explain it in the context of explaining below the identification of the six branches. [75b]

As for master Ekādashanirghosha's explanation of retraction as the foundation of the body isolation, he is thinking of the import of the *Illuminating Lamp*'s explanation of retraction as that to be purified and of contemplation as the means of purification.

The claims that the two [lines] "independent" and so on indicate endurance to be the mind isolation, that "separately illuminated" refers to the magic body, that the three lines indicating the last branch refer to the two contemplations, that communion is explained apart from the samadhi branch, and that the last three lines refer to a path of spontaneity different from communion—all these are not good. They will be easy to understand when I explain them below in the context of explaining the text on the six branches.

[VI.B.3.b.ii.c'3'a'ii'b''2'' – Analyzing the accuracy of the Tibetan explanations]

When we refute the claim of a certain Tibetan, [the scholar] Lan, that "retraction" refers to the conduct, the argument "the normal order is contradicted if the conduct comes at the beginning of achieving the supreme" can be applied equally well to our own position. Thus, it is incorrect for "retraction" and "contemplation" to refer to the magic body, because it is contradictory for the magic body to come at the beginning of achieving the supreme. By explaining "at the beginning," we are saying "it must not come at the beginning," and this is the same when used about the conduct. If we indicate the fault of contradicting the normal order, it applies the same way to either the six branches or the five stages, and it is very contradictory for a retraction and contemplation [branch] magic body to develop before the vitalizing energy-control vajra recitation, for there to be a mindfulness [branch] mind isolation after the endurance [branch] clear light, and for the [premature] arisal of the third stage magic body. Furthermore, since it is certain that there is a vitalizing energy-control path in the five stages and that mind isolation and magic body arise developed in sequence, [76a] in the *Time Machine* system also both the vitalizing energy-control vajra recitation and the mindfulness mind isolation would have to come before the retraction and contemplation magic body, and one part of mindfulness would have to develop before endurance; because they are accepted as synonymous.

Such faults are not properly explained as the same in meaning, so we should not insist on explaining them as the same. Likewise, we ourselves assert that the magic body is the eleventh stage, and clear light the twelfth, or the thirteenth [stage], if we count from the stage of faith, and the twelfth stage is the stage of becoming noble. Such being the case, it seems contradictory [to claim] such views as that the noble stage eleventh stage magic body will be attained through retraction in the beginning of the achievement of the supreme, that the *Time Machine* samadhi branch will be attained from the alienated individual's stage, that it could be understood as communion, and so forth.

As for the reason why it is incorrect for contemplation to refer to body isolation, to state that "it is because no benefit of the lessening of subject and object [dichotomy] will develop in body isolation" will not apply to that fault, since the opponent did not claim that, and it seems that the opponent does claim that the one-pointedness of mind of lessening of subject and object is [a benefit of] mind isolation. Therefore, both "self-consecration" and "superficial reality," as explained by the noble father and sons and by the *Time Machine* literature, are nominally the same but different in meaning. For example, there are many [differing interpretations of the two] such as when Ghaṇṭapāda's *[Supreme Bliss] Five Stages* explains the self-consecration as the meditation on the drop in the heart center.

As for how other Tibetans seem to take the position that the *Time Machine* way of reconciling the six yoga branches with the six stages has the same meaning, their [76b] incorrectness can be understood from what has already been explained.

Therefore, Nāropa explained the texts on the six yogas of the *Further Tantra* according to the explanation of the *Illuminating Lamp*, but in his *Commentary* on the *Summary of Initiations*, he explained according to the *Time Machine*. Thus, even though such things are not properly explained as the same in meaning, it is good to investigate what is the equivalent, since if you do that, you will determine the practical instructions of each individual tantra.

To explain a little more, the *Time Machine* system's retraction and contemplation [branches] are the means of purifying the central channel preliminary to the vitalizing energy-control branch's injection of the two [side channel] energies into that central channel. So even if you do not meditate according to how it is explained there, if [what you do meditate] seems to serve as a means of purification of the central channel to prepare for injecting the two energies there, it is the equivalent. Likewise, the *Time Machine*'s vitalizing energy-control [branch] is the means of injecting the energies into the central channel, and [its] endurance is the holding those injected energies immobile in the hubs of the channel wheels; so even if you do not meditate vitalizing energy control and endurance exactly as it is explained in that source, if [what you do meditate] seems a means to achieve that purpose, it is the equivalent of those two. Likewise, [the *Time Machine*'s] mindfulness is, by the art of meditating depending on the prior means, burning the furor fire, melting the spirit of enlightenment, and experiencing the joy of its falling to the tip of the secret place, and [its] samadhi is the changeless bliss of holding that enlightenment spirit without emission; so even if you do not meditate exactly as explained from that source, if what you do serves as a path able to achieve that purpose, then it serves as the equivalent of those two. Therefore, from the perspective of the ability to achieve a particular purpose, the five stages and so on can be matched with other paths and one can mutually reconcile the paths; [77a] though you do not explain them as having the same meaning, the point of the context is accomplished, and you will attain fearlessness about where the keys of the paths of different tantras fit. And such reasoning can also be understood to apply to other paths as well. So you should hold on to this exceptional way of analyzing of those of great genius.

As for Lan's interpretation of retraction as the conduct, though there is a mere similarity of definition, it does not work out since the *Further Tantra* mentions the conduct entirely apart from the six branches. Therefore, avoiding that, if you connect the six branches to the six stages of the perfection stage, it is better to follow Ekādashanirghosha and connect retraction and contemplation to body isolation. According to the *Illuminating Lamp* explanation, there are three vitalizing energy controls meditated on the three nose tips, so, though there is a vitalizing energy-control [practice] that is neither the actual speech isolation nor vajra recitation, those two are given the name as they are the chief kind of vitalizing energy control; so [vitalizing energy control] is included with those two, [speech isolation and vajra recitation. Mind isolation, except that it can be understood to be the one-pointedness of contemplation and has similar characteristics with the three voids prior to entry into clear light, is not mentioned explicitly. Endurance is explained by the *Illuminating Lamp* as the same in meaning as clear light, so it does not work out for it to indicate mind isolation and magic body. Mindfulness refers to the way of arisal of the luminances coming during the re-emergence from clear light. Samadhi is very clearly explained in the *Illuminating Lamp* as communion, so there is no point in explaining it otherwise, as I will explain in detail below. The third stage magic body, except that it can be understood from its having similar characteristics to the communion magic body, [77b] is not mentioned verbally among the subjects explained by the commentaries of the texts on the six branches. And as for the fact that "actuality of all buddhas" does not refer to the magic body, I will explain it below. If I explain their meanings in detail, the magic body and the mind isolation will also be brought out, so there is no fault of not reconciling the important things about the achievement of the supreme of the perfection stage with the path of the six branches.

[**VI.B.3.b.ii.c′3′b′** – Certification of their order]

As for the statement in the *Five Stages* about the two stages being like the steps of a ladder, the five stages of the perfection stage are similar; for it states that by abiding in vajra recitation, the mind objective will be attained, [then] the magic body will be purified by the reality-limit clear light, and arising from that, nondual communion will be attained. And one can also understand thereby that by abiding in the mind objective the magic body will be attained. That is the order indicated, in that each later stage arises depending on each previous stage. This is not detailed in the *Five Stages* but is detailed in the *Integrated Practices*; where it states the order of the progress of the two spiritual conceptions, [including] the aspiration to the buddha vehicle, the single-minded awareness of the coarse deity yoga, the subtle conceptual yoga, the training in each previous stage from body isolation to communion leading to the learning of each subsequent stage; and it also states the order of the reverse, how from body isolation on, if the former is lacking, the latter will not arise. So from this one must accept the certainty about the progressive order. Except for just that explanation, the *Root* and its explanatory tantras and the treatises of the noble father and sons do not provide clearly the reason for the certainty of such an order.

The Kashmiri Lakshmī [78a] explains [the process as] first the necessary purifying of the ordinary body, which is accomplished by the creation stage from the first beginning up until the body isolation of the hundred clans. Then the speech isolation purifies the speech, and the mind isolation purifies the ordinary mind. Then in order to bring to fruition one's former vows, to abandon the nihilistic tendency gotten from the teaching of the god Maheshvara, to accomplish beings' aims until the end of the eon and to abandon the cessation truth accepted as enlightenment by the disciples, one attains the magic body.[64] Again, if one is attached even to that, one will become objectivity oriented, and one uses clear light to purify that. And finally, communion is taught in order to abandon any nihilistic extremism related to clear light.

Previous Tibetan scholars have said that, just as a flute will not give a pleasant sound until its insides are cleansed, the speech isolation will not arise until the ordinary body is isolated by the body vajra samadhi, and it will arise in the opposite case. Just as, until the horselike energy mounted by the mind is tamed, the riderlike mind will not be under control, so mind isolation will arise when speech isolation has brought the energies under control. In mind isolation, if even at the coarsest [level] one does not understand all things as merely self-aware mind, if at the subtlest one does not understand superficial reality as mere magical illusion, or if one has not [attained] the self-aware bliss samadhi in mind isolation, then the magic body will not arise; for the magic body is achieved from just those. For example, if the cognition cannot pick out a vase it cannot determine its property of impermanence. Likewise, without going to the limit of the subject of magical illusion, [78b] one will not realize the clear light of [its] dissolution by the two [holistic and dissolving] contemplations. If the

64. This is a very interesting way of defining the role of the creative art of the magic body, as the special means for fulfilling the bodhisattva vow, and avoiding the temptation of escaping into the bliss of the clear light, which is seen either as a tendency of the great Shiva or as a trap into which the individual vehicle adept might fall through attachment to a dualistic notion of the third noble truth.

invisible clear light is not first attained, one will not realize the communion of vision-void indivisible, just as before one's cognition can determine a mirror image as vision-void indivisible, one must have determined that a mirror reflection lacks the substance of the reflected object.

A certain Marpa tradition scholar holds the same position as Lakshmī on the first two, posits mind isolation as it is taught to include body and speech, posits magical illusion in order to abandon truth-insistence, posits clear light in order to abandon insistence on mere magical illusion, and posits the teaching of communion in order to abandon nihilistic extremism.

In regard to that, the first interpretation seems to say that the three isolations are the means of purifying the three doors [of body, speech, and mind], since from the coarse level there must be abandonment, considering the certainty of the order of those three doors; that since there is nihilistic extremism in mind isolation, one achieves the magic body in order to abandon it; that clear light purifies any orientation of absolutist extremism toward that [magic body]; and that communion is taught to abandon any lingering nihilism in that [clear light]. [This system] does not contain the necessary indication of the exceptional way in which the former develops the latter among the three isolations. Its procedure of developing an absolutist path to abandon nihilism and then a nihilistic path to abandon absolutism is, like an elephant washing himself [with mud], not truly appropriate. As in the *Integrated Practices*:

> If you lack understanding of the superficial reality, you cannot directly realize the ultimate reality!

[Āryadeva] teaches that you must understand and attain the magic body before you can experience the clear light, [79a] so he must show a reason for the position that magic body must be developed before clear light can be realized—and how can "one must enter clear light to abandon insistence on magical illusion" count as a reason? Reasons must be shown in that manner for the order of mind isolation, magic body, clear light, and communion; showing them in other ways seems to miss the essential point.

Furthermore, as for the statement that mind isolation is taught in order to understand the inclusion of body and speech into the mind, it shows the fault of not investigating carefully how the orientations of mind isolation are produced. [Āryadeva] states in the *Integrated Practices* that having understood properly the true import of the mind, one can engage in the achievement of the magic body, which does not mean that one could fail to eliminate doubts about the truth-habit concerning the mind while in the mind isolation and subsequently eliminate them by means of the magic body; for it is stated that one must thoroughly ascertain the import of voidness [long before], even in the time of meditating the creation stage.

The second interpretation is quite excellent in stating its reasons, in that speech isolation develops mind isolation by the power of its controlling the energies, that mind isolation serves as the foundation of achieving the magic body, that the magic body must realize clear light, being immersed in it by the two contemplations, and that clear light must precede the achievement of the [magic-body-clear-light] complementary communion. But as for its statement of example and import of the lute as the reason for the order of the first two isolations, it is insufficient, since it seems that the analogy between example and import remains to be established.

As for our own system's reasons for making the order certain, I will explain them in the context of proving the certainty of the enumeration.

[**VI.B.3.b.ii.c′3′c′** – Certification of their number]

The third [79b] has two parts: [i′] The actual meaning; and [ii′] How to reconcile other paths with this path.

[**VI.B.3.b.ii.c′3′c′i′** – The actual meaning]

The *Integrated Practices* explains as above the way of learning the path in stages. It states that after having attained communion there is no new learning of any stage of the path. The *Five Stages* also states—

> Dwelling in the communion samadhi,
> There is nothing at all further to learn

—that there are no stages of the path not included in these and that one must learn them [all in order]. Thus, since no other paths not included there are needed, a larger number is eliminated, and since without them one cannot [achieve the goal], a smaller number is eliminated. Therefore, we must accept the certainty of their enumeration. Even so, a clear reason for the certainty of the number [of the stages] is not explicitly stated in the two kinds of tantras or by the father and sons.

In this regard, Lakshmī says that the three isolations isolate [from ordinariness] and so purify body, speech, and mind; the clear light isolates and so purifies superficial and ultimate realities; communion causes the attainment of vajradharahood where the two realities are one in taste; and there are no more things to learn after that—so six stages are not needed. And since by just this explained above our desired goal is achieved, and since there are not only four stages, the number of five stages is definite.

Bhavyakīrti is the same in regard to the first three. The self-consecration is in order to accomplish the aims of beings with the purified three doors. Insistent adherence to that is abandoned by clear light, and any [temptation of] nihilism in that is abandoned by communion. There is nothing beyond that to learn, so there is no sixth stage, nor are there any less stages, since without those two the aims of [80a] self and other would not be accomplished.

Another former Tibetan scholar determines a count of six stages in terms of suppressing the manifestations of obscurations and eradicating the seeds of them. He locates the three isolations in the suppression of the manifestations of addictions and conceptual notions: body isolation, as the support of the tranquility of bliss-void, and speech isolation, as controlling the energies and thus not allowing conceptual notions to arise, are the conditions and mind isolation is the actuality, since that bliss-void is developed in the mind process by depending on the consort. He further states that magical illusion is there to abandon, through its realization of objective voidness, the seeds of objectivity notions insisting on objects in the private process, that clear light is there to abandon, through its realization of the voidness of the mind, subjectivity notions insisting on the subjective mind, and that communion is there to abandon the seed of insistence on the difference of the two realities; and that there are no more things to be abandoned than these.

The first two [of these interpretations], except for some differences of expression, seem the same in meaning; and I have already examined whether they are correct or not. They do not appear to claim that [the different stages] are like the transcendent wisdom explanations of tranquility and insight as different in meditative mode while similar in orientation toward voidness, so I do not think their interpretations are satisfactory; since one can't make the paths of quiescence and insight different, and one cannot determine the latter three paths [of the perfection stage] as individual remedies for different notions. [80b]

Well then, one wonders, relying on what can one achieve the determination of the number [of stages]?

Relying on the ultimate thing to be achieved, [one can determine the number] by the procedure of "because to achieve that, these are necessary, and it is not necessary not to include them here." Just to do that, we will explain further below the already explained fruit of communion, which unites the wisdom truth body and its support, the extraordinary matter body. In order to attain such a communion, you must create on the learning path the learner's communion that combines the ultimate clear light, which is the direct application of the great bliss wisdom to the import of thatness, and the utterly pure superficial magic body, which is developed from the cause of the five light rays of the energies that carry that wisdom. Prior to that communion of the two realities, you must achieve each side of the pair individually; because, as [Āryadeva] says in the *Integrated Practices* that:

> without realizing ultimate reality, you cannot realize the stage of communion . . .

and it is stated that you cannot realize clear light without having previously attained the superficial magic body. Therefore, first you must create the magic body as the support for the direct realization of clear light, the reason for which will be explained.

The third stage, magic body, and the fourth stage, clear light, no longer exist at the time of communion, and so are not the two parts of the time of communion. Yet in general, superficial magic body and ultimate clear light become the parts of communion; and so the two former things are explained thinking of their becoming those two [parts of communion].

As for the energy and the mind that serve as the basis from which such a magic body is achieved, [81a] they are the mind created as the three wisdoms of the mind isolation and the energies serving as their mount, arising from the dissolving process of the energies collecting in the heart center by the process of earth dissolving into water and so forth, and of the energies that move the eighty natural instincts themselves dissolving and so forth; therefore you must attain mind isolation before the magic body.

By such arts, to achieve the distinctive process of compression in the heart center, you must have the two meditations of the outer vitalizing energy control uniting with the evolutionary and wisdom consorts and the inner vitalizing energy control meditating on the energies and drops and so on; therefore, before mind isolation you must achieve the process of speech isolation vajra recitation. "Speech isolation" and "vajra recitation" are designated by the name of one side of vitalizing energy control, but the general name of this stage is mentioned in the *Further Tantra* as the "vitalizing energy control" that is third of the six branches. It has three vitalizing energy controls that meditate the substance drop at the lower nose tip, the indestructible mantra drop at the heart center nose tip, and the light drop at the facial nose tip. While it teaches the union with the two consorts by meditating the substantial drop outside the two lower nose tips of the art and wisdom, there are two occasions of vitalizing energy control of union with the two consorts, one performed before the consummation of vajra recitation and one after such consummation.

The chief reason for the necessity of the energy-mind arisen from the energies gathering and dissolving in the heart center *dhūti* channel as the basis for the achievement of the magic body has already been explained. I will explain below the detailed reasons for that and the procedure by which the two consorts become the means for compressing the energies in the heart center. Thus, before achieving the path of vitalizing energy control that is a distinctive procedure of collecting the energies in the heart center, [81b] you must meditate aiming your visualization at other key points of the body. And so you must meditate the body isolation that meditates the development of orgasmic bliss arising from the general injection and dissolution of the two energies in the *dhūti* channel, which views all that arises as the play of that [bliss], and meditates all of that in the form of divinity. As there is no certainty of specific channels and wheels in terms of the other key points of such a body, here you focus your meditation on the drop in the lower door.

As for the development of the roots of virtue underlying the generation in your mental process of such a complete perfection stage, you must first meditate the single-mindedness of the coarse yoga of the first stage that cleanses the mind process through conversion of birth, death, and between into the three bodies and the four-session yoga that constructs the subtle mandala. And as for achieving fitness as a vessel of meditating the two stages, you must attain complete and pure initiations, and must maintain carefully the undertaken vows and commitments. And in order to become fully qualified as a vessel of maintaining the initiations and commitments, you must, as I have previously explained, cultivate the common path stages to cleanse your two spirits of enlightenment and their accessories. And as for the conducts that heighten the impact [of the practices], as they are taught by the example of the outer vitalizing energy control, such is the ascertainment of the number of all paths, of the two stages, and of the stages of the two stages.

Thereby, you can know the ascertainment of their order as well. A single person needs all of those to become enlightened, and so Lakshmī, Bhavyakīrti, and so on are right to say that one person must meditate all five stages, [82a] and each stage is not taught in terms of each different personal process. The *Moonlight Commentary* is not correct when it explains that the best person needs the last two stages, the medium person needs the third and fourth stages, the inferior person needs the creation stage and vajra recitation, and the most inferior needs those two and verbal recitation, asserting that others' system is that "best, medium, and inferior" are posited in the context of one mental process gradually progressing from higher to higher and that its own system is that this intends different personal processes; since this [interpretation] contradicts the noble father and son treatises' indications of order and also the *Rosary of Complete Yoga*.

This ascertainment of the number [of the stages], if you apply it to other tantras, the last three stages should be interpreted as above. Since the heart-center compression processes exist openly in such texts as the *Supreme Bliss Five Stages* [by Ghaṇṭapāda] and Kukuripa's [*Heruka Sādhana*] instruction [based] on the *Mahāmāyā [Tantra]*, it is easy to understand the way of focus on it. Without that [heart-center compression], you should understand the procedure of finally focusing on compression in the heart center even on the paths of penetrating the vital points in the navel and so on. And you should understand what is explained here as the reason how elsewhere even when the name "body isolation" is absent, if its referent is present, it is the same, and if its referent is absent it need not be contradictory, as a part of understanding the easy compression in the heart center. And you should supply the same principle also to the creation stage. As for the common path, it is similar in all [these principles of progression].

[**VI.B.3.b.ii.c′3′c′ii′** – How to reconcile other paths with this path]

[Chandrakīrti] states in the *Illuminating Lamp*—

> This is the supreme branch of practice,
> The condensed import of all tantras . . .

—that in these five stages including the first stage all imports of all tantras are included. [82b] You should not understand this as meaning merely all *Community* tantras, but must understand it as referring to all tantras; because the same text states that the *Community* is the root of all tantra categories and the vessel of all sutras. Therefore, the statement from the same text—

> The divisions of this stage—
> Who understands how all the many
> Elaborated stages truly fit into them—
> That one does know tantra

—should not be understood as referring only to *Community* tantras, but to all tantras.

Here you wonder, "Well, what is the meaning of the statement that who knows the path stages of other tantras, as stages elaborated from here and also as included here, knows [all about] tantra?"

This, as explained above, does not mean they are included because they are exactly the same in meaning, but that they are included because they have corresponding functions. Further, you must understand how, while it is according to the interpretation of purposes from mind isolation up to communion, the chief art of developing mind isolation is the process of compression in the heart center, and how, even if the heart center compression process is not explicitly clear, compressions in other places such as the navel end up focusing on the heart center. But I have not written more than this little bit [on this], fearing prolixity.

Even though [another tantra's creation stage] might be somewhat dissimilar from this [*Community*'s] creation stage, if you understand how it must serve as the means of developing the roots of virtue to complete the perfection stage, its meaning must be similar. Therefore, if you understand well the way of reconciling such a path, you will attain fearlessness in regard to all imports of tantra.

Here someone [claims] that, just after the above quoted "you should meditate in a single sitting," the *Concise Five Stages Elucidation* goes on to say:

> In order to truly realize thatness,
> The supreme [83a] path with the five stages,
> The transcendence and the various other vehicles
> Are explained connecting them upon a single mat,
> In an existent life, in a single day.

As for the meaning of the beginning, [that someone claims that] in the *Transcendent Wisdom Sutra*, the Teacher sitting with body erect indicates the creation stage, his body's radiating millions of light rays, the vajra recitation, the eighteen voidnesses, the mind objective, the illusoriness of matter, the magic body, the identitylessness of matter and so on, the clear light, and nonduality, nondualism, and so on indicate communion. Furthermore, as for the meaning of "connected to various vehicles," [Serdingpa's] *Five Point* explains that:

> The disciple vehicle is included in the creation stage, because the appearance of coarse atomic conglomerations asserted by the disciples and the constructive yoga of the creation stage qualitatively correspond; the vajra recitation includes the hermit buddha vehicle, because the vajra recitation of the twelve energy transits qualitatively corresponds with the twelve relativity [links] of the hermits; the mind only vehicle is included in the mind objective stage, because both of them emphasize the mind; the illusory centrists are included in the magic body, because both assert that all things are illusory; the nonabiding centrists are included in clear light, because both assert all things as void; and all secret mantra vehicles are included in communion, since all tantric views are the equal taste communion of the two realities.

[Serdingpa's] *Wheel Endowed* and the *Father Tantra Quintessence [Five Stages Single Session]* agree also.

As for the meaning in that treatise of "explaining in connection with the *Transcendent Wisdom [Sutra]* and the various [83b] vehicles," it is not connected as in the above explanation, connecting the basic time five stages to the process of existence, birth and death, and to a single day. Well then, what is it connected to? "Explain them as connected to them" indicates that in general the sutras of the various individual and universal vehicles, and specifically the keys of all the profound *Transcendent Wisdom Sutras*, are incorporated in the *Community Tantra*, since their vital points are included in the five stages of the *Community*'s path; because the same text explains:

> That which serves as the path with its five stages
> Is indicated by various words such as
> The accessories of enlightenment, import of sutras,
> The three secret things, and the two ultimate [imports of the tantras]

—that is, that the verbal meanings of the various sutras that teach the accessories of enlightenment and of the various tantras that teach the three secrets and the two ultimates indicate by example the five stages.

As for the way they are included, although those paths as explained in other treatises are not explained here, the vital points of the paths of those [vehicles] are the means of achieving the liberation of deliverance from the life cycle and the exaltation of buddhahood. And the meaning of [this tantra] serving as their root is that they are completely, with their accessories, present within the path taught here, and also those other paths must focus here in the end. And as for others' systems' reasons for incorporating other paths into this path, they seem uncertain and unestablished.

4. Body Isolation

[83b.6–107b.1]

[VI.B.3.b.ii.c′3′d′ – The import of the individual divisions (of the perfection stage)]

The fourth has two parts: [i′] How to learn the samadhis of the three isolations; and [ii′] How to learn the samadhis of the two realities.

[VI.B.3.b.ii.c′3′d′i′ – How to learn the samadhis of the three isolations]

The first has three parts: [A″] How to learn the body isolation body vajra samadhi; [B″] How to learn the speech isolation [84a] speech vajra samadhi; and [C″] How to learn the mind isolation mind vajra samadhi.

[VI.B.3.b.ii.c′3′d′i′A″ – How to learn the body isolation body vajra samadhi]

The first has six parts: [1″] Analysis of which of two stages has body isolation; [2″] Sequence of creation stage and distinctive body isolation; [3″] Identification of body isolation; [4″] Typology of body isolations; [5″] How it serves as retraction and contemplation branches [of the six branches]; and [6″] How to put the body isolation into practice.

[VI.B.3.b.ii.c′3′d′i′A″1″ – Analysis of which of two stages has body isolation]

The first has three parts: [a″] Setting forth individual interpretations; [b″] Analysis of their correctness and incorrectness; and [c″] Setting forth our own interpretation.

[**VI.B.3.b.ii.c′3′d′i′A″1″a″** – Setting forth individual interpretations]

There are disagreements about where to place body isolation on the two stages. While many such as Abhaya, Munishrī, Lakshmī, and Bhavyakīrti explain body isolation as [belonging to the] creation stage, both mentors Tsunmojen and Abhijña claim it to be [part of the] perfection stage, and master Gö reports in his *[Great] Voidness Session* that Kṛshna Samayavajra believes the body isolations of the hundred clans, the five clans, and the three clans to be creation stage and the body isolation of one clan to be perfection stage. Some of the Marpa tradition scholars say that Nāropa considered [body isolation] to be creation stage; but this is not true, since the *Concise Five Stages Elucidation* explains those two [creation stage and body isolation] separately.

As for how such disagreements arose:

[First of all,] based on the *Integrated Practices* statements that

> one remains in the beginner's samadhi when learning the yogas of conceptuality and single-mindedness and one learns body isolation after having already so remained . . .

and that

> beginning from the creation stage up to the culmination [84b] of body isolation . . .

wherein the two are treated as separate, [body isolation] is posited as [included in the] perfection stage. One is considered a "beginner" here in this system from beginning the creation-stage meditation until completing it; as *Five Stages* says:

> By the yoga of the beginner, one will attain the eighth stage . . .

and the *Integrated Practices* says:

> In this vajra vehicle one trains in the creation stage and attains the eighth stage.

Then again, on the strength of the *Integrated Practices* statements:

> As for the just explained aggregates, elements, and media, one isolates the body; one sets a deity there, common to all, since it is a coarse yoga . . .

and just after that in the text:

> . . . speech isolation is not creation stage, because it is extremely subtle . . .

—[here,] "common to all" indicates [body isolation] to be common to both stages; depending on which it is interpreted as having parts belonging to each stage. Those who posit it as creation stage seem to think its way of meditating the aggregates as deities has the same import as the pure meditation on the individual deities of the creation stage.

If one wonders, "well, those who advocate body isolation as creation stage, in which context of that [stage] do they claim that body isolation is being taught?"

Abhaya accepts the mere visualization of the body of the creation-stage-generated vajradhara as the body isolation, stated in the context of creation stage, thus accepting it as the chief of visualizations. Though others do not explain clearly, when other visualized deities are set in the body, they must be imagined as indivisible from the aggregates and so forth, [85a] so it seems that they interpret those [practices] as body isolation. As they explain them as generated by mere visualization, it seems they do not claim the body mandala created from seed [syllables] as body isolation. Munishrī is not clear about the way in which body isolation is indicated, except for the statement that "the 'creation stage' mentioned in the *Condensed [Sādhana]* indicates the body isolation."

The latter two pandits accept body isolation as creation stage because they explain that one practices it after already learning the three samadhis of the *Condensed [Sādhana]*, but they do not accept it as the [whole] creation stage explained in the *Condensed [Sādhana]* itself. Most Tibetan scholars of the Gö tradition assert body isolation to belong to the perfection stage. Lan interprets the coarse body isolation that does not discriminate finely the five [buddhas] in the five aggregates and so forth as observation, and interprets the body isolation that finely discriminates from the hundred clans to the one clan as examination, holding the former to be a body isolation in common with the creation stage, since the creation stage [texts] also explain such meditation in the context of "extreme yoga," and holding the latter to be the perfection stage's distinctive body isolation.

[VI.B.3.b.ii.c′3′d′i′A″1″b″ – Analysis of their correctness and incorrectness]

Which should we accept of those different interpretations?

If you accept the whole of body isolation as the creation stage explained in the *Condensed [Sādhana]*, you cannot avoid the contradiction with the *Integrated Practices* statement that one must train in body isolation after already having learned the beginner's samadhi. It is very incorrect to not include body isolation within the three samadhis mentioned in the *Condensed [Sādhana]* and to locate it on a different creation stage: because [85b] the three samadhis of the *Condensed [Sādhana]* indicate all the creation stages needed as preliminaries of the perfection stage, except for some creation stages [implemented] on the occasions of conducting ritual activities; because you cannot posit that "this is the way of learning the arisal of deity forms of the previously unexperienced body isolation creation stage, after completing both subtle and coarse creation stages of the *Condensed [Sādhana]*"; and because there do not appear [in those creation stages] any ways of meditating the body isolation other than meditating the forms of deity bodies.

It is incorrect to posit the whole of body isolation as perfection stage: because it is stated that "body isolation is common to all"; because speech isolation is specially picked out and stated "not to be in the province of creation stage [practice]"; and because you can understand [it is so] from the statement that coarse and subtle are the means of achieving the common and the distinctive. Therefore, as "establishing the deities" refers to the establishing of deities as the aggregates and so forth, which is common to both stages, you cannot explain that the body isolation is never said to be common [to both stages], and you should divide body isolation into two body isolations belonging to the two stages.

Such being the case, you should not interpret this according to the view of Damtsig Dorjey, since the *Integrated Practices* states that all body isolations, from the hundred-clan body isolation to the three-clan body isolation, are included in the one-clan body isolation, and it is improper for that included to be of the creation stage and that which includes to be of the perfection stage.

As this meditation of aggregates and so on as deities of body isolation is a meditation of the arisal of the deity form, and, since it is taught that [86a] you meditate this after having found extreme stability of the vivid vision of the complete habitat and inhabitant mandalas within a mere mustard seed, you could not gain the experience of this without having already experienced the preceding, it would be incorrect to explain in some other way this stage of the path, [which must be] learned after having learned that [preceding stage]. Though there is no clear explanation in the context of the first stage concerning this division of each aggregate and so on into five, when you complete the coarse and subtle creation stages, you aim your mind at whatever arises and you can immediately generate stable vivid vision of the arisal of the deity, and you cannot say you cannot generate the division into fields; therefore, Lan does not seem to be correct in his way of differentiating the body isolations of the two stages.

Some scholars say that while the creation stage is the new creation [of a deity], the body isolation meditation of aggregates and so on as deities is the method of deity meditation of the perfection stage, which sees the deities as if primordially established. This seems to be an account based on failing to differentiate clearly between the two procedures of mantra body and wisdom body, [both used] on both stages. Just as, on the occasion of the perfection stage, drops and syllables and so on are indeed visualized in mind without existing as they are visualized, since they can create the nonartificial perfection stage without having to develop into other homogeneous visualizations, they are included in the perfection stage [in spite of involving conceptualization]. So you cannot achieve such [a nonartificial perfection stage] just by thinking "aggregates and so on are deities primordially," and such a method of deity meditation [as the perfection-stage body isolation] seems greater than the creation stage with its method of mental imagination and artifice; so you cannot differentiate the two stages just by [equating them with] those two [86b] ways of viewing deities.

Similarly, even though the objectification of the mind that realizes voidness can be taken as the arisal of a deity, it cannot thereby be distinguished from the creation stage; because that occurs even on the occasion of the creation stage; and because, while it is stated that one should purify [reality] in voidness by the [mantras] "*shūnyatā* . . ." and so on before creating a deity, it is improper to interpret its meaning as merely the retraction from perception without any proper understanding of the view of voidness.

[**VI.B.3.b.ii.c′3′d′i′A″1″c″** – Setting forth our own interpretation]

Well, then what is the way to differentiate body isolations in terms of the two stages?

In regard to this body isolation that meditates aggregates and so on as deities, there are two ways of meditating it; one where the objectivity aspect [involved] in the realization of voidness arises as a deity, and one where it does not. When it does arise [as a deity], it has two varieties; one where it is a distinctive bliss that is realizing voidness, and one where it is not. And when it is the distinctive bliss that is realizing voidness, there are again two kinds; one where it is the bliss arisen from the *rasanā* and *lalanā* energies penetrating and dissolving into the *dhūti* channel, and one where it is not [the bliss] thus arisen.

Of those, on the creation stage there are body isolations where voidness is realized in the second ways of the first two alternatives—voidness being realized without being realized by that bliss of melting, and where the aggregates and so forth are meditated as deities through the second ways of the last two alternatives. The body isolation that meditates the aggregates and so forth as deities through the first ways of the latter two alternatives is posited as being the perfection stage itself.[65] The creation-stage body iso-

65. This rather brilliant analysis deserves a schema:

Body isolation that meditates aggregates as deities
- *a) Seeing voidness as a deity*
  - *i) Seeing the void-deity through bliss*
    - *x) Central channel bliss*
    - **y) Noncentral channel bliss**
  - **ii) Seeing the void-deity without involving bliss**
- **b) Not seeing voidness as a deity**

Creation-stage body isolation (bold) = b, a-ii, a-i-y.
Perfection-stage body isolation (italic) = a, a-i, a-i-x.
This way of differentiating shows distinctiveness while allowing overlap.

lation wherein aggregates and so on are meditated as deities is said to consist of the occasions of the visualization of one's own body mandala and the mandala retraction, and of the viewing of all objective appearances as Vajradhara; and this is indicated by the statement about how the creation stage employs the pure art and wisdom that views the five sense spheres as male and female deities. Therefore, [87a] learning such a body isolation occurs on the same occasion as learning the creation stage. As for the statement that "after having already learned the beginner's samadhi, one learns the body isolation," it refers to the perfection-stage body isolation.

Well then, if you wonder, "where is it taught that the body isolation meditates the aggregates and so on as deities from the perspective of great bliss?"

It is taught by the *Integrated Practices*' quote, in the context of meditating the five-clan body isolation, from the *Equal to Space Tantra:*

> All this living world has the nature of five buddhas,
> Appearing like actors or like lovely paintings;
> Wherein "great bliss" itself alone,
> Alone performs through many moods.

Here just as a single actor performs using different masks and costumes and a single color such as blue arises in many forms of color, so the single great bliss itself is stated to perform in many kinds of aesthetic mood. This is not to be understood as referring to such a performance by Buddha Vajradhara alone, but is used in terms of all great blisses of path and fruition times.

Thus in the occasion of body isolation, great bliss alone is meditated as arising in the manifold play of the five clans and so forth, and that is not in terms of visualizing the bliss of other beings without having that bliss in one's own continuum, but is so meditated having generated that bliss in one's own spiritual continuum. Therefore, in that context, the *Integrated Practices* states [quoting the *Magic Supreme Bliss Tantra*]:

> The yoga will not arise
> From a cast statue and so forth,
> But striving in the spirit of enlightenment, [87b]
> The yogi/nī will become a deity.
> Oneself the nature of all buddhas!
> Oneself the nature of all heroes!

Thus one joins the divine,
And thereby should realize one's nature.

Thus one should not just visualize the form of an external deity but should establish oneself in unity with the deity through striving in the spirit of enlightenment; the "spirit of enlightenment" quoted [here] in the *Magic Supreme Bliss [Tantra]* is the bliss-void-indivisible spirit of enlightenment.

The *Hevajra Tantra* also states:

Definitely the purity of all things is called "suchness";
Then distinguishing each one, one should call them deities.

And also:

Oneself self-aware is purity, not freed by another purity,
Objective things being pure, self-knowing, bliss supreme.

Thus, three purities are stated: a general purity called "suchness purity," when you determine all outer and inner things to be void of intrinsic reality status; a purity of individual deities from meditating the matter aggregate and so on as deities; and a purity of natural awareness, the supreme bliss of each yogi/nī's natural awareness. The middle of these is said by the same text—

In the realm of the creation stage,
This should purify the aggregates.

—that the purity of individual deities, lacking the great bliss deity meditation, is in the creation stage. Therefore, great bliss is the purity of the perfection process, and the suchness purity is common to both stages.

Therefore, if you do not know the above-explained way of deity meditation of perfection-stage body isolation, since in this context you will lack the way of deity meditation that creates the wisdom body, [88a] though you posit it as perfection stage, it will show no difference from the way of creating the mantra body deity, and you have not understood the vital point of this.

Well then, one wonders, if this kind of great bliss is not posited on the creation stage, and its art of creation does not appear until the creation stage is perfected and body isolation arrived at, and moreover if even in the context of body isolation the way of producing this does not appear, how does great bliss emerge in this context?

By the reason that this seems to be one of the greatly difficult points, very hard to sort out, I will explain it in the context of the sequence [of the stages].

[VI.B.3.b.ii.c′3′d′i′A″2″ – Sequence of creation stage and distinctive body isolation]

How do you ascertain the sequence of the creation stage and the perfection-stage body isolation?

Generally, as for the complete meditation of the coarse and subtle creation stages, it is the means of developing the root of virtue that produces all the perfection stages, so it also serves as the means of developing the arisal of the perfection-stage body isolation. In particular, the meditation of the subtle [symbolic] implement or drop within the jewel is the method of collecting the *rasanā* and *lalanā* energies into the *dhūti* channel. Depending on that, when you develop the above-explained great bliss, it becomes the meditation of the actual body isolation, and that is how it is connected with the subtle creation stage.

One wonders here, "from what does one know that the meditation of the subtle at the lower door becomes the art of collecting the two energies into the *dhūti* channel?"

Although vitalizing energy control is taught in both the action and performance tantras, it has previously been explained how these cannot collect the two energies into the *dhūti* channel. As for the meditation of vitalizing energy control taught in the unexcelled [yoga tantras], "vitalizing energy" means the *rasanā* and *lalanā* energies and "control" means their insertion into the *dhūti* channel, having blocked their movement in the *rasanā* and *lalanā* [channels]. [88b] Much has been said about this in the *Time Machine* literature. Though the *Illuminating Lamp* does not so explain the meaning of "vitalizing energy" and "control," it is similar [there] since the meditation of vitalizing energy control accomplishes that very task. Therefore, the *Personal Instruction [of Mañjushrī]*, commenting on the meaning of the *Further Tantra* statement that the meditation of the subtle at the secret nose tip is vitalizing energy control, states:

> In the way of the strong-hearted,
> The drop falls from the heart lotus,
> And abides in the center
> Of one's vajra jewel;
> Supreme form of five elements,
> Reality of five wisdoms,
> Visualized as the subtle sign of one's divine self,
> Ablaze with the five light rays.

That is stated more concisely as "stopping the breath is the branch of voidness," saying that this is the branch of creating the void by stopping the expanding and contracting of the breath exhaling and inhaling from the nostrils, showing that the vitalizing energy-control branch and the breath-stopping branch are the same in meaning. Tathāgatavajra also states [in his *Art of Achievement (Lūyipa's Sādhana) Commentary Autocommentary*]:

> Having caused the vital energy with its nature of the five elements to move downward, by the way of enfolding it into a drop of spirit of enlightenment the mere size of a mustard seed, having it descend to the nose tip of the vajra, you should visualize with the previously explained process of retraction and the five-branched contemplation. This is the drop yoga; for the sake of reversing the outward flow of vitalizing energy, because of that very reason, the *Esoteric Community Further Tantra* called this "vitalizing energy control." And this again is merely an illustration; the yoga of subtle *āli* and *kāli* [letters] at the navel, or the contemplation of the yoga of drops and so on at the heart and so on, [89a] whatever works toward blocking the emission of vitalizing energy is called "vitalizing energy control." Especially, on the strength of such contemplation as this, the control of the vitalizing energies moves intensely into the central channel, having reversed their flow in the *rasanā* and *lalanā* channels; and this again is called "vitalizing energy control."

Thus the *Further Tantra* states that "vitalizing energy control" is the meditation on the subtle [drop] of the lower door, as it blocks the inhalation and exhalation flowing in the nostril from the *rasanā* and *lalanā* and injects them into the central channel. And that is merely a partial example. For this extremely clear explanation that vitalizing energy control is what accomplishes that function, by meditating the visualization of drops and letters and so on at the navel and heart and so on, must be understood as applying to all statements about meditating the perfection stages that place letters and so on in whatever channel wheels there are. As for the statement about meditating [the yoga branches of] retraction and contemplation, as those two are accepted as creation stages, it means they should be meditated on by one who possesses [expertise in the] creation stage.

Some of the Indian treatises on the six yoga branches of the Jñānapāda tradition also explain in this same way. The *Sheaf of Instructions* says there is an eight-petalled channel wheel inside the jewel, and the *Initiation Summary* mentions "the lotus of the jewel" intending that. Thus, meditating the subtle [drop] therein, one can withdraw the energies into the *dhūti* channel. The *[Vajra] Rosary* statement "by seeing the place within the jewel" resembles the statement about changing [this place] into the lotus in a woman; one must understand [the statement in this context] as referring to that support, [the channel wheel in the jewel, or in the lotus].[66]

In the noble system, it is said that first you become stable by meditating the subtle in the jewel [89b] and [then] you can meditate the mandala within the expansion into the lotus of the mother. Thus, except for those of the type who can easily collect the energies, even if you stably meditate the mandala of the subtle of the creation stage it is hard for the two energies to dissolve into the *dhūti* channel, so usually when you enter the body isolation having stabilized the subtle mandala, and you meditate the subtle drop or implement in the jewel, only after having injected the two energies into the *dhūti* channel should you meditate the actuality of the body isolation, the union of bliss-void and so on.

As for the *Further Tantra* explanation of vitalizing energy control that meditates the drop in the heart center and the lower door, its meaning explained by the *Personal Instruction* as a branch of stopping the breath is clearly elucidated by the two Indian treatises, especially explaining that all

66. I am uncertain about this; it refers to the need to be in a controlled sexual union posture with a consort to bring the drop into this position, and both partners in the union must be able to focus in this way, in the jewel for a male and in the lotus for a female.

meditations of letters and drops in the places of the channel wheels serve as methods for compressing the energies into the *dhūti* channel. This is a marvelously eloquent detailed explanation of vitalizing energy control.

If you do not understand this, as your [understanding of] vitalizing energy control will be too narrow, you will not understand the need to employ the vitalizing energy control of the six branches in many of the unexcelled [yoga] perfection stages. And if you do not understand the vital point of meditating by having visualized channel wheels and having set letters and so on in them, you will not understand the vital points of the meditations of the two *Community* systems and Ghaṇṭapa's *[Supreme Bliss] Five Stages* and so on, where drops and letters are set in those places without clearly visualizing the channel wheels. Thus it seems that the great certainty about the ultimate points of the instruction will not arise. But if you understand this pattern, it seems that it can develop the wondrous certainty about the vital key points of the private instructions about all of these [practices]. [90a]

If you still do not know properly the way of meditating the perfection-stage body isolation of this system, the problems lie in failing to know the way in which subtle drop meditation serves as the vitalizing energy control that collects the two energies and the way in which that develops the great bliss. Relying on the wisdom consort, having completed the subtle and coarse creation stage, you can bring your enlightenment spirit down from your crown to the tip of your secret place. You can stop it there with the PHAṬ letter, with extremely stable visualization, and relying on that you can generate the four joys. But that cannot be posited as the perfection-stage great bliss, since it does not arise from the dissolving of the two energies into the *dhūti* channel. Therefore, even the meditation on the aggregates and so on as deities from the perspective of uniting voidness and such a bliss [of four joys derived from visualization of the wisdom consort without dissolving the energies] is not accepted as perfection-stage body isolation.

[**VI.B.3.b.ii.c′3′d′i′A″3″** – Identification of body isolation]

The third has two parts: [**a″**] Others' interpretations; and [**b″**] My interpretation.

[**VI.B.3.b.ii.c′3′d′i′A″3″a″** – Others' interpretations]

Many Tibetan mentors consider there to be four body isolations, and [consider that the quote] from the *Integrated Practices*, from:

> . . . this acquired body abides like a heap, piled up as a mass of things, such as the measure of flesh . . .

up to:

> . . . the eyes and limbs and so forth . . .

explains that the verbal meaning of body is "pile," a mass of thirty-six impure substances, and refers to the "material body isolation," which is an object also common to the disciples, since it is an "isolation" from the fundamentalists' and so on reifications of the body as pure and happy.

[They also consider that the *Integrated Practices* statement:]

> . . . the five aggregates, four elements, six media, five objects, and five wisdoms are called a "heap," just like calling many grains such as rice and barley and so on a "heap," and so the body [90b] is said to be a heap of a mass of limbs and members . . .

refers to the "natural body isolation," which is an object also common to the followers of the transcendence [vehicle], since it is "isolated" from the notion of the singular self, since it is composed of a multiplicity of aggregates, elements, media, and so on.

[They also consider that the *Integrated Practices* statement:]

> . . . [the body-mind] is called an "accumulation," since, due to the meeting of [minds and] elements, it forms a continuum of intelligence, views, mentality, misknowledge, instinct, craving, and addiction, and this heap or mass of consciousnesses cannot be perceived [ultimately], since it is not located [spatially] . . .

refers to the "consciousness body isolation," since it is isolated from subject and object [dichotomy], consciousness not being perceived; which [isolation] is an object common also to the idealists.

[And finally, they also consider that the *Integrated Practices* statement:]

> . . . since aggregates, elements, and media have been present from the beginningless due to the pride of ordinariness, they are shown to be a reality created from the subatomic particles of all transcendent buddhas . . .

refers to the "samadhi body isolation," since that body devoid of the two selves serves as an object of pride as created from the subatomic particles of all transcendent buddhas, manifested as the hundred clans and so on; and that is the uncommon object of [only] the tantric practitioner.

[**VI.B.3.b.ii.c′3′d′i′a″3″b″** – My interpretation]

As for explaining the three first [types] as body isolations, it does not occur anywhere in the translated Indian treatises in the noble tradition literature, neither does it seem to be the intention of the *Integrated Practices*.

Well, then, how should we interpret the intention of the *Integrated Practices*?

You posit a body isolation only after having identified the body that is to be isolated, [91a] and the verbal meaning of "body" is "heap," "pile," and "mass." Thus, the first [*Integrated Practices* statement] shows it to be the mass of "the measure of the flesh element and so on," as that is the way of "piling" up many things such as rice and barley and so on, and among those three; and this statement is also made in the *Vajra Rosary*.

Then, as for the way of piling up shown in piling up the twenty-five [elements], such as the five aggregates, as one calls it a "pile" when many grains of rice or barley are piled up, he shows it to be a pile, a mass including the body's limbs and members. Among the twenty-five the mind and mental functions are also included, and the way they are piled up is different from the way grains of rice and so on are piled up; i.e., mind and mental functions are not spatial objects, each occupying its individual spatial location. So [Āryadeva] mentions "because of the meeting of the elements" in order to differentiate the [two ways of piling up]. Because the eyes and so on, the faculties, and the objects such as form meet one another, the mentality and the sixfold assemblage of the mind and wisdom and so on, the mental functions, occur. And as for their way of accumulating, assembling, and piling up, it is through collecting many parts of an uninterrupted continuum of former and later moments. So he says it is not a collecting of many spatial objects each occupying its location at the same time, since he specifies that "accumulation" refers to continua. While he says that the piling up of consciousnesses cannot be directly observed, as it does not stay still, and argues that consciousness is not embodied, by the reason that it does not reside in the eastern etc. spatial locations, and so is not a collection of many objects occupying space, [91b] he does not refute substantial subject-object dichotomy.

Now, as for what such a to-be-isolated body is to be isolated from, he indicates it by saying that it is present from the beginningless through the pride of ordinariness. As for what is meditated as the antidote of that, he indicates it by showing its reality as created from the subatomic particles of all transcendent buddhas. And so it does not appear that the above explanations of the system of isolation, and also the many other [such] explanations, are in accord with the meaning.

[**VI.B.3.b.ii.c′3′d′i′A″4″** – Typology of body isolations]

The fourth has four parts: [a″] Body isolation of the holy hundred clans; [b″] Body isolation of the thatness five clans; [c″] Body isolation of the secret three clans; [d″] Body isolation of the great secret single clan.

[**VI.B.3.b.ii.c′3′d′i′A″4″a″** – Body isolation of the holy hundred clans]

The first has four parts: [i″] Body isolation of the five aggregates; [ii″] Body isolation of the four elements; [iii″] Body isolation of the six faculties; [iv″] Body isolation of the five objects.

[**VI.B.3.b.ii.c′3′d′i′A″4″a″i″** – Body isolation of the five aggregates]

From the *Root Tantra*:

> In short, the five aggregates
> Are well known as the five buddha-clans.

Thus, the body [that is] isolable in the aggregate-body isolation is stated to be the five, the matter aggregate etc., and its "isolation" to be the perception of those five as the five buddhas.

If we analyze the matter aggregate Vairochana, there are five forms:

internal and external shape forms, such as long and short of both; aspectual forms, such as self, other, and both; color forms, such as blue etc. of the internal and external; luminant forms, such as sun and moon of the internal and external; and noninformative forms. These are [really] the five clans, respectively, Vairochana-Vairochana, Vairochana-Ratnasambhava, Vairochana-Amitabha, Vairochana-Amoghasiddhi, and Vairochana-Akshobhya.

If we analyze the sensation aggregate Ratnasambhava, there are five sensations: those of equality or neutrality: of phlegm-energy origin; of pleasure; of pain; and of bile and [92a] combination origin. These [also] are the five clans, Ratnasambhava-Vairochana and so forth.

If we analyze the concept aggregate Amitabha, there are five concepts; those of the immovable unchanging; the four footed; the footless; the many-footed; and the two footed. These are respectively the five, Amitabha-Vairochana and so forth.

If we analyze the creation aggregate Amoghasiddhi, there are five creations; those of the body, the three realms, of speech, of liberation, and of mentality, which are respectively Amoghasiddhi-Vairochana and so forth.

If we analyze the consciousness aggregate Akshobhya, there are five consciousnesses; those of eye, [ear, nose, tongue,] and body, which are respectively, Akshobhya-Vairochana and so forth.

[**VI.B.3.b.ii.C′3′d′i′A″4″a″ii″** – Body isolation of the four elements]

The *Root Tantra* states:

> Earth is Lochanā,
> Water element is Māmakī,
> Fire is Pāṇḍarāvāsinī,
> Energy is renowned as Tārā.

The body isolable by the elemental body isolation is the [sum of the] four elements such as earth; and its isolation is explained as the realization of those four as the goddesses Lochanā and so forth.

If we analyze the earth [hardness] element Lochanā, concerning the internal, out of internal and external, there are five essences; the hair-bone-excretion-liver-essence, the body-hair-nail-pus-essence, the teeth-skin-flesh-essence, the ligament-muscle-rib-essence, the excrement-intestine-bile-essence. The "five essences" in this context have their source in the *Integrated Practices* [quotation from the *Vajra Rosary*]:

> [Lochanā] definitely dwells in the five heart-essences,
> Emerging in the five processes,
> Endowed with the five [dream] energies,
> Causing the function of five desires.

As for the meaning of the second line of this quote, it is according to the statement from the Darma Tsöndru translation of the *Vajra Rosary*, "Originating from the five senses"; due to the further statement, after the "causing the function . . . ," [namely:] "By the path of whatever sense faculty, [92b] the practitioner attains the object."

Further, the *Vajra Rosary* states:

> Stuff of bliss, staying in the heart center,
> Buddha, light of brilliant sun,
> Through form of subject and object,
> That is the twelve light rays.

Here this states that twelve energies come from the heart center, rely on the paths of the sense faculties, and become the energies of the six subjectivities and six objectivities. Therefore, the interpretation of five "essences" is arrived at by analysis according to the fact that the support of the five sense energies is the heart center.

As for the five external earths, they are Sumeru, and the continents of the south, west, north, and east. And the five external-internal classes [of buddha-clans] are Lochanā-Vairochana and so forth.

If we analyze water [liquidity] Māmakī, the five internal waters are phlegm, including mucus, sweat, blood, saliva, and urine; the outer waters are waterfalls, streams, canals, pools, and oceans; and the five clans are Māmakī-Vairochana and so forth.

If we analyze fire [heat-energy] Pāṇḍarāvāsinī, the inner are the heats of head, navel, all limbs, belly, and heart; the outer are stone fires, fire-crystal fires, wood fires, forest fires, and constant fires; and their clans are Pāṇḍarāvāsinī-Vairochana and so forth.

If we analyze wind [motility] Tārā, the inner are pervading, evacuating, ascending, metabolizing, and vitalizing energy-holding; the outer are zenith, south, west, north, and east winds; and their clans are Tārā-Vairochana and so forth. If outer and inner are separately counted for four elements there are two sets of twenty. However, they are taken as one twenty, taking both outer and inner elements together in each element such as earth.

[**VI.B.3.b.ii.c′3′d′i′A″4″a″iii″** – Body isolation of the six faculties]

[93a] The *Root Tantra* states:

> The vajra sense-media themselves
> Are the supreme mandala of bodhisattvas.

This states that the six senses are the isolable body of the inner media body isolation, and their body isolation is the realization that they are the bodhisattvas.

If the eye Kshitigarbha is analyzed, there are the eye's perceiving threefold form, the white of the eyeball, the form of the eye glancing sideways, eye movement, and the precisely grape-size eye sense; and their [clans are] Kshitigarbha-Vairochana and so forth.

If the ear Vajrapāṇi is analyzed, there are the ear nature, its perceiving threefold sound, the ear hole, the ear root, and the cut-twisted-birchbark-like ear sense; their clans are Vajrapāṇi-Vairochana and so forth.

If the nose Ākāshagarbha is analyzed, there are the nose's nature, the center of its inner part, its perceiving threefold smell, its nostril holes, and the fine eye-medicine-spoon-like nose sense; these are the clans of Khagarbha-Vairochana and so forth.

If the tongue Lokeshvara is analyzed, there are the tongue nature, its root, its tip, its perceiving threefold taste, the half-moon-shape tongue sense; these are the clans of Lokeshvara-Vairochana and so forth.

If the body Sarvanivaraṇaviṣkambhin is analyzed, there are the body sense, the body's bones, the flesh nature, the skin nature, and the perceiving of texture; and these are the clans of Sarvanivaraṇaviṣkambhin-Vairochana and so forth.

If the mind sense faculty Mañjushrī, in which luminance, radiance, and imminence are collected, is analyzed, there are the mirrorlike, equality, individuating, all-accomplishing, and truth-realm wisdoms; and these are the clans of Mañjushrī-Vairochana and so forth.

In regard to these [five wisdoms], [93b] [Āryadeva] in the *Integrated Practices* describes them, after the purification of virtuous and nonvirtuous instincts, [respectively:] as the simultaneous knowledge of all things as reflections in a mirror; as the realization of all beings of the four types—footless etc.—being of the single aspect "merely mental"; as the abiding, doubt-free individual discernment of all inner and outer things, knowing that if investigated "all have the nature of buddhas," yet distinguishing these "members of the class of all things" as separate, like the petals of a lotus; as the full accomplishment of self and other's duties of body, speech, and mind; and as the deliverance from affliction and evolution, purifying the obscurations of body, speech, and mind. These descriptions concern the fruitional stage of the wisdoms.

The *[Stage of] Arrangement* describes them—intending to accord with the explanation of the process of the dissolution of the four wisdoms—as the clear appearance of objects like clear reflections in a mirror, as the equality of class unity among the three sensations, as the individual remembrance of the individual names of beings such as father and mother, and as the mindfulness of mundane activities and necessities. These are the first four, and the fifth is the actuality of the mental sense, ready to be transformed upon abandonment of the taints.

Here, the *Integrated Practices* explains:

> The samadhi of Mañjushrī has already been explained . . .

thinking that, after explaining also the five, Rūpavajrā and so forth, he explains the five wisdoms. So to take the explanation of Mañjushrī as incidental, then to additionally explain the five wisdoms would be incorrect: because [the hundred clans] is [reached by] making each deity into five clans, leaving out of the thirty-two deities the ten terrifics and Samantabhadra and Maitreya; [94a] and because the five wisdoms counted as five clans of the hundred clans are collected in the mental consciousness; and because, even in the context of the sense-media, though those sense-media are not openly there, many occasions of placing them in the clans of those contexts are [elsewhere] evident.

[**VI.B.3.b.ii.c′3′d′i′A″4″a″iv″** – Body isolation of the five objects]

The *Root Tantra* states:

> The mantrī always realizes
> Form, sound, and so forth as deities.

Thus, the isolable body of objective body isolation is the five objects, and their body isolation is their realization as the five vajras.

Now, if the visible form Rūpavajrā, associated with the seeing of forms through the moving energy operating through the eye, is analyzed; there are mere general form seen based on the assembly of three conditions; passionate form; pleasant, unpleasant, and neutral form; work-accomplishing form; and alluring—seductive, playful, and charming—form. These are the clans of Rūpavajrā-Vairochana and so forth.

If the sound Shabdavajrā, associated with the hearing of sounds through the permoving energy[67] operating through the ear, is analyzed; there are sounds inside ear, head, and hair; sounds of songs and continuous sounds of palate and lips and speech; musical sounds of clay drum and so on; sounds of forest, streams, and palms clapping; and sounds of the mild and fierce HŪṀ letter. These are the clans of the five, Shabdavajrā-Vairochana and so forth.

If the smell experience Gandhavajrā, associated with the smelling of scents based on the commoving energy operating through the nose, is analyzed; there are general smell, auxiliary scents, specifics of threefold smell, [94b] smells of tastes, and inexhaustible smells. These are the five clans of Gandhavajrā-Vairochana and so forth.

If the taste experience Rasavajrā, associated with the tasting of tastes based on the surmoving energy operating through the tongue, is analyzed; there are sweet, astringent, salty, hot and sour, and bitter tastes; these are the clans of Rasavajra-Vairochana and so forth.

If the texture experience Sparshavajrā, associated with the experience of textures based on the ultramoving energy operating through the body-sense, is analyzed; there are textures from staying in one seat, embrace,

67. Regarding the terms “permoving,” “commoving,” surmoving,” and “ultramoving” in the passages below, see note 73 below.

sucking, kissing, and sexual union. These are the five clans of Sparshavajrā-Vairochana and so forth.

As for the way in which those deities, thus taken as five for the twenty [above] arise as deities, if we use Vairochana as an example, the five [Rūpavajrā-Vairochana and so forth] are similar to Vairochana in number of faces and arms and implements, and yet become five by differing in colors; by this the others can be understood.

If one wonders, "Well, having explained twenty out of thirty-two, why not elucidate the other twelve?"

The *Root Tantra* clearly explains the contemplation of each of the twenty from matter aggregate to texture as a deity, while the ten limbs, the joints, and the muscles and channels are not clearly explained to be meditated as the ten terrifics and the two bodhisattvas. Therefore, the *Integrated Practices* explanation was given in the same terms; because [Āryadeva] stated that "If each of the four sets is completed, it explains the meaning of this summary in the *Root Tantra*." The *Integrated Practices* quotes the *Moon Esoteric Drop* as the textual source of such a hundred clan [teaching], or its derivatives, the five-clan practice, or the three-clan practice. For example, in the *Further Tantra*:

> Thatness [practice] is explained in five forms.
> Secretly it is explained in three forms:
> The archetype deity is the great secret; [95a]
> The hundred clans are a hundred.

This statement shows the meaning.

The *Explanatory Tantra Vajra Rosary* also teaches the hundred clans. Again in that tantra, in the context of the body isolation explained in the hidden meaning manner in the preface, the ten limbs are explained as the ten terrifics; and in the actual explanation of eye Kshitigarbha and so forth, Maitreya and Samantabhadra are also picked out, so that all thirty-two deities are completely accounted for: because it is stated [in that way] in the context of meditating the body as a deity in other sections [of the text]; because there is no difference on making each of the twenty deities suitable for analysis into five clans, while leaving the others unsuitable; and because they are equally used or not used in the body isolation [practice].

Therefore, even though one is concerned lest the hundred clans become too numerous if one applied the above explanation of the ten terrifics to the body isolation, it would not be correct to omit the complete explanation of the thirty-two deities, by not seeing how to arrange the passion-practice-concealing explanation, which had previously included them. Therefore, all should be included in the section of the body isolation. You practice your body isolation using those twenty and, since you rely on the deities of the five clans dividing out into the hundred parts, it is stated that "your own body becomes realized as made with the subtle atoms of all transcendent buddhas." Here "subtle atoms" is a name of having divided [the body] into a hundred separate parts and realizing them as a hundred deities.

[**VI.B.3.b.ii.c′3′d′i′A″4″b″** – Body isolation of the thatness five clans]

If one [can] compress those classifications among the holy hundred clans, they can be compressed into five clans. Here, the isolable body five clans are comprised of the four elements such as earth and the realm of consciousness. The twenty from the matter [95b] Vairochana clan to the Sparshavajrā-Vairochana clan are included in the earth realm. Likewise, the twenty Ratnasambhava clans are water, the twenty Amitābha clans are fire, the twenty Amoghasiddhi clans are energy, and the twenty Akshobhya clans are included in the consciousness realm.

Here the *Integrated Practices* explains the matter aggregate and so on as derivative elements. Now, the matter aggregate, except for the four elements and the form in the objective sense-medium, does consist of actual derivative elements, and the four nominal aggregates are also designated as derivative elements as they just depend on the elemental body.

It is good that the five realms that compress the hundred clans should be taken as the clans of the five transcendent buddhas.

[**VI.B.3.b.ii.c′3′d′i′A″4″c″** – Body isolation of the secret three clans]

The same [hundred-clan isolation body] compressed into five clans is again compressed into the secret three clans; which is accomplished by the process of including the Ratnasambhava clan in the body vajra Vairochana clan, including the Amoghasiddhi clan in the speech vajra Amitābha clan, and including the Vajradhara clan in the mind vajra Akshobhya clan.

Here the *Integrated Practices* statement that the buddhas and bodhisattvas from the hundred clans to the five clans are collected within one's body, speech, and mind does not contradict the above analysis into the hundred clans wherein are mentioned many things contained in the processes of persons other than the practitioner as well as many things not contained in the personal processes of either self or other but only in the inanimate universe: because the way in which they are contained is not only by the way in which the matter aggregate contains the four elements. [96a] This will be explained [below]. Here the isolable body consists of the three: body, speech, and mind.

[**VI.B.3.b.ii.c′3′d′i′A″4″d″** – Body isolation of the great secret single clan]

If one again condenses what is thus included in the three clans, it becomes the great secret single clan. And that, from the perspective of taking body, speech, and mind as the three vajras, becomes the sixth archetype deity, Vajradhara, the indivisibility of the three vajras; and this is the ultimate in body isolation.

[**VI.B.3.b.ii.c′3′d′i′A″5″** – How it serves as retraction and contemplation branches (of the six yoga branches)]

The fifth has two parts: [a″] How retraction is contained within body isolation; [b″] How contemplation is contained within body isolation.

[**VI.B.3.b.ii.c′3′d′i′A″5″a″** – How retraction is contained within body isolation]

In regard to "retraction," the *Further Tantra* states:

> "Retraction" occurs,
> When desires concerning
> All of the ten faculties' natural functions
> And habituation to them are withdrawn.

Generally, "desires" can mean both "the desirer" and "the desired"; here it is the latter that is desired and craved, namely the five sense objects, matter, and so on. Toward them, the sense faculties withdraw again and again from each [object], and by taking each one by one, [the process] is called "retraction." Designating the objects also with the word "sense faculty," they are explained as the ten sense faculties. "Natural function" is the natural action of the five sense organs, eye and so on, as apprehender, and form and so on as apprehended. "Habituation to them" is natural habitual action. "All" means habituated to lesser, greater, and medium differences. "Concerning" means the dative [or locative] case. The sense faculties function for all those. The Chag translation says "of the ten sense faculties," [96b] and in the commentary there is no meaning of again and again.

The semantic equivalent for [the Tibetan] *so so* is [Sanskrit] *prati*. In the context of relativity, in the *Lucid Exposition*, it is explained as meaning "to meet" or "to repeat." The meaning of *pratimoksha* as a semantic equivalent for *so sor thar pa* is explained in the *Treasury [of Clear Science]* as "primary liberation." The meaning of *pratīchha* is explained as "specific acceptance." Here, the meaning of "repeat" is to "repeat again and again, and memorize." Further, in the context of the expression "I will repeatedly memorize firmly" other commentaries likewise explain it in the sense of "again and again." Therefore, it is not necessary to mention each and every different sense of *so so*. Here, we are not postulating the explanation in the *Illuminating Lamp [Intention] Elucidation*: "It functions in each—matter and so on," and "It is withdrawn from the respective [objects]—form and so on." There are also many meanings for "withdraw," but here they have the sense of "retract" and "collected retraction." Gathered things are said to be the five objects of desires, so the sense faculties enjoy five objects.

Furthermore, completing common familiarization practice—the four vajras, the sense faculties of the yogi/nī who enters the supreme familiarization practice do indeed enjoy objects, but just this alone is not the path of "retraction" meditation, because that must be posited as for the mental consciousness itself alone. Therefore, in the *Illuminating Lamp* fifteenth chapter it is stated, [quoting the *Root Tantra*]:

> "Eat the vow of excrement and urine!" Here, "excrement" means the sense objects—form and so on. "Urine" means the sense organs—eye and so on. The "vow" of those is the coming together of the object and subject. "Eating" that is the gradual experience of the stages of retraction [97a] and so on.

Thus [Chandrakīrti] says that the sense faculties enjoying the sense objects is what is to be eaten, and "retraction" is the process of eating. Therefore, as explained above, the expression "retraction" is used for some special methods of enjoyment of sense objects by a yogi/nī's sense faculties, but the "retraction" member of the six-branched yoga is, when the sense faculties are enjoying the sense objects, the yoga of enjoyment that is sealed by the bliss-void great bliss of meditatively entranced body isolation. Thus, "retraction" is body isolation as an aftermath practice.

Well, someone might ask, "What is the meaning of the statement in the *Illuminating Lamp [Intention] Elucidation* that teaches the second branch [contemplation] for the purpose of purifying retraction?"

Even though retraction and contemplation are similar in taking the senses' enjoyment of desire objects as the path, the meaning [of the above statement] is that in retraction there is no enjoyment through realizing those [senses and objects] as deities as there is in the contemplation [branch]. Further, that being the case, there is no fault of them not counting as body isolation, because great bliss itself is the definitive meaning deity, and meditating as sealed by that [great bliss] is the great art that isolates one from notions of ordinariness.

[**VI.B.3.b.ii.c′3′d′i′A″5″b″** – How contemplation is contained within body isolation]

In the *Further Tantra* it is explained that:

> In sum, the five desired [sense-objects]
> Are connected to the five buddhas;
> By this they are discerned and contemplated,
> That contemplation becoming fivefold:
> [A process of] examining, analyzing, being joyful,
> Having the great bliss of suchness,
> And actualizing one-pointed mind—
> Contemplation is comprised of these five.
> The *Esoteric [Community] Tantra*
> Explains all [these] [97b] in many different ways.
> Examining is the arisal of the three secrets,
> Analyzing is the enjoyment of those;

> Third is the touching of joy;
> Fourth is being concentrated through bliss,
> Ending the arisal of subjects and objects;
> And knowing your own mind is the fifth.
> The actuality of all buddhas is peace,
> Which permeates everything desired.[68]

As for the statement that "The five desired [sense objects], form, sound, and so on, are concentrated and made one with the sense faculties," it means that both sense faculty and object are included as both faculty and object.

In the statement in the *Illuminating Lamp* "The five buddhas are the eye and so on in union with them, true union, by uniting with them as the five buddhas, thereby even form and so on are buddhas," the phrase "The five buddhas are the eye etc. in union with them" it is intelligible, though the translation is a bit awkward.

As for the true uniting of the five [sense organs], eye and so on, with the five buddhas, from Vairochana to Akshobhya, the five [sense objects], form, sound, and so on, are also connected to the five clans. Thus, to say that both the faculties and objects are buddhas is to designate them as totally purified deities; that is contemplation. That is [broken down] into five—examination and so on. In this context of explaining the general definition, when it is explained that the contemplation [branch] is that which meditates objects and faculties as deities, it is just for illustration. According to the context of the body isolation, one should understand that one also meditates the aggregates as deities. Therefore, do not think that it is only the body of the deity that one meditates on. One must also meditate the reality of the deity, as one can understand from the context of the extensive explanation. [98a]

In the *Elixir Secret*, there are the five desired [objects] and the five aggregates, and each has [further] internal classifications, but that does not mean that they are classified as five for the sake of abbreviation. The sense faculty, the object, and the faculties' cognition are the three secrets; and the idea that "the three sets of five have the nature of the five buddha-clans" is [the contemplation component called] "examination." The analysis [com-

68. This part of this verse resembles verse 41 of Nāgārjuna's *Letter to a Friend* (thanks to Dr. Lozang Jampal for this information).

ponent] is that these three sets of five are analyzed as of the nature of the five clans. Patsab and Chag translate "the three secrets are examination," which is appropriate, since there is no point in bringing this up further in the commentary. Then one enjoys that examination, dwelling further on that object by analyzing it; and that is [the contemplation component of] analysis. Since the *Elixir Secret* explains that analysis is meditating through distinguishing, the components of examination and analysis are differentiated by fineness of discrimination, while both of them are body isolations cultivated in aftermath states.

Thus, first on the occasion of retraction, you learn to view things such as objects and senses as the transformations of bliss-void. As that stabilizes, you learn contemplation wherein those bliss-void transformations arise as deities.

Here, the *Illuminating Lamp* says:

> Thus having analyzed, when one confronts the entry into thatness, that having the nature of mental bliss is the contact with joy. Then, when one enters manifestly into thatness, that bliss which one attains with the nature of body fluency, and so on, is comprised as bliss.

Joy is said to be mental bliss, and [pure] bliss is body fluency. "And so on" indicates the bliss of mental fluency. The former is attained by confronting entry into thatness, [98b] and the latter is attained having entered into thatness. Patsab's translation says "while thus analyzing," and Chag's translation says "from thus having analyzed." The two old translations say "thus having analyzed." The meaning there is that both examination and analysis are referred to by saying "thus having analyzed." "By entering thatness, joy and bliss will be attained" indicates the future attainment of the latter [components of contemplation]. "Entering into" thatness and "confronting" thatness are similar in import, but as for the way in which joy and bliss are attained by that process; first you attain great bliss by the power of meditating the subtle [drop] in the lower door [of the central channel], and then you meditate with that [bliss] being focused on the ascertainment of the import of thatness. Thereby you will attain contact with the distinctive mental bliss of realizing voidness and you will attain the physical and mental fluency that arise from realizing voidness.

Actual physical fluency is a special kind of tangible experience that makes the body become extremely adept, but here it is not that [type]. This is the bliss of fluency that becomes the property that causes both body and mind to become extremely adept. It is a mental function that is a correlate of the previous mental bliss.

By practicing as previously explained or by becoming accustomed to that, thereby you terminate the six [subjective] consciousnesses, visual and so on, and the six objects, form and so on, and [you realize] voidness with respect to the mind's perception of the subject-object dichotomy. Therefore, [such] one-pointedness of mind, defined as primal wisdom, is called one's "nature of mind." [99a] Here, the Chag translation [of the *Illuminating Lamp*] says:

> The nature of all buddhas is peace; all of them totally abide in space . . .

and

> Such a yogi/nī's mind is peace, the nature of all buddhas.

[The mind of contemplation] is said to be "peace" because it has eliminated the notions of objects and so on, and is merely vision. Previous statements, such as "This ultimately occurs in unity with universal voidness," are good, but the Patsab translation's "that culminates only in universal voidness" is better. As for that previous one-pointedness of mind, it means the entry into voidness, the nature of all buddhas, and the word "merely" means peace in that it cuts off all ideations at that time. "Space" means void, and "universal void" is the fourth void. When you wholly abide there, you enter by going through the three previous voids. These two lines explain one-pointedness of mind. Therefore, what Lan said—

> If one interprets one-pointedness of mind as mind isolation, then, in short, by the expression "the actuality of all buddhas" one means the magic body, and by the rest of that one refers to clear light . . .

—is incorrect. In the context of the body isolation of the elements, there is the cryptic explanation of the prologue [of the *Esoteric Community Tantra*] in the *Vajra Rosary*:

> Wind, fire, water, and earth
> Are the four, Lochanā and so on,
> Known as three types of natural primal wisdom,
> They grant the buddha enlightenment.

It states that the four elements—realized as Lochana and so on—should be understood as having the nature of the three wisdoms of the three voids, [luminance, radiance, and imminence]; [99b] and therefore the path-time three voids' primal wisdom is present during body isolation.

The previous mention of the fourth void is metaphoric clear light, and its arisal is never precluded from body isolation up to the magic body. However, the mention of the three voids being present before the magic body intends that metaphoric clear light be included in the great void of imminence. Therefore, in these contexts, the entry of imminence into clear light should be understood as the imminence in which you become unconscious, after which you enter into the cloudless-sky-like absorption in universal voidness.

Well here you might think that the above general definition of contemplation seems to account for examination and analysis, but it does not seem to describe joy, bliss, and one-pointedness of mind; so would not those three become severed from that sort of contemplation?

This is not a problem, since that explanation of contemplation as the meditation of the senses and objects and so on as deities includes both the meditation of the deities with forms of faces and hands and also the meditation focusing on the thatness of the deities. In the *Illuminating Lamp [Intention] Elucidation* it is stated that when one engages objects, the idea that the senses and so on, the three, have the nature of the five clans is "examination," the idea that those are the nature of the five primal wisdoms is ideational "analysis," the arisal of a distinctive joy from thinking "I am a realization of thatness" is "joy," and "bliss" is explained as physical fluency coming from attaining that mental bliss. And examination and analysis are explained to be luminance, joy to be radiance, and bliss to be imminence. And this [text] does seem to claim the presence [here] of the three primal wisdoms of mind isolation.

In this regard, the meaning of the three primal wisdoms [100a] as stated in the *Wisdom Vajra Compendium* is the objective explained in the *Integrated Practices* in the context of mind isolation, where there is the problem of not being thoroughly explicit about the way in which what sort of habit pattern holds that object. And Nāropa's explanation of these two branches [retraction and contemplation] appears just to consist of his quoting of the *Illuminating Lamp*.

Although one should explain in detail this six-branched yoga of the noble system, since my predecessors did not seem to give the details, here I explained in detail, and will do so [even more] below.

[**VI.B.3.b.ii.c′3′d′i′A″6″** – How to put the body isolation into practice]

The sixth has three parts: [a″] How to concentrate the energies by meditating the subtle; [b″] How melting bliss arises from that; and [c″] How to cultivate samadhic and aftermath [body isolations] when [bliss] arises.

[**VI.B.3.b.ii.c′3′d′i′A″6″a″** – How to concentrate the energies by meditating the subtle]

Having discovered the stable yoga that visualizes the subtle mandala, you then become able to develop a distinctive melting bliss. Once that has emerged, then you already know how to produce joy, and you should cultivate it as will be explained. However, if you discover that, but [melting bliss] does not emerge, in the interim you should meditate abiding in the yoga of the lord and lady. If that also is not there, if you practice the entry into the present, you should meditate after concluding a preliminary meditation of the yoga of the retinue of [the deities of] the mandala. As it is explained in the *Concise Five Stages*:

> One should know the four kinds of essential points,
> Those of body, time, object, and energy.

The essential point of the body will be explained in the speech isolation. The essential point of time in general is continuity, but in specific it is when awareness is clear and you meditate in the afternoon in the time of fire. The essential point of energy is sufficiently [explained in] our own system. As for the essential point of object, the place where one aims one's perception, the sixth chapter of the *Illuminating Lamp* says that [100b] "For the male, in the hole of the vajra there is a mere barley-grain-size hand symbol; and for the female there is the mere measure of a chickpea[69] in her vagina." The third chapter of the *Illuminating Lamp* explains that one should meditate the superficial spirit of enlightenment, the size of a grain of mustard, in the mouth of one's vajra, as having the nature of the five clans. And in the *Personal Instruction [of Mañjushrī]* it says "As previously quoted, one should meditate [it] in the center of the jewel"; so there is no disagreement with the statement "Meditate [it] in the hole of the vajra." "Meditate in the mouth of the vajra" intends the lower opening of the *dhūti*; those two are similar. The *Personal Instruction* explains that with the clear light of the seed at the heart center one invites the mandala, melts those absorbed into the heart center, whence they descend as a drop and abide in the jewel.

The *Illuminating Lamp* explains that you should meditate in harmony with the process of birth in existence, as when the basic time male and female sexually unite and the fire of passion melts the drop and it falls into the lotus; which makes plain the meditation of the drop thus produced descending to the lower door. The *Illuminating Lamp* intends that the color of the drop should be the color of your deity. If you hold the mind in the extremely subtle drop, it is easy to cut off conceptual thoughts, because it is easy to terminate the evolutionary energy that drives those [conceptions]. However, if it seems that you cannot hold it like that no matter what you do, then let it be a little bigger, and when you can hold it, then make it subtler. This could be a problem of jumping a stage of meditation, not having stabilized [well enough] on the creation stage. If one makes it stable, then there is no problem of not being able to hold the mind on such an object.

The distinctive way of holding the mind, the way of cultivating without depression and elation, not desiring the termination of the energy even though the object is well-held, [101a] how to proceed when you are not ready to generate such an intense bliss and so on, and the way to dispel the arisal of some odds and ends of previous discomfort in desiring to terminate the energy, etc.—all these private instructions are explained in detail elsewhere. Thus, you meditate by aiming your vision toward the place of the great vitalizing energy of the body, either the lower door of the *dhūti* or the center of

69. Sanskrit *caṇaka* means chickpea.

the channel wheel of the jewel, and you hold your mind there by means of the vital point of getting the energy and mind to function in unity. At that moment, you terminate the energies' movement in the *rasanā* and *lalanā* channels and move them into the *dhūti*. After that, it begins to dissolve there, and first the five signs will arise. In the *Personal Instruction* it is stated:

> Thereupon [in] the great secret drop
> Very subtle, like a lump—
> Hold your own mind—gently, gently—
> And reach the place of thinglessness.
> There again, by cultivating this object,
> The deceptive earth disappears,
> You perceive hallucinations
> And you must know the first of the signs.
> Likewise, when water disappears,
> You perceive the smokelike [sign];
> You must know it as the second [sign].
> When fire disappears in turn,
> You have the third [sign] like fireflies.
> When energy likewise disappears,
> You perceive a butter-lamp-like flame,
> And you must know it as the fourth sign.
> Likewise, deceptive consciousness is gone,
> The nonduality of depth and clarity
> You see clear as a cloudless sky—
> That sign you recognize as the fifth.
> With [the arisal of] those five signs
> You will attain nonlocated nirvana.
> The yogi/nī thus should strive in this—
> This being the branch of endurance.

As for the *Further Tantra* statement that these five signs emerge in the context of the yoga branch of endurance,[70] [101b] the four signs emerge before

70. In the quote just given, "endurance" is spelled in Tibetan as *gzung ba*, perhaps an old-fashioned way of spelling it, whereas Tsong Khapa correctly writes *'dzin pa* in his gloss.

entering into clear light, and the fifth at the time of clear light. This intends that the entry into clear light is an entry by the power of meditating the three vitalizing energy-control practices. The *Personal Instruction* also says that the five signs emerge in the contexts of meditating the subtle [object] in the lower door and the indestructible [drop] in the heart; so you should understand that these signs emerge then by performing those two [types of] vajra recitation.

As for the *Illuminating Lamp* explaining the entry into clear light through the door of the five signs, though it should be explained that the entry into clear light comes [only] after having attained mind isolation and the magic body by completing the three vitalizing energy controls, nevertheless it is not that [Chandrakīrti] does not accept the arisal of those signs on the lesser occasions of entering into the metaphoric clear light. So there is no contradiction in explaining the branch of endurance as an entry into the clear light that abides in insubstantiality by the progression of the signs on the occasion of meditation on the subtle [drop] in the lower door.

Tathāgatavajra explains that by meditating the HŪṀ letter at the heart center, you meditate the energy entering its drop, and holding that, you will attain clear light—it is explained just so. It is explained that you will achieve the clear light of endurance, either with the yoga of the subtle vowels and consonants abiding in the navel channel, or meditating the drop in the tip of the vajra, or meditating with the furor yoga, and so on, whichever [of these] are suitable. It is explained in agreement even in the Indian treatise of the six-branched yoga of the Jñānapāda system. So this is excellent. Therefore, when one holds the mind in the point of the great vitalizing energy of the channels of the body, it is not like other foci of the mind. The practice of meditating the subtle in the lower door [102a] exists up to there, but as explained above, if one doesn't know the advantages of meditating on that, then it seems one will not find certitude about the personal instructions. This is well explained depending on the *Further Tantra* and the statements of His Holiness Mañjushrī. Thus, this path should be understood as the instruction that is an unerring, distinctive method of vitalizing energy control. Therefore, it is said that the yogi/nī should make effort in this. Make a fierce effort in this meditation.

[VI.B.3.b.ii.c′3′d′i′A′′6′′b′′ – How melting bliss arises from that]

Second, there is a normal experience of joy that comes from the melted enlightenment spirit descending to the secret place of those both meditating and not meditating the path in general, and it can happen that a melting will emerge from the blazing of furor fire both in the navel and the secret place. So it is not necessary that the vitalizing energy dissolve into the *dhūti* for the furor fire to burn and melt the spirit of enlightenment. Therefore, certain types of persons meditate as above and so experience the bliss of the melting of the spirit of enlightenment, though their energies do not dissolve into the *dhūti*.

This kind of similar [experience] can happen to [people in general], as [those that are achieved by yogi/nīs] meditating other personal instructions for penetrating the vital points in the body. When such a drop reaches the vajra jewel, it seems to be very difficult to retain. So one must first, by the outer and inner descending methods, forcefully reverse the descent of the enlightenment spirit from those places [higher in the system] before it reaches the jewel. As soon as it reaches the vajra, if it cannot be diffused within the body, the many [redirecting] strains [needed] to instantly reverse it and the forceful methods of reversing it seem to produce sickness. And even if [some] have already implemented many procedures of such diffusion, [102b] it does not seem that they know the systems of distinguishing the enlightenment spirit melting with the energies dissolving into the *dhūti* from its melting without [the energies dissolving there], and thus how to determine the difficulty or ease of retaining the enlightenment spirit, the necessity of its forceful reversal or lack [of such necessity], and whether or not one will become sick by not spreading the reversed [spirit] within the body.

About that, as for the necessity of the melting of the enlightenment spirit by burning the furor fire by the power of meditating the path, it is for the sake of generating the orgasmic intuitive wisdom. In generating that [furor-fire], the enlightenment spirit melts and falls; if it does not generally reach below the navel and particularly reach into the jewel and stay there somewhat without emitting, you can never develop the fully defined orgasmic [wisdom]. And to equate this orgasmic [wisdom] with the great bliss of the perfection stage, it must be one that abides by the power of dissolving the energies. If the enlightenment spirit is melted by the power of dissolving the energies into the *dhūti*, then it will be held in the tip of the jewel and will not emit outward until the fully defined orgasmic [bliss] has been generated. This is because, when the enlightenment spirit descends from the crown [wheel] by stage after stage, as the energies become weaker and weaker and it reaches the jewel, the energy's function that would push that enlightenment spirit outside becomes calmed. At that point, it will not emit until one arises from the orgasmic samadhi.

When you do arise, as the energy can become greatly agitated, you must know the art of not emitting [the enlightenment spirit]. In that case, even if you do not practice the method of reversing [the spirit] at the first occasion when you are not accustomed [to the experience] and the method of reversing it later [when you are accustomed], again, when it goes back upward [in the body] at both times of naturally going in reverse again, there is definitely no arisal of sickness by its not having spread out within the body. If you melt the enlightenment spirit by meditation on the subtle and so on, not by the power of dissolving the energies, [103a] you cannot hold it more than a bit in the jewel, so you must reverse it right away, and you must understand the height of the place to reverse it to. If the melting is weak, it is easy to reverse it. If it is intense, it must be spread in the body. If you meditate on this for a long time, even though you don't reverse it right away, you will get the ability after a while.

As for the fact that, in the tantras and the great Indian treatises, these subjects do not occur as they do in other practical instructions, it is because of the essential point that the principal [jewel-like] disciple of this teaching will quickly generate the energy-dissolving perfection stage, [and so] such practical instructions are not necessary.

As for the process of generating the four joys in descending order, as the enlightenment spirit melts and reaches from place to place, the *Vajra Rosary Tantra* says:

> Then one should teach the emerging order:
> In the crown of the great bliss wheel,
> It is said to be "joy";
> In the wheel of beatitude it is "supreme joy";
> In the Dharma wheel it is "ecstatic joy";
> And in the emanation wheel "orgasmic joy"—
> All these are caused to be experienced.

Here, "joy" is assigned [to the movement] from the crown to the throat.[71] The other three should also be understood in that way.

As for the way of generating [the four joys] welling up from below, according to the same text [the *Vajra Rosary*]:

> In the emanation wheel there is joy,
> Supreme joy dwells in the Dharma wheel,
> Ecstatic joy dwells in the beatific wheel, and
> Orgasmic [joy in the] great bliss [wheel]—
> These are declared the stages in the reverse order.

The places of this should be understood by the reasonings previously explained.

This also agrees with the *Great Seal Drop*. [103b] In that text also, it says that, by making each of them, upper and lower, have four parts, there are sixteen parts of the moon, and from the solar point of view in each there are three and [thus] there are twelve parts. To quote that same text:

> These parts of the "rabbit-marked" moon
> Are the sixteen drops of joy
> To be known as actually the *āli* [vowels].
> From the stages in the four wheels
> Just as has been explained,
> We say there are twelve solar parts.

Here when the spirit of enlightenment streams up and down, it streams together with the blood. Here you experience a bliss in each of the sections that you made of the four parts of each of the four places. In each of the four places from the point of view of particles streaming in each of the four sections made into three parts, respectively, there are small, medium, and great bliss discerned in one's experience, and one who has that should understand it, said to be [quite] subtle. In the *Sheaf of Instructions* it is explained

71. Here the movement down from each wheel to the next is where the joys are experienced, not merely in the wheel itself. Tsong Khapa is here improving a bit on the original text. The genital wheel is not mentioned in this passage and the following, though the emerging order joys end in it and the reversing order joys begin in it.

that the four upward-surging orgasmic blisses are differentiated into small, medium, great, and intensely great. The upward-surging four blisses are said to be more intense than the downward-falling four blisses. When surging from below, until the reversal has become firm at the crown, bliss is not stable. When it is firm in the crown, then it is stable, it is said. The same text [*Sheaf of Instructions*] says:

> Upon the vitalizing energy is mentality.
> Going against that, it will descend.
> Abiding in the center of the navel of the lotus,
> It stabilizes outside of that.
> At that time the savior will not go.
> Just as in a vessel with no holes
> Water will remain inexhaustibly.
> At that time bliss will be firm.
> When firm, there is orgasmic joy.
> Thus, buddha inexhaustible—
> The yogi/nī will definitely [104a] achieve.

The *Sheaf of Instructions* explains that here, "mentality" means "semen." "Going against" means "the reverse order." "Firm" means "reaching the crown."

Here, Lakshmī explains that when the enlightenment spirit drips from the crown, it is luminance. When it descends into the joints of all the limbs, it is radiance. When the one drop emits from the tip of the vajra, it is imminence, and when it is firm in that very tip, then that is the arisal of clear light. Again, the first two [stages] are similar, but its going into the vajra tip or center being imminence, and abiding within the jewel being the arisal of clear light, are also explained as the four joys. There are many [explanations] like this, [all of] which are similar.

Munishrī explains that when it reaches the root of the vajra, it is luminance; when it reaches the center of the jewel, it is imminence, and when it reaches the tip of the jewel, it is clear light. This implies that he must claim that when it reaches from the root of the vajra to the throat of the jewel, it is the arisal of radiance.

The *Great Seal Drop* explains that the four joys are the same as luminance, radiance, imminence, and clear light. The *Root* and its explanatory tantras of the *Esoteric Community* and treatises of the five noble literatures do not contain explanations of the four joys as the four voids, and the five noble father and sons do not say that when [the enlightenment spirit] melts and reaches this place, the four joys or the four voids arise, they just explain the arisal of luminance by dissolving the energies and the arisal of radiance by the dissolving of mind and so forth. As for most of the other followers of the five noble literatures, except for mentioning the four voids generated from the process of the descent of enlightenment spirit from the crown to the secret place vajra, they do not explain any other way in which the primal wisdom of the four voids is included in the path. [104b] Not to accept [the reticence of these sages] is a misunderstanding of the great vital point of this system, as will be explained below.

Here, someone says, "Which should be accepted among these ways of generating the four joys by the process of the streaming of the enlightenment spirit?"

The distinctive types of the four voids that will be taught emerge from penetrating the vital point in the heart center. Although these are not produced here, a simulation of the four voids is produced. If one practices like Munishrī it is clear that there is a very important correspondence here. Here, great bliss is the life of the path, and making it firm, as it depends on the upward-surging bliss, is the extremely important way to produce it. Again, the *Sheaf of Instructions* says:

> With the arisal of that enlightenment spirit, beginning from the jewel until it reaches the navel, it increases without emitting, and proceeds upward.

Taking this literally, [we would think that] when it does not emit from the jewel, it is as if it naturally reversed itself; but it is not so. Even though it does not emit, it can happen that it goes indivisibly where it will, without entering the very same path as it came down. And it can happen that even if it reverses direction, there is no certainty it will reach straight to the crown and it may spread out into the lower part of the body. Therefore, if it is necessary that it go to the crown by winding itself upward, the yogi/nī must do that purposefully. As the *Vajra Rosary Tantra* says:

By the preceding of the thatness
Of the energies, it is driven upward.
The yogi/nī causes that achievement,
And therefrom in the emanation wheel
One realizes what is called "joy."

It [further] says that the yogi/nī makes it go upon the [heart's] Dharma wheel [105a] and then up to the beatific wheel.

Thus, by meditation on the subtle, as for all those processes—dissolving the energies, the arising of the signs, the melting of the spirit of enlightenment by burning the furor and it coming downward, its reversal upward, and the production from both of those [processes] of the downward streaming and the upward firming joys in their sixteen [lunar] portions and, from the solar perspective, twelve portions—they are all similar in involving the blazing and the dripping of the furor in the navel and the secret center, meditation by setting letters and drops there, and meditating there on vase breathing, and so on. All of those are very important, and especially they are methods that do not mistake the vital points of the path of the yoginī tantras; so you should understand them well.

This meditating of the subtle drop in the lower door is very powerful for burning the fury fire, as it easily reverses the evacuative energy upward, and can demonstrate well the downward streaming orgasmic joy. In this it is necessary that the spirit of enlightenment abide for a long time in the jewel. Although there are many [other] necessities such as its long abiding there, I do not write about them for fear of getting too lengthy.

[**VI.B.3.b.ii.C′3′d′i′A″6″c″** – How to cultivate samadhic and aftermath (body isolations) when (bliss) arises]

When you are able to generate the orgasmic joys of the upward and downward order, it is necessary to unite them with the completely decisive view of selflessness, the purity of suchness. Therefore, you must generate this with the two minds functioning as one, and you must meditate in the equipoised trance on the union of voidness and great bliss as object and subject. When you arise from that [trance], moved by the force of energies, the way you meditate is described in the *Vajra Rosary Tantra*:

As for the sense engaging the object [105b]
Binding whatever abides there,
You should intensely engage the superficial relative,
The magic [body] and so on, nondual with voidness.
Such as the wisdom-intuition initiation,
It is the bliss of [that] experience.
By remembering great bliss,
Your senses reverse the objective body.

This means that "voidness" is clear light transparence; "nondual" is communion; the "superficial" is the magic body and so on. Included in the "and so on" are also the ways of engaging sense objects in the context of less advanced [practices]. You should understand according to what is explained here that, in all the occasions of developing the four voids, from speech isolation on, whatever arises is sealed with bliss-void. Thus, when you enjoy an object, you seal it by remembering [both] the bliss taken as the actuality of the third initiation and the previously explained great bliss according to the explanation of what is included in the "and so on." You restrain any attitude that is in disharmony with that, and abide there with all objects appearing as bliss. After that, conditioned by the blazing of bliss the energies that function through the doors of the senses are reversed within and the sense consciousnesses also are retracted, the energies dissolve, and, as before, bliss arises.

In that regard, just as in first stage one must learn that everything outer and inner that arises, arises as divine, so in the second stage all that arises must [be experienced to] arise as a transformation of great bliss. But again, that is only after having discovered the orgasmic great bliss of the perfection stage, so here the statement that you should see everything that arises as the play of great bliss from the perspective of body isolation [106a] is made in order that all visions should arise as bliss.

In that regard, through determining the pure nature of all things, you first must understand all substantial things as transformations of voidness, and then through the process of uniting bliss and void, you must meditate them as transformations of great bliss. To explain those, in the *Integrated Practices* it says:

> "I am pure by nature!" which means "My nature has been firmly created." And as for having visualized yourself as the great Vajradhara, with the nature of the three vajras, it is explained as the "yoga of blessing."

On this occasion of the single-clan body isolation, yourself the yogi/nī develops a firm visualization that knows your natural purity, and are said to have meditated yourself as Vajradhara. And not only yourself, but also all the whole body that is to be isolated, and not only on the occasion of the one clan [body isolation], but likewise on the occasions of the hundred-clan body isolation, and so on.

Therefore, when all things to be isolated [from routine ordinariness] are primally determined to have the nature of the pure reality devoid of intrinsic identifiability, that very realityless voidness is known to arise as all those substantial things—and that is the meaning of things being the transformations of voidness. Although there are many different kinds of things, since they are no different in being void of truth [-status], the negandum of which they are devoid, they are all of a single aesthetic taste, without any multiplicity of different voidnesses. Therefore, when such voidness is taken as the object by orgasmic bliss, then, even though subject and object may not [yet] merge like water poured in water, one can imaginatively practice that way. [106b] At that time, by the vital point of imagining bliss-void as a single aesthetic experience, it is easy, by the power of visualization, to focus [on things] as the transformations of bliss just like they are the transformations of voidness. And this is the real reason for sealing everything that arises [with great bliss] by remembering the bliss-void trance concentration.

Thus, in terms of seeing all substantial things as the transformations of the uniform aesthetic experience of bliss-void, even the appearance of the life cycle, the effect, and of evolution and addiction, its cause, become the play of great primal wisdom, and so the routine life cycle and its cause have no place of origin. In the passage [from the *Vajrashrīvara King of Nondual Tantras*] quoted in the *Integrated Practices* in the context of the hundred-clan body isolation:

> The aggregates, elements and likewise the media,
> Having been divided into five classes and again five,

Are blessed individually by the transcendent lords—
Whence could the life cycle evolutions emerge?
Likewise, each one of the five outer objects,
Individually by the five bliss-lords,
Are always specially blessed,
Always truly standing as the three and five wisdoms.

Chag's translation in this way is excellent.

Seeing the implication of this, Saraha said [in an *Enlightenment Song*]:

Don't take it as two, take it as one;
Don't distinguish the various specific clans.
Transform all of the three realms—all of this—
Into the color of the single great passion!

There, there is no beginning, middle, or end.
It is not existence, and it is not nirvana.
In this supreme great bliss
The self [107a] and the other do not exist.

In the front and back, in the ten directions,
Whatever you see is that itself.
That bliss itself, your savior, right now ends all error.
Now, you need not go to ask for anyone else.

Here, "great passion" is primal orgasmic wisdom.

Thus, according to the explanation of the hundred clans and so on, at first this is determined by learning and reflection. Then at the time of practice, you preliminarily learn the [yoga branch of] retraction wherein you see everything that appears as the play of bliss-void. Having learned that, then you learn the ultimate body isolation wherein all that arises is the single great secret Vajradhara, and you meditate yourself as bliss-void in the form of arising as Vajradhara. And again you there have union with your consort. The treatises of the noble father and sons are not explicit as to whether Vajradhara is blue or white.

If you cannot create the great bliss as just explained but can create the melting bliss, then meditate on that. If even that is lacking, you should create it through understanding well the process of joining bliss and void and the process of cultivating the entranced and aftermath [samadhis]. In order to take great bliss as the path, there is no other art than, by the power of firm familiarization with this method of cultivating great bliss in trance and aftermath [samadhis], associating everything that arises with the blazing of bliss. And so there are many explanations of it in many tantras and treatises. In this [noble] system, it is clearly explained in the context of body isolation, so having thoroughly understood it, turn your mind toward it again and again. And this is how you should inherit the extraordinary ability of the class of [the practitioners of] this path. [107b]

5. *Speech Isolation in General*

[107b.1–143b.1]

[**VI.B.3.b.ii.c′3′d′i′b″** – How to learn the speech isolation speech vajra samadhi]

The second has six parts: [1″] The order of body isolation and speech isolation; [2″] Refuting the assertion that speech isolation is a creation-stage path; [3″] Teaching the reality of energy, the knowable object of speech isolation; [4″] Teaching the ultimate reality of mantra; [5″] The way that speech isolation becomes a component of breath control; and [6″] The way to put speech isolation into practice.

[**VI.B.3.b.ii.c′3′d′i′b″1″** – The order of body isolation and speech isolation]

One might wonder, "What is the meaning of the statement that one should learn the speech isolation after learning the body isolation; [since] without the body isolation preceding, speech isolation will not succeed?"

The *Integrated Practices* states when one learns the gross and subtle creation stages, one abides in the beginner's samadhi, and when one learns the body isolation, one dwells in the body vajra samadhi. There is also a "body vajra samadhi" in the first stage, but what is called "body vajra samadhi" here is the body vajra of the perfection stage, where the body vajra is distinctive. Further, though the "vajra body" and "wisdom body" explained to be the magic body are not [yet] present here, this is a body vajra that arises as the play of the perfection-stage orgasmic bliss one has [here] attained. Thus, "vajra" here has the meaning of inseparability from great bliss.

Further, [the body isolation must be attained as] the prerequisite of speech isolation; because, since speech isolation is the special mantra recitation of the perfection stage, if that [deity] body is not present in the deity meditation of the reciter, the potency of that recitation will not develop. Further, [since speech isolation aims] to cause the energies to collect and dissolve in the distinctive place of energy contraction, the *dhūti* channel in the center of the heart complex, by the reason that [108a] in general such contraction is very easy when preceded by [body isolation's] initial generation of bliss from contracting and dissolving into the central channel and is difficult when not so preceded, the order [of the two isolations] is so [determined]. This is because, as the *Vajra Rosary* states that the releasing of the channel knot at the *dhūti* of the heart complex is harder than the releasing of the other channel knots, first contracting [the energies] into the central channel in other locations is easier than doing so at the heart complex.

[**VI.B.3.b.ii.c′3′d′i′b″2″** – Refuting the assertion that speech isolation is a creation-stage path]

The *Moonlight Commentary* states:

> As the vajra recitation also is a meditation of that [creation stage] type, first mentioned as a component of that [creation stage], it is assigned to the creation stage. However, the *Integrated Practices* locates it at the end of the speech isolation, as it abides in the speech vajra samadhi; and so [Āryadeva] says that one should seek the mind isolation, going beyond the creation stage. Now, the instantaneous visualization [of oneself] as a fully developed deity body is the [procedure used on the] perfection stage; and since [speech isolation] depends on that [procedure], the *Integrated Practices* states, "The speech isolation is not the province of the creation-stage practitioner."

Thus, it is explained that, when one abides in the speech vajra samadhi, one is seeking the mind isolation beyond the creation stage, and the speech isolation does not differ from that [samadhi]; and since the instantaneous perfection in the deity body is the referent of the designation "perfection stage," which is not the gradual creation as a deity [of the creation stage], [the speech isolation] is not the province of the creation stage. That statement of the *Integrated Practices* is to show that dwelling in the speech isolation samadhi is beyond the creation stage, and not to show that the mind isolation is beyond the creation stage. [108b] Thus, both translations [of the *Integrated Practices*]—[the usual] "going beyond the creation stage," and that of Chag, "having gone beyond . . ."—are good.

Again, one should not think that [speech isolation] is creation stage because of the *Integrated Practices* statements that "the creation stage leads to attainment of the eighth stage," and that "one who abides in the speech vajra samadhi is lord of the eighth stage." This is because, though both are placed on the eighth stage, as there are many [ways of arranging the] prior and later stages, it is not necessary to interpret them both as referring to only one state. I will explain [below] the layout of these stages.

The *Integrated Practices* states:

> Speech isolation is the primal wisdom of the yogi/nī; extremely subtle, it is not the object of the [exoteric] universalists, nor is it the object of those who, though on the vajra vehicle, are practitioners of the creation stage; since it is extremely subtle.

As for the meaning of this *Integrated Practices* statement, it is not properly cited to show that, while [the vajra recitation] is not the province of the creation stage of a gradually created deity, it is the province of the creation stage of an instantaneously created deity: because it is or is not equally the province of those two; and because, when the *Integrated Practices* explains separately, at the beginning of the speech isolation, the meaning of the [*Root Tantra*] third chapter's mention of the meditation of the five-colored jewel at the nose tip for the two stages' subtle yogas, it explains the vajra recitation as the subtle yoga of the definitive meaning perfection stage; and because the *Five Stages* also states the explanation of the five stages such as vajra recitation for [the benefit] of those who have already practiced the creation stage and desire subsequently [to enter] the perfection stage.

As for the statement that it is "not the province of the [109a] creation-stage practitioners," it does not mean that such a person can have no understanding of it, but that it is not such a person's path [of practice]. Therefore, one should not be confused by the fact that other authoritative treatises also explain the vajra recitation in the context of creation stage, since there is not any contradiction at all between explaining it in such a context and [holding that it] is not the path [of such a practitioner]. And this also refutes the assertion that Gad pa [kīrti] accepted the vajra recitation of the energy inhaling and exhaling as an instruction of the creation stage.

[**VI.B.3.b.ii.c′3′d′i′b″3″** – Teaching the reality of energy, the knowable object of speech isolation]

The third has seven parts: [a″] The import of gradually learning energy, mantra, and vajra recitation; [b″] Advantages and disadvantages of knowing and not knowing the reality of energies; [c″] Analysis of energies; [d″] Explanation of each type; [e″] How energies transit; [f″] What sort of functions the energies perform; [g″] Teaching how to know the vital key of practice relying on that.

[**VI.B.3.b.ii.c′3′d′i′b″3″a″** – The import of gradually learning energy, mantra, and vajra recitation]

[Nāgārjuna] states in the *Five Stages*:

> After [engaging] the reality of energy
> One should fully enter the reality of mantra.
> Having realized the objective of mantra,
> One learns well the vajra recitation.

Thus, by the process of engaging the reality of the energies, one enters the reality of mantra; and realizing that, one learns the vajra recitation.

Here, Kalden Drakpa explains the meaning of "engaging the reality of energy" as the meditation by means of the yoga of the three vajras having the three poisons, the substance drop of enlightenment spirit at the nose tip of the secret place, the mantra drop at the nose tip of the heart complex, and the light drop that compresses the energies into drop form at the nose tip of the face. The meaning of "entering the reality of mantra" is meditating by visualizing the compression process of the crown OṀ into the throat ĀḤ, the throat ĀḤ into the heart HŪṀ, the HŪṀ's drop into the crescent, into the head, into the HA body, into the vowel hook, [109b] and the vowel hook becoming the short A. Lakshmī and many others likewise accept this. Nevertheless, those [interpretations] are not the meaning of the *Further Tantra* and the *Vajra Rosary*; nor are they seen as the meaning of the *Five Stages* and the *Integrated Practices*.

Therefore, as for the statement about "gradually entering into the three realities," it means, according to the interpretation of master Gö, that, beginning with the knowledge of the reality of energy, one next comes to know the reality of mantra; and after knowing well those two with learning and critical reflection, one meditates the vajra recitation.

[**VI.B.3.b.ii.c′3′d′i′B″3″b″** – Advantages and disadvantages of knowing and not knowing the reality of energies]

The *Vajra Rosary Tantra* states:

> Listen! Next I will explain the ultimate,
> The supreme reality of energy.
> If the yogi/nī meditates on energy,
> S/he will swiftly attain the powers.

And the *Vow Arisal* states:

> Who doesn't know the yoga of energy,
> And who knows but doesn't meditate—
> They are harmed by various sufferings,
> And become insects in [future] life cycles.

To know and meditate the yoga of energy, it is very important to know well the vital points of the energies. And one must know them thoroughly not only to meditate directly on the energies, as in the vajra recitation, but also to meditate by visualizing the drops etc. in the vital points in the body, and to generate the path through the door of the external vitalizing energy control.

Therefore, having well understood that all the perfection-stage meditations that penetrate the vital points in the body are systems that function as mechanisms of energies, you should realize that the direct and indirect meditations on energies [110a] are indispensable on this path.

[**VI.B.3.b.ii.c′3′d′i′B″3″c″** – Analysis of energies]

"Well just how does one ascertain the details of the energies?"

The *Buddha Union* and the *Wisdom Vajra Compendium* refer to the ten energies by the ten nonliteral [jargon] expressions "koṭakhya" and so forth. The *Vajra Door Tantra* uses the literal expressions vitalizing, evacuative, digestive, ascending, and pervasive, and upmoving, permoving, commoving, surmoving, and ultramoving.[72] The *Vajra Rosary* and *Revelation of the Hidden Intention* use the same expressions for the first five, and for the latter five, Nāga, Kurma, Kṛkalāsa, Devadatta, and Dhanujit [Dragon, Tortoise, Chameleon, Devadatta, and Dhanujit]; for this last, some commentaries also call it Dhanajit (*nor las rgyal*). The terms for the two sets of five, the "root energies" and the "branch energies" are not explicit in the other writings of the noble tradition, but they are used by Ekādashanirghosha.

If one wonders, "Well, do the hundred and eight energies taught in the *Vajra Rosary*, called 'sender,' 'holder,' etc., include the ten energies or not?"

Some Tibetan scholars say that there are ten synonyms for each of the ten energies and eight names for them in common. However, in the *Vajra Rosary Commentary*, it is explained that, except for the pervasive energy, which lacks [a localized] activity and circulates throughout the body, each of the other nine energies circulates in each of the six wheels, emanation, Dharma, fire, beatific, wind, and great bliss, giving fifty-four in the day and [110b] fifty-four at night, giving one hundred and eight. There, the vitalizing energy circulates from the centers of the six wheels, and each of the eight energies, from evacuative to ultramoving, circulates in the petals of the four [main wheels], not counting the fire and wind wheels. The fire wheel under the beatific wheel is taught as three-petalled and the wind wheel at the brow as six-petalled. Thus the former has eight [sites], the three knots relative to the central channel, the channels of the right and left breasts, and the [channels in the] three petals; and the latter has eight [sites] also, including the six petals and the two channels of the right and left brows: in those [sixteen], the other eight energies circulate.

In a different translation of the *Tantra*, it is taught that there are fifty-four from midday to midnight and fifty-four from midnight to midday; but this does not appear in the translation of the commentary.

As it seems that the hundred and eight is explained as derived from nine

72. Tib. *rgyu ba, rnam par rgyu ba, yang dag par rgyu ba, rab tu rgyu ba, nges par rgyu ba*; Skt. *udvāha, vivāha, saṁvāha, pravāha, nirvaha*. These are yogic jargon words anyway, so I don't mind creating jargon translations in this case: upmoving, permoving, commoving, surmoving, dismoving.

energies circulating in six wheels, the previous explanation disagrees with the *Tantra*. If each of the nine energies such as vitalizing and evacuative circulates in each of the six wheels, and if [they also] circulate in others, then it is still necessary to explain the system of deriving the hundred [and eight] count; and if [they] do not circulate [elsewhere], it is incorrect, as [a energy] circulating from the navel to the nostrils must circulate through the heart and throat centers and so forth.

Furthermore, the sutra quoted in the *Commentary* as:

> Beginning from the half session, having the nature of nine in the six wheels, until the very end of the half session . . .

also does not seem to be correct. Whatever the case, though it seems to be the meaning of that tantra that the hundred and eight energies are not non-comprised of the ten energies, as it also seems difficult to posit the pattern of circulation of each of nine energies in order in each of six wheels, [111a] we must still investigate this [question].

[**VI.B.3.b.ii.c′3′d′i′B″3″d″** – Explanation of each type]

The fourth has three parts: [i″] Explaining the meaning of the five root energies; [ii″] Explaining the meaning of the five branch energies; and [iii″] Explaining the meaning common to the two energies.

[**VI.B.3.b.ii.c′3′d′i′B″3″d″i″** – Explaining the meaning of the five root energies]

As to where the five energies stay and which energy belongs to which savior, the *Vajra Rosary Tantra* states:

> Vitalizing energy stays in the heart center,
> Born from the specific clan of Akshobhya.
> Evacuative energy stays in the genitals,
> Born from the Ratnasambhava clan.
> Ascending energy stays in the throat,
> With the nature of Amitābha.
> Metabolic energy stays in the navel lotus,

> With the nature of Amoghasiddhi.
> Pervasive energy stays in all parts,
> The actuality of Vairochana.

The *Integrated Practices* also states it in that way.

The statement, "this illumination of the reality of the five energies has the actuality of the five wisdoms," that the [energies] are the five wisdoms, should be understood as referring to the five clans.

Now the vitalizing energy circulating from the nostrils is the gross vitalizing energy, and the "indestructible energy" staying in the heart center is the extremely subtle vitalizing energy. As the *Vajra Rosary Tantra* states:

> In the sky of the chamber of the heart lotus
> The wisdom vajra always dwells . . .

And:

> The world realm of the great Lord
> Akshobhya is that very reality.
> The place where he always dwells
> Is called the "life-wisdom."

Thus, the energy that always dwells in the heart center as long as one lives is explained as the vitalizing energy. So one must posit both a gross and subtle vitalizing energy. As the *Four Goddess Dialogue* states:

> Supreme subtlety of just the half-[mustard-seed]-measure,
> The actuality of the mentality in the form of a drop—
> It always [111b] dwells in the center of the heart,
> Ablaze with magnificent rays of light.

This refers to the indestructible energy that blazes with five light rays. And the *Vajra Mandala Ornament Tantra* also teaches the indestructible energy:

> Indestructible in the center of the heart,
> Brilliant like a pure butter lamp,
> Unchanging, supremely subtle,
> *A*—the holy Lord.

In general, there are many "heart center indestructibles," such as white and red enlightenment spirits, the ground clear light, and the subtle vitalizing energy, etc. This one is explained in the *Vajra Rosary Commentary* as "clear light energy." And it is the same one mentioned in the *Reality Accomplishment* as [involved in] the:

> . . . realization of ultimate reality when the orgasmic energy abides in its own place after the other energies have dissolved.

Therefore, as the *Vajra Rosary* explains that the energies at the time of death dissolve from below upward in the sequence of their original birth, and as it is taught that in the original [fetal] development the vitalizing energy [is the] first [to] develop, it happens that in the end the energies dissolve into the subtle vitalizing energy. Thus, also the *Integrated Practices* explanation that the energies enter the indestructible in the end means that they dissolve into the heart center's indestructible energy.

While the heart center's indestructible energy and drop stay within the *dhūti* central channel of the heart-center channel knot, the vitalizing energy that circulates from the nostrils, though abiding in the heart center, does not abide [exactly] there [in the center of the channel knot].

As for the "Body Speech Mind Essence" chapter of the *Vajra Rosary* statement that the evacuative energy abides in the anus, in the middle of the secret center, the actual place is the lotus of the secret center, intending that the evacuative energy evacuates "great dirt" from the anus. [112a] The *Illuminating Lamp* explanation of the earth energy abiding in the lotus of the anus also refers just to that secret center lotus.

Here one objects: "There is a statement of the *Vajra Rosary*, that:

> Both the sixty-four- and eight-petalled [wheels], as they face up and down [respectively], cause the vitalizing and evacuative [energies] to circulate by relying upward and downward.

Is it to be understood as [referring] to above and below the eight-petalled heart center? Or is it referring to the above and below of the sixty-four-petalled navel center? If the former, it contradicts the locations as explained above; if the latter, it contradicts the statement made after the two lines 'chamber of the lotus of the heart, etc. . . . ,' namely, 'relying upward and downward, the vitalizing and evacuative great energies abide.'"

[In response,] "upward and downward" is taken as above and below the channel knot of the heart center. "Abide" means "cause to circulate," referring to the path of circulation, not to a fixed place; so the first fault does not apply.

Here one may wonder: "Well, as it explains that the earth energy, the evacuative [energy], circulates in the two nostrils, how can it be said to 'circulate relying downward' from the heart center?"

That means that the evacuative energy cannot go up through the *dhūti* path since it is blocked by the heart-center channel knots; and the same [vice versa] for the vitalizing energy. Just as the vitalizing energy enters and exits from the nostrils from the heart upward through the throat, so the evacuative energy enters and exits from the navel to the anus and the urethra. As the *Red Yamāri Tantra* states:

> Beginning in the navel, the evacuative [energy]
> Goes on the lower path to stop at the secret center;
> Having departed the heart to the throat,
> The vitalizing [energy] goes from the nostrils. **[112b]**

The metabolic [fire-equalizing] energy abides equal with the furor of the navel. By reason of the *Vajra Rosary* statement that, blocked by the channel knot in the middle of the heart center, the vitalizing energy cannot go down from that place and the evacuative energy cannot go up, the three energies that abide in the other three wheels also cannot likewise enter and exit through the center of the channel knots. As the *Vajra Rosary* states:

> Coming and going are manifested in the lotuses
> Of throat, heart, navel, and secret centers . . .

—excluding the pervasive energy, such is the pattern of the coming and going of the other four energies in their abodes. Further, those abodes are determined by their first arisal and their final place they return to once completing their circulations, and it is not that their overall circulation always goes out only from those places and enters into only those places.

When there is coming and going of the energies, as for from which nostril they move, which energy they are, from which elemental sphere, and what color they are; the *Vajra Rosary* states:

> Dwelling in the clans of the five buddhas,
> Emerging from the nostril hole,
> The five energies truly move upward.
> They always change, acting in the body,
> By moving in the superficial nose,
> They emerge from that door.
> Four kinds—moving from left, right,
> From both [nostrils], and gently moving.
> The right [nostril energy], its elemental source
> Is the actual sphere of fire;
> Its good red color
> Marks the movement of the lotus savior.
> The left [nostril energy], its elemental source
> Depends on the sphere of energy;
> Its greenish gold appearance
> Marks the movement of the karma savior. The double [nostril energy] [113a]
> Has a golden color,
> Is the actual sphere of earth,
> And is the movement of the jewel savior.
> The gentle [energy], unmoving,
> Is the elemental sphere of water,
> Its pure crystal appearance
> Marks the movement of the vajra savior.
> [Energy] emerging from all elements,
> Objects constituting habitat and inhabitant,
> Is the nature of Vairochana,
> It will emerge [only] at the end in death.
> Entranced on these four elemental spheres
> Always recite [their mantras].
> The mantrī, by the very count of recitation
> Always recites all day and night. . . .

As for the meaning of this, the *Integrated Practices* explains that one should always recite [in the vajra manner], once light rays have emerged from the tip holes of vajra and lotus and gone upward, by the process of engaging [by inhaling] etc. the lord of the three-syllable mantra in each elemental sphere of [energy] moving from the right and left nostrils of the superficial nose. In regard to the fourth line, another translation says "always truly moves in the body." The pervasive energy also is said to circulate from the nose door along with the other energies, thus being shown to emerge from the nostril. And as for "gently moving," though elsewhere it is taught to move from both left and right one by one, here it is understood to be moving from both nostrils. "Unmoving" has the meaning of "barely moving," according to the *Integrated Practices*. This statement about "emerging from the right, etc." is explained by the *Integrated Practices* as referring to the right and left nostrils and also both nostrils. The *Vow Arisal* similar statement is to the same effect; not meaning, as [thought by the author of] the *Vow Arisal Commentary*, as referring to the movement [113b] from the left, right, and center of each nostril.

That the *Vajra Rosary* teaches thus does not contradict the *Personal Instruction*'s teaching that energy moves from the right nostril, water from the left, and earth and fire from both. This is because the former statement intends the movement in terms of the lord [of the buddha-clan], and the latter, even when it mentions equal movement [means] movement in each nostril, and when it mentions movement in each nostril means movement in both nostrils, so its [statements on this are] never sure. The statement of movement in the left explained as movement in the right is for the sake of showing the uncertainty about the energy of each of the two nostrils. Finally, it will be explained that, when each energy of a primary element moves, the other three move in its retinue. Though these four—"movement from the right nostril, etc."—are not explained clearly from the *Tantra* or from the treatises of the father and son as "this is the root energy," still you can understand if you combine this explanation of the energies of the four saviors and the previously quoted explanation that "the vitalizing energy etc. is this savior etc."

The *Illuminating Lamp* explains that the four [kinds of] energies of earth, water, fire, and wind [elements] respectively circulate from the lotuses of secret, heart, throat, and navel centers.

In regard to color, from the quotes of the translations of the *Vajra*

Rosary and the old translations of the *Vajra Rosary* and the *Integrated Practices*, the energy of the left emerges as green-yellow, and in its explanation that green-yellow is described as the "actuality of black light rays." From the quotes from the Patshab and Chag translations of *Integrated Practices* it is called green-blue, as also in the commentaries. In the *Integrated Practices* [114a] the four energies are respectively described as really being black, red, yellow, and white light rays, which agrees with the description given in the fourteenth chapter of the *Illuminating Lamp*. In the third chapter of the *Illuminating Lamp* the colors of the four energies are explained as red etc., and the *Revelation of the Hidden Intention* explains the same. And in the *Illuminating Lamp* sixth chapter, except for explaining the right energy as actually red light rays, the other three colors are as explained above.

Thus, though there are various explanations, vitalizing, evacuative, ascending, and metabolic energies' independent colors are, in order, white, yellow, red, and black, as determined for each. As for there being light rays of five colors in each of them, one holds this as the meaning of the *Integrated Practices* statement:

> Granted that is so, each light ray that emerges, itself surely has five-colored light rays; since even a single elemental sphere pervades all four elemental spheres.

Karunashrīpāda explains that *shyāma* can mean both green and black, so it should be taken as green-blue or green-black and not as green-yellow. Lakshmī, depending on the statement of the pervasive energy as Vairochana and the vitalizing energy as Akshobhya, explained them as white and black; but the latter contradicts many treatises, and though there is no clear word on the former, it is better to take it as clear blue according to master Gö. As for one sphere of element of the energies pervading the four [others], when each energy, the vitalizing etc., circulates [114b] it brings the other three with it; so in each time all four circulate.

Because the *Illuminating Lamp* sixth chapter states:

> When one engages in the process of the sphere of each [elemental] sphere, the other three spheres operate as retinue, and thus [each] one radiates as including [others] within it;

because in elucidating its meaning the same point is made in the *[Root] Tantra*:

> It radiates along with its particular retinue;

and because the "four spheres" of that context are explained as being the four spheres of right, left, and [strong and gentle winds in] equally functioning nostrils, you must take them as the four energies, vitalizing etc., [so that] when the ascending energy circulates in the right nostril, vitalizing, evacuative, and metabolic energies circulate also together [with it]. And by this one can understand the other three as well.

As for the way in which the other three energies circulate by being incorporated within the ascending energy, they are generated like a single rainbow; as those other three are under the power of the fire energy, they are reddish white, reddish yellow, and reddish green. By that one can understand how the metabolic energy etc., [plus] three, circulating from the left etc., with a main energy and three accompanying energies included in each case, operate. Thus, the statement that the ascending operates from the right, the metabolic from the left, and the vitalizing and evacuating from both equally is in terms of them operating as main energies; it does not restrict their circulation as subordinate energies.

When the ascending energy moves the energies of the four principal saviors in the right nostril, there are first 225 Pāṇḍarāvāsinī energies, and then three sets of the same number, respectively, Tārā, Lochanā, and Māmakī [115a] energies.[73] Further, in each of the goddess energies there are four savior energies. Likewise, when the metabolic energy in the left nostril moves the energies of the four principal saviors, [there are four sets of goddess energies], beginning from Tārā [working round through Lochanā and Māmakī to Pāṇḍarā]. From this one should understand that, when the vitalizing energy equal from both nostrils moves the four principals [savior energies], [there are four sets beginning from] Māmakī [energies going around to Lochanā energies]. When the evacuative energy moves [from

73. Thus, a 900-breath-long session of red fire Padmanātha energies (with Karmanātha, Ratnanātha, and Vajranātha retinue energies) moving from the right consists of 225 Padmanātha-Pāṇḍarāvāsinī energies, 225 Padmanātha-Tārā energies, 225 Padmanātha-Lochanā energies, and 225 Padmanātha-Māmakī energies.

both nostrils equally slowly] the four savior energies, there are four sets of goddess [energies] beginning from Lochanā energies. The *Revelation of the Hidden Intention* explains that:

> Pāṇḍarā and so forth in order,
> Above and on the side, in front and below,
> Having the spheres of fire and wind and earth
> And water. . . .

Thus, Pāṇḍarā energies operate above, Tārā energies on the side, Lochanā energies in the front, and Māmakī energies below; and those four are explained respectively as four energy-planes from fire to earth.

Such being the case, as for each energy, the ascending etc., in each set of the circulation of four energies of the clans, there are four goddess energies to be distinguished, which do not operate at one time. As the four energies distinguished as savior (*nātha*) energies operate at one time and the goddess energies only operate successively, and there are no energies other than the savior energies that operate together, the assertion of Kṛshna Samayavajra, that one energy operates in the center and the other four abide in the directions, and that the five all operate at one time, is not good; and the position of Tsunmojen that the four energies do operate together indistinguishably like a single rainbow is good. Thus, the explanation of the other [115b] system that takes the five subordinates [energies] as operating simultaneously in the center and directions is again different from this; so the "operating from the above" etc. is explained as successive and not simultaneous.

According to the expression in the Chag translation "above, on the side, equal below . . . ," when four goddess energies are explained in each set of nine hundred energies, the fire Pāṇḍarā energies operate in the upper part of the nostril, the wind Tārā energies operate from the side of the nostrils, the earth Lochanā energies operate equally from the middle of both left and right nostrils, and the water Māmakī energies operate from the lower part of the nostrils. That agrees with Shridhar who, having posited energies of the four elements in the energies of each of the transits, explained the operation of the earth energy in the center and the wind energy from the two sides. The *Sampuṭa [Tantra]* explanation of operation from the side, and others' explanation of operating from a facet, are taken as "operating from the side," while the meaning of "operating equally" and "frontally" is "operating from the center." If there is operation from the two sides of the nostril, it should be successive.

In the context of the comment in the *Tantra* "upon the five energies," it is mentioned that the pervasive energy also emerges from the nostrils, thinking about the explanation below that it emerges in the end at death; so except for its circulating there at the time of death, it does not circulate there in life. This is the position of Lakshmī, Alamkakalasha, and many former Tibetans. Ekādashanirghosha explains that in the present life it emerges in the pattern of whatever elemental sphere emerges, and at the time of death emerges in the pattern of being principal. In the *Sheaf of Instructions*, there is a third explanation, that the energies operating in the Devil-free channel, [116a] as they are life-exhausting energies, are pervasive energies. Though there are those three explanations, the pattern of whether or not the pervasive energy that pervades all the joints operates in the nostrils is better [understood] according to the first explanation. Therefore, though one can contract [in meditation] the energies that cause inhalation and exhalation through the nostrils, there are many pervasive energies that cannot be contracted—and yet they must be contracted [eventually]; because the *Sheaf of Instructions* explains the meaning of the *Sampuṭa [Tantra]* teaching about practicing vase-breathing and contracting the energies of the twenty-four places as referring to the contraction of the pervasive energies.

[**VI.B.3.b.ii.C′3′d′i′B″3″d″ii″** – Explaining the meaning of the five branch energies]

The *Integrated Practices* explains the five branch energies as residing in the five sense faculties such as eye. And the *Vajra Rosary* states that [the five energies] operate from the five channels:

> "Moon-part," "Luminance,"
> "Reverence," "Hidden crystal," and "Liver"—
> These are the names of the five channels.
> The energies that operate from the five channels are
> "Dragon," "Tortoise," "Chameleon,"
> "Devadatta," and "Dhanujit."

Again, from the same text [the *Vajra Rosary*]:

> Reality of bliss dwelling in the heart center,
> Light illuminating the Buddha-sun,
> With the form of subject and object—
> That constitutes the twelve light rays.
> Light-increase, Light-ray, Refulgent,
> Clear, Blaze, and Light-blaze—
> Depending on eye and so forth,
> They hold all outer [objects,] form etc.
> Light-ray, Light-full (*'od ma*), Luminant,
> Clear-beauty, Clear-light, Solar-clear—
> The aspect of outer forms etc.,
> These six are proclaimed as light.

Thus, the energies emerging from the heart center, depending on the six sense faculties, are called the six subjective energies that mobilize the six-fold [consciousness] cluster and the six objective energies **[116b]** that distinguish forms etc. So those channels are obviously channels that abide in the heart center. One must investigate whether these refer to the same channels in the heart center, such as "Triply twisted," explained as the channels for the five objects.

The five branch energies are mainly branches of the vitalizing energy, and so the heart center is the principal location in which they both arise and decline. As the *Illuminating Lamp* declares:

> The five blazes are the five kinds of light such as "clearly shining," and "having the nature of the five light rays such as 'many sparkles shaking'" and "a wheel, as it ceaselessly turns day and night like a water wheel. 'Vajra' has the five colors . . ."

Thus the five branch energies each have the nature of five light rays, and they enter and exit the sense doors all day and night. As for their colors, master Gö explains that the upmoving energy is red, the permoving blue, the commoving yellow, the surmoving white, and the ultramoving is green. And as for the way in which the fifth energy abides in the body sense faculty, it abides wherever that sense faculty pervades.

[**VI.B.3.b.ii.C′3′d′i′B″3″d″iii″** – Explaining the meaning common to the two energies]

The Integrated Practices explains the ten energies as becoming the inhalation and exhalation, as developing in the womb, as not involving respiration until birth, and as involving it from birth. Again, the entry and exit of the five main energies has already been explained. Some of the five branch energies function together with the energies that operate in the nostrils; or else they apply themselves whatever way is appropriate. And those [117a] [also] become the four elemental spheres such as wind, the four goddesses, and the five elements, as above explained. And the root energies have already been explained as becoming the five clans and the five wisdoms. If we do the same for the branch energies, it should be done in accordance with the way they are distributed among the five senses, the five objects, and the five clans.

The statement about using them for vajra recitation, basing on the three letters, refers to all ten energies. The statement "all those energies, based on the letter *A*, cause all words to be expressed" is not precluded to apply to all ten.

Again, those become insubstantial when attaining the indestructible, meaning that in the end at death, they dissolve into the indestructible in the heart center and enter the clear light; that can also be done in the same way through the path. In the *Integrated Practices*, thinking of the statement in the context of answering the questions about these, as to what the ten energies do and where they abide, the functions of the energies are explained:

> However, as to their functions, the five root energies abide in the parts of the bodies and perform the functions of the body. And the five branch energies abide in the eye etc. and perform the functions of the senses.

This is what is stated. For more details, it has already been explained in the body isolation, so it should be understood from that.

Therefore, "becomes inhalation and exhalation," and so forth, is understood as conveying their identities. In the *Five Stages*, the comments such as "this is the mount of consciousness" declare that the energies are the mounts of consciousness, meaning that the energies mobilize the consciousnesses. It is also stated that: "... for that reason all of us living beings [117b] are a world in movement ..." And if one said that the physical body caused all movement and agitation, giving that as the reason, it would not apply to "all of us" living beings, [since some do not have gross bodies, but all are moved around by gross or subtle energies].

If one wonders: "As for the material body being moved by energy, it is not the same with consciousness, so what is the meaning of that [energy] moving [consciousness]?"

Lakshmī et al. say that the discernment of objects by the six consciousnesses depends on their being impelled by energies; otherwise, [without] them, one would not see at all, like a blind person. And therefore these two when connected together, like a cripple [consciousness, who can see] and a blind person [energy, who can walk], can achieve their purposes.

The *Revelation of the Hidden Intention* states—

> Going, performing acts such as [seeing] objects,
> Here, they depend on that [energy function] ...

—that performing the functions of going and moving etc. and perceiving objects all depend on the energies. Since the *Integrated Practices* states that the five [branch] energies abide in the sense faculties and perform the functions of the objects and senses, one does have to accept that the function of consciousness in holding its objects depends on energies. Nevertheless, one cannot use that reason to posit that energy is the mount of consciousness, just as the senses and objects themselves [are not mounts of consciousness].

Furthermore, the *Integrated Practices* states that one gradually moves out of the immersion in the subtle realm of luminance, and, conditioned by that, one experiences all the natural instincts day and night. And the Great Brahmin [Saraha] also said [in an *Enlightenment Song*]:

> This, [luminance-] mentality once withdrawn,
> Is energized by energy;
> It moves, is agitated, and becomes very disturbed.

That is, when energized by the energy, the mind is produced in a very agitated form. Thus, though they accept that all agitations of the mind, either conceptual or nonconceptual, are caused by energy, still you should not think that just for that reason you have discovered the meaning of positing energy as the mount of consciousness.

If one wonders: Well then, how is it [so posited]? [118a]

As consciousness is not embodied, it has no independent power to come and go in relation to objects; but when it functions together with energy, then it becomes capable of relating to objects. The *Integrated Practices* states that the three luminances are free of coming and going; and again, in answer to the questions, "How does it expand and contract in the body day and night? What is witness to this?" it states, after explaining how those three [luminances] are formless, that:

> Granted it is so; but as it is endowed with luminance, thus one can witness it when [it is] together with the element of wind.

The meaning of that is that, granted that the three consciousnesses are disembodied, as they have the luminance [that goes along with subtle] energy, they are caused to come and go, just as the witness together with the energy comes and goes without resting. Therefore, its going to objects by way of the energy is the meaning of the "mind going mounted on the energy." And in that regard, there are instances of the mind both serving and not serving to pick up the object. Further, when progression in the energy itself upon which one is mounted occurs from prior to later, although there is no progress from one objective area to another, it is not that there is no objective progression.

[Āryadeva] states in the *Integrated Practices*:

> The subtle element and the consciousness luminances, as they are immaterial, they become mingled like butter poured in butter, and they cause the completion of all activities, mundane and transcendental.

Here, energy and mind are stated to be mingled like butter in butter; hence Lakshmī's pronouncement that they are one actuality is excellent.

As for the *Integrated Practices'* calling the energy "immaterial," [118b] it intends a lack of the materiality that functions as the gross elements, and does not intend an absence of the five light ray [energies] of the subtle realm,[74] just as before that "immateriality" was mentioned in reference to the lack of the forms of hands and feet in the external energy. Also, the statement that consciousness causes the movements of the body is made [intending consciousness's working] together with the energies, as mind cannot move [the body] without the energy. This can also be understood from the *Four Hundred Commentary*.

[**VI.B.3.b.ii.C′3′d′i′B″3″e″** – How the energies transit]

The fifth has two parts: [i″] The way [the energy] transits or does not transit from one nostril to another; and [ii″] The way it transits from one petal and elemental sphere to another.[75]

[**VI.B.3.b.ii.C′3′d′i′B″3″e″i″** – The way (the energy) transits or does not transit from one nostril to another]

From the *Time Machine* literature, six energies—energies of earth, water, fire, wind, space, and consciousness—move from the right and [the same] six energies move in reverse order from the left. So there are twelve transits from the right earth to the left space and so forth. And in each transit interval, fifty-six breaths move from the central channel in each quarter. So in one day, 675[76] energies move from the central channel,

74. This underlines a crucial difference between exoteric and esoteric physics of consciousness, in that the "nonmateriality" of consciousness—the radical dualistic interactionism of mental and physical—is here stated to apply only on the coarse reality level; and on the super subtle level, mind and energy—material yet super subtle energy—are said to be ultimately indivisible, making the mental and physical also ultimately indivisible.

75. These sections are among the most dense and confusing in the work. In navigating through them, one must remember that this is the vajra recitation section, so the aim is to understand the natural circulation of the body's inner energies (breaths and other energies) throughout the nervous system, in order to fuse their functions with the transformative energy of mantra, to isolate all speech and subtle energies from ordinary naturalness and experience and manifest it as the play of enlightened divine beings. Thus, by cultivating a minute awareness of the way energies circulate in the body at the ground level, their transmutation into divine functions can become complete. Tsong Khapa here may frustrate the would-be practitioner, because, as a scientific investigator, he is concerned to show the variety of interpretations and systems of the great texts and masters, and does not hasten to present a single, unified system as the one to memorize and implement.

76. In fact, 12 x 56 = 672, so there should be 56.25 central channel breaths per transit for it

and the rest of them move from the right and left channels. Again, if you divide one day's 21,600 energies by twelve, the resulting amount in each is eighteen hundred, explained as the energies of each transit—though each will not be quite that much if you count separately the energies moving from the central channel. One "breath" (*dbugs*) is an inhalation and exhalation together. The *Vajra Rosary* and the *Vow Arisal* also agree with that. According to the *Sheaf of Instructions,* there is no separate space energy apart from the four element energies. This is supported by the *Vajra Rosary*, the *Revelation of the Hidden Intention*, and the *Nondual Triumph [Tantra]*. [119a] Thus, those things stated in the *Time Machine*—such as the space [energy] moving apart from the four element energies, the energies of the five small elements moving in each nostril in the four directions, and the center, the throat and crown petal numbers switching, and four of the sixty-four navel petals being empty—all these are interpretable meaning [teachings] for the benefit of disciples such as Sūryaratha; they are not definitive in meaning.[77] As [the *Sheaf of Instructions*] explains, it is just like the teachings about the arrangement of the environment universe of the three realms in the upper boundary of Sumeru, by following the claims of [the astronomer] Varaha, etc.

In regard to the *Moonlight Commentary*'s statement about the *Revelation of the Hidden Intention*'s mention of twenty-four transits, some say that since, after two transits move uninterruptedly in one nostril, [the energy] transits to another nostril, in one day there are twelve transits in the nostril, just as in the external year there are twelve transits of the sun. As for the explanation in the *Two-Part [Hevajra Tantra]* about sixteen transits, the sixteen petals of the throat are intended.

Others say, after one and a half transits of the twenty-four have moved in one nostril, [the energy] transits into another nostril and another two and a half move there. Thus in one day there are sixteen transits, having left four of the sixteen petals in the third row out of the navel lotus, that leaves twelve transits; so [the count of the internal transits] should agree with the external [transit count].

---

to work out—very subtle energy movement from that central channel!

77. The idea that much of the *Time Machine Tantra* inner technology is interpretable meaning level, in order to attract the outsider yogi/nīs, may be a distinctive interpretation of Tsong Khapa's tradition, also turning up in Khedrup Jey's extensive *Time Machine* commentaries.

Otherwise, all outer and inner things need not be placed in agreement. In both sides, one and a half transits in inner and outer [dimensions] [119b] constitute half a session. The *Vajra Rosary* and so forth explain that there is no contradiction with having each [outer] transit constitute a half a session of the inner. Every two transits of the twenty-four transits, according to the system that takes each transit [as movement in] the nostril, makes an explanation of sixteen transits, intending the [sixteen] throat petals and not the nostril transits. And by the system that takes one and a half transits of the twenty-four as a single nostril transit, the explanation of the twelve transits intends the twelve petals of the navel chakra, thus harmonizing with the outer transits, and not intending the nostril transits. There is also the *Vajra Rosary* etc. explanation of each transit as a half session and the *Revelation of the Hidden Intention* explanation of one and a half transits as a half session—all these inconsistent explanations are accepted as noncontradictory.

The *Sheaf of Instructions* statement of twenty-four is explained as twenty-four half sessions. These must be explained as twenty-four [referring to] each transit of the four goddess energies. Munishrī interprets the *Revelation of the Hidden Intention* explanation of the twenty-four nine hundreds in a single day in terms of the nostril transits and the statement of twenty-four transits as interpretable in meaning, and the *Hevajra* explanation of sixteen transits as definitive in meaning. Further he accepts them as nostril transits, saying "because of agreeing with the statement 'as without, so within.'"

In that regard, the *Esoteric Community Root Tantra* and its other explanatory tantras do not explain clearly the duration of the four elemental sphere energies moving from the nostrils, and in the present translation of the *Revelation of the Hidden Intention*, each of the four energies, white, yellow, red, and black, has four [120a] 225 [breath] goddess sets, totalling nine hundred, which by twenty-four sets moving in a single day gives 21,600 movements of energies. To reconcile that with the *Vajra Rosary*, the four energies are root energies, and, taking each as a principal one by including the other three within it, each moves nine hundred times. The *Vajra Rosary* explains that when the four energies move, they abide in each half session. About the meaning of that, Tibetan scholars explained it as the duration of each set of nine hundred energies moving. And Munishrī also explained a *Community* system half session in the same way.

The *Illuminating Lamp* fifteenth chapter explains that in the time of each set of nine hundred energies moving, the vajra recitation accomplishes the activities of peace and so forth. The *Illuminating Lamp* fourteenth chapter, with a quote said to be from the *Explanatory Tantra*, elucidates the meaning of the statement that "the four element energies last each a half session," by explaining that the four elemental sphere energies emerge from the four centers such as the secret center, and explaining that the period of maintaining a half session is a performing of the four activities such as peace. Thus, the period of each half session is a set of nine hundred; and the four element energies, when moving in the nostril, seem to measure each in their period of duration as a half session. Thus, it does not intend to explain that nine hundred in the former half session and another continuous nine hundred give eighteen hundred motions and [only then] transit to another nostril. Nor is it interpreting there to be twelve transits in left and right nostrils in the energies of one day, due to the fact that the two elemental energies [120b] that move evenly in both nostrils do not transit the nostrils.

The *Illuminating Lamp*'s mention of the *Explanatory Tantra* refers to the *Revelation of the Hidden Intention*, according to Shraddhā and Kalden Drakpa, and though it is not in the present translation, it is included in appendices, and so it is not inconsistent.

Well, but from the *Liberation Drop*, it is stated that:

> Each set connected to [one of] the four seals
> Comprises two hundred twenty-five,
> Multiplied by four makes nine hundred;
> And the twenty-four transits,
> Thus make twenty-one thousand
> Six hundred [breaths] . . .

—how does this reconcile with the above statement of the twenty-four transits?

Both here and in the *Personal Instruction*, two elemental spheres in each nostril and two spheres of equal movement are explained. So in regard to the two elemental spheres, there are twelve transits in right and left nostrils, and in regard to the other two elemental spheres, though there are no transits in the nostrils, the treatise's meaning is interpreted as referring to twelve transit events of the elemental spheres. So also the *Liberation Drop*

Commentary [by Vitapāda] does not state that the treatise's intention is to explain there being twenty-four transits in each of the right and left nostrils.

Here one might imagine: "Well, if one allows the *Revelation of the Hidden Intention* system to be like that, the *Vajra Rosary* measure of the half session is not the same. To quote:

> By the division of the session boundaries,
> Then one will recite in conforming order;
> In each session boundary, the vitalizing energies
> Are discerned as controlled;
> And by count of two thousand seven hundred
> They should be fully incorporated
> [In vajra recitation practice].

And also, it is [not consistent] because it explains that there are 2,700 energies in each session measure, and so there should be 1,350 in each half session. To quote again: [121a]

> Those, through the application of enthusiasm,
> Gradually become eight sessions . . .

And therefore [it is inconsistent] because it states there to be sixteen half sessions in a day."

[In response to this:] As for the meaning of the first quote, the *Vajra Rosary* here is talking about—having taken out six months for vajra recitation after completing the creation stage—such an above-stated measure of constructs about the energies during the second month of the conforming order recitation, since the yogi/nī through purposeful control effort has made the energies of a single day into eight equal segments. This is what is meant, and the statement does not apply to the movement of energies in others not [having reached that stage]. As for the meaning of the second quote, it indicates [the energies] radiating from the three channels, *rasanā*, *lalanā*, and *dhūti*, and becoming the eight channels of the session at the heart center, and does not indicate the measure of the duration of [ordinary] energy movements. And, as for the statement that the energies of the four spheres moving in the nostrils abide each for half a time-period, it indicates the duration of energies moving naturally in the occasions of basic time and path-time. Thus, a "half session" in that context and the "half period" of the 2,700, though nominally similar, are different in meaning.

Therefore, one should reconcile the "half sessions" of the two explanatory tantras and the explanation of the *Nondual Triumph [Tantra]*, which is quoted in the *Five Stages*. In this regard, Lakshmī, Kalden Drakpa, and Alaṁka[kalasha] [all] said [words to the effect] that there arise eight sessions in the measure of the process of energies, sixteen half sessions, with eight hours in each session, and a half hour of clear light free of inhalation and exhalation in each session. Thus in one day, four hours of clear transparence arise, and if one holds the mind on the drop during [121b] that time, the mental one-pointedness with the nature of clear light is produced.[78]

While other tantras of the *Community* literature do not explain the number of hours in a day, the *Vajra Rosary* states there to be sixty hours in a day,[79] which does not mean that there are sixty-four hours in this system. In that tantra "period" (*dbyu gu*) and "hour" (*chu tshod*) have similar meanings, and, as other tantras talk of sixty-four "periods," if one tries to avoid contradictions between sixty and sixty-four, [one needs to know] the meaning of others' explanations of thirty-two hours and sixty-four periods. This tantra differs in meaning from the above explanations of both the *Vajra Angel* and the *Four Seats*, which [therefore] must be abandoned. Thus, as the time of half an hour free of respiration in the beginning of the session of movement in the nostril is refuted by not being perceived when it could be perceived, [such explanations] are not good. And if one thinks it refers to the *Time Machine* explanation of four empty petals in the sixty-four navel chakra petals, that is not the meaning.

The *Vow Arisal* says:

> The energies of the sixteen
> Transit factors happening in a day,
> Always in [one or both of the] nostrils,
> Truly move a half session each.[80]

78. This count would give sixty-four "hours" (Tib. *chu tshod*) in a day, therefore the "hour" here is 22.5 of Western "minutes" long.

79. In this case the "hours" of a sixty-"hour" day would be twenty-four minutes long.

80. In this section on the energy-control practices, Tsong Khapa frequently quotes the *Vow Arisal Tantra*, parts of which have been beautifully translated from the Sanskrit by

Thus it sets up sixteen half sessions per day and explains the sixteen transits taught as moving in the nostrils in each half session; but this is not to be interpreted as the sixteen transit-arrivals in the left and right nostrils. For, in that tantra, it explains the fire and wind sphere [energies] as each moving [respectively] in the right and left nostril, and the earth and water sphere [energies] as moving equally in both nostrils. Thus one should recognize eight transit-arrivals in each of the right and left nostrils and [122a] eight elemental sphere transits, which do not transit the nostrils.

[Shrīdhara's] *Black Yamāri [Tantra]* commentary, *Orgasmic Luminance*], explains as "eight day-times" and "eight night-times" the transits of energies from one nostril to another, [the energies] having stayed in either nostril for half a session; and Damtsig Dorjey and Munishrī also accept that.

[**VI.B.3.b.ii.c′3′d′i′B″3″e″ii″** – The way it transits from one petal and elemental sphere to another]

The *Vow Arisal* states:

> The channels are thirty-two,
> And four quarters of one session
> Are [together] called "root" and "hour."
> The measure of "day" and "night" periods
> Becomes sixty-four.
> Half a "root," half an "hour," a "period"—
> These are remembered as an eighth of a session.[81]

Astronomers make an eighth of a day the measure of a "session" [three Western hours]. So [a day has] an eight-session duration, and, taking half

---

S. Tsuda, whose Sanskrit edition is cited in the footnotes to the Tibetan text edition. His English translation often differs from mine, as the Sanskrit and the Tibetan have some differences beyond English styles and terminologies. When those differences occur, I have followed the Tibetan Tsong Khapa is citing, as his commentary depends on that version. In some cases, Tsuda's interpretations have been of great help in understanding the quite complex energy-control systems in both texts.

81. Tib. *Thun*, "session," seems to be 3 Western hours. "Transit" (Tib. *'pho ba*) is 90 minutes. An "hour" (*chu tshod*) is 45 minutes, and a "period" (*dbyu gu*) is 22.5 minutes.

a session as one "transit" [ninety minutes], [there are] sixteen transits, and, taking one quarter of a session as an "hour" [forty-five minutes (*chu tshod*)], thirty-two hours, and, taking a half an hour as a "period" [twenty-two and a half minutes], sixty-four periods. In the *Vow Arisal Commentary*, using the Bhasati[82] mathematics, [the author] puts a hundred periods in a day, and he explains that the various astronomers make the length of the period according to their own wish; and the same goes for the hours. Accordingly, in the *Tantra*, its states that for some, a day has thirty-two hours, for some sixty, and for others in each hour there is one period.

As for internal [time], as for [the claim that] 2,700 transit-arrivals move in each channel petal of the heart center as the energies of each session; and that each transit in one channel petal [122b] of the throat center consists of the 1,350 energies of each half session; and that the 675 energies of a quarter of each heart center channel-petal moving in a single channel-petal of the crown as each hour; and the 337.5 energies of an eighth of each heart-center channel as the energies of each period move in each channel petal of the navel center; and that the energies of the channel petals of each center, navel, crown, throat, and heart, each is the double of the previous, and falls each to the latter—such is the *Vow Arisal Commentary*'s explanation of the import of both the *Hevajra* and the *Vow Arisal*—with the *Sheaf of Instructions* also explaining that to be the meaning of the *Hevajra*.

As for through which of the three main channels the energies of the four [element] mandalas move, the *Vajra Rosary* states:

> Vitalizing and evacuative are made to move;
> Those two are clearly stated as the energies
> Endowed with conceptualization.
> Two essences of body and speech,
> The *lalanā* and the *rasanā*—
> *Avadhūti* the supreme channel,
> In the center of those two, supreme of supreme.
> The energy which is devoid of conceptualizing,
> Always moving, all-pervading.

82. An Indian astronomical system, the history of which I have not yet found.

Thus, vitalizing and evacuative are said to be concept-generating energies, and the energy entered in the *dhūti* channel is said to be conceptuality negating energy:

> The two conceptualizing energies
> Thus having been cut off, then proceeds
> The great energy without conceptualizing,
> Having cut off body and speech vajras.

Thus, in cutting those two energies, one cuts the body and speech vajras, it is said, thus the "two essences of body and speech" are the vitalizing and evacuative. Further, they are shown to move in the two channels. Thus this is the system wherein the vitalizing and evacuative are forced into the *dhūti* channel by the power of yoga, and wherein they do not move in the *dhūti* channel [123a] except at the time of death. Again from the same text [the *Vajra Rosary*]:

> The two conceptualizing energies
> Emerge from the nostrils
> Truly the sun and moon
> Are made to move from within the hidden.

This is also stated, so those two move from within the sun *rasanā* and moon *lalanā*; so in this system, it cannot be presented that one can make them move in the central channel by equalizing their moving.

Although there is no clear explanation about the metabolic and the ascending energies, those two also move from the two *rasanā* and *lalanā*. Thus, in moving from the *rasanā* and *lalanā*, there are both alternating and simultaneous movings. When the fire [ascending] and metabolic move as the principal energy, they move from *rasanā* and *lalanā* one by one, and when the vitalizing and evacuative energies move as principal energies, they move simultaneously from the *rasanā* and *lalanā* together. When [any of them] move as subordinate energies, there is no definite [pattern].

As for the transiting from one energy elemental sphere to another: in terms of the major elemental spheres, there are six transit-arrivals in each in a day, making twenty-four, and in terms of the minor [elemental spheres], in each of the previous six transit-arrivals there are four [minor transit-arrivals], making ninety-six; such is the system of the *Community Explanatory Tantras.* As for the system of the *Vow Arisal,* one must take it that there are sixty-four minor elemental sphere [transits], and so the commentary's explanation of there being ninety-six is out of context. The *Revelation of the Hidden Intention* states that the transit measure of each of the energies of the four elemental spheres is nine hundred alike. The *Vajra Rosary,* the *Vow Arisal,* and the *Personal Instruction* explain that two elemental spheres are in each nostril and two in both nostrils equally, hence, [123b] the energies of the two movings in each nostril alone are able [to account] for half a day's energies, and the energies moving in both nostrils equally account for the other half. That being so, as the equal moving from the two nostrils and the individual nostril moving are equal in time, the way of counting each as a nine hundred set of equal moving must be interpreted as indicating one cycle of inhalation and exhalation as one energy together. So one must reflect critically as to whether one must employ a different method of counting when dealing with the energies moving from each nostril individually.

Thus, the equal moving of the two energies of left and right, when their degree of force is similar being short in duration, while equal moving of alternating strength and weakness seems to take longer duration; so both of them are considered as equally moving. As for the way of equal moving in the transit-interval from the right to the left, as the right energy becomes weaker, in the interval when it is not manifest as just that, the moving in the left comes somewhat weakly, and it is held from that; and when its moving [in the left] becomes a little stronger, the right becomes proportionately weaker, with finally even the subtlest moving ceasing, at exactly which time the left begins to move alone. The transit from the left to the right is just similar. So though it is a case of the energy newly moving actually in a nostril where previously there was no energy moving, there are both transited and untransited energies that were actually previously moving.

If one wonders here, "Well, but then, according to the *Community Explanatory Tantras,* in half the energies of a day there are twelve nostril transits and, according to the *Vow Arisal* there are eight, and according to the *Time Machine,* not counting 675 [energies], there are twelve [124a] nostril transits in the energies of a day taken as a whole—so how do we understand whether or not there are contradictions?"

Here one should take these [different countings] as noncontradictory, since stated in terms of [the needs of particular] disciples, by setting apart the explanations of that *Community* system elucidated by the *Personal Instruction of Mañjushrī* and by the noble father and sons, and by seeing how the *Vow Arisal* explanation seems to be the import of that tantra; so the meanings of those references are not properly explained as the same. And as it seems difficult to make a difference saying that "in regard to the energies moving in the nostrils, this system is established by experience and that other is not so established."

Granted that other such [apparent] inconsistencies indeed seem to be there in the literature on the channels and energies etc., if you know what is necessary to determine their meanings, when you penetrate the vital points in the body, you concentrate the evolutionary energies in the *dhūti* channel and dissolve them, which generates great bliss that is united with voidness. In all those systems, it seems that this is taken as the essence of the path; and so those [differences of numbering etc.] do not become a condition for disagreement about the vital points of the path.

Though Kalden Drakpa explains that the fire energy of the right nostril moves at the beginning of a day, the *Vow Arisal* states that:

> From the first day of the white fortnight
> Beginning to move in the moon [channel]
> For three days in a half session.
> Then total moving in the sun [channel]
> [For three days] as long as energy [lasts, and so on]
> Until the fifteenth day of the white fortnight.
> From the first day of the dark fortnight
> Beginning, one says one moves in the morning
> For three days in the sun [channel],
> [And so on] until the fifteenth [dark] day . . .

But this also is not contradictory. [124b] "Moving in the moon" means from the left nostril, and "moving in the sun" means from the right nostril. "Day" means from sunrise to sunset, and "night" means from sunset to sunrise. The *Sheaf of Instructions* says that "beginning moving" means predawn twilight.

That energy sign of the pattern of first moving of the waning period is six days, and one [waning] phase is a fortnight, and two phases is two fortnights, and three phases is three fortnights. If the order is reversed, some problems arise, concerning which the same text [*Vow Arisal*] states:

> In one, two, three, four, five,
> And six days, reversing, from that,
> If the energy moves wrongly,
> Then a great argument will happen.
> From one fortnight of moving wrongly,
> Great illness originates.
> From two fortnights of moving wrongly,
> Beloved relatives will decline.
> Three fortnights of moving wrongly,
> One will die in six months.

Although in regard to death signs, there is much else stated, there is no error in explaining as a death sign the mistaking of the energy signs of balancing elements; if that happens, it is said one should perform inner and outer death-averting rituals.

As for the way in which benefits and problems arise during the moving of whichever of the major element energies, the *Vow Arisal* states:

> By the earth [energies], there is dominion,
> By water [energies], aims are truly fulfilled.
> When the fire energies move,
> There is thirst, hunger, poison, suffering, illness,
> And all activities become ruined.
> So said supreme Vajradhara.
> By energies, arguments, fatigue, confusion,
> Loss of wealth, and addictions overwhelm.
> Earth [energies] bring wealth and grain and so on,
> Profit is gained and collected.
> By water energies moving, [125a]
> Desired accomplishments are all performed,
> So the supreme application of that
> Is what Vajrasattva mainly declared.

The same text [*Vow Arisal*] also mentions what should be done during energies moving from the nostrils individually and equally from both:

[Energies] with wisdom nature are highly praised
To conquer poison etc. for abundance,
And to create glory and good fortune.
Always the power of glorious compassion [energies]
Wins battles, plays games, and feasts;
For cutting and breathing,
And in work of cooking and making,
The compassionate [energies] are highly praised.
Further, those of both natures, the Vajra-holders,
Should be known as doubtful,
Indeterminate as virtuous or nonvirtuous,
By the knowing of energies, this is an example.

"With wisdom nature" means those moving from the left nostril alone, and "having compassion nature" means those moving from the right nostril alone; "having both natures" means the time when energies move from both nostrils equally. In the commentary the import of the above is explained to be that the energy a yogi/nī should practice by performing the activities of growth during the earth energy moving, of peace during the water energy [moving], of terror during the fire energy [moving], and of expelling fierce qualities and so forth during the wind energy [moving].

The master Shrīdhara explained [in his *Orgasmic Luminance*] that one should act according to the statement about virtuous and nonvirtuous actions, going and coming, and so on:

In earth and water energies, virtuous actions,
In fire and wind energies, the dark side;
One should truly know the moon,
In sharp light it is medium.
If one does nonvirtue in the day [breath],
It definitely brings death;
That same, if it happens in the moon-[time],
It does not bring extreme suffering.

Here, "moon" means the time of the moving of the energy of the left. [125b] "Sharp light" means the time of the energy of the right, the energy of the sun. At that time, if one does terrific activities, it brings death—that is, the activities are accomplished. In short, gentle activities of peace and so on, if done during earth and water energies, are good; and they are unhappy if done at the time of fire and wind energies. They are good if done during left nostril energies; and medium if done during right nostril energies. And when one performs terrific activities, it is the reverse of the above.

The four energies are explained by Shrīdhara as the minor elements. Further, if your energies are moving through the *āli* [vowels], the left, and the requester's are moving from the *kāli* [consonants], the right, when you are requested [about something], or vice versa, the aim is not accomplished. If both [energy circulations] are corresponding, that aim is accomplished. And if one is requested when both are moving from both, then whether the goal is achieved or not is indeterminate. And if your own energy is being inhaled within and another makes a request and one begins the activity, it is good; and bad if it happens while one exhales; and indeterminate if it happens when one is holding the breath within. From the same text [*Vow Arisal*]:

> When the savior moves in the *āli*,
> If someone abiding in *kāli* should ask;
> Or if [the savior] moves in *kāli*, and one abides in *āli*—
> The desired goal will be lost.
> From where the savior is moving,
> If someone who asks abides there,
> Their purpose will be truly achieved.
> From abiding in both, it is doubtful.

And again:

> [For] the requester or oneself, whichever,
> The truth body is all virtue,
> The beatific body is indeterminate,
> The emanation manifests conflict.[83]

83. The Tibetan differs from Tsuda's Sanskrit text, but accords better with Tsong Khapa's commentary.

"Truth body" means inhalation, "beatific body" means holding within, and "emanation body" means exhalation.[84] [126a]

[**VI.B.3.b.ii.c'3'd'i'B''3''f''** – What sort of functions the energies perform]

If one knows the first [of the two functions] mentioned in the *Integrated Practices*, as to how all mundane and transcendent actions can be completed by mixing the subtle element energy and consciousness-luminance, one understands what is common and uncommon with other vehicles in [describing] the process of entering the life cycle. And if one understands the second [activity], relying on already understanding the [first], one comes to understand well what is common and uncommon [with other vehicles in describing] the process of departing from the life cycle.

Well then, one might wonder how the energy accomplishes all mundane life-cycle functions.

According to the *Vajra Rosary*:

> As the moon is gripped by the planet [Rāhu],
> So the energies gradually decay.
> Previously from full to full, its nature is to dissolve,
> [So the energies] give forth, are held,
> Are made to move with ease or difficulty.

Thus at the time of death, as the moon becomes invisible when seized by a planet, so the previous energies dissolve serially into the later ones, "giving forth, being held" states that the process continues until it reaches the vitalizing energy. This has the same meaning as the *Integrated Practices* statements:

> Again, those [coarse energies] attaining the indestructible, become nonsubstantial . . .

84. A tremendously focused mindfulness is involved in this vajra recitation practice. One's mindfulness of the breath goes way beyond merely being mindful that one is breathing, moving into just how one is breathing, from which nostril, which part of which nostril, which involves being aware of the exact time of day and month and so on.

and:

> Thus all having been done on the occasion of abiding in the body; finally, [the energies] enter the indestructible.

That is the energies, in the conclusion of death, dwelling in the indestructible [drop] of the heart center, enter into the clear light transparence of nonsubstantiality. Further, when earth, water, fire, and wind dissolve, the former into the latter, at the end of the movement of wind becoming progressively slighter, when the [subtle] energy that mobilizes the natural instincts dissolves into the first consciousness-luminance, **[126b]** the natural instinctual thoughts are eliminated and the first void arises. Then the second void, the third void, and the fourth void clear light transparence arise; again they arise by the power of each having progressively less movement of energy. Then, when the energy increases more greatly than the clear transparence [super-subtle] energy, imminence emerges, and then radiance and luminance again emerge each by force of the energy progressively increasing. And when the energy moves more coarsely, greater than the luminance energy, the instincts are produced.

Such being the case, the process of birth and death is caused by energy, and the arisal of the four voids is during the period between the dissolving and arising of the energy mobilizing the natural instincts. Thus, the natural instincts are derived from the increased movement of the three luminances, and thus it is said that the three luminances are the root of the natural instincts of all beings. As the *Vajra Rosary* states:

> Who hears here of the three consciousnesses
> Having the nature of the three luminances,
> This is the natural root of the entire realm
> Of all living beings.

And:

> This is the great realm of energy,
> The mount of the three consciousnesses.
> Thereby the natural always
> Proceeds accordingly.

And the *Five Stages* states:

When endowed with luminance,
One moves mounted on the energy,
Then all those instincts arise completely.
Wherever the energy abides,
There it bears along the natural instincts.

The natural instincts [127a] create the addictions; thereby evolutionary action is accumulated and one is born into the life cycle. As the *Vajra Rosary* states:

Just as there is nothing left when burned by fire,
Without moving, it dissolves and departs.
Again when the vitalizing energy arises
There are the various evolutionary energies.
Together with that is consciousness
And again one lives in the three worlds.
Therefrom is evolution and likewise birth,
Therefrom instincts such as lust,
And therefrom again death and birth.
Thus, it is like a revolving wheel.[85]

Such statements are not to disagree with the statements that the self-habit is the root of the life cycle, by teaching that the energy is the root of the life cycle. The *Integrated Practices* also makes the same statement. Depending on the self-habit and the property-habit, one performs virtue and vice, and one thus enters into the life cycle revolving between heavenly and hellish realms; this process is established by three sutras such as the *Eight Thousand*. And Nāgārjuna declared [the following] to clearly show their meaning:

If all this is naturally void and unproduced
How could one circle throughout [the realm of] evolution,

85. Except for the introduction of the energy role in the process, this closely resembles Nāgārjuna's description of the life-cycle process in his *Jewel Rosary*.

Here where pleasure and pain, and so on, function?
At once, on the claim of self,
One is stuck with the taints of lust and so on,
One becomes other-controlled—
And that fool is afflicted with suffering.
All of these are merely mind,
Truly arising in the form of illusion;
Wherein by virtuous and vicious evolutionary action,
One is born in heaven and hell.

This is the system common to the sutra and tantra texts. [127b] Therefore, the statement that one is born in the life cycle through the energy should be understood as referring to the auxiliary condition of being born in the life cycle through the afflictions of the self-habit and so on.

That is the general function of the energies, but as for their individual functions:

The function of the vitalizing energy is stated in the *Vajra Rosary*:

From the continuum of the door of sense,
Vitalizing energy and exertion move,
And as it totally moves at all times,
It is explained to be "vitalizing energy."

In regard to this, there are many different translations in other translations of the *Vajra Rosary* and in [other texts] where it is cited. It means that the continuous activities of energies entering and emerging from the doors of the five senses are mainly energized by the power of that [vitalizing energy] and are nourished by this, which is the meaning of the "vitalizing energy" [function]. The meaning of "exertion" being their long-term expansion, it has the function of long-term expansion; that it has these two functions is the interpretation of Abhayākara. The *Elixir Secret* explains it[s function] as making the energies go out and in the door[s] of the sense[s].

The function of the evacuative energy [stated in the *Vajra Rosary*]:

Of vitalizing energy, energies, excretions,
As well as semen and so on,
All these down-drives as evacuative [energy],
The yogi/nī should recognize.

So it is stated that the driving in the downward direction of semen and so on is the function of the evacuative energy. Other translations have "urine" in place of "vitalizing energy," which is better. And the drawing down of the energies brings them specially to the two doors of the genital region and also to the navel as explained above.

The function of the metabolic energy [stated in the *Vajra Rosary*]:

> Laughing, eating, licking,
> Drinking [128a] and sucking,
> Whatever always [makes it] equalized
> Is called "metabolic energy."

The Chag translation explains its function as making food and drink homogeneous, and the verse quoted in the *Sheaf of Instructions* reads:

> It is homogenizing as it draws into equality
> Food and drink and so on at the navel region.

This means that, as the *Elixir Secret* explains:

> . . . food and drink and so on are simultaneously digested

—[this energy] causes food and drink enjoyed to be digested into equal taste at the navel.

The function of the ascending energy [stated in the *Vajra Rosary*]:

> Going upward, gathering,
> Eating food and tasting and so on,
> Knowingly joining [things] together—
> Recognize as the functions of the ascending [energy].

There are also translations "knowing and joining together," and "joining together with knowing." This means that, agreeing with the *Elixir Secret*'s explanation that the previous [energies] leave [this one to] recognize food with the tongue consciousness, and the explanation of the *Sheaf of Instructions* that this one causes the ten energies to descend. Although the *Elixir Secret* explains this energy as radiating the evolutionary energies at the sense doors, "ascending" is a going upward of the energy, and the text mentions "gathering" to indicate it is not only that rising function, indicating that it also functions to cause entrance within. By knowing the way of enjoying food, it joins together with the tongue, which shows its function of chewing and so on.

The function of the pervading energy [stated in the *Vajra Rosary*]:

> Pervading and maintaining,
> Going and coming back and so on,
> As it pervades all the joints,
> It is said to be [128b] "pervading."

In the first line the Chag translation says "nourishing."

As for the individual functions of the branch energies, it is to accompany the five senses holding their objects, as above explained.

Having explained the way of executing functions in common between ordinary persons and yogi/nīs, now I should explain particularly how the energies function for the yogi/nīs. Having practiced vajra recitation of the four root energies, one executes the functions of achieving the four ritual activities such as pacification and so forth, causing the achievement of the ordinary accomplishments. Again, practicing vajra recitation of those four energies, one develops the four voids and creates the magic body with the subtle energy thereby causing achievement of the supreme accomplishment. Practicing the vajra recitation with the five branch energies, one is caused to achieve the five clairvoyances such as the divine eye, and one is caused to have all objective perception become the blaze of great bliss. Practicing vajra recitation with the pervasive energy one achieves the supreme in the between, causing the experience of clear light transparence, according to the word of the ancient sages.

[VI.B.3.b.ii.c′3′d′i′B′′3′′g′′ – Teaching how to know the vital key of practice relying on that]

Here one might ask, "Thus, relying on the explanation of the natures and functions of the energies, how does one understand the keys of penetrating the vital points in the body?"

In the *Vajra Rosary*, after the statement that one wanders in the life cycle by the deceptive force of the instincts and the instinctual natures created by the energies—the vehicle of consciousness having mingled with the consciousness's instincts and put it in touch with objects—there being no life cycle other than that, Vajradhara states:

> Thus, in order to abandon the life cycle,
> Illuminate the state [129a] of discerning the drop
> And strive to meditate [on it]—
> Ignorance will not be known by other [means];
> Thus opening up that central knot,
> You will gain the [supreme] accomplishment.

Thus it teaches that to purify the instincts for wandering in the life cycle, you "discern the drop that causes the opening of the ignorance knot that binds the heart center *dhūti* channel," which means you should meditate the vajra recitation.[86] As explained above, at the boundary between the moving and unmoving of the instinctual notions, you recognize the arisal of the four voids, and you understand the need to meditate a vitalizing energy control such as the vajra recitation in order to generate such a sequence in your life-process; and this is the unexcelled knowledge of the key of spiritual practice that relies on the explanation of energy.

Further, having well negated the object held by the two self-habits, having sought the wisdom realizing selflessness decisively certain of the import of selflessness, then you meditate on that and radically overcome the two obscurations—all the supreme experts in all that [process] agree [on this point]. However, when meditating profound voidness, already having well determined it thus by learning and reflection, other vehicles and the lower tantra types do not teach the need for the distinctive subjectivity of great bliss as taught in this [unexcelled] vehicle; and thus it is the distinctive characteristic of this unexcelled vehicle.

Whatever the special art you use to develop the four joys and four voids, it is through the door of the great bliss that it is developed. And since that

86. Here we have a very clear description of the connection, through the concept of the subtle body, with energies, channels and their knots, and awareness drops, of the process of critical wisdom unraveling the confusions of the self-habits and identity-habits as parallel to the process of energy and channel-structure meditation unraveling the sixfold heart center knot, called the "knot of ignorance." You could say this is the mind-body key point of unexcelled yoga tantra.

cannot be completely produced until the energies that drive the instinctual notions are blocked, you should strive in the art of blocking the energy.

Therefore, [129b] as it is stated that the mind stays steady by using energy meditation to eradicate the energy's readiness to move, if you entertain such ideas as "even without meditating the energies if one knows how to cultivate the thoughtless mind-setting free of depression and agitation, and by that practice itself one discovers firm samadhi, what's the use of energy meditation?" or "if one stabilizes the mind abiding thoughtless, that itself is the insertion of the energies into the *dhūti* channel, so one need not meditate anything else!"—then you must explain the following. In general, the mere stable abiding of the mind in thoughtlessness is shared in common with outsiders and insiders and individual and universal vehicles, and in particular the immaculate samadhi abiding thought-free on the import of voidness is shared in common with the vehicle of the transcendences; so for them, how can the energy yoga involving meditating on the penetration of the vital points in the body be necessary? However, even though one has attained such a samadhi, that does not mean that one has attained the great bliss by power of the energies dissolving in the *dhūti* channel. Therefore, the "stable mind" meant in the expression "stable mind attained by blocking the movement of the evolutionary energies" is the mind of orgasmic bliss. As Saraha declared [in an *Enlightenment Song*]:

> Here, mentality contracted, the energy energizes,
> It moves and lifts and grows quite uncalm.
> When one realizes the orgasmic nature,
> [Only] thereby does one become stable.

To generate that requires the dissolving of the evolutionary energies into the *dhūti* and the blazing of the furor fire; and the minds of those [yogi/nīs], while nominally also being "thoughtless" and "blissful," are definitely different [from those of yogi/nīs in ordinary meditative trances and blisses]. But this has been much explained above.

Once you have decisive insight into the view of voidness, [130a] when you meditate, if you enter into the perfection stage because of the key of needing to meditate by means of that melting bliss, first, there are many doors taught for penetrating the vital points in the body, which is the art of generating great bliss. Therefore you should not persist in thinking that "the perfection stage is not profound with its channel-energy-drop yoga, energy yoga, and so on, and has no meditation on voidness." Thus the stopping of the evolutionary energies by meditating energy yogas is a stopping in general of the ten energies that cause entry and emergence in the doors of senses relying on the two channels, and a stopping in particular of the two main energies, vitalizing and evacuating, from moving in the right and left channels. For those [two main] energies, when not pushed into the *dhūti* channel, rely on the other channels and cause entrance and emergence, and thus drive the eighty instinctual patterns—[all of] which creates an obstacle to the realization of the four voids. To fully generate the universal bliss requires a powerful melting of the enlightenment spirit, which itself requires a powerful blazing of furor, and its special blazing requires the evacuative energy to dissolve into the *dhūti* channel from below. For that you need to stop the entry and emergence of the evacuative energy in the lower door, for which, as explained above, you must perform the procedures of entry and emergence in the upper and lower nostril apertures.

If you understand the previously explained process of entering into the life cycle shared in common with both vehicles, you know the need to eliminate its root, the self-habit, and you come to seek the decisive insight into the view of selflessness. If you know the uncommon process of entry to the life cycle by power of energies, you see the need to stop the evolutionary energies [130b] that drive the instinctual notional patterns, and you come to develop a decisive insight into the instruction of penetrating the vital points in the body, the art of stopping that [evolutionary energy]. You then come to practice, taking as the essence the path that joins bliss and void, ascertaining the import of voidness with the great bliss developed from that art [of stopping the evolutionary energies]. In this way you do not miss the essential key of the [mentor's] personal instruction. And if you do otherwise, you do not distinguish the subtle differences between great bliss and other blisses, you do not discover the ultimate view by distinguishing the coarse and subtle voids, and though you praise the bliss-void-union, it is no more than delighting in the mere name. And that essence explained in both [unexcelled yoga] tantric categories is chiefly the distinctive means to attain the truth body. The distinctive means of attaining the material body is explained [especially] clearly in this [father tantra] system, as has been explained above and will be further explained below.

[**VI.B.3.b.ii.c′3′d′i′B″4″** – Teaching the ultimate reality of mantra]

The fourth has five parts, explaining: [a″] Collecting the mantra; [b″] The symbol of mantra; [c″] The import of mantra; [d″] The ultimate of mantra; and [e″] Short *A*, root of mantra.

[**VI.B.3.b.ii.c′3′d′i′B″4″a″** – Collecting the mantra]

In regard to the basis from which the mantras are collected, implicit in "collecting the mantras," the *Triple Rite* mentions:

> From the city of *āli* and *kāli*,
> The root of the emergence of mantra . . .

[These *āli* and *kāli* are] the sixteen vowels and the thirty-four consonants. As for the fact that the *Integrated Practices* mentions only thirty-three, eliminating the letter KṢHA, it intends that it is not other than the KA and SHA [already enumerated]. As for the mantras collected from there, these are all those stated in the tantras such as essence-, close-essence-, and rosary-mantras [of various deities] and so forth. [131a] As for the way they are collected, the tantras state numerous ways of collecting mantras.

As for the reality of all such mantras, it is the three letters OṀ ĀḤ HŪṀ. The *Integrated Practices* states:

> The mantras for snakes and so on actually arise from vowels and consonants. Their reality is the three letters emerging from the indestructible. Therefore all mantras, of male, female, and neuter nature, are activated in the three letters according to the personal instruction attained. Therefore, the three letters are the lord of mantras.

The sentence from "Therefore [all mantras . . .]" gives the reason why the three letters are the lord[s] of all mantras. The *Root Tantra* also declares:

> That same collected essence of all mantras is celebrated as the secret of body, speech, and mind . . .

—that is, the three syllables are the essence or chief of all mantras.

Here if one wonders how the three, "female" and so on, are applied to the base of collection, vowels and consonants, to the mantras, for snakes, and so on, and to the three letters, the Chag translation of the *Integrated Practices* translates [the above phrase as]:

> All mantras with nature female, male, and neuter;

the two old translations of the *Illuminating Lamp* sixth chapter translate:

> Mantras come from *āli* and *kāli* are actually for snake [prevention] and so on, and by being female, male, and neuter they become the base of the three letters; hence mantras are the three syllables; [131b]

with the two new translations translating:

> . . . being concentrated in the three syllables.

Also from the *Illuminating Lamp* tenth chapter, there is an explanation of the three mantras, male and so on, being collectible into the three syllables, which takes the collected mantras as the three.

The way of interpreting mantras as male, female, and neuter and the way to collect them into the three syllables was mentioned "according to the personal instruction attained." Aside from that, they are not clearly explained in the treatises of the five father and sons, and it does not seem that other explanations can afford confidence of mind. As for our own interpretation, mantras are classed as threefold when they pertain to a male deity, a female deity, or used for both, and since all mantra deities taught are collected in the three vajras, all mantras are collected into the three letters. Thus the three letters are the essence of all mantras. The essence of all body vajra clan deities being the letter OṀ, the OṀ letter is the chief of all mantras of that clan. And the other two [speech and mind] should be understood in the same way.

If one interprets according to the basis of collection, one should do this according to the *Vajra Essence Ornament Tantra* statement that the twelve *ālis* are female, the KA, CHA, ṬA, TA, and PA groups are male, and the four [semi-vowels] *Ṛ* and *Ḷ*, [each short and long,] are neuter. As for the three letters, it is obvious that OṀ is male, ĀḤ is female, and HŪṀ must be neuter.

Such scholars as Kalden Drakpa claim that the vowels and consonants are collected into the first letters of the eight groups, A, KA, CHA, ṬA, TA, PA, YA, SHA, and those eight into A, KA, YA, SHA, and those four into A, KA, YA, and those three again are transformed into female ĀḤ, male HŪṀ, [132a] and neuter OṀ. Thus there are measureless ways to collect mantras from the mantra base, but in this context they are collected into OṀ ĀḤ HŪṀ, and each of those comes from three syllables along with the indestructible, and so to collect all mantras into the three syllables is to concentrate mantras.

As for the need to show all mantras as concentrating in the three syllables, it is to make it understood that the ability to attain accomplishments of all other mantras exists in the three syllables, and so theirs is the ultimate recitation of all verbal recitations. For, as both *Root* and commentary of the *[Esoteric Community]* tenth chapter state, the creation stage practitioner, if s/he does not attain the powers after incorporating the experiences of the three conducts, s/he can command the heart essence of all deities by the three-letter recitation mantras. And [it is also the case,] since, as will be explained, the creation-stage practitioner becomes able to achieve all four ritual activities from the door of this [three-syllable recitation].

Such being the case, when [the three mantras] are recited, connecting the definitive meaning three-letter recitation indivisibly with the three energies, that is the vajra recitation. What need to mention that it has the power of all verbal mantra recitations to induce the heart stream of all deities to cause them to bless the practitioner? Thus, not only does vajra recitation have the excellence of collecting energies in the *dhūti* channel through applying energy yoga, but it also generates a distinctive power from the door of reciting mantras. And so you must become certain about the way in which it is unexcelled, different from [132b] other energy yogas.

As for what one should do with such a sort of three syllables, there are two *Integrated Practices* statements. First, concerning the way of performing activities common to the ordinary person and the yogi/nīs: on strength of engaging [vajra recitation] through the process of inhaling, holding, and exhaling those same three syllables, one can maintain [the practice] through making the body abide [just by breathing OṀ ĀḤ HŪṀ] through the day and night. At the time of sexual union, the same three syllables, together with the semen-nature *āli* [vowels] and ovum-nature *kāli* [consonants], face downward and emerge from the secret nostril hole in the form of a seed and cause the creation of a being's body. And the same [three letters] again, combined with vitalizing energy control, going upward, cause the awakening of the sense doors such as eye. When semen and ovum merge with energies and go downward, the three letters are taught intending that you cause the energy to enter and exit from the lower (*dhūti*) tip door and also keep it in its own place. When the vitalizing energy goes upward as well, some part stays within and some goes without, after which it comes again within, hence becoming fit to be counted as the three letters. A letter with the sound of the energy has gotten the name "together with the energy." Having performed all the activities already explained and to be explained below in the context of dwelling in the body, at the end in death, it enters into the indestructible, and once again you rely on [getting another] ordinary body that performs all the activities previously mentioned—and the meaning of this statement has already been explained.

[Second,] for the yogi/nīs in particular, there are two ways to perform activities. The creation-stage person's way to perform [133a] [the practice] is to create the deity body from the true application of the three letters, which here are the three letters having the form of colors and shapes. The same, having placed them in the heart center and so on in the form of letters having color and shape, you perform whispered and vocal verbal recitation, relying on an activity color and facing a direction and so on, and you accomplish activities such as the peaceful; and in this practice there are both audible and visible three syllables. The perfection-stage practitioner's way to perform the practice is to make the effortless vajra recitation come out of the nostrils, and it purifies previous karmic obstructions; as the energy moves in the four elemental spheres through vajra recitation in each half session, you accomplish mainly one of each activity of peace, prosperity, power, and terror, and incidentally [you accomplish] the other three activities—so that you accomplish both main and incidental activities. Both [creation and perfection] yogi/nīs use the three letters while enjoying food and drink to purify the faults of the food through the process of purifying, transforming, and expanding. In these cases also the mantras have sound and form both.

Such is stated in terms of both outer and inner. However, the main thing here is [to realize] the three syllables as the very tones of the energies emerging, entering, and abiding in the heart center indestructible. As the *Integrated Practices* states:

> One should not hesitate to engage with the mantra syllable having the inward nature.

And each of them is also there stated to emerge from the indestructible.

[**VI.B.3.b.ii.c′3′d′i′b″4″b″** – The symbol of mantra]

The symbol of a mantra is the name [133b] of the mantra. There are four kinds of mantras: those that have OṀ at the beginning and SVĀHA at the end, called "snake"; those with OṀ at the beginning and no SVĀHA, called "tail-less"; opposite to that, the "head-less"; and the "collected" kind, which have neither. Then there are many others, the essence mantra, the secondary essence mantra, and so on. Here, it is stated in the *Revelation of the Hidden Intention*:

> The three realities abide with the symbols;
> They have the character of a natural recitation.

Therefore, it is shown that one should understand that, with the symbols, the three realities of the energy—exhaling, inhaling, and abiding—abide from the beginning in the character of a natural recitation. The symbols of the three inner mantras stay the same as those three. The reality of entering is the symbol of OṀ. The other two should be known in the same way. In that [same] tantra, it states [the mantras to be aligned with] the symbols of "quickening, compressing, and going slow." Thus, when collecting the mantra to be recited in vajra recitation, the three letters emerge. When one indicates that named sign, one knows them as the letters that are the tone of the energy, and those two [energy and mantra] are taken to be indivisible. As the *Revelation of the Hidden Intention* says:

> When the mantrī is alone without a seal,
> S/he does not become a person of mantra.

If the mantrī and the seal are not united, you will not accomplish [your aim]. Here, in the *Esoteric Community*, in answer to: "If one does not employ the seal of the hand, how will one achieve just by the mantra alone?" [the *Revelation of the Hidden Intention*] says:

> Having the three—quickness and so on—
> Is explained as achieving the seal.

Here, if one does quick exhalation, compressed inner inhalation, and leisurely holding in, along with counting, then this serves as the seal, binding that [practice]:

> Definitely employing in mantra [practice]
> The quick, [134a] the compressed, and the leisurely
> The master says it with effort
> Close to the ear of the disciple.

Uniting the mantra of three letters with those three [breathings] is using the mantra and the seal of the hand. It explains that one will achieve the great seal. It is shown that the excellences of all of the bonds of the seal are collected in this. These answers are as quoted in [Nāgabodhi's] *[Stage of] Arrangement*.

Again, somebody asks [in the *Revelation of the Hidden Intention*]:

> How can one well express
> Inviting and asking to go?

In answer to this it is stated:

> The continuous practices
> Of quickness, entering, and abiding
> Are inviting and asking to go—
> These truly serve as the seals.

"Bound in the hand gesture" is to invite the deities, to enter is to keep them in the place, and then asking them to go. This is in order to invoke them each to do their own divine activity. That purpose is also achieved by vajra recitation. Thus, by the three recitations of inhaling within and so on, they are invited, requested to stay, and exhorted to go. This achieves the purpose.

[**VI.B.3.b.ii.c′3′d′i′b″4″c″** – The import of mantra]

In general there are many meanings of mantra, but here we must explain the meaning of mantra in the context of the three letters of the vajra recitation. Further, we have already explained how that is understood as the tone of the three letters; but [this meaning] is not that.

Well, what is it? It is the three things, body vajra and so on, of the perfection stage. Here, the *Revelation of the Hidden Intention* states:

> That is the fully transformed form here
> Perceived as a deity.

In the *Integrated Practices*, to explain the statements from this explanatory tantra, [134b] [Āryadeva] explains four [things]; the summary of the mantra, the symbol of the mantra, the meaning of the mantra, and the thatness [reality] of the mantra. This is the same as the four things explained in the tantra: the pronunciation, the visualization, the symbol, and the ultimate reality.

Further, the *Root Tantra* second chapter states that you should create the magic body, which is the indivisible union of the three, body, speech, and mind, in the verse, "The body is like the mind, etc." In answer to the question about how to create the magic body, those two lines show how to create it. Thus, that [magic body] has the actuality of insubstantiality, and is the energy-mind arisen from the clear light transparence indestructible. From the total transformation of that it is visualized as the body of a deity. From the energy-mind it arises as a buddha. That same thing is the magic body of the indivisibility of the three vajras. Thus, there are two magic bodies.

[**VI.B.3.b.ii.c′3′d′i′b″4″d″** – The ultimate of mantra]

[That same *Revelation of the Hidden Intention* states:]

> Unceased, extremely peaceful,
> Beyond permanence and annihilation,
> Not made by the three-times-knower,

> The nature of thought-space-indivisible—
> This only is the ultimate reality,
> Its nature is introspective intuition.

The ultimate reality of things, like space, is not created by buddhas, and thought, or knowledge, becomes indivisible with it, in uniformity of experience. This is the clear light transparence spirit of enlightenment. This shows the reality, or the ultimate reality, of mantra. Here, the two—concentrated mantra or the recited mantra, and the symbol of the mantra—indicate the manner of performing vajra recitation. Having performed that, one creates the spirit of enlightenment in relation to the two realities. What these two—the meaning or visualization of mantra [135a] and the ultimate reality of mantra—indicate, you should understand as the meaning of the *Explanatory Tantra [Revelation of the Hidden Intention].*

[**VI.B.3.b.ii.C′3′d′i′B″4″e″** – Short *A*, root of mantra]

In the *Five Stages*, [Nāgārjuna] teaches the reality of mantra by quoting the *Root Tantra* tenth chapter stating that those three syllables [OṀ ĀḤ HŪṀ] concentrate all mantras, and he explains that same thing by the verses stating the expressed mantras in the second chapter of the *Revelation of the Hidden Intention*—those are the sources he quotes. In the *Integrated Practices* also, the way that those three letters generate all other letters is shown by those verses, which [Āryadeva] also quotes. In that quoted treatise, after showing how to concentrate all mantras in the three letters, there is a statement that says:

> In the short [letter], there is the totality of speech;
> It is not one, and it is not many.

And, except for the explanation in the *Integrated Practices*—which states that:

> In the short [*A*], there is the totality of speech . . .

—this meaning is not explained at all in other treatises. The reason for this is that [the father and sons] intend that in order to understand the reality of mantra, it is indispensable to understand well the difference between the interpretable and the definitive about the statement that the short *A* is the root of all speech; and, that if one knows that, it will be easy to understand the definitive meaning of the other treatises. Therefore, you should determine well the meaning of [Āryadeva's] statement in the *Integrated Practices*, made in answer to the question about the way in which the short *A* is required to be attached to all other words:

> In regard to this, the explainers of the Buddha's sutras, first knowing the words through grammatical analysis, follow[87] merely the verbal meaning and do not understand what is expressed by letters, why it is [so expressed], and what is to be attached to them. They don't understand the reality of letters correctly, [135b] because that is the sphere of knowledge of buddhas. You should listen, then, in order to understand that through the stages of teaching!

The "explainers of the Buddha's sutras" are all the Buddhists who explain the import of sutras without understanding the reality of mantra, which is the definitive meaning short *A*, which must become attached to all speech, relying on the *Explanatory Tantra*. In the *Integrated Practices*, [Āryadeva] states:

> About the so-called reality of mantra: root tantras such as the *Reality Compendium* and so forth, and the *Further Tantra*, mention only "mantra," and do not teach the concentration of mantra. Therefore, in the *Explanatory Tantra*, the Divine Lord [Buddha] states only the truth, the concentration of mantra, the symbol of mantra, the meaning of mantra, and the reality of mantra. Therefore, not understanding the *Explanatory Tantra*, those who insistently adhere to the outer secret mantra will never understand this.

The meaning of the quote from "grammatical analysis" up to "follow

87. Available Sanskrit editions (Pandey and Wedemeyer) have *anusmaranti* ("memorize") for Tibetan *rjes su 'brang* (*anusāranti*) ("follow"), but I have followed the Tibetan cited by Tsong Khapa.

merely" is that one just understands the import of the pronounced word, having ascertained the meaning of the word explained by the system of grammar to be attached to whatever by the power of the word, the meaning of the word of speech. As for "expressed by letters," the *[Revelation of the Hidden Intention] Tantra* says:

> The short [*A*] becomes all speech.

That is the definitive meaning, which is something other than the mere literal achieved sound. There is also the meaning of where it is attached, why it is attached, and how it is attached.

Some Tibetan mentors explain this as "when one attaches speech to words, one attaches it to the meaning of what it expresses." [136a] "Why," is "by which reason," [asking about] how it is attached from the point of view of short *A* becoming the cause of [speech]. "How" does one attach it? When one collects many letters there is a name, when those are collected there is an expression, when many of those are collected there is speech, and when many of those are collected there is a treatise. That is the explanation up to there. But this is not the meaning. If that were so, the statement that those who explain sutras according to works on grammar do not understand would be extremely incorrect.

Well, what is [the meaning]?

Here, the attacher is that example of what is said to be speech that has the nature of *āli* and *kāli*, which is Vairocana, who is the energy of vowels and consonants. Where is that attached? It is attached to the heart center indestructible. This has already been explained previously, quoting from the *Integrated Practices*. Why is it attached? Because by achieving the indestructible, one realizes insubstantiality. This is what the *Integrated Practices* says. This is because clear light transparence is interpreted as insubstantiality. How is it attached? By means of the [death or yogic] dissolution process, as by earth dissolving into water, etc. Thus, the reality of that short *A* letter of such three processes is only the realm of buddhas, and is kept secret from the lesser disciples, as they do not understand it. In the *Integrated Practices Commentary*, in the context of the passage "at the time of learning, getting involved in the meaning of the syllables" and so forth, it is explained that "those who are not holy do not understand; like pointing at the moon with a forefinger," they do not see the meaning. In the process of teaching, regarding the way of making it understandable, it says "all speech." This refers to all of the forty-nine letters, the sixteen vowels and the thirty-three consonants. Gradually concentrating [all speech], all the treatises, both sacred and mundane, such as the sutras and tantras emerge and enable one to perfect all accomplishments. [136b] If one knows the import of the specific letters connecting such speech to words, etc., this is because short A is their vitalizing energy, because such a letter as *K*, etc., which does not have the short *A* [which makes it KA] does not exist. Because it would simply be a stop, it would not become an expression. That explanation is the literal interpretable meaning of the expression [in Nāgārjuna's *Five Stages*] "the short one becomes the totality of speech."

Therefore, just as is stated in the *Hymn of the Names [of Mañjushrī]*:

> *A* is the supreme of all letters. It has great import; it is the supreme letter. It arises from within; it is unproduced. Abandoning the pronouncing of expressions, it is the supreme cause of all expressions. It illuminates all expressions.

This is not quoted as a means of making known the instruction of the previously mentioned point that short *A* contains all other letters. Therefore, the Divine Lord said:

> The *A* is the door of all things, because it is unproduced; and it is the word, the seed of the door of all contemplations.

It is also called "the [natural] orgasmic letter." Also, in the *Vajra Mandala Ornament [Tantra]* it is said, in order to clearly indicate *A*:

> Indestructible in the center of the heart . . .

etc., as quoted above.[88] And just after that quote [the *Integrated Practices* says]:

88. See p. 230, above (Tib. 111b).

> Therefore, all buddhas become the clan of *A*—*A* becomes the cause, and they are released through *A*.

These three references are given. Taking this as a reason, [137a] it is established that all buddhas arise from *A*; it is not proven that all speech has short *A*.

After that, the *Integrated Practices* says:

> In the *Mission to Laṅka [Sutra]* it says to rely on the import, but do not rely on the letter; if one goes after the letter, one will lose the ultimate meaning; furthermore, it will not cause understanding. Thus, it is like someone pointing out something to another with a fingertip and the other just looks at the fingertip; even so, foolish persons, attached to the literal meaning of things, will not be caused to seek the ultimate meaning. Therefore, if one desires [to know] the import, do not just depend upon the [letter], but get rid of insistence on the literal, and seek the [deeper] meaning.

This is the [*Mission to Laṅka*] quote. If one holds just the literal meaning of showing the short *A* applying to all expressions, one will not find any other import represented by that. One will just be looking at the fingertip, and one will not see the meaning pointed out by that. Similarly, it means that beyond that literal meaning, one must look for another meaning. What is that [other] meaning? Here, Tibetan mentors say that all speech words arise from vowels and consonants, and all of those arise from short *A*. Short *A* arises from the clear light in the void interior of the body. Therefore, all words are like space, and have voidness as their root. Therefore, in regard to all aggregates etc., the import of being expressed by that sound should be understood as like space, without intrinsic reality. This is the explanation of the reality of the word. [137b]

Our own system, according to the quote in the *Vajra Mandala Ornament [Tantra]*, is that:

> *A* means the indestructible that blazes like a butter-lamp flame in the center of the heart.

In the *Hymn of the Names* it is explained that *A* is the supreme of all letters. Other tantras state that *A* is the door of all teachings; in this context, these must be explained as having the same meaning. Further, in the *Integrated Practices* it is stated that after death, the ground where the energies dissolve is the indestructible. If one explains the definitive meaning of short *A* in that way, the definitive meaning of the vowels and consonants mentioned there are the energies arising in dependence upon the subtle energies of the indestructible, which energies go and reside in the places within the body. This is taken as those vowels and consonants that are explained as arising in the form of vowels and consonants, and does not refer to those vowels and consonants that are produced from the effort of the tongue and palate.

The *Sampuṭa [Tantra]* says that in the center of the eight-petalled lotus of the [heart wheel's] hub the supreme syllable *A* abides. All mantras of all beings are said to be produced from there. That short *A* mentioned there is the furor-fire atomic[-level] *roma* channel! In this context, in answer to the question, "What is the abode from which the 108 energies you mentioned arise and which of them is supreme?" the *Vajra Rosary* states:

> The nature of the place of energy,
> Energy that pervades the six channel wheels,
> Always abides in the Dharma wheel.
> Called "vitalizing energy," it pervades all beings.
> Free of thought, at midnight,
> Arising from the supreme space,
> It opens up the nature of energy. [138a]

In general, the place of the energies is the six wheels. Especially, that vitalizing energy that arises from the void space in the heart center, opens all energies, moves and makes the energies arise. The statement "by that energy all the energies of beings are pervaded," and the statement "when [an embryo] is first conceived, the vitalizing energy is developed from the heart center, and [at the end] is finally collected there," are explained as [meaning that the energy] previously arises from the indestructible short *A*. As for that, the vitalizing energy that abides in the heart center and the short *A* is the indestructible [drop] of the spirit of enlightenment.

In regard to the *Sheaf of Instructions* statement that "the eight divisions of the letters stand at the navel," it is explained that they stand [there] while actually being invisible, and that they arise invisibly when pronounced as being the birthplace of energies in the lotus of the vagina, and that they are visibly produced from the functioning of the palate, etc.

The short *A* of the heart center is the supreme ground of the arisal of clear light. It is the supreme of all syllables, it has great import and is the best letter. It emerges from within, and is unproduced. The Chag translation says "The great vitalizing energy has no letter." "Life energy" means "the vitalizing energy." "Great" means "supreme." "No letter" means the "the indestructible does not exist in the form of a syllable." "Abandoning verbal expression" means that "it does not have the actuality of expression." "The cause of expression" means "all energies in general, but the chief cause is the indestructible." "It illuminates all expressions" means that when the energies that come from there go to the throat they produce expressions that are articulated sound. The door of all teachings is the door of all contemplations [138b] because bliss-void clear light transparence is the essence of all samadhis.

In regard to the indestructible *A*, when samadhi collects the energies together, the naturally unproduced voidness is ascertained by the great bliss [awareness]; that is the dawning of clear light transparence and that is what is "primally unproduced." It is not merely the voidness of nonproduction with respect to intrinsic reality. That being so, as was explained before, about the three elements, "where it is attached, etc.," that [clear light] constitutes that very same import of short *A*. It is the supreme key point of the path to buddhahood; thus it is said that all buddhas arise from *A*.

In summary, the heart indestructible [drop] is understood to be the root of all energies that have the form of inner vowels and consonants. When the energies dissolve into that [indestructible], you realize the manifestation of clear light transparence. This is the extraordinary way of understanding the reality of mantra in the context of the vajra recitation. This is said to mean that the definitive meaning, described as other than the literal meaning, of the statement "The short ['*A*'] becomes the totality of speech," has been discovered. Therefore, just as we explained the meaning of the statement, "When somebody points something out to one with the tip of his finger, you should look at what is being pointed out, and not be obsessed with the means of pointing," it seems that many still persist in behaving in that way. Thus, do understand this thoroughly with wide analysis of the details, and do not be too easily satisfied.[89]

[**VI.B.3.b.ii.c′3′d′i′b″5″** – The way that speech isolation becomes a component of breath control]

In order to show how speech isolation serves as a branch of vitalizing energy control of the six [branches of] yoga, [consider] how that branch is described in the *Further Tantra*:

> Breath, with nature of the five wisdoms,
> Is the reality of the five elements, [139a]
> Arising in the form of a lump,
> Imagine it on the tip of a nose.[90]
> That five-colored jewel [drop]
> Is called "vitalizing energy" and "control."
> Visualize your mantra in your heart center,
> Place the vitalizing energy changed into a drop.

The meaning of this is explained by [Chandrakīrti in] the *Illuminating Lamp*. The first four lines explain the meditation on the substance drop on the nose tip of the secret [wheel]. The first two lines [again] and the lines starting from "[That five-colored] jewel" etc. up to "your mantra" describe the meditation on the light drop, the practice of vajra recitation in the upper nostril. The two and a half lines after "in the heart center" indicates the meditation on the indestructible drop at the nose tip of the heart [center indestructible], and its purpose.[91] These are meditations of three vitalizing

89. This whole section on the ultimate reality of mantra, connecting the short *A* to voidness, clear light, and so revealing it to be the source of all language, meaning, creation itself, really, reminds me of the idea of voidness as enabling the functions of both the world and liberation from the world, as stated classically by Nāgārjuna in his *Wisdom*, as "What works with voidness, works; what doesn't work with voidness, doesn't work"; and on the mantric level, the mysterious paradox of the part of the famous mantra, ŚHŪNYATĀ-JÑĀNA-VAJRA, where the intuition of voidness is likened to an unbreakable diamond.

90. "A nose" can be either the nose on the face, or a point at front of the heart center, or a point at the tip of the genital organ, penis or clitoris.

91. Tsong Khapa's text must have been slightly different from the versions available to us, which only have one and a half hemistiches after "in the heart center."

energy controls meditating on the three drops in the three "nose" tips. As for them, the breaths of the five wisdoms [are listed in passages] from "the pervading breath is the mirrorlike wisdom" up to "the vitalizing energy is the truth realm [purity] intuition." The five elements, from earth to space, are [also listed in passages] such as "the evacuative energy is of the nature of earth." That very breath of five wisdoms that have the nature of earth etc.—you should meditate it in the form of a lump-like drop of enlightenment spirit, emerging from the hole of your vajra into the nose tip of the lotus of the science-[consort].

The way in which the energies become the actuality of the drop is explained in the *Illuminating Lamp* sixth chapter as being that, when the art [male] and the wisdom [female] unite, the controlled vital energies that dwell above are developed by the joy of entrancement in union and melted by the fire of passion, and thus become a drop. In all the translations where the *Further Tantra* is quoted, in the *Illuminating Lamp* sixth chapter, [139b] in the two new translations of the commentary on the twelfth chapter, and in the *Five Stages* and the *Integrated Practices* translated by Chag, all say "on the nose tip of the lotus." In the two accurate old translations of the commentary on the twelfth chapter, and in the *Further Tantra*, the *Five Stages*, and the *Integrated Practices*, all translated by the Great Translator [Rinchen Zangpo], there is no "lotus." Thus, it is clear that in the Indian texts there are both [those] with ["lotus"] and without it. This is clearly described by six lines in the *Integrated Practices*:

> You perform the vajra recitation of the three letters on the energies of the four elemental spheres at the upper nose tip. The five wisdoms, etc. . . .

Therefore, it is clear that not mentioning "lotus" is correct. Though Kānhapa explains that this means "In the nose tip of the lotus of the face," it is incorrect.

When you apply yourself to practice the vajra recitation in the face nostril, according to the statement of the *Integrated Practices*, the four energies other than the pervading [energy] emerge at the nose tip—the upper "nose door"—in the form of a lump—each in turn moving as principle, enfolding the other three together with it. The *Elixir Secret* explains that the inhaling, exhaling, and abiding of these energies emerge in the form of a lump and in the form of the three letters. Kalden Drakpa says that "meditating on the lotus nose tip" is just for illustration, and meditation on the vajra nose tip is also taught; this being the system in which male and female each meditate on their respective nose tips. Here, you meditate on both your own and the science consort's nose tip, since meditating on each individual nose tip has already been explained in the contexts of the subtle creation stage and the body isolation. [140a] In regard to the statement in the *Integrated Practices* sixth chapter that says that these verses teach the creation-stage meditation on the subtle drop in the lower door, this shows that they have similar characteristics; but the actual meaning concerns the perfection stage.

Meditating on both nose tips is discussed in the *Vajra Rosary*:

> Streaming down through the channels,
> The spirit of enlightenment made firm,
> In the moment of holding the energies
> In the tips of the vajra and the lotus,
> Expressing the syllable in the palate
> And expressing the syllable KṢHMAṀ,
> It is taught that supreme yoga will be achieved.

This means that the art—which will be explained—for melting the spirit of enlightenment that streams through the channels, having stabilized [that spirit] in the two nose tips, will accomplish the supreme yoga. As for the art for stabilizing that, according to the *Commentary*:

> The "palate" is an extremely long channel in the center of the vagina, and to connect with that is to constrict it very tightly, meditate KṢHMAṀ at the vajra tip, and at the instant of holding the energy . . .

This statement explains that it will be attained by the supreme yoga of meditating on the vitalizing energy. That being so, "connection with the palate" will be achieved. In other translations it says "Held by the energy." This is good. "Application of the letter in the palate, and by the yoga of the mantra PU KṢHMIṀ" is not good. Holding in this way in the vajra nose tip is also holding it in the nose tip of the lotus, as it is at the meeting point of the two channels. Also, since in the *Root Tantra* it is stated:

Enjoying all desire fulfillments,
Recite, not losing the mantra branches . . .

—[140b] on this occasion also, as for certain great yogi/nīs who have great distinction, it is not prohibited that they should rely on an evolutionary seal [consort]. Here also, some meditate on this relying on a wisdom consort. If you know how to apply this statement in the *Illuminating Lamp* to the five stages practice manuals, it seems to be the supreme vitalizing energy control for dissolving energies into the *dhūti* channel. The *Illuminating Lamp* translation says:

The very thing, the breath which moves upward, has five colors.

Patsab's translation says "That breath itself," which is better. That very energy, previously explained as the wisdom and elemental breaths, goes upward to the door of the sense faculties. It is five-colored, thus having the nature of the five transcendent buddhas. Therefore, it is a precious jewel. "Vitalizing energy" is translated in the old translations as "life" (*jīva, 'tsho ba*), and "control" (*āyāma, rtsol*) as "long-radiating effort," but Patsab translates "'Vitalizing energy control' causes extension and long expansion." This is better. This means that the vitalizing energy, the energy that causes one to sustain one's life for a long time, is called "vitalizing energy control." The linguistic equivalent of "control" is *āyāma*, which means "effort," also "cessation," and it is also used for "length and breadth." Here, it is the latter. The translation "vitalizing energy and effort" is wrong, because it would be a redundancy, an equivalency compound, as the Tibetan experts say. In the *Time Machine* literature, it is taken in terms of the middle [of the above three meanings], as "vitalizing energy control," explained as "vitalizing energy cessation." In Tibetan the word "control" (*rtsol ba*) does not work well for both "terminating" and "sustaining," but due to its linguistic equivalents, [141a] those both do work. Likewise, in the Tibetan, the "retracting" of [literally] "concentrating together" (*pratyāhāra, sor sdud*) can be used as "taking." The "together" (*prati, so sor*) can mean "repeating," and though it does not apply here, it is not precluded as a linguistic equivalent. The reality of the entry, exit, and abiding of that very energy which goes into the upper door is your own mantra for natural recitation day and night.

In the two old translations of the *Commentary* on that it is stated:

> Because you will do [vajra] recitation day and night, you think of your mantra in your heart, i.e., in the lotus in [your] heart center . . .

but in the two new translations of the *Commentary* it is stated in a better way:

> Because you will recite it, it is your mantra.

Here, "because" gives the reason, but it is not the previous reason for energy being practiced as vitalizing energy control, nor should it be employed for any other reason; because you must consider it [itself] to be the reason for your mantra, and because the *Illuminating Lamp* eleventh chapter states that:

> "Your mantra" consists of the three letters that have the nature of inhaling etc.

In this context, Nāropa states in his *Further Tantra Commentary*: "'Vitalizing energy and control' are thinking that one has short *A* in the lotus of one's heart center." As for the fact that the quotations from the *Illuminating Lamp*, "The explanation of 'vitalizing energy control'" and "reciting day and night, inhaling with the energy, etc." and the expression "your mantra" do not occur [in Nāropa's text], this is an incorrect text or a flawed translation, because the other contexts of the six branches [of yoga explained by Nāropa] appear just as they are in the *Illuminating Lamp*. The teaching that you should think of the short *A* in the heart center **[141b]** is either in certain Indian texts of the *Illuminating Lamp* or else does fulfill the intention of the *Commentary*. The explanation in the *Illuminating Lamp* [of the short *A*] as "the indestructible drop" is good because it is in agreement with the explanation with the reference quoted in the *Integrated Practices* that says that "the short *A* is the indestructible [drop] in the heart center."

In regard to the statement that "Vitalizing energy should be set to become a drop," the *Illuminating Lamp* states no more than: "you set it by attaching it to the indestructible." That means that the drop is the indestructible, to be considered present in the heart center. "Vitalizing energy" consists of the energies. "To set them to become . . ." means to focus them to be incorporated in the indestructible. This refers to concentrating the energies in the indestructible. This is the all-purpose function [accomplished] by meditating the three vitalizing energy controls. Here, it is explained in the *Elixir Secret* that "Your mantra is the three letters . . . ," and "consider it as present at the heart center" refers to those three [letters] dissolving into the three—the exhaling, inhaling, and abiding energies—and to those three [letters] dissolving into the vitalizing energy.

As for the meditation of the vitalizing energy dissolving into the indestructible drop, it is explained as the meaning of "setting the vitalizing energy to become a drop." Munishrī says that:

> Meditating your mantra at the heart center, you visualize the letter HŪṀ there. The channel emerging from the HŪṀ is "the indestructible." [Here,] the subtle *A* letter is in the form of a drop. The mind is set to become a drop, meaning that you should meditate the mind having become that there.

The *Moonlight Commentary* states:

> In your heart center you visualize your mantra as the samadhi hero, and upon that as a drop, you should visualize the mind in the natural form of a channel as [142a] the actuality of the mentality.

And Lakshmī explains that in the *dhūti* channel in the center of the lotus of the heart, you visualize your mantra as the drop of the HŪṀ letter with the cloud sound. Setting the vitalizing energy in that, you should set [there also] your consciousness, which rides on the energy.

Here, other systems explain this otherwise, but in this system in this context, in the heart center it is suitable to meditate either a HŪṀ or the letter *A* in the heart center. However, the meaning of "your mantra" is not those [letters]; but rather, the taking of the vitalizing energy as the mind and aiming that at the drop atop that letter. Nor does this refer to "set the vitalizing energy to become a drop." [Rather,] this is the context of the distinctive purpose of meditating the three types of vitalizing energy control; because it is to develop the four voids through concentrating and dissolving the other energies into the heart center indestructible.

You might think that: "Allowing the other two types of vitalizing energy control to be like that, still, as for the meditation on vitalizing energy control in the lower door, if, as previously explained, you hold the spirit of enlightenment when it descends to the tip of the genital, then this does not produce the four voids that come from gradually concentrating the energies in the heart center!"

This is true—but that is not a fault, since that [practice of focusing rather on the genital tip continues only] until you are steadily able to hold the drop on the tip of the secret place, and after that, even when you unite with [either of] the two [kinds of] consort, then still you must apply the distinctive instruction that serves as the art of concentrating the energies in the heart center.

When it explains the meaning of the statement in the *Root Tantra* that you should meditate on the tip a five-colored jewel the size of a mustard seed, the *Vajra Rosary* refers to the three nose tips and the three drops that are to be meditated there, [the energy drop, the substance drop, and the mantra drop]:

> Defining **[142b]** the three nose tips—
> They are named secret, heart center, and face nose

And:

> The three drops of energy, mantra,
> And substance are unexcelled.

As for meditating the substance drop at the secret nose tip, this is indicated by the previous quote. As for meditating the mantra drop at the heart center nose tip, there is the statement:

> At the center of the heart lotus hub,
> You establish a HŪṀ.

After that, there is the statement:

> This explains the mantra drop.

As for meditating the energy drop on the face nose tip, it is indicated by the statement:

> The energy drop, the supreme yoga,
> The great clear light, of five colors,
> By the yoga of fixing it at the nose tip
> You should totally meditate.
> And the yogi/nī should recite
> The supreme mantra of such a kind.

Furthermore, [the half verse]—

> This very mantra drop is supreme;
> The [other] two drops are light and substance.

—states that the mantra drop that is the heart center indestructible is superior to the other two drops; and it refers to the energy drop as "the light drop." As for meditating on the light drop, it is stated that "There is vajra recitation on the coming and going of the energy on the nose tip." This is the yoga practiced and the vitalizing energy control of the *Further Tantra* previously explained, and does not have the meaning given by such as Kalden Drakpa.

Here you might wonder: "Well, if the previously explained three vitalizing energy controls are to be meditated by one person, then this does not seem to agree with the statement from the *Vajra Rosary* that says in answer to the question 'Should one yogi/nī meditate this or different yogi/nīs?' 'The answer is that one with great lust should meditate on the substance drop, one with great anger should meditate on the mantra drop, and one with great delusion should meditate on the light drop.'"

In general, the *Esoteric Community* is taught for the sake of the person who has lust [143a] for the union of the two organs, mentioned as "For the sake of a lustful person." Although all three kinds of meditation are applicable to this person, there are three subdivisions. [The *Vajra Rosary*] cites three [types of persons] with regard to whom [meditation should be used] principally to lead them to the path. They are not stated to show that a single person should not meditate all three of them, saying only that these three paths, again, are for those disciples to achieve liberation in this lifetime, and that this is very quick for [achieving] liberation. Here, a "delusive" one is one whose passion and hatred are equal. When reciting your mantra, which is done by connecting the three letters with your inhaling, exhaling, and holding, you visualize the indestructible drop in the lotus of your heart as you recite. However, even without that connection, you must meditate the mantra drop at the heart center. In this system, [the "vitalizing energy" in] vitalizing energy control is the energy that makes the life system endure. Just that does not make it a branch of the six branches of yoga; the term "vitalizing energy control" only refers to the vitalizing energy control yoga branch.

As for meditating on the two drops in the tips of the heart and the secret place, although it is not a direct meditation of vitalizing energy control, it does not prevent [the effect of] vitalizing energy control, since it is still [virtually] the distinctive art of compressing the evolutionary energies into the *dhūti* channel. "Speech isolation" and "vajra recitation" are names that are designated from the perspective of the unique distinctiveness of the yoga of vitalizing energy control. Their specific names may be erroneously designated to the general, and so, in the context of vajra recitation, if the other two vitalizing energy-control meditations are eliminated, it is a very great error. Therefore, you should understand thoroughly how you need to meditate on all three vitalizing energy controls. **[143b]**

6. Speech Isolation—How to Practice

[143b.1–176a.6]

[**VI.B.3.b.ii.C′3′d′i′B″6″** – The way to put speech isolation into practice]

The sixth has three parts, explaining: [a″] The stage of meditating the three vitalizing energy controls; [b″] The uncommon function of vajra recitation; and [c″] Having meditated vitalizing energy control, the stage of generating experience.

[**VI.B.3.b.ii.C′3′d′i′B″6″a″** – The stage of meditating the three vitalizing energy controls]

The first has three parts, explaining: [i″] Meditating vitalizing energy control of the mantra drop at the heart center nose tip; [ii″] Meditating vitalizing energy control of the light drop at the face nose tip; [iii″] Meditating vitalizing energy control of the substance drop at the secret nose tip.

[**VI.B.3.b.ii.C′3′d′i′B″6″a″i″** – Meditating vitalizing energy control of the mantra drop at the heart center nose tip]

The first has two parts, explaining: [A‴] The way to meditate the partial mantra drop; [B‴] The way to meditate the mantra wheel.

[**VI.B.3.b.ii.C′3′d′i′B″6″a″i″A‴** – The way to meditate the partial mantra drop]

As for the place where to meditate, it is according to the *Vajra Rosary* statement:

> A person will achieve the chief of mantras
> In a solitary, divine place, without demon problems,
> Free of piercing sounds, and far from crowds,
> Delightful to the fortunate, a peaceful pleasure grove,
> While enjoying the five desires, full of great bliss.

A "divine place" here means a chapel and so forth.

As for the [topics of the] vital points of the body, which conducts are useful for meditation, and the vital points of the energies, they are, according to the same text:

> The path of conduct is the place of great bliss,
> Whereby supreme accomplishment will develop;
> The practitioner sits upon a comfortable seat
> And having aimed the two eyes to the nose tip
> And placed the nose in line with the navel,
> Keeps shoulders level, tongue pressed on palate,
> Teeth and lips left relaxed
> Exhalation and inhalation loosened,
> Bit by bit freed of control,
> Breathing naturally,
> And sits well in the spiritual hero posture.
> Maintaining such a path of conduct, [144a]
> One should constantly recite the two letters.

Such statements made in the context of the two-syllable vajra recitation apply similarly to the three-syllable vajra recitation. Other translations have "the vajra [instead of 'spiritual hero'] posture."

As for the key point of time, it is as previously explained.

As for the supporting embodiment, one should perform [vajra recitation] by visualizing [oneself] as the body isolation, great secret, single clan father-mother [in union]. In the *Five Stages*, quoting the *Further Tantra*, [Nāgārjuna] states:

> By visualizing the heart center, put the vitalizing energy into dwelling in the drop.

The *Illuminating Lamp* explains the meaning of this to be meditating on the indestructible drop in the heart center. And [other] *Five Stages* commentators also explain it as meditating the mantra drop in the heart center. Just after the *Four Goddess Dialogue* passage quoted in the *Five Stages*, such statements as "Supreme subtleness, the mere size of a split [pea]," like the above quotes, have the same meaning as the above reference from the *Further Tantra*. In the *Integrated Practices*, [Āryadeva] also quotes a reference from the *Vajra Mandala Ornament [Tantra]*, and states that the short *A* of the heart center indestructible and the indestructible [itself] are the places for compressing the energies, in order to make the meditation on the heart-center indestructible understandable.

Further, in the *Illuminating Lamp* third chapter, [Chandrakīrti] states:

> The precious jewel of five colors with the nature of the five transcendent lords is renowned as the indestructible, because it creates the precious jewel of buddhahood. It has the precise measure of a grain of mustard seed, because that is the form of the drop. "On the tip of the nose" indicates the hub of the heart center lotus. "Intensely" means that you should meditate constantly day and night by focusing on it and using the yogas of inhaling, holding, releasing, and compressing. [144b]

Thus the text states that you should meditate the heart center indestructible day and night through the yoga of inhaling and so on.

As for the sequence of the meditations of the indestructible and the vajra recitation, the following [*Illuminating Lamp* passage, coming right after the one above, teaches, in commentary on a *Root Tantra* passage, namely,] "Having made the jewel stable, one radiates, and one does not radiate without its becoming stable"[92]—

> "Stable" is constant. What is that? The indestructible. From it you should massively radiate "jewel," or five-colored, light rays, and you should engage with it by inhaling, holding, and

92. The *Root Tantra* passage and the commentary on it are in reverse order in the Tibetan texts, due no doubt to scribal error, so I have reversed the order back to make it clearer.

> releasing. "Without its becoming stable" means that you should practice this yoga with [constant focus on] the realization of the thatness of the indestructible, and not otherwise.

The meaning of this is as follows. Meditating on the indestructible drop mentioned previously in the statement that "you should constantly meditate the indestructible by the yoga of inhaling and so on," you develop firmness. Thereby you should practice the yoga of making the energies enter etc. within [the central channel]. Thus, by any other way than by having realized the natural experience of the thatness of the indestructible and developed stability in taking the indestructible as object, you should not perform this yoga of inhaling etc. Such being the meaning, first you must stabilize a constant and unchanging meditative indestructible, and after that you can practice vajra recitation.

This explanation is said by [Chandrakīrti in] the *Illuminating Lamp* to be an ultimate [meaning] explanation. To that, a certain objector argues that this is the way of explaining the vajra recitation [only] for a person who has [already] embodied the ultimate communion. [145a] Others do indeed explain the "indestructible" as the fourth stage clear light. However, from the extensive explanation of this point in the commentary on the [*Root Tantra*] third chapter, after explaining the energies of the four [elemental] spheres emerging from the indestructible, the Chag translation has the statement:

> By achieving such a body, speech, and mind, the body and so on are created; and "emerging from the vajra" refers to the creation of the divine circle that has the nature of the two realities arisen from clear light transparence.

Thus the explanation is said to be "ultimate" in terms of [its referring to] the objective of vajra recitation, which is the creation of communion by the energies through the practice of vajra recitation. This is similar to the seventeenth chapter's explanation of the three voids being called "ultimate."

As for the place where the indestructible is meditated, its objective vital point is the hub of the heart center lotus; and it is the same in meaning as the *Vajra Rosary*'s statement to meditate the mantra drop in the hub of the eight-petalled Dharma wheel [of the heart center]. Lakshmī's statement that you should meditate within the center of the heart center's *avadhūti* [channel] is good; and it does not mean the [same thing as] the *Five Point*'s mention of the black and white boundary in the heart, or the *Four Point*'s mention of the empty space in the heart center. As for the *dhūti* channel, it is stated in the *Great Seal Drop* and the *Wisdom-Intuition Drop* to be stabilized as the "staff of the vitalizing energy" and the root of the vitalizing energy. Since the hub of the heart-center channel wheel is in front of the vitalizing energy channel at the height of, and in the center between, the two breasts, you should visualize it there.

In regard to such reasonable instructions as this [concerning] the meditations on the drops and so on as accurately penetrating the vital points of the body, if you know well the vital points of the body, when you aim the mind there, [145b] it will reach those vital points; and otherwise not.

As for the drop meditated in that place, the *Vajra Rosary* does not explicitly mention a drop other than the syllables, but the *Illuminating Lamp* teaches the meditation on the indestructible in the form of a drop. In this context, some followers of the Gö tradition wish to meditate the short *A* in the center of a drop that is an interlaced sun and moon. The *Concise Five Stages* teaches the meditation of the indestructible drop together with the short *A*. In both of the personal instructions of Serdingpa, the drop is explained as white and the short *A* as black. In one, a half-white, half-black short *A* resides within a white drop; again in another, a bar-shaped *A* resides within a half-black, half-white drop; yet another recommends meditating a white, reddish-tinged drop. As for a red-white-interfaced drop, it is in agreement with the great adept Kukuripa's statement [in his *Vajrasattva Sādhana*] about the drop used as support for vajra recitation:

> Visualizing in its hub
> A sun disc, a drop, and a moon disc,
> Shaped like a closed [round] shrine-box,
> The sun of art, and the moon of wisdom.

However, here [in the noble system], a syllable is used in place of the drop in the center of that [heart center]; the *Personal Instruction* explains it as a slightly reddish white. The heart center is explained to be the place where the between person's consciousness enters in the center of the semen and ovum of father and mother in the womb; and is also explained as the support of the mind. And that is the key of the basic reality cultivation foundation of both those [noble and Jñānapāda] systems of meditation.

The measure of the drop is said to be just that of a mustard seed; for if you hold the mind on a subtle object, it is easy to eradicate thought constructions and compress the energies.

As for the syllable, [146a] the *Vajra Rosary* mentions both *A* and HŪṂ as the syllable in the heart center, and the *Integrated Practices* mentions the *A* syllable; and they are meditated as representatives of the indestructible. Since there is something established there in the form of a syllable, there is indeed no certainty [about which one], so here one can meditate either *A* or HŪṂ. In either case the color should be dark blue; or the *Vow Arisal* also suggests white. Here, "energy" stands for the indestructible, and the "white-red drop" stands for the indestructible enlightenment spirit. In this context the five-colored jewel is blazing with the five light rays, which is proper to connect with either syllable or drop. Other traditions explain the drop as being on top of a syllable itself located on a hand symbol; but here [in this noble system] it is better as above.

Thus one should focus the mind, practicing free of the faults of holding the mind either much too tightly or much too loosely on the heart center indestructible.

This is highly praised in the *Liberation Drop*:

> That brilliant form of the indestructible drop,
> Just the measure of a grain of mustard,
> Dripping and blazing with five light rays,
> Properly always stands in the heart center.
> Gazing on that, great wisdom will blaze up
> In the yogi/nī in just an instant—
> There should be no doubt about it.

It is also praised in other tantras, as in the *Unexcelled Clear Articulation*:

> Always dwelling in the heart,
> Unchanging in the sole drop,
> The person who meditates on that
> Will definitely generate wisdom.

And from that [tantra's] meaning commentary [by Ghaṇṭapāda], called the *Supreme Bliss Five Stages*:

> The mind that has the drop and the sound, [146b]
> You should place it in the heart center:
> This will dispel the fog of delusion—
> You will become a master divine lord buddha.

Thus depending on the meditation of the indestructible drop in the heart center, the orgasmic [wisdom] that radically cuts off ignorance will arise. Also the *Vow Arisal* states:

> The energy gone into the heart-center lotus,
> In the likeness of a white HŪṀ letter—
> You should visualize and be entranced with that,
> And you will not be bound by objects.
> The energy moving up into the life cycle
> Will progress downward into nirvana.
> The totally nonlocal nirvana
> Dwells in the heart-center lotus' anthers.

Thus, if you can collect, stop, and stabilize the energy—by the distinctive arts such as explained above—in the center of the heart-center channel wheel, you cannot be bound any more by the mental constructions engaged with objects such as form and sound, and it will grant you the exalted state of nirvana not located in the extremes of existence and peace.

Again, as explained above, the twelve subject-object energies are said to arise in the heart center. If you practice the art of penetrating the body's vital points and holding the mind therein, those energies will compress back there, and by the key process of their dissolving there, you can easily cut off the constructions of subject and object. By such a procedure, you generate the great certitude about this that is praised in the many treatises of the great adepts and in many tantras. Thus you should strive to meditate the vitalizing energy control of the mantra drop, the indestructible in the heart-center nose tip.

[**VI.B.3.b.ii.C′3′d′i′B″6″a″i″B‴** – The way to meditate the mantra wheel]

The *Concise Five Stages* [attributed to Nāropa] states:

Since the various memories and mental constructions
Arise from the mind as evolutionary actions,
Meditate the mantra wheel at the heart center, [147a]
The base where consciousness and vitalizing energy converge.

Thus [it is explained that] the various mental constructs arise from the mind, and the place where the energy and mind gather together is the heart center, so the meditating of the mantra wheel should penetrate the vital [point] in the heart center. Further [the *Concise Five Stages* states]:

As for the wheel of mantra syllables;
First, contemplate an eight-petalled lotus
Containing rows [of letters],
In a pattern of outer, inner, and secret.

[This explains] the meditation of an eight-petalled lotus with three rows [of letters on it] in the heart center.

Further [the *Concise Five Stages* states]:

The outer row is marked by wisdom-vowels,
The middle row by the art-consonants,
And the nondual letters stand within—
This samadhi of rows in cardinals and quarters,
Has the nature of the three yogas,
With the indestructible drop in the center,
With its A-syllable that becomes vitalizing energy,
Essence of all, radiating and gathering back.

Thus, this teaches that you should meditate the outer [row on the] eight petals of the lotus as marked with the twelve vowels [that are] the actuality of wisdom; the middle [row on the] eight petals as marked with the consonants that are the actuality of art; and the inner [row] with the four neuter letters [*Ṛ*, *Ṝ*, *Ḷ*, *Ḹ*], which are the actuality of art and wisdom nondual; and the center as the indestructible drop, together with a short *A*.[93]

In this regard, three [texts by Serdingpa] explain that you should meditate the mantra wheel as a preliminary of the vajra recitation: the *Five Point*, the *Wheel Endowed*, and the *Five Stages Single Session*. Though the *Four Point* [by Serdingpa] explains this in the context of mind isolation, in the *Root Text* [of the *Concise Five Stages*, attributed to Nāropa] it explains that you do the vajra recitation after previously meditating the mantra wheel; so you should do it according to the previous three texts.

Serdingpa said that the lotus petals should be red, the shape should be [convex] like an upheld mirror. [147b] From some of the other instructions of the Marpa tradition, it is explained that on the channel having a form like a lotus and which is white with a reddish tinge, the letters are white. With regard to the lotus that is the place established in the heart center for the drop that is the support of the vajra recitation, Kukuripa says that that lotus should be thought of as having the nature of the four elements, with four white petals and four red petals. This is to think of them as being the actuality of the four channels of the directions of the heart center. From some other treatises also, on the occasion of the perfection stage, the lotuses in the navel etc., whereon are established the drop and the letters etc., are explained as "channel petals," and that is how one should take them, or else one can also visualize that the lotus petals themselves are the actuality of the channels.

There being uncertainty about the color of the heart-center lotus, and there being many explanations of the eight-petalled [lotus] of the channel wheel, it appears that there are two explanations; and a third explanation is not often found elsewhere. If you visualize it like a lotus-flower petal, then there is no point in [visualizing it] like a raised mirror. Serdingpa has the consonants established on the outer [rows on the] petals and the vowels on the middle [rows]; but this does not accord with the *Root Text* [of the *Concise Five Stages*]. Therefore, you should establish [them] according to

93. The way this commentary is written, one could think that this eight-petalled heart lotus is actually twenty-four-petalled, since it seems as if the three rows are marked each on a different row of petals. I believe that is because in the shorthand way of dictating, Tsong Khapa assumes his audience knows the heart lotus has only eight petals, and the letters are arranged in three rows on the eight petals, vowels near the tips of the petals, consonants in the middle, and the four neuter semivowels on the base of the four directional petals.

what appears elsewhere in the Marpa tradition, which accords with the *Root Text*, [Nāropa's *Clarification of the Concise Five Stages*], which says that the vowels are luminance, the consonants radiance, and the neuter syllables are imminence. That being the case, it is good if you make the outer letters white, the middle letters red, and the inner letters blue or black. The *Root Text* says "Twelve letters having drops . . . ," meaning that on the eleven vowels, excluding the four neuters, there is a drop, [148a] so you should place a drop on the head of those eleven.[94] It does not mean that you should accept that you place the drop in front of them, [or that] you establish them with no drop.

As for the way of setting the [syllables] up, you begin from the east; and in the four directions you put two-two, then starting from the southeast in the four quarters you do one each, or else you arrange them in continuous order from the east, according to Serdingpa's instruction. The consonants are also like that.

As for setting up the consonants, the *Root Text* says:

> From KA up to HA,
> leaving out KṢHA, having four.

This [is explained by some to] mean that one should start from the east, on five petals, and place the five sets [beginning with] KA CA ṬA TA PA. Then, on three petals put the YA and SHA sets [on two of them], and then, on the last petal, put the four letters KLA BLA SLA SHLA, these four being called the "hidden," or "the four tongue-rooted letters." But that comes from not knowing the meaning. What the text [actually] means is [that] on each of eight petals, leaving out KṢHA from KA to HA, you put four. In this way, the five sets of four KA CA ṬA TA PA, the NGA NYA ṆA NA set of four, and the two YA and SHA sets of four are eight [sets in total]. The MA letter is the drop on the vowels.

On the inner lotus petals of the four cardinal directions, *Ṛ*, *Ṝ*, *Ḷ*, *Ḹ* are placed, and the quarter petals are left empty. When you put them on the channel [of the] petals, and the letters are not alone [on that part of the petal], you set [the four consonants] sequentially in the channel [of the

94. Tsong Khapa interprets the statement about twelve letters as referring to eleven letters, apparently meaning that the short *A* is in the center and not repeated in the outermost row.

petal] from outer to inner, and have them standing up. If you set them in the [circular] plane of the petal itself, put them in the form of the arrangement of a garland. [148b]

As for setting the indestructible in the center together with its *A*, it is as already explained.

The *Root Text* says:

> Present in the center of the realm of space,
> You should visualize the brilliant mandala.

As for the meaning of this stated in the context of the mantra wheel, it does not mean, as some people assert, to meditate that, from within voidness, awareness arises as a mere *nāda* [channel] and transforms into the moon disk of the heart center. With regard to the definitive meaning of that statement in the *Root Tantra*, the *Illuminating Lamp* says that the realm of space means clear light transparence, and the moon disk that stands in its center is said to be the indestructible. That very [explanation] is to be applied here, because by that it is shown that the supporting body of the vajra recitation is the indestructible [drop].

As for meditating the mantra wheel in this way, except for the personal instruction of Nāropa, it does not occur in the treatises together with the personal instructions of the noble tradition. In some of the instructions of the lineage from Jñānakara to Nagtso there are things disagreeing with this. Even in the instruction [manuals] of the Marpa tradition, dissimilar things sometimes appear. What is explained above, [coming from Nāropa], is correct.

In regard to what Serdingpa says—that the *Revelation of the Hidden Intention* quotes cited in the *Five Stages*, "Five having truly five," and "Four definitely attached in threes," and "Sixteen abiding in parts," show the ways of establishing the letters on the petals—that is not what they mean; because, although those letters—OṀ ĀḤ HŪṀ—are collected from the vowels, they do not show how you meditate when you place the vowels on the lotus petals.

In other tantras there are statements [to the effect that one] sets up many letters in the wheels and then meditates; [149a] [thus,] they are taught in order to compress the energies there; here it is similar. Thus, if, for the sake of compressing the energies in the heart center, you visualize setting up letters there in the cardinal and quarter directions, you do so in order to collect the energies gradually into the indestructible; so this is just the personal instruction for doing that.

In that context, first you visualize the lotus petals, and then gradually from without, in sequence, you visualize the letters of the directions and quarters and hold the mind [on them, until] the energy is collected in the indestructible. In this way, [the energies] easily go closer and closer [to the center]—that is the key to the way they teach. It is not definitely necessary for the mantra wheel to be very elaborate. Just as in the five stages instruction manuals of the Marpa tradition there are explanations of practicing vajra recitation by establishing no wheel at all, [by visualizing] the triply-nested spiritual heroes, all three simultaneously without any mantra wheel, [or visualizing] the indestructible drop with the short *A* and setting up the HŪṀ syllable—according to [whichever of] these explanations, [you can perform] the vajra recitation.

Nevertheless, it is definitely necessary to meditate the indestructible drop together with [its] letter as explained above, [but] whether the mantra wheel is necessary depends on whether one does it extensively or briefly. For example, in the *Sheaf of Instructions* you establish both hub letters and petal letters in the four wheels, [although] a second way is [also] explained that requires the four letters only in the centers [of the wheels].

[**VI.B.3.b.ii.c′3′d′i′B″6″a″ii″** – Meditating vitalizing energy control of the light drop at the face nose tip]

The second has two parts: [A‴] In what place and with what energy does one practice the vajra recitation; and [B‴] The way of uniting energy and mantra, showing the way to differentiate [various types of] vajra recitation.

[**VI.B.3.b.ii.c′3′d′i′B″6″a″ii″A‴** – In what place and with what energy does one practice the vajra recitation]

Thus you meditate either the indestructible together with the mantra wheel, or the indestructible together with the letter, [until you] become stable without vacillating; relying on that you should practice vajra recitation. Now, if the perfection-stage practitioner performs the vajra recitation for the sake of the ritual actions of either pacification, prosperity, [149b] dominion, or destruction, s/he performs them with the four root energies; and if this perfection-stage practitioner performs the vajra recitation for the sake of the five higher knowledges of "divine eye" etc., then s/he should do it with the five branch energies. If the body isolation has preceded, and if one practices the vajra recitation for the sake of achieving the [four] voids of the mind isolation, first [you practice with] the four root energies; and from the point when you discover the power there, you then practice with the five branch energies. On the three occasions of practicing vajra recitation stated in the text, this refers to the latter.

Here, one might inquire, "If that is the way you practice vajra recitation with regard to such-and-such energies, is it certain or not about the place in the body about which one might say 'you should practice through this spot that is the vital point in the body'?"

In this regard, most people, except for their mere making the energy enter in and go out of the nostrils from the inner hollow of the body, have no certitude that they should practice from such and such a spot in the channel wheels of the body. Again, some people say that the four root energies should be understood as residing in the four elemental spheres in the four [wheels]—the throat and so on.

In regard to the first of these [two opinions]: although it allows that there exist the union of the three letters with the three [processes] of the energy—exhaling, inhaling, and abiding—if you lack the personal instruction that says that "you should practice in this vital channel wheel of the body," however much you strive, it will not happen that the four voids will develop through the dissolving of the energy injected into the *dhūti*. Otherwise, [if that were not the case,] you could not avoid the logical absurdity that by counting the exhalations and inhalations of the energy as explained in the *Disciples' Stages*, you would get the same result.

In regard to the second opinion, though it has the idea that there is a mere penetration of the vital point of the channels, it has not discovered the import of the key of how the vajra recitation of this system penetrates the vital point in the body. Therefore, in our own system, the three—inhaling, exhaling, and holding—are done from the [150a] indestructible drop, along with its letter, itself in the center of the heart.

So to first establish this point with the [statements from] the *Illuminating Lamp*; compared to the previous *Illuminating Lamp* quotation, giving the meaning of the passage that you should meditate by the yoga of inhaling, exhaling, and holding, the later passage makes it more clear, and states that it is from within that indestructible drop that one should perform the exhaling, inhaling, and holding of a mass of five-colored light rays. Also the *Illuminating Lamp* third chapter, when it explains the definitive meaning of the statements that "you should draw a moon disc standing in the center of space," and "standing in the center of the sphere of clear light transparence, you should visualize a wheel mandala and a lotus mandala and a jewel mandala," and "you should draw a yoga mandala," [it identifies] "the sphere of clear transparence" as the indestructible, "standing in the center," and as arising from that; and it states that you should know the four elemental spheres that arise from that as the emerging four energies of the four spheres of water, fire, earth, and wind, in that order. Again, in comment on the *[Root] Tantra* sixth chapter statement that you should meditate the four discs as standing in the middle of the realm of space—sun, clear light transparence, jewel, and light discs, "the realm of space" is the indestructible, "standing in the middle" [means] emerging from there, and the four discs that are emerging are explained as, in order, the energies of the four elements. [150b] It says that in those you should practice the vajra recitation of the three letters, and also that you should command with vajra recitation the Vajrasattva who dwells in the heart center.

As for the explanation of the vajra recitation of the four energies that is taught in the [*Root Tantra*] third chapter, [the *Illuminating Lamp*] explains it by quoting the explanatory tantra *Revelation of the Hidden Intention*. Especially to eliminate doubts arising from the *Vajra Rosary*'s statement that you should perform going and coming of the four energies from these four places, "at the adam's apple, the heart center, the navel, and the lotus of the secret [center], manifest coming and going"; the *Four Goddess Dialogue* states that "the going and coming of the energies" is from the indestructible of the heart, which fits with the above-explained meaning of the *Illuminating Lamp*; therefore you should understand that from the detailed analysis in the [*Lamp's*] subcommentary.

From the *Integrated Practices*, it says:

> In the context of the vajra recitation of the three letters, mantras such as "the snake" and so on are those that arise from the vowels and consonants. The reality of those is the three letters that arise from the indestructible.

This also means that the recitation of the three mantras of the vajra recitation should be recited by the method of coming [in and out] of the indestructible. It does not mean that one should recite by the method of causing them to enter and exit from the [central] places of the four chakras. As for the reason of needing to do it that way: as explained above, the four voids emerge from the compression of the energies in the indestructible, and the vital key of vajra recitation is that it is the means of compressing the energies into the indestructible of the heart center; because the principal method of causing the entrance of the three explained above, such as entering, [holding, and coming out] etc. [151a], is the vajra recitation. Therefore, Ekādashanirghosha explains:

> Coming out from the indestructible drop, which abides in the center of the lotus in the heart center, is the exhalation, HŪṀ, entering inhaled there is OṀ and held abiding there is the nature of ĀḤ. These depend on the color white etc. having the characteristic of the elemental spheres of water etc. They occur with the process of [normal breathing] through the superficial right nostril etc. Thus you do the vajra recitation that effortlessly accomplishes the activities of pacification etc., and effects the purification of all previous obscurations.

Also, from Bhavyakīrti's *Five Stages Difficult Point Commentary*, he correctly explains that you should do the vajra recitation of the triple process of having all four elemental spheres leave, enter, and hold within the indestructible drop.

In the *Root Text* it is explained that in the central indestructible, the essence of the whole body, energies etc. are first radiated and then finally gathered back, so that is how you should do the vajra recitation, as it is a repetition of the [natural] process of all things arising from the indestructible [in the first place]. The *Four Point* explains that from that indestructible abiding in the center of the heart, you should do the recitation connecting the letters with the entering, leaving, and standing still of the five root energies radiating in their five colors of light. That is the meaning of the *Root Text*, and also it is the ultimate key point of the practice of vajra recitation. Nevertheless, it seems there are still those who do not understand the good explanations in those texts, mainly because of their not understanding the need to know well the vital point of the heart center in this system.

Some others of the Marpa tradition [151b] claim that, by visualizing in order from the outside the letters in three rows on the lotus petals, you should do the vajra recitation of the three energies of entering, abiding, and exiting in those ranks; thinking that is the meaning of the phrase, "the nature of three kinds of yoga." But that is incorrect, because the meaning of [the passage from Nāropa's *Concise Five Stages*]—

> The samadhi of the rows in cardinal and quarter directions
> Has the nature of the three kinds of yoga.

—is the actuality of the three yogas that practice the three samadhis visualizing three rows [of letters] in the cardinal and quarter directions. Kukuripa teaches that you should practice the vajra recitation of exhaling and inhaling from within the kiss of the [two halves of the] drop set in the heart center. Although the *Personal Instruction [of Mañjushrī]* teaches [variously] that you should practice the vajra recitation by meditating the three vajras in the center of the two breasts, in the heart center, in the throat, and in the crown, [by meditating] the three letters abiding in the moon in the center of the elemental spheres of wind, water, fire, and earth standing in order in the symbol in the heart center of the meditated wisdom hero, and [by meditating] the seed-syllable of your own deity; nevertheless, you should not do it through the heart center of each individual deity, but through the indestructible [in your own heart]; as [Jñānapāda] says, "you should do the actual vajra recitation of the indestructible drop by these [various] procedures."

Therefore, when the *Liberation Drop* says that you should practice the vajra recitation of the four energies that emerge from the upper nostril as light rays radiating from the four [element] letters, [meaning that] the right-side wind [element] is the body vajra, the left-side water element is the speech vajra, and the both-together fire element is the mind vajra, and the both-together earth element is the nature of all deities, it is explaining in that way wishing to show that those four energies are the energies of the four elements, and [152a] not that you do the vajra recitation by having the entrance, exit, and holding go from there. It is just like [the way you should understand] the explanations, in both this text, [that you should do vajra recitation] in the nostrils with the elemental energies,] and in the *Personal Instruction*, that [you should do vajra recitation as] the inhalation, exhalation, and holding of the energies as the four letters set in the heart center of the deity, and [the many other explanations elsewhere that you should do vajra recitation], apart from those two [ways]. [At least] those [two texts] are mentioning [procedures] that correspond with this [noble] system, while other systems teach that you should practice vajra recitation in the navel center.

[VI.B.3.b.ii.C′3′d′i′B″6″a″ii″B‴ – The way of uniting energy and mantra, showing the way to differentiate (various types of) vajra recitation]

As for the way of uniting energy and mantra, while there is the teaching of the *Illuminating Lamp* that the white OṀ, [red ĀḤ, and blue HŪṀ], having certain forms, shapes, and colors, and being established in the places of the body, are [identical with] the energies' being inhaled, held, and exhaled, and the symbolic meaning of the three letters is these [movements of the] three energies, nevertheless, it is not the case that those [symbolic] meanings of the [three letters as placed in the body etc.] are to be meditated as the [movements of the] three energies. Also, this is not in the context of the vajra recitation.

In the context of the vajra recitation, in [the literature] of the noble tradition and from the tantra, it seems that there is no explicit teaching of any sound or form of the three letters and, in regard to the reality of the energy connected with them, [no clear mention of] which energy and which tone. Although master Gö gave [an explanation] of the resonance of the sound, he did not give [an explanation] of the syllable as a shape, and so skilled persons who follow this [noble system] also accept [the OṀ ĀḤ HŪṀ] in that way. Many Marpa followers assert that the energy is like a rosary-cord and the syllables are arranged like rosary-beads, having that form if you drew them. In the *Root Tantra* seventh chapter, it is said, "Do not recite while eating alms-food," and the ultimate meaning of that statement is given in the *Revelation of the Hidden Intention*, as quoted in the *Illuminating Lamp*:

> A separate syllable is the alms-food, and to recite those [syllables] is to eat. That is accepted as [the meaning of] "eating alms-food."

This passage explains that practicing recitation with energy and mantra being different is the opposite of vajra recitation; [152b] so that means you must understand them as not being different. Here, the [Sanskrit] word for "alms-food" is *bhiksha* and by way of etymological analysis, *bhinna* means "different," and *akshara* means "syllable." So to recite with energy and syllable as different is "to eat alms-food." Even when you practice dividing energy and mantra in two, the mantra is pronounced as a sound; it is not taught that you should think about its written form. Therefore, when you take energy and mantra as nondifferent, you must take the mantra's sound as what is nondifferent [from the energy], but you do not take the mantra's form as nondifferent from the energy. Though it is a sound, if it is recited as a word, it becomes an outer speech; this is not [what Āryadeva means] in the *Integrated Practices*, by saying it is an inner word. Even when it is not spoken as a word, it is not a sound that is mentally thought in the form of a spoken word. Therefore, the natural sound of the three energies that enter, abide, and exit are here taken as the three syllables. The meaning of the expression "uniting energy and mantra indivisibly" is that indivisible union of the sound of the mantra with just the natural sound of the energy. When you recognize that your energies sound like the sound of the three letters, aiming the mind without distraction toward that [recognition], you are practicing this [vajra] recitation. And on this, even though the *Illuminating Lamp* refers to it as "mental recitation," you should make a clear distinction, since it is very different from the "mental recitation" that is the mental imagining of the form of the pronunciation of a word by the efforts of the palate and tongue. The meaning of "energy and mantra indivisibly united" must be that they arise as one in mental experience; but if you do it as above, they will not arise as the same in mental experience.

Concerning the *Private Instruction*[95] statement, "When the energy abides within, you should make it longer each time"; certain scholars state [criticisms] with reference to the intention of the *[Root] Tantra* commentary [153a] "you should leave the energy just as it is, without any artificial effort!" Their statement is incorrect: because there would be no practice

95. Tib. *gdams ngag*, not elsewhere cited as a text name in this way by Tsong Khapa.

of the vajra recitation of exiting, entering, and abiding, since it is taught that there are no more than 21,600 [breaths] per day, taking inhalation and exhalation as one [breath], so if you were to leave it [as natural] without any artificial effort, there would be no abiding, which is neither inhalation nor exhalation. Therefore, if you practice according to the statement of the vajra recitation of just the two letters, it would be sufficient to do it without any special effort, nevertheless, in the personal instructions of both Marpa and Gö, you must practice with a special intention to hold the breath in between, to fit with the [practice with] three letters. For the *Personal Instruction [of Mañjushrī]* explains four times to "hold gently at the time of abiding with the nature of ĀḤ."

Though many people desire to hold it a long [time] inside, apart from when one is exhaling or inhaling, it is good to [do it] according to master Gö who maintains that all three should be equal. The *Personal Instruction* says that when you exhale the energy, you purify all things and they become elixir, and reaching the nature of OṀ when inhaling you purify the instincts of your own inner process, and by the nature of ĀḤ you purify your inner process. The *Liberation Drop* says:

> With a HŪṀ, when you emanate buddhas etc., you achieve [the perfection of] all inanimate phenomena. With OṀ at the time of collecting all buddhas, you achieve [the perfection of] all animate things. With the letter ĀḤ at the time of upholding the buddhas etc., you cause the entry into nondual wisdom of all things animate and inanimate.

As for "achieve," the commentary explains that it means "purify." The noble tradition [153b] does not teach that way of practicing it. Though some people want to [think that it is saying] "from the *Five Stages*, the verse 'The HŪṀ letter truly radiates living beings,'" that's not the meaning. The *Five Point* says [words to the effect that] "Practice just twenty-one vajra recitations of the three letters each time. When you count more than that, as for the actual vajra recitation, when you feel well and it is easy to hold the energy, the upper energy is pressed down by OṀ, the lower energy is drawn up by HŪṀ, and you should practice visualizing the kiss of the energies in the heart center." In the *Four Point* it is taught that "When by doing the vajra recitation of the three letters the energy enters into the central channel and no longer flows, you should do it up to the perfection of the vajra recitation where you generate the experience of bliss-void." In the *Wheel Endowed* also it explains that by doing the vajra recitation again and again 108 times, and so forth, the five signs arise.

Thus, the first of those [three passages supposed to be from Serdingpa], which seems to disagree, presents the vajra recitation of the three letters as practiced only a bit more than twenty-one times etc. That appears to be a great error, which contradicts the *Root* and its explanatory tantras and the treatises of the father and sons. And, the explanation of the vajra recitation as the holding of the energy in an [inner] kiss appears to be just a fabrication. Our own system contradicts many [of others'] claims about the energy yogas of the mind isolation. Therefore you must practice according to the *Four Point* teaching, and interpret the *Wheel Endowed* as in agreement.

In the *Condensed [Sādhana]*, quoting the *Four Goddess Dialogue* as authority, it is explained that at the time of eating one uses this kiss [of the two energies]; but except for some commentaries that do teach this as a kiss [of energies], it is not so taught in any Indian treatises of the noble tradition. Even if you use personal instructions, if you interpret them in accord with the other personal instructions of our own system's teaching in the context of the mind isolation, it will agree with our system. [154a]

In regard to the vajra recitations, if we divide them according to their objects, the energies, there are the two kinds of vajra recitations, focusing [respectively] on root and branch [energies]; and each of those also can be divided into four and five [respectively]. To divide them according to the recited mantras, the *Vajra Rosary* teaches both the vajra recitation of the two letters HŪṀ and HO and the vajra recitation of the three letters. The *Revelation of the Hidden Intention* and the *Further Tantra* teach the vajra recitation of the three letters.

Lakshmī and Kalden Drakpa et al. teach eleven [types of] six-clan, fierce, three-poison, and neuter *vajra* recitations, claiming that to be the meaning of the root text and commentaries of the *[Root Tantra]* thirteenth chapter.

As for the intention of the *Illuminating Lamp*, you should understand its meaning by analyzing the thatness of the three letters; [Chandrakīrti] teaches the vajra recitation of the body, speech, and mind. Then there are the "jewel recitation" and the "unobstructed recitation," said to be the main vajra recitations.

Therefore, just the previous three do not constitute the full-fledged vajra recitation. They teach those [previous three] vajra recitations to be mental recitations, and teach the fierce recitation to be a verbal recitation; so it is very clear that these do not constitute the vajra recitation. As for the three-poison recitation, this is taught as a visualization of all beings possessing the three poisons as being placed in clear light; but this is not an energy recitation. As for the neuter recitation, it seems to be interpreted as a meditation on clear light transparence, so this also is not an energy recitation, and those are also not said to be vajra recitations.

Declaring the principal vajra recitation, the *[Root] Tantra* says:

> Recitation following the [ultimate] meaning, [154b]
> Through the goodness of realitylessness,
> Discerning the three times buddhas—
> This is taught as the jewel recitation.
> The buddhaverses everywhere,
> Radiating clouds of embodiments,
> Inviting them back and forth is the meaning of "vajra"—
> That is called the unobstructed recitation.

For the second line, the Chag translation has "Through the goodness of reality itself," which is better. As for the meaning of those, the recitation that follows after the three—inhalation, exhalation, and retention—as the meaning of the three letters, is said to be the recitation following the meaning. By the goodness that arises from the reality of the indestructible means that by that cause that radiates uninterruptedly one discerns the buddhas that arise in the three times to be [identical with] the three-fold [energy control], inhalation, exhalation, and retention. In that regard, this means that one comes to realize that which is the actuality of all the transcendent buddhas is the reality of the indestructible drop. That is what is called the "jewel recitation." This is explained in accord with the good translations of the commentaries. And that means that the vajra recitation compresses the energies into the indestructible.

Thus compressing them, they dissolve there; and when you exhale from the buddhaverse, your own heart-lotus indestructible, you gush forth everywhere, through all the doors of your eye sense-medium etc., clouds of [buddha-] embodiments and invite them back within; and all of this radiation, which has the nature of what is meant by "vajra," standing within [the indestructible], is the "unobstructed recitation."

As for calling the previous one the "jewel recitation," it intends that the vajra recitation of the root energy brings the energy into the jewel of the indestructible, and does not indicate a recitation related to Ratnasambhava of the five clans. [155a] Similarly, the "unobstructed recitation" is called that because, having developed the ability to compress the energies, it practices the branch energy vajra recitation, entering without obstruction the door of each sense faculty; it does not indicate a recitation related to Amoghasiddhi. From a quote in the *Five Stages* the former are called vajra recitations. Except for the *Illuminating Lamp*, in the treatises of the father and sons and the *Concise Five Stages* etc. there is no teaching of the branch energy vajra recitation. After that previously indicated boundary, if you then practice the recitation of the branch energies, then you must recite by way of emerging from the indestructible of the heart center; and by doing it that way, master Gö maintains that it serves as an ancillary cause for bliss to burn in the perception of all objects. This seems to be the supreme intention of the *Vajra Rosary*.

Now in regard to the verbal meaning of vajra recitation, though certain Tibetans and Indians seem to explain various things, the *Illuminating Lamp* says:

> Their meaning is the three syllables. Reciting them, it is the three, entering etc. Their existence is symbolized by the indivisible three vajras. And that is called the "vajra recitation of their reality."

Therefore, "vajra recitation" is the reality of the indivisible union of the three sounds of the three energies with the three syllables of the three vajras. Therefore, in trance meditation, from within the experiential reality of having [in mind] the four vital points, the above taught points of the body etc., getting rid of all faults that could turn into depression or elation, by the enthusiastic force of seeing well the excellences of both the energy yogas and the recitation yogas, [155b] you should properly learn how to have the sound of the three energies arise as mantras; and you should also keep on learning in the aftermath states. [You should practice] according to the *Revelation of the Hidden Intention* statement:

> In every kind of activity,
> By staying aware of this yoga, even sleeping, etc.,
> Always recite, leaving the three times,
> The nameless and inexpressible.

As for the meaning of the latter two lines, Shraddhā explains that it means that you recite in all three times the three syllables, free of any nominal or verbal expression.

[**VI.B.3.b.ii.c′3′d′i′B″6″a″iii″** – Meditating vitalizing energy control of the substance drop at the secret nose tip]

There are two parts to meditating on the substance drop at the nose tip of the secret center.

[First,] although the *Vajra Rosary* mentions that "the meditation on the drop involves holding the enlightenment spirit without emitting it in the boundary where there is the meeting of the consort's lotus nose tip and your vajra's lotus nose tip," it is not the case that you meditate by visualizing the form of a drop there. The *Illuminating Lamp* states, when explaining the *Further Tantra*, that meditating by visualizing the drop is "when the energy emerges with the form of a drop from the hole of your vajra and is imagined with the form of a drop in the nose tip of the lotus of the consort." Now clearly that is inside the wisdom seal, and moreover, that is meditated at the boundary where the two nose tips meet, so it is not the same as meditating on the nose tip of each one.

In general, in meditating relying upon the wisdom seal, there are three main types of meditation explained in the literature of the noble tradition. These three are: a creation of bliss by uniting with that [wisdom seal]; a meditation upon the mandala [environment] within the drop that is settled within the lotus [of the consort], which is the objective spirit of enlightenment that [melts down] through uniting with that [consort]; and a meditation visualizing the drop at the juncture of meeting of the two nose tips of the secret places of the father and mother. Here, [we are discussing] the latter. [156a]

While the need of that [practice] is for the sake of compressing the energies into the *dhūti* channel, it does not mean that you can compress [through this practice the energies] you were previously unable to compress in the *dhūti* channel; because when you learn the body isolation you gain the ability to compress the energies. Therefore, the meditation of the vitalizing energy control in this context is the means of compressing [energies] you were not able to compress in the heart center by the two previous [methods]. Thus, this [vajra recitation] serves as a way of heightening the impact of compressing [the energies] in the heart center.[96] On other [subsequent] occasions also, you should apply the same reasoning.

[VI.B.3.b.ii.c′3′d′i′B′′6′′b′′ – The uncommon function of vajra recitation]

The second has two parts: [i′′] Showing how the vajra recitation releases the channel knot at the heart center; and [ii′′] Showing how that release of the heart-center channel knot is the principal channel-knot release.

[VI.B.3.b.ii.c′3′d′i′B′′6′′b′′i′′ – Showing how the vajra recitation releases the channel knot at the heart center]

Thus, the reason why it is necessary to practice vajra recitation through the indestructible in the center of the heart-center wheel is clearly stated in the *Vajra Rosary*:

> Abiding in the center of the urna,
> The drop is truly taught as energy,
> And is opened through the reality of mantra.
> The yogi/nī upon releasing the [heart] knot,
> Knows the reality of energy;
> [But] to apply a distinctive opening,
> [If] the yoga itself is not understood;
> This yoga of holding the energy,
> For those who see wrongly and unclearly,
> Transcends expression and expressible,

96. Here we can see why Tsong Khapa considers that the *Esoteric Community* and its noble tradition of investigation and practice is unparalleled in the father tantra context of unraveling the heart knot, opening the indestructible, and creating the magic body.

> Lacks contemplation and meditative object,
> And is hard even for buddhas to attain.
> Yet by the kindness of the yoginī,
> It endures transmitted face to face.

As for the import of the first two phrases, same text says:

> The *A* dwells in the Dharma wheel lotus,
> And pervades the wheel of wind.
> This only is the great energy
> "Vitalizing energy" is thus declared.

By stating that there is a six-petalled wind wheel at the place of the urna-tuft in between the eyebrows, **[156b]** this shows the *dhūti* channel as the abode of the vitalizing energy, which pervades up to there from the heart center.

Here, in regard to [the knot] that is opened through the reality of mantra and energy, "mantra" is the one [mentioned]. Another [one mentioned] is the yoga of the opening of the knot of the *dhūti* channel. But if you do not understand the distinctive means of opening, which comes from having the reasoning of the reality of [both] mantra and energy, that objective will be hard to achieve by the yoga of holding the energy. That is the meaning additionally supplied in the section of the verse from "energy" up to "hard [even for buddhas] to attain."

The translation by Zhiwa Öd—

> If you did not also know that yoga
> By the yoga of supreme differentiation

—is better, and there he also translates, "Understanding the reality of energy."

As for not being able to understand that meaning without the personal instructions of the mentor, [it is because] "it transcends expression and expressible." "Unclearly" means that you will not understand it clearly. As for apprehending wrongly the meaning of the textual reference, that is "wrongly seeing." Thus having known [wrongly] the reality of mantra and energy, since you lack the meditation of contemplating that [correctly], it is difficult even for buddhas to release the knot at the heart center by the power of yoga. The translation of Zhiwa Öd says:

Even buddhas find it hard to attain.

In this *[Vajra Rosary] Tantra* it is said that the reality of mantra is to be understood by the kindness of the yoginī and the speech of the mentor. Therefore, "yoginī" does not mean the mentor. "Who then?" if you ask. In this tantra's chapter on the characteristics of the formation of the channels, it says that by condensing the seventy-two channels, they become the channels numbered according to the twenty-four holy places such as *Pulliramālaya*; [157a] again condensing those [into] the eight channels that are the exact measure of the heart center; those eight again [are condensed into] the three channels of the center of the heart center; and those three again are united to become the single *dhūti* itself. You should understand this pattern through the yoginī tantra, according to [this *Vajra Rosary Tantra*]. And that tantra teaches the reason for the necessity of the vajra recitation, the reality of mantra and energy, to open the heart-center channel knot; in that way, it intends the instruction in the *[Unexcelled] Clear Articulation 100,000* and so forth, given in response to the inquiry of the yoginīs, about the first formation of the channels and the final ultimate places of compression [of the energies].

As for the above statements of that kind, the vajra god Vajrapāṇi implored [Vajradhara] with [this] vajra petition [in the *Vajra Rosary Tantra*]:

O Savior of beings, I pray you to teach
The opening of the drop, with its rationale.
Who knows it, quickly practicing the supreme yoga,
Will accomplish the opening of the knot.
These beings of the three realms
Will go quickly to supreme accomplishment.

"The opening of the drop" refers to the means of opening the reality of energy and mantra; by knowing which, you can open the heart-center knot through the practice of the supreme yoga of meditation, and thus you will proceed quickly to the supreme accomplishment. So he prayed to the Savior of Beings please to teach it. As for the answer given to that request [in the *Vajra Rosary Tantra*]:

The Vajrin thus having been asked,
He said to the Vajra Lord:
"The nature of the supreme secret
That is not stated clearly anywhere,
That opening of the drop—
I will explain—you listen to it!
In the sky chamber of the heart lotus,
The intuitive wisdom vajra always dwells,
Showing truly the lower and the upper, [157b]
Home of the great life and evacuative energies.
There again, in the center of the hard to open,
It is wrapped up by three knots.
These defeat the evacuative energies,
Which do not succeed going upward.
These also defeat the fivefold energies;
The vitalizing, evacuative, ascending,
Pervading, and metabolic energies.
These flow from the five tips,
And depend on the five channels.
The expansive, the extremely expansive,
The crazy, the falling, and the friendly—
You should know these as the five channels;
Under the vajra, they clearly spread.
In the center of the upper vitalizing energy [channel],
They go into the vajra hub realm of space.
"Vitalizing," the great energy,
Emerging depending upon the knot,
Is also defeated and moves fivefold.
On the tips of the five channels,
The moon-portion and luminance . . .

So it continues as previously quoted.

Here, what is not clearly stated in any other tantra, the extremely secret point, is this yoga of opening the channel knot of the heart center by the vajra recitation. As for the knot that is to be opened, it is in the void space in the chamber of the *dhūti* channel in the center of the channel wheel of the heart center, at the height of the home of the wisdom vajra indestructible, and it is wrapped three times by three extremely hard to open knots. From the right, the *rasanā* channel, and from the left, the *lalanā* channel, each wrap three knots. Although that makes six, there are three if you take both in common.

That knot blocks the evacuative energy and does not allow it to go upward, meaning that it does not release it upward within the *dhūti* beyond the boundary of the knot, though I have already explained above the general upward movement [not in the *dhūti* channel] of the evacuative energy. Defeated by the [knot], it becomes fivefold; [158a] it is not that the evacuative energy moves in the five energies, but below the block by the knot the five energies move downward. They move pervasively below the previously mentioned wisdom vajra. That is according to what is stated in this tantra about drawing downward the evacuative energies.

The word "again" shows that the five energies also move upward. In regard to the five, the vitalizing energy etc., in order, proceed from the five channels called "expansive" etc. In the upper center of the hub of the vajra, the vitalizing energy emerges from the sphere of space of the channel-chamber of the life energy, and also one should add that it moves in its five forms.

As for being defeated depending on the knot, because the upper vitalizing energy is blocked by that knot, within that [*dhūti* channel] it is not allowed to go downward. As the same [text, the *Vajra Rosary Tantra*,] states:

> The upper ones also go downward;
> Even though defeated by the vitalizing energy,
> They also are within the life-channel,
> Entering and facing down,
> They do not go downward,
> Bound by the knot of ignorance.

As for the defeat of the vitalizing energy's movement, to translate it "defeated by the vitalizing energy" is not felicitous. Although the upper energies do go downward, they do not go downward within the central channel from the level of the knots. Because it is taught that ignorance is the reason, the translation of Zhiwa Öd, "the machine of the knot of ignorance," is not good.

It is said that the vitalizing energy moves with the five energies that are "Dragon" etc., from the upper channel chamber [above the heart knot], and that it drives the five energies upward to the doors of the senses. Here, the *[Vajra Rosary] Tantra* states that the energy, the chariot of consciousness, mixing with the instincts of consciousness and engaging with objects, **[158b]** generates the [eighty] instinctual natures, that it wanders in samsara by the power of being polluted by the instincts, and that "without that, there is no life cycle." Just after that it states:

> Thus, in order to abandon the life cycle,
> Meditate with the greatest effort
> The clear state of the opening of the drop;
> Not known [usually] due to other unknowing [senses],[97]
> When you have opened that central knot,
> You will become [the supreme] accomplishment.

Thus, this tantra states that, in order to purify the instincts for wandering in the life cycle, you should "open the drop," that is, cause the opening of the chamber of the egg of ignorance that binds the heart-center *dhūti* channel, meditating on the reality of energy and mantra. Until you dissolve the vitalizing energy and evacuative energy, which generate the [natural] instinctual constructs, into the heart center indestructible, the clear light will not fully arise. For that purpose, you must open the heart-center channel knot. "Opening that" means opening it by [meditating on] the reality [of mantra and energy].

Thus, the *Vajra Rosary* sixth chapter expresses the need for opening the heart-center channel knot; that, if you open that with the reality of mantra, you will achieve the superknowledges of sword and pill etc. and the great seal accomplishment; that the reality of mantra is the recitation combining HŪṀ and HO with inhalation and exhalation; and that if you practice it for six months, you will certainly achieve [accomplishments].

Here, you might wonder, "Well, is it the teaching of reality that the vajra recitation of the two syllables opens the channel knot? Or is it the vajra recitation of the three syllables?"

97. Thanks to David Kittay for helping me clarify the meaning of this line, with the help of Alaṁkakalasha's commentary.

Of the two types of "reality of mantra" stated to "open [the heart knot] by the reality of mantra," one is stated in the [*Vajra Rosary*] sixth chapter and the second is stated in the [*Vajra Rosary*] fifteenth chapter:

> The vajras of body, speech, and mind,
> You should pronounce reciting three mantras; [159a]
> Thereby you will swiftly achieve accomplishments,
> And will transcend the reality of mantra.

And:

> As for teaching the reality of mantra,
> It illuminates the unperceivable stage,
> The cause of Vajrasattva himself,
> Possessing all the virtues of mantra,
> The vow of body, speech, and mind.
> Supreme wisdom generates that reality,
> Reality that concentrates the sense of all,
> The reality of mantra that is unexcelled—
> Repeat it for six months, you will achieve
> [Accomplishments]; otherwise no way.

Thus, it is very clearly stated that by practicing for six months through the lotus of the heart center the three-syllable reality of mantra and energy, you will achieve [accomplishments]. Therefore both the two-letter and three-letter vajra recitation are undoubtedly intended by the *[Vajra Rosary] Tantra* to open the channel knot.

As for how to open it, from the same text:

> Having named the sound HŪṀ and the drop HOḤ,
> By opening with the two energies
> You cause the opening of the ignorance-knot.

For example, just as when the chamber of a bamboo is blocked, putting a long spoon in there and pulling it in and out opens it up, the inhalation and exhalation of the energy also opens up [the knot] like that.

The same [text] states:

> The being who is lacking the A HAṀ
> Is like a tree whose root is cut.

If you lack the knowledge of the definitive meaning of A HAṀ, it is like having the root [of your practice] cut off. [It continues]:

> *A* is explained as the vitalizing energy,
> And likewise the evacuative energy is said to be HAṀ.
> As for those two becoming one,
> That is renowned as A HAṀ.

That is what is stated [in the *Vajra Rosary Tantra*]. This method merges the vitalizing and evacuative energies in the home of the heart center indestructible.

[**VI.B.3.b.ii.c′3′d′i′B″6″b″ii″** – Showing how that release of the heart-center channel knot is the principal channel-knot release]

Of the two ways [—interpretable and definitive—] of collecting the mantras of the three letters, **[159b]** as for collecting the mantras of interpretable meaning: according to the *Vajra Rosary* fifteenth chapter, there are three [syllables]: the first vowel, which is *A*; the fifth vowel, which is the letter *U*; and the last syllable of the last division of KA CA ṬA TA PA, which is MA; then from *A* and *U* comes *O*, the *U* becoming nonmanifest, and then, putting an *O* sign upon the MA letter you get OṀ.

Then, according to this tantra's chapter on the essence of body, speech, and mind, in place of *U*, *O* is written in all three translations, which is not correct; according to the commentary an *U* syllable is written, which is correct. At the beginning of the vowels there are two *A*'s; and there is the warmth factor, which is the warmth [sibilant] division's last letter, HA; and as for the first two of three, with regard to similar syllables, the former becomes long, and the latter is erased, leaving one long *Ā* [with a visarga terminal *Ḥ* sound attached]. As for the *H* letter having no [vowel to give it] life, the commentary explains that it should be put in the place of a strong [terminal] point; on two occasions the *H* letter is mentioned.

The heat factor *H* letter, by being adorned with the sixth vowel—long *Ū*—becomes HŪ. By adding the *Ṁ* letter, which is the end of the PA division as an *anusvāra* terminal point above, there is HŪṀ.

In the text of the commentary, "Having the last part of the heat [sibilant class"—here, the commentary explains this indicates a crescent moon. In that way, you should interpret it according to the *Integrated Practices*' statement that each of the three letters arises from three syllables.

As for the definitive meaning collection of the mantras, there are three.

As for the way of bringing together the definitive meaning OṀ, in the same *[Vajra Rosary] Tantra* it says:

> *A* abides in the lotus of the Dharma wheel,
> Pervading the wheel of energy.
> Only this is the great energy,
> Everywhere it is called "the vitalizing energy."

Thus, as for the definitive meaning of the *A* letter of the three letters of the letter OṀ, it is explained as the vitalizing energy. [160a] In the translation of the *[Vajra Rosary] Commentary*, [the last line of the verse] is given [in Tibetan] as:

> The so-called vitalizing energy collects everything.

It is explained that this means that all energies are collected in it.

[The *Vajra Rosary Tantra* states:]

> As for the [*U* in the][98] OṀ, it abides in the beatific wheel,
> With its likeness of fire and sun,
> Home between the limits of throat and crown,
> It pervades as the body of radiant energy.

This means that the definitive meaning of the *U* letter is that it pervades from the beatific wheel up to the great bliss wheel. Its color is like fire and like sunlight, and it is a body of blazing energy, its actuality shown to be the

98. This should be *U*, not OṀ, as the following commentary indicates, since it explains the definitive meaning of the *U* in the middle of the OṀ. Derge printing has *Ū*.

ascending energy. In the translations of the commentary, Zhiwa Öd and [the translator] Ra write *U*, which is correct.

[The *Vajra Rosary Tantra* states:]

> In the place called "the great bliss wheel"
> Is the MA letter, just as a drop.
> Its height is twelve finger-widths.
> It dwells in the place of a royal ushṇīsha.

Thus, the definitive meaning of the MA letter is the spirit of enlightenment drop, located from the brow level measured twelve fingers up to the place of the crown protuberance. In Zhiwa Öd's translation [of the *Vajra Rosary Commentary*] he writes:

> As for its height, it is across twelve fingers,
> Dwelling within the ushṇīsha.

Just as the OṀ is placed on the crown in the interpretable meaning, in the definitive meaning three things—[namely] the vitalizing energy, the ascending energy, and the HAṀ drop—are collected in the interior of the channel knot of the *dhūti* channel at the great bliss wheel.

As for the way of collecting the definitive-meaning ĀḤ letter, [the *Vajra Rosary Tantra* states:]

> The letter *A* has already been explained;
> It is the supreme vitalizing energy . . .

and:

> *A* from the lotus of the Dharma wheel,
> Becomes a double letter *A* at the throat.
> Vitalizing energy itself and the evacuative energies,
> Are wholly bound by the HA letter
> To dwell in the center of the throat [wheel].

Thus, the heart-center vitalizing energy, [160b] combined with the throat-center ascending energy, the two becoming a double *A*, is the [definitive] meaning of "long *Ā*." The third, the evacuative energy, is the meaning of what is symbolized by HA. The meaning of the ĀḤ letter placed in the throat is said to be the collection [of these energies] inside the central channel of the channel knot of the beatific wheel.

As for how to collect the definitive-meaning HŪṀ, [the *Vajra Rosary Tantra* states:]

> As for HA, it is the energy named "evacuative."
> It dwells in the center of the anal secret place.
> The [long] *Ū* letter is the ascending energy,
> Dwelling in the lotus of the throat.
> The *Ṁ*[99] letter is the vitalizing energy.
> In the wind-wheel of the forehead
> They become one. When in the heart center,
> They are declared to be the heart seed.

So here the meaning of HA is evacuative [energy], and the meaning of *Ṁ* is the vitalizing energy pervading the wind wheel in the interval from the heart center to the brow. The meaning of the [long] *Ū* is the upward-going or ascending energy, the third [of these three energies]. As the HŪṀ syllable is set in the heart center, it is said that it compresses [all three energies] within the *dhūti* channel in the center of the Dharma-wheel channel knot. Saying twice "they become one," [you should] apply this also in the same way to the definitive meanings of OṀ and ĀḤ.

As for thus explaining the definitive meanings of the three letters, it indicates a merging of the vitalizing energy, evacuative and ascending energies within the *dhūti* channel, having released the three wheels' channel knots. To consecrate body, speech, and mind by setting in the three places the three definitive meaning syllables OṀ ĀḤ HŪṀ, as taught in many authoritative mantric treatises, that is the way to give a blessing.

In [response to] that statement [in the *Vajra Rosary Tantra*], Vajrapāṇi [says]:

> I understand the verbal meaning of three vajras
> And the opening of their places—

99. Tib. here and below reads MA, the scribe failing to block the vowel.

[Now,] who is the master in their center?
What does the Lord declare?" [161a]

Thus, though he has understood the merging of the energies as the definitive meaning creation of the three syllables by [each] uniting three syllables [and energies], and also, where in the body's channel wheels the mergings occur, he asks about what sort of master is there within the center of those three. In answer to that [the Lord declares]:

You ask for the hidden meaning
Of the supreme secret of secrets,
Which is not taught in all the tantras—
I will fully explain; so do you listen!
The master of the seed of the heart
Within it all, is mental-construct-free;
Whereby the other [two] lords
Will also be obstructed and removed.

The [Lord declares that], in the place of the released channel knots of the three channel wheels of heart, throat, and crown, within the merged three energies of vitalizing energy, evacuative, etc., "this is the great key point." [It is] the point that is the greatest secret of secrets, hidden within other tantras. So [while I] explain this, you should listen. Within all three of those, the definitive meaning HŪṀ syllable, the seed of the heart, is the master merger within the *dhūti* channel [central chamber] of the released heart-channel knot. Why? The release of the heart-channel knot is the freedom from mental constructions. It is the supreme of causes of cutting off [the instinctual constructs]; because, unless you hold the energies there without moving, those energies become the chief thing that moves the constructs to obscure and deprive [you of accomplishments].

Or else, as for the other lords, the body and speech vajras other than the mind vajra, and the places of those two, their crown- and throat-channel knots are [automatically] destroyed by the release of the mind-vajra channel knot, [161b] which you should understand is what is meant by "obstructed and removed." This refers to the key point that is taught below that when you release the heart-center channel knot, by the power of that the other knots are released. The commentary [says] that "among the three letters the

HŪṀ letter is chief, because all things depend upon the mind." However, that explanation [is too simplistic, and] comes from not properly discovering the definitive meaning of the three syllables.

Then, [the *Vajra Rosary Tantra*] states:

> Third, you, the yogi/nī, realize
> The thought-free great miracle.
> By stopping all energies,
> You realize [reality] in this very life.

As for the "third," it is the entry of the energy into the place of the release of the heart-center channel knot, which is the verbal meaning of the mind vajra. As for "realize," that [mind vajra] becomes manifest to the yogi/nī. At that time, the freedom from mental constructions is a miracle, and [you should] add that you generate the miraculous orgasmic wisdom. "Realize reality" means that it is miraculous. As for the reason, it is because all energies and thoughts cease, since you can collect them in the heart center indestructible. Here [Buddha Vajradhara] makes more explicit the reason previously explained that the heart seed is the master.

That shows that compressing the energies in the heart center is the great vital key for ceasing all thought constructs and the energies that move them, which shows that compressing them in other channel centers does not have that much power; since this [*Vajra Rosary*] is the authoritative text that teaches the reason why compression in the heart center is the main practice. Then, it [goes on to] state:

> In the center of the emanation and Dharma wheels,
> [The Buddha] said there are two lotuses;
> One of sixty-four and one of eight petals,
> Their blooms facing upward and downward.
> Relying on the above and the below,
> Life and evacuative energies [162a] circulate.
> Just those two are clearly stated
> To be the energies of instinctual notions,
> The two essences of body and speech,
> The *lalanā* and the *rasanā* [channels].

The emanation center has sixty-four petals, and the truth [Dharma] center has eight. In regard to the fourth line, the commentary aptly states, "they dwell like a jewel sack," which means that the heart center lotus facing downward and the navel center lotus facing upward, as explained in the *Sampuṭa [Tantra]*, stand in a shape like a jewel sack with its two halves joined together. These verses teach the condition of the heart and navel center wheels, and also that the circulation of the vitalizing and evacuative energies located above and below produce the [eighty] instinctual notions. Thereafter, [the *Vajra Rosary*] continues:

> [In] the supreme channel, the *avadhūti*,
> Supreme supreme, central between those two,
> Lies the energy free of instinctual notions,
> Always circulating, all-pervading.
> The yogi/nī, whatever s/he attains,
> Always can accomplish the aims of beings.
> The specific natural pattern of energy,
> Whichever prevails of the hundred and eight,
> At all times remains prevailing.
> Not understood by the childish yogi/nī,
> In one instant, manifestly perfect enlightenment
> Is attained thereby, according to this tantra.

Instinctual notions are cut off when you inject the energy into the *dhūti* that lies in the center of the two [side] channels. That channel is superior to the two side channels. A yogi/nī who attains that can benefit others, prevailing over the energies that generate the 108 notional patterns. This is not understood by a creation stage [yogi/nī], that by injecting the two energies into the *dhūti*, [162b] in an instant, that is quickly, you are said to attain the clear light of manifest buddhahood. In order to inject the energies into the *dhūti*, first you must perfect the creation stage, and then there is the stage where you must practice the vajra recitation; [as the *Vajra Rosary* states:]

> Further, however you effect attainment,
> It is pronounced to be rational.

First the great yogi/nī,
Good-hearted one, meditates quiescence.

By the yoga of the creation stage,
Having made the seal of ferocity,
In the nine doors of the faculties,
All of them are entirely bound.

Repeating HŪṀ, perform the peerless,
Supremely uninterrupted,
Practice for six months;
Afterward, you will attain in an instant.

Here the "seal" is the great seal, the deity body developed in the creation stage. The commentary calls the "ferocity seal" the "blazing seal," which refers to the creation stage's burning away conceptual notions of ordinariness. "Reciting HŪṀ" is one aspect of practicing the vajra recitation. Thereby, you compress within the energies back from the eye and so on, the nine sense doors, which [process] is described in the two lines from [the one with] "faculties." Thereafter, it continues:

Wherefore, having recited that [HŪṀ],
The heart lotus [knot] is destroyed,
[And the navel center knot also], by gazing up.
Then, though you performed the embrace
Of the lotus of the secret [center],
The two conceptual notion energies
Still go, along with their patterns.
Freedom from thoughts bestows the bliss—
[Then,] you will attain by the reality of mantra,
And you will stay in the *avadhūti* stream.
Energy having opened the center of the brow,
You attain—and the joy of such attainment
Continuously arises and does not end.

Thus, the first two lines teach the destruction of the heart-center channel knot by practicing the vajra recitation for six months. The translation of the commentary by Zhiwa Öd and [the translator] Ra says, "the heart-center lotus goes by looking upward"; [163a] and Darma Tsöndru translates it as above. The commentary explains that the meaning of "goes by looking upward" is that the [jewel sack's two halves] break open their cover as they join together the [heart and navel] channel wheels, and that such opening, taking the "lotus of the secret [center]" as the emanation wheel, is the undoing of the binding of the jewel sack; so it does not seem to differ from the previous [translation.]

The heart and navel wheels face downward and upward respectively, but are not united [forming an enclosure], so it is not a question of opening each of them individually.

In this tantra's teaching of the six channel wheels, the secret [genital] center wheel is not mentioned; yet in the verse "It manifests coming and going in the throat center, heart center, navel center, and secret lotus," a "secret lotus" is mentioned apart from the navel [center], which does not indicate the emanation wheel. This tantra teaches that the vajra recitation "opens" the knot, "destroys" the knot, and "conquers" the knot; here again it teaches the "destruction" of the knot by the vajra recitation; therefore "destroying the heart center lotus" refers to the releasing of the heart-center channel knot. "Destroyed by looking upward" refers to the navel channel knot. In releasing the heart-center channel knot, it must happen in the sequence of the death process. The *Sheaf of Instructions* explains that you reverse the heart lotus upward at the time of practicing [soul-] ejection, and the *Great Seal Drop* states:

> The vitalizing energy in the heart-center channel,
> When it does not function even for an instant,
> Its lotus is turned upside down,
> And in an instant it goes upward.

Thus, it seems the heart lotus must be reversed upward. In that tantra, the navel seems not to be mentioned explicitly, [163b] and the heart center is widely recommended; or else it is, as mentioned, the "navel of the heart center lotus." In some texts it reads "if you don't eliminate it for a mere instant," supporting the interpretation that it means binding the vitalizing energy there and stabilizing it. The "secret center lotus union" refers to the knot by the *rasanā* and *lalanā* channels uniting around the central channel.

So here it is taught that the navel and secret center's knots are released when the heart-center channel knot is released. "The midbrow is opened by energy" shows that the energies open the wheels' channel knots, meaning that all the other channel knots are opened by opening that [heart center] knot. When the [heart] channel knot is released it cuts off the vitalizing and evacuating energies' circulation in other channels, causing them to circulate only in the central channel *dhūti* alone, giving rise to the unceasing stream of great bliss free of thoughts; thus it declares that the reality of mantra is realized by the vajra recitation.

Those explanations, just as the *Vajra Rosary* repeatedly states "you will achieve by means of the reality of mantra alone," and also [as] the noble father and sons [teach], do not explain any other explicit yoga of meditation of energy, but explain the vajra recitation itself. Thus it seems to be the indispensable method that grants the great certainty; and so I have explained it extensively.

[**VI.B.3.b.ii.C′3′d′i′B″6″c″** – Having meditated vitalizing energy control, the stage of generating experience]

The third has two parts: [i″] How to produce experience by meditating on the heart center indestructible; and [ii″] How to produce experience by meditating on the other vitalizing energy-control practices.

[**VI.B.3.b.ii.C′3′d′i′B″6″c″i″** – How to produce experience by meditating on the heart center indestructible]

As explained above, it is taught that by gathering the energy into the heart center, clear light arises. In the *Illuminating Lamp* it is stated that, before entering into clear light, the process of dissolving earth into water, etc., [164a] gives rise to the five signs, mirage etc. And it states that this happens not only on the occasion of entry into objective clear light but also on all occasions of the arisal of the four voids, after the energy has been collected into the *dhūti* channel and has dissolved there. Thus, meditating on the indestructible in the heart center gives rise to the five signs.

In the *Personal Instruction* it says:

You should set the mind in the drop.
Holding your faculty there,
The earth element enters into water;
In turn, that water enters into fire;
Then the fire enters into the wind,
And the wind enters into the [subtle] mind.
When your mind just enters into nondual wisdom,
The signs [of dissolution] ensue.
Because Vajrasattva enters [your central channel],
The five signs arise, appearing
Mirage-like, like smoke,
Like a candle and like fireflies,
And like a cloudless sky.

Also, Kukuripa says [in his *Vajrasattva Sādhana*]:

With the intention of great effort,
Regard the drop of shape itself.
Again, entering into that,
The five or eight signs will emerge.
Then you will abide in clear light,
Abiding as long as you like,
A day, a month, a year, etc.
Then all your activities such as the aims of beings
Will effortlessly be accomplished.

The five signs are the [usual] five—mirage etc. The eight signs add the three luminances, [with signs of] moon, sun, and darkness, onto those. Since Vaidyapāda explains that there are three signs [within each sign], as the false earth etc. are ready to be eliminated, slightly eliminated, and totally eliminated, [164b] you must understand that there are many degrees of these signs.

It is taught that these signs become more clear [as you progress] from the earlier to later [stages], being mirage-like, etc. However, among the three opinions of various persons, expressed as "It is not that they arise seeming just like them," "The consciousness that has the signs has various degrees of stability or variability," or "The smokelike etc. visions arise," the latter one is best.

Further, the visions of [the signs] like moon, sun, and darkness happen at the very time of the [states of] luminance, radiance, and imminence. The vision of a cloudless sky is the time of the universal void. The signs such as mirage-likeness, etc., are the preliminary signals of the wisdoms of the four voids being produced in your mind-stream.

In the tantras, infinite praises are lavished on the clear light of the universal void and the orgasmic joy, which, as explained above, is the yoga of bliss and void practiced by one who is expert in the way of indivisibly uniting bliss and voidness. As for the first development of such distinctive bliss, it is definitely necessary that you gather the left and right energies and dissolve them into the *dhūti* channel.

As for that [development], you will never produce it no matter how long you practice, if you lack the direct meditation on the energies in paths of outer and inner vitalizing energy control, which is the art of penetrating the vital points in the body, and the yogas of the drops, etc., even though you have incisively determined the view of voidness and know how to cultivate it unerringly. Thus, you need definitely to meditate on what is taught in the authoritative treatises about the art of penetrating the vital points in the body. When you meditate on that, if you are one of those who wish your meditation to reach the vital point unerringly, you must definitely experience the signs that are the preliminary signals of the production of the orgasmic joy or the universal void wisdom. [165a] And that is the key point of why so much praise is lavished on those signs.

However, you should bear in mind that even when you practice only the settling of the mind in nonconceptuality, some simulation of those signs will arise. Thus it is extremely difficult to tell precisely the difference between such [simulations] and the signs that arise by meditating on the art of penetrating the vital points in the body—[so] you must be skillful! As for the [genuine] signs that arise from penetrating the vital points in the body, they begin with the signs from the initial slight inward reversal of the energies, which [usually] move totally outward from the doors of the senses, from their [actual] slight reversal, from their being slightly injected into the central channel, and so forth. There are many stages of distinctive [energy] reversal signs and actual [energy] reversals on the occasions when the path has become advanced. So do not be content with thinking [wrongly] that all of the benefits explained for the true [signs] fully function with the [merely] simulated signs, and, even though you have the real signs, do not be content with just having found the tip of the nose [of the full experiences]. But, understanding clearly the lower and higher stages, you must seek the distinctive excellences of the highest stage.

If you understand all of those procedures well, in the many treatises of the great adepts, such as the *Personal Instruction* of His Holiness [Mañjushrī], [and the treatises of] Nāgārjunapāda, Kukuripa, Ghaṇṭapāda, etc., there are statements regarding the perfection stage that explain the art of penetrating the vital points in the body such as energy, drop, and letter visualizations, statements that you must definitely generate wisdom meditating on the drop in the heart center, and statements that there is no doubt that you will blaze with wisdom. Finding the marvelous certitude from these, [165b] you will develop the resolve from your heart to make these practices your essential [purpose]. People of inferior discrimination, who don't understand this accurately, do not understand the key points of the tantras by means of the instructions of the great adepts, practice the perfection stage as a partial meditation on voidness, and even though they might try out numerous samadhis properly described in those [treatises], they tend to think that "This is not the supreme perfection stage," and then, [tragically,] they take a false path as the essence of their lives.

Therefore, since the unerring voidness is extremely difficult to realize, and the tantras and adepts' treatises are very deep when it concerns the extraordinary bliss, very hard to subtly understand, it seems that uniting bliss and void is extremely difficult. Nevertheless, if you know their vital points roughly and do not mistake their distinctive arts, you will correctly develop great bliss by the power of cultivating them. Even meditating only that is an extremely wondrous samadhi, very different from other things claimed to be profound.

About the vision of the cloudless sky, the fifth sign, two types arise; one from the meditation that depends on the personal instructions on how to penetrate the vital points in the body and another from mere one-pointed samadhi meditation without those [instructions]. This is very difficult to differentiate for those unskilled in the key points of the tantras. Even as for what is taught in the tantras, there is one version [of the cloudless sky samadhi] explained in other tantras concerning [its arisal on] the occasion of slightly withdrawing the energies within, and another here. [Here,] when we talk about the fifth sign, we are talking about the time of the universal voidness clear light that is the last of the four voids. Before that, it is necessary for there to be the three states of luminance, radiance, and imminence, which arise with the signs of moon-like, sun-like, and dark-like, and those can only arise by dissolving the energies into the central channel. Thus, the meanings [of the two types of arisal] are different. [166a]

Now some followers of the Marpa school have said that there is no certainty about the precise arrangement of the eight signs and the awarenesses holding the signs. Nevertheless, the intention of the treatises is that they should arise in a certain way. And it seems that they do arise in that way for those who have incorporated the vital points of the art of compressing the energies. Now if you understand well the key point of meditating the indestructible in the heart center and you meditate on it for a long time, from the time when you first generate the wisdom of the four voids, it is called the "simulated mind isolation." Thus from that point of view, though it is fine to call it "mind isolation," it is not mind isolation true to its definition.

Further, as for that, there are the two arisals of the four voids, in the emergent order and in the reverse order; and of those, the former is easier and the latter is a bit harder. As for that [arisal] of the four voids, you must let [the process run its course], just as long as you stay steady in each [void]. When you arise from them, you visualize your embodiment as before [you entered], which is to perceive [yourself] as just a drop. As Kukuripa says [in his *Vajrasattva Sādhana*]:

> At the time you arise from that samadhi,
> Do not think of some other thing,
> But always hold [yourself as] that same drop.

By that artful method, once you compress the energies and dissolve them into the *dhūti* channel, you get the ability to generate the four voids. When you visualize [yourself as] a drop, compressing the energies is very easy; without spending a long time at it, you are able to develop the four voids. By the very holding of the mind aimed at the visualization of [yourself as] the drop, and so on, in the most greatly vital point of the body, you compress the energies into the *dhūti* channel and generate the orgasmic wisdom; and this seems to be the extremely wondrous point that fascinates the wise. So you should understand the qualities of the extremely great differences involved when you use forceful methods of compressing the energies, such as being capable or not and being stable or not, depending on whether you [know well or] do not know well this key point of the energy yoga—[166b] which is not even [slightly] rivaled by any other ways of holding the mind.

[**VI.B.3.b.ii.c′3′d′i′b″6″c″ii″** – How to produce experience by meditating on the other vitalizing energy-control practices]

The second has three parts: [A‴] How to generate month-by-month experience by practicing vajra recitation; [B‴] How to make the energies dissolve into the central *dhūti* channel by vajra recitation; and [C‴] How to make the furor fire ignite.

[**VI.B.3.b.ii.c′3′d′i′b″6″c″ii″A‴** – How to generate month-by-month experience by practicing vajra recitation]

When you have completed coarse and subtle creation stages and have practiced the body isolation, as for how you should practice vajra recitation in the first month, the *Vajra Rosary* states:

> First, exhalations and the inhalations,
> Having the definite count of twenty-one
> Thousand and six hundred
> In the course of a day and a night,
> Focusing 'til you achieve that count
> Throughout twenty-seven days—
> That continuous yoga
> Is considered [successful] counting.

As for the last part of this verse, the Zhiwa Öd translation says "you should consider the number again and again."

In a single day [and night], counting inhalations and exhalations as one, you have 21,600 breaths. Then, over twenty-seven days, until you gain the certainty of the count of just how much the energies move in a day and night, it is taught that you should count them again and again, and that, during the count of each day and night period, you should keep [inhalation and exhalation] even, without increase or decrease, excluding holding [the breath]. When the breaths of each time period are even, the great elements of the body become equalized, and when that happens, the virtues produced depending on the body are easily produced—that is the necessity [of this practice].

As for the way of practicing the second month, [the *Vajra Rosary* states]:

> Then after that you should recite accordingly,
> [With] the vital life-energies
> In each session and break;
> You should mark [your] control of them. [167a]
> Then, counting 2,700 [breaths],
> You should hold them truly.
> Then with the form of determination,
> Over twenty-seven days,
> Dividing into the four wheels,
> With certainty day and night . . .

Thus, in the second month, in each of eight time periods, you should keep [your breaths even], using the procedure of [counting the] moving of the 2,700 energies. The former month's practice was easy; this one is difficult. Now the commentary explains that in each of the sessions there is a set of 900 breaths multiplied by three as they are inhaling, holding, or exhaling, that being how it derives 2,700; but that is not a good [interpretation].[100] Because then the [valid] teaching that in one day there are 24 [sets of] 900 breaths would be incorrect; because there are only eight sessions.[101] "You should make it definite in 27 [days]" means that you should practice the vajra recitation with the four energies that emerge from the four wheels.

As for the way of practice in the third month, [the *Vajra Rosary* states]:

> By making effort staying with that,
> You should attend to it differently.

100. The correct interpretation is that each of the 2,700 breaths include inhalation, exhalation, and retention.

101. This means that 900 times 24 is 21,600 and so each hour has 900 breaths, and each of the eight sessions is three hours.

By moving in the channel wheel
Ascertaining inhalation and exhalation,
By the yoga of certain holding
You should investigate the channel wheel,
And by opening the wheel channel
During twenty-seven days . . .

From that kind of equalizing the energy in sessions, by the art of ascertaining the moving of the energy of exhalation and inhalation in the channel wheel, the place where the energy moves, you should analyze the differences in the channel wheels during the 27 days. This means that you should clearly see individually the channels within the channel wheels.

Now the way of practicing in the fourth month, [the *Vajra Rosary* states]:

Then, you should discern the true sign
By the opening of its places,
And to the places that are individually noted, [167b]
You should strongly move 108 times.
The supreme practice that is thought-free,
Its nature being the abandoning of thought,
Master of the natural instincts of all things,
Move it strongly 108 times.
This is truly the supreme yoga,
Through which, during 27 days,
The yogi/nī who meditates its nature
Meditates intensely as it stands.

This states that, having individually determined the channels, the yogi/nī meditates the nature of the energies as they stand, sees the 108 energies moving in the channel in the fourth month, and so they are ascertained.

This teaches the supreme yoga of the vajra recitation that is the means of cutting off habitual thoughts, the art of entering into clear light that abandons notions of the instinctual natures of all things, while mentioning "conceptual thoughts" three times, and "this" once.[102]

102. Tsong Khapa is perhaps suggesting here that the mention of "conceptual thoughts" (*rnam rtog*) three times (I can only count two in this quote, unless we take *rang bzhin* as

As for the way to practice in the fifth month, [the *Vajra Rosary* states]:

> The yogi/nī who has instinctual thoughts,
> Then turns the yoga away from them,
> And the great energy of thoughtlessness
> Is moved into the channel wheel.
> Then, having been fully bound by the addictions,
> S/he determines the ultimate reality [of energy],
> And during the twenty-seven days,
> The intelligent [yogi/nī] should eliminate
> The practices of the beginners.

Zhiwa Öd's translation reads, "The intelligent one, through eliminating. . . ."

In the fifth month, depending on the consummation of the vajra recitation, the energy yogas posited as [for] beginners are given up by intelligent yogi/nīs, along with the energy-driven instinctual thoughts, and they then make the great energy that develops instinctual thoughtlessness move in the channel wheel. And this is the occasion when you begin to reverse the energies [168a] into the place of the indestructible.

As for "the ultimate reality of energy," you should add that the ascertainment of reality eliminates being driven by the binding addictions.

As for the way of practice in the sixth month, [the *Vajra Rosary* states]:

> Then those purifications,
> By the power of true yoga,
> Those conceptual notions of vitalizing energy control
> Are totally abandoned,
> The reality of energy moves,
> And you should meditate the supreme yoga.
> By this supreme nondual yoga,
> During the twenty-seven days,
> You stabilize the reality of energy.
> And the vacillating mind is purified.

---

rang bzin rtog pa) refer to the three states of the subtle mind—luminance, radiance, and imminence—and "this" to the clear light transparence.

In the sixth month, by the power of meditating vajra recitation that has stability in its moving of the reality of energy, you abandon instinctual thoughts and the life-energies and controls. And you also purify the mind bound by its instinctual thought, which gets distracted toward objects. As for those [procedures of the sixth month] they are given the designations of [1] counting, [2] conforming, [3] notions of the difference of places, [4] notions of the difference of times, [5] reversal of the energies, and [6] total purity.

As for [this statement about] the complete release of the heart-center channel knot at the end of practicing the six months of vajra recitation, it is intending the disciple of extremely sharp faculties.

In many contexts in this tantra, [the Buddha] does not mention holding [the breath], as other than just exhaling and inhaling. But when he mentions "teaching coming and going," the commentators explain that it refers to the going and the not going [of the breath]. Nevertheless, they [go on to say] clearly, "The yoga of the perfection stage is entering, holding, and exiting."

According to master Gö, the criterion for completing the training of the coarse energies is the clarity of their movement; **[168b]** which [amounts to] the clarity of the sense-faculty direct experience of the forms of the colors [of the energies], the clarity of the lack of confusion and error in regard to the forms of the counting, the clarity in the nature of the sounds of the form of the three letters [OṀ ĀḤ HŪṀ], and the clarity about the nature of the places [in the body], and the degrees of subtlety, of speed, and of weight. The sign of completing it is that no sudden illness can occur.

The criterion of completing the training of the subtle energies is that you become able to mix external and internal [worlds] by causing the energies of the outer universe to enter through the hair-pores of your skin and fit within your body, and by causing the inner energies to go out and fill the universe; and that you feel contact and bliss by the mere touch of the outer energies.

The criterion of completing your training of the branch energies is said to be that you become able to project [all] your sense faculties through each sense door, and to bind them [there] in freedom from any harm, according to the system of Abhijña. When the four energies of wind, fire, earth, and water move, and you bind them within, without allowing them outside, respectively then, without any harm to yourself, you will fly in the sky, you will not be hurt by outer cold, you will not be pushed around or even assaulted by a champion wrestler, and so on; and finally you will not be hurt by fire etc.

[**VI.B.3.b.ii.c′3′d′i′B″6″c″ii″B‴** – How to make the energies dissolve into the central *dhūti* channel by vajra recitation]

As already explained, when you practiced the recitation that indivisibly connects mantras and energies, you experience not mere imagination but an intense mind-transforming feeling where in your mind the energies' tones resound as the three syllables; just as, for example, [169a] the creation-stage practitioner first has to accustom himself or herself to meditate by imagining the deity, but later his or her mind does not have to be expressly contrived but naturally transforms itself into the pride of the deity. When that happens [in vajra recitation], you can terminate both perception and conception of the difference between energy and mantra; and furthermore, having recited with the entry, exit, and holding at the level of the center of the *dhūti* channel, by the key [practice] of the energy and mind functioning in unison, you can make the energies move directly through the *dhūti* channel. Here again, while first you have to construct this on purpose and make the energies enter and exit in such a way, when you become accustomed to it, conditioned by your vajra recitation, you have experienced the properly defined injection of the energies there [in the central *dhūti* channel].

As for the sign of that [happening], when you have not practiced vajra recitation, the [energies] move in each of the left and right nostrils. When you practice vajra recitation, before very long the energies definitely begin to be drawn into an equal flow, as the vajra recitation merely injects the energies there [in the central channel]. You should understand that this also [happens] when you meditate on the subtle [drops] in the lower [genital center] door and in the heart center. Although thus you may have the mere ability to inject the energies into the *dhūti* channel, the problem with having only a slight bit of practice is that before long it will migrate to each of the left or the right nostrils. If you have a practice, as already explained, of injecting [the energies there] and making them enter and exit, and the heart-center channel knot little by little has become slightly looser, then finally you become able to release the heart channel knot.

Now here you might suspect, "Well, although it can happen that the vajra recitation practiced within the *dhūti* channel depending upon the vital point of the heart center can allow the energies to be injected into the *dhūti* channel and the channel knot to become looser, the vajra recitation is incapable of stopping the energy in the central channel; because vajra recitation is set up as having the function making the energies go in and out without stopping. [169b] Therefore, if you lack the stopping of the exit and entry of the energies by holding them compressed together within, your vajra recitation is unable to cause the energy to dissolve into the *dhūti* channel."[103]

It is true that such doubts arise for those who are satisfied with some biased [understanding] of the perfection stage, who in general do not understand how to compress the energies by the yogas of the drop etc. as explained in the authoritative treatises, and in particular who do not know the literature of the *Community*, which explains all the keys of that [dissolution process] emphasizing vajra recitation. However, there is no such fault [in this system of vajra recitation]. When, as already explained, you have become accustomed to the vajra recitation that equalizes the three [movements], entering, holding, and exiting, of the energies, though you do not purposely cause them to hold still at a certain threshold, the energies stand still on their own momentum. Their [stillness] gets longer and longer, and then, though you do not purposely block the inhalation and exhalation of the energies, they become shorter and shorter. So when you first practice, in the process of breathing naturally you do not need to purposely lengthen exhaling and inhaling, but still, anyway, when you work on vajra recitation, the in-and-out movement of the energies will eventually stop completely and [the energies will] stay within.

Thus, further, the *Revelation of the Hidden Intention [Tantra]* declares:

> By [such a] sign, [energy-]reality stays [all] three,
> The nature of natural recitation;
> Nameless and inexpressible,
> This is supreme enlightenment spirit.

103. This refers to the vase breathing called *kumbhaka*. What it means is you take the upward energy and the lower energy and unite them at the navel center or heart center or wherever and hold them there, one pressing up and one pressing down in the central channel.

Those very three become one,
And neither go nor come.

This teaches that, after having practiced the recitation as energies of the spirit of enlightenment, with the realities of mantra and energy indivisibly united, being the natural recitation inexpressible in naming words, the three [energy movements], inhalation, exhalation, and holding still, [170a] become a single experience without any separation; and then there are no more going out and coming in of energies.

In that [same] tantra, it states that "the spirit of enlightenment becomes energy," and this means that here the spirit of enlightenment is energy. In that tantra, it states that the reality of energies entering, exiting, and abiding becomes of one experiential taste, and thus the other [tantras] have a similar meaning.

The *Vajra Rosary* also states:

By practicing vajra recitation,
Knowing its own nature,
You cut off the instinctual energies.

This means that the vajra recitation stops the movement of energies. And again:

At the nine sense doors,
All of them are totally bound,
Repeating HŪṀ, become incomparable!

This states that vajra recitation binds the energies within, not letting them move out from all doors such as the upper and lower nostrils etc.

As for the meaning of those *Vajra Rosary* statements, the *Personal Instruction [of Mañjushrī]* states:

Then you exhale with HŪṀ,
Collect with OṀ, hold with ĀḤ,
And holding still the reality therein,
You discover the intuitive wisdom,

> Free from inhaling, exhaling, and holding,
> And you need have no doubting ambivalence.

Thus it very clearly states that by practicing vajra recitation from the dissolution of the energies getting free of the threefold inhaling, exhaling, and holding, you attain wisdom, and about that there need be no doubt or ambivalence.

Here you might wonder, "Well, how do you get the energy to dissolve within by the vajra recitation of two letters?"

By practicing that [vajra recitation], injecting the energy into the *dhūti* channel and releasing the channel knot is similar to [the same process with] the three letters. So then the energy finds the path to go to its own root place, [170b] and it enters into its own place, as in the time of death. The tantra explains the two kinds of vajra recitation, while the noble father and son set forth the vajra recitation with the three letters just as an example. The *Personal Instruction* states that not only can you be liberated from both inhalation and exhalation, but also you are liberated from holding; what that means is that you need first to reverse the moving of the exhalation and inhalation and to hold the energy within, and then you have also to dissolve the holding within.

By practicing recitation of exiting and entering you reach the nonmoving of energy, and since there is a type of nonmoving under the influence of depression, you must be able to tell them apart. When you stop the nostril movement of energy, if it stays within without dissolving [into the central channel], then the body will seem to be inflated; but this is eradicated when it dissolves. As already explained, when the definite signs of the energy entering the *dhūti* channel by its own force occur, and the energy naturally stays within for a long time and then dissolves into the *dhūti* channel, what arises is like what is taught about [the four] voids. On dissimilar occasions, although there is an inner dissolution, it is not a dissolution into the *dhūti* channel, and so [the experience] will not match what is taught about the voids. In order for the energies to dissolve into the actual indestructible heart center, you need to have loosened the channel knot of that [heart center]; before that, even if you [seem to] compress [the energies] into the *dhūti* channel by means of the art of compressing [energies] into the heart center, that is a dissolution into the near-*dhūti* channel, but not into the *dhūti* itself.[104] Similarly, although it can happen that your energy can dissolve into the *dhūti* channel, you are unable to make it come and go from the *dhūti* channel in the [exact] place of the channel knot. As the *Vajra Rosary* says, "Little by little, free of effort"—and what is meant there is that you should not make a strenuous effort [to force] the energies to enter and exit [the heart center]. [171a]

The *Personal Instruction* also says that when you cause the energy to abide within, you should hold it very gently. The vajra recitation [should be] performed gently with the three, exhaling, inhaling, and abiding energies, as it is highly critical that, when the energies begin slightly to stop, the elements of the body are not disturbed and remain balanced. The production of those excellent virtues that must be produced [only] through penetrating the vital points in the body is different from other [kinds of] productions.[105]

Thus [penetrating the vital points precisely] is extremely necessary for extreme power in developing the voids, for ease of gaining greatly increasing impact from the moment of the first time of developing the voids, and for the great stability of your bliss and [furor] heat, and so on. Therefore, when you have had a whiff of the experience of the blaze of bliss and heat and have become enthusiastic and see the need for the ability etc. to cultivate positive practice, even if you practice the system of cultivating forcefully, you must keep at it until you have achieved the purpose [of penetrating the vital point precisely]; and if you follow the teaching of the treatises, it is [even more of] a joy.

Here also, though there is a bit of intensity [used in practicing] the energy yoga of vajra recitation and in cultivating by aiming your visualization at the drop etc., if you use the forceful yoga for such as meditating energy compression, it is said to cause untimely death. And though it seems to have the benefit of slightly greater speed, you should be careful to keep it

104. So there is a way of dissolving the energies into the *dhūti* channel under or above the very central part of the heart center where the indestructible is, without them dissolving right into the indestructible, because that is still sealed off by the knot.

105. To be able to inject the energy and make it enter into the central channel in the navel or heart center, you have first to have a clear visualization of exactly where that center is and put your focus right on the spot in the various strategic places. Doing that is "penetrating the vital point," and energy-pressure focused there produces the true dissolution experiences. Pressure aimed vaguely nearby can seriously disrupt the nervous system.

within bounds.[106] I previously quoted Kukuripa saying that the signs arise from meditating on the heart center drop, intending the signs of the vajra recitation, so here the signs such as mirage will arise.

Until you have well released the heart-center channel knot, [171b] you will not attain the actual voids of mind isolation. Nevertheless, it seems that those on lower stages will definitely experience voids conforming to [those of the] mind isolation; so you should carefully differentiate these [two kinds, actual and conformative]. If you do not distinguish between them, you might hold the three voids developed by vajra recitation on the lower stages to be the actual mind isolation, the fourth void to be the fourth stage clear light, and the two arisals in deity bodies after those two to be, [respectively,] the third-stage magic body and the fifth-stage communion body. Thus you will become excessively proud of such attainments when you have not really attained any of their excellent qualities, and you will lose your drive to attain the higher excellences not already attained. Then, since you have none of the distinctive transformations coming from them, some of you might generate a false view and think, "I attained a path such as this, but did not experience any sort of benefit of that attainment such as light rays; so these teachings are just words!" And some of you might think, "Relying on the fact that, in the literal texts of the treatises of the [noble] father and sons, not much is taught about the arisal of the voids of the path until the attainment of mind isolation, so until then the voids of the path will not arise [for me]"; and so you will not make effort in the methods of producing those and you will lose out on the great purpose.

Therefore, by meditating the perfection stage and dissolving the energies into the *dhūti* channel, you generate the four joys and the four voids, without having to consider this a very advanced path. So you strive in order to generate them as already explained. [172a] When the energy dissolves and the three voids together with the metaphoric clear light arise, if you remember your [realistic] view and set yourself in that as long as it lasts, then when the energies move and you arise from that again, you do vajra recitation again; and so you should increase your meditation on the method of compressing the energies.

106. He emphasizes the gentleness of this practice with this warning, that if you do energy compression with a power yoga, it can be fatal; so even though it might be quicker, you should be skillful about knowing the limits.

[**VI.B.3.b.ii.c′3′d′i′b″6″c″ii″c‴** – How to make the furor fire ignite]

Now here someone says, "Well, even if we allow that the vajra recitation is able to inject the energy into the *dhūti* channel and to cause that injected energy to dissolve there, this vajra recitation is not able to make the spirit of enlightenment melt by stimulating the furor, and it thus becomes unable to unify bliss and void; or, if it is able to do that, then please tell how it does it."

Already, the *Vajra Rosary* taught how this [vajra recitation] develops great bliss. And that great bliss is the bliss of the melting of the spirit of enlightenment of the crown center. And it is very true that melting that requires the navel furor fire to blaze. As for how that is done, the *Vajra Rosary* says:

> Since the ḍākinī compresses,
> She is the "pressure ḍākinī."
> She always stays in the navel center,
> And has a light like a thousand suns.
> Emitting the fire of great wisdom
> She conquers all instinctual thoughts.
> By her arisal aggregate-notions burn,
> And the body becomes unobstructed.
> After that the element-notions
> Are compressed, and again, naturally,
> The subject and object notions
> Afterward are again compressed.
> Thus, when like a moth [by flames]
> All bondages are consumed,
> By the yoga of the reality of energy,
> And by knowledge of the reality of mantra,
> The mere instinctual notions
> Are doubtless **[172b]** just consumed.

Now the first four feet of that [verse] show the actuality of the navel furor fire, which is said to be the actuality of the union of all ḍākinīs. This is just like the statements of the *Samputa [Tantra]* calling it "Nairātmya" and the *Spring Drop* calling it "the actuality of Varāhī," since those two are the actuality that unites all yoginīs such as Gaurī and Pracaṇḍī; so mentioning any [particular goddess] is by way of example. Showing that the blood of the reddish furor is the actuality of the union of all ḍākinīs means that the activity of the science consorts is to develop the great bliss in the yogi/nī, and that is achieved by the blazing of the furor fire.

Thereupon two feet [of the verse] show in general the burning of the conceptual notions by the blazing of the furor fire. And then two feet, one and a half feet, and two and a half feet, respectively, discuss the suppression of the conceptual notions about the aggregates, the elements, and subject-object [dichotomy]. Here "suppression" means burning or conquering. "Unobstructed" here has the meaning of again and again or continuous. And "body" here means burning in the body. Now again two feet unite the metaphor and the import of the burning of the conceptual notions. Then again two feet refer to that burning of conceptual notions by the blazing of furor fire, and then again two feet explain how the knowledge of the union of the reality of mantra, the three or the two letters, with the reality of energy, the three, exhalation, inhalation, and abiding, or the two, inhalation and exhalation, is what accomplishes the burning of the notions by the blazing of furor fire. [All this] thus means that the vajra recitation accomplishes [the furor fire] just like that. Again the last two feet state that even the subtlest conceptual notions are consumed without any doubt.

Again [173a] the same text [the *Vajra Rosary*]—saying:

> Depending truly on the reality of energy,
> Exhorted by the syllable HŪṀ,
> The wheel of fire is very much awakened . . .

—thus states that furor is made to awaken by the reality of mantra depending upon the reality of energy. And HŪṀ here expresses a single aspect of the vajra recitation of either two or three syllables. Other translations have the phrase "by the yoga of the body of mantra," and in the commentary the meaning of that is explained as being a meditation on the creation stage. In the Indian texts also it is clear that there were two discordant readings, and so Darma Tsöndru's translation, like the previous reading, is better.

The furor blazes moved by what sort of energy? The *Personal Instruction [of Mañjushrī]* says:

Vowed effort, by moving the bow-shaped,
The wisdom fire blazes in the triangle,
And the element melts. . . .

The bow-shaped located in a triangle is the energy, which is stated to ignite the furor fire, and it is the evacuative energy. Also the *Great Seal Drop* states:

The way being located in the navel,
The limit of the way is the secret lotus;
There the self-blazing energy
Circulates and so refreshes.
By the union of the two organs
The energy ignites the fire.

—declaring that the energy located in the lotus of the secret place ignites the furor fire.

You might wonder, "If the furor fire is ignited by a particular motion of the evacuative energy, how does that movement function?"

The *Sampuṭa [Tantra]* says:

In the mandala of the navel furnace,
Agitated by the evolutionary energy,
The brahma-fire burns in the triangle.

Concerning that statement, the *Sheaf of Instructions* explains that [173b] [the furor fire] is ignited by the energy impelled by the evolutionary force of the action of the union of the two organs and the action of the meditative entrancement. The first [action] refers to the meditation [either] on the energy or the drop and so on that have been injected into the vital point in the body. The second [action] is explained by the [union of the] two organs. As for the blood, the actuality of the fire-atom to be ignited, though it abides in many parts of the body, the main ones are the blood of the navel symbolized by the short *A* and the "brahma-fire" symbolized by the syllable KṢHA, both dwelling below the navel in the secret place; and further they abide within the *dhūti* channel. As for the evacuative energies that ignite them, one kind enters within the *dhūti* channel and one kind does not, and the former is the main one. As the *Vajra Rosary* says:

In the left descends the moon, enlightenment spirit,
In the right, blood and sun descend.
Knowable in the center, the energy moves,
And you should know that wakens up the fire.

Thus it states that when the energies move through the central channel, they make furor fire awaken. From the threshold when the vajra recitation injects energies into the central channel, a slightly heated special furor fire burns. When it increases, it melts the crown enlightenment spirit. As the *Great Seal Drop* says:

By the true burning of that fire,
The great bliss wheel will melt.
By melting, all the channels
Will drip with the supreme nectar.

As for the meditation of blazing and dripping, it happens that there are many meltings of the spirit of enlightenment by the burning of furor fire even without injecting energy into the central channel. And even if you meditate energies and drops etc., without meditating in such a way [as by penetrating the vital points], furor fire can blaze and enlightenment spirit can melt before the energy has been injected into the *dhūti* channel and dissolved there. [174a] For example, it happens even in ordinary sexual union of the two organs. In those [experiences], as the enlightenment spirit melts, just due to its intensity it is hard to hold it without emission, whereas when this occurs from the [energies] dissolving into the *dhūti* channel, it is very easy to hold it.

Again, as for the blazing of warmth, there are two kinds, with and without the ability to melt the spirit of enlightenment. As for the warmth that is able to melt the spirit of enlightenment, there are kinds arising from the energies being and not being injected into the *dhūti* channel. As for those when [energies are] injected, there are kinds where they dissolve and do not dissolve therein. And even bliss has a kind where bliss happens from the energies merely becoming serviceable, which does not turn into melting bliss. And melting bliss also comes in many stages. Therefore, you should be very skillful in distinguishing well these [various types of experiences].

When the evacuative energy first ignites the main furor fire, it ignites the two fires of secret place and navel, and as evacuative energy in the two lower doors goes in and out like [energies do] in the two upper nostrils, those energies must be injected into the *dhūti* channel. Just as the injected vitalizing energy dissolves [therein] without going in and out of the upper nostrils, when the [evacuative energy] dissolves and does not go in and out of the lower doors, the powerful blazing of furor fire increases the power of the melting of the spirit of enlightenment.[107] Even if such a thing should happen once, it frequently happens in alternation that the energy arises again and starts to go in and out; it is not the case that once it dissolves it does not arise again, as is the case when you eliminate seeds by transcendent paths.

As the *Vajra Rosary* teaches that the vajra recitation binds the energies within all the nine doors of the senses, not only does it terminate the entry and exit of the upper nostril doors but it also terminates [174b] the lower nostril door entry and exit. When you do this by pulling up with a fierce physical effort, although there is some slight speeding up of the blocking of the energy, it tends not to go to the vital point. It is better if you stop the [energies'] movement by gentle exertions such as vajra recitation; so you should know that [fact], even about holding the energies in a compression lock.

You might wonder, "since the evacuative energy enters and exits the two lower doors, is it proper to use vajra recitation in relation with that entry and exit as you do in the two upper doors?"

Concerning this, Tibetan mentors give a personal instruction about the yoga of closing and opening the lower door as a way of generating bliss. Although this is not called "entry-exit recitation," if you know how to discern its meaning, it is like performing [the vajra recitation] in the upper door. About this way, from Atīsha's *Dharma Song*:[108]

> Conquer the progress of sun and moon—
> Otherwise in the door of the great sky,

107. Just as the upper energies dissolve in the *dhūti* without the upper energy breathing in and out, this lower energy dissolves so there is no more going in and out of the lower doors. It thus becomes stronger in melting the enlightenment spirit.

108. This quote has not yet been identified in an original. Perhaps it is from an older version of Atīsha: **Dīpaṁkaraśrījñāna-dharma-gītikā* (*d'i paṁ ka'a ra shr'i dznya' na'i chos kyi glu*) (Tōh 2374; rGyud 'Grel, ZI, 10a–10b); or *Caryāgīti* (*spyod pa'i glu*) (Tōh. 1496; rGyud 'Grel, ZHA, 215a–216b), wherein it was not found.

Berampa[109] will not enter.
By the yoga of opening and closing,
You should compel that fierce goddess.
The five buddhas and the four goddesses—
You should burn them again and again.
The ten directions' heroes and yogi/nīs
Gather and dissolve into Jalandhara.[110]
The four drops in the four lotuses
Will generate the sixteen blisses.
The self-luminous wisdom dwells
In the center of the formful lotus navel.
When enlightenment dwells in the jewel tip,
You gain nirvana like a butter lamp.
When you win nirvana there
In the tip of the jewel,
The host of notions such as self and other,
I no longer see them at all.
When the planet [Rāhu] seizes sun and moon,
The mind and the Bera[m]pa do not proceed.
When all notions fully melt and dissolve,
The mind becomes pure experience of the [reality] realm.

[175a] Here he declares the distinctive art of injecting the energy into the *dhūti* channel. This same meaning is also expressed in the *Great Seal Drop*:

109. *Berampa* (*be raṁ pa*) = *Vairambha[ka]* = *Beraṁbha* (*be raṁ bha*) = *Bairambha* (*bai rambha*). Tōh. 1413 (Indrabhūti, *Cakrasaṁvara-vṛtti*, fol. 115a.3–.4); Tōh. 1427 (Lūyipa, *Bhagavad-abhisamaya*, fol. 187a.4–.6); Tōh. 1449 (Vanaratna, *Vasantatilaka-tika*, fol. 336a.7–b.4). These texts identify this term as referring to the bow-shaped energy-disc that forms the base of the mandala universes of various tantras, which can only be visualized or projected by the yogi/nī after having dissolved the ordinary universe by melting all energies into the central channel via its lower door, either navel or genital wheel. I am indebted to Paul Hackett for these references.

110. Jalandhara is one of the twenty-four holy places of the *Chakrasamvara Tantra* and also is the crown center of the yogic nervous system; the idea here being that the fire blazing from the energy at the closing of the lower door of the central channel causes the furor fire from the navel center to blaze up and melt all heroes and yoginīs into the moon disc of bindu drops at the crown center.

> By closing and opening [the lower doors],
> The energy encompasses the fire.
> With the wood of the organ of the truth,
> Thereby the furor fire burns,
> Consuming the body entirely,
> And all materials of the heap of notions.
> And by the true burning of that fire . . .

So it declares just as before.

This enables you to understand that there is a [vajra] recitation of the exit and entry [of the energy] through the path of water, and although the upper [body] vajra recitation accomplishes both these purposes, if you want to take it in terms of singling out the evacuative energy of the lower parts, you should perform it relying on your attainment of the already present base of personal instructions. If you perform the reversal of the evacuative energy by forceful methods, there are great hindrances such as the blocking of excrement and urine. But if you perform the gentle yoga with the skill in the vital points taught in the oral instruction and reverse the movement [of the energy], you need not lessen excrement and urine and have to eliminate them time and again. You will not experience the slightest discomfort, your furor fire will burn with much greater power, you will have a superlative bliss, and however intense your melting of the element, you will have no need of caution about emission, and so on—such are the signs that will occur.

You might say, "Well, by meditating the heart indestructible and the vajra recitation etc., and the spirit of enlightenment melts by the blazing of furor fire, as is explained by the yoginī tantras, and falls down to the jewel—relying on that, are the four joys developed? Or else do you generate the four voids compressing [all energies and drops] into the heart center from above and below?"

This I am going to explain [175b] in the section on mind isolation.

Here, many [yogi/nīs] have performed the yoga of blocking the energy etc. with intense force, seeing that to be a bit quicker and not knowing how to discern well the differences of how the immediate and long term advantages are generated from gentle and rough yogas. Once they perform the arts of penetrating the vital points in the body, they meditate considering that they must practice with very intense force. Now, some of them experience extremely great hindrances, and they then stop meditating those [methods]. Others, although their hindrances are also very great, accept the need to meditate with skill in the methods of dispelling them.

As for the way of dispelling hindrances, some might say, "Well, when you compress the energy and it generates shooting pains before it becomes peaceful, you should meditate the yoga of many holes and thus expel them outside. And many others alleviate the shooting pains of energy compression with other methods."

To that someone says, "When striving in order to compress the energies, if you then quiet them without performing the method of entering them into the central channel, your efforts will be pointless, as you lack the personal instruction." But our own system is that you enter the [energies] into the central channel by the yoga of the art of squeezing the two waves of enjoyment;[111] and this is recommended also for pacifying shooting pains. Everyone seems to agree about using a forceful yoga at the beginning of meditation.

Once you have meditated combining channels and energies etc., it is not certain that a great hindrance will arise that either will deprive one's vitalizing energy or come close to doing so. Such would be the fault of not knowing decisively well how to cultivate at first, because if you do know [well the key points], [such dangers] will just not occur. Thus if you know well how to practice, [176a] and how to avoid great hindrances through meditating, you are an expert. If you stubbornly produce great hindrances, even though you know ways of getting rid of them, you are not expert.

When you compress the energies with gentle yoga, in general, hindrances are less. And if at first you compress the energies without having first purified them, there is a way of clearing away slight shooting pains that may arise—I will explain this elsewhere.[112] Do not think that [these concerns] just have to do with pacifying the shooting pains. Rather they are to make

111. I have not previously encountered this expression *longs spyod kyi rlabs gnyis 'tshir bai thabs kyi sbyor bas*, and cannot quite yet figure it out.

112. One place in Tsong Khapa's Collected Works where this is somewhat explained is in the *Zhu Lan bDud rTsis Snying po*, a text recording the 1399 CE conversations between Vajrapāṇi and Hlodrak Namkha Gyaltsen about Tsong Khapa, wherein the dispersal of the neuralgic pains that can come from some kinds of energy meditations is extensively discussed. I translated this long ago and published in the *Life and Teachings of Tsong Khapa*, LTWA, Dharamsala, 1982; second edition, Wisdom Publications, Boston, 2018.

sure that you know how not to let the compression of the energies become difficult somewhat later, and moreover how to dispel any failure to inject the previously compressed energies into the central *dhūti* channel—this is then to be an expert.

Therefore if you practice according to the two former systems, it seems that while it might happen that you might alleviate the shooting pains of compressing energies, it will not benefit your injecting the previously compressed energies into the *dhūti* channel.

The third method of dispelling [obstructions] can still work well with the forceful yoga, but our own system is that you must perform [the practice] with the gentle yogas as the [best] method of dispelling [obstructions], not using the forceful yogas at all.

Thus, as for [my composing] this detailed explanation of the vital points of the vajra recitation: though there seem to be very many ways to perform vajra recitation given in the oral instructions, nevertheless, since the literature of the *Esoteric Community* explains vajra recitation exhaustively in ways that are not present in other tantras or treatises, since it seems that good explanations of the system of the *Esoteric Community* are rare, and since the noble father and son do not explain the other energy yogas but explain this one quite a lot, [I have written this] in order to interpret decisively [their explanations].

7. Mind Isolation

[176a.6–203b.5]

[**VI.B.3.b.ii.c′3′d′i′c″** – How to learn the mind isolation mind vajra samadhi]

The third has five parts: [1″] The reason you must understand the reality of the mind; [176b] [2″] The way the natural pattern of that mind is declared in the sutras; [3″] Demonstration that the especially excellent art for realizing the nature of the mind is the unexcelled [yoga] tantra; [4″] Teaching the tantra's import, the three luminances and the instinctual natures; and [5″] Showing the dangers and the advantages of not knowing and knowing that [import] correctly.

[**VI.B.3.b.ii.c′3′d′i′c″1″** – The reason you must understand the reality of the mind]

If you desire buddhahood, generally staying on the vajra vehicle and specifically learning and practicing the vajra recitation, you must seek to discover the actuality of your own mind. According to the *Integrated Practices*, the *Reality Compendium* states:

> noble child, with meditative absorption, you should introspectively realize your own mind.

The *Vairochana Enlightenment* states:

> Enlightenment is the total understanding of the reality of your own mind.

And;

> Even as stated in *Three Baskets' Way*,
> "Going alone, one wanders far,
> Living in the cave of the bodiless Lord;
> But taming the mind so hard to tame—
> [I say such a one is a Brahmin!]
> Who will be freed from the devil's chains."[113]

And then, [the *Integrated Practices* concludes, in words to the effect that]:

> Wanting to realize the magic body, you abandon all five obstructions such as vacillation and sleep, you propitiate the teacher who has truly obtained the personal instruction of all transcendent buddhas, you follow the explanatory tantras such as *Wisdom Vajra Compendium*, and you should then experience the three consciousnesses of natural luminance.

All three references, cited as reasons why one who wants to learn the [177a] mind isolation must seek the reality of the mind, teach the need to experience the reality of the mind. Thus they refute certain Tibetan and Indian [scholars] who claim that the mind isolation wisdom knows the subjective mind and does not know the reality of the mind, since if it did, it would become indistinguishable from [the later stage of] clear light [wisdom]. While the fourth stage clear light wisdom directly experiences the reality of the mind, mind isolation [wisdom] knows that ultimate reality without fully experiencing it; hence they are not indistinguishable. Although the [above] three supporting references from a sutra and the two lower tantras do not indicate the three mind isolation wisdoms, they still serve as reasons for the need to realize the reality of the mind.

113. This seems to be a case of a tantric commentary quoting a sutra verse, perhaps one similar to one from the *Dhammapada* (ch. 3, v. 5): "[The mind] travels far, moves alone, has no form, sleeps in a cave—those who restrain the mind will escape the bonds of evil." (Thanks to Dr. Lozang Jamspal for noticing this.)

[**VI.B.3.b.ii.c′3′d′i′c″2″** – The way the natural pattern of that mind is declared in the sutras]

You may wonder, "If I must investigate the reality of the mind, just what is it like?"

Here the *Integrated Practices* explains both transcendence and tantra vehicle types of statement. First, it quotes the *Mission to Laṅka* to the effect that your mind desires to know subject-object-constructed appearance as the sphere of buddhas, [then it] teaches that the obscurations such as gregariousness and sleep must be abandoned, and [finally] that mind, mentality, and consciousness are the root of the whole world of beings and environments. Though the old translation of the *Integrated Practices* says "sphere of mental construction," the Chag translation is better, translating "mental construction the sphere of buddhas." [177b]

[The *Integrated Practices*] goes on to quote the *Inquiry of Bhadrapāla*, [the *Consciousness Migrating Sutra*], showing that consciousness, even when taking a body and entering lower birth-places, is not polluted by their faults; that wherever consciousness migrates, its evolutionary fruition, the sensations of pleasure and pain, also migrates; and that one who does not see the truth does not know that consciousness, abbreviating the meaning by saying that:

> Thus, consciousness has a nature free of color, sign, and shape, said to be sheer introspective wisdom in the universal vehicle sutras.

"The sphere of buddhas" refers to the ultimate reality of mind. The demonstration of its being the root of all refers to its natural pattern of subjectivity. It is taught as entering various birth-states without change in its reality, and as not experientially knowable by any non-noble person. Thus, that mind is declared ultimately to be devoid of all signs, conventionally colorless, shapeless, not depending on other means of knowing, and sheer knowledge, itself knowing its object.

As for the way it is described in the vajra vehicle, the same text [the *Integrated Practices*] continues:

> The Divine Lord declared in words found in all the tantras, "That mind investigated as the buddha-sphere is in reality rootless,

> placeless, groundless, signless, shapeless, colorless, transcending the senses, and beyond the scope of the dogmatists."

This refers to [178a] an import shared with the transcendence vehicle about the actuality of that mind, investigated in the context of learning mind isolation, and not to mind isolation [itself].

[Nāgārjuna] states, in the *Reason Sixty*:

> The world seems to be illusory,
> Placeless, imperceivable,
> Rootless, non-enduring,
> Originated from the cause of ignorance,
> Abandoning beginning, middle, or end,
> Coreless like a plantain tree,
> Like a city of fairies,
> An intolerable city of delusion.

And in the *Commentary*, [Chandrakīrti] explains that "place" refers to the six media such as eye, "perception" refers to all things, "root" refers to the seed patterns of causal conditions, and "illusory" refers to its lack of intrinsically real existence by reason of its relativity. Groundless is meant by its [ultimate] "imperceivability."

[**VI.B.3.b.ii.c′3′d′i′c′′3′′** – Demonstration that the especially excellent art for realizing the nature of the mind is the unexcelled (yoga) tantra]

The *Integrated Practices* states:

> Without entering the great yoga tantras such as the *Community*, you cannot realize the actual condition of your own mind, even if [you try] for as many eons as there are grains of sand in the Ganges riverbed; nor will you see even the superficial reality.

I have already explained that this does not teach that you cannot determine the [authentic] view of the ground [reality] without entering into the unexcelled [yoga tantras]; nor does it mean that, having determined it and meditated on it, you cannot experience it. No reasonable person says that the transcendence vehicle does not enable you to attain the stage of nobility; [178b] because if you can attain that [stage], it precludes your not realizing actuality experientially. Nor does [Āryadeva] teach the ultimate actuality of the mind intending the truth body; since this is the context of the analysis of realizing the true import of the mind in terms of mind isolation, which you can also understand from the statement "nor can you see even the superficial reality."

Therefore, the meaning is that the main subjectivity realizing the reality of the mind is orgasmic bliss, and, as for such intuitive wisdom realizing that object, it cannot be realized if you do not enter the door of the unexcelled [yoga tantras], but enter any other door of the transcendences or the lower tantras. This exaltation must be attained through other paths [only] after many immeasurable eons, but is attained in a single lifetime on the path of the unexcelled. As for this special distinctive speed, is because of [this path's] being practiced after orgasmic great bliss has ascertained the import of reality. As the *Sampuṭa [Tantra]* states:

> Thus, what need is there for lengthy explanations.
> In brief, buddhahood is [usually] gained
> After millions of immeasurable eons;
> [But] you, by means of noble bliss,
> Will attain it in this very life.

As for the mere termination of addictive obscurations, it can be attained by some [individual vehicle] disciples in three lifetimes, and the experiential realization of the import of reality is common to both vehicles. Thus, this distinction of speed does not just concern the speed of liberation from the life cycle through the speed of experientially realizing voidness. Therefore, this path requires an extreme speed in terminating cognitive obscurations.

In that regard, [179a] according to the transcendence vehicle, if you lack the dimension of art in practicing the infinite different clear categories of the infinite stores [of merit and wisdom], even if you understand penetratingly the view of voidness and meditate however so much, except for becoming free from the life cycle, you cannot terminate the cognitive obscurations. Hence, universal vehicle persons' developing such infinite stores over long times is for the sake of turning that realization that understands voidness into the means for terminating the cognitive obscurations. On the unexcelled path, though you do not, as in the case of the transcendence-vehicle practitioners, develop the infinite different clear categories of the stores, it is declared that your [progress] is extremely swift, since you meditate on the incisive import of voidness by means of the orgasmic bliss. Thus, it is by the key point of the distinctive subjectivity of great bliss that you can understand that the purification of the cognitive obscurations, which constitute the instinctive dualistic error about the realization of voidness, is so very accelerated. Therefore, in this path's initiation and first stage with their auxiliary rites, the declarations of great praise about its excellence, distinctive from other paths, are not just gratuitous, but aim to establish receptivity for the path of the union of bliss and void and serve as means of developing the fulfillment of that [union].

Now the proof of the supreme distinctiveness of speed on the path of bliss and void in union turns on the understanding that venturing upon it provides an extraordinary cause of attaining the buddha matter body, which [extraordinary cause] is recognized as a substitute for the infinite different clear categories of the store of merit. [179b] Further, that [extraordinary cause] is none other than the magic body, hence you will not find the keys of both [father and mother] tantras completely until you become expert in both perfection stages, that of the void-side great bliss and that of the vision-side magic body.

[Here,] the *Community* explains:

> Formerly, before as many eons as subatomic particles in incalculably many buddhaverses, from the time when the Buddha Dīpaṁkara passed away until the time of the Buddha Kashyapa, the great secret was not taught, since the beings during those times had no fortune to learn the import of the great secret.

However, that enlightenment that is not attained by those bodhisattvas, even though they strive and seek for as many eons as grains of Ganges' sand, is attained in one single lifetime by those bodhisattvas who delight in the *Community*. As for the meaning of the reason for that, the *Illuminating Lamp* states:

> During that time, the beings aspired for the inferior goal, they educated themselves by means of the passionless teaching, giving gifts, being moral, and so forth, and their minds were afraid of

> the teaching of the profound. Thus they had no fortune, and [the buddhas] did not explain the import of the great secret during those times. At this present time, exclusively the Transcendent Lord knows that beings are involved with passion and their inclinations are overwhelmed by the five corruptions, [and so he] visits the world and teaches [the secret teaching].

According to this, it depends on whether or not [a bodhisattva] has an aspiration for the outer [180a] art of developing the great bliss. If you unite bliss and void by the art that fully incorporates void and bliss, you can [still] feel fear about its bestowing enlightenment in this life, though you have no fear about voidness alone. As for the cause of fearing that conduct that is passionate and skilled in art, granted that it is also a weakness of passion, mainly [that cause] is the [erroneous] idea that since the fruit of buddhahood has boundless excellence, it is suitable [to attain] after infinite different clear categories of stores and time, and is not suitable without them; and that, since the great treasures of excellence who reside on the high stages are required to spend a long time, a statement about attainment in a short time, a lifetime or so, is in order to attract certain disciples, and is not to be taken literally. Even among those who have great faith in this path and in voidness, two ways of proceeding must be distinguished, beneficial and faulty; you must get clear the arrangement of the two paths, seeing the distinctive means of attainment, and then, with intense aspiration, it is very important that you firmly determine [yourself to wield] the extraordinary ability of the type of person suited for this path.

The teaching—that the mind isolation wisdom's realization of the reality of the mind and its experience of the superficial magic body are extremely difficult to find on any other path—is put forth from the wish to teach as an extraordinary path the process in which the mind isolation of great bliss—derived from meditating the above-explained three vitalizing energy controls—meditates the reality of the mind and achieves the magic body. [180b] As for the statement that, without entering upon the great yoga tantras such as the *Community*, you will not see the superficial reality even for many eons, it rejects the claim that the superficial magic body is a samadhi that realizes the nonreality in apparent things, and the claim that it is the mere nonreality of the appearance of the deity body. I will explain below how other paths do or do not bring you ultimately into this process and the reasons for those [results].

[**VI.B.3.b.ii.c′3′d′i′C″4″** – Teaching the tantra's import, the three luminances and the instinctual natures]

The fourth has three parts, explaining: [a″] Luminance; [b″] The instinctual natures; and [c″] How to generate luminance intuition.

[**VI.B.3.b.ii.c′3′d′i′C″4″a″** – Luminance]

The first has two parts, explaining: [i″] Synonyms of the three luminances; and [ii″] Definitions of each of the three luminances.

[**VI.B.3.b.ii.c′3′d′i′C″4″a″i″** – Synonyms of the three luminances]

The *Integrated Practices* mentions two kinds of synonyms of the three luminances, those in common with the transcendence universal vehicle, and those uncommon, of renown in the vajra vehicle only.

[Synonyms in Common with the Transcendence Universal Vehicle]

The first are the synonyms "art" and "wisdom," clearly mentioned by the Teacher, and the third, "neuter," which is implied. Also "mind," "mentality," and "consciousness"; and "imaginary," "relative," and "perfect"; and "lust," "hate," and "delusion"; and the "three realities." Here, "art" is "radiance," "wisdom" is "luminance," and "neuter" is the concentration of both [in] "imminence." In regard to bliss and void, it is said that luminance has the stronger [181a] awareness of void, radiance the opposite, and imminence has a balanced proportion. However, this does not indicate that all sets of art, wisdom, and their combination refer to those three. That also is in terms of the three luminances of the path, the three basic reality luminances also being termed the same, from [the fact of] their aspects being similar.

As for calling luminance "mind," radiance "mentality," and imminence "consciousness," there is no indication that those three correspond [directly] to these three. And further, "mind," "mentality," and "consciousness" are not considered mutually exclusive as are the three luminances. In some other treatises, based on equating "mind" with fundamental consciousness, "mentality" with addictive mentality, and "consciousness" with the sixfold functioning consciousness, they seem to explain luminance as functioning consciousness, radiance as afflictive mentality, and imminence as the fundamental. But this seems incorrect. For, if you claim that radiance and imminence are the afflictive mentality and the fundamental consciousness, then the two [claims] would have the imperative consequences that an alienated individual could ascertain as manifest a fundamental consciousness and an afflictive mentality as different from the sixfold consciousness; [which is] not [possible]. And then there would be the extreme incongruity of positing perceivability for luminance and lack of perceivability for the other two. And then it would contradict the frequent explanations of the new generation of the luminances by the path of outer and inner vitalizing energy control. Finally, if you adopt [this theory] because there are occasional reasons to apply the name "fundamental" [to the luminances etc.], then, as that also is not taught, [181b] it is also incorrect.

Well then, how is it?

In general, in the discourses it is stated that mind, mentality, and consciousness in general are the root of all purificatory practices. Thus, as he wished to teach a special set of the three, mind, mentality, and consciousness, as serving as the root of all purificatory practices, [Nāgārjuna etc.] applied the terms of those three to the three luminances. As Āryadeva quotes the *Wisdom Vajra Compendium* in the *Integrated Practices*:

> Consciousness emerges from clear light. That very thing is called "mind" and "mentality"; and it has the root of all things whose nature is afflictive and purificative.

As the *Vajra Rosary* states:

> Having the nature of the three luminances,
> Who here learns of the three consciousnesses,
> This is the root nature
> Of the entire realm of living beings.

As for calling the three luminances "consciousness," as "mind" and "mentality" are similar, each of the three luminances can be called by all three names. But as for calling the three luminances individually by one of those three terms, they should be assigned in terms of temporal sequence corresponding to the homogeneity of mental consciousnesses. As for the verbal meaning, [luminance] is called "mind" because of its accumulating, [radiance] "mentality" because of its serving as support, and [imminence] "consciousness" because of its dependence. Those [three functions] are completely present in all three luminance minds, they do not differ in intensity, nor can they be differentiated according to such etymologies.

From the *Five Stages*, [Nāgārjuna] states that luminance is the relative, radiance is the imaginary, and imminence is the perfect. [182a] Such an explanation realizes [luminance as] the apparent ground of perception of dichotomous subject and object, as the relative; the reification of substantial subject-object dichotomy as the imaginary, and the changeless as the perfect. And in the face of that, one should analyze, thinking "Is it luminance that is the ground of the beginning of the voids as isolated from both the imaginary and dualistic appearance? Is it radiance that emerges as based on that? And is it imminence when both the above are abandoned? Are they [so designated] depending on such corresponding properties of the interpenetration of art and wisdom?"

As for calling luminance "anger," radiance "lust," and imminence "delusion," it is from the perspective of their functions as slight bliss, big bliss, and medium bliss; and their states at times of basis and path are as above.

As for the names of the three realities, as the three natures are already explained, it is not that [same set of] the three realities. Thus, the reality of the void side and that of the vision side, and the reality of the two in equality [is referred to] as above explained.

In the transcendence vehicle, there is no assignation of such names to the three luminances; so while the names designated are common [to both vehicles], such designation of the three luminances by those names is not common.

[Uncommon Synonyms, of Renown only in the Vajra Vehicle]

Second, [they are called in the *Integrated Practices*] luminance, luminance-radiance, and luminance-imminence; voidness, extreme voidness, and great voidness; mind, mental functions, and misknowledge; dispassion, passion, and medium passion; [182b] and:

> *OṀ* is the cause of confirming [luminance intuition,] the seed using the door of speech; since those beings of little faith will

> not understand the Transcendent Lord's intentional statements, they will visualize it as "the form of a moon disc," and as "the clear form of the superficial reality of the mind in the actuality of "softness," or "lotus," "female form," "left," and "night."

And:

> ĀḤ is the cause of confirming [radiance intuition,] the seed using the door of speech; since those beings of little faith will not understand the Transcendent Lord's intentional statements, they will visualize it depending on a solar disc, in the form of the superficial reality of mental function in the actuality of "roughness," as a "five point vajra," "jewel," "day," "male form," and "right."

And:

> [HŪṀ,] the perfect, [as the cause of] confirming [luminance-imminence intuition,] the seed using speech, is luminance-imminence.

So it is stated. In the Chag translation it is stated: "Depending on [short] *A*, the seed of speech."

Thus, it is incorrect to take the three voids as the realities of the three luminances but not as the three luminances themselves, just because it is said that "the three voids are the serial dissolutions of the three luminances." For the *Integrated Practices* states that the three luminances themselves are the three voids, and that very fact is clear in the *Wisdom Vajra Compendium*.

Therefore, the three luminances are called: "luminance," since it is perceived as like moonlight after the dissolving of the imaginative thought-moving energy, [183a] and that same [luminance] being void, devoid of the eighty imaginations together with their energies; "luminance-radiance," since it is very brilliant like sunlight, being extreme void, devoid of luminance with its energy; and "luminance-imminence," since it is perceived extremely indistinctly like a [night] between-time dark fog, close to clear light, and is a great void devoid of radiance with its energies, or "ignorance," since it is not clear, ["ignorance"] naming an aspect of imminence.

Here, "the door of speech" refers to the path through which speech emerges; the seed produced depending on that constitutes the three syllables. The "cause that confirms them" [means] that the three terms cause the ascertainment of the three intuitions.

From the *Five Stages*:

> The name of the left is that very one.
> Having the moon disc and lotus,
> Serving as cause of the confirmed,
> The first letter with a drop [OṀ].

And also:

> Likewise, with the name of vajra,
> Adorned by two drops [ĀḤ],
> Know that very thing in that part.

Thus the luminances have meanings illustrated by the verbal signs of those letters.

As for "those of little faith," coming to perceive them depending on sun and moon, it refers to the creation-stage person, who cannot accomplish the development of the magic body from the three intuitions as can the perfection-stage person who has attained the mind isolation. So here the symbol "moon" means luminance, "vajra" means radiance, and so forth, and imminence, the union of mind and mental functions of luminance and radiance, [is symbolized by] the union of moon and vajra etc., which means [it causes] the creation of the deity body. From the *Five Stages*:

> Just this reality of wisdom [**183b**]
> Is imagined as a pure moon disc;
> The mind just sees itself,
> Just itself in the form of a moon.
> Then perceiving the moon,
> Imagine [there] the vajra sign,
> Symbolizing the liberative art
> Of the yogi/nīs who create the vajra etc.
> The moon and vajra etc. in union,
> Combine mind and mental functions.

By uniting wisdom and art,
The deity form is born.

Here the fifth line is better in the Chag translation: "From perceiving the full moon, etc."

As for referring to the first two luminances by the words "moon" and "sun," "day" and "night," it comes from the sky appearing to be filled with moonlight and sunlight. Referring to them by "lotus" and "vajra," "female" and "male," "left" and "right," is in terms of their referring to art and wisdom. As for "soft" and "rough," it relates to inferior and not inferior blisses, and to objective appearance being extensive and not extensive.

As for "superficial form" expressing the moon etc. being symbols of the two intuitions, it is the nature of the "artificial." As for luminance-imminence, it is signified by names such as "neuter," "day-night-boundary," "left-right-between," "soft-rough-between," "wisdom-art-commingled," and "moon [-sun] and day-night-combined."

[**VI.B.3.b.ii.c′3′d′i′c″4″a″ii″** – Definitions of each of the three luminances]

[Āryadeva states] in the *Integrated Practices* that:

> The concise definition of the three luminances stated in the *Wisdom Vajra Compendium* is to be taught as the mentor's precept.

Regarding that statement [in the tantra, Āryadeva says]:

> If you ask "What is the definition of luminance?" [we reply:] its nature is formless, [184a] without body or speech; it is like a taintless autumn sky filled by the illumination of light rays from the moon disc, perceived in the form of natural clarity in all things—this is the ultimate spirit of enlightenment, the first void, the wisdom-luminance.

And:

> "What is the definition of luminance-radiance?" That has the form of freedom from subject and object, and is without body

> and speech; being the perception of all things in the reality of extremely brilliant taintlessness, like the autumn sky flooded with sunrays, it is the second spirit of enlightenment, the total goodness, having the character of the second stage, that of extreme void.

And:

> "What is the definition of luminance-imminence?" It has the form of nothingness, the character of space, lacking body and speech; as if pervaded in a state of fog-bound-midnight, subtle and selfless, motionless, with no movement of vitalizing energy control; without mind, unwavering and . . .

In this system, a proper determination of the four voids is very important, yet although the *Root Tantra* and the other four explanatory tantras frequently mention just their names, their identifications are very unclear. And the *Wisdom Vajra Compendium* does not describe them otherwise than just mentioning them as "ignorance-darkness," "mental-function-sunlight," and "mind-moonlight." Further in the other treatises of the other four [of the noble] father and sons, the identification is very [184b] unclear. So it must be understood relying on the *Integrated Practices* itself.

While the *Wisdom Vajra Compendium* explains the three voids as the stages of the reverse process from the clear light of death, the *Integrated Practices* explains the voids of path-time in common [with the luminances].

Thus, the four voids are shown as symbolized by the example of clear sky, and since the autumn is the time when there are many conditions, such as the summer rains having controlled the earth's dust from rising into view and such as the lack of obscuring clouds, the autumn sky is taken as the example. In daytime that clear sky is filled with sunlight; it is filled with thick, black darkness from evening until the night darkness clears [at dawn]; it is filled with moonlight from moon-rise until dawn; and it is free of these three causes of deviation from the sky's own color in the predawn when moonlight is gone and sunlight is not yet arisen. These are the four occasions.

As the latter of them is the example of the fourth void, universal void, [let us] leave it aside for the moment. The first of the three examples applies to radiance, the second to imminence, and the third to luminance. When those three intuitions arise, experiences like those three skies dawn.

In the context of the third, in place of "having the form of nothingness," the Chag translation is better "in the nature of formlessness," as corresponding to the first definition. And that has the same meaning as the "free from [185a] subject and object" in the second definition. Further, except for the dawning as in the three modes of perception explained above, it means that all other coarse, dualistic perceptions have declined in that state. In all three, "without body and speech" refers to the lack of physical movement and verbal expression in that time. From "just as . . ." up to "like . . ." is already explained. "The character of space . . ." applies to "like dark fog filling the sky." "Perceived in the form of natural clarity" refers to the clear arisal of that objective appearance [of luminance], and "extreme clarity" refers to even greater clarity than before. "Perceived in all things" means that the objective luminance pervades all directions and quarters; and the scope of the perception comes out as appropriate.

"Actual ultimate spirit of enlightenment" refers to the intuition of path-time bliss-void-union, metaphorically designated also upon other paths and also basis-time. As imminence becomes unconscious, it does not experience bliss-void-union, but it is not that imminence lacks that in general. "Subtle" refers to difficulty of realization, and "selfless" to having the form of intrinsic realitylessness. "Vitalizing energy control not occurring" refers to the lack of respiration. Although those traits are present in all three, they are mentioned about imminence by predominance. For "free of mind" the Chag translation of "samadhi unmoved by unconsciousness itself" is preferable.

Thus, when the energies that move the imaginations dissolve, the sign of lamp-flame occurs, and [185b] the luminance that arises next is a pure voidness, very clear like a clear night autumn sky pervaded by risen moonlight, arising in the form of a white luminance of light; and no extra coarse dualistic perception arises there at all. For example, though the sky is filled with moonlight, one sees without the sky being obscured by that; so in that state, the form of white light luminance arises without obscuring that clear, void-like pure space.

When that luminance withdraws, luminance-radiance dawns, like the clear autumn sky filled with sunlight, even much more transparent pure voidness than the previous, arising with a red or orange color; and the rest are as above.

Then, after that radiance has withdrawn, imminence begins, the stopping of energies becomes great, and the object perception arises in the form of black[ness] like night-fog pervading void perception; the subjective consciousness declines and becomes unconscious; it is not a weakening of a faulty consciousness.

Those signs completely arise at the time of death, but only partially similar states arise at sleep, as the nostril respiration does not cease.

In the time of the path, the energy is injected into the heart center *dhūti* channel and dissolves there, and the signs completely arise; when they dissolve elsewhere their mere suggestion does not arise.

By influence of practice of those three and the intensity of the concentration and dissolution of the energies, many different degrees of extensiveness and solidity and duration of the object perception can occur. [186a] In the context of energy meditations and so on, if a black-out unconsciousness arises without being preceded by the first two luminances, then it is not imminence.

As for such kinds of three voids, granted they can arise between magic body attainment and objective clear light realization, on the occasion of arising in reverse order from objective clear light, and between attaining the learner's communion and attaining the nonlearner's communion; and yet they are not mind isolation. Likewise, even before attaining mind isolation there is an occurrence of the wisdom of the three voids, so you should differentiate the three void wisdoms and the mind isolation void wisdoms by their degrees of pervasiveness.

Some former Tibetans advocated all nonconceptual cognitions such as sense cognitions as whichever of the three luminances, claiming that luminance was such a cognition's first apprehension of an object, radiance was the progressive clarification of its seeing the details of the object, and imminence was the final approach to obscurity in its termination. This interpretation is not explained in the *Root* or explanatory tantras or in any of the treatises of the noble father and sons; and it seems to contradict the *Integrated Practices*' above explanation of the definitions of the three luminances.

Now, as for the previous mention of "mind, mentality, and consciousness" and the "three realities" and so forth as synonyms of the three luminances, it is because there is some reason for the attaching of each of their names to the three luminances; but it is not that all of them indicate the three luminances. If it were, there would be many inconsistencies, such as that the eighty instinctual natures would also become luminances.

Well, but how about the *Five Stages'* statement—

> With the nature of twilight, [186b] day, and night,
> There are luminance, luminance-radiance,
> And likewise luminance-imminence;
> Thus the mind is said to be threefold,
> And thereby its basis is explained.[114]
> The energies, in their subtle form
> Having become fully mixed with consciousness,
> Emerging through the paths of the senses,
> Thus cause the perception of [all] objects.

—that consciousness, mingling with the subtle energies emerging from the sensory doors such as the eye and so perceiving objects, is what constitutes the three luminances?

As for the meaning of that, in place of the statement that "after explaining the three [forms of] mind, I must announce their attainment," the *Integrated Practices* translations of the Great Translator [Rinchen Zangpo] and [the translator] Chag read "their basis," meaning "let us express the energies that support those three minds." Further, "the three minds having mingled with the energies," they mingle or are moved by the energies, which means that such movement produces cognitions apprehending objects through

114. An ambiguity emerges here with the use of Tib. *mtshams* (usually "boundary") to translate Skt. *saṁdhyā,* "twilight," aligning it with luminance-imminence, the third of the three luminance intuitions, the state at the boundary between the subtle mind and body and the extremely subtle body-mind, between the dualistic universe and the nondual clear light. The simile used to convey the experience of imminence is that of the dark night sky, opposite to the moonlit and sunlit skies of luminance and radiance. Then, the predawn morning twilight (Skt. *pratyusha*, Tib. *tho rangs*) is used as a simile for the clear light transparence, being a state of inconceivable nonduality of dark and light, mind and body, self and other, etc. So the "twilight" aligned with imminence is to be connected with evening twilight, which is when light of day merges into dark of night. This ambiguity comes up again below (p. 465), in discussions of the fourth stage clear light clear enlightenment. (Thanks to David Kittay for focusing my attention on this issue.)

the sense doors and also the instinctual natures. Just after the above reference, [the *Five Stages*] continues:

> When you have luminance
> Mounted on energies,
> Then all the instinctual natures
> Fully arise without remainder.
> Wherever the energies remain,
> There the instinctual natures function.

This is quoted in the *Integrated Practices* along with the previous quote, with the statement that the concise meaning of these is that:

> Having entered the subtle realm, luminance moves in a second, a moment, an instant, an eye blink, a handclap, and in that same [187a] second, moment, instant, eye blink, and handclap the instinctual natures also function.

Further, this is mentioned for the sake of repeatedly merging [the cognitions arising] from the voids of sleep with those that are gradually produced from the arisal of the three voids in the reverse order at the time of taking birth. And this does not indicate that the occasional arisals of instinctual natures in conjunction with functioning cognitions are directly produced from the three voids. Though one can exhaustively divide cognitions into conceptual and nonconceptual, there is no need to exhaustively divide them into luminance and instinctual nature, and therefore it is not necessary for sense cognitions to be instinctual natures since they are not luminances.[115]

115. In the context of considering the arguments that support the idea of the coordination of sutra and tantra (*mdo sngags zung 'brel*), dear to the heart of Tibetan scholars, I am attracted to the theory that the four "formless" or "immaterial" realms (*ārūpyadhātu*) described in basic abhidharma and universally accepted in the cosmology of exoteric Buddhisms are Shākyamuni Buddha's way of providing a hint of what is scientifically and technically taught to be the four luminances and four voids in unexcelled tantra. Thus infinite space hints at luminance, infinite consciousness at radiance, absolute nothingness at imminence, and beyond consciousness and unconsciousness hints at clear light transparence. Of course, outsider and nontantric insider yogi/nīs who attain these immaterial states through advanced samadhis without deep knowledge of voidness, without unraveling the heart knot, and without awakening the great bliss mind, experience them

[**VI.B.3.b.ii.c′3′d′i′c″4″b″** – The instinctual natures]

If such are the luminances, how do the eighty instinctual notions become instinctual natures? And how are they produced from the luminances?

There are thirty-three instincts in the first luminance. The *Five Stages* states:

> Its natures arise distinct—
> Now I should clearly explain.
> They are known as dispassion,
> [Small], medium, and great,
> Internalizing and externalizing;
> [Small, medium, and great] sorrows;
> Peace, and mental construction;
> Fear, small, medium, and great;
> Craving, medium craving, great craving;
> Appropriation, nonvirtue, hunger, thirst,
> Sensation, medium, intense sensation moments,
> Knower, knowing, knowable,
> Discernment, conscience, compassion,
> Love, small, medium, and great,
> Anxiety, greed, and envy; [187b]
> These are the thirty-three natures,
> Introspectively known by embodied beings.

As for those, "dispassion" has the aspect of not desiring objects, with three degrees of small, medium, and intense. The mentality "externalizing" is going out to objects and "internalizing" is engaging with internal objects. The followers of the Gö tradition claim "this applies in general to all." "Sorrow" is the mental pain of lacking pleasurable objects, with degrees of slight, medium, and intense. "Peace" is explained in the *Clear Meaning* as the mind abiding peacefully, previous [Tibetan commentators] explaining

as objective realms, and hence can get stuck in them without realizing the workings of their subliminal conceptualities. And Buddha was clear that these states are not nirvana —but he taught their existence as a hint of what everyone passes near at every death, and what he discovered when he attained communion.

it as the leisure of the mind staying within its essence. "Construction" is explained by the *Clear Meaning* as abiding in agitation, previous [Tibetans] explaining it as the construct of combative mind. "Fear" is the mind's fright when encountering the unpleasant, "craving" is longing for an object, and each has three degrees. "Appropriation" is the appetitive holding to sense objects. "Nonvirtue" is explained in the *Clear Meaning* as indecisive hesitation about virtuous action, previous [Tibetans] explaining it as depression in one's mind. It can also be translated as "ignorance." Previous [Tibetans] explain "hunger" and "thirst" as desire for food and drink. The Chag translation condenses hunger and thirst into one [instinctual nature]: but the previous [Tibetans'] interpretation is better. "Sensation" includes pleasure, pain, and indifference, and there are three degrees depending on the object. "Knower," "knowing," and "knowable"—these three functions are the three "concepts." "Discernment" is the investigation of the rational and irrational. "Conscience" [188a] is the avoidance of the reprehensible for personal or religious reasons. "Compassion" is the desire for freedom from suffering. "Love" is the desire for the beloved to be protected and to meet with happiness; and it has three degrees. "Anxiety" is the lack of certainty in the doubting mind. "Greed" is the thought to accumulate properties. "Envy" is the disturbance of mind at the fortune of others. "Avarice" is mentioned in the *Clear Meaning* and in the Chag translation, but the *Five Stages*' and *Integrated Practices*' old translations' use of envy is better.[116]

As for the forty instinctual natures [of radiance], the *Five Stages* calls them:

> Desire, attachment, pleasure,
> Medium pleasure, intense pleasure,
> Delight, indulgence,
> Amazement, excitement,
> Satisfaction, embracing,
> Kissing, sucking,
> Stability, zeal, pride,

116. Tsong Khapa does not reduce the thirty-five instinctual functions here to the thirty-three that should be here, though his comment, without approval or disapproval, that the translator Gö considered "internalizing and externalizing" not to be instinctual functions but properties of all thirty-three of them may be a hint that he might agree.

Activity, covetousness, aggressiveness,
Enthusiasm, natural [boldness],
Small, medium, and great,
Hostility, charm,
Resentment, virtue,
Lucid truthfulness,
Untruthfulness, certitude,
Non-appropriation, generosity,
Initiative, heroism,
Shamelessness, deceitfulness, sharpness, wickedness,
Ungentleness, and crookedness;
These forty natures constitute
The instant of extreme voidness.

"Desire" is mental desire for the unobtained object. "Attachment" is the mental desire for the obtained object. "Pleasure" from the experience of the [188b] pleasant is slight, medium, and intense. "Delight" is the mind happy with achieving a desired aim. "Indulgence" is such a mind's repeating its experience over and over. "Amazement" is explained by the *Clear Meaning* as wondering about various stories "Is it? Or isn't it?"—but the previous [Tibetans] explain it as the experience of a mind at an unprecedented event. "Excitement" is the movement of mind when experiencing a pleasant object. "Satisfaction" is the notion of satisfaction by an object, though the *Clear Meaning* explains it as the distinct experience of happiness. "Embracing," "kissing," and "sucking" are minds that desire to do those things. "Stability" is the mind of not changing its process. "Zeal" is exertion in virtue. "Pride" is the haughty mind. "Activity" or "action" is full enaction of routine activities. "Covetousness" is the desire to rob wealth. "Aggressiveness" is the desire to conquer others' armies. "Enthusiasm" is the mind that activates practice on the path of virtue. "Natural" stands for the Sanskrit *sahaja*, which the former scholars said was not found in the Indian texts, but rather *sahasa*, which should be translated "hesitant," or "engaged with the difficult." The commentary *Clear Meaning* says it means "nonhesitant," explaining its meaning as engaging in nonvirtue through arrogance. Old translations of *Integrated Practices* have "engagement in difficulties," the Chag translation of the *Five Stages* has "potency," his translation of the *Integrated Practices* has "nonhesitant." [189a] The ancient scholars defined it as "slight, medium, and intense engagement in striving after an objective." "Hostility" is the unprovoked desire to contend with superiors. "Charm" is the desire to play or possess when seeing a beautiful person. "Resentment" is the mind of resentment. "Virtue" is the desire to initiate such action. "Lucid truthfulness" is the desire to speak understandably and without distortion of idea. "Untruthfulness" is the desire to speak distorting the idea. "Certitude" is a very firm determination. "Non-appropriation" is the disinclination to seize an object. "Generosity" is the desire to give things away. "Initiative" is the desire to arouse lazy others. "Heroism" is the desire to triumph over enemies such as the addictions. "Shamelessness" is engagement in nonvirtue, not avoiding it for personal or religious reasons. "Deceitfulness" is deceiving others with artificiality; when "sharpness" occurs [in texts], it describes [this instinct] as a mind of sharp pickiness. "Wickedness" refers to [a nature] steeped in evil convictions. "Ungentleness" is mischievousness toward others. "Crookedness" is dishonesty. In the Chag translation, the last two quarters read, "The instants of the forty natures are produced from extreme voidness."[117]

As for the seven instinctual natures [corresponding with luminance-imminence], the *Five Stages* says:

> One instant of medium attachment,
> Forgetfulness, mistakenness,
> Reticence, fatigue,
> Laziness, and doubt.

"Forgetfulness" is the loss of memory. "Mistakenness" is holding a mirage as water and so on. "Reticence" is heartfelt [189b] disinclination to speak. "Fatigue" is mental exhaustion. "Laziness" is disinclination for virtue. The other two are immediately understandable.

117. The count is even further off here, with forty-six instinctual functions listed, though if pleasure and boldness, the only two instinctual functions with three degrees, are counted as one function, the count is exactly forty. If we use the same method on the thirty-three previous, however, we would have only twenty-one functions. Neither the Indian noble writers nor Tsong Khapa are of much help with these enumerations, as apparently these counting questions were not thought of as interesting, in the context of the exalted paths of the perfection stage. What is interesting is the relation of the *prakṛtikalpana* to the lists of *kleśa* and *upakleśa* in the abhidharma, though Tsong Khapa does not accept the effort of the author of the *Commentary Jewel Rosary*.

As for these three divisions of instincts, though they seem similar in explanation as collected into three classes as determined by their extreme desire for objects, their extreme aversion to objects, and their neutrality, [respectively], they are explained as above relying on the commentary *Clear Meaning* [attributed to Nāgabodhi] and the ancient Tibetans. The commentary *Jewel Rosary* [also attributed to Nāgabodhi] seems to explain a way in which these instincts are interconnected with the fifty-one [Abhidharmic] mental functions. However, since it does not seem plausible, I do not set it forth.

In regard to the *Integrated Practices*' mention of such three sets of instinctual notions as the nature of the three luminances, "nature" comes from Sanskrit *svabhāva*, which can be used for element, nature, and thing, and can also be quoted in the meaning of element. The *Integrated Practices* declares it to refer to the natural identity of the three luminances, saying "in short, as for nature . . ." and "in summary, it is these thirty-three natures, and the forty, and the seven." Lakshmī's statement that the meaning of "nature" is "of the nature of that" and the *Clear Meaning*'s explanation that it is "included in the category of that" are incorrect. For, as the *Self-Consecration* of Āryadeva states:

> The earth element dissolves into water,
> The water dissolves into fire,
> Fire into the subtle element.
> Energy dissolves into the mind,
> Mind dissolves into mental functions,
> Mental functions into ignorance,
> And that goes into clear light transparence.

That energy dissolves before the mind produces luminance, and, since that energy is the mover of the instinctual natures, [190a] the instincts must also dissolve at that time; hence, luminance and the instinctual natures are extremely incompatible.

Also in the context of the creation stage, as the *Wisdom Vajra Compendium* states that the instinctual notions are generated after generating the three luminances, and the *Terminal Action Investigation* states that the 160 instincts arise after generating the three voids, and that the first group of instincts are effects having the cause of the luminance wisdom and the other two groups are similar. In some of the editions of that

[text], the explanations that the seven instincts [of the last group] occur at the time of ignorance [here intending imminence], are the result of textual error.

Here one might wonder, "As it is said that energy dissolves into luminance, since there is no luminance before it is generated, it is impossible to dissolve into it!"

Since such statements are made in terms of luminance, radiance, imminence, and clear light, such assertions as that "after the latter is produced the former must dissolve so they are not cause and effect or else they would become unlocatable in any order at all" cannot be accepted. For the *Five Stages* states:

> Void and extreme void,
> Third, great void,
> And fourth, universal void—
> These are distinguished as causes and effects.

Therefore, "the former dissolves into the latter" is just a designation for the process wherein the former's potency withdraws and becomes unclear and that potency seems to transfer to the latter. Therefore, the claim such as that "at the time of dissolving, the thirty-three instincts cease; [190b] then luminance arises, and after that, the forty instincts cease, then radiance arises and so on," the similar claim that the instincts and luminance are coordinates, and the claim that at birth first imminence arises and then the seven instincts and so forth—all these are irrational and contradictory positions. I have already quoted the *Integrated Practices* statement that the instincts emerge from luminance. The Chag translation of the *Five Stages*, just as in the above explanation of the definition of the three luminances, holds them not to be non-different actualities. Just as in marking a mansion by [the fact that there is] a crow [on the roof], an actually different definer is given as the definition.

Further, the statement of the *Integrated Practices*—

> Likewise, consciousness luminance is formless, yet can be inferred from the instinctual natures such as attachment, detachment, medium attachment, and so on.

—is a means of defining luminance saying that luminance is inferred from the instinctual natures. As for how it is inferred, seeing that instinctual natures have degrees of minor, medium, and intense, the luminance that generates them is mounted on energies, and it can be measured that their movements are weak, medium, and intense. [191a] Thus, of any of the seven instincts with the weakest [energy] movement, there is an imprint of the weakest movement of the energy-mounted luminance, which can be posited as the effect of imminence. You should extrapolate the same reasoning for the others.

As for the yogi/nī who can develop the three wisdoms by the power of meditation on the path, s/he can ascertain those three in manifestation, not inferring them from their signs. Therefore, the persons who must infer luminance from the instincts is not one of these; and so it is inaccurate to claim that any of the three luminances [appear] to the sense cognitions. Sense cognitions need not infer from signs but can ascertain things directly. As for the ordinary person, s/he experiences the three luminances along with clear light at the time of birth and death and so on. But such a person cannot induce certitude [about them] through direct perception.

As for the 160 instinctual natures, they are set forth from the perspective of having a set of eighty engaged in each of day and night. Also, the *Vajra Rosary* explains that there are 108 instincts agitated by 108 energies.[118]

Thus, in basic reality there are two states, one in which the instinct-moving energy is dissolved and another in which it is not dissolved. The undissolved state is the time when the instincts emerge. In the dissolved state, there are two states, one in which the three luminance energies are dissolved and another in which they are not dissolved. The undissolved state is the time of the three voids. The dissolved state is the time of the arisal of clear light. In the time of the path also they are generated in that

118. This comment may provide a clue about Tsong Khapa's disinterest in counting too strictly—there are numerous ways of counting and various numbers put forth by various authors. All such enumerations are heuristic devices used in meditative practice to develop introspective awareness of the workings of one's conscious and unconscious levels of mind. Just as in the case of the famous "five aggregates"—Jamyang Sheyba mentions in his *Clear Science Final Analysis* textbook that there could be three aggregates or a hundred aggregates, and that the five are used as convenient for a specific context.

manner; and that is the necessity to determine the arising [191b] and dissolving processes of the four voids and the instinctual notions.

Such as the above, it is an import that comes from the literature of the *Root* and its explanatory community tantras. It is not explicit in writings other than the commentaries of the noble father and sons. And further concerning them, the private instruction of all buddhas, praised in the *Integrated Practices* as taught by the kindness of [Āryadeva's] own mentor, Nāgārjuna, is the way of achieving the clear light and the extraordinary magic body. Thus, [the greatness of these teachings] comes from the vital point of relying on their knowing [of these extraordinary private instructions].[119]

[VI.B.3.b.ii.c′3′d′i′c″4″c″ – How to generate luminance intuition]

The third has two parts: [i″] Setting forth the separate systems; and [ii″] Setting forth the correct opinions among them.

[VI.B.3.b.ii.c′3′d′i′c″4″c″i″ – Setting forth the separate systems]

Lakshmī, Bhavyakīrti, and the rest, set OṀ in the hub of the eight spokes in the wheel of the navel, have OṀ, ĀḤ, and HŪṀ radiate from that, to be set in the crown, throat, and heart centers; then OṀ radiates white light and attracts OṀ's, which dissolve into the navel letter, upon which one focuses

119. This whole section remains somewhat unclear, since Tsong Khapa starts off by saying that the luminances and the instinctual natures are not the same thing, since the instinctual natures must be mobilized by energies, which have dissolved by the time of the arisal of the luminances. Without distinguishing coarse and subtle energies, he goes on to say that the three luminances are driven by energies, obviously subtle energies, since the wind energy that dissolves into space and luminance in the fourth stage of eightfold death and mind-isolation dissolution processes are the coarse energies. The luminances-mounted subtle energies dissolve only at the transition from imminence into clear light transparence and universal voidness. Tsong Khapa's interest here is surely in the practice, and the mind isolation practitioner need not concern herself or himself with the eighty instincts—which disappear upon entering actual luminance—but rather with the four voids and joys marking the dissolving process. The alignment of the eighty instincts in three batches with the three luminances seems rather pertinent only to the ordinary person who is subject to their surgings at death, failing of course to perceive the luminances or transparency except as a flash of light here or there.

one-pointedly, generating the luminance wisdom-intuition. Likewise, they visualize a red ĀḤ in the hub of the [navel] wheel and a mere drop. Its red and black light rays attract ĀḤ's and HŪṀ's, respectively, cause them to dissolve into the navel, and focus on that one-pointedly, thereby generating the intuitive wisdoms of luminance-radiance, and [luminance-] imminence, [respectively]. Then, they explain that you meditate the drop and even the wheel as dissolving into the space of the navel, and thus create the clear light preceded by the five signs. The first two intuitions are said to be synonymous with OṀ and ĀḤ. In the context of imminence, they use the private instruction of the *Five Stages*:

> The seed is not endowed with a drop;
> It does not go out [192a] the door of energy.
> Who attains the luminances
> Has the character of full perfection.

This is called the generation of mind isolation by the art of the stage of mantra. As for the generation by the stage of the seal, it is according to the statement in the *Five Stages*; I have already explained the way the voids are produced there.[120]

Master Gö explained two methods of generating mind isolation, the systems of Kṛshna Samayavajra and of Tsunmojen. Concerning the first, as for the path of the lower door [of the central channel], rely on a consort; and as for the upper door, by generating great, medium, and small bliss of the natural melting of the inner enlightenment spirit though the emanation and retraction of the light from meditating a crown HAṀ, a throat AṀ, and a heart center A, you should meditate bliss-void from ceasing the three degrees of subtle to coarse natures. They explain that to be the measure of the ancient sages' practice of tantra, and they give that meaning by quoting a reference from Āryadeva. However, the quoting of that reference and the making of that explanation seem to be quite inconsistent, and so that explanation seems very unsuitable. It is clear that it emerges from the speech of the mentor Samayavajra, and such an explanation does not appear anywhere in any treatise of Āryadeva. Concerning the second of the

120. In the *Great Stages of Mantra*.

systems, except for generating it depending on the consort, it seems to lack any meditation on seed-syllables. The disciples of Gö, Ngog Yeshey Sengey and company, [192b] explain it according to that latter system.

Certain others who uphold the interpretation style of Gö maintain a Tsunmojen method relying on the lower door as previously explained. As for their reliance on the upper door, with the energy made fit by vajra recitation, they visualize an AṀ on a lotus upon a moon in the heart center, from which extremely subtle light rays, white and cool like moonlight, enter into the central channel, energizing the crown HAṀ, from which white spirit of enlightenment cascades down abundantly onto the AṀ, which gets brighter and brighter, and finally the mind-bliss develops into the wisdom-intuition of luminance clear as moon[light]. In a similar manner, visualizing an ĀḤ on the hub of a vajra on a sun at the heart center and visualizing a lone A not depending on any base, emitting from the central channel light rays hot as sun and very subtle black light rays, [respectively,] and so on, you proceed as before and develop the latter two intuitions.

Gö's mentor Saraha advocates developing the three wisdom-intuitions from visualizing the three letters, without practicing emanating and retracting. All those explanations of the moon, sun, and syllables, and so on as the modalities of the intuitions are accepted as private instructions, saying that Abhijña[121] has simply explained those as nominal synonyms, yet claim that "he does not teach meditation in that way." As for this explanation, if you compare it with Gö's [own text,] the *[Great] Voidness Session*, it does not match his explanation of Tsunmojen's [instructions].

According to the private instruction of Nāropa expressed by Serdingpa as received through Marpa, [you can use either of] two [methods], using or not using a wheel center, the way of setting up a wheel center being as above. [193a] You do not retract the wheel center during the time of vajra recitation, but do retract it during the [practice of the] mind objective. As for holding the upper and lower energies in kiss-connection while you are learning the mind objective, it is taught in the four great and three lesser private instructions; doing it at the heart center is taught in the *Five Point*.

They teach also that you create the first void by meditating holding the energy and visualizing the [row of] letters on the outer [part of the] lotus

121. Abhijña ca. 1000, was a teacher of the translator Gö (ca. 1030), and was a student of Atīsha (982–1054).

petals, the extreme void by then meditating compressing the letters into the middle and visualizing the middle [row of letters], and the great void next by meditating compressing those again into the four inner letters and visualizing them. Again, "from the beginning causing the first lotus petal to dissolve"; and "visualizing at the beginning after already having experienced the sign-possessor of luminance white like the moon and meditating having dissolved the first lotus petal into the second and so terminating the thirty-three instinctual natures"; and "at the time of visualizing the letter of the latter lotus petal, it is better to collect the deity body into that"; and again, "after creating the three voids collecting the deity body into the drop of the central channel"; and "radiating light from the letter of the first lotus petal, cultivating vessel and essence, and collecting that into the consonants"; and again, "collecting them into the vowels"; and so on—many different instructions appear, but the real position is clearly as above.

In regard to the three of those, respectively, they are explained in the *Wheel Endowed* and the *Four Point* as being the experience of bliss just from the arrival of the spirit of enlightenment at the root of the vajra, at its throat, and at its vase. [193b] The *Five Point* says that at the beginning you experience bliss from merely the enlightenment spirit's movement from its abode, but this becomes the same as the previous two. In the *Wheel Endowed* it explains that, having prepared with vajra recitation, you alternate with holding the energy in kiss-connection, and since therein there are many different methods of arisal of signs and sign-possessors, I do not write them here.

In the [procedure] without a wheel, there are three. The first of these is explained as follows: in the heart center of oneself as a luminous deity, in the center of a mirrorlike light, meditate on a drop marked by a short *A*. Then, practice vajra recitation as above. Then, for the mind objective, hold the upper and lower energies kiss-connected, compressing the deity body, light, drop, and short *A* one into another and meditate to produce the three voids. This is called "wheel-less," designating it influenced by the general name. [Second,] from the *Five Stages Triply Nested Spiritual Heroes*, it is explained that you meditate a thumb-sized wisdom hero in the heart center of yourself as luminous devotee hero and in its heart center, in the hub of a mustard-seed-size vajra, a samadhi hero of a blue-black HŪṀ, as if drawn by a single hair brush; you do vajra recitation as above, and for the mind objective you hold the energies in kiss-connection, you compress the two heroes and the vajra and HŪṀ one into another and meditate to produce the three voids. [Third,] from the *Five Stages Simultaneous* it is explained that you meditate in the heart center of yourself as luminous deity, in the navel of a four petal red lotus, a white drop with a black short *A*, [194a] you do vajra recitation as above, and for the mind objective, you aim the mind at the deity body, the lotus petals, and the drop to produce the three voids. Though it teaches you to compress the deity body, lotus petals, drop, and short *A* one into another, its not setting the dissolving process of those as [equivalent to] the three voids can be understood as an error, by the key of the other two versions. You should produce the three voids through the three dissolutions as in the previous versions. It seems that the intention here is that you should do vajra recitation until the five signs such as mirage arise, which is excellent.

By the system of these extensive and concise instructions, in developing the mind isolation, it is accomplished by bringing together two arts, the holding of the energies in kiss-connection and the compression process of the visualizations. The development of the mind isolation relying on the consort is explained in the *Five Stages*; while that is not stated explicitly in the *Concise Five Stages* or among the personal instructions of Serdingpa, the general way to develop bliss relying on the great seal consort is obvious in the instruction that appears there.

Some others who follow Marpa's tradition assert that, without holding the energies in kiss-connection, visualizing the three kinds of letters, practicing vajra recitation in order and purifying the three kinds of instinctual natures, the three wisdoms are created. From the private instructions of Nāropa transmitted through Nagtso, in regard to the condition of the mind needing to be realized by combining with bliss, there are two ways; the first is the passionate relying on the lower door, which involves relying on a consort, and [the second] is the dispassionate relying on the upper door. [194b]

Then there are the three methods to develop bliss, relying on a garland of letters, on a mere letter, and on no letter. In terms of the first of these, you meditate that, by the light rays radiated from the three kinds of letters in the heart center, the crown HAṀ melts and fills the heart center, and when bliss develops the energy is taught to be held only for brief intervals; and otherwise there does not seem to be the instructions as before to hold the energies in kiss-connection and to visualize the compression process.

[**VI.B.3.b.ii.c′3′d′i′c″4″c″ii″** – Setting forth the correct opinions among them]

The second has two parts: [A‴] Analyzing how are those systems; and [B‴] Setting forth the enduring opinion.

[**VI.B.3.b.ii.c′3′d′i′c″4″c″ii″A‴** – Analyzing how are those systems]

As for the energies, to first collect them in the central *dhūti* and dissolve them, you must have the definite vital key of the body. Having meditated the art of penetrating the vital points in the body through vajra recitation and so on, you inject the energies into the *dhūti* and they dissolve, and you practice by developing the four voids and joys, and then visualize whatever objective and hold the mind [there; then] the energies collect and those experiences as appropriate seem to arise. That occurs by the force of the previous, and it is not certain that there is any imprint of that later objective. Therefore, [though you may] have learned well the vajra recitation, once having learned [a bit about the mind objective], if you hold the visualizations as above explained and those experiences happen to develop, by that reason [alone] one cannot prove that that instruction is the [full] import of those treatises. As for the *Five Stages*' and *Integrated Practices*' explanations of the three letters and moon, sun, and vajra as synonyms of the three luminances, they mean that those names are designated to the three luminances of the perfection stage, and that "you should meditate imagining those, as in the creation stage [195a] you cannot develop the three luminance intuitions." Therefore, what the mentor Abhijña asserted is correct, that it does not mean that [you can reach the mind objective just] by meditating through the perfection stage, having set up letters on moon and sun and so on. Even if you cause it to be produced, you must do it in the heart center; if you do it in the navel center, you do not understand the key point of this system. As for statement that "they originate from the intuition of luminance and from radiance . . . ," it indicates that the instinctual natures originate from those [luminance states], and does not teach that the intuitions originate from meditating on letters and so on. By making effort to meditate the letters and the white, red, and black colors of the light rays the objective perceptions arise in those colors; but that is not the way of the arisal of the colors explained in the treatises. Though the *Concise Five*

Stages explains the three sets of letters in order, as illustrative of luminance, radiance, and imminence, it does not need to teach that the intuitions are produced by holding the mind in front of those letters set up [in visualization]. As that text says:

> Bind the mind in equanimity,
> You will evenly see the intuition
> Of the hub of the wheel in equipoise,
> And imminence is great void

—it does not agree with the explanation that you bind the mind from distraction toward other objects while visualizing the letter set in the wheel, equilibrating the mind as if it dwelt in the letter; [then,] from habituating to that equilibrium, [195b] the mind enters into the indestructible along with its short *A* in the hub of the wheel, and the great void is produced from that turning into uniformity of experience.

Therefore, even if you compress the wheel, once you have reached stabilized vivid vision in the letter, first visualize the outer, then compress into the intermediate, then compress into the inner, and then compress into the indestructible, and then become habituated to visualizing that. Or, setting up the letters as above, if you alternate doing that, the compression into the *dhūti* is quick. Whereas if you do not compress into the interior of the *dhūti* but habituate on the outside, the definitive paths of void will not arise, since they emerge from compressing and dissolving into the *dhūti*. From the *Concise Five Stages*, there is no explanation of holding the energies in kiss-connection beyond those of the meditation on the letters and the vajra recitation. Though the *Vajra Rosary* often states that "you achieve by the reality of mantra alone!"—if you meditate knowing the vital points of that, it has the meaning that you achieve even though you do not combine it with any other energy connection.

Here, not having realized the complete vital points of vajra recitation, if you think that "if there is no holding the energies in kiss-connection, I won't be able to accomplish the dissolving of the energies into the *dhūti*"; [you are right, as] it is explained that if you hold them in kiss-connection it seems you do not realize the key point of this practical instruction; but this does not mean in general that the vajra recitation meditator is at fault if s/he holds the energies in kiss-connection. Here [in mind isolation context,] [196a] holding in kiss-connection requires that you perform the vase-pressure at the heart center. What is stated in the *Vow Arisal*, "in first meditating energy connection, heart-center vase-pressure is a great hindrance," is a message for those who are inexpert in that yoga; if you know what you're doing it is not a big hindrance.

By that explanation of the energy compression process taught in the *Wheel Endowed*, you can understand also the compression process of the three wheel-less [instructions]. Though it is not sure that the three wisdom-intuitions will be produced immediately in front of the set-up of the letters, the voids are not posited as occurring from the stages of the descending of the enlightenment spirit from the crown to the jewel. And as for the Marpa tradition personal instruction that the voids are produced from the stages of compression in the heart center, it is the vital point of the word, "consciousness is the support of the compression of vitalizing energy, meditate the wheel of mantra in the heart center"; and this seems to be the unexcelled vital point also of the father and son personal instruction.

[Chandrakīrti] states in the *Illuminating Lamp* that the four signs from mirage to burning candle flame arise from the dissolution one into another of earth, water, fire, wind, and consciousness. It has been explained above how when wind dissolves, luminance is produced, which does not mean that those many signs arise at the time of the three luminances, and so it should be accepted according to [Āryadeva's] explanation in the *Integrated Practices* as expressed in the *Concise Five Stages* passage:

> First the mirage-like experience
> Arises with its five light rays,
> Second there is the moonlike luminance,
> And third there is embrace by the light of sun;
> And from the night luminance there is imminence.

[196b] Here, not mentioning the three signs other than mirage is for the sake of brevity; it can be understood more extensively according to the *Further Tantra* and other contexts in the *Illuminating Lamp*. In short, as the previous various systems did not newly add visualizations such as meditating letters here in the context of the mind isolation, it is not good to newly add visualizations as arts of developing mind isolation, without examining whether, having first achieved body isolation, you are or are not able to

develop how much of the four voids in general by the speech isolation vajra recitation. This is because it would seem to be a case of explaining subtle arts while leaving out the principle of penetrating the vital points in the inner body where mind isolation is developed. The things explained above in the category of the arts of generating bliss through the visualizations given in the private instructions descending from Nagtso seem to be rendered in view of the need of the swift generation of bliss; nevertheless, they do not seem to convey the import of the authoritative treatises.

[**VI.B.3.b.ii.c′3′d′i′c″4″c″ii″b‴** – Setting forth the enduring opinion]

The second has two parts: [1‴] The way the intuitions are produced from outer and inner conditions; [2‴] The way such bliss and void are united, and so forth.

[**VI.B.3.b.ii.c′3′d′i′c″4″c″ii″b‴1‴** – The way the intuitions are produced from outer and inner conditions]

[Nāgārjuna states] in the *Five Stages*—

> The mantrī/nī staying in vajra recitation
> Will attain the mind objective . . .

—that the vajra recitation develops the mind isolation void, but is not explicit about how it develops. [Āryadeva], in the *Integrated Practices*, states that you will attain mind isolation by abiding in speech isolation and that mind isolation will not arise without speech isolation, but in this context is also not explicit about how that mind isolation arises. However, [197a] if you know how to investigate the statements that explain the three [experiences] that you enter in the context of the detailed explanation of speech isolation and those about the arisal of clear light at the conclusion when the energies enter the indestructible, you can comprehend how the voids are produced from the vajra recitation's compressing and dissolving the energies into the indestructible; which I have already explained. Further, the *Vajra Rosary* states often and explicitly how the mind isolation voids are generated from the perspective of the vajra recitation's blocking the circulation of the energies:

> By strong application of vajra recitation
> Having known the nature of energy,
> You cut off the instinct-driving energies,
> And will attain the objective in the mind.

I have already explained how in general the vajra recitation develops the voids. As for the particular boundary whence the mind isolation voids are developed, it is from when, having well released the heart-center channel knot, you are able to compress the energies into the heart center indestructible, and it is not before that.

Well then, you may wonder, are any other visualizations for the compression process needed to develop [the voids] from that boundary, or are there not?

Since, from the above quote from the third chapter of the *Illuminating Lamp*, "you should meditate always day and night with the yoga of entry, abiding, emergence, and compression," the "yoga of emergence, entry, and abiding" is the vajra recitation, the "compression yoga" clearly must be taken to apply to being able to develop the four voids by means of vajra recitation and the indestructible. Nāropa's [197b] private instructions also sometimes mention the development of the voids as "compression yoga." As for the way of compression, according to the *Five Point* statement "it is the practice by means of the two contemplations," it should be practiced by means of the holistic holding and serial dissolving [samadhis]; since the Lawapa *Commentary* on Lūyipa's *Arts of Achievement* explains the compression by serial dissolving from the lower part of the perfection stage, the *Personal Instruction* also explains through binding the compression by serial dissolving into the heart center indestructible, and there seems to be no difference about that here in this context. Also the private instructions from Nāropa as inherited from Nagtso explain the way to generate mind isolation without any letters, and mantra wheel letters do not appear in the three *Concentrated Personal Instructions* of the Marpa tradition; thus even in that tradition mantra wheel letters are not indispensable.

If you wonder, "If we take the method of developing the mind isolation to be the meditation of the three vitalizing energy controls and the compression yoga, will that be sufficient?"

Here the *Wisdom Vajra Compendium* states:

> Uniting the vajra and the lotus serves as the method of mind and mental functions. Uniting mind and mental functions serves as the art of the great bliss samadhi. That is indicated by the simile of magical illusion.

And:

> Just as without thoroughly combining milk and sesamum you won't get butter and sesame butter, [198a] so without uniting vajra and lotus that thoroughly combine mantrī/nī and consort you cannot approach the three consciousnesses. Through such inability to unite vagina and phallus, the samadhi of great bliss is not discovered.

Here the positive inference is that the three luminances are produced from the union with the consort and the negative inference is that those three are precluded when that union is eliminated. In regard to the "great bliss" mentioned where wisdom is the art of great bliss, [Āryadeva] says in the *Integrated Practices* that it is the magic body; therefore you need the external consort in order to fully generate the three intuitive wisdoms of mind isolation that are the base for achieving the magic body. As for that import, it is stated in the *Five Stages*:

> Of all magics, woman's magic is most excellent.
> This clearly marks the distinct three wisdoms—
> Attachment, detachment, and that between—
> All three come from the union of two organs,
> The connection of vajra and lotus.

Thus, this does not mean that, in order to generate mind isolation, the specifying of the lustful and the lust-free refers to the practice of the lower door and the upper door. Bearing in mind that statement in the *Five Stages*, [Āryadeva] in the *Integrated Practices* did not mention the external art for generating mind isolation. As for Lakshmī's explanation of this marking of the three intuitions from the consort in the time of the third initiation, though in general such does apply in the time of the third initiation, this is the context of the path of learning [198b] the mind isolation.

Here you might wonder, "If, in the case of a properly qualified person, the actual anointment with the third initiation is preliminary to meditating the path of the two stages, is it necessary or not that in this context the three intuitions are marked through relying on the evolutionary consort?"

Previously, in that initiation the four joys are there from the perspective of the outer vitalizing energy control that dissolves the energy into the *dhūti*. In this context [of mind isolation], it is taken as referring to the proper discovery of the ability [to dissolve the energies] by meditating the three vitalizing energy controls. Thus, here it concerns the generation of the mind isolation three wisdom-intuitions, much more distinctively excellent than the former; so it is not unnecessary that again it be marked [in that way] here.

You may then wonder, "Here, is that generating of the three intuitions relying on the evolutionary consort a matter of generating it from the enlightenment spirit melting from the crown and falling to the tip of the phallus at the secret center? Or is it a matter of compressing the melted enlightenment spirits from the upper and lower parts of the body into the heart center?"

[Chandrakīrti says] in the *Illuminating Lamp* that the mandala triumph is generated from the enlightenment spirit melting and falling into the path of the vajra. However, other treatises' clear explanation that when the enlightenment spirit melts and reaches this center in the body, this joy and void are produced, does not appear in the treatises of the five father and sons. Nevertheless, it is explained that when wind dissolves, there is mind luminance, when mind dissolves, there is mental function radiance, when mental function dissolves, there is imminence, and when that dissolves, clear light arises. As [Āryadeva explains] in the *Integrated Practices*:

> From the union of the vajra and the lotus, beginning from the crown, the enlightenment spirit melts from the 72,000 channels [199a] and descends gradually through the lustful, lustfree, and their medium states.

By force of the melting of the enlightenment spirit the three intuitions are produced. Thus, the four voids arise by the force of both the process of dissolving the energies and the melting and falling of the enlightenment spirit. In that regard, I have already explained that the best place for dissolving the energy of this system is the interior of the heart center *dhūti*; and I will explain it further. Thus, through vajra recitation and so forth, the fury-fire blazes and the enlightenment spirit melts, and the place wherein compressing it produces the four voids is the heart center. Again, it is not that the four joys cannot be produced in the emergent order through the falling of the melted enlightenment spirit to the sensitive tip of the secret place and the reverse order of its reversing back up to the head crown. That does indeed take place as already explained in the context of the body isolation. Here you are developing the four voids of extremely great impact according to the death process, and so it is an emergent order coming from the process of compressing the energies hither into the heart center and a reverse order coming from a process of expanding back out from the heart center. Thus, by the inner condition of the method of meditating vitalizing energy control however you do it, and by an outer condition of relying on union with the consort, the energies and enlightenment spirits are both compressed into the heart center from the top and bottom of the body. As [Āryadeva says] in the *Integrated Practices*:

> Together with your consort, by the process of the holistic holding or serial dissolving, you enter into ultimate reality.

Thereby, he explains that by uniting with the outer consort [199b] you enter into ultimate reality by the process of the four voids, using the compression yoga of whichever of the two contemplations, which amounts to compression in the heart center; because, when you rely on previous habituation to the compression process in the heart center, when you unite with the consort and practice the yoga of the two contemplations, the union with the outer consort serves as a condition for the compression of the energy-mind into the heart center.

As for the arisal of the voids from compression of the enlightenment spirits melted down [and up] from upper and lower body through the vajra recitation's ignition of the furor fire, it can be understood as applying from the boundary of being able to generate the voids from the dissolving process compressing the energies into the heart center through vajra recitation, even though it is not yet perfected. Thus, you can understand correctly the generation of the voids by melting the enlightenment spirits through the condition of the outer consort, serving as the condition of compressing [energies and enlightenment spirits] into the heart center from the top and bottom of the body. By this you should understand also how by uniting with the wisdom consort you can compress energy and enlightenment spirit into the heart center. If you can generate the voids through the process of compressing the energy and enlightenment spirit in the heart center, you can also be able to practice either way to develop the distinctive voids, through the process of the joys of downward descending and upward stabilizing, or the process of compressing into and expanding out from the heart center.

Some others who follow the father and sons do not grasp the vital point of generating the distinctive four voids of this system, since they interpret according to the explanation that in general the voids emerging from melting the enlightenment spirits and especially the voids emerging from union with the outer consort, all of them are the same as the four joys, [200a] whether of falling from crown to secret place sensitive tip or of rising back up to the crown. They have made the mistake of not determining precisely the need to achieve the magic body according to the between [process] and the need to generate the voids systematically according to the processes of death. Here, [Nāgārjuna states] in the *Five Stages*:

> Who finds not vajra-lotus union,
> Even superficially,
> Will [still] achieve [mind objective] once by experience,
> Due to the potency of the yoga.
>
> Through the actuality of the wisdom function,
> Understanding accurately the distinctions,
> The yogi/nī should always discern that
> Just that also is the instinctual nature.

In regard to the meaning of this, [Vīryabhadra's] *Clear Meaning* explanation is not correct in saying that this refers to the precept holders and the hermaphrodites who have no union of two sex organs yet can generate the three wisdoms from the vivid contemplative stabilization. Damtsig Dorjey explains that if the devotee vajra experiences [this deep dissolving] one time [already] at the time of initiation, it will be achieved on the strength of his/her inner yoga; such also are the positions of the *Moonlight* and of Lakshmī. The explanation of master Gö [of this] as the Tsunmojen system, that the yogi/nī, even without uniting with the outer consort in constant reliance, if s/he recognizes [the mind objective] naturally a single time, afterward s/he learns in other ways; that is the meaning of the treatise. ["Not finding even] superficially" is claimed by some to refer to not finding according to common knowledge. However, the meaning is that, [200b] just as the "superficial" nose tip refers to the facial nose tip, even though there is no continuous union of the superficial [outer consort's] lotus and vajra, by experiencing [such union] even once [imaginarily], depending on that, by accustoming yourself to a wisdom consort and so on, you can develop the mind isolation.

Here, one might wonder, "If reliance on the outer consort begins from the boundary of perfecting the vajra recitation, then the *Esoteric Accomplishment* statement:

> Having an evolutionary consort,
> Through the union of vajra and lotus,
> A truth speaker can experientially
> Proclaim such a meditation.
>
> A beginner practitioner
> Who gives up such an evolutionary consort,
> [Even] showing [mastery of] the enlightenment spirit,
> By other-shown [arts] will not see [the mind objective]—
> As should be understood from the beginner's case.

and the *Five Stages* also will be in contradiction; since from that [text above] it states that in the case of the beginner, if s/he abandons the method of the outer consort, s/he will not be shown [the goal] by other methods, and so s/he must be shown by that [method]. And here the beginner is defined as the yogi/nī who cannot inject the energies into the *dhūti* by the force of meditating the inner vitalizing energy control."

There is no such contradiction, since the explanation in the *Five Stages* intends the generation of the three intuitions of mind isolation, and the intention of the *Esoteric Accomplishment* is the generation of the orgasmic wisdom of the four joys. As for a fully qualified embodied person as stated in the definition of such a beginner, it is extremely rare; so since the object is like that, you should not make a mistake in regard to what is a "beginner." [201a] In regard to that embodied person as a vehicle of bliss, though there seem to be other arts of developing it up to the secret center, "if you abandon the above-explained art other [methods] will not show [the objective]" intends its serving as an art for injecting the energies into the *dhūti*. Further, as for the reason for that, though you can develop a little assurance if you apply the references from the *Vajra Rosary*, the *Great Seal Drop*, and the *Personal Instruction*, a decisive assurance is extremely difficult. As for the art for such an embodied person to be able to hold [back the energy and spirit of enlightenment] without emission until the orgasmic [bliss] is shown, it is the meditation of the reversal of energy and the [placement of the] PHAṬ syllable, and so on.

Here you might wonder, "it is not necessary to reverse the energy in relying on an outer consort, since the *Vajra Angel*, the *Red Yamāri Tantra* eighteenth chapter, and the *Achala Unexcelled Tantra* and so on state many techniques for arresting the substance seed."

Such statements are for the general purpose of causing one not to emit the enlightenment spirit. If you apply them to the context of the outer consort, statements such as "if enlightenment spirit falls after having held the showing of orgasmic wisdom, take it with the tongue" are for the purpose of not allowing enlightenment spirit to be emitted, and are neither stated when one cannot inject the energies into the *dhūti* and dissolve them nor stated when one can dissolve the energies in the *dhūti* by the force of meditating vajra recitation and so on. As for this, for many who can hold [enlightenment spirit] without emission, there is no fault, and though [the practice] can be claimed to produce great excellent qualities, if there is no art of uniting this [practice] with the view of voidness that decisively ascertains reality, the purpose for generating bliss is lost. Hence, [201b] there are very many statements that it [can] become a cause of endless horrible migrations; but I do not recite them, fearing prolixity. Further, since it is not enough either, just to have such a view of voidness, you must realize with precision the purposes for fulfilling many other qualifications.

In terms of the objective [consort] mentioned, you should understand, from the *Personal Instruction* and the *Vow Arisal* and so on, the mention in general of the three yoginīs, the orgasmic, the local, and the mantric, and chiefly the latter; those of the buddha-clans such as Lochanā, who are of four types, the "lotus-possessing," the "conch-possessing," the "elephant-possessing," and the "deer-possessing"; and who individually have general and specific characteristics and so forth of body and mind. Just as in inner vitalizing energy control there are many ways of developing distinctive qualities from the procedures of penetrating the vital points in the different channel wheels, there are the same [variety of ways] in the outer vitalizing energy control. As for the reason why such an art must mark such a special beginner, the remembering and cultivating that bliss-void in the context of the creation stage has served as a special means of developing the roots of virtue that generate the realizations of the perfection stage; and when s/he meditates the arts of penetrating the vital points in the body of the perfection stage, there are many purposes, such as [giving] an extreme ease of compressing the energies.

[**VI.B.3.b.ii.C′3′d′i′C″4″c″ii″B‴2‴** – The way such bliss and void are united, and so forth]

Thus, in relying on an outer consort, you must unite the bliss developed by that method and the void you have precisely understood. As for the bliss developed by meditating vajra recitation and so on, if your voidness view is well developed, you must meditate uniting it with that. [202a] In this regard, in other tantras when the four joys are generated, they usually do not teach uniting the first three joys with the voids, but often mention uniting [universal voidness] with the fourth, orgasmic joy. Here, as above explained, mind isolation is generated as a means of realizing the reality of the mind, and therefore it is a union of bliss and void in the context of all four voids. Since you will not realize selflessness if you do not unite the bliss and void of the three wisdom-intuitions, they will not arise in the mode of nonelaboration, and only the luminances themselves of white, red, and black will arise. If you do unite the bliss and void of those three, in the actuality of the certain knowledge of the view you must eliminate the subject-object dichotomy in the three luminances. Thus, though the three luminances arise in that awareness, they do not arise in the experiential actuality of the conceptual differential of certainty. For example, when the noble equipoise arises in the mode of nonelaboration in conceptual consciousness, though it arises as having the form of the decline of dualistic perception in the experience of certainty, in general there is no decline of dualistic perception in that conceptual consciousness.

Here you may wonder, "Just after having recovered from the unconsciousness of imminence with its aspect of darkness, if there is at the least the arisal of the void like the clear predawn sky, why in the context of mind isolation is the procedure for developing the three intuitions taught and the universal void not taught?"

This is true. Intending the nonproduction of objective clear light wisdom anywhere short of the magic body, [only] the three voids are explained; but it is not that the metaphoric clear light is not generated.

Here you may wonder, "Well, when one accomplishes the three wisdom-intuitions, [202b] where does the metaphoric clear light come in?"

It is compressed into imminence. Thus, in the first part of imminence there is a dark-like aspect but awareness is not lost, in the middle part you lose awareness, and in the end that unconsciousness is cleared away and a seeming clear sky happens, free of the three causes of deception. If you interpret metaphoric clear light as universal void, in terms of the four voids the first two parts of imminence are interpreted as great void. In general, in the first three voids, by just the proportion of how great is the momentum of termination of energies, just so dense and long are the clarity and nonconceptuality of the clear light. Especially in the occasion of imminence unconsciousness, by just how great is the momentum of the loss of consciousness, just so much is the elimination of the mind's ability to distract itself to other objects and the development of immersion into clear light itself. As [Āryadeva says] in the *Integrated Practices*:

> By that very iron hook-like ignorance itself you do not cause there to be any mixture in consciousness, but openly reacting to clear light itself, there is the immaculate actuality.

At the time of the arisal of clear light, except for remembering the view of voidness and focusing one-pointedly on the import of reality, you must concentrate consciousness completely, unmoved by energies, without any thinking about other objects. As [Āryadeva says] in the *Integrated Practices*, "as long as consciousness is unmoved, even sleeping you behold the clearly luminous." He mentions here the sleep clear light just as an example. When your mental consciousness develops into the great bliss, by then remembering the import of selflessness, [203a] you achieve the subject-object union of bliss and void, without requiring any other way of union. As for the bliss-void-union of the three intuitions as explained, that is the "mind" that is the basis to be isolated; and the elimination of [both] the sign-habit [holding] that apart and any non-immersion in the experience of universal bliss is the meaning of "isolation." And as for these explanations of the arrangement of the voids in the occasion of mind isolation, you should understand it also [as applicable] to other occasions higher and lower.

[**VI.B.3.b.ii.c′3′d′i′c″5″** – Showing the dangers and the advantages of not knowing and knowing that (import) correctly]

If you do not realize correctly the true nature of your mind in terms of the eighty instinctual natures and the three luminances, relying on the tantras that explain them in that way, you will be bound like a silkworm by the evolution and addictions stemming from egoism and possessiveness, and finally, having experienced the fruition of the two kinds of evolutionary momentum previously accumulated, by the process of entering the ultimate reality clear light of death, you will abandon your old body-mind complex, you will adopt a between body of mere energy-mind as the homogeneous effect of the truth-realm death clear light, and, driven into the five migrations by whichever of the two kinds of evolutionary momentum in the pattern of the rattling buckets on a water wheel, again and again you will be reborn and suffer the miseries of the egoistic life cycle. [On the other hand, Āryadeva says] in the *Integrated Practices* that, if you possess the intuitive wisdom of realizing mind isolation through the process of [knowing] the instinctual natures and the three luminances, at the time of the homogeneous [emergent] order, you will dissolve the energies that move the virtuous and nonvirtuous natural instincts and the voids will dawn in sequence and you will enter into the clear light transparency. [203b] At the time of the reverse order, relying on the strong movement of the luminance energies, you will realize the movement of the instinctual natures, you will orient yourself at the door of the self-consecration, and you will achieve liberation.

To abbreviate the import, understanding the self-habit as the cause of migrating in the egoistic life cycle and as the means of supporting the instinctual cognitive obscurations, you decisively determine the view of selflessness that eradicates the objective of the self-habit. You see that if you do not develop that view into the experiential actuality of great bliss you will not have completed the extraordinary cause of the wisdom truth body, so you generate bliss by dissolving the energies that drive the instincts. You see that if you do not develop that bliss into the experiential actuality of the four voids that come from the energies dissolving according to the process of death, you will not complete the magic body, which is achieved like a between [embodiment] as the extraordinary cause of the beatific body; so you achieve the generation of the mind isolation through such procedures. This explains that very statement above, that if you do not enter this path, even over limitless eons you will not discover the extraordinary realization of the reality of the mind, and you will not be able to manifestly actualize the superficial magic body.

8. The Two-Reality Perfection Stage

[203b.5–242b.1]

[**VI.B.3.b.ii.c′3′d′ii′** – How to learn the samadhis of the two realities]

The second, the two-reality perfection stage, has two parts: [A′′] The perfection stage of the two realities severally; and [B′′] The perfection stage of the two realities inseparably.

[**VI.B.3.b.ii.c′3′d′ii′A′′** – The perfection stage of the two realities severally]

The first has two parts: [1′′] The perfection stage of superficial magic; [2′′] The perfection stage of ultimate clear light.

[**VI.B.3.b.ii.c′3′d′ii′A′′1′′** – The perfection stage of superficial magic]

The first has two parts: [a′′] The actual instruction of the magic body; [b′′] The associated instructions.

[**VI.B.3.b.ii.c′3′d′ii′A′′1′′a′′** – The actual instruction of the magic body]

The first has two parts: [i′′] What should what sort of disciple do; and [ii′′] The teacher's teaching process. [204a]

[**VI.B.3.b.ii.c′3′d′ii′A′′1′′a′′i′′** – What should what sort of disciple do]

[Nāgārjuna says] in the *Five Stages* that, in order to obtain instruction in the magic body, a disciple with four qualifications should first praise the mentor and then petition him [or her]. The four qualifications are: [1] that one has obtained initiation suitable for the creation stage and has practiced it; [2] that one possesses the wisdom that knows the intention of the four kinds of tantras, having the wisdom of experience of all four kinds of tantras; [3] that one should be learned about the three isolations, having well practiced the path of the three vajras; and [4] that one should have intense aspiration for the two realities, with a very firm ambition for the separate and indivisibly combined two reality perfection stages.

Such a person should first long propitiate a mentor, and after pleasing him [or her], should make host offerings and offer the mentor a sixteen-year-old consort. One then should praise, "There is no hollowness in your body!" and then petition, "Omniscient one with a wisdom body. . . ." Here the *Five Stages* old translation says that, after obtaining the private teaching on the magic body, one gets the nine initiations such as garland initiation along with the secret initiation, and then one praises and petitions. Nevertheless, the Chag translation says that in order to attain magic body instruction one gets the secret initiation with the nine initiations [204b] and then one praises and so on; this translation is better, as the Lakshmī commentary is similar.

The early [scholars] were greatly unreasonable in their claim that the ancient treatises taught that since one learned in the three isolations should receive the secret initiation, if one gets the vase initiation fully even without getting the higher initiations, it is alright to meditate the three isolations. [They are wrong] because, without getting the higher initiations to make one eligible for the perfection stage, one should not properly be taught the perfection-stage secrets, and also because the treatise seems to mean that one learned in the three isolations should praise and petition in order to get the magic body instruction. Otherwise, to say that one learned in the three isolations would petition upon [only then] receiving the secret initiation along with the nine [vase] initiations has the fatal flaw of considering such a one eligible to meditate the three isolations without having received the rosary and so forth initiations. It is Nāropa's explanation that one is eligible for magic body [instruction] once one has received the secret initiation; and this is this treatise's meaning.

Having already obtained initiations, when one requests this instruction, having pleased the mentor and so on, [having performed] the three things [mentioned above], one should praise and petition [again], as that is required in common for both initiation and request for instruction. Having thus petitioned, the procedure through which the disciple petitions the mentor for the magic body instruction should be understood according to [Āryadeva's] explanation in the *Lamp of Integrated Practices*:

> Beginning from the creation stage [205a] up until the completion of the body isolation, one just aspires to the nature of the three vajras and so forth. Thus, in the body isolation there is no form of the deity, as the body is only a mass of subtle atoms. The culmination of speech isolation also, by the process of entering and so forth, is acknowledged as just the vajra recitation, wherein there is no deity aspect either, as sounds are just like echoes. The culmination of mind isolation also amounts to just mere recognition of natural luminance, wherein one does not discover the actuality of the deity body supreme in all respects, since that mind is pure luminance. By this reasoning, relying on the superficial, one will not discover the abode. Therefore, one should seek to understand the creation of the deity from mere wisdom, [conveyed] from the presence of the mentor.

As for this inquiry: from the time of the creation stage, within the experience of purging all ordinary concepts and percepts within clear light, while it seems to be explained that your mind must be generated within a deity's body, when the discerning investigate, it must be [only] from a certain boundary on the path that there is [the actual] creation from pure wisdom in a deity body, and not just in [your] wishful imagination. There is a reason that from the start of the creation stage up to complete mind isolation it does not happen, or that by this [205b] process, one does not arrive at reliance on the superficial magic body and at abiding in that samadhi on those occasions. For that reason, [Āryadeva] said that for the actual creation—not mere imaginative deity-body visualization—of the magic body from sheer wisdom, one must realize it from the live speech of the mentor.

To prove the [three] reasonings [for why body, speech, and mind isolations are not the magic body] in order: from the beginning of the creation stage until one reaches the great secret single clan [body isolation], and the three body vajras etc.—"etc." here including the merely imagined visualization creation of the five- and hundred-clan deity bodies —[there is no actual deity body]. Thus, in body isolation there is no magic body deity body, "because the body is a mere mass of atomic particles." This means that, when the mind imagines one's deity body, the measure of its objectively becoming such [a body]—the form that is imagined and about which one generates one's deity-body pride—is no more than just that former body of aggregates and elements that are [now visualized as deities infused in] the masses of subtle atoms. This also shows that mere visualization of that magic body deity body does not create the divinity, and that the yogi/nī needs a deity form other than the coarse body form as a basis for generating pride. Not only that, the magic body deity form is not a body even up to the culmination of the speech isolation, as the word "also" shows that there is no deity creation by the above "mere imagination."

Well then, what does the vajra recitation accomplish?

By the process of entry, abiding, and exiting, [206a] words are just caused to be known as echo-like, by settling the energy, the vajra recitation base, to become extremely serviceable. The *Integrated Practices* explains in the procedure section that the vajra recitation causes one to recognize the vitalizing energy; and the *Vajra Rosary* also says that it makes the energies known. The word "just" in that context excludes any deity body creation other than mere imaginary visualization. Even up to mind isolation culmination one does not discover the magic body deity body endowed with all supreme aspects of signs and marks; the word "also," as above, including the previous reasons.

Well then, what does [mind isolation] accomplish?

One must understand "natural luminance" as the name of luminance and the name of the natural instincts of the luminance [state], and so [mind isolation] amounts to knowing natural luminance as just the three voids; since on that occasion the yogi/nī comes to know his [or her] own mind as mere luminance devoid of instinctual constructs.

Here a certain ancient *Community* practitioner,[122] explaining the lack of a deity body as a lack of the communion deity body, does not understand the meaning in context and does not see the import of the explanation of the last three reasons as proof of the lack of a deity body in body, speech, and mind [isolations, and of the fact] that the superficial, artificial, conceptual mind does not reach the communion body relying on meditating on

122. Butön Rinpochey?

the three isolations. Although the Chag translation says "not relying on the superficial," here the previous translation was better.

If one does not know how to decide the meaning of the *Integrated Practices* [206b] inquiries, one will not understand the meaning of the answer teaching the keys of the magic body of this noble tradition. So one should understand them well.

[**VI.B.3.b.ii.c′3′d′ii′A″1″a″ii″** – The teacher's teaching process]

The second has two parts: [A‴] How to explain the preliminaries to the actual magic body; and [B‴] Explaining the actual stage of magic body.

[**VI.B.3.b.ii.c′3′d′ii′A″1″a″ii″A‴** – How to explain the preliminaries to the actual magic body]

When the mentor hears the petition to teach the magic body, he feels compassion for the student and [so] teaches, and this precept is one not found elsewhere than in the mentor's personal instruction. According to the *Five Stages*:

> The so-called "stage of self-consecration,"
> The teaching of the reality of the superficial,
> That is obtained by the grace of the mentor's foot;
> And not in any other way.

And the *Integrated Practices*:

> The inconceivable deity reality is explained by all the buddhas; coming from the sequence of the lineage of mentors—that which is beyond the scope of even the lords of the tenth stage—I should come to realize it!

And [Āryadeva states] in the *Self-Consecration*:

> The Dharma like a dream and magical,
> Proclaimed by all the Buddhists,
> Though true, thereby is not understood.

Looking away from the self-consecration,
Your own wisdom does not see
The bow-like nature of mentality,
Being consciousness endowed with energy.

If you are confused about the simile of magic,
Even though you have perfected learning
For immeasurable eons,
Without the holy word of the mentor,
You cannot experientially realize that magic.

Thus, if you wish the fruit of buddhahood,
Having totally let go of your arrogance,
You should mount the vajra vehicle, [207a]
And strive to propitiate the mentor.

According to the *Integrated Practices*' and the *Five Stages*' statements that attaining mind isolation brings one to abide on the tenth stage, one cannot experience [magic body] even on that occasion. Or, if one interprets it as referring to one who attains the tenth stage on the transcendence vehicle, one cannot realize it on that stage of one's own path. According to the *Illuminating Lamp*:

> The totally pure deity yoga surpasses all notions, is individually realized, is the sphere of the buddhas, abides in the jewel sack of the body, is beyond tendencies of existence and non-existence, is beyond the scope of literalists and dogmatists, and should be known exclusively from the mentor's precept.

Here [Chandrakīrti] declares that the magic body, which is beyond the scope of those literalistic textual scholars who have not been taught well the tantric import by means of the six parameters, must be understood only from the mentor's precept; and that such [a teaching he received] from the personal explanation of the savior Nāgārjuna. It is necessary to realize the pure magic body from the mentor's precept itself; and the third stage magic body is just the same. The ultimate of the instruction of the need to understand the magic body from the mentor's precept is in the *Five Stages* and the *Integrated Practices*; but it also comes up a bit in the other instructions given by the [other] sons [of Nāgārjuna]. And further, what is unclear in the *Five Stages* is clearly taught in the *Integrated Practices*; so it must be realized [207b] from the *Integrated Practices.*

Though there are many details not included in those treatises, the main imports are what they contain. So if you know well just as many points as they do contain, you will not mistake any of the crucial keys. If you do not work at them long, but work at other smaller precepts, your notion that you have come to see the thrust of the key of the instruction that states that you must know [the magic body] from the mentor's precept will not work out. However, if you know how to investigate connecting the greater and smaller instructions, that will make a great difference; so those [smaller keys] also are necessary. From among the difficult points of mantra, most of which are stated to require reliance on the mentor's precept, the reliance on the mentor's precept in the case of the magic body instruction seems to have an extremely great impact completely different than other [instructions].

Now here you might wonder about the need to realize it exclusively from the mentor's precept, as well as about what are the benefits of realizing that and the dangers of not realizing that.

According to the *Five Stages*:

> The practitioner not finding
> The self-consecration stage,
> His [her] trouble over
> Sutras, tantras, and rites is in vain.
>
> Who obtains the self-consecration stage,
> He [or she] is the chief, personification of all buddhas,
> And doubtless will attain buddhahood
> In this very life.

It is as [Nāgārjuna] declares, that if you do not discover the way to attain this body from the mentor, you will not achieve the buddhahood that is the point of all your trouble; and if you do know that compellingly, and then you practice it, you will definitely, in this very life, [208a] attain buddhahood. In regard to the supreme distinction of the speed of attaining buddhahood in a single life, of the two, the path of bliss-void-indivisible and the magic body, the latter is very much more difficult to realize. And if you investigate it through this supreme system [of Nāgārjuna etc.], you will necessarily know how to apply it to other [traditions of tantric practice].

[VI.B.3.b.ii.c′3′d′ii′A″1″a″ii″B‴ – Explaining the actual stage of magic body]

The second has two parts: [1‴] How to establish the basis of the magic body precept; and [2‴] Relying on that, explanation of the way to attain the magic body.

[VI.B.3.b.ii.c′3′d′ii′A″1″a″ii″B‴1‴ – How to establish the basis of the magic body precept]

In order to attain the magic body, you must know how to abide on the foundation on which it is achieved. According to the *Five Stages*:

> All beings are powerless,
> Not born voluntarily.
> The cause of that is clear light,
> Universal void, transparency.
>
> The mind that serves
> To bind fools in the life cycle,
> That same mind takes yogi/nīs
> To the bliss-lord exaltation.
>
> Here there is no birth at all,
> There is no death at all;
> So should you understand the life cycle itself,
> Constituted [only] by instincts of the mind.

The first verse teaches that beings do not arise independently without depending on their prior descent into the clear light of death, and so are born [involuntarily] from the clear light of universal voidness. The second verse shows that the very mind by power of which the being takes birth, the death clear light energy-mind, that very life-cycle-involving mind arises for the yogi/nī skilled in liberative art as the magic body [with which s/he] becomes a buddha. Although some *Five Stages'* commentators explain the meaning of that [208b] verse otherwise, that the meaning is as I have explained it is known from the *Integrated Practices'* statement that "the existence-between, the cause of the alienated individual's life cycle, becomes the magic body for one who has the private instruction." The third verse teaches how just that [energy-mind] cycles in the life cycle, since there is no agent causing birth and death except for just the natural instincts of energy-mind.

The *Self-Consecration* clearly teaches the foundation for achieving the magic body:

> The elements such as earth
> And the four voids
> Should be known as the eight things,
> Causes of birth and destruction.
>
> From clear light, great void;
> From that art truly arises;
> From that wisdom is born;
> From that energy emerges;
>
> From wind, fire truly comes;
> From fire, water originates;
> From water, earth arises—
> Such is the birth of beings.

And "Then, earth element dissolves into water . . ." from there up to "the triple existence is thus concealed" as already quoted above.[123]

> Thus, from the beginningless,
> One enters in the life cycle of existence.
> As long as by the samadhi of the magical,

123. See above, p. 375 (Tib 189b). Note that the final phrase cited here ("the triple existence is thus concealed") occurs in the *Self-Consecration* immediately *after* the last line Tsong Khapa cited above; so that line does not appear in the current text.

> One does not experience one's own self-eminence,
> Then, as for the self-realization of the magical,
> It is beyond the sphere of the dogmatist,
> Even though it abides in one's own body,
> Those small in merit will not discover it.

These statements clearly teach the basis for achieving the magic body.

As long as you have not experienced your own nature by means of the magical samadhi, that long will you be engaged in the life cycle; [209a] and in this engagement in the life cycle, there are both the wandering in the life cycle and the uninterrupted engagement with the instincts of the life cycle. To eliminate the first, the magical samadhi is necessary, this referring to the magical samadhi common to mantra and transcendence vehicles. In regard to the magical samadhi needed to eliminate the latter [instincts for the life cycle], there are both common and uncommon [samadhis]; and in regard to the uncommon again, there are the two [samadhis], the union of bliss and void and the magic body. And here it is the latter that is intended. In the context of explaining the basis for achieving the magic body, it is declared that there is no person living in the life cycle other than the mere energy-mind: which [shows Nāgārjuna's] claim that, while the energy-mind is not the [real] referent for the designation of the term "person,"[124] the designative base is identified as the being's subtle body.

According to the *Vajra Rosary*:

> Than your vitalizing energy vital essence,
> There is nothing other in the three realms;
> By the magical energy, the three realms
> Are seen as like dreaming [in] a dream.

Thus, the vital essence of beings is their own vitalizing energy, there being no other body of [beings of the] three realms than energy; hence the magically illusory body of the three realms achieved by energy is stated to be like a dream body. Here in the verbal expression mostly there is indication

124. This very subtle point shows how even in the esoteric area of the indestructible drop, the extremely subtle body-mind, etc., care is taken to avoid reifying this deepest level of personal continuity as any sort of intrinsically identifiable "person" or "thing."

of the foundation for achieving the magic deity body; nevertheless one can also apply it to the [magical] body itself; therefore [Chandrakīrti] in the *Illuminating Lamp* quotes [this verse] as a source for the fact that the magic deity body is produced from the mere energy-mind.

Therefore, as the *Vajra Rosary* states:

> Birth, living, [209b] and dying,
> And abiding in the between existence,
> Whatever [states] the world constructs,
> Are the emanations of the energy of mind.

Beings' births, lives, deaths, and between states are the emanations of mere energy-mind. And as the *Revelation of the Hidden Intention* states:

> Conscious or unconscious, all those designated "beings" are arisen from energy; and again they are terminated by energy. While the unrealized mind abides in the ocean of the life cycle, it goes in the wrong directions, and as dog, fox, and elephant, that mind continues thus.

—the energy and mind both progress in various states of being. Now this teaching that all beings have this body of energy-mind, [indicates] the subtle body that serves as designative base of the term "being," amounting to no more than the body of mere energy-mind, indicating that there is no other subtle body substantially different from that; which is not to indicate that there are no external objects or that the coarse evolutionary bodies are not beings' bodies. Thus, the bodies of beings are of two types; the temporary and the subtle. The first of these is the evolutionary, elemental, coarse, and so forth body other than the body of mere energy-mind; and the second is the body established from mere energy-mind. Though the coarse body is not produced in the contexts of first connecting into conception and so forth, it is not that it is not the body of a being. Likewise, [210a] though at death the elemental body is eliminated, the being's body is not eliminated, hence [such an elemental body] is not the subtle body; [it rather stays only temporarily imposed upon the subtle body,] like salt in water. The energy-mind body is never eliminated in all of those occasions, and so it is the subtle body; like wetness in water. Now even in this present occasion of the coarse matter body, the subtle body is a body of just energy and mind, with the coarse body being like its residence. And although there might be other purposes for so stating that fact [in other contexts], the main reason [here] is in order to identify the subtle body that is the foundation from which the magic deity body is achieved. Its mind is not the sense-consciousness [mind], but is just the mental consciousness; and its energy also is not the other four root energies and the five branch energies, but is the vitalizing energy; and of its forms, coarse and subtle, it is the subtle.

Basis time beings have bodies achieved from just that, having the forms of legs and arms and so forth, appearing as the separate bodies of the between and dream states. And bodies achieved from just that which does not appear having the forms of arms and legs and so forth are as previously explained. Intending the existence of such a foundation, [Āryadeva in the *Self-Consecration* above] said "even abiding in one's own body."

As such a supportive embodiment of consciousness, there are both extremely coarse, elemental matter body and subtle energy body; and so one must understand that there are not two continua [of the person], there is no need for the subtle body to abide after abandoning its location in the coarse body, and that although the main designative base of the term "person" is both the energy and the mind [210b] that does not contradict the coarse body also being [the person's] life-support.

[**VI.B.3.b.ii.C′3′d′ii′A″1″a″ii″B‴2‴** – Relying on that, explanation of the way to attain the magic body]

The second has three parts: [a‴] Explaining how it is expressed in the treatises of the father and sons; [b‴] Explaining very clearly the way it is achieved, along with its excellences; and [c‴] Explaining what comes from the mentors' precepts.

[**VI.B.3.b.ii.C′3′d′ii′A″1″a″ii″B‴2‴a‴** – Explaining how it is expressed in the treatises of the father and sons]

Here you might wonder, "If such is the basis time condition of the foundation on which the magic body is achieved, in what way is it achieved at the path time, produced upon that foundation?"

The *Five Stages* declares:

> Again that same threefold consciousness,
> Endowed with energy,
> Arises as the yogi/nī's form,
> Called "magic body."
>
> Thus, all beings here
> Are said to be like magic illusions;
> Staying in the magical samadhi,
> One sees everything as just like that.

The Chag translation here is better, saying "That very threefold consciousness endowed with energy, again. . . ."

The first verse states the magic body as arising from the art of the outer and inner vitalizing energy control as the yogi/nī's body, being both the foundational mental consciousness' mind isolation [subtle] mind of luminance, radiance, and imminence and the energy carrying it. "Again" means that the yogi/nī does not only take a body of energy-mind at the time of first taking birth. The next two lines, on account of such an interpretation of how to achieve the magic body, in explaining all beings as illusory in this unexcelled vehicle, [211a] indicate that here there is a distinctive meaning of "magical" not shared with the transcendence vehicle, the lower tantras, and the creation stage. As for that explanation of "magical," the *Vajra Angel [Further Tantra]* states the same similes used in the *Five Stages*:

> One is taught to be the Lord,
> Who sees [things] to be like mirror images,
> Dreams, magical illusions, bubbles,
> And hallucinations;

and this shows that here one must interpret according to the uncommon elucidations the import as explained even in other unexcelled tantras. Then two lines state that the yogi/nī achieving the magic body sees all beings as just like that; as already explained, seeing them as their subtle bodies; and that even the inanimate world is experienced as like his or her own magic body, all of it as emanations of energy and mind. As for the way it is expressed in the *Integrated Practices*, it states:

> "The thorough realization of one's mind's reality" does not exist in the aggregates, elements, and media, but appears as mere wisdom-intuition, apprehended as the deity body fully endowed with signs, as illustrated by the twelve similes such as magic and dream—being the body of the [mere] nature of the mentality of buddhas.

The "realization of one's mind's reality" refers to mind isolation. Its not existing among aggregates, elements, and media **[211b]** precludes the magic body being produced from any [material] body other than the mere energy-mind of mind isolation. The first "mere" excludes the achieving [of the magic body] from mental construction and the latter excludes its achievement from a coarse body, saying that the magic body endowed with signs and marks, illustrated by the twelve similes, is achieved from the mere intuitive wisdom of mind isolation.[125]

Here there is an inquiry [in the text], as follows:

> "As without a body support there is no nature of mind, and without mind also, body is not apprehended," this is stated in an expression of the scripture; so then how can a deity body with arms and legs and so on, endowed with all signs, be completed from mere mind alone? Those having discriminating views will not believe it without scriptural reference and realization. Therefore, as a method of easily making perceptible the unapprehendable deity reality of those, O Divine Lord, Vajra Master, Teacher, please explain it!

125. It occurs here that the experience of those who uphold the view of "other-voidness"—that ultimate reality voidness is not itself devoid of the buddha-qualities, that therefore the buddhas' material bodies of beatitude and emanation come from the nonvoid absolute itself and so do not require a laboriously-developed-over-eons causal store of bodhisattva merit—are devotionally absolutizing an absolute activity for the role of the real, relative "other" of the unexcelled tantras, which is the father-mother mentor him- or her- self, whose "word" of consecration transmits the laboriously evolved compassionate bliss power of the timeless tradition that implants holographically the relative, compassionate, artistic, buddha-material qualities that enable the buddha embodiments.

Here, if one understands the "mere" word, used in the statement above that the sign-endowed deity body was achieved from mere wisdom, as excluding any other cause not the mind, then it is incorrect for the mind alone to complete a deity body endowed with arms and legs and so on; since the sutra states that, [as concerns] the supporting body and the supported mind, if one is missing the one, the other does not exist. "Having discriminating views" refers to those thoughtful doubters, and "reference and realization" to [the fact that] those [persons] will not gain trusting certitude free of doubts without good reasons. "Unapprehendable" refers to the signless reality [212a] of the deity, which must be realized as the magic body—as a method of doing so, please teach [us] to remove all doubts.

As the answer to that, [Āryadeva] states that:

> Those engaged in the way of the sutras and those meditators abiding on the creation stage, though they may intensely imagine and use the similes of all things as being magical, dreamlike, and reflection-like, they will not understand by these similes the self-consecration precept by which sheer intuitive wisdom completes the deity body of the nature of mentality. Therefore, I, following the yoga tantra, will let you understand the cause and condition for perfecting Vajrasattva[hood].

He states that [though] sutra followers express all things as "illusory," they reflect on its meaning and imagine its reality, but still cannot understand the magic body self-consecration. This refutes that the magic body can be identified by those who understand penetratingly the import of superficiality and illusoriness as taught in the central way, who meditate on that, and who attain freedom from truth insistence. Although such is a general illusory samadhi, it does not have the import of the hidden meaning third stage magic body and the ultimate [meaning] fifth stage magic body. Creation-stage meditators do visualize all things as illusory, yet they are still declared to not thereby understand the magic body self-consecration precept, [212b] which refutes the possibility that the magic body self-consecration can be identified by detached contemplation of the apparent deity body as abiding in the actuality of realitylessness. In the unexcelled [yoga tantra] creation stage, though one might experience many extremely stable samadhis wherein [deities] appear transparent, very vivid, unobstructed like a rainbow, and simultaneously many freedoms from truth-habits connected with the view of voidness, just by that, he declares, one does not know the perfection of the deity body by sheer wisdom, [through] the instruction of the self-consecration of the magic body. [To judge] from this, what need is there to mention the practitioners of the three lower tantras who have not received any instruction?

If one understands those well, one will completely get rid of errors of holding the self-consecration magic body as being actualized in the experience of detachment at the time of the samadhi developed when holding one's mind on the reflection of a deity body in a mirror, meditating it ultimately as dissolving into one's body, and focusing on just that much vividness and clear light.

Thus, having taught that the realization of superficial illusoriness apart from contemplating a deity body, the deity body of the creation stage where one meditates everything connected with deity body meditation, and not only those but also even the deity body of the occasion of the three isolations that discovers great bliss in the perfection stage; none of these are the self-consecration magic body; based on that, he mentions the "yoga tantra" wherein one comes to know the [magic body] precept, meaning the *Root* and its explanatory tantras of the glorious *Esoteric Community.*

As for the way of making completely understood the cause and condition of completing the magic body vajradhara body, [213a] the same [*Integrated Practices*] states:

> In truth, the mind is just luminance apart from shape and color, its reality like space, hard to touch like ultimate reality. That being granted, the three luminances of mere luminosity come to depend on energy, and becoming common become light; therefore, the energy binds the consciousness. Then the two luminances of wisdom and art, endowed with light rays, come to arise as the illusory deity body endowed with all variety and excellence. What is its mount? It is [super subtle] energy, which the mind vajra rides like a horse, traveling wherever it wishes.

In the *Commentary* of this same text, the word "truly" occurs, and, so one questions if the illusory cause and condition is ultimately established. Here the answer is that though the mind is not ultimately established, superficially the three luminances coordinate with energy, the energy binds the consciousness and causes it to wander. But this answer is in terms of the two realities, which does not help at all to resolve the above doubts, and that "energy causes it to wander" is an irrelevant answer, and so useless. Therefore, the mind being free of color and shape and equal to space means that it is not a body. Like ultimate reality it is hard to touch or understand. "In truth" means "truly." One can understand these expressions easily as they resemble those given [from the *Integrated Practices*] in the context of the mind isolation. Granted that it is so that the mind is not embodied, [213b] the three luminances of the mind isolation rely on energy, and so energy binds consciousness, or holds it. Most of the old translations are as above. But some of them say "becoming common, they mingle . . ." and the Chag translation says the threefold luminance uses energy as its element, and so its support is lightness." Some say that the meaning of the above is that since energy and consciousness mingle, and energy is lightness, so consciousness becomes lighter and lighter. But the meaning of "light" is that energy is much subtler than the other elements and so has a common quality that makes it fit to mingle with consciousness. This fits with the *Integrated Practices*' section on mind isolation. From that merging of energy and mind, wisdom luminance and art radiance, being endowed with fivefold light rays, arise as the magic deity body endowed with the excellence of signs such as arms and legs and so on.

To summarize their meaning, although if the mind were alone without energy, it could not be made into a deity body with faces and hands and so on, since the five-light-rayed energy and mind exist as one actuality, there is no problem in producing the deity body. This indicates that if it was exclusively a consciousness that perceived the aspect of a deity, the aspect of form would exist, but it could not directly achieve the magic body. Though "wisdom and art both" are mentioned, just before all three luminances are mentioned, its theory on the foundation of the magic body is like that of the *Five Stages*. "Cause and condition" here refer to the material cause of the mind achieving the magic body—the previous mind—and the coordinating [214a] condition—the energy; while of that body [itself], the material cause is energy and the coordinating condition is the previous mind. "The mind vajra that is the three intuitions mounts its mount like a horse and goes where it wants" means that, at the time when the subtle body of mind isolation energy-mind is made into the magic body, it separates apart from the coarse body and goes where it wishes either outside or inside. As for this meaning, the *Integrated Practices* states that "the *Consciousness Migrating Sutra* also states it very clearly." In that sutra, it is stated that the arms and legs and so on of the between being, achieved just after death, are like the shadow of a man on the water, having no sensation of cold and heat, pleasure and pain, fatigue and rest and so forth, without flesh and so forth, as if unable to be destroyed by elements. The Chag translation says "after having quoted such statements as 'this consciousness abandons the interior of the body of the previous migration and becomes the shape of another body'; and 'thus the between existence of the childish alienated individual, etc.' becomes the cause of the life cycle"; thus it explains [the between body functions] as in the above quotes. [Āryadeva] states that, though that sutra does not describe the magic body clearly, it does describe clearly its intention of how a complete body with limbs and so on is made from just energy-mind, how the magic body splits from the old body and so forth as made very clear in the similes that define it, how that energy-mind becomes a cause of the between for one who does not have the art, and how the magic body arises for one [214b] skilled in that art.

The *Vairochana Enlightenment* statement that "the pure body like a rainbow will be attained by meditating reality" is quoted in the *Integrated Practices* in the magic body context, which, though not teaching the way of achieving the magic body, is still suitable to quote as being useful to confirm generally that meditating the import of reality one achieves a rainbowlike body, and to confirm specifically that if one meditates the reality of mind isolation one achieves the rainbowlike magic body.

[**VI.B.3.b.ii.c′3′d′ii′A″1″a″ii″B‴2‴b‴** – Explaining very clearly the way it is achieved, along with its excellences]

Thus, in order to achieve the magic body, it is necessary to be able to separate the coarse and subtle bodies by force of meditation. Further, regarding the art of separating those two through the yogas of transferring consciousness heavenward and taking possession of the body [city] of another, as the *Sheaf of Instructions* explained the import of the *Sampuṭa [Tantra]*, one must preliminarily practice the energy yogas such as vase-breathing and one must visualize again and again consciousness mounted on energy emerging from the heart-center seat of consciousness. But here, one does not do such [practice]; one does it with another, distinctive, art. As for that, for example, when the death sequence occurs, from earth dissolving into water up to the death clear light, those stages naturally serve to separate the coarse and subtle bodies. Likewise, when the necessary preliminaries of the mind isolation, such as vajra recitation and so forth, the inner and outer vitalizing energy-control meditations, have been consummated, that very same complete [215a] generation of mind isolation, from the perspective of generating earth dissolving into water and so on as in the process of death, itself separates the two bodies, and the self-consecration magic body is achieved from the mere energy-mind of the voids. The self here is the energy-mind that serves as base of the designation thinking "I." That very thing is created as the vajradhara body, which is the consecration.

When one separates apart [into another body] the energy-mind body through the power of body-possession, it is extremely different from creating [oneself] in the vajradhara body by imaginative attention. This is not just mere imaginative mind, but the energy-mind itself is created as a deity body, which is dissimilar from the deity body of meditation where the mind is just envisioned in that form. Once one has attained the magic body of the learner's communion, as its homogeneous continuity is uninterrupted, one is said to "live in reality," and the characteristics of the "vajra body" are complete.

The third stage magic body proceeds purifying itself by realizing objective clear light; so though it is called "vajra body," it is not full-fledged, [with characteristics complete]. Hence there is no contradiction in calling it "a wisdom body" that abides according to the yogi/nī's experience, intending that it does not abide as in the previous case. However, except for using the expression "third-stage magic body" without differentiating actual and virtual,[126] one should not hold that the actual self-consecration magic body is a deity body that is a mental state alone perceived as distinctly apart from the coarse body. Except for explaining that the magic body is achieved from the energy-mind of the mind isolation three luminances, [215b] it is not clear from the treatises of the five father and sons at which point in forward and reverse voids the magic body is achieved. Lakshmī and so forth explain an art of a sudden process where one arises in the vajradhara body

126. *dngos dang rjes mthun pai sgyu lus.*

suddenly from clear light like a fish from water, and an art of a gradual process through imminence and so on where one arises in the vajradhara body from the point of entering luminance, having gone from clear light to imminence and from imminence to radiance. I will explain my own interpretation in the section [below] on communion.

In regard to separating from the old body, it is understood from the above explanation that having abandoned the position of the old body it does not follow that it must abide [therein], and from the *Illuminating Lamp* explanation that the pure magic body dwells in the jewel sack of the body and so forth.

If the magic body were achieved by the yogi/nī who has achieved mind isolation by a procedure of preserving both the subtle and coarse bodies, the father and son treatises' explanation that the magic body is achieved from just the energy-mind would be incorrect; for example, if cloth were made from the whole ball of yarn, the explanation that the cloth is made by specially picking out two separate threads from the ball of yarn would be inappropriate. Although at the first time of achieving it, it must be achieved from the energy-mind of the voids, when one abides in it after achieving it, there are many occasions when the magic body exists even when the three wisdoms of luminance, radiance, and imminence are not manifestly realized; hence it does not follow that the magic body is eliminated when those three are eliminated, or that those three [216a] are present when the magic body is present.

As for the way to achieve the magic body by what sort of will-projection, as it is not explicit in other treatises of the father and sons, one must know to apply the reasoning given by the *Integrated Practices* explanation that one should project the will that "[just as] on the occasion of attaining buddhahood in the between, one dwells in clear light, rejecting the ordinary body, I should resurrect [myself] by the process of self-consecration!" This should be applied also in the case of those things conforming to the magic body pattern. Such a body is said by the *Wisdom Vajra Compendium* to be illuminated by the twelve similes of magic. These twelve are magic, water-moon, hallucination, mirage, dream, echo, fairy city, illusion, rainbow, lightning, water-bubble, and mirror-reflection. They are called the "twelve similes of magic" even though "magic" is used only once as a simile, intending that the first simile stands for the rest, or that they are similes for the magic body.

In that regard, as the vajradhara body is created just from energy and mind, it is like a magic human, as it is just energy-mind even though limbs and members are complete. As it pervades everywhere, it is like the moon in water. As it is devoid of flesh and bone and so on, it is a hallucination, like a body of human shadow. As it moves in an instant, it is like a mirage. As it is a body made of just energy-mind, it is like a dream body separate from the evolutionary [coarse] body. [216b] Though included in one continuum with the evolutionary body, it appears as other, like an echo. The habitat and inhabitant mandalas of that body are like the fairy city. Though it is one, it appears as many, like an illusion. As the body's five colors appear unmixed and unobstructed, it is like a rainbow. As it abides within the aggregate of the evolutionary body, it is like lightning flashing within the thick of a thundercloud. As it arises suddenly from the experience of voidness, it is like a bubble bursting forth in very clear water. As its limbs and members are perfect, it is like the image of Vajradhara arising in a mirror.

Now these are how the learner's magic body is illuminated [by the similes]. When used to illuminate the master's magic body, the sixth and the tenth similes are used in a similar way. The *Self-Consecration* mentions "shadow" in the meaning of "hallucination," and uses "cloud" in place of "illusion." As for its various synonyms, it is according to the statements [in the *Five Stages*:]

> It is explained as "self-consecration,"
> With its nature taught as magical.
> This same thing is designated,
> Superficial reality, magicality,
>
> And the perfectly beatific body.
> That same becomes the fairy being,
> The vajra body is that same thing,
> Vajrasattva, the eminent personage.

As for the excellence of attaining that magic body, it is said that one definitely will attain buddhahood in that same life. Again, from the *Five Stages*:

> Gone into that [magic body] state, [one becomes]
> A lord, great spiritual hero, made of every bliss,
> And one gets home, clothes, [217a] food, and so on
> Instantaneously, just from space.

Static living is cut off,
One is teacher, supreme person,
Worshipped by all, including the gods,
And is saluted again and again.

The *Integrated Practices* also states that one will obtain the consecration of the Buddha. And the *Root Tantra* also declares:

Meditate vajra gentle
In body, speech, mind vajras,
Elaborating body, speech, and mind,
Become like vajra gentle.
By lights of blazing vajras,
To the extent of a hundred leagues,
You shine, the personification of joy,
Adorned by every ornament;
And gods like Brahmā and Rudra
Are never able to behold you.

In comment on which the *Illuminating Lamp* says:

"Vajra gentle" refers to the magic body with its mental nature; and not only does one meditate that as one's body, speech, and mind, but also when one meditates having elaborated it into the body, speech, and mind of the three realms, it all becomes like vajra gentle. Vajras blazing to the magnificent extent of hundred leagues and through countless world realms indicate the illumination by your body's light, adorned by the ornaments such as the thirty-two signs. And if the discovery of such a wisdom body is never even experienced by deities such as Brahmā, what need to mention others; since it is the sphere of irreversibility. That great seal of Mañjushrī [217b] is not experienced or touched by [even the greatest] alienated individual beings; and so this samadhi is called "unperceivable."

And just after that it also says, "that very magic nature body, because it is achieved by purification by means of clear light. . . ." Thus it explains this [impure magic body] entering into clear light by means of the two contemplations, and does not explain the communion magic body entering clear light by means of the two contemplations; therefore this refers to the third-stage magic body. Since it will not be explained that the noble stage is not attained by abiding in that, here the mention of "not beheld by alienated individual beings" refers to [alienated individual beings] other than oneself; and that accords with the above explained "not beheld by Brahmā and so forth," [meaning that it] is not beheld by alienated individual beings who have not attained the magic body.

In regard to a certain samadhi that does not even have the partial tendency to such excellences as these, as for the [false] sense of relief from identifying it as the actual attainment of the wisdom body magic body, it has the fault of not knowing the criterion of attaining this body, the way of attaining this body, and the excellences belonging to the attainment. Since other treatises are not clearly explicit about the two procedures of creating the deities of the creation-stage mantra body and the perfection-stage wisdom body, all explanations of the procedure of deity creation in the perfection stage context are claimed by many who hold other systems to be [only] pertaining to the creation stage. As for those who do practice this system also, though they have differentiated the two [kinds of] deity bodies, it appears that their precise differentiation is extremely rare. Therefore, thinking that this very [218a] greatly secret issue should not be lost, I have made it explicitly clear.

[VI.B.3.b.ii.C′3′d′ii′A″1″a″ii″B‴2‴c‴ – Explaining what comes from the mentors' precepts]

The third has two parts: [i‴] How it is given in the personal instruction tradition; and [ii‴] Explaining that import in connection with the treatise[s].

[VI.B.3.b.ii.C′3′d′ii′A″1″a″ii″B‴2‴c‴i‴ – How it is given in the personal instruction tradition]

From the way mentor Serdingpa gives the Marpa tradition instructions, as for the way to identify the actuality of the magic body, the *Four Point* explains:

> As for the magic body, the noble father and sons claim that the "magic" is that it appears without intrinsic reality, and the "body" is the deity body; so it is a deity body that appears without intrinsic reality. As for its originating cause, the creation-stage deity-body meditation and the creation-stage deity-body-upholding habit are purified by the three voids, and hence the art and wisdom deity body freshly arises uninterruptedly like a bubble bursting forth in water or like a fish leaping from a clear stream. Further, the four neuter syllables dissolve into the indestructible drop, causing the drop to arise as the deity body. The mother symbolizes void, the father symbolizes vision; their mutual kiss is the taste of vision-void arising as bliss. Like the linear short *A* that abides endowed with the five light rays; it is the energy-mind body, hence one meditates by compressing down to that. Further that magic body deity body is meditated within a reality source triangle white outside and red inside.

Again, in the *Wheel Endowed*, [Serdingpa] explains that:

> It is meditated as the drop, which has been compressed into the indestructible drop in the center of the inner lotus, which arises as the father-mother deity body like a mirror reflection.

In the *Five Stages Single Session*, there is an error that seems inconsistent with that tradition's two great and [several] lesser precepts, namely:

> One should aim the mind to the drop [218b] and meditate, that being the learner's clear light; and, when that is stable, one should engage in the paths of the conduct when one arises from the void drop as the deity body.[127]

Again, the *Five Point* explains:

127. This is slightly confusing, as very subtle. The error may be that one, presumably the yogi/nī, is here described as arising *from* the "void drop" as if "one" were something other at this point than the drop itself, which is energy-mind indivisible, bliss-void-indivisible, etc.

> That abiding with five light rays like the linear *A* is the reality condition, the energy-mind body, and one meditates compressing the mind to that. It does not exist apart from that identification, yet is not non-existent as it appears even without intrinsic reality—that is the identification of "magic." "Body" is explained by Āryadeva as the deity body, and so that "magic body" is interpreted as that deity body, unidentifiable, so vivid and void, apparent without intrinsic reality. It is said to be illustrated by the twelve similes of magic illusion; thus identifying it as like a mirror-reflection and so on identifies that magic body.

In that source, though it is written that the magic body is actually the indestructible drop, one can also understand that it is really that drop arisen as the deity body. Therefore, one can also understand the explanation in the two lesser private precepts of the short *A* and the HŪṂ letter as the magic body. The *Five Point* explains:

> In the magic body practice, there are the magic equipoise and the magic liberation. The first of these: in the southwest of your dwelling place make a skylight, suspend a sword above a copper kettle filled with lac-water; and place a mirror before you that reflects a painting of Vajrasattva; thus aim your mind and meditate. Since truth insistence [219a] will not emerge toward these things, they identify magic illusion. This is said to be the instruction for purification in the creation stage.

This is accepted as corresponding to the meaning of the *Five Stages* explanation: "A well-shaped Vajrasattva" and so on. As for the way to terminate truth-insistence based on that, Serdingpa explains in the *Personal Instruction of the Triple Continuum of Magical Illusion*:[128]

> Of the three magic illusions, explain those of equipoise, dream, and between: as for the former, the first of the three solely purifying activities; holding magical illusion one should sit before a mirror image and, examining whether pleasure or displeasure,

128. This text has not been identified among the works of Serdingpa; it may be lost.

> attachment or anger arise there from praise and blame, one should see to it that they do not. One should contemplate just like that. Again, look to see [in the mirror] whether attachment or anger arise from praise or blame. When they do not arise, [the reflection] should merge into one and one should meditate oneself as like a magical deity body. One should practice not being happy and attached when one is praised, anointed with sandalwood unguent from the right, and offered wealth and so on. And one should practice not being unhappy and angry when one is blamed, poked with an axe from the left, and one's wealth is robbed.

Some people who uphold the personal instruction of this system, having set apart the designation "magic illusion" for equipoise, set up the way of meditating as holding the mind, having set the mind immobile by strict body-vital-point [penetration] and gaze; by holding it, energy is held; from that, experience develops. Earth, water, fire, wind, mind, mental events, misknowledge, and universal void—the former dissolves into the latter [219b] with the signs of mirage up to darkness. Then, from the cloudless sky-like universal voidness in reverse order up through the three luminances, the mind along with its energy-mount arises immeasurably with the vivid vision of the experience of the magical deity body and so forth. Even though you meditate that way, if it does not develop that intensely, there is a method to develop the impact, extensively described in the *Five Point*. Or if that doesn't work, by meditating aiming one-pointedly at the heart center of the deity body reflected in the mirror, the first vividness of the image is luminance. Then, when the image seems to split apart, it is luminant radiance. Then its disappearance into darkness is luminant imminence. Then its total sky-like clear light transparence experience gives rise to a variety of experiences as above explained.

Concerning this [outlook], as for the former [instruction], it seems as if these people are considering the "self-consecration" explained as the visions of various luminance experiences in the space of the retraction [yoga branch], cited previously from the *Stainless Light* and the *Supreme Bliss Eulogy Commentary* to be the same as this "self-consecration" of the occasion of magic body. As for the method of intensifying the impact, it seems to be based on some former Tibetans' explanation of the process of looking at any object, wherein the first vividness is luminance, its refinement is radiance, and its final unclear approach to termination is imminence.

In the learning of the magical liberation, the *Five Point* explains its daytime waking practice and its night-time dreaming practice. As for the first, [220a] within the experience of deity-body vividness, one meditates integrating energy and mind by the experience of bliss-void in the throat center, thus generating the experience of engaging in the vital point of vitalizing energy control; this develops the magical liberation. In sleep, dreams come, but here they do not, so these two are dissimilar. As for the transcendent liberation, one goes to Akanishta heaven and is blessed by the mentor, and one has visions of many emanation bodies and listens to the Dharma and so on. As for learning the mundane liberation, it is said that one sees heavens such as the Thirty-three, the [joyous] Tushita, and the [highest] Akanishta, one goes to them, one is worshipped by gods and goddesses, one holds the drop from such as those, and it happens that one manifests various miracles. It is claimed that such things happen as if in a dream, caused by meditating the vase-breath-holding in the throat center preceded by focusing the will to engage in those liberations.

The *Equipoise Magic Illusion Instruction* explains that one meditates the energy-kiss, aiming one's visualization at the heart center drop along with its short *A*, thus developing the experiences, such as flying in the sky, that generate the magical illusion liberation, thus cultivating direct experiential voidness without glee and pride and so on and without obstructions such as deep ravines and precipices and so on.

The *Four Point* explains that the liberations happen as above explained, relying on worshipping the victors by radiating lights from the urna hair-tuft of one's vivid deity body, purifying the two obscurations by manifesting embodiments as needed to tame beings and then compressing the lights back into oneself, [220b] then, having melted one's self-creation into a deity body into light, one collects the light within by the two contemplations.

[**VI.B.3.b.ii.C′3′d′ii′A′′1′′a′′ii′′B′′′2′′′c′′′ii′′′** – Explaining that import in connection with the treatise(s)]

As for that short *A* with its five-colored light rays in the *Five Point* and the *Four Point* being called the "energy-mind body, reality of things," it is not properly considered just that form of the short *A* that appears to the mind's eye in meditation; it is rather the energy-mind subtle body consisting of the subtle vitalizing energy indicated by that [short *A*] and the mental awareness adhering to that [short *A*]. And that [short *A*] is also explained as generating the magic body from the experience of bliss-void in the arisal of the [four] voids unobstructed by anything else, which means that the totally unobstructed magic body is generated from the energy-mind of the three voids. Thus, the intent of the instructions that explain the drop arising as deity body to be the creation of the magic body, and the drop and the syllable to be the magic body should be understood as meaning that the magic body is created from the subtle energy-mind body indicated by those [drops and syllables]; so the magic body should not be interpreted as the mere deity body creation from the transformation of the drop and syllable appearing in the mind's eye.

If one understands it like that [avoiding such misinterpretation], [one can rightly understand] the *Concise Five Stages* [passage], just after its explanation of doing the vajra recitation once the mantra wheel is established:

> Ordinary conception-instincts
> Are visualized as the mind of mantra itself.
> Purifying the body purifies conceptions,
> Purifying energy, one becomes taintless,
> And manifests the wisdom superficial magic [body].

This teaches [221a] the procedure of creating the magic body by purifying the energy by means of vajra recitation preceded by visualizing the mantra wheel. Concerning that, the forms of the mantra-letters set on the petals of the wheel are the means of indicating the mind of the eighty ordinary conceptions and the energies that move them. The bodies or forms of those indicative syllables are serially collected and purified, which purifies the conceptions and their attendant energies. When the conception-mobilizing energies are purified, that means the realization of the intuitive wisdom body, the superficial reality magic body. As the same text states:

> The magic body, along with its luminance,
> Arises from mere energy and mind

—which accords with the explanation that the magic body is made from mere energy and mind purified of its eighty conceptions and their energies. And that procedure seems to agree in import with the *Root* and *Explanatory Tantras* and the treatises of the father and sons.

Further, as for the twelve similes of magic illusion characterizing the magic body, I will explain a few of the correspondences between simile and referent, as it is said that "by recognizing them one recognizes the magic body." I approve the explanation that the ascertainment of the correspondence between simile and referent here is the means of determining the magic body, and also, the personal instructions' explanation that such [ascertainment] is also the means of empowering the clarity of creation stage practice when it is unclear. In the magic body section of the *Five Stages*, if one so interprets the meaning of the passage beginning with "A well-formed Vajrasattva appears,"[129] and if one meditates while perceiving a mirror image, then one sets the mind for a while having moved mentally out [of the mirror]; and [221b] finally one takes the creation stage deity body merged into oneself as the magic body. This then contradicts the [author's own previous] statement that "from one's experience of bliss-void by intuitive wisdom of voidness one generates the magic body without interference by any other," and it disagrees with all authoritative treatises, and also appears to contradict [the author's] own root verse. The mentor Marpa had many different private instructions from many mentors, among his instructions on each tantra, so it is not sure that all of his instructions come from Nāropa.

Well then, one asks, what is the meaning of the *Five Stages*' statement:

> Free from existence and non-existence,
> A well-formed Vajrasattva appears,
> As if reflected clearly
> In a flawless mirror.
>
> Endowed with all the best forms,
> This body that always fascinates
> Should be shown to the good disciple;
> That is called "self-consecration."

129. The full verse is cited just below.

This means that it is a body like the accurately drawn image of Vajradhara, free of two extremes, dawning in clear vision in the pure surface of a mirror, which is superior in all aspects and always delightful to the beholder. And the meaning shown to the disciple by connecting the simile and the meaning of the reflected image and the magic body is explained as "self-consecration." It is not that one meditates while visualizing oneself as reflected in a mirror or that the magic body is shown to be the deity body extracted from the mirror and drawn into oneself. Otherwise, one would have to literally follow [as meditation instructions] the other similes.

As for the "reflection" simile, [222a] among the three out of twelve similes mentioned in the *Five Stages*, it is the reflection of a vajradhara image and not reflections in general. And it is a simile for the body's parts all being completed simultaneously. The rainbow simile indicates unobstructedness and the nonmixture of colors. The water-moon simile indicates the singularity of the magic body itself, being nevertheless capable of creating multiple emanations to accord with the disciples. And as for the *Self-Consecration*'s statement—"By them one meditates the body!"—that one meditates on the magic body through those three similes, it means that one should meditate on the magic body as ascertained according to the description by those [similes].

According to the two ways of achieving the magic body by meditating visualizing a mirror reflection, it does not mean that one must complete the creation stage and the three isolations to achieve it. As for advocating the magic body depending on the explanations in the *Stainless Light* and so on that the luminance of the experience of retraction is self-consecration, it would force you to claim that the eight [signs] from mirage up to the Rāhu-like black luminant [imminence] are the magic body, and that the explanation of the deity body only arising during the reverse order [of the signs] after that as the magic body is incorrect. The *Time Machine* mentions the [eight death] signs such as mirage in the context of retraction as the signs of the time of approaching [initial] reversal and [final] inward reversal of the sense-faculty energies' engagement with ordinary objects. The four signs such as mirage that arise in the context of mind isolation and so on are the signs that arise immediately after those [reverse order] four voids, since it has already been often stated [222b] that the energies must have entered and dissolved into the *dhūti* channel for them [to have arisen]. Therefore, the visions of the aspects of moon, sun, and Rāhu in the context of retraction do not amount to the same thing as the moonlight and so on of the three voids. In short, if you know well the samadhi wherein the sense consciousnesses proceed to dissolve well before the natural instincts, and their motor energies dissolve at the time of generating the mind isolation voids after completing the vajra recitation, then you will not feel any doubt such as "will there be any meditating while seeing with the eyes when the magic body is achieved?"

In general, as for the aftermath arisal of whatever appears as false magical illusion, if you develop great bliss on the occasion of the three isolations and the magic body, it should be a source of intensifying your meditation itself by combining it with penetratingly understood voidness. There is little importance [of using such bliss] in the aftermath context [to direct] the notions and so on of liking or not liking or being or not being reflections to terminate the truth-insistence habit. Here, if you develop certainty through the rationally aware wisdom that has completely eliminated the truth-habit-objectification pattern concerning inner and outer things, subsequently the process of objective appearances arising as magical illusions by their own momentum depends on the excellent understanding of the centrist reasonings. And the *Five Stages*' pronouncement [to the effect] that, after attaining the magic body, one sees everything as illusion no matter in what activities refers both to the vision of illusion that is common with the transcendence [vehicle] and to the previously explained vision of the extraordinary magical illusion [body] wherein the subtle bodies of all beings are seen as no more than mere energy-mind and so on.

By meditating on the energies and becoming pure fluency, while accepting the arisal of all objects of the buddhaverses and realms and so on, [223a] letting the momentum of that precede, if you practice the kiss-union of energies, although such and such appearances will arise illusorily, the explanation about meditating in such a way in the noble literature will not have taken effect. They do not explain the retraction of objective appearance by means of the two contemplations in the context of meditating on magical illusion, and in fact that is not the goal to be attained.

[**VI.B.3.b.ii.c′3′d′ii′A″1″b″** – The associated instructions]

There are two parts in explaining the instructions connected with that: [i″] Providing the context for explaining the sources of the instructions;

and [ii′′] The actual explanation of the instructions of sleep, dream, and so forth.

[**VI.B.3.b.ii.c′3′d′ii′A′′1′′b′′i′′** – Providing the context for explaining the sources of the instructions]

If one wonders, "Are these explanations in this system of the instructions of sleep, dream, death-point, and between made in reliance on the tantras and the treatises of the father and sons?"

Here, master Gö explains both the merger with death and the merger with the between in order to attain buddhahood in the between, and explains the merger with sleep in order to attain buddhahood indirectly through rebirth; the merger with dream is lacking in his private instruction. He does not explain those mergers in order to attain buddhahood in this life, though they are explained quoting the texts of the *Integrated Practices*. These mergers are not there [either] in the private instructions from Nāropa transmitted through Nagtso, though many instructions on all four of them are there in those transmitted through Marpa, explaining sleep and dream mergers in attaining buddhahood in this life, [explaining] sleep, death, and between mergers in attaining buddhahood in the between, and [explaining] all four of them in attaining buddhahood in the next life. This treatise, except for mentioning a mere portion of the teaching, [223b] does not seem to express them clearly.

The *Concise Five Stages* gives the dream instruction:

> To purify the dream body,
> From the time characterized as magical,
> All apparent superficial objects one sees
> Are the stage of superficial reality magic . . .

and:

> Cultivate the dream as solely magical . . .

and it teaches just briefly the sleep, death, and between merger instructions:

> Merge with the three forms of the between . . .

and, as mentioned above, it says to meditate the five stages, connecting existence, birth, and death [between] stages with [the processes of] a single day.

In savior Nāgārjuna's treatises, the mergers are not literally clear, except for the explanation in the *Five Stages* of the magic body as the between and the suitability of explaining the merger of those two. Nāgabodhi doesn't mention utilizing the between, sleep, and dream, except for mentioning the use of the death process in the perfection stage, and the use of birth, death, and between in the creation stage. Chandrakīrti explains the death and between mergers in attaining buddhahood in the between, and, except for the context of explaining the dreamlikeness of all things in the fifteenth chapter, where he quotes a reference from the *Integrated Practices* to establish the equality in truthlessness of the things of dream and waking, he does not openly explain the sleep and dream mergers. Thus, this does not mean that one can claim that this system gives the instructions of holding the dream and so on in the fifteenth chapter explanation of the dreamlikeness. Therefore, the explanation of merging sleep and the four voids is not in any other treatise of the father and sons [224a] except for the *Integrated Practices*. The *Integrated Practices* states:

> Having familiarized from birth to birth and having learned the teaching of selflessness, understanding the yoga of merging, one should merge together with the natural luminance; and through this process one should perceive it in the ultimate reality. The process is as follows: Plunge the aggregates and so on into the subtle element. Plunge the subtle element into the mind. Plunge the mind into mental functioning. Plunge mental functioning into misknowledge. Thus uniting things, fall into sleep. At this time, awareness is forgotten in the instant of mind, mental function, and misknowledge. Afterward, the reality of intuitive wisdom free from unconsciousness also is clear light transparence. There being liberation, through energy, natural instincts are discovered, whereby other things emerge in one's dream. As long as consciousness does not move, one sleeps and beholds clear light; that is called "the interior manifest enlightenment, introspectively realized ultimate reality free of body, speech, and mind." Through this process, the transcendent buddha-hosts abiding in the mandala of the body are to be killed and merged

> into suchness, and one attains the accomplishment of the well-destined; and without relying on either the elaborated or unelaborated activities one totally exchanges one's form. This is what it means. [224b]

Chag's translation here is better, saying "energy moves the natural instincts, if other dreams do not arise. . . ."

Just after the above quote, [the *Integrated Practices*] states:

> This very meaning, from the great yoga tantra called *Revelation of the Hidden Intention*, is expressed:
>
> > Seeing inner things such as form
> > Is pronounced to be "critical insight,"
> > While counting Akshobhya and so on,
> > Abide in quiescence of all notions.
> >
> > These are explained as peace,
> > The suchness of insubstantiality;
> > And the yogi/nī merges the buddhas
> > In the mandala of suchness.

Thus, the yogi/nī who generates sleep into the experience of the samadhi of the four voids is one who lives with the extremely unelaborated conduct. Such an embodiment has two procedures of developing the four voids, at the times of falling asleep and waking from sleep; here the first is not described. When that [procedure] develops the four voids, it is said to develop them thus. Again, the *Integrated Practices* states, "By this process one engages in just the acts of *bhu su ku*," meaning that one simply lives by eating and drinking, urinating and defecating, and otherwise merely meditating clear light by constant sleeping. If one understands the point of this explanation to be that there is no meditation of clear light other than by falling asleep, one will come to understand the ultimate points of the other mergers.

Well then, while the *Revelation of the Hidden Intention* teaches that the yogi/nī should plunge the buddha-aggregates and so on into the clear light mandala of suchness, [225a] how can that be interpreted as substantiating the plunging of the aggregates and so on into clear light by the process of the four voids of sleep?

Though the yogi/nī's producing the experience of the four voids of sleep is not explicitly stated in the tantra's words, it can be understood by Āryadeva's elucidation that uses the personal instruction by Nāgārjuna. Thus, concerning such a process of plunging into clear light, the meaning of the *Revelation of the Hidden Intention* statement about the aggregates and so on being plunged into clear light completely serves as a means of understanding [that process]. For example, the expression that states that the definition of a pot is "round-bellied" does not explicitly show, mixing up round-belliedness and that specific object, that a jade's round-belliedness is [also a kind of] pot; nevertheless, it does show completely the round-belliedness of that specific object.

As for the statement that "the well-destined accomplishment will be achieved when one kills the hosts of transcendent buddhas," it is the same as the *Root Tantra* statement that

> Killing the hosts of transcendent buddhas,
> One will attain the very supreme accomplishment!

And that quote, by its similarity of character, is also properly applied to the clear light of sleep. Relying on that personal instruction of Āryadeva, that mention of which scriptural text the [practice of the] clear light of sleep relies on, can make other [points] understandable. As for such holding of the clear light of sleep, it seems to be part of the activities of attaining buddhahood in that life. Thus, the supreme of merging sleep and clear light intends the buddhahood in this life of the most developed person. Attaining buddhahood in the between or after rebirth in another life require that [instruction only] according to the personal instructions of the mentors. [225b] Thus, if such explanations in personal instructions and the process of generating the four voids of sleep depending on them do not have effect, when one sees that the *Integrated Practices* states that the extremely unelaborated practitioner should use them, one can understand that they are teachings accessible [only] for such a person. So such a person nowadays should not neglect such teachings, or the great import will be lost. The *Integrated Practices*' stated process of merging sleep and the four voids, though it is beyond the ability of the inferior person, it is not that they cannot develop the merely general samadhi merging sleep and the four voids. So one must accurately distinguish the differences of the paths. Therefore, that source in the *Integrated Practices* can be applied by contemporary persons to the holding of the voids of sleep.

Well, what is the source for the instructions of dreams?

That also, since it is not explicated in the tantra and in the other texts of the father and sons, must be understood from the *Integrated Practices*, as follows:

> Why? Sleeping a long time. Why? One abandons the body's interior, and in the dream one goes to the Thirty-three Heaven or to other countries and regions, experiencing the five sense-experiences. Again, coming here into the body, one will attain the fruition of experiencing virtuous and unvirtuous dreams.

One should thus inquire into dreams, "Are nonsleeping states the same or different from sleep-states?" As for "Why? Sleeping a long time," it investigates the cause of long sleep without dreams arising. [226a] As for "Why? Abandoning the interior of the body," it means as above, at the time of dreams arising after falling asleep, a dream body separates from the interior of the previous body, and going to other countries and places it comes again to this body. "Why does it come back?"—again inquires into the cause of its entering there.

According to the wording in the Chag translation, "in the dream, with all senses, to the abode of the Thirty-three, or . . ." it means that the separate dream body seems to have a complete life-support for all senses. As for the meaning of "Why? Dreams virtuous and . . . ," it inquires into the cause of experience, at the time of awakening, of the fruits of the good or bad signs of the dream. As for "Is sleep different or not from the waking?" it inquires into whether there is the difference that the objects seen in dreams are false and those seen on waking are real. In answer to that, it is said to be excellent to inquire into the nature of dreams, in order to eliminate doubts about perceptions viewed as substantial in the body that has the nature of beginninglessness, and in order to illuminate the explanations of the self-consecration. And so [the *Integrated Practices*] states:

> Therefore, from the perspective of dream[likeness], you should introspectively realize all deity bodies explained as mirror-reflections, you should thoroughly understand following the tantras and sutras, and you should attend with a single-pointed mind.
>
> Aggregates, elements, media, faculties, and so on,
> Collecting here both those awarenesses,
> Who becomes the great void and falls asleep, [226b]
> Experiences the dream by the power of energy.
> Desirous of fruition in the dream,
> Noting no difference between dream and waking,
> Beings fall asleep all day and night,
> Dense as earth, they sleep so long.
> By acts performed with effects undeveloped,
> Their energies engage them again in this life.
> As effects develop, this very energy
> [Makes] people die and swiftly go elsewhere.
> The victor lords of the ten directions,
> Though their bodies have no marrow, flesh, or bones,
> They enter the elements to benefit sentient beings,
> Performing deeds with emanation bodies.
> To a mind awake from sleep through such a process,
> Though caught in the net of thoughts desiring fruits,
> Thereby all things are like a dream,
> And true and false do not exist.

Here, [the task is] to dispel the "doubts about perceptions held as substantial in the body," namely the doubts about whether one can or cannot achieve the magic body like a rainbow, not understanding the coarse and subtle bodies separately, but holding the mere coarse body as substantial and depending on it as life support. The Chag translation has "like a mirror-reflection." As for how the tantras cause realization by means of the dream simile, it is expressed from "aggregates" up to the "mind awakened." And as for how the sutras cause realization, it is explained quoting the *Purification of Evolutionary Obstructions Sutra* regarding differentiating true and false in regard to the waking and dream states. [227a] As for gaining realization through the tantras, the magic body is taught relying on the *Root Tantra* and the *Wisdom Vajra Compendium*.

As for the meaning of the first line, according to the *Vajra Rosary* statement, [beyond] the first four aggregates, the four elements such as earth, the four objective media, the four faculties such as eye, the words "and so forth" include all the rest. As for them being included here in the body, one gradually collects consciousness [normally] involuntarily engaged with objects. Thus collected, the two consciousnesses arise, those of luminance and radiance. Of those two, the former collects into the latter and dissolves into imminence, and one becomes a great void and falls into deep sleep. As for "dense earth," from the *Community* explanatory tantra the *Four Goddess Dialogue*, when it establishes the four mandalas in the body, the heart center is called "earth." Other tantras also assign earth to the heart center. Collecting the energies in the heart center, it becomes dense, and on strength of that, dreams do not arise and one sleeps long. These express in general the cause of going to sleep and in specific the cause of long remaining sleeping. When the imminence unconsciousness after dream experience begins to clear, a sleep clear light will dawn; and when that is released dreams arise, so that clear light is included in imminence. In the old translations, "beings [going]" here refers to sleep, and the Chag translation has "persons experience dreams day and night." As for "energies," it should be understood by the key of inquiring into the dream body made of mere energy-mind going to other places. [227b] As for effects developing and not developing, it has to do with the power of evolution being exhausted or not exhausted when that energy-mind is separate and not separate from this coarse body. Thus, when it is not exhausted, it says "again one engages here," expressing the cause of repeated engagement.

As for the answers to the third question, one can understand that the separated dream body still has one continuum with that shown functioning in the previous body. And the second "awakening from the dream" and the third "desiring fruition" show the nondifferentiation of the truth and falsity of dream and wakefulness. The Chag translation says "all those things are dreamlike." By the five lines "just as" and so on it shows that the beatific body has no flesh and bone and so on, yet it dwells in a body of coarse elements in order to be seen by beings, and the emanation body performs deeds for the sake of beings, and this enables one to understand how the dream body goes to other places when one sleeps, and how the waking mind functions again in the old body. Thus since the dream body is like the beatific body, one understands [it as like] the magic body, and that body entering in the coarse body is understood as like [the beatific body entering] the emanation body, and this shows how to understand the magic body beatific body upholding the coarse body emanation body. The Chag translation says "the mind waking from sleep by that process."

Therefore, since the three voids that precede the magic body are exemplified by the three voids of sleep that precede the dream [body], [228a] the actual magic body is exemplified by the dream body, and the [waking in the coarse body] after the dream exemplifies the magic body incorporating the emanation body. You should understand from the personal instruction of Āryadeva that the dream example, out of the twelve examples, is peerless in exemplifying the magic body. Except for the fact that by connecting the corresponding elements of example and referent in the other similes you get a mere idea of developing certainty about the magic body, you cannot develop the metaphoric magic body as an actual path through the exemplification from those examples; but such power does reside in the dream example, and so it is superior.

Further, as for the teaching that the yogi/nī develops the four voids of sleep that occur prior to the dream into the actuality of samadhi, it is the instruction in the merging of sleep and clear light, so you can understand by irresistible reasoning the instruction that the body of the dream that occurs after those is merged with the magic body. You can know it with certainty through the key point that there are explanations for [both] creation-stage practitioners and perfection-stage practitioners (of three each)[130] of the path three bodies and the basis three bodies to be purified. Thus, this is how this supreme system becomes the instruction about the dream, and that process is necessary for all three [types of] persons.

The *Apparitional Nondual Triumph [Tantra]* states:

> The place of ejection with the energy
> Develops in the throat of all beings,
> Abiding there with the letter OṀ,
> That which is called "unexcelled."
> By holding, changing, growing,

130. My text has *lam gyi sku gsum gsum*, but I think the second *gsum* is an error.

> Remembering magic, and sealing,
> Both become the path of samadhi.

Though it thus explains how to hold [228b] the dream, it is hard to believe.

As for the mergers of death and between, the *Integrated Practices* and so on explain buddhahood in the between, which is also fit to be interpreted as buddhahood after a rebirth depending on that, as in the case of the sleep merger. As for the system of relying on the sources for the continuum and so on of sleep and dream, it can be inferred from the foregoing. Thus, if you understand well how to explain these merger instructions, which are Marpa's distinctive specialty, as leading back to the treatises of the personal instructions of the noble father and sons, it seems to be the unexcelled distinctive specialty [of the tradition]. Thus, in the context of the magic body of the metaphoric illusion, exemplifying depending on the dream example, in terms of the statements of the *Integrated Practices*, the dream instructions are connected with the magic body context; and so the instructions of holding the sleep voids are also connected to that context. In terms of their import, from the boundary of being able to develop at least the four voids during waking time, you can enter into the void of sleep. After that, when you meditate the instructions of dream, this [practice] can occur either in the context of body isolation, or in those of speech or mind isolation.

As for merging with actual death and between, that happens on those occasions; and developing in correspondence with those two is designated "mergers with those two," but actually the practice is done as appropriate in waking time or in sleep time.

[**VI.B.3.b.ii.C′3′d′ii′A″1″b″ii″** – The actual explanation of the instructions of sleep, dream, and so forth]

The second has two parts: [A‴] Explaining the sleep and dream mergers; and [B‴] Explaining the death and between mergers.

[**VI.B.3.b.ii.C′3′d′ii′A″1″b″ii″A‴** – Explaining the sleep and dream mergers]

The first has two parts: [1‴] The sleep merger; and [2‴] The dream merger.

[VI.B.3.b.ii.c′3′d′ii′A″1″b″ii″A‴1‴ – The sleep merger]

Here one might wonder, "is it definite or not, that, as the basis of purification, [229a] according to the definite sequence, first the voids of dreamless sleep occur and after them the arisal of dreams: so in the time of the path also, first one meditates the sleep and clear light merger, and after that there is a definite sequence of the dream and magic body merger?"

Here some latter-day Marpa followers, thinking about the *Five Stages* statement that the magic body is third stage and the clear light is the fourth stage, separate the two mergers and interpret the dream magic [body] meditation as third stage and the sleep clear light meditation as fourth stage. However, the *Five Point* explanation is better, that the four voids are held first at the time of sleep, and then after that the dream body resurrects as the beatific body. The essence of the instruction of dreams is that the dream body rises up as the beatific body: because for that to happen, the voids must first be produced; because the sequence must correspond to the basis-time sleep and dream process; because, as the voids of the mind isolation must precede the third-stage magic body, the clear light voids must precede the communion magic body; and because the sequence is always the same, the between arising from the death void, and the [creation stage] primal savior being created from the dissolving of one's visualization into clear light and so on. Here, although the "sleep clear light" has the name of "clear light," I have already explained that it is not [the real clear light, which is not experienced] short of the metaphoric clear light after the occasion of magic body.

Here you might wonder, "If, before meditating on the magic [body] of the dream, the sleep clear light [229b] is held, how is it held?"

In this regard, in general there are two ways to create sleep as an experience of samadhi. Thus, first, if one finds a stable samadhi of the quiescence common to the philosophical individual and universal vehicles and to the mantric and transcendence vehicles, even if one does not make a purposeful effort to create sleep as a samadhi, when one experiences waking state samadhi at the point of falling asleep, and then falls asleep right after that, one might pass into many samadhis without experiencing an ordinary sleep. Again, second, at the time of falling asleep after the arisal of the four signs such as mirage by the power of forcing the energies into the *dhūti* channel, the three voids such as luminance like moonlight first arise, and then one generates sleep into clear light like a cloudless open sky. In the first of these [two ways], without any prior arisal of the four signs such as mirage or the three voids such as moonlight-like luminance, though there is an arisal of a transparent clarity of pure voidness, still it does not mean it is the sleep clear light. In order to produce such a [samadhic sleep,] it is not necessary to have the arts of holding the sleep clear light taught in the mantra vehicle and one does not need to enter into this vehicle. Therefore, to generate sleep into clear light here, it must be developed in the latter manner by the force of dissolving the energies into the *dhūti* channel. Therefore, having meditated during waking time on the instructions of penetrating the vital points in the body, from the boundary of at least being able to develop the four voids, those voids can be merged with the four voids of sleep; since otherwise, though one wants to merge [230a] [the clear light] with sleep, there is nothing there to merge with it.

In that regard, as in the occasion of sleep, usually the subtle breathing in and out in the nostrils is not eliminated. Though there is no basis-time void of sleep according to the void of dissolving in the *dhūti* channel, cutting off even the subtle respiration, it is not that there are no four voids [at all]. Even so, there are great differences between the sleep before any dreams have arisen and [the sleep] after they have arisen in [terms of] the intensity of dissolving the energies into the heart center and in the dissolving and not dissolving of the coarse [energies]. The yogi/nī who is capable of merging the waking-time voids and the sleeping-time voids, at the time of developing the sleep void, must approach eliminating even the subtle nostril respiration and dissolving it into the central *dhūti* channel. For such a person, when they begin to go to sleep, at first though the four signs such as mirage might not arise in definite sequence, as they cultivate further they must definitely arise in neat arrangement. Therefore, a sleep that is not preceded by the arisal in definite sequence of the three voids, when it is produced as an actual samadhi, is still not the sleep clear light; because such an arisal of universal void clear light must definitely be preceded by void, extreme void, and great void, since each is the cause of the succeeding one that is its effect.

Therefore, in the Marpa system's personal instruction of the forceful method of [attaining] clear light transparence, though there is an explanation of holding the sleep void in a month's retreat by visualizing the setting of the white and red drops in the center of the four petals of the heart center lotus, if you concentrate on that visualization during one month and meditate continuously night and day, [230b] it could happen that the energies might concentrate somewhat easily. And that is the vitalizing energy control of meditating the indestructible in the heart center. Further, as a preliminary to that, when you can develop the four voids during waking time, you can then merge them with sleep; it is not that you will develop this ability by meditating this only at going to sleep, not meditating anything else day and night.

Further, on the point of falling asleep, if you meditate again and again by aiming your visualization, it can happen that you can identify the basis time sleep void, but the fully defined voids from dissolving energies cannot arise. As the *Five Point* states [in words to the effect that]:

> Before merging with the dream, in order to hold the sleep void, you must set the [unexcelled] *anuttara* in the throat. Meytson asserts meditation on the throat center, and Tsurton asserts meditation on the heart center; these meaning that for meditating clear light focus on the heart center and for meditating the dream magic body focus on the throat center. Visualizing the petals' four letters, connect each of them with holding each of the voids.

Thus, prior to merging with the dream, it is better if you hold the voids of sleep. If you hold them alternatively, the lotus with the drop should be held in the heart center according to Tsurton's position, and the throat center meditation is not good. If you meditate clear light, due to its connectedness with the heart center, you must meditate in the heart center. Without being able to enter the merging with the dream by the power of dissolving the energies, if you hold the dream by the power of will, it seems you must have a great distinction of connecting with meditating in the throat center. According to the explanation that the "meditation of A NU TA RA" is from the *Nondual Triumph Tantra*, this can be thought of as [231a] the position of some Indians. But to accomplish the meditation of the mantra wheel at the heart center according to the instructions of Nāropa, not to practice by this [way], it does not seem there is cause to practice by those four letters [alone]. Therefore, when you hold the sleep clear light, it is better to meditate on visualizing the white and red drop in the heart center according to

Marpa's personal instructions. That seems to be the orientation of the mind toward the indestructible in the center of the mantra wheel in the heart center. So if you want to expand from that, you can set the mantra wheel and contract it as previously explained. As the *Five Stages Single Session* explains, you should visualize the four letters along with the central drop in the heart center and practice the vajra recitation to hold the sleep clear light. Here the need or lack of need to set up the four letters has already been explained; and the holding of the sleep clear light by practicing vajra recitation having visualized the drop in the heart center is the marvelous instruction; since it is also the import of the *Revelation of the Hidden Intention*. As the *Revelation of the Hidden Intention* states, just after the passage explaining the recitation of the energies of the four mandalas:

> One explains it all in the eighteen;
> Again, that abides in these themselves.
> Just as milk pervades
> And comes to be new butter,
> So Pāṇḍarāvāsinī, and so on,
> Abide there in peace itself.

—and after that, from "The inner things such as form . . ." up to "the Buddha enters"—and after that:

> In and out breathing of the yogi/nī,
> The reality of uniting is sameness.
> Wisdom abiding in art,
> Recite without losing the limbs [231b] of mantra.
> Knowing the yoga in the actuality
> Of all activities, lying down and so on,
> [As the] nameless, the inexpressible,
> Transcending three times, always recite.

The first six lines here state that in the vajra recitation of Pandāra and so on, the clear light of the actuality of the eighteen voidnesses abides like fresh butter emerges from the milk; thereby explaining the development of the four voids through vajra recitation. From "matter and so on . . ." up to "enter the Buddha . . ." the aggregates are explained as entering into clear light, the meaning of which also applies to the sleep clear light, as I have already explained. "The yoga" and so on the four lines describes the recitation uniting energy and mantra indivisibly. The next four lines teach one to perform the recitation also at the time of lying down. Thus, it teaches that at the time of lying down at night, doing the vajra recitation develops the four voids, since that also means that vajra recitation can develop the sleep clear light. In short, whichever art develops the four voids during waking time must be merged to develop the four voids at the time of going to sleep. The supreme art during waking time is the meditation of the indestructible at the heart and the vajra recitation, as I have already extensively explained.

Those two arts of holding the clear light of sleep come from the personal instructions of master Marpa and must be understood as the instructions of the *Root* and *Explanatory Tantras* and the unexcelled intention of the father and sons. It is of crucial importance to distinguish the mutually intermingled, scattered personal instructions. [232a] If you understand this, when the *Integrated Practices* states that sleep emerges as the actuality of the four voids, you can fully eliminate the arisal of the doubt that wonders "where was this art of holding the clear light of sleep stated?"

In general, in regard to whichever path, if you know how to turn with methodical skill whatever exists in the basis reality into the path, it is swift[er]. Thus in this time of sleep also, the base reality is that the energies naturally withdraw and a void is produced. So if you know how to turn it into a path through the instructions of merging, it is extremely swift. Though there are voids in the base reality, since there is no void of very great intensity and sleep has a great tendency to destroy mindfulness, you will not be able to develop a certitude of recognition [of the four voids] until you can turn the process into a path. Here, if there is no diminishing at all of the force of mindfulness, sleep will not come; and if the loss of mindfulness is too severe you just fall asleep and never ascertain the four voids of sleep. Thus you must practice through the personal instruction, when going to sleep, doing it without losing mindfulness and so losing ability to ascertain the void.

The obstruction of this virtuous practice through not falling asleep is rather weak in intensity; and among the personal instructions there are many ways to dispel that [insomnia] and too deep a sleep, as well as other methods not explained there. After the arisal of the voids of light, moderate, and deep sleep, at the time of clear light, having remembered the [realistic] worldview, you must cultivate it for a long time. Thus, quick waking and quick dream arisal become obstacles; so I will give a definite explanation of the basic way of dispelling those. The yogi/nī who inserts and dissolves the energies in the *dhūti* [232b] can produce the four joys and the four voids; but if s/he does not know such an instruction of merging, when s/he meditates by merging sleep with those experiences s/he will not develop intense understanding of the path in this life and will not attain the supreme [accomplishment]. And at the time of death, not only will s/he not be able to be immune from the suffering of death by having taken the four voids of death as the path but s/he will not know how to intensify the understanding of the path. Therefore, you should become expert in the instructions of merging. If you know them well, though you won't develop the power [to accomplish these things] just by that, by applying them to your mind again and again you will develop a marvelous strong instinct.

Thus, this thorough explanation of, even when you cannot create sleep as an actual samadhi, having or not having the ability to ascertain the corresponding voids of sleep of the base reality; of, even when you can create that, producing or not producing it in the reality of the voids of sleep; and of the genuine and spurious methods of creating that—this is a method of developing a rough understanding that is not misled about the key of the instruction of holding the clear light of sleep. The rest of them I will explain elsewhere in fine detail.

[**VI.B.3.b.ii.c′3′d′ii′A″1″b″ii″A‴2‴** – The dream merger]

Thus, one who can merge the voids of sleep, having held the dream by the force of energy, when the voids of sleep arise in sequence, s/he can ascertain "this and this is the luminance and so on of sleep." Thus, from the perspective of understanding the process of arisal of dreams after the clear light of sleep, you should well distinguish the boundary between the void of sleep and the arisal of dream. In that regard, [233a] there is no need for any other method of recognizing dream as dream, and so Āryadeva did not state any other method of holding the dream than the method of holding the clear light of sleep. As for holding the dream, not being able thus to hold the dream by the force of energy, since one cannot hold the dream through the door of previously ascertaining the four voids of sleep, other methods of holding are explained from the personal instructions. Here, without requiring meditation on the path, from the base reality time itself, there are many times it happens that one recognizes dream as dream. Whatever activities one concentrates on with intense will repeatedly in the daytime usually come out also in the dream. By the key of that, it is not that difficult to develop the knowledge that the dream is a dream, and it is recommended that the cultivation of intense will in the daytime can lead to holding [consciously] the dream. In this regard, since if there is no sleep, dreams will not come, though it is possible to carry over [the intention to another] day, still this [problem] will only cause a slight obstruction of the virtuous practice of merging the dream [with the magic body]. When sleep does come, if it is too deep, the dream will not emerge. In some cases where there is excessive habituation to mind focusing only in the daytime, there are no dreams. Or it can happen that even if there are dreams, one does not remember to say at the time of waking, though that is also less intense [as an obstruction]. If such problems should occur, one should use the methods to dispel them as given in the personal instructions, which will be easy if you know how to apply the reasoning behind them.

Now, to hold the dream when it is not the case that sleep does not come and it is not the case that even with sleep coming dreams do not come, thinking that "the current perceptions in the day [233b] are a dream," and especially creating the instinct that projects the strong intention "I will recognize the dream as a dream," these are crucially important in order to awaken [to consciousness] within the context of the dream. In that case, if things do not become clear even when there are many dreams and they are enduring, that kind of instinct cannot have been awakened, so it is crucial that the dreams are clear. If the dreams are clear from the beginning, it is easy to hold them; if they are not clear there must be a method to make them clear. These are to aim the mind and so on at drops in the throat and mid-brow and so on. If one awakens [completely] when the dream had just been recognized or not long after it has been recognized, this obstructs the virtuous practice of merging the dream. One needs to know a method for prolonging the dream. Many of these are not taught, [but] the main one depends on the statements from other tantras that drops at the heart and jewel-tip centers cause deep sleep, at the throat and secret center below the navel cause dreams, and at the forehead and navel cause wakefulness. When you go to sleep, due to the intensity of the energies collecting at the heart, the jewel sleep without dreams occurs, which stays that way as long as the drops stay there. When the binding of the energies there opens up a bit, they go to the throat and the secret place, and the *Community* says the dream emerges, which lasts as long as they stay there or as shortly as they stay there. When the binding of the energies there opens up a bit, they go to the other two places, and one begins to awaken. Upon that, [234a] if you know how to prolong softly the awakening, that serves as the key point. Thereby you can understand the method of prolonging the not long remaining [in the dream], once you have identified the sleep clear light.

In the instructions of the mentor Marpa, the heart center is the vital point for holding the clear light of sleep and the throat is the vital point for holding the dream. As for the explanation of how greatly vital are these two vital points during sleep time and the meditation of the navel in furor fire meditation while waking, it must be understood relying on the explanations above. As for the emphasis on the throat as the vital point for holding dreams, it intends the holding of the dream for one who cannot hold the dream that is [normally] unholdable by the force of the energies. At the time of equipoise, one aims the mind at the drop in the crown, explained [among the] two vital points for waking time. By that one who holds the dream by the force of will, though one cannot ascertain the sleep voids before the dream, when one practices by confirming the recognition of dream, one can find in the Marpa system a special instruction for holding the four sleep voids during that occasion of dreaming. And if you can do that, having stabilized long familiarity with it during the sleeping time, it gets easier to collect the energies during waking time; this is a powerful side-effect for developing the four voids during waking time, which should enable you to understand this as a special exception of the above explanations.

Thus, in the best case, you first develop the four sleep voids by the force of energy and then you arise in the dream beatific body. Or in the worst [case], by the above-explained method you might develop [234b] the sleep four voids, but if you do not know an instruction to merge the dream body with the dream arising in the beatific body, you don't have the superior essence of the instructions of the dream. The statements about the way the dream body arises in the beatific body from the experience of the sleep truth body, and once that happens, [the teaching] that you can definitely merge with the between, occur in the *Five Point* instruction of the Marpa system. The vital point here is extremely great. The later [teachers] engage with this without engaging the fine distinctions; and once they do engage, it is very hard for them to understand that there are the two distinctive systems of arisal; and that, especially, there is a system providing a distinctive certainty through the instruction of merging the [magic body with] the dream and merging the [magic body with the] between.

That is the supremely holy among instructions about merging the [magic body with the] dream; and its common distinctiveness emerges from the personal instructions about emanative transformation and viewing visions of pure and impure objects and so on. As for viewing visions of pure and impure objects, when you recognize [you are in] the dream by some means other than recognizing the dream by the force of dissolving energies into the *dhūti* channel, among good visionary experiences in waking time occur visions of pure lands and deities and so on. However, those are not the real deities, but merely virtual simulations of them, and the pure-land visions are not real either but only simulations. As for the scriptural reference establishing that, though they are stated in the *Samadhi of Direct Experience of the Present Buddhas* and so forth, [235a] fearing prolixity I will not recite them. Although visionary objects seen in a dream recognized through the force of energy are very much different from the above visions, until you reach a high degree of forceful ability of merger, though you might see the mere forms of pure lands and their inhabitants, it is [only simulation] as in the above case. Thus, though occasional unerring clairvoyances about past and future might occur, many erroneous ones will also occur, it is hard to rely on them one-sidedly.

As for stabilizing your habituation to recognizing the dream by force of energy, it seems after a certain stage to be an excellent method for developing unerring clairvoyances about past and future. These nonprincipal distinctions about merging with the dream, though they are not explicit in the great authoritative treatises, seem to be helpful to contemporary persons. As for thus holding dreams by force of energy, it is the principal thing, so you must strive in that procedure. And as it seems very hard to develop this even if you strive, you should hold the dream with other procedures; and then strive further to stabilize those by holding it through the force of energy, and not rest content with just that [progress made with the other procedures]. If you do not know the uncommon instructions of merging [the magic body] with the dream, you will not know how to achieve the realization of the metaphoric magic body that illustrates it in waking time. Or else, even if you know about it, your realization does not intensify and does not become supreme, and you won't know the distinctive procedures of merging [the magic body] with the between at the time of death. Thus, [235b] you should become expert in that, as explained above.

In holding [or recognizing] the dream, if you begin to comprehend the two times of base and path, and in the latter both what is common and what is uncommon with other vehicles, and in that latter again both what is principal and what is commonplace and so on, having then well distinguished the main and accessory points in the dream and magic body merger, you won't get confused about the rough vital points of personal instruction. As for the fine details that remain unexplained about the [nine] mergers here, I must explain them elsewhere.[131]

[**VI.B.3.b.ii.C′3′d′ii′A″1″b″ii″B‴** – Explaining the death and between mergers]

The second has three parts: [1‴] The way of merging buddhahood in the between; [2‴] The way of merging buddhahood after becoming reborn; and [3‴] Demonstrating the analysis and the synthesis of the mergers.

[**VI.B.3.b.ii.C′3′d′ii′A″1″b″ii″B‴1‴** – The way of merging buddhahood in the between]

In general, in developing a path according to the base-reality processes of death, forming the between, and taking birth, there are the expressions, "the conversion of birth, death, and the between into the three bodies" and "merging with birth, death, and the between." Thus, you set up as the paths of the three mergers the attainment of buddhahood in this life, in the between, and after being reborn in another life; and that path again is set up in terms of both creation and perfection stages.

As for the merger of clear light with actual death, the *Integrated Practices* and the *Illuminating Lamp* explain it as attaining buddhahood in the between. You might wonder, "Well, just how much realization of the path does that person attain here in this life?"

The *Integrated Practices* says "seeing the truth, realizing the perfection

131. This intention may have resulted in Tsong Khapa's *bsre ba dgu'i gdams pa*, TKSB, Zhol, vol. cha, no. 34.

stage, and understanding reality," and the *Illuminating Lamp* says "realizing the process of perfection." The followers of Gö explain [236a] that the person [who attains buddhahood in the between] is one who has attained communion but not practiced it, calling such [a person] "one who has abandoned birth but not death." However, the *Third Stage* [chapter of the *Five Stages*] states that if you attain the magic body you will surely attain buddhahood in this very life, and the *Second Stage* [chapter] states:

> Having attained manifest enlightenment,
> [One] proceeds to the pure abodes,
> Not turned back from the buddhaverses,
> In this very life [one will become] omniscient.

—that when you attain the fourth stage [manifest enlightenment, or clear light transparence], you will become a buddha in this life, [but] when you attain buddhahood in the between, magic body and clear light are not attained [in this life].

Further, it is said that attaining the fourth stage [of clear light], you purify the three luminances, which is to realize reality in intuitive experience. If—as the *Ultimate Continuum* [by Maitreyanātha] states:

> The noble one eradicates the miseries
> Of death, aging, and sickness;
> No longer born under power of evolution and addictions,
> He lives free of [the miseries of the life cycle].

—the transcendence universal vehicle noble one abandons death under the power of evolution, what need is there to mention the mantric universal vehicle noble one's abandoning it? [And after all,] this [transcendence vehicle noble] one has not even [fully] abandoned death [itself] under the power of evolution.[132] However, the *Integrated Practices* states that, of the two kinds [of noble ones] mentioned, one of them has no wealth of possessions for performing the [tantric] conducts; but that [statement] is refuted by the statement [by Nāgārjuna] that "once you attain magic body, food

132. Although Maitreya states that the miseries of death etc. are abandoned, evolution-dominated death itself is still driven by untamed instincts even in the noble one.

and clothing are instantaneously obtained from the sky." The *Bodhisattva Stages* says that once you have attained the joyous stage you will never lack for possessions, and so a universal vehicle noble being cannot be lacking in possessions, then that also refutes [the possibility that a noble one can be poor]. [Thus, the mind-isolation-realized mantric] practitioner cannot have attained either of the last two [perfection] stages. Therefore, the meaning of saying "seeing the truth" [during mind isolation] [236b] is that, at the perfection of vajra recitation, one realizes the reality of thatness by the intuitive wisdom of mind isolation; since it does not follow that any experience of reality is a direct experience.[133]

Here again, the *Integrated Practices* explains that some are distracted by farm work, trade, and devotional practices, and are not able to perform the conduct; others lack sufficient wealth and cannot perform the procedures according to the prescriptions in the tantra, and [it further] explains by implication that since the conduct has not been performed those [persons] attain buddhahood in the between. This shows that if one can perform the conducts, one attains buddhahood in this life, so it is clear you must be ready to perform the conducts of the occasion of the perfection stage, and for that you must have at least the definite attainment of mind isolation. This [person] ready to perform the conducts, if s/he does not attain the magic body, knows that s/he must perform the conducts in order to attain the magic body. And if s/he does, the *Vajra Rosary* quote is pertinent:

> Knowing to separate instincts from luminance,
> Then [you] should perform the conducts.
> Abandoning the evolutionary body,
> [You] will attain the vajra body.

Since this states that such a [person], if s/he does not perform the conducts, s/he won't attain buddhahood in this life, it shows that to attain buddhahood in this life, the conducts are definitely necessary and that to represent the conduct that is the art of achieving this magic body, you

133. Tsong Khapa uncharacteristically takes issue with Āryadeva's statement that one out of the two types of noble ones (attainers of the third path and first bodhisattva stage, and of the mind-isolation realization of the mind objective but not yet the magic body, respectively) lacks the wealth to pursue one of the three types of tantric conduct.

should perform [it] by taking the four voids of this life and the four voids of death to be the same. Therefore, in general, as in the case of the performance of the yogas of soul-ejection and body-possession, though the conducts are not needed to separate the coarse and subtle bodies by the force of meditation, the separation of the two bodies by habituation to the samadhi that develops the four voids through the dissolving process by compressing the energy-mind at the heart center [237a] and the creation of that separated subtle body again into the magic vajradhara body adorned with all the signs are extremely difficult to achieve; and so you must engage in the conducts for the sake of that achievement.

Since such is the case, in regard to the merger of [clear light with] death, the *Integrated Practices* does not teach more than the mere transmitting of the projected will for the merger of death and ultimate reality. The followers of Gö very appropriately recommend merger through vajra recitation at the time of death, also using the visualization of the heart center indestructible and the arts of compression through the two contemplations. In regard to such performance, except that the actual process of dissolution, such as earth dissolving into water etc., developed from samadhi, becomes the dissolution process of the compression process of death, there is no other sort of death process [performance]. Therefore, at the time of the death clear light, the import of reality is not [yet] directly realized: because the magic body has not been realized up until then, and because the magic body definitely must be attained in a supporting embodiment that has the experiential realization of the objective clear light; and because the *Five Stages* states:

> The samadhi of self-consecration
> And likewise the state of clear light,
> Distinguished as effect and cause,
> Indicate the two realities.
> By the process of self-consecration,
> The clear light transparence is attained . . .

and also because the *Integrated Practices* states:

> Apart from realizing superficial reality, you cannot directly realize ultimate reality. [237b]

Here, the *Integrated Practices* mention of "superficial reality"—used in the expression of [the yogi/nī's] projected will "This life is to be superficial reality!"—refers to the third-stage magic body. And the *Illuminating Lamp* statement:

> At that time, having taken the time in the very continuum of the being, one arises, and realizes the magical samadhi . . .

also supports this point, since there is no magic body [creation] prior to [realizing] the objective clear light.

As for the way the magic body is realized, it is not done after first arising in the characteristic between state [after death]. That very energy-mind of the death clear light is what is born as the magic body; otherwise, that [very] energy-mind that goes into the between would automatically emerge as the magic body vajradhara body.[134]

Here some people think, first one achieves the full between state, then you meditate and transform the between body and it becomes the communion body. Others think that when you achieve the between, you meditate it as the vajradhara body. These both are at fault by not understanding well the way of achieving the magic body. Here the *Integrated Practices* states:

> Truly understanding "dying is ultimate reality and birth is superficial reality," at some point you develop a determined mind, "having entered clear light and abandoned the ordinary body, I shall arise by the process of self-consecration!" Put that in your mind and stay with it, and that impression will not quit even in another life; then you will become omniscient. Therefore it is said [in a sutra]:

134. This discussion clearly presents the view that tantric enlightenment is finally not about "powering one's way" to buddhahood, as it has often been misrepresented. In order to attain the special cause that accelerates the material buddha-body to full evolutionary perfection, the practitioner has to fully go through death, either virtual or actual, which means a complete surrender of all egocentrist will, with the only ticket forward being a strongly projected will to emerge as embodying the universal love and compassion for all living beings, transmitted with determination in the time of complete surrender to the experiential annihilation of any controlling subjectivity.

> By which and which intention, [238a]
> Humans truly apply their minds,
> That becomes their nature;
> Just as the varied [colors tinge the crystal] jewel.

Thus, [Āryadeva] supports with a sutra reference his contention that whatever willpower concerning the two realities is projected at the time of death, one will develop in that way. Since this does not refer to birth in coarse existence, "birth" in regard to the energy-mind that becomes the between in the case of another person, there is the projected will "I must resurrect in the superficial magic body," and it is said one will achieve according to that projected will. So this must undoubtedly be accepted as the very energy-mind of clear light not being born as a between being but being born as the superficial [reality] magic body vajradhara body.

"Well then," you might ask, "if there is no between here, is it not unsuitable to refer to this as 'buddhahood in the between'?"

If that were [wrong], since there is no [real] clear light present in the imaginative visualization of compressing [energy-mind] into clear light, and there is no [real] vajradhara in the creation of the primal savior through the five enlightenments, it would be wrong to use those expressions for those states; and there are many such parallel reasonings. Therefore, since just as there is a [kind of] between at the end of the death clear light, one attains buddhahood creating it from the mere energy-mind, there is no contradiction in designating that as "buddhahood in the between." If you claim that buddhahood in the between is a practicing of the path after having achieved a full-fledged between after the clear light of death, you are in disagreement with both this system and the personal instructions.

Further, by that vital key of attaining the third stage magic body at the end of the death clear light, since this person does not directly realize the reality of thatness at the time of the death clear light, s/he [238b] attains buddhahood after having achieved the [third stage] magic body, and then [achieves] the two last stages in that embodiment. This way of achieving the magic body gives a great certainty also about the way of achieving the magic body in the process of buddhahood in this life.

"Well, in this case," [you might further object,] "there is a connection with the previously existent coarse body, so there is no such certainty about buddhahood in this life."

In such a case, even if one cannot last the measure of the between of forty-nine days, there is no point counting them, as, going into the presence of the buddhas, one can listen to [their] personal instructions. The *Personal Instruction [of Mañjushrī]* states that performing as a yogi/nī of the self-consecration stage, one should be taught for several eons. Then it states that having propitiated a mentor and attained well the initiation, pledges, and vows, having fully attained the suchness discovered from the speech of the mentor and having understood the secret and the supremely secret, if you cannot meditate by means of the ritual activities as explained, you should meditate thatness through this stage. According to that statement, if you practice the private instruction of [soul-]ejection again and again, conditioned by such aspiration, it is stated [further in the *Personal Instruction*]:

> When the self enters the mind-reality-realm,
> You realize clear intense delight like the sky;
> Then having the force of magical manifestation,
> You achieve the form of a five-year-old boy,
> And you realize incomparable perfect bliss.
> Then when you project [your will] toward other births,
> You will truly realize an emanation [body] form.
>
> Thus, by whatever wishes beings have,
> Truly joining with the minds of humans,
> You become just like what [they need],
> Like the variegated jewel of the sutra.
> You will experience a truth body like the sky
> Of intense delight, like death, fainting, [239a]
> Falling asleep, yawning, or the moment of orgasm;
>
> Intensely meditating on it, you cultivate
> The mentalities of embodied beings.

"You enter the mind-reality-realm" here means entering the death clear light, and realizing the thatness reality at that time. "When you achieve the form of a child" here means the time when you would otherwise achieve the [ordinary] between. "Then you realize incomparable perfection bliss" means that you attain the beatific body as previously explained. "When you take another birth existence you attain an emanation body" indicates the two bodies of the path. Although this latter [point] is not stated in the *Integrated Practices*, this fills in its intention. The one who achieves the magic body is capable of maintaining an emanation body that is perceived by the fleshly eye. "Therefore," [and following] is similar to the *Integrated Practices'* [quote above]. And the five lines from "truth body . . ." teach the taking as the path of the arisal of the ground clear light in the previous context of the ground reality. In this case where otherwise you would attain the between, as for this attainment of the beatific body, it refers to assuming the magic body without taking up the full-fledged between. Again from that same text, [the *Personal Instruction of Mañjushrī*]:

> If you do not attain the three bodies,
> You will [at least] become the chief of scientists,
> And gradually achieve the universal seal.

Thus, it states that, even if you do not attain the three bodies of the path, you will achieve a body of the chief of scientists, a distinctive embodiment for the mantric conduct; and it does not explain that one who does not achieve the three bodies then has a way of practicing the path in the between. Further, it is clear that such an embodiment [of chief scientist], without needing to take any further rebirth in another existence, is going to be born in a [celestial] buddhaverse.[135]

[**VI.B.3.b.ii.C′3′d′ii′A″1″b″ii″B‴2‴** – The way of merging buddhahood after becoming reborn]

Although the *Root* and *Explanatory Tantras* and the treatises of father and sons [239b] do not clearly explain the way of merging death and the between [with truth and beatific bodies] for one who attains buddhahood

135. This whole section is fascinating in the context of Tsong Khapa's biography, as the Buddhajñānapāda quote from the *Mañjushrī Personal Instruction* describes in a startlingly precise way the account given of Tsong Khapa's death in 1419, when his assembled disciples witnessed him transform into a small boy amid a dazzling explosion of light and energy. It is said he postponed his full body (as well as mind) buddhahood in his life for twenty-one years from his profound realization of 1398, because he could not engage in the tantric conducts without resigning as a monk. So he then attained the magic body, clear light transparence, communion buddhahood at the time of death, twenty-fifth day of the tenth lunar month of 1419.

after taking rebirth, that explanation of the *Integrated Practices* and the *Illuminating Lamp* can be applied to those two mergers illustratively [by interpolation], and in this tradition, such an explanation from the private instructions of the mentors is excellent; just as in the case of the sleep and dream mergers.

If you wonder here, "in order to merge [the clear light with] the actuality of death, what sort of realization must you have right now?"

As for this, taking as a base the proper obtainment of initiation and the keeping of the vows and pledges, you then establish the foundation through practice of the creation stage. This is of extremely crucial importance in all three of the patterns of buddhahood, in this life, in the between, and in the next life. Then, by meditating on the methods of penetrating the vital points in the body, you compress the energies into the *dhūti* and dissolve them, and then stabilize the development of the four voids. Then, if you are capable of applying the view that accurately realizes the import of selflessness, you are capable of merging [the clear light with] the voidnesses of death. Remembering the view at the time of the death clear light, you can also realize the import of the reality of thatness. If you have the former ability without the view, though you can merge the death voids, there is no realization of thatness. So there are two ways. If you can merge as in the former way, it develops with extremely great effectiveness that you cut off the elaborations of coarse dualistic perceptions, and the realization of the thatness reality develops with extremely great intensity. And if it is [only] as in the latter case, there is a very great difference. As for not gaining the ability even as much as that, if you from now remember in your mind again and again the stages that happen at death and constantly meditate on them, [240a] the force of such familiarity clearly will enable you to recognize the death voids by being able to remember [the stages] on the point of death; since it is stated in the *Stages of Yoga Practice* that whatever you emphasize in mental habituation in this life, you again will engage with the same thing on the point of death. In this regard further, by the influence of whether or not there is a connection with the [realistic] view, one does or does not realize the thatness reality when one recognizes the base clear light. And in regard to these again, as for the private instruction about the time of death, through the dissolving processes such as earth dissolving into water, you have the impressions from mirage up to candle-flame, then you should remember the private instructions about the three voids, and then you should meditate the private instructions about the two vitalizing energy controls and the two contemplations, the methods of developing the voids through the path.

As Lūyipa's *Arts of Achievement [Sādhana, Clear Realization of the Divine Lord]* states:

> The yogi/nī who restores the mind does not rely on nirvana. At the time of migration, these yogi/nīs, greeted by such as the Glorious Heruka and the yogi/nīs, carrying various flowers in their hands and various standards and banners, with the sound of cymbals and various delightful songs, recognize death, and are led to the paradise of the ḍākinīs.

This means that the yogi/nīs at time of death are visited by heroes and heroines carrying various symbols in their hands and are led into the ḍākinī paradise; that is, are plunged into the clear light, according to the three commentaries such as the Lawapa *Commentary*,[136] stating that later [240b] one should employ the arts of entering the clear light through such conditions. As to the meaning of the first two lines, "nirvana" refers to an ultimate death, which this is not, explaining that this is a restoration of the mind like going from house to house. Here the statement from the *Supreme Bliss [Tantra]* is just as an example; it is visibly evident in this life that being greeted by one's own chosen deity at the time of death is a benefit of those who have the intense devotion of keeping vows and pledges pure, revering the mentor, and meditating as archetype deity the creation stage of the chosen patron deity.

Here you might object, "If one who gets lost in the full-fledged between without attaining the magic body after the clear light of death does not attain buddhahood in the between, then what about the *Concise Five Stages* explanation? [As follows:]

> Attaining the abode of clear light, manifest buddhahood,
> The diligent will reach the supreme in this very life,
> The indolent [will reach it] on the point of death,

136. The three commentaries are by Tathāgatavajra (Tōh. 1509), Vīravajra (Tōh. 4577), and the one mentioned here by Lawapa (Tōh. 4578).

And the worst one, in the existence between;
And their supreme [emanation] bodies will accomplish the
aims of others.

[To answer,] this refers to attaining the supreme through that clear light of buddhahood from realizing clear light, realized at best in this life, at medium realized at the time of the death clear light, and at worst realized in the between. It does not refer to attaining buddhahood at the same time as the clear light of death or to attaining buddhahood in the actual between state; since the "worst" case must be interpreted as the one who attains buddhahood after another birth. Thus, as for the merging [the beatific body] with the between, when you get the ability to merge [the truth body] with death, you will also get the ability to merge the between by the force of projecting the will as above explained in the between. However, in that case one is practicing by using the imagination of self as a deity body after attaining the full-fledged between. [241a] As for the special method of recognizing the between, it can be developed properly by the force of meditating the four voids during the waking and sleep states. After that, there is the personal instruction for developing the illustrative, metaphoric magic body; and even without that much ability, there is a good method in holding the dreams by willpower. Without any of those, when you impress in mind the private instruction of death, you must habituate yourself to impressing in mind the ways of achieving the between after death and the meditations on the form of the magic body.

[**VI.B.3.b.ii.c′3′d′ii′A′′1′′b′′ii′′B′′′3′′′** – Demonstrating the analysis and the synthesis of the mergers]

As the *Concise Five Stages* explains "you should merge the three kinds of between," by that example you should understand the three deaths and the three births. Though these mergers' designations do not occur clearly in the treatises of father and sons, they are meaningful.

The three betweens are the existence between, the corresponding dream between, [and the path between]—and here many persons in the Marpa tradition interpret the meaning of the expression "birth-death between" as this present body from birth until death—however, taking the two base reality betweens and the one path between[137] as the third corresponds better with the father and sons' treatises. Further, in the *Five Stages* there are mentionings of the magic body as a between, in regard to which there are both actual and virtual understandings. As for the three deaths, there is the well-known death, there is the sleep death, which is the sleep voids prior to the key explanation of the dream body as a between, and in the perfection stage there is the path death, which is developed according to the base-reality death dissolution process. [241b] Thus there are two base reality deaths and one path death. As for the three births [or lives], there is the birth maintained as womb-birth from the existence between, there is the waking-time birth when the dream betweener again enters into the coarse body, and there is the birth when the magic body betweener [re-enters and] maintains the coarse body. Thus there are two base births and one path birth.

As for the first of those sets of three, the merger of between and beatific body is the magic body merger. As for the middle three, the merger of death and the truth body is the clear light merger. And as for the final three, the merger of birth and the emanation body [is the magic body entering the coarse body or any other emanation for the sake of beings].[138] In regard to those, if you synthesize them, they are called "the three merger cycles." If you separate them, they are called "the nine mergers."

Here, relying on the explanation of the *Concise Five Stages*:

> By the energy of the furor-fire yoga,
> The mind objective is great bliss.
> Uniting dream and magic as one;
> You should merge the three betweens.
> Addictions become the path of wisdoms.
> The path of swift cutting is ejection,
> And body-possession is a branch.

137. This seems to be the third-stage magic body itself.

138. As Tsong Khapa out of reticence did not maintain the parallel of the previous two sets of three by equating a line of mergers (death-truth body etc.) with a path, I supplied the bracketed emanation path from his immediately previous listing of the third birth merger.

Serdingpa connected the furor meditation in the private instruction literature of the *Community* with the five stages and also gave the private instructions of ejection and body-possession. As for the explanation in the *Concise Five Stages*, in regard to meditating the furor fire taught in the yoginī tantras, it is claimed that it is taught in the terms substituted in the five stages of the father tantras. Doing it that way is in order to show how to synthesize all the paths of both types of tantras, the actual five stages or their analogous [six branches or other stages]. Interpreting that way, the analogue of developing mind isolation by the energies in vajra recitation [242a] is the very same yoga of furor fire. The analogue of mind isolation itself is the four joys of the great bliss derived from dissolving the energies into the *dhūti* channel depending on the meditation of furor fire. Both of those do occur in the mother tantras. Thus the meaning of that treatise is that one constitutes the five stages by adding [to the isolations' analogues] the father tantras' magic body, clear light, and communion; and it does not mean to explain things otherwise.

"Uniting dream and magic as one" means that the personal instructions about dreams should be combined with the personal instructions about the magic body. "Between" refers to the three mergers of the magic body. As for this very merging of the two base reality time betweens with the path between, it is in order to purify the impure, the latter referred to as "addictions." If you do not attain the supreme in this life or in the between, then, having attained a distinctively excellent embodiment for practicing mantra in another life, the way of not prolonging that path is soul-ejection yoga, and body-possession is a distinctively excellent branch of soul-ejection yoga. Those two are clear in the yoginī tantras. Or else, body-possession is the branch of swift cutting the path by exchanging in this life one's own embodiment with another's embodiment because of differences of their qualities of good and bad. The reason for mentioning these two here is to say, "add those two to the father tantra." Or, since, once you are capable of creating the illustrative, metaphoric magic body of the father tantra, if you meditate the personal instruction of body-possession, you can develop an especially excellent ability, [the two are mentioned] in order to make that understood.

Many ways of merging the nine mergers have been explained. Yet there seem to remain some vital points [242b] that are very hard to understand, and they seem to require some further determination.

9. Ultimate Clear Light Transparence

[242b.1–263b.3]

[**VI.B.3.b.ii.C′3′d′ii′A″2″** – The perfection stage of ultimate clear light]

Second, the perfection stage of ultimate clear light, has two parts: [a″] The import explained in the *Five Stages* and the *Integrated Practices*; and [b″] The import explained in the endurance branch statement of the *Further Tantra*.

[**VI.B.3.b.ii.C′3′d′ii′A″2″a″** – The import explained in the *Five Stages* and the *Integrated Practices*]

The first has three parts: [i″] Procedure to ascertain the sequence, along with how to become eligible; [ii″] Explaining the practical instruction in clear light to such a person; and [iii″] The way that stage also reaches the end of other paths.

[**VI.B.3.b.ii.C′3′d′ii′A″2″a″i″** – Procedure to ascertain the sequence, along with how to become eligible]

Here you might wonder, "As previously explained in the context of confirming the sequence [of the stages], what is the reason for the statement that you cannot attain the clear light of this stage if you do not previously create the superficial reality magic body?"

In general, since according to the system of the noble father and sons the direct realization of the import of the thatness reality that is objective selflessness is shared in common with the noble disciples and hermit buddhas, what need is there to mention that there is a direct realization of that ultimate reality on the joyous stage of the transcendence vehicle? Since the achievement of the magic body is the uncommon distinctive excellence of the unexcelled mantra vehicle, it is not claimed that such a magic body must be achieved merely as a prerequisite of the direct realization of the ultimate reality clear light. However, the claim is that the achievement of the magic body must precede that objective clear light which consists of the orgasmic bliss's direct realization of the extremely subtle import of thatness. This will now be explained in detail.

In that regard, according to the systems of other vehicles, the realization of voidness, chief cause of the wisdom truth body, serves as an interactive condition for the matter body, and the infinite store of merit, chief cause of the matter body, [243a] serves as an interactive condition for the truth body. Nevertheless, you do not travel the path by taking these two chief causes as art and wisdom indivisible in actuality and combining them into one in a concentrated samadhi. In the context of this unexcelled vehicle, I have already explained the unerring union of bliss and void and their union in one actuality with the magic body. And I have also already explained the import of how, though there is the similarity here in the mere general outline of the path of learning the six transcendences, having conceived the spirit of enlightenment, there is a distinctive way of learning each of the separately categorized types of merit stores and there is a distinctive process wherein the realization of voidness is able to purify the objective obscurations.

According to that vital key point: the quickest individual vehicle [practice] causes the exhaustion of the addictions with their seeds in three lifetimes; and in the transcendence vehicle, there are very different long and short timespans, such as the statements that it takes much time to attain the joyous stage where you directly realize the nature of reality, that the addictive obscurations are exhausted on the eighth stage, and that there are many different ways of abandoning and not abandoning addictions. Thus, in this path, the magic body is not created [only] in order to produce the intuitive wisdom that is just the direct realization of the reality of thatness by the orgasmic bliss. It is developed [also] in order to master the distinctive ability to purify the objective obscurations by the intuitive wisdom of objective clear light; since it is the chief cause of the uncommon matter body. Although when orgasmic [243b] bliss takes voidness as its object, there is a door for developing a distinctive ability to purify objective obscurations through that subjectivity, in this context of the perfection stage, the magic body is the substitute of the infinite stores of merit of the other vehicles. Recognizing the combination of those two is the ultimate vital key point.

Thus, though the [various ways of] achieving the matter body are similar in the sense of enhancing the distinctive ability of the chief cause of the wisdom truth body to purify the objective obscurations, there is a very great difference in regard to what you take as the chief causes of the two bodies. Thereby you can understand the difference between how on the other vehicles you attain the body adorned with signs and with that support you meditate only voidness in concentrated samadhi, and then, aroused by the buddhas, you engage in gathering the magnificent stores in the aftermath; and how in this context when you attain the magic body you do not have to proceed in that way. In regard to these reasons for confirming the sequence, without easily being satisfied, you must deeply investigate the general arrangement of the procedures of the path in the other vehicles, in the other tantra classes, and in the two [categories of unexcelled] tantras, and all the subtle vital key points of those. For, due to the extreme difficulty of understanding it, there are many likely but spurious explanations about the magic body such as "to purify the taints of holding magical illusion you must plunge it into the clear light!" and so on.

Therefore, the *Fourth Stage* [chapter of the *Five Stages*] states:

> This self-arisen Divine Lord,
> Alone is just the greatest of divinities;
> The vajra master is even greater,
> Since s/he bestows the personal instructions.
>
> Having truly pleased him or her,
> Over years or also months,
> Having satisfied that mentor,
> Worship [244a] as much as you can.
>
> Having well instructed the consort
> With whom you join, she should be given away,
> And you should make offerings with proper rites
> Amid the mandala of the host.

It declares that, since s/he bestows the personal instructions about this, you should view the mentor as greater than the Buddha, and you should propitiate him or her for a long time. After that you should make offerings with the secret and other offerings to the mentor who teaches this. And [Āryadeva also in] the *Lamp of Integrated Practices* says that you will not realize clear light without the personal instruction of the mentor, and that, having obtained the verbal transmission from the mentor who teaches indivisibly the causal and the fruitional teachings, you should make offerings to that mentor as before. Though this is said [previously] in the context of receiving initiation, it is just the same in the context of receiving the practical instructions. You should understand that these, even if you perform them by mental imagination, are praised as the causes of arranging the favorable auspicious conditions for the distinctively excellent path.

After that, as for the *Five Stages* and the *Integrated Practices* declaration that the mentor confers the secret and third initiation preceded by the nine initiations [of the vase initiation], if you have previously attained once the initiation that makes you a fit vessel, a second initiation to become fit is not necessary. In the *Fourth Stage* [chapter of the *Five Stages*] statement that, in the predawn twilight[139] of the night when the initiation was conferred at midnight, the disciple propitiates the mentor by offerings and praise, the offerings are as before. The praises are the four and a half verses beginning with "Liberated from the three realms. . . ." After that praise, it is stated that the disciple petitions the mentor with the three verses from "Liberated from evolution and birth. . . ." [244b]

As for the reason behind the statement that you should praise and invite the mentor in harmony with the personal instructions in the contexts of magic body and clear light, it is good to assert that you should meditate the mentor yoga, having also used it in the contexts of the other stages, and that you should pray with those procedures. Therefore, you should pray in that way not only on just the occasion of hearing the practical instructions but also on other occasions. Therefore, in general in all vehicles and in specific in this vehicle, you should not break your commitments to the mentor, you should make offerings while considering him or her as a buddha, you

139. Here the PK verse Ch. IV, 7 mentions the predawn twilight (Skt. *pratyuṣa*, Tib. *tho rangs*) in connection with the attainment of clear light transparence, after praising and pleasing the mentor.

should please him or her with all methods of propitiation and abandon all unpleasing things; this seems to be the superior vital point.

[VI.B.3.b.ii.C′3′d′ii′A″2″a″ii″ – Explaining the practical instruction in clear light to such a person]

The second has three parts: [A‴] Explaining both outer and inner manifest enlightenments; [B‴] Explaining the two contemplations, the art of realizing them; [C‴] Explaining their synonyms, along with their greatness.

[VI.B.3.b.ii.C′3′d′ii′A″2″a″ii″A‴ – Explaining both outer and inner manifest enlightenments]

The first has two parts: [1‴] The actual meaning; and [2‴] Rebutting objections.

[VI.B.3.b.ii.C′3′d′ii′A″2″a″ii″A‴1‴ – The actual meaning]

As for what is taught out of compassion to such a disciple who prays in that way, [Nāgārjuna says] in the *Fourth Stage* [chapter of the *Five Stages*]:

> Luminance is part of the night, day where bright sunrays spread is luminant radiance,
> Twilight [evening darkness] is luminant imminence, and gradually one's instinctual natures go [away].
> Freedom from instincts is nor night, nor day, nor twilight dark,
> It is just the instant of enlightenment taught by the best mentor, the goal of the yogi/nīs themselves.
>
> Twilight limit[140] not ended, [245a] but its deep black darkness fully past,
> Yet the sun not risen—this moment is proclaimed the taintless limit of reality.

140. Skt. *samdhyā-tejas* (perhaps "energy of twilight") here oddly translated as Tib. *mtshams kyi mtha*, seems to mean that the ambiguous state between light and dark, "extreme

> The supreme master free of confusion shows the outer enlightenment to the disciple,
> Who attains untroubled inner bliss by this instant of buddha-enlightenment.

Thus both an outer and an inner enlightenment are taught. The Chag translation reads "Those are endowed all at once with freedom from instinctual natures," and "the end of darkness is finished and the splendor of twilight is entirely transcended, as long as the sun does not arise in that immaculate instant, here is taught the reality limit."

Also [Āryadeva states] in the *Integrated Practices* that

> There are two kinds of manifest enlightenment. The outer manifest enlightenment is the clear light universal voidness in the boundary-state of the predawn when the ignorance luminance is transcended and the sun has not yet risen. Therein is the clear light universal voidness.[141]

The import of this is explained as in the *Five Stages*, that passing beyond the times of imminence and the luminance night, while the sun has not yet risen, it is the predawn twilight [of clear light transparence]. [The *Integrated Practices* continues]:

> When the sun rises it is radiance,
> When the sun sets it is ignorance,
> When the moon rises it is luminance.

As for teaching the inner manifest enlightenment: first, in the mirage-like state one sees an assemblage of five-colored light rays. Second, there is luminance like moon rays. Third, there is luminance-radiance like sunrays. Fourth, there is luminance-imminence like darkness. Then in the instant

---

twilight," so to speak, inconceivably bridges over into predawn dark-light-nondual clear light. See above, p. 369 n. 115; and again, see D. Kittay's translation of *Jewel Rosary Tantra*, Twilight chapter 15.

141. Tsong Khapa abbreviates this quote from the CMP, especially the last phrases, but keeps the essential point .

free from darkness, there is clear light transparence, [245b] extremely clear, having the nature of constant luminance, seen by the intuition eye as the intrinsic identity of the ultimate reality.

Here you might wonder, "Here the mentor teaches the disciple the two enlightenments, outer and inner. As for the first, dividing an outer day into four parts, if you interpret separately the explanation of the four voids, it is incorrect that the fourth void is the instant of enlightenment and that it is the object of the yogi/nī him/herself. If I interpret him [or her] as explaining the four voids taking as example the four skies of those times, since the inner four voids are also like that I will not be able to differentiate the outer and the inner; since in the inner occasion also, they are taught using the examples of moon, sun, and darkness. If I interpret it as producing the four wisdoms of the four voids in the four times, it would happen that in the time of each of those four times the four voids would not develop in one time, and so how then would I distinguish the difference between the outer and inner enlightenments?"

In this regard, master Gö set forth two systems, the position of Nāropa and the position of both Tsunmojen and Kṛshṇa Samayavajra.

The first of these [systems] is the explanation of the four parts of the day as the four voids, which refers to the interpretable meaning, outer enlightenment, since it is the example of reality, the time, the sign, and the means of indication. The definitive meaning is the inner enlightenment; if you meditate by uniting with the consort, bringing the enlightenment spirit into the root, shaft, and vase of the vajra and sealing those three blisses with voids, then ensue the three path luminances and the universal [246a] void clear light, when there is the wisdom of the bliss that eliminates the reality [habit-grounded] instinctual constructs at the time of two drops releasing and two drops abiding.

The second of these [systems] is the outer enlightenment [that occurs] when the four outer examples indicate the negandum from the part of the four freedoms from adventitious instinctual constructs, and the inner enlightenment is when that is shown from the side of the experience of immersing the magic [body] in the clear light through the two contemplations.

As for Lakshmī explaining the four parts of the day as the four voids, it is claimed that these are the four inner voids that have those names, and the inner enlightenment is explained as the four voids relying on the evolution consort and the four voids relying on the wisdom consort, or the four voids attained through the progression of the five signs such as mirage. The *Moonlight Commentary*, the *Clear Meaning*, the Samayavajra *Commentary*, and Munishrī explain the four voids of the outer occasion as the inner four voids, without clearly differentiating outer and inner voids. If you analyze as before explained, those who differentiate outer and inner have no cogent answer, neither do the explanations of those who do not differentiate seem to have a cogent answer.

This point is very hard to understand and seems to be important, so it must be investigated. It must be understood relying on the statements from the *Illuminating Lamp* fifteenth chapter. The *Root Tantra* states:

> [With] a girl from the priest, warrior,
> Merchant lord, and commoner classes,
> You should practice as the vajra Dharma-lord.
> This is the means to attain the secret.
>
> When the vajra sun sets
> You should initiate all achievements.
> At the time when the dawn light arises,
> It will be achieved by the supreme meditation.

Explaining the meaning of this, [246b] [Chandrakīrti's] *[Illuminating Lamp] Commentary* explains as follows: The perfection-stage practitioner takes a female consort from any of the four castes; relying on her, the Dharma unbreakable as a vajra diamond is the perfection-stage yoga. As for the nature of that, the practitioner endowed with that understanding should achieve the means of attaining the vajra secret that is Vajradhara. And that must be perfected by means of the progression of manifest enlightenment. The method of that is shown by the four lines beginning with [the one containing] "vajra."

In that regard, as there are two processes of outer and inner enlightenment, as for explaining the first; the vajra sun is the actual sun. "When it sets" refers to the passing of the time when the red sun is cut off; you should propitiate the mentor with whatever possessions are at hand. Then when you have attained initiation by the kindness of the mentor at midnight, at the time of dawn, since the parts of the night that indicate luminance have passed, at the time just before sunrise, you are struck by the transmission of the process of clear enlightenment, and you will achieve it—meaning it will become pure. All this explains the process of the outer enlightenment. If one explains according to the process of inner enlightenment, the vajra sun emerges as the nature of union of the art [male] with the intuitive wisdom [female], and its setting is its cessation as the reality of wisdom emerges. Thus when luminance and radiance have set, you should initiate the imminence, the means of achieving clear light—that is, it emerges. Dawn arising is ignorance; when that is passed, the practitioners, by the cause and condition of the three voids, realize the supreme meditation that is the clear light, and thereby they will achieve the universal seal [embrace]. Here the universal seal [embrace] is [247a] the communion [stage].

Since this is stated as the means of the direct realization of clear light, both outer and inner enlightenments should be applied to objective clear light. As for the reliance on the external seal [consort] in the occasion of the proximate cause of realizing that, it is the meaning of the first verse. As for the way of reliance, at midnight the mentor confers the initiation relying on the evolution seal, as a means of indicating clear light. After that, when hit by the personal instructions of the way of meditating predawn clear light and of the system of achieving communion after that, you will attain objective clear light, and after that achieve communion. Thus, since the realization of objective clear light specially relates to the predawn time, it is called the outer enlightenment, and since the realization is accomplished by the process of the four inner voids it is called the inner enlightenment. Therefore, having taken the other three segments of time in a day as the other three voids, explained above in the mind isolation context, it is indicated by the examples of the sky of those times, and so there is no fault of being unable to differentiate outer and inner. The nonlearner's communion is also stated [by Nāgārjuna] in *Five Stages* and [Āryadeva] in *Integrated Practices* as being attained in the predawn time.

[**VI.B.3.b.ii.c′3′d′ii′A″2″a″ii″A‴2‴** – Rebutting objections]

[Here, you might] object, "As for the fact that the *Five Stages* and the *Integrated Practices*, for the sake of that one who has achieved the magic body and aims for the clear light, state the private instructions of the predawn after midnight initiation [as] two enlightenments and two contemplations, is it that you can produce the objective clear light in that very predawn, or not? If not, it contradicts what was said above from the *Illuminating Lamp*. If so, [247b] since before obtaining such ability, one would be unfit to be taught the personal instructions of clear light, though one fully attains all four initiations before achieving the magic body, one would become unfit to learn completely the perfection stage that explains the tantra by the six parameters and four procedures. Or, if one were fit, then explain the intention of teaching as above the way of learning the personal instruction of clear light having completed the magic body!"

Let us explain. In regard to that statement in the *Five Stages* and the *Integrated Practices*, there are two contexts, one that of achieving basic fitness and the other that of having attained the magic body and having such an ability. The *Illuminating Lamp* statement intends the latter context and is not made in terms of all such statements. A qualified disciple will prepare for attaining the complete fitness initiation by developing understanding from a complete explanation of the tantra. A fully qualified mentor thoroughly develops in his spiritual process a realization of each phase of the path and so will explain the personal instructions that are developed in the disciple's spiritual process by the stages of the path teachings. Now since that disciple must still rely [on the mentor] even more intensely, how could it be the case that the personal instruction on the clear light previously explained would not now have to be explained [more deeply]? Therefore, since there are naturally limitless disciples for achieving the magic body, and there are even more limitless persons worthy of being their mentors, it does not suffice to count them by the masters and disciples of nowadays.[142]

Just having attained the magic body, you cannot develop the objective clear light within a single day; [248a] since the *Wisdom Vajra Compendium* states in the context of ultimate clear light as follows:

> "Divine Lord! What happens after the three voids and clear light?" The Divine Lord replied, "Just as fire burns wood to ashes, so in clear light, wisdom-intuition causes purification over a long time. Just as the tala leaves become ashes, the art intuition causes purification. Just as the petals of cotton plants

142. This is a rather amazing statement, considering the usual view of then and now being ever deeper in a dark age.

burn, so the intuition of luminance attained causes purification supremely quickly."

And the *Five Stages* also states:

> In a year or in a month, having propitiated that mentor . . .

Thus, even having attained the magic body, having heard the instruction of the clear light from the mentor, after having meditated many methods of entering into the clear light through the two contemplations, you should then do as the *Illuminating Lamp* statement recommends. You must differentiate how orgasmic bliss becomes the objective clear light that directly realizes the import of the reality of thatness and how it well understands the qualities of the metaphoric clear light even when it does not [yet] become that [metaphoric clear light].

[**VI.B.3.b.ii.C′3′d′ii′A″2″a″ii″B‴** – Explaining the two contemplations, the art of realizing them]

As previously explained, one who has well achieved the magic body must strive to develop the objective clear light in her or his spiritual continuum. When objective clear light manifests for you, you must be taught the way the outer and inner enlightenments occur, and before [**248b**] that the way to meditate the two contemplations of the holistic holding and the serial dissolving. Of these, the former has already been explained; so here I will explain the two contemplations.

Nāgārjuna explains these in the *Fourth Stage* [chapter of the *Five Stages*]:

> The disciple who has gotten the private instruction,
> Then learns the two kinds of yoga:
> The processes of holistic holding
> And of serial dissolving.
>
> From the head or the feet,
> Until it reaches the heart center,
> The yogi/nī should enter the truth limit—
> That is called the holistic holding.

> First having made animate and inanimate
> Into clear light,
> [The yogi/nī] should make [his own] nature such—
> That is the dissolving process.
>
> As breath on a mirror
> Completely dissolves,
> So the yogi/nī should enter the truth limit
> Again and again.

And [Āryadeva, in] the *Integrated Practices*:

> Thus having realized directly universal voidness one should visualize the two contemplations through this stage. The procedure is as follows: As a lump [of snow] placed in an immaculate stream or pond, so the yogi/nī should gradually meditate a process of serial dissolving. S/he should regard it as like breath-vapor gradually fading in a mirror. And also in the case of holding holistically, s/he should visualize also in this stage.

Here, as for "having realized the fourth void and accomplishing the visualization in the two contemplations," it describes the realizations of the two enlightenments and the two contemplations, after what has already been explained. The two verses beginning with "the disciple who has gotten the private instruction" [249a] refers to one who has gotten the private instruction and is in training. For that person, holistic holding proceeds "reaching up to the heart center" by compressing down from your head and up from your feet, [bringing] both ends into your heart center. Kānhapa explains that you compress everything between your head and your feet into your heart center seed and that into a drop and that into the void. Thus compressing into the heart center the yogi/nī enters into the truth-limit clear light transparence. As for the example of that, it is given by the four lines beginning with "of the breath. . . ." As the vapor smudge left on a mirror by breath collects from all its limits into the center, so you compress into the center of the heart center from the up and down, left and right, back and front of the body.

As for dissolving, first you compress animate and inanimate into clear light and after that compress yourself into clear light. As for "according to your nature," it is correctly explained by Kānhapa as performed in the same way as holistic holding. "Again and again" refers to the need for practicing those two repeatedly. The example of dissolving is the gradual melting of a ball of snow in a pond. Here the old Chag translation is more apt in mentioning "drops" (*thigs pa*).

Both these practices involve a gradual destruction of your aggregate, being distinguished merely by whether or not they first compress the rest of the animate and inanimate environment. The verbal meaning of "dissolving" is as [already] explained. Abhaya explains that "holistic" refers to the body and "holding" to its being held by voidness. The body enters, or is held, into clear light. [249b] That the two contemplations both realize the objective clear light having made the heart center the final place of compression is the marvelous position of the noble father and sons, as you must understand according to the many reasons already explained.

In regard to this visualization of a process of compression, though it is not openly and clearly explained as a compression of energy, you should understand that when you perform that visualization it in fact serves as the unexcelled energy compression process. Here, the *Four Goddess Dialogue* says:

> Always abide in the center of the heart,
> Endowed with the blaze of great light,
> Up to reaching the nine,
> Abiding in the forehead and down to the foot soles,
> Compress it all into that drop,
> Abiding in the center of that hub.

Thus, from the "brow," that is the head, down to the soles of the feet, everything is compressed into that very heart center drop, which means it states that you should make it stay in the hub of the lotus of the heart center. Therefore, in the speech isolation context, you must understand that all three meditations of vitalizing energy control are methods of developing the four voids by compressing the energies and light-spirits into the heart center. By the force of habituation to that, here by the process of compressing the sphere of vision, you cause the energy and enlightenment spirit to compress into the heart center and enter into clear light; and that is the reason why the two contemplations are stated as the meditation that is the method for the magic body yogi/nī to enter into clear light.

Moreover, the necessity of uniting with the outer seal is stated in the *Wisdom Vajra Compendium*, since it has the same function [as the two contemplations]. As for the statement that the two contemplations cause the magic body to enter the clear light—having [250a] meditated on the energy and mind again and again compressing into the heart center and developing the four voids—at the time when the objective clear light is manifest, it means that it serves to purify the magic body as well. As for the magic body person meditating the two contemplations, though the followers of the Marpa tradition do not teach the meditation of the triply stacked spiritual heroes of the three vajras, the private instructions of the Gö system claim that the meditation of those three is the meaning of the *Root [Tantra]* and commentaries of the eleventh chapter. Thus it is especially excellent, in that something lying in the tantra commentary is taken out and used as a private instruction. That again is stated in the *Root Tantra*:

> Buddha abiding in the center of the mandala,
> Place Vairochana in my body.
> Visualize the letter OṀ in the heart center,
> Meditate consciousness in the mantra.
>
> The cessation vajra in the very mind,
> When it develops there,
> Hold the supreme of all buddhas,
> Like the glorious wish-fulfiller.
>
> Buddha abiding in the center of the mandala,
> Meditate Vajra Akshobhya,
> Meditate the HŪṀ letter in the heart center,
> Place the mind to become the drop.
>
> Buddha abiding in the center of the mandala
> Meditate Amitāyus.
> Visualize the letter ĀḤ in the heart center,
> Place the vajra in becoming the drop.
>
> This is that supreme of supreme commitments—
> Meditating the three vajra unbreakables,

The cessation vow intuitive wisdom,
You will attain the power of buddhahood.

Here "buddha" means "buddha-realization," what is to be realized, the mandala [250b] of knowable objects, the body, speech, and mind of the three realms. "In the center of that" means the reality of those things. "Abiding there" means you imagine the actuality of your body, speech, and mind. As for meditating Vairochana, Akshobhya, and Amitāyus, it means meditating Vairochana as the inseparability of the two bodies, Akshobhya as the inseparability of the two minds, and Amitābha as the inseparability of the two speeches.

As for meditating the three, OṀ ĀḤ HŪṀ, in the heart centers of the three meditated devotee heroes, they are the wisdom hero. As for the mantra, OṀ is assigned as consciousness, the samadhi hero drop, HŪṀ is assigned as the natural mind of the samadhi hero become a drop, and ĀḤ is assigned as the vajra of the samadhi hero, the natural mind become a drop. The yogi/nī who meditates in that manner injects his/her natural mind into the center of the cessation vajra, the clear light. Thereby, when s/he abandons meditating the drop and the ultimate clear light is developed, s/he holds or achieves the supreme of all buddhas, becoming like a wish-fulfilling gem that fulfills all aspirations, endowed with the glory of both stores [of wisdom and merit]. As for this meditation of the indivisibility of your own body, speech, and mind and the three vajras of body, speech, and mind of all beings, it is the supreme commitment, superior to the creation stage, generating the intuitive wisdom that is understood by the private instruction that holds the commitment to the clear light transparence of cessation. Therefore, the Buddha, [251a] that is the accomplishments of the aggregates, free from the ordinary body, the profound, magnificent wisdom body, will be attained. Such is the explanation of the *Illuminating Lamp*.

Thus, having attained the magic body, for the sake of immersing your body, speech, and mind into the clear light, first you meditate, as triply nested, the body vajra, then the speech vajra, and then the mind vajra. You truly meditate not only the first two heroes, but also the samadhi hero as the drop, and thereby cause your own immersion in the clear light. The samadhi hero as the three drops is claimed by the followers of Gö as being within the short *A* and the place of focus, the triangular drops.

After that, the tantra explains the meditation of the three vajras by the passage "the vajra abides in the realm of space . . ." and so forth, which some people connect with the dissolving and the former holistic holding; since it is stated that the previous import is illuminated by the later statements by different expression, the previous meaning itself is divided into the two, the holistic holding and the dissolving. As for the way to meditate that, you radiate light rays from whatever seed in the heart center, you compress the devotee hero into the wisdom hero of the heart center through a process of descent from the head and ascent from the foot-soles, you compress the wisdom heroes again gradually into the short *A*, the samadhi hero indestructible drop, and then you compress that into clear light and hold the mind there undeviating, similar to both the contemplations. **[251b]**

As for the way that dissolving preliminarily compresses into clear light all animate and inanimate things other than oneself, it is according to what the *Illuminating Lamp* says:

> Moving and unmoving things, taking the letter KHAṀ as sky, are made insubstantial by the process of serial dissolving, then one is made to enter gradually therein, the vajra wisdom becoming equal to space, and one becomes one who has the nature of the three spiritual heroes. KHAṀ is clear light.

The Patsab and Chag translations explain that dissolving makes all things invisible and enters oneself therein gradually. Thus one's heart center seed radiates light rays that melt all animate and inanimate things into light, which mass of light gradually dissolves into oneself, making it also invisible. In general the OṀ letter is meditated on the crown and the ĀḤ on the throat, but here all three letters are stated to be meditated at the heart center; the reasons for which have already been stated, which does not accord with the meaning of Lakshmī's instruction to have the radiation and compression in the navel from the letter in the hub of the wheel established at the navel. As for the statement that, as the benefit of this, one attains the wisdom body free of the ordinary body, though one has attained a wisdom magic body separated from the ordinary body, it does not preclude one's attaining a previously unattained communion vajra body free from the ordinary body. As [Nāgārjuna says] in the *Five Stages*:

> The magical illusion samadhi
> Is purified by the limit of reality.

And [Āryadeva says] in the *Integrated Practices*:

> Superficial reality is purified [252a] by the ultimate reality.

Do not think that [Chandrakīrti's explanation in] the *Illuminating Lamp*—that the magic body is immersed in clear light by the two contemplations—contradicts the fact that the meditation of the three vajras here immerses you in the clear light, since the magic body is the vajradhara body. Although that body achieved as the magic body abides in the beatific vajradhara body, by habituating its repeated compression into clear light by the meditation as the emanation body of the three vajras, when the objective clear light is directly realized, the magic body also disappears like a rainbow in the sky. Further, the body achieved by the energy purified by the objective clear light is not eliminated at the time of direct realization of clear light, and there is the difference that this differs from the [body] achieved by the energy purified by the metaphoric clear light.

Here, relying on the two contemplations and the seal [consort], at the time of repeating the fourth void, if you do not meditate by conjoining as subject and object that bliss and the void of decisive insight into reality, however you accustom yourself to the four voids coming from the mere process of compressing the energy and mind, it is impossible to realize the objective clear light. Thus it is necessary to have the way of uniting bliss and void of the sages. And in that context, though many predawn-like clear skies may arise, purged of coarse dualistic appearance, the extremely subtle dualistic appearances will not be eliminated, and the direct realization of voidness coming from the one taste of the two things, subjective bliss and objective reality, will not arise. [252b] Thus you must well distinguish between [real clear-transparence-purified communion bodies] and these conditions of the magic body that have not been purified in clear light.

If you do not differentiate them properly, then you are likely to consider the dawnings of the three voids from the low state of not yet reaching mind isolation as the actual mind isolation; to consider the divine body that arises after that in mental experience as a transparent, very clear, rainbow-like, luminant body as the actual magic body; to consider as the actual clear light the state of obliteration of imaginative aiming that manifests with the thought of "This is it!" when you meditate the two contemplations and purify that body in the clear sky; and to consider that the arisal in a deity body after that is the actual communion. Those states are categorized as the virtual simulations of the four stages such as mind isolation, hence fit to be merely designated by their names in contexts where authentic and virtual are not distinguished. But if you hold them as being the actualities of the four out of the five stages, then, [even] with the key of the ultimate private instruction of the *Five Stages* and the *Integrated Practices*, you can never open up the vital points of the *Root* and *Explanatory Tantras*.

Therefore, you must understand properly the way these accomplishments are developed in the spiritual process of the disciple by the teaching of the way the former paths are completed and the way that the later paths are then entered into, using the teachings of the *Root* and *Explanatory Tantras* and the treatises of the noble father and sons, mostly applied in terms of the jewel-like person who is the chief disciple. Then you must also distinguish properly how the other four persons who do not have such an ability and especially the contemporary persons who meditate do develop in their spiritual processes the virtual simulations of those previous paths; [253a] and thereby you will not consider whatever virtual realizations of the five stages they develop to be the same as the actual path of the five stages as defined. Thus, having become habituated through the two contemplations, when you discover well the signs of approaching very close to the realization of the objective clear light, through the teaching of the midnight initiation and the predawn private instruction you will realize objective clear light.

[**VI.B.3.b.ii.c′3′d′ii′A″2″a″ii″c‴** – Explaining their synonyms, along with their greatness]

The nominal synonyms of that objective clear light transparence of the direct realization of the meaning of the reality of thatness by the orgasmic bliss are many, such as clear light and universal void and so on. In the *[Root Tantra]* second chapter the six transcendent buddhas each express the spirit of enlightenment, and other unexcelled yoga tantras make statements such as [the following from the *Nondual Triumph Tantra*]:

> Transcending meditation of all branches,
> Abandoning conceptions of conceptions,

> Transcending the augmented drop [vowels]—
> This is the supreme mandala.

In sum, these expressions are those mentioned in the *Integrated Practices* as:

> These words uncertain in what they name, being the most difficult of the literal meanings of all eighty-four thousand teachings, are renowned as based upon ultimate reality

because such teachings dispel the intellectual insistence that insists on different meanings for each name. As the *Second Stage* [chapter of the *Five Stages*] says:

> In the various sutras and tantras,
> Whatever of thatness reality is taught,
> Other than this very abode of universal void—
> Nothing is there declared!

Thus, in the sutras and tantras, whatever of the import of thatness reality [253b] is taught, it is explained that no other thing is expressed than universal void clear light transparence. As for the meaning of such a statement, though great bliss intuition is not mentioned, there are very many expressions of the import of thatness, therefore the clear light that is the realization of thatness reality by orgasmic bliss is not that which is taught in every case. Nevertheless, [the above statements intend] the teaching of the ultimate clear light that is the object of that intuition and the clear light of realizing thatness by the intuitive subjectivities other than great bliss as being what is taught by all the sutras that teach thatness from the orientation of the transcendences and by the lower tantras. Such a clear light is the general image of clear light. The realization of thatness by great bliss is classified as whichever, the hidden meaning and the ultimate [meaning] clear light. Therefore, in regard to the intuition that enters into experiential uniformity with the import of thatness reality, it has two forms: one that is and one that is not the intuition of the perfection stage.

Thus having cut the doubts about the two kinds of enlightenment, the practical instructions of the two contemplations that are the arts of [realizing] those, and the synonyms of clear light, as for the way in which the disciple performs the eulogy invocation that aims to the mentor who teaches that and the teaching itself, with countenance very clear, palms joined together:

> Emaho Buddha! Emaho Dharma!
> Teaching Dharma—the great wonder!
> Realistic meaning, pure meaning!
> Homage to the enlightenment spirit!

It is to be expressed thus, as stated in the second chapter [of the *Esoteric Community Root Tantra*]. The two "Emaho" exclamations praise from the conventional and ultimate perspectives respectively. [254a] The meaning of the second line is to praise from the perspective of teaching the union of the two realities. The "realistic meaning" refers to the clear light and the meaning purified by that refers to the fully purified divine body; which two phrases together mean "Homage to thee, great Vajradhara who has such qualities!" Such as this illustrates the culmination of teachings explained on other stages.

[**VI.B.3.b.ii.c′3′d′ii′A′′2′′a′′iii′′** – The way that stage also reaches the end of other paths]

The *Integrated Practices*, after teaching the personal instruction of clear light, continues:

> By this very stage, all the transcendent buddhas stirred the Divine Lord, Glorious Shākyamuni, by the sound of a finger snap, and he arose from his immovable samadhi, went and sat down near the enlightenment tree, and at the time of midnight directly realized clear light. He then arose from the magical samadhi, and manifested the teaching of the Dharma for the beings. From that beginning, for as long as the noble Dharma lasts, it has descended from mentor's mouth to mentor's mouth.

The Chag translation here renders it:

> . . . Then arising with the magical samadhi, he turned the wheel of Dharma for the tamable beings. . . .

"This very stage" refers back in the *Integrated Practices* to the predawn teaching of the personal instruction, having been initiated at midnight. And before that, if you connect it to "just after that one should confer the wisdom and intuition initiations," the meaning is similar. Also, the *[Five Stages'] Second Stage*, after showing that the unexcelled yoga mantrī/nī's own path is the way to buddhahood:

> Then from the pure clear light,
> Intuitive wisdom's expression [254b] emerges,
> Holding the thirty-two signs,
> Endowed with the eighty marks,
> Supreme in all aspects,
> Thus, becoming omniscient;

it continues:

> As the *Magnificent Play Sutra* states:
>
> "The Transcendent Shākyamuni,
> Wishing this manifest enlightenment,
> Formed the intention 'I must attain
> Buddhahood by the great void.'"
>
> On the bank of the Nairañjana river,
> He entered into the immovable samadhi.
> Then the victors sitting in the space vajra,
> Just as sesame seeds fill their pod,
> Snapped their fingers and spoke in unison
> To the bodhisattva:
>
> "This contemplation is not perfect.
> You won't reach the ultimate by this.
> You must perceive the clear light,
> Supreme like the face of the sky.
> Attaining the abode of clear light,
> You will be born in the form of intense joy.
> That time you will attain the lordship over all,
> The superjoy vajra body."

> When he heard that expression,
> He gave up the immovable samadhi,
> And thus, at that midnight time,
> The victor-child perceived thatness.

And also:

> Universal void the great amazement!
> Great intuition clear and transparent!
> By the kindness of the mentor himself,
> Then that is clearly seen.

And:

> By the vajra-like samadhi,
> At the time when gray light arises,
> He is adorned by the qualities of magic,
> Such as water-moon and hallucination.
> Seated at the essence of enlightenment,
> He conquered all the devils.
> The Shākya Savior well attained
> The realistic [255a] unexcelled intuition,
> Saving and helping beings,
> Here he taught all thatness.[143]

Thus is taught the procedure of buddhahood by the unexcelled path at the culmination of the universal vehicle transcendence path.

The Chag translation renders it, "from that pure clear light" and "likewise also the universal vehicle sutra," of which the last is better. This means to show that, just as one attains buddhahood through clear light and communion by one's own path, one uses that same art to attain buddhahood at the culmination of the other paths; since this is not put forth as a means of proving the previous teaching. The six lines beginning with "Shākyamuni"

143. This quote from the *Lalitavistara Sutra* is not in the Sanskrit or Tibetan versions of that work, but seems to originate in a quote from the *Five Stages*, presumably cited from an earlier recension of the sutra. Tomabechi, in his erudite "Étude du Pañcakrama" (2006, p. 139, n. 158) states that there are some terms in the existing *Lalitavistara* that correspond to this account, but no actual narration. However, he traces the account to Jñānapāda's *Pearl of Liberation*, and to the tantra *Sarvatathāgatatattvasaṁgraha*.

show that Shākyamuni wished to attain buddhahood through the great void and entered the immovable samadhi on the bank of the Nairañjana river. That much was stated in the *Magnificent Play*. As for the rest, from "That time the victors' space vajra" and so on was not taught as stated in that sutra. "Great void" is explained by some commentators on the *Five Stages* as referring to the stage of imminence, but in that sutra it states that he entered the space-pervading samadhi of the fourth [immeasurable] contemplation, and so if we interpret it as referring to that, it is better, as that also is called the "immovable samadhi." In the *Integrated Practices*, it only mentions that "Shākyamuni was stirred up," but then the four lines beginning with "that time" explain how he was impelled to sit on the bank of the Nairañjana river.

In the *Reality Compendium*, it says no more than, "when the bodhisattva Siddhārtha sat near the enlightenment tree, the transcendent lords stirred him up," and is not explicit about the Akanishta [255b] and the desire realm. The *Vajra Summit* says that he was at the Akanishta Dense Array buddhaverse. As for the way he was exhorted by voice, "this samadhi" and so forth, the four lines exhort him by saying that the previous contemplation is incapable of purifying all the obscurations, and will not lead to the attainment of the ultimate exaltation, therefore you must realize clear light. The next four lines exhort him to realize the vajradhara exaltation, the communion with its eight divinities, how it serves as an exhortation being clearly explained in the Chag translation. As for being exhorted by voice, except for the *Reality Compendium* statement:

> Are you thinking of attaining buddhahood through asceticism,
> without realizing the thatness of all transcendent buddhas?

the way of exhortation and the way of realizing the fruition after being exhorted here [in the *Integrated Practices*] are absent in the *[Vajra] Summit* and the *Reality Compendium*. Thus, it seems that this explanation is set forth as occurring in some other unexcelled yoga tantra.

The four lines beginning "Thus . . ." and the *Integrated Practices* passage from "immovable" to "realized" must be explained as the same in meaning, so he was exhorted while sitting on the riverbank; after arising from there he sat at the enlightenment tree, and at midnight [in Akanishta] he relied on the seal consort, was initiated, and realized clear light. The four lines beginning with "universal void" makes more explicit "he perceived thatness." The four lines beginning with "vajra-like" describe how he attained the nonlearner's communion body in the predawn twilight, the two lines beginning with "enlightenment" describe his conquest of the devils, and the four lines beginning with "Shākya" describe how he taught others, once he had attained the fruition. [256a]

The *Terminal Action Investigation* states that:

> Even through limitless eons of giving
> [Great] gifts of one's own head and treasures,
> One will not attain the fruition of enlightenment,
> Because one's visions have not been purified.
> Likewise, even throughout limitless eons
> Of practicing justice and tolerance and so on . . .

And after that as above, and then:

> Even throughout limitless eons,
> By the samadhi of the mantra body, . . .

with the conclusion as above; but then finally:

> When you purify the three visions
> There will be no doubt of omniscience.

Here the intention is that, as the first two verses mention the transcendence vehicle, and the next verse mentions the paths of the three lower tantras and the creation stage alone, these do not have the ability to purify the three visions, and thus will not lead to attainment of the unexcelled enlightenment. Thus, since there is the dualistic perception error in the occasion of the three visions, that dualistic perception will not be eliminated until the erroneous instinct has been entirely purified. And in regard to conduct, up to the way of the definite elimination of that [dualistic perception], what is required is meditation with orgasmic bliss realizing the import of thatness reality; and the meaning is that outside of the unexcelled vehicle there is no other way.

As the *Liberation Drop* says:

> Wherefore, Shākyamuni, having gathered stores for countless eons, not realizing that meaning, dwelt in the samadhi of nothingness on the Nairañjana bank. That time all the transcendent buddhas eliminated that crushing attitude, and like the mandala of sky, manifested the taintless profound clarity of total purity. At the time of midnight, [256b] as if fainting, meditating on thatness reality, at the time of predawn twilight, in an instant, thatness was realized.

Thus it agrees with the two former passages. As for "nothingness," the commentary explains it as the [nihilistic] voidness that crushes to dust, and that he realized thatness as if fainting, having been blessed by the orgasmic master; the "master" here explained as the science consort.[144]

The *Sheaf of Instructions* states:

> By means of the knowledges of private instructions, he will come to understand totally clearly this excellence, it being sufficiently [shown] by this very detailed [account]; "You should declare that the supreme culmination depended on this art!" For example, from the initiation of the wisdom [consort] given by the perfect buddhas seated in the sky, the Shākya Savior sat near the enlightenment tree, and relied [on her] at midnight in order to attain enlightenment, just so, only by this, O Divine Lord, at the vajra essence [site], the conferral of initiation was given through the supreme consort of the [indestructible] drop.

As for the *Hevajra* statement:

> Erecting the mandala
> Vibrating the garland of blazing flames,
> Because of giving initiation at the vajra essence,
> The supreme drop is compelled.

It is the scriptural source for the fact that the tenth-stage bodhisattva is initiated relying on the actual science consort.

144. "Master" does not seem to be included in the quote as we have it, only mention of the transcendent buddhas, so Tsong Khapa here seems to anticipate the next quote.

Here you might wonder, "It is stated that the Buddha would not have manifested the buddha-deeds in the desire realm without having previously attained buddhahood in the matter realm Akanishta. In the great transcendence vehicle, it is stated also that the Shākya Savior attained buddhahood many eons previously. The *Stage of Arrangement* [257a] also states that the next-to-last life bodhisattva [Shvetaketu] did not use a beatific body to accomplish the aims of humans, and thus entered a mother's womb in order to manifest the emanation body [of Siddhārtha]. And the *Magnificent Play* indicates that Shākyamuni was already a buddha before he manifested the [twelve] deeds such as asceticism. Therefore, how is it that attaining buddhahood by the path of mantra at the end of the path of transcendences is stated here to come after he performed the ascetical deeds on the banks of the river?"

Let me explain. First, at the end of the path of the transcendence vehicle, at the time of both the final existence before buddhahood in the beatific body embodiment in Akanishta and the final existence before buddhahood in the emanation body in the desire realm, there are respectively the actual buddhahood through exhortation as explained above and the manifestation of the way of attaining buddhahood. Therefore, the latter is not a fresh buddhahood of someone who has not already attained buddhahood; and such a demonstration shows in general that an embodiment of a final existence of a tenth-stage bodhisattva of the transcendence vehicle must attain buddhahood by creating the mantra path in their continuum.

The *Vajra Rosary Commentary* states that the bodhisattva Siddhārtha was initiated by the buddhas, once they had prepared and emanated the mandala; and [then, that by] relying on the teaching of three samadhis, the hundred-clan body isolation, and the private instructions of the five stages, at midnight, [he attained] buddhahood; and at predawn, the devil conquest. This latter [explanation] contradicts both the *Five Stages* and the *Integrated Practices,* [257b] contradicting their statements that at this time no other private instructions than those of the clear light transparence and the communion were given.

The followers of Gö claim that the progression through the transcendence path up to the tenth stage is the substitute for creating in one's continuum the progression from the creation stage to the mind isolation, because the *Five Stages* states:

By the beginner's yoga
One should attain the eighth stage;
And who sees the three luminances
Is exalted on the tenth stage.

Therefore, that final existence of the transcendence vehicle is equal to meditating onward from the magic body [stage]. In the evening receiving the secret initiation, the magic body is realized. At midnight receiving the third initiation, clear light is realized. In the predawn twilight, the fourth initiation is received and the nonlearner's communion is realized—it is claimed that he attains buddhahood in a single night. The boundary at which one enters the mantra at the end of the transcendence vehicle is the tenth stage, which is equivalent to the latter of being both a next-to-last-life bodhisattva and being a final existence [bodhisattva, Shvetaketu and Siddhārtha], which can be understood from this [process] being equated to attaining buddhahood in a single night.

As for how one enters, it is not by rejecting one's own path, but rather by adding the mantra path to that path; it being correct as the Gö school maintains that in this case you do not need to create the progression from the creation stage up to the mind isolation. As for the reason why you don't need the magic body of the third stage, you can understand that from the teaching of the reason why the person who engages in the unexcelled yoga from the beginning needs to achieve the magic body before s/he [258a] can realize clear light.

Having conferred the third initiation, there is mention of giving also the fourth; and those are the two initiations given. When the third initiation is given, the subtle dualisms of the prior experiences of luminance, radiance, and imminence, and the transition from imminence into clear light are purified and the objective orgasmic [bliss-wisdom] is realized. This bodhisattva had already realized reality from the first stage, but had not previously experienced directly the voidness with the orgasmic great bliss, which is what is created here. Then, meditating on that import, in the predawn magic samadhi he is said to achieve the body characterized by the examples of magic, such as water moon; which means he attained the orgasmic intuition of objective clear light and the mere energy on which it rides, the totally pure magic body of the nonlearner's communion.

In the transcendence vehicle, one attains the body adorned with the signs from the first stage and, at the end of the progressive improvement of the stages, one attains the culmination of the learner's signs by that method. But by the unexcelled art, by reason of not attaining the nonlearner's matter body by just that, one must first create the basis on which that body is achieved, the extraordinary clear light intuition along with its energy. Knowing this, you can well understand whether you can achieve or not the magic body [just] from the evolution of the coarse body in the occasion of the third stage and the learner's communion. Therefore, until you have meditated on the direct realization of the import of thatness with the orgasmic great bliss, you will not attain the truth body that completely abandons the objective obscurations. [258b] And until you have attained the magic body from the mere energy-mind cultivated by the objective clear light, you will not attain the nonlearner's matter body. Since these are taught, that teaches that the union of bliss and void and the achievement of the magic body are the ultimate essence of the unexcelled vehicle and these two are the two extraordinary causes of the two bodies.

In this context, that very meditation relying on the consort of the third initiation substitutes for the conduct, and so the reason that he did not need to learn the other three conducts can be understood by the previous reason. Likewise, these are the means to understand how the conferral of the two final initiations without having previously conferred the vase initiation and the secret initiation, and this creation of the two final stages without having first created the [unexcelled] path below the third-stage magic body, are exceptions to the rule. So that the previously explained sequence of the two stages, the determination of the number needed, the fact that the mantra path needs the embodiment of the desire realm, and the necessity of the passion of the union of the two organs are all taught in terms of the definite category of practitioner who enters the unexcelled path from the beginning. As for the statements such as that the desire realm deities and so on never emit the jasmine-like enlightenment spirit, they intend ordinary desire-realm and matter-realm gods and do not intend exceptional embodiments such as that of the final-existence bodhisattva.

Just as one can postulate three temporary definite categories without postulating the definite categories of the ultimate three vehicles, though one enters the unexcelled path at the end of the transcendence vehicle, this does not contradict [259a] one's being definitely categorized by one's own path prior to the tenth stage. Though arhat saints and nonregressors are free of attachment to food and clothing, they can purposefully wish for food and clothing. Tenth-stage bodhisattvas have ended addictions and so have ended craving for the bliss of sexual union; yet this does not prevent them from producing the purposeful desire for that bliss. Otherwise, since the outsiders hold that where there is desire there is passionate attachment, it would not refute [the view] that any one speaking a word must be counted as one passionately attached. Therefore, to hold that "since the *Analysis of Tradition*[145] explains separately the causes of making fit a [sexual] organ to be free or not to be free from attachment to desire, so therefore it is impossible for one who has terminated craving for sense objects to rely on a consort!"—this is an opinion that betrays a lack of learning whether in mantra or in transcendence [vehicle literatures]. As for the two paths—[wherein one being] at the end of three incalculable eons on the transcendence vehicle then relies on the mantra path and reaches the universal illumination eleventh stage of buddhahood, and [the other being] enters the mantra vehicle from the beginning and thus reaches the universal illumination stage of buddhahood in a single lifetime—though neither is inferior to the other [intrinsically], that doesn't mean that the difference between the two paths is negligible, since it is obvious that there is a great difference of distance [in time], and another path must be added finally to the transcendence vehicle path.

Such being the case, finally, relying on the mantra path does not contradict the attainment of buddhahood through countless eons. For that [transcendence vehicle bodhisattva] did have to add the [mantra] path at the end of the three incalculable [eons], in order to manifestly attain perfect buddhahood. As the *Vajra Summit* says:

> Previously [259b] in the past,
> Having upheld the spirit of enlightenment,
> He became a bodhisattva
> Endowed with art and wisdom.
>
> Great delight! Great wonder!
> He performed measureless hardships,

145. *lung rnam 'byed,* identified with the *Vinaya-vibhaṅga* (see *Blue Annals,* I, 36; II, 490).

In order that he would attain well,
Until he became initiated.

He consummated the stage by the great wisdom.
Having attained the raiment initiation,
He experienced joy in the dense array of Akanishta,
Entering the great intelligence.

Thus, he completed the learner's stages, and while sitting near the enlightenment tree, he was exhorted by the buddhas, and meditated the five illuminations and became a buddha.

Again, the same text continues:

Through three incalculable eons,
Giving and the good fruit of giving,
He attained treasures like space,
And was initiated by the wish-granting jewel.

In the third incalculable eon,
Performing ordeals of other [paths],
He achieved the fruition through enterprise,
And was initiated through the vajra.

And:

Being initiated by the four secrets,
He attained enlightenment as a perfect buddha.
Then, being anointed with the name initiation,
That sage became Vairochana.

Thus, being initiated as Vajrasattva, Vajradharma, Vajraratna, and Vajrakarma, he attained, respectively, the reality body, the beatitude body, the signs and marks, and the emanation body, thus becoming a buddha. Further it explains that he was previously such a bodhisattva and attained those paths in three incalculable eons. Thus, this text explains both the single lifetime [260a] buddhahood of the jewel-like practitioner who enters the path from the beginning by the unexcelled arts, and the buddhahood attained by adding the mantra path at the end of the transcendence path.

So the yoga tantra method distinguishes its own path and others' path, and the previously explained connection with the transcendence path does not appear, and further, neither does the other procedure of buddhahood at the end of one's own path. So you should wonder whether the interpretation of one's own path is the above-explained consummation of the stage attaining buddhahood after exhortation by the buddhas—this should be well examined.

According to the unexcelled tantras, those two additions [creation and perfection stages] to the above-explained path, if not generated in one's continuum, cannot produce buddhahood, and since those two are absent from the path of the three lower tantras, they must be added as well to those who have engaged in the paths of the three other tantras. As for the intended basis of the two [unexcelled] tantras' statements about buddhahood relying on the five illuminations such as moon and vajra when the stages are consummated, it seems it must be taken as [equivalent to] the *Five Stages*' statement that in place of the creation-stage person's creating the mantra body through the moon and vajra and so on, the perfection-stage person creates the totally pure deity body from the four voids. Thus interpreting it, that import which is thought of as the intended basis of the statement, though it is distinctive to the unexcelled yoga, that does not prevent it from serving in the lower tantra's path as the literal import thought of while taught in other words. In many contexts here, this [principle] seems to be very necessary [260b] in commenting on scriptural statements.

As for this analysis of the way the main things of the perfection stage of this tradition serve at the end of other paths, it discovers the exceptional certitude about the chief distinctive excellences of our path. Relying on it you can become certain about the power of the reason of this path, so it seems the marvelous cause of the art of not regressing into other paths. And since it seems to be extremely hard to understand, I have explained it.

[**VI.B.3.b.ii.C′3′d′ii′A″2″b″** – The import explained in the endurance branch statement of the *Further Tantra*]

This *Five Stages*' explanation of the stage of clear enlightenment of the fourth stage clear light transparence is mentioned as the endurance branch of the six branches given in the *Further Tantra*:

It is said to be the holding of the object
Of the ceasing of the independent jewel;
The mind becomes the cessation vajra,
And the close holding of the sign happens.
The realm of the sign is fivefold,
As stated by Bodhivajra.
The first is like a mirage,
The second is like smoke,
The third is like fireflies,
The fourth is like a burning butter lamp.
Like a cloudless sky,
Constant luminance is the fifth,
Stabilizing, from the vajra path,
Shine forth into the realm of space.

In the Great Translator's translation of the *Illuminating Lamp*, just after completing the explanation of the first two lines, there is the passage "this is 'endurance,' the fourth branch." Patsab's translation is similar. Gö's translation, right after the complete explanation of the passage from "independent" to "radiate out," is the statement "those are the endurance branch, the fourth." Thus, all these treatises take this as the authority for the endurance [261a] branch, and the Chag translation also does. Thus, though there seem to be two [versions] in the Indian text, the Gö translation is understood to be preferable from the explanation in the commentary.

As for oneself, both the visible objects and so on and the eye organ and so on cease and dissolve, and after that the jewel, i.e., the object, as [coarse] mind along with vitalizing energy ceases and declines, is held, and that [jewel] is the reality-limit, clear light. As for mind dissolving along with vitalizing energy, it is the sequential dissolving of the three minds [luminance and so on]. Sense organ and object dissolving happens according to the death process. As the *Elixir Secret* states, "independence" refers to isolation from ordinariness, and the "jewel" is the jewel wisdom-intuition of buddhahood, which knows the mind's isolation from subject and object and the fault of not realizing that isolation from the mind's roaming in the life cycle by clinging to subjects and objects. "It is explained as holding the object of ceasing . . ." refers to not experiencing the meaning of "teach the mind isolation," [or experiencing many imports of] the mind being isolated through the yoga of the three luminances arising from the vajra and lotus entering union and the enlightenment spirit arriving in the root, stalk, and tip [of the vajra organ]. "The cessation vajra" is clear light, and the "mind becoming that" means going there. Entering there, one perceives the signs such as mirage and so on, thus the signs are experienced and are produced. The signs appearing are said to be fivefold, three perceptions from mirage up to fireflies, arising from the four, earth, water, fire, and wind [261b] dissolving one into another. "Sky-light" (*khadyota*) means fireflies as Patsab correctly translated, and is not correctly understood as seeing ripples in the sky. From among the movement into the three total illuminations of the subtle realm, the arisal of butter-lamp flame is the subtle realm mentioned in the *Illuminating Lamp*, which is the energy that intensely moves the natural instincts, and when that dissolves, a vision arises like a butter lamp flame not being agitated by the energy.

As for the *Integrated Practices* statement:

> The aggregates and so on enter into the subtle realm. The subtle element enters into the mind.

The first refers to the earth and following dissolutions up to the wind, and the second's explaining the subtle realm entering the mind does not contradict the *Illuminating Lamp*'s explaining the subtle element entering into the three luminances. The former is a coarse arrangement and the latter is a subtle analysis arrangement. For example, it is like the *Terminal Action Investigation* and the *Vajra Rosary* statements about consciousness, not analyzed into three, entering into clear light, and the *Integrated Practices* analyzing them into three and mentioning imminence as subsiding into brilliant clear light. Most of the old translations have the final natural total illumination come into the cloudless sky, with the statement "becoming constant illumination, mere clear light is fifth." Compared to some texts' and some translations' "dissolving into total illumination," the former is correct, since for clear light to arise the three luminances must dissolve. The *Illuminating Lamp* speaking as it does is an abbreviation; if you analyze things, [262a] you must accord with the *Self-Consecration* and *Integrated Practices* statements that mind dissolves into mental function, mental function into mental imminence, and imminence into clear light. As for the process of arising of the time of the three luminances, you should interpret according to the previously quoted *Integrated Practices* statements such as:

> Second, luminance is like moonlight.

When the *Integrated Practices* mentions:

> First one sees such as mirage endowed with the mass of five-colored light rays

it is abbreviating, not mentioning smoke and so on, the three [other signs]. For a more detailed presentation, you must have the four signs as mentioned in the *Further Tantra* and the *Illuminating Lamp*.

By those five signs you will attain nirvana, objective clear light. To provide evidence for earth dissolving into water and so on, the *Illuminating Lamp* follows [Nāgabodhi's] the *Terminal Action Investigation*:

> As previously occurred,
> One dissolves by this process,
> First earth enters water,
> Water dissolves into fire,
>
> Fire dissolves into wind,
> Wind dissolves into consciousness.
> Consciousness proceeding into holding,
> And from there enters into clear light.
>
> Then becoming a gandharva fairy,
> One is reborn, driven by evolution.
> Thus being born thousands of times,
> One is born again and again.
>
> Totally erring as the natures cycle,
> This is not the sphere of the dogmatists.
> Total knowledge of luminance,
> Is not to be known by [ordinary] beings.

This quote [262b] is from the text of Nāgabodhi, and is not, as Bhavyakīrti thought, from the *Terminal Action Investigation Sutra*. Here, consciousness entering into clear light is total luminance dissolving into clear light, and is not the dissolution of the instinctual natures. This shows the basic death process, which is similar with the path entrance into clear light in the arisal of the signs of mirage-likeness and so on, so it is not good to say they are not similar: because, in attaining buddhahood in the between, the forms of mirage and so on [also] arise; in the measure of stabilizing or not the sign-experiencing awareness engaged in this life's process of entering into clear light, there is the distinction of its being similar to the five signs such as mirage; [in regard to] the measure of stabilizing or not as stated in the *Integrated Practices* the distinction is accepted of arising in the form of mirage and so on as stated in the *Illuminating Lamp*; and in the *Personal Instruction [of Mañjushrī] Commentary* [Vitapāda mentions how] the four signs each become more clear than the other.

These signs arise at the times of the evaporating earth element and so on, of the sense energies being ready to reverse within—of the reversing, and of the ceasing. That process also has a base-reality-time and a path-time, and the latter occurs on many lower and higher occasions such as body isolation and so on; so all mentioned should be specifically distinguished. Further, when the energy that moves the instinctual constructs dissolves, the vision like a butter lamp arises. At the time of the luminance intuition there is a vision like moonlight. Those two are sequential, and at the time of the emerging order, from luminance intuition up to clear light, and at the time of the reversing order, from clear light up to luminance, mirage, and so on, [263a] the four arise, at the former time before luminance and at the later time after luminance. In this context, when the mind is held, contracting again and again through the two contemplations, though [the signs] occur, it is not good [either] to connect each sign to the specific contraction of the three holistic contemplations [or] to connect each sign to the specific contractions of the three spiritual heroes of each holistic contemplation.

On the occasion of the illustrative, metaphoric clear light, within its experience, the objective aspect of clear sky arises, while on the occasion of the objective clear light, even the subtle dualistic perception declines and the simile of sky applies to its lack of fabricative taint, but it does not arise in such a form [of clear sky]. When the genuine intuition of the three voids of the path is produced, whatever is experienced appearing as an object is perceived as like moonlight, undivided in any direction, but it is not the perception of a specific round orb, as moonlight-likeness and so on is the perception of moonlight-likeness that arises at the time of the three voids' intuition. As soon as the luminance that is moonlight-like contracts, it is not certain that sunlight-like radiance is produced, since it can happen that there is a [moment of] staying between the two. Since in that case also it happens that a clear sky-likeness arises, in regard to the process wherein that and the fourth void arises, there is a great difference. Entering clear light by the sequence of five signs not to be surpassed by the vajra path, there is stability, and [there is] purity, as sky radiates out into the world realms. It should be explained according to the Chag translation, "By the process of the truth body [263b] it should be pervaded." As for the meaning of radiating out into the world realms, it is that the intelligence pervades the nature of all inanimate and animate things.[146] As for the statement not to surpass the sequence of the five signs, though it is possible that at the first time there might be a slight indefiniteness about one or two of them, when one knows well how to meditate on the voids of the corresponding or noncorresponding orders, they will definitely arise in the proper order.

Here mainly this should be contextualized within the objective clear light, but before one reaches there one must familiarize oneself again and again with the illustrative, metaphoric clear light, so one should understand these explanations also at the occasion of the lower path.

146. The attainer of this clear light transparence no longer sits like an alienated individual within her or his skin apart from sky or void or other relative beings and things, but perhaps amazedly within orgasmic bliss intelligence merges nondually with all relatives and absolutes.

10. The Perfection Stage of Communion

[263b.3–277b.2]

[**VI.B.3.b.ii.c′3′d′ii′b″** – The perfection stage of the two realities inseparably]

The second has two parts: [1″] Explanation of the meaning of the *Five Stages* and *Integrated Practices* passages; [2″] Explanation of the two branches coming from the *Further Tantra*.

[**VI.B.3.b.ii.c′3′d′ii′b″1″** – Explanation of the meaning of the *Five Stages* and *Integrated Practices* passages]

The first has two parts: [a″] Question; and [b″] Answer.

[**VI.B.3.b.ii.c′3′d′ii′b″1″a″** – Question]

From the *Integrated Practices*:

> Divine Lord! How do you enter the ultimate reality, become insubstantial, and then resurrect yourself? What is the experience once you have confronted this? What is it to become immune to regression? What is the import of freedom? Why are you liberated? Who is liberated?

These are six questions asked in order to determine the stage of communion.

In regard to the first of these, it is "What is the process through which the third stage magic body enters ultimate reality, becomes purified, and once again arises from the clear light?"

The second [264a] question is "In this unexcelled vehicle one gains experience through confrontation [with reality] by means of the stages such as the first bodhisattva stage; what is the stage of producing experience of the path of progress, through confronting the fruition?" Here Chag's translation has "What is the coming to the experience of the noble bliss here?" But the previous version is preferable.

The third question is "What is the boundary between regressing and not regressing into the life cycle?"

The fourth is "What is the freedom, where you are free from what?"

The fifth asks the reason, "What is the reason you become free or liberated?"

The sixth asks the actuality of the person, "Who is the liberated one?"

There the Chag translation leaves out the two latter, and asks "From what is there liberation?" But the old translations are better.

[**VI.B.3.b.ii.c′3′d′ii′B′′1′′b′′** – Answer]

> The vajra master spoke. "Great being! Excellent! Excellent! The stage of arising from clear light is not the sphere of those who look away from the transcendent buddha's private instruction. It should be realized following the glorious *Esoteric Community*. Listen with mind one-pointed!"

Thus, [in the *Integrated Practices*,] having instructed the disciple to listen, he explained the meaning inquired into. There are four parts to his answer: [i′′] The answer to the second question; [ii′′] The answer to the third and fifth questions; [iii′′] The answer to the first question; and [iv′′] The answer to the fourth and sixth questions, along with some remaining thoughts.

[**VI.B.3.b.ii.c′3′d′ii′B′′1′′b′′i′′** – The answer to the second question]

First: the *Integrated Practices* explains:

> In this vajra vehicle, by learning the creation stage, [264b] you will attain the eighth [bodhisattva] level. Until the perfection stage is attained, you should propitiate the spiritual friend. By clearly realizing body, speech, and mind, you attain the tenth level and

> specifically attain the magical samadhi. By truly realizing the magical samadhi, you specifically attain the clear light that purifies the three luminances. Arising from the nonluminous clear light transparence,[147] by the process of abiding in the communion, you evidently manifest the buddha-deeds, and will abide being adorned by all the excellences of the vajra-like samadhi.

Here the Chag translation says:

> . . . You attain the tenth level, having realized the isolation of body, speech, and mind, and then you specifically attain the magical samadhi . . .
>
> . . . having actualized the buddha body. . . .

This makes the previous translation clearer.

Except for merely mentioning "ten stages," there is no mention in the father and son treatises of any name of the level or any meaning of the name. In the *Vajra Rosary statement*:

> The vase initiation is the eleventh [level], and the higher three initiations [go up] to the fourteenth, each initiation [representing] a level;

except for [giving] a mere enumeration of fourteen levels, it does not state the name or meaning of any level whatsoever; and the *Revelation of the Hidden Intention*, except for stating:

> Where the buddhas rely
> Is the thirteenth level

gives neither the names nor the meanings of the thirteen [levels]; nor are

147. This is why I occasionally substitute or add "transparence" for or to "clear light." Clear light can be understood as more light than clear, and its nonduality beyond light and dark can too easily be missed. Transparency is the key to the inconceivability of the vajra realm, not luminosity.

they stated in any other root or explanatory tantra. By the key point of that fact, [265a] disagreements arise. The *Integrated Practices Commentary* says:

> When one reaches the heat at the end [of the application path],
> [Before the moments of] tolerance and world triumph,
> With great and medium [degrees], the application [path has] twelve levels,
> And the extremely joyous [level] is the thirteenth.

And also:

> From the extremely joyous [level]
> To the Dharma-cloud [level],
> Those who have attained them, afterward
> Develop them through the communion [stage].

Thus, by dividing each of the branches of the application path, heat, peak, tolerance, and triumph, into three, small, middle, and great, there are twelve levels [therein], with the extremely joyous level being [counted as] the thirteenth, [at the beginning of the vision path]. And the vajra recitation leads to the attainment of the eighth level, the medium tolerance, the mind isolation to the small or medium triumph, the magic body to the great triumph, the clear light to the first of the noble ten stages, the extremely joyous, the thirteenth in relation to the twelve levels of the application path. Finally, he says that the communion [stage] purifies the already attained levels. Thus, it is evident that the creation stage carries one through the seventh level.

Lakshmī takes the ten [bodhisattva] levels, such as the extremely joyous and so on, saying that:

> The creation stage along with the body isolation as the eighth level, and by implication the vajra recitation as the ninth level, the experience of the three luminances, since they master intuitive wisdom, as attainment of the tenth level, and the magic body, since it is the aftermath attainment of that is also only the tenth level, since it is not the stage of a [separate] level. The clear light [stage] is attained as the eleventh, all-luminous, level, and the communion, being its aftermath attainment, is also only the elev-

> enth level. As for the beginner's level, it is attained by meditating the [four divine] abodes of Brahmā and so on. As for attaining buddhahood in that very life, that is the thirteenth level.

The *Moonlight Commentary* explains the ten stages of the extremely joyous and so on [265b] but does not clearly give a way of connecting the levels. A certain ancient expert in the *Community* takes the ten stages such as the extremely joyous and so on, and considers that the consummation of the creation stage leads to the attainment of the immovable and the Dharma-cloud [levels]. His intention is to hold that these are not attained by way of completing all the qualities of those levels, but only that these [unexcelled yoga stages] are substitutes [for the levels].

A certain Tibetan expert claims that those paths attain the actualities of those levels: [applying] to the ten stages such as the extremely joyous the meaning of the *Unexcelled Clear Articulation* quote:

> The unexampled, the endowed with wisdom,
> And the vajra level is the thirteenth;

—and [following] Abhaya's transcendence-vehicle explanation of the ten stages, that the tenth level is threefold, including the tenth level [alone], its distinctive path, and its unobstructed path, [he equates] the distinctive path with the "unexampled," the unobstructed path with the "endowed with wisdom," and the all-luminous with the "vajra level." That kind of thirteenth level is accepted [by this expert] as the *Revelation of the Hidden Intention* explanation of the thirteenth [level] of universal void clear light, and also [he claims that] the intention of the *Integrated Practices* is that the magic body is the eleventh level and the clear light is the twelfth level, the very same thing [taken to be] the thirteenth, when counted from the positive orientation practice level. He also explains that the thirteenth stage intended by the *Vajra Rosary Tantra* is the stage of clear light. According to this, the communion [stage] must be taken as the fourteenth level.

Concerning this, in the transcendence universal vehicle it is frequently stated that the learning levels for the nobles are the ten stages such as the extremely joyous, and the nonlearning [level] is the eleventh, the all-luminous; and there is also a mention of the alienated individual's positive orientation and beginner's levels. From the mantra [systems], there are enumerations of twelve, thirteen, [266a] and fourteen. As for their names, the *Vajra Essence Ornament Tantra* mentions twelve, including the all-luminous, and the elixir-luminous. The *Hevajra* and the *Sampuṭa [Tantra]* and so on mention a different twelve and also a corresponding twelve such as the extremely joyous. The *Sheaf of Instructions* and other such works explain that the positive orientation and all-luminous levels are included by implication, but I wonder if this latter [arrangement] is maybe the same as the previously mentioned twelve stages.

There are three different naming systems for the thirteen, as mentioned by Abhaya, and since they are nobles' levels, if you add the positive orientation level to them, you have the fourteen vajra levels. Thus, the number of levels is more than in the transcendence vehicle, but this does not mean there is a level [of buddhahood] above the [transcendence vehicle's] eleventh all-luminous level. The *Root Tantra* states:

> One becomes a bodhisattva,
> Abiding on the ten stages

in the context of the communion stage. The *Illuminating Lamp* gives the meaning of this as "the ten stages are the ten light rays, where one totally abides." And these ten stages should be taken as the extremely joyous and so on, the [usual] ten. The creation stage is stated to lead to the attainment of the eighth level and the vajra recitation also. Of these the first can be understood as referring to the bare attainment of the eighth level, and the second should be understood as connecting to the ninth level, as exemplified by the transcendence eighth level, intending that the perfection-stage body isolation is categorized within the vajra recitation. The *Five Stages* explains that by experiencing the three luminances one abides on the tenth level [266b] and the *Integrated Practices* has a second statement that by realizing body, speech, and mind one attains the tenth level. These two can be taken as the same in meaning, as the sixth chapter of the *Illuminating Lamp* explains that body, speech, and mind are luminance, radiance, and imminence. All of this connects mind isolation with the tenth [bodhisattva] level.

Kānhapa, in comment on connecting the experience of the three luminances with the tenth level, explains it as attaining the self-consecration, which can be taken as attaining the magic body relying on mind isolation;

and connecting that with the tenth level is the import of the *Integrated Practices.*

That adds some upper part to the transcendence tenth level. As for placing the clear light [stage] and learner's communion [stage] below the tenth stage, it is understood by the previous explanation of the system of adding the unexcelled path upon the ten stages of the transcendences, whereby placing the nonlearner's communion stage in the eleventh all-luminous is also understood.

As for the two tantras explaining clear light as the thirteenth level, it depends on counting the positive orientation level, and also is exemplified by the learner's communion.

If, you might wonder, such is the way of connecting the levels, when you complete the path of each occasion such as the creation stage and so on, are you attaining completely the excellent qualities of those levels such as the extremely joyous? Or are they connected from the perspective of some corresponding qualities of similarity, like connecting each of the fourteen levels with initiations conferred, connecting the five paths to a single session of a creative contemplational performance, or connecting the three bodies to the visualization of contracting into clear light?

Though you attain the third stage magic body, if you do not realize clear light, since it is stated that you eliminate cycling under the power of addictions, just by the fact that the path has been consummated [267a] in its own context, it is not only that you do not attain the tenth level, you do not even attain the noble level. Hence, those ways of connecting do not imply that you attain by the way of perfecting the qualities of the levels such as the extremely joyous. There seem to be many other fatal flaws in the position that consummating the creation stage leads to the actual attainment of the immovable level. Therefore, the proceeding to the tenth level by means of the transcendence vehicle is explained as being substituted for by proceeding from the creation stage of this path to the magic body stage. Accordingly, these paths of this vehicle can substitute for proceeding up to that stage by other vehicles for buddhahood. Thus it is said when these [mantric] paths are attained, one has attained up to the tenth level, and it is not necessary for it to be attained in a complete mutual matching up of the qualities of the paths.

Further, the creation stage is the means of evolving toward the complete generation of the realization of the perfection stage, and the developing of the last of that is like just barely attaining the eighth level. The previous developments are connected to the seventh level, but not connected in the way where it can be said [with precision that] this distinctive quality of the creation stage is this quality of the seventh level.

Furthermore, when you finalize the creation stage, in ordinary [reality] you can enter at will into an extremely stable nonconceptual samadhi and attain total purity of perception of animate and inanimate worlds as measureless mansion and deities; and this is just like the eighth bodhisattva level. With that as preliminary, relying on body isolation and then moving to practice speech isolation, as the *Integrated Practices* says, you can accurately attain the tolerance of the birthlessness of things. Then having purified the energy, the root of speech, you attain mastery of that, just as in the ninth level you master the intuition of the purity of speech in teaching the Dharma. [267b] Relying on completing speech isolation, you achieve the magic body from the energy-mind achieved in the mind isolation, and you will attain the conferral of initiation from the buddhas, just as on the tenth level you attain mastery of evolution, and you apply the bad evolutionary instincts that cause an inferior body to become the cause of the perfected body, and also you attain the conferral of the initiation by magnificent light rays, since you transform the energy-mind that causes the ordinary body into being the cause of the beatific body.

Just as on the tenth level, you complete the stores of the path that cause you to have the powerful ability to overcome the obscurations to the realization of voidness and you have nothing new to learn on your own path, so depending on attaining the magic body you enter into clear light. Also, since subsequently attaining communion is similar to that [tenth level], those stages are connected to the tenth level.

Paths are dividing into [those of the] alienated individual and [those of the] noble based on whether one has or has not attained the noble levels by realizing or not realizing reality directly. If you make the alienated individual paths into the two, of accumulation and of application, and so begin from the common paths, as long as one cannot develop direct experience of the void by forcing the energies into the *dhūti* by the power of meditation and dissolving them there, one is on the accumulation path. When one can do that, it becomes the application path up until [having become] a magic body one still cannot realize directly thatness through bliss. Then, until one attains communion by means of the objective clear light, it is taken as the vision path and the joyous level. And finally, until one attains the nonlearner's union by means of the learner's union, it is taken as the meditation path and the ninth level.

[**VI.B.3.b.ii.c'3'd'ii'B''1''b''ii''** – The answer to the third and fifth questions]

Those who have attained a magic body can still regress as long as they have not clearly realized ultimate reality. The reason for that is explained in the *Integrated Practices* in saying that:

> As long as the three luminances have [not] purified it, [268a] consciousness is [still] imaginatively constructed, and as long as that obtains, there is the continuum of the instincts of addictions, and thereby rebirth continues to take place.

To not clearly realize [ultimate reality] means to not directly realize [it]. Not realizing in such a way, one cannot completely abandon the seeds of the addictions, thus cannot abandon birth under the power of addictions; which means that rebirth continues to take place by the continuum of the instincts of the addictions. These instincts are the seeds of the addictions, and not the instincts that are posited as objective obscurations. When the magic body is attained, it is certain that buddhahood will be attained in that very lifetime. Therefore, though it is not that there will again be birth under the power of evolution in the life cycle, "if thatness is not directly realized" is setting a hypothetical limiting case; as for example, saying that if Shuddhodhana's son Siddhārtha had not renounced the home life he would have become a universal monarch.

Thereby it shows that until one attains the fourth stage one does not directly realize the import of thatness. In that context, when the three luminances are purified, even subtle dualistic perception is purified, and intuitive wisdom enters into experiential unity with the reality of thatness just like water flowing into water. As the *Integrated Practices* states just after the previous quote:

> When one is free from any other thoughts, that is the state of purity . . .

—citing as evidence the *Glorious Supreme Prime* statement that the place of purifying the three poisons is the place of the spirit of enlightenment, and quoting the statement of master Kambala that, as a method of achieving the inner reality;

> Freedom from the coarse nature of sound, from the subtle nature of thought or intention, [268b] and from [all] thoughts and intentions, that is the place of the supreme of yogi/nīs.

Here the Chag translation reads "that freedom from all thoughts," indicating the clear light that purifies the three luminances, which is the place that purifies somewhat the seeds of the addictions. Attaining that, there will be no further rebirth under the control of evolution and addictions and so no regression back into the life cycle.

In the individual vehicle, though there is direct realization of voidness, if one has not become an arhat, rebirth controlled by evolution and addiction is not eliminated. In the universal vehicle, once one directly realizes voidness, rebirth and death controlled by evolution and addiction is eliminated; in this regard, both [esoteric and exoteric] universal vehicles are the same.

In the *[Five Stages'] Second Stage*, just after mentioning the connection between the creation stage and the eighth level and that one attains the tenth level by means of the three luminances, [Nāgārjuna] states that:

> Having attained perfect enlightenment,
> One fully realizes the pure abode,
> Irreversible here in this life,
> One becomes omniscient in the buddhaverse.

He indicates that through the clear light [stage] one becomes nonregressing, implying [one could] regress before that. Since the "pure abode" is as just explained, the Chag translation here is preferable; and I have already quoted the older translation.

[You may well] wonder, "What is the reason that in this vehicle once one has directly realized the thatness reality, one is liberated from rebirth controlled by evolution and addiction?"

[The *Integrated Practices*] gives the reason just after the previous quote from Kambala:

> Wherefore, by this reason, by this stage of clear enlightenment, one truly attains clear light, the taintless [269a] nature of one's body, speech, and mind becomes universal voidness—the reality of transcendent wisdom that purifies the three consciousnesses, and that thought-free and inexpressible condition is the realm of nirvana, formless, hard to know, delivered from evolution and birth, extremely clear like the light of sun, moon, fire, and jewels.

"Wherefore by this reason" refers to the process of the art of plunging the three luminances into clear light. That is the one who has attained the magic body employing the art of entering clear light by relying on the two contemplations and the physical consort. That one uses the magic body as the substitute for limitless stores of merit and realizes thatness directly with the distinctive subjectivity of great bliss. And that one is shown thereby to be capable of stopping birth in ordinary existence under the control of evolution and addiction. This means that, although the thatness that is realized also by the individual vehicle practitioner and second [by the exoteric universal vehicle practitioner] is not objectively different, the subjectivity [engaged here in the unexcelled vehicle] is very much more powerful.

Such being the case, the insight-path practitioners of the transcendence vehicle and of the individual vehicle do not differ in regard to their realization of thatness. Yet the universalist practitioner, once s/he has that [realization], is able to block regression into the life cycle under the influence of evolution and also obtains twelve hundred excellent qualities, while the individualist does not come to have these things. This is because the former produces and the latter does not produce a greater intensity of that realization by the power of developing or not [269b] the infinite stores of merit on the accumulation path and positive orientation practice level. There also is a great difference [between the two] in the swiftness of the direct realization of voidness; and the qualities derived from it are as [different in quantity as] space and the palm of the hand. By this reason you should understand why the universalist does not rush like an [individualist] disciple to achieve a direct realization of the thatness reality.

Herein, the direct realization of thatness is very much swifter. And not only swift, but also the store of excellent qualities is obtained in a fashion much superior to other universal vehicle paths. Therefore, this path is miraculous! Just as this path and the other two paths differ in abandoning objective obscurations, the latter requiring an incalculable eon and the former a single human lifetime of the degenerate age, there is also an extreme difference of speed in abandoning the addictive obscurations. Further, by the key point of there being such supreme, exceptionally distinguished properties of effectiveness in abandoning obscurations different from other paths, it is not necessary that this path correspond to others' systems of abandoning the conscious [obscurations] on the insight path and the unconscious [obscurations] only on the meditation path. Likewise, granted that according to the transcendence [vehicle], there is a difference [between individual and universal vehicles] in that the individualist is quicker to abandon addictions and the universalist not so quick; herein, from the juncture where one can predominantly meditate by uniting orgasmic bliss and voidness and one practices meditating that, combining it with [the realization of] thatness, it proceeds by the way already explained that is different from other paths. Therefore, this path is different from other universalist [paths] in that it terminates addictions extremely much more quickly.

Therefore, it is stated that the fourth [270a] stage clear light wisdom-intuition abandons the seeds of addictions, and since there are no contaminations left in the subsequent attaining of communion, those seeds of addictions are the "instincts" referred to in the stated excellent quality of "liberation from all instincts of addictions." Thus, they should not be taken as merely conscious addictions, but are [also] the instinctual addictions. The objective self-habits explained as objective obscurations by other systems, and not only those but the more subtle instinctual objective self-habits considered to be addictive [obscurations] by the noble father and sons—as for those, I have already extensively settled them in other works such as the *Discrimination between Interpretable and Definitive.*[148]

[**VI.B.3.b.ii.C′3′d′ii′B″1″b″iii″** – The answer to the first question]

At the time of entering the objective clear light of the fourth stage, the previous magic body is purified and no longer exists—then how does one accomplish the way of resurrecting in the communion body?

148. See my translation of this work in *The Central Philosophy of Tibet*, Princeton University Press, 1980.

The *Integrated Practices* states, after its statement about how imminence comes from objective clear light, from [imminence] comes hot-sunlight-like radiance, and from [radiance] comes cool-moonlight-like luminance:

> Therefore, by such sky-like illumination, from the store of luminances that remain the same reality as voidness, all the world realms are illumined. The actuality of the indestructible vajra body, inseverably and indestructibly together like a shadow with its subtle elements, without transmigration and uncontaminated, liberated from all instincts of addictions, accomplished in mastery of whatever one wishes, like a fish leaping from water, or like suddenly sleeping and awakening, a form of a reality body of supreme joy [270b] arises; such a form being named "great Vajradhara," and "freedom," since one is definitively delivered from all bonds of the life cycle.

And the *Esoteric Community* ninth chapter says, giving the example of how fire is kindled by rubbing fire-sticks together, but cannot be found by searching in each of your hands:

> . . . likewise, you should accurately understand the going and coming and so forth of the vajra-commitment of all transcendent buddhas!

In comment on that, the *Illuminating Lamp* explains that this statement shows that this vehicle is distinctive from all others in its art of producing the vajra body from clear light; that "all transcendent buddhas" refers to universal voidness, "vajra" refers to great voidness, "commitment" refers to extreme voidness, and "accurately understanding" after the three is voidness. "Going" is the going into ultimate reality by the process of those three voids. "Coming" is the coming through the three voids in the reverse order. "And so on" is explained as indicating that there is no going and coming of entering [reality] and resurrecting in the context of the perfection [stage]. This teaches that there is no going and coming in the arisal of the three voids in reverse order in the context of [first] achieving communion and in the forward and reverse order of the four voids in the context of the nonlearner['s communion]. The *[Five Stages'] Second Stage* also has a quote, already cited, that explains the arisal of the three intuitions from clear light in the context of achieving the communion [body].

Here, you might argue as follows: Is the communion body achieved immediately upon arising from the objective clear light of the fourth stage? Or is it not? If it is, then it contradicts the previous quote [271a] that states that the three voids arise in the reverse order from the clear light of the occasion of achieving communion; for if the communion body were not achieved from the energy-mind of the three voids arising in the reverse order, then there would be no point in such an explanation. And the explanation of the magic body as achieved from the three luminances along with their energies during the third stage would be incorrect; since the three luminances are required as the cause of achieving that, and a distinction of not requiring them would be incorrect. [On the other hand], if [the communion body] is not achieved in that way, and, not being achieved immediately upon arising from the fourth stage objective clear light, but only after the three voids in the reverse order have already arisen, it necessarily means that it is achieved from the mere energy-mind of the first void; and so what is the point of mentioning that "it is achieved from the three voids"? The *Integrated Practices* statement that the "four voids become one" would become meaningless; since the objective clear light does not exist during the first luminance or its immediate aftermath, the attainment of union would become incorrect, and the process of purifying the achieved between state without any other obstruction after the clear light of death would be contradicted. If you claim that communion is achieved at the time of once again entering clear light after the last luminance, it contradicts the *Five Stages*' statement:

> Arising from the truth limit
> One will attain the nondual intuition;

and also the many statements of the *Integrated Practices* and the *Illuminating Lamp* that communion is achieved upon arising from clear light. And if it is achieved upon arising from that, then the previous many faults obtain. Thus, you must explain what is this transition where the communion body [271b] is achieved from clear light.

[To respond:] In order to understand well the communion [stage], the chief subject of the *Glorious Community*, you must first understand conclusively the process of achieving the learner's communion. To that end, by having set forth the above doubts, you can eliminate doubts that could possibly arise concerning other final points—this being necessary, [this inquiry] is very good.

In regard to this, the followers of the father and son, commentators on the *Five Stages* and so on, do not seem to make such a determination. However, master Gö, relying on the above-taught explanation of the voids in the reverse order, explains that the communion body is achieved from the three luminances along with their energies arising from the clear light in the reverse order, and Lakshmī also explains a procedure wherein the magic body is achieved from the voids arising in the reverse order. Accordingly, I have set it forth in that way in another treatise.[149]

However, we should determine this difficult point in fine detail. The *Five Stages* states:

> The aim of beings may sometimes be [realized]
> By the process of the self-consecration,
> Which yokes consciousness with energy,
> And releases corresponding light rays.
>
> Just as from clear stream water,
> The fish leap up so swiftly,
> So from the universal void clear light
> The net of magic expresses itself.

Thus, this body also emerges from the mere energy-mind through the process of self-consecration. As for the meaning of the example wherein the pure magic body emerges like a fish suddenly leaping from clear light transparence like clear stream water, it is employed to illustrate that it arises from clear light [272a] without being obstructed by anything else. As the *Integrated Practices* states that, as for the sleep used in the example taught of awakening suddenly from deep sleep, it illustrates clear light, and the awakening is the example for the emergence of the communion body. This also highlights non-obstruction. And as for the four voids becoming one, this fits with the fact that at the emergent order time, the former dissolves into the latter and finally all go into the clear light as one, and does not fit

149. The *Great Stages of the Mantric Path*, its final chapter on the perfection stage.

with the reverse order. This is extremely in agreement with the process of the purified base reality, wherein immediately after the death clear light transparence the between is achieved together with the [reverse order] imminence. Hence the communion body is achieved immediately after resurrecting from the fourth stage objective clear light. This still does not contradict the above birth of imminence and so on from clear light. So though it is stated that in the time of achieving the communion body the three voids emerge in the reverse order, that is not stated for the purpose of achieving that body.

Here one might object that "Is not communion the simultaneous combination of the objective clear light mind and the pure magic body? Though it is posited that the pure magic body is achieved immediately after arising from the fourth stage clear light, how can it be posited as the [perfect] communion, since at that time there is no direct realization of the clear light intuition?"

True enough! In this regard one must understand the many *Five Stages* explanations of the process of attaining communion, which explain twenty-one communions, running from:

> Abandoning the two notions
> Of life cycle and liberation,
> When all becomes one reality—
> That is said to be communion . . .

up to:

> Having abandoned the two notions
> Of material and immaterial,
> The [272b] lord of yogi/nīs who realizes peace—
> Thereby attains communion.

Here taking the verse "the holistic contemplation . . ." to indicate two communions, and the verse "equipoise . . ." to indicate two communions, it is also correct to interpret these passages as teaching twenty-three communions. As for the main communion thus explained, as the Chag translation reads:

> The knower of thatness sequentially
> Understands self-consecration and clear light;

> And when just those become united,
> This is the stage of communion.

the pair here is self-consecration and clear light, and their coming together is explained to be communion. Further, his translation reads:

> Having critically understood apart,
> The superficial and the ultimate,
> When you truly commingle the two,
> That is pronounced to be "communion."

—indicating that the pair here consists of the superficial and the ultimate, and their mingling is explained to be the communion.

In that regard, before attaining objective clear light, when the magic body achieved from the five energies' light rays is present, the mind is not the clear light of the same taste as ultimate reality. Before attaining communion, when the clear light of the same taste as the bliss-mind ultimate reality is present, there is no superficial reality body that serves as the magic body. Thus, there is no communion since these two [realities] are merely alternating. When the body is consummated as the superficial reality magic body called "self-consecration," and the mind is consummated as the "clear light" ultimate reality, and these combine at one time in one continuum, coming together equally without alternation, then communion is attained.[150] When the main communion of that kind [273a] is first attained, though it is required that those two be combined, there are still other ways of positing it as communion; so any kind of communion attainment need not be posited as achieved by that way of positing. The Sanskrit

150. This explanation so much reminds me of Tsong Khapa's explanation of the realistic view in the *Three Principles of the Path*, I cannot resist quoting it as an example of how Tsong Khapa's understanding of these profound perfection-stage attainments influences the way he teaches the exoteric dialecticist centrist view: "Appearance inevitably relative, and voidness free from all assertions—as long as these are understood apart, the Victor's intent is not yet known. But when they coincide not alternating, mere sight of inevitable relativity secures knowledge beyond objectivisms—and investigation of the view is perfect. More, as experience dispels absolutism, and voidness clears away nihilism, you know how voidness dawns as cause and effect—then you will not be deprived by extremist views."

for communion is *yuganadva*, where *yuga* is a pair and *adva* is nondual;[151] interpreting that as meaning that the two mates [of the pair] are not separate through a process of alternation but are completely [present] at one time—[such] is the above-explained communion.

This will be attained when once again entering clear light after arising from the final luminance of the reverse order. The *Five Stages* often mentions the communion that becomes nondual undisturbed by any ideas, having abandoned dualistic instinctual notions in regard to dualisms such as life cycle and liberation—this is an example of another way of positing a communion different from the previous way. Taking it that those dualistic ideas subside in the face of the direct realization of the import of thatness, it is already attained from the time of the fourth stage clear light. Thus it is incorrect to say that it is inevitable that this kind of communion must be achieved relying on that being previously present. If you take it that one must have totally abandoned whatever kinds of notions, then that would not be attained until one attained the nonlearner's communion, and that does not fit with the learner's communion. Therefore, communion in this context is just the nondual intuition that abandons all ideas that adhere to truth-status perceived in persons and objects, along with their instinctual propensities.

Here you might object, "Well then, since communion is achieved just after [273b] resurrecting from the first realization of this fourth stage objective clear light, how can such a single session of objective clear light have the power to conquer all the unconscious addictions?"

As for the cause of such an achievement of objective clear light intuition acquiring the mighty power to abandon [addictions], it comes from the force of the frequent contemplation of the magic body and the exemplary clear light, while engaging in the conduct of that occasion. And that is not abandoned at the time of the fourth stage. At the time of the first attainment of the learner's communion, it is posited as abandoning unconscious addictions. When such a clear light is realized, one can remain evenly entranced for a long time—it is not like you get no [water] from the first water-scoop;[152] since, if even before

151. Here Tsong Khapa takes the Sanskrit *naddha* (deriving from *naddha* "binding") for *nadva* or even *adva* (nondual). Meaningwise, it is a good play, and surely Tsong Khapa found etymologies in the Indic tantric literature suggesting "nondual" binding of the pair (*yuga*), magic bliss body and clear light mind.

152. *Khyem pa cig las med pa min*—not too sure about what this means. Perhaps a proverb, sort of like "a thousand-mile journey begins with a single step!"

that one can focus for a long time on the exemplary clear light, what need is there to discuss [one's ability to focus on] the objective clear light?

The *Personal Instruction [of Mañjushrī]* says:

> Not perceiving passion, dispassion, and neutrality,
> The wisdom deity becomes clear in that instant—
> You should experience that wisdom for eight hours,
> A day, a month, a year, an eon, or a thousand eons.

That is, a person should meditate the orgasmic wisdom-intuition for as long as his or her strength endures. Here also, the *Concise Five Stages* explains it very well:

> Having attained the abode of clear light,
> One will cross beyond the life cycle.
> For the time of one session, one day,
> One fortnight, one month, or one year,
> One eon, or a thousand eons,
> One abides there moment by moment—
> And wisdom-intuition yoga keeps on coming.

I have already explained the meaning of the *Integrated Practices* statement about the four voids [274a] becoming one. As for the meaning of the passage from "the store of luminance" up to "having illuminated," the light rays of the body achieved from the clear light energy-mind fill the world-realm, just as the sun illuminates the realm of space. As is stated in the *Illuminating Lamp* fifteenth chapter—in the context of elucidating the achievement of communion as previously explained, after manifesting the objective clear light of the predawn twilight—the tantra's statement that the light rays shine only a hundred leagues around is merely for illustration, and so it is said that light illuminates the world even throughout the billion world universe. As for the statement that there is where one obtains the ten strengths and so on, this should be interpreted appropriately as intending the simulation [of the attainment] during the learner's communion and the actual attainment during the nonlearner's communion. Among the *Integrated Practices*' and the *Five Stages*' mentions of communion, there is need of [both] common and specific explanations of both [learners' and nonlearner's communions]. As for the [communion bodies'] lack of [further] soul-migration, having attained that body, its homogeneous [further emanations] can manifest without interruption; [since] this is the attainment of the fully characterized vajra body [of a buddha]. As for its being uncontaminated and so on, it is the abolition of all addictions.

The *Illuminating Lamp* states that for the nonlearner's [communion] there is no coming back from clear light in the three voids of the reverse order; hence here these things explained in the context of arising in the reverse order should be interpreted as referring to the learner's communion.

[**VI.B.3.b.ii.c′3′d′ii′B″1″b″iv″** – The answer to the fourth and sixth questions, along with some remaining thoughts]

In accord with the Chag translation's comment on the line "as for the name that has the nature of matter," "who has the nature of name and matter, that is great Vajradhara," [274b] the *Moonlight Commentary* states that "name" is the remaining four processes, and "matter" is the material process. Since that again shows that the communion vajradhara has the nature of merely the energy-mind, it is the answer to the previous "Who is liberated?" As for the lines "the life cycle" and so on, it is explained as meaning the liberation that abolishes all addictions that cause bondage, in answer to the question "What is the meaning of liberation?" And both these teach that the perfect abolition of the addictions begins from the first attainment of the learner's communion. When you first attain this communion body, you attain it by way of living in a different locus than the previous body. [So,] as for the *Illuminating Lamp* eleventh chapter statement that, past the attainment of communion, you maintain an emanation body that is visible to the ordinary eye, though there are other ways of maintaining an emanation body, a maintaining of an emanation body that enters into the old body is hard to understand as being [just] like a between being's entering the womb and being seen by everyone after being born outside. Hence, it should be understood as something [built up] upon that [old gross body]. That is what is meant by the *Illuminating Lamp* first chapter's statement, "Having attained communion, entering into the processes and so forth, you maintain [the old body as] the emanation body." Because the *Illuminating Lamp* also states that "the totally pure deity body abides in the jewel sack of the body"; and Nāgabodhi also states:

The true savior, striving
In thatness, stays hidden
In the jewel sack of the body.

Therefore, [275a] though the ordinary person does not perceive the range of an irreversible communion body bodhisattva such as Nāgārjuna, [such] ordinary persons can see their former [gross] body. That being the case, the magic body also is achieved at the end of arising in the reverse order from the metaphoric clear light. As for the statement that "it is attained from the three minds," it is attained indirectly through the upper and middle [sectors] of imminence and the other two luminances, and directly attained from the lower part of imminence.

You should understand according to this previous explanation the way in which the beatific body is at first achieved in a separate locus than the old body and then maintains an emanation body by re-entering into the old body. If you understand it well, you will discover the great certainty about the definitive meaning of meditating the triply nested spiritual heroes and will dispel many doubts about all such things as how the magic-bodied person and the communion-bodied person perform deeds by mounting upon their old bodies and how the vajra recitation accomplishes activities. In regard to the statement about how the communion-bodied person abides in the beatific body and accomplishes such things as the meditation of the mandala triumph of the emanation body, it is not that you meditate having purified the perception of the beatific body, and it is not that thereby having realized clear light you proceed away from those bodies; and this reasoning should be understood [as applicable] also to all not included in the occasion when the magic-bodied person enters into the objective clear light.

Though the *Five Stages* and the *Integrated Practices* say that once you attain communion there is no more new learning on your own path, it is not that you do not meditate on what you have already learned. The *Five Stages* says:

The great yogi/nī, while still learning,
Abiding in the state of communion,
Should meditate it as communion, [275b]
Also nondual with his or her conduct.

—that is, that you should perform the conduct while meditating communion and abiding within it. Nāgabodhi also says:

> Nonconceptual, profound,
> Magnificent, the body of buddhas;
> This is explained as the two realities,
> The superficial and the ultimate in import;
> Having analytically known them separately,
> Having then merged them into one,
> You should meditate the uncontaminated place.

And he also says, just after the above-cited passage:

> Therefore, striving, you should realize,
> By the kindness of the foot of the mentor,
> When mentality comes clear by thatness,
> Then you should engage in the conduct.

As for the nominal synonyms of learner's and nonlearner's communions, the *Five Stages* and the *Integrated Practices* mention them extensively, by such as "perfect buddhahood through the magic net," "transcendence of the ocean of the life cycle," "the great yoga that has done its duty," and "living the way of the two realities."

[**VI.B.3.b.ii.c′3′d′ii′b″2″** – Explanation of the two branches coming from the *Further Tantra*]

As for the same way that the *Five Stages* and the *Integrated Practices* explain the way of achieving communion, the *Community Further Tantra* teaches it in terms of the [last two of the six yoga] branches, mindfulness and samadhi. As it states:

> When you meditate on mindfulness,
> You should delight like that!
> Thus "mindfulness" is explained—
> Individual illumination is born of that!

By uniting together the art and the wisdom,
All things gathered into an epitome
Are concentrated in the pattern of a lump;
Meditate the form in the middle.
In an instant, intuition is made perfect,
And that is called "samadhi."

Thus, the eminent person meditates, having entered into clear light. [276a] Having manifestly perceived it, then by the forms previously mindfully recollected, the mirage-like [vision] and so on, it is like that attainment of clear light as the reality limit. Hence by the stages of thatness you should create delight. Those things just explained should be understood as explaining the fifth branch known as mindfulness. Chag's translation:

Having meditated who remembers mindfully,
Should delight in that way;
That should be understood as mindfulness.

here accords with the sequence of the commentary. Previously at the time of entering into clear light in the emerging order, like entering through the forms such as mirage and so forth, it is explained that one resurrects again with the same kind of process in the reverse order, which begins from creating imminence from clear light, and, after luminance, creating the signs of lamp-flame, fireflies, smoke, and mirage-likeness. "Individual illumination" refers to true endurance, "from which the mindfulness branch is produced, and not elsewhere." This is how the two old translations translate it and also the Chag translation. Though the Patsab translation here translates, concerning "created from that individual illumination," "'from that' means that from the mindfulness branch, true insight, that is true experience, will be created"; the three previous translations are better, since this is the context of showing how the mindfulness [branch itself] is created from clear light.

In case you wonder, "Well, since it is said 'mindfulness is thus explained,' and that completes the mindfulness branch, does this show how communion is produced from mindfulness?"

That [276b] is just the sequence of explanation; but if you follow the order of meaning, the third line follows the fourth.

Further, if you wonder, "Therefore, as for the insistence that the true insight of mindfulness is produced from clear light, and not elsewhere, as there is emergent order and reverse order in the entering into clear light, in the context of which is mindfulness discussed?"

It must be that since it is explained in the order of resurrecting in the reverse order from clear light, [the phrase "it is not elsewhere"] is explained in order to make certain that this does not occur otherwise in the emergent order. So one must explain this instruction of the *Illuminating Lamp* in conformity with the explanation of the *Integrated Practices*.

"Art" is the magic body that is the purity of the superficial reality, and "wisdom" is stated to be the ultimate reality, it being the clear light intuition that is of one taste with that [reality]. "Uniting together" is uniting indivisibly in actuality. All things are stable and moving. Their epitome in the form of a lump is, having made them one in the form of the great seal deity body, in the center of that vessel and essence you should meditate the form of the communion vajradhara.

By this process, in a moment, that is a mere split second, the intuition body is made complete, which is explained as the samadhi branch, the sixth [yoga branch], according to the intention of the *Illuminating Lamp*. The two realities being the pair, and the indivisible uniting of their actualities the communion—this is the main communion, which gives meaning to the other communions. As for the way in which all vessel and essence worlds are condensed into the single communion body, the root of all animate and inanimate things is no more than mere energy and mind, [277a] and that is what arises as the single communion body. "This process" refers to resurrecting from clear light like a fish leaping from the water. The "mere" of "a mere split second" excludes any obstruction by any other thing [in arising] from clear light. This process of [universal] communion has already been explained.

By really understanding the commentarial explanations in this way, you can understand the incorrectness of the different explanations in such works as the *Elixir Secret*, since they do not explain this way. Here the *Illuminating Lamp* cites the *Magic Net* as the source of the statement of the three deity yogas of blessing, constructively imagining, and completing the form, the first two being [constituted by] the means of instantaneous arisal in the deity body, the sequential arising by means of the seed-syllable and so on, and the intuition three bodies arising in the communion body.

Though Kunga Nyingpo[153] indeed elucidates this tantra as [authority for this interpretation of the unexcelled] yoga [tantric form of communion], here that is not acceptable, according to the *Esoteric Community*. The first two of those, as above explained, are deity body arisals by means of mere imaginary mental formations, and are not deity body arisals like the [arisal of the] two forms of the magic body. Though the latter, [the third of the above] is indeed the main pure magic body and also the third stage magic body, it still does not seem best to assert that all instantaneous arisals in deity bodies by those perfection-stage practitioners capable of meditating the orgasmic great bliss have the meaning of the instantaneous completion of the intuition body stated by those two tantras, [*Magic Net* and *Esoteric Community*,] and other tantras like them. Rather, you should recognize that, although one can take as source the *Vairochana Enlightenment* statement about pure [277b] and impure deity bodies and interpret that they thus resemble the mantra and intuition bodies mentioned in the unexcelled yoga tantras, insofar as they are impure and pure deity bodies; or one can posit that the performance tantras mention deity bodies intending with hinting intention the deity bodies of the unexcelled [yoga tantras]; the way of meditating the deity body of that [*Esoteric Community*] *Tantra* is not accessible from the literal meaning [of those other categories of tantra], as previously explained.

153. Presumably, Sachen Kunga Nyingpo (1092–1158), a great scholar and one of the five great patriarchs of the Sakya Order, especially known and appreciated as a practitioner and commentator on the mother tantras.

11. The Conduct, the Art of Heightening Impact on the Two Stages

[277b.2–312b.6]

[**VI.B.3.c.** – The conduct that is the method of heightening impact on the two stages]

Third, in explaining the conduct as the art of developing impact on the two stages, there are two: [i.] The general arrangement of conducts; and [ii.] Specific explanation of unexcelled [yoga tantric] conduct.

[**VI.B.3.c.i.** – The general arrangement of conducts]

The first has two parts: [A′] Explaining the divisions of conduct in general; and [B′] Eliminating scriptural contradictions with the distinctive conduct.

[**VI.B.3.c.i.A′** – Explaining the divisions of conduct in general]

The Teacher descended to the human realm from Tushita heaven. Manifesting the four, continuum, context, and so on, he emanated the dispassionate body. He caused those with aspirations for the individual vehicle to understand the four noble truths and [he manifested] the dispassionate conduct. As for those with broader aspirations on the universal vehicle, he caused them to understand objective selflessness by teaching the eightfold assemblage of consciousness and so forth, manifesting the conduct of the stages and the transcendences.

Additionally, he emanated himself in the form of an imperial wheel-turning monarch, and for those with intense aspiration toward the profound, he employed the passionate conduct, manifesting the conduct of the teaching of passion right up to the above-explained realization of the two realities.

All paths going to liberation and omniscience that do not employ passion for the objects of sense maintain the conduct that is dispassionate. The *Integrated Practices*' statement that the dispassionate conduct [278a] was taught for the individual vehicle person is just by way of example. Though the three lower tantra categories do not teach union with the evolutionary consort or the visualized goddess, in general they do just use as the path the passion that perceives the five sense objects of the goddess visualized as present in front of you, and so their paths are included in just making a path of passion for sense objects.

For those disciples who totally engage with all objects of the extraordinary two realities and who delight in the supreme fruition of the great bliss, the dispassionate conduct appropriate for those of the disciple vehicle and the transcendence sutras is not taught. The disciple tamed by those [vehicles] does not understand the perfection stage of great bliss of taking as the path the passion for sense objects, and though by means of the hard conduct of the twelve ascetical practices and so forth they may seek enlightenment for a long time, they have a conduct that cannot attain ultimate enlightenment without relying on another path.

Therefore, the *Vajra Angel* states:

> To one who is an actual mendicant,
> To anyone who likes various ideologies,
> To one who has become old,
> Do not teach thatness to them.

A renunciate who is tamed by the dispassionate path is not capable of aspiring to the passionate path. An old person whose seeds have weakened is not capable of uniting bliss and voidness. A devotee of outsiders' ideologies does not enter this teaching. Therefore, the text explains they are not vessels of the supreme path. [278b] Thus the distinctive fruition must arise from a distinctive cause, and the great bliss of the fruitional occasion should be understood as achieved from the distinctive bliss of engagement with the sense qualities in the occasion of the cause. Those who are ascetical, engaging with other things, will not obtain the one-pointedness of great bliss, since the melting bliss comes from the flourishing body, and those ascetical activities punish the body that has the five senses and their supports.

Thus again, the *Vajra Angel* says:

> Illusory things
> May create the distinctive enjoyment.
> While that bliss is transforming,
> One will attain the distinctive fruition—
> Why should one not desire it?
> There are no animate or inanimate things,
> Their nature is mere appearance.
> Who has that distinctive meditation,
> The fruition of pleasurable bliss,
> The power of the unexcelled clear mind
> Achieving the cause of ambition for fruition—
> There, who would turn away a goddess?
>
> Therefore, by all efforts,
> Make offerings of the ubiquitous.
> By intolerable ascetical vows
> The body dries out and suffers.
>
> That suffering distracts the mind,
> Causing accomplishments to go elsewhere.
> Having stabilized body and mind,
> Always strengthen your bliss.

And the *Root Tantra* says:

> You won't achieve by relying
> On unbearable ascetic vows—
> Relying on enjoying all desires,
> Very soon you will achieve.

As for asceticism, by yogas that wear out and tire the body one practices in a[n abandoned] temple and so on. As for vows, [279a] they are the twelve ascetical practices such as living at the foot of a tree and so on. As for unbearable, it refers to hanging from cliffs and entering fire and so on. As for not attaining enlightenment while suffering by relying on those things, those things desiccate the body, oppress it and torment it, weaken the jasmine-like enlightenment spirit, divert the mind from great bliss samadhi to other states, and make sure that the supreme accomplishment will not be attained in this lifetime.

As for the meaning of the *Integrated Practices* quote of the *Glorious Supreme Prime* statement similar to the above, it should be taken as the meaning of the statement that intended a general explanation or an explanation like the foregoing; since it is not explained as having a verbally literal meaning.

Again, from the *Root Tantra*:

> Keeping body, speech, and mind
> In happiness, enlightenment is attained.
> Otherwise one will surely die an untimely death
> And will [eventually] be burned in hell.

Here the meaning of the previous [lines], the benefits of blissful conduct, is implicitly shown by the last two [lines], while they explicitly indicate the dangers of maintaining ascetical conduct.

As for that, some part explains the faults of the ascetical conduct of the fundamentalists, and some part explains the faults of incurring the eighth root transgression of maintaining an ascetical conduct, abandoning what one understands of the reality, [after] having received initiations and taking vows.

As for the unexcelled path's affording enlightenment in this lifetime, it depends on the union of bliss and void, and that bliss comes from the flourishing of the enlightenment spirit in one's body, and for that one must take care of one's body along with the senses and their supports. For that purpose is taught the conduct [279b] wherein the five senses rely on the five objects as one desires.

The *Illuminating Lamp* seventeenth chapter states that whatever commitments exist, [are fulfilled through] women [or male] consorts such as the "lotusful" and so on. They are [essential] for the commitment of the three vajras, and you should respect and delight in them by all activities of body, speech, and mind. "Don't despise the mind vajra" intends that their minds should not separate from passion, since the mind is the root of the body, and since the body is the root of the spirit of enlightenment.

Relying on the body of the "lotusful" and so on, one's enlightenment spirit increases; and since the root of the body of that one is the mind of that, if that mind is eradicated, the cause of the root of great bliss is injured, and the text thus intends that this causes obstruction to the increase of the great bliss samadhi. Therefore it states that one should protect such a mind. And the infraction of the fourteenth root transgression intends that same thing. By that reason you should understand not to harm your body but to make it thrive. The two new translations of the *Illuminating Lamp* are correct in explaining that the mind is the root of the body and the body is the root of the spirit of enlightenment. Should it be translated in the reverse it would be incorrect.

Thus, as stated, one should follow the conduct of the six transcendences, though there are statements that one's conduct should accord with one's path. Here, "conduct" refers to conduct from the perspective of knowing the nature of the five sense objects as the cause of great bliss. Therefore, if you do not live blissfully in body, speech, and mind through sense-enjoyments, you will not attain one-pointedness of mind, and your mentality will not become evenly entranced, and so you must keep [280a] a conduct of bliss for that purpose. And that statement is not just for achieving a mere stability of one-pointed mental equanimity, but is for the purpose of achieving the samadhi of orgasmic great bliss.

[**VI.B.3.c.i.B′** – Eliminating scriptural contradictions with the distinctive conduct]

The second has two parts: [1′] Setting forth the *Integrated Practices* statements and explaining their meaning; and [2′] Rebutting others' objections to that.

[**VI.B.3.c.i.B′1′** – Setting forth the *Integrated Practices* statements and explaining their meaning]

Well, then, [someone objects,] if it is said that you attain buddhahood by relying on sense objects as much as you want, how does it not contradict the statement [from the *Glorious Supreme Prime*] that passion for the five sense objects is a poison to be avoided:

> Desire, hatred, and delusion,
> These are the world's three poisons!

and the explanations from the sutras that show the dangers of desire as the cause of the horrible migrations, since relying on the sense objects causes the production of addictions?

In answer to this objection, [Āryadeva] in the *Integrated Practices* says:

> The addictive energies serve as condition for the addictions of those with objectifying views such as the disciples, since they do not understand the reality of the addictions. If they know the reality, those energies could become the cause for enlightenment.

The *Glorious Supreme Prime* says:

> Desire, hate, and delusion,
> Holding them they become poisons.
> When the poisons are eradicated,
> Poison has been made poisonless.
> Relying on them with an elixir process,
> They become elixir itself.

The *Jewel Heap Sutra* says that just as the city's manure enriches the fields of sugar cane, the manure of the bodhisattvas' addictions enrich their becoming enlightened. And [it also says that] just as poison combined with medicine and mantra is no longer able to kill, [280b] so addictions combined with art and wisdom are not able to cause wrong downfalls. The *Discipline Amoghasiddhi Tantra* also says:

> "That which binds the foolish person,
> Fully liberates the wise."
> When the bodhisattva meditates on this,
> All these wrong things,
> Which imprison the confused,

Sending them to the howling hell,
The same things liberate [the bodhisattva]
Who attains bliss by the power of wisdom.

By this reason, one enters into a delightful situation where there is a distinctive incentive, a distinctive transformation, and a distinctive fruition, and one can achieve the goal of the fruition of the unexcelled great bliss—and not any other way. For the sake of that, by that very one, the pleasures of eating and living and so on cause the realization of omniscience that includes the eight masteries of excellent qualities and so on. The *Magic Supreme Bliss [Tantra]* also says:

Therefore, by bliss there is bliss itself
And all buddhas thus attain themselves.

As for "serve as conditions for addictions," the two new translations of the *Integrated Practices* are correct to translate "become the cause for the horrid states." Concerning that, to the argument that "relying on the five objects, addictions are produced, and that again leads to the bad migrations," he answers that in regard to the addictions produced by relying on sense objects, they are analyzed into two, a cause of bad migrations for those who do not understand reality, such as the disciples, and a cause of buddhahood for those who understand reality. He does not answer that relying on sense objects [281a] will not produce addictions.

In general, as above explained, the person free from attachment to sense objects is not precluded from taking interest in getting desire objects such as food and clothing. In regard to pleasant, unpleasant, and indifferent sense objects, they do not become addictive just by the five senses experiencing them or just by the mental sense's having an interest in sense objects. However, in this case, the main point is made in terms of not separating from passion for sense objects, and from among sense objects this is examining whether or not it is correct that one can take the passion for the union of the two sex organs as the path. If you are not free of passion for the desired, you do not have the realization of reality, and you still rely on sense objects as much as you want, you will feel the passionate addictions. Those [addictions] will also become the cause of your going to horrid migrations; thus, the addictions will not at all be transformed into the cause even of liberation, and therefore they are not allowed. Neither does the individualist who does possess the understanding of reality have the ability to transform any addiction into a cause for enlightenment: since such a person does not have the art element of such a transformation, which is taught in either the [exoteric] transcendence or the secret mantra universal vehicle; and since such transformation requires both the distinctive art and [distinctive] wisdom. Therefore, the statement that understanding the thatness of addictions serves as the cause of enlightenment shows that in such a case the addictions can become a cause of enlightenment [281b] and does not show that for all those who understand thatness, the addictions that rely on sense objects become the cause of enlightenment; otherwise the many statements of the necessity of elements of art beyond the view of voidness would be meaningless.

The reference quoted from the *Glorious Supreme [Prime]* shows that the three addictions can become either poisons or elixirs, which shows that the one-sided statements that the three addictions are only poisons to be eliminated are for the sake of a certain type of person and not for everyone. The previous reference from the *Jewel Heap* shows that some of the addictions of bodhisattvas create the buddha-qualities, which teaches that not all addictions obstruct the attainment of enlightenment. The second reference [from the *Jewel Heap*] shows that addictions combined with the distinctive art and wisdom cannot lead one into the wrong downfalls into the horrid migrations, showing that the same addictions that obstruct the higher rebirths for those not expert in [the distinctive] art cannot obstruct those who are so expert. As for the meaning of that *Jewel Heap* reference, it states that just, while the transcendence vehicle bodhisattvas could eliminate craving for the addictions that cause rebirth in existence, when they purposefully leave them uneliminated, those addictions become a cause of buddhahood by driving them to take rebirth with the ability to complete the magnificent bodhisattva deeds.

Elsewhere, there is the story about the addictive desire to commit sexual misconduct in the case of the distinctive embodiment of the brahmin boy "Star," where the point is that if he did not pursue his desire [for a certain woman] it would have the preventable consequence of [her] death; and if he did pursue his desire he could uphold virtue [282a] as he wished.[154] This is

154. Have not yet been able to trace the source of this story about Bram ze'i khye'u skar ma.

completely different from such addiction becoming the cause of enlightenment and the system of making passion into the path in this [tantric] path. Nevertheless, as this is a source for certain addictions combined with expertise in art becoming a cause of enlightenment, you can rebut the criticisms argued against [this path] that producing addictions from relying on sense objects must [inevitably] lead to horrid migrations, must become obstacles to enlightenment, and that various references are mutually contradictory.

In the *Dialogue with the Householder Ugra*, while the Buddha did recommend the deeds of the bodhisattva householder to one who could not eliminate the household desires, since there was no aspiration there to follow the path with the vehicle of passion, that [householder] was told to engage [in those deeds] with the idea of the dangers of relying on desires, which is different from the passionate discipline of the path of the unexcelled. The reference from the *Glorious Supreme [Primal] Yoga Tantra* is suitable for support here since, though it does not show that there is no fault [at all] in making passion into the path, [as it can be a problem for an ordinary person,] it does show in general that it is possible in certain cases to take as a path the three addictions, relying on sense objects combined with expertise in the arts in order to increase one's spirit of enlightenment relying on the body of another and to increase the spirit of enlightenment of one's own body.

Here you might wonder: "Well, it might be conceded that it can be permitted to use desire, but how can there be permission for hate and delusion?"

As for hatred, when you practice fierce activities such as killing or banishing, there is no anger at the time of the causing motivation, yet it is said that a rough mind is developed [**282b**] on the occasion of the continuing motivation. In the context of the initial [creation-stage performance] meditation of the defense wheel and so on, compassion is developed in the time of the causal motivation, but in the time of the continuing motivation it is explained that a hateful mind and so forth is developed toward the obstructive demons. So there is some allowance for hatred and its associated patterns. Further, since every passion or hatred occurs in coordination with addictive delusion, delusion is permitted as incidental to the permitting of other addictions, though it is not by itself permitted expressly. As for "by what," it is the stupidity through passion for sense objects and specially passion for the union of the two sex organs; being a confusion about the meaning of thatness, it binds in the life cycle.

By that very passion that leads to the hells such as the howling hell, the expert in art can become liberated in great bliss by the power of wisdom that realizes thatness. Thus, when you meditate the enlightenment spirit of bliss-void [-indivisible], the artistically inept find a cause of bondage and the artistically expert become liberated.

The *Hevajra Tantra* says:

> By passion the worldling is bound,
> But by passion one becomes liberated.

Therefore, there is cause both for bondage and for liberation in the same addiction of passion for sense objects. As the *Vajra Rosary* says:

> Abandoning duty and deviance,
> But performing the prohibited,
> Like the lotus unsullied by the mud,
> Understanding reality, one is not infected.

Even though there is passion for the desire objects, one is "not infected," that is not crushed by its faults; it is not that passion does not arise.

Here you might wonder: "Well, [283a] if there is a way as that above in which other vehicles make addictions into a cause of enlightenment, and if the other types of tantras make it into a path, making into a path just the passion of visualizing the five objects in the goddess who is meditated without [actual] union, then what about the way of making passion for sense objects the path in the unexcelled [tantras]?"

When your mind is attracted by intense faith from seeing clearly the exceptional excellence of the path that meditates on the decisively understood meaning of thatness by means of the intuition of the orgasmic bliss of melting, you then desire to develop the great bliss for the sake of meditating on thatness. That is to make a path out of the passion for the sense objects [involved in] uniting with the outer evolution consort or the [inner] intuition consort, as a means of developing that [great bliss]; and that is not only for that [purpose,] but is also in order to achieve the magic body. These I have already explained many times.

As for making a path out of passion for desire objects for the sake of developing the distinctive subjectivity for meditating on voidness, it does not exist in any other vehicle than [that of] the unexcelled [yoga tantras].

"By this reason" and so forth is translated by Patsab as "By this way, [there is] a distinctive presumption, and," which conforms to the [related passage in] the *Reality Accomplishment*. The "meaning" is the creation of the deity as [desire-] object and support. "Abiding" is well [translated] as "transforming." And all those [expressions] concisely express the path of the [advanced tantric] conduct.

By the art of penetrating the vital points in the outer and inner body, one melts the spirit of enlightenment and produces the distinctive textures of the body as inner object, and by that serving as an objective condition you create a distinctive bliss of sensation in the body consciousness. With that serving as the immediately preceding condition, [283b] the mental consciousness then develops a superlative experiential bliss. At that time, just by remembering the meaning of the reality of thatness that has been ascertained, bliss and void become united. That is declared to be the meditation on voidness by the art of creating the mentality as the experience of bliss. Relying on that, the discerning person can understand the key point of this path as being the distinctive subjectivity that [focuses on the] nondifferent [object of] voidness.

As for that process of generating bliss in the sense consciousness and mental consciousness, it can be understood from the reasonings stated by the Lord of Reasoning [Dharmakīrti, in his *Treatise on Validating Cognition*]:

> When passions etc., expanding, increase,
> They are produced from pleasure and pain;
> And again, elements being equal, and so on,
> From approaching the inner object. . . .

And:

> Because a mind arising from a special inner object
> Can also be made to change it.

Therefore, you should understand that the sense consciousnesses arise in the actuality of bliss from the immediately preceding condition of the mentality becoming the actuality of great bliss.[155]

155. Tsong Khapa seeks the backing of the great epistemologist Dharmakīrti to show how a mind that is dominated by the inner object of subliminally enlightenment-spirit-grounded deep bliss perception becomes a bliss-subjectivity that can transmute any sense experience

[**VI.B.3.c.i.B′2′** – Rebutting others' objections to that]

[Someone here might object,] "Since the *Integrated Practices* states that 'disciples and so on, by being convinced about the object,' and 'causing those who aspire to the magnificent to realize objective selflessness,' doesn't it contradict the [dialecticist centrists' distinctively special] statement that the followers of the individual vehicle can understand objective selflessness?"

Since among disciples there are both those who understand thatness and those who do not, here mention of the "convinced about the object" disciple specifies which among them is being considered. As the noble [Nāgārjuna]'s statement was quoted [by Chandrakīrti] in the *Introduction [to the Central Way] Commentary*:

> You said that without understanding signlessness,
> One will not attain liberation;
> Therefore, you completely taught [284a]
> That in the universal vehicle . . .

he was thinking that, although objective selflessness is explained in both canons, it is more extensively explained in the universal vehicle; thus, he states that it is in the universal vehicle that one is caused to understand objective selflessness. Likewise, from the *Disclosure of the Spirit of Enlightenment*, [Nāgārjuna] says:

> Those who desire to benefit,
> Explain to the disciples the five aggregates
> Of matter, sensation, conception,
> Volition, and consciousness.
>
> The supreme human always says
> That matter is like a ball of foam,
> Sensation like a water bubble,
> Conception like a mirage,

into bliss, whether ordinarily pleasant, unpleasant, or neutral; a compelling epistemology of sublimation.

Volition like a plantain tree,
And consciousness like an illusion.
Teaching the aggregates in such a way,
He explains them to the bodhisattvas.

Thus, he was intending that there are many explanations to the bodhisattvas of the intrinsic realitylessness of the aggregates by means of such examples, and not so many similar recitations in the individual vehicle canon. But, [he was] not [intending] that the individual vehicle follower was never taught the applicability of those five examples; since in the *Introduction [to the Central Way] Commentary* those five examples for the aggregates are stated, quoting from a sutra taught to the disciples.

If it was the interpretation of [Nāgārjuna] that the individual vehicle lacks the understanding of voidness as intrinsic realitylessness, he would have been incorrect in stating in that same [*Disclosure of the Spirit of Enlightenment*] text:

Who do not understand voidness,
They do not approach liberation,
And those confused persons will wander
In the prison of existence through the six migrations.

—since followers of the individual vehicle [284b] do have liberation from the prison of existence. Likewise, the *Integrated Practices* statement that by teaching those aspiring to the magnificent they are made to understand the eightfold aggregate of consciousness and so on, is merely referring to what was stated in the sutras, since in [Āryadeva's] own system he does not accept a fundamental consciousness apart from the sixfold aggregate of consciousness. According to the noble system of the *Esoteric Community*, the mind of death clear light universal voidness is the death mind and the mind of imminence arising therefrom in the reverse order is the birth mind, neither of which is suitable as the fundamental consciousness. Though [Nāgārjuna] mentions the mere name "fundamental consciousness" in the *Disclosure of the Spirit of Enlightenment*, it is only for the sake of declaring that the mental consciousness is the root and foundation of all purifying things, as I have already explained extensively in my *Wisdom Vajra Compendium Commentary*.

One may here object, "By meditating on the import of thatness with the bliss from relying on the consort using passion for sense objects as a cause, are all addictions terminated or not? If it is the latter, then there is a contradiction between the realization of voidness progressing to the extreme ultimate and some addictions not being terminated. This is because, having terminated all truth-habits, it is not appropriate that the termination of the cause, the truth-habits of misknowledge, would not eliminate the effect, passion, and so forth; and because it is contradictory for liberation to be attained without terminating all addictions. If it is the former, [it is contradicted] since, as you need the passions as the cause of the path that terminates the passions, there is the absurd consequence that light serves as the cause of darkness; [285a] and it is contradictory for passion to serve as the cause of that path's radical elimination of the truth-habit misknowledge. This is because it is contradictory for the cause of radical termination of a cause to be affected by the effect of that [cause]; and all other addictions are made to arise by the truth-habit misknowledge."

This I have already explained extensively elsewhere.[156]

Furthermore, you may wonder: "The 'passion' concerned in the context of wishing to make passion into a path, if [on the one hand,] it is just a matter of attaching the name 'passion' to some other virtuous quality, it contradicts the *Integrated Practices* proof with evidence of something serving as basis of addiction either becoming or not becoming a cause of enlightenment, and it makes the statement that for some other person such a passion serves as the cause of going to bad migrations. A virtuous quality will not become the cause of bad migrations and will be the cause of enlightenment, so where is the excellent artistic skill distinctive from other vehicles? If [on the other hand,] it is real passion involved here, you would have to clearly pronounce how it becomes a path; [which you cannot do,] since you cannot express how a means of destruction eliminates its target from the perspective of being discordant in habit pattern, as for example, 'This becomes the remedy of this kind of addiction.' Therefore, the artistic skill of the unexcelled vehicle is no more than a mere object of [unfounded] faith!"

Here I should speak plainly. I do not accept the second alternative, but do accept the gist of the first. As for how the objection does no harm [to my position], the statement "addictions are terminated by meditating the

156. Tsong Khapa has refuted this argument earlier in the context of self-consecration.

import of thatness by means of the bliss of relying on the consort" [285b] refers to the termination of misknowledge, the cause of all other addictions. Eliminating that means eliminating all addictions, but there is no fault [of contradiction,] since it does not eliminate that through a path that is manifestly contradictory in habit pattern to the passion that is attached to sense objects. The causal truth-habit is not terminated until you attain the learner's communion, so therefore there is no contradiction for a single continuum to alternate for a while the meditation of a path that is directly contradictory in habit pattern to the truth-habit and the using as a path the attachment for sense objects [that is not contradictory in habit pattern]. When you rely at will on a distinctive sense object without parting from attachment for sense objects, the two blisses, from passion for desire and from relying on a consort, are [related as] cause and effect; and as they are temporary cause and effect, if that attachment did not precede, such bliss [of contact with a consort] would be eliminated, though the mere bliss of relating to a consort would not be eliminated. For example, sweet myrobalan soaked in milk would not be produced without the milk, though the mere myrobalan would not be eliminated.

Here, in terminating addictions on this unexcelled vehicle, I have already established that there is the enjoyment of sense objects through the union of two sex organs. As the *Sampuṭa Further Tantra* says, in answer to the argument that you must eliminate passion by meditating offensiveness, which has its contradictory habit pattern:

> When you make use of the reality of passion, you separate from passion. Thus, the Divine Lord says: "Noble child! Emaho! The buddhas' passion is without turbidity; conquering dispassion by means of passion, [286a] they grant the bestowal of all bliss."

When the stream-winner experiences desire it does not become a natural transgression [for her or him]. When an incense-elephant eats the ketaka flower, the digested product becomes musk, while when an ordinary elephant eats the same flower its product becomes manure. Likewise, addictions such as passions are explained to produce a distinctively excellent fruition from a distinctively pure continuum. Master Shāntarakshita also explained this point clearly in his *Reality Accomplishment*. Therefore, it is not a case of affixing the name "passion" to what is not real passion.

Though one engages in making a path out of passion for desire objects, at the time of the causal motivation, through one's intention being captivated by the spirit of enlightenment and the orgasmic intuition, one engages by perceiving [objects] for the sake of developing those [wisdoms] and one does not adulterate that [intention] with addictions. Since it is not otherwise than that body and speech become virtuous and nonvirtuous by the power of that [motivation being good or bad], when you engage in such activities with such an intention, acts such as self-creation are explained as happening without addictive intention; and this does not intend only the context of the time of motivation [but also the whole time of action].

When you make a path out of such a kind of passion, it does not dislodge other addictions by way of maintaining a contradictory habit pattern.

Well then what [does it do]?

One who has that distinctive embodiment makes it into a path with a view [first] to suppress the dangers of being led into the bad migrations by those passions and [second] to cause the swift development of the excellences of the superior [286b] path.

In regard to the first, such [practitioners] have become suitable vessels by the power of the stability and purity of the twofold spirit of enlightenment of the ordinary vehicle. They then defend properly the vows and pledges. They inquire into the decisive meaning of the view of selflessness, thereby confirming their vision of the magical [nature of reality]. They create the deity body as the universal seal from within the experiential nonperception of the three sectors of object and support. They thereby develop the potency of aspiration blessed by mantra and seal. [Such practitioners] have many [accomplishments], such as restraining the tenfold nonvirtuous actions with regard to objects, purifying their continua by means of initiation, guarding properly their vows and pledges, cultivating the samadhi of the first stage, and being expert in the science of the control of passion.

In regard to the second, it is not enough to consider a meditation on voidness to be merely a thought-free stabilization of the mind that produces bliss derived from such passion. Rather, enlightenment is quickly bestowed by meditating on orgasmic wisdom-intuition realized by placing the mind on the great bliss, above and beyond the view that is superlatively decisive about the import of selflessness. Further in that regard, it is not sufficient that the enlightenment spirit melted by the condition of the consort be made by other means not to emit; rather [it is required] that—since the orgasmic [great bliss] can only arise from such union causing the energies of [right] *rasanā* and [left] *lalanā* channels first to be injected into the *dhūti* channel and then to dissolve there, as the art of orgasmic bliss—it is necessary for the energies to dissolve [into the *dhūti* channel] and hold the melted jasmine-like spirit of enlightenment. In making such a sort of passion into the path, though there is no offensiveness meditation, [287a] a habit pattern diametrically opposite to that of passion, finally passion is terminated [anyway]; because [this orgasmic intuition] is a path that corresponds with a validating knowledge of a habit pattern diametrically opposite to that of the root cause of [such passion, namely the deluded truth-habit].[157]

Without uniting with the void that is known as the voidness of the intrinsic reality of all of the samsaric life cycle and of nirvana, achieving the bliss of mere non-emission of the enlightenment spirit produced by the joining of the two sex organs does not at all damage the truth-habit of misknowledge, the root of existence. Thus, however much you engage with such bliss, the craving derived from that truth-habit only becomes more increased, just like a thirsty person plunging into the perceived water of a mirage, such a thing is inferior. However, in the case of being able to unite the bliss and void as previously explained, without such an art [of restraining emission by injecting the energies into the central channel], one will not quickly attain the buddhahood that fulfills the hopes of the beings of the three realms. Thus, [that art] is praised from the angle of its being the swift path. As Saraha says [in an *Enlightenment Song*]:

> Who does not fully know things' reality,
> Achieving great bliss when in sexual union
> Is [still] like a thirsty person finding a mirage,
> Even dying, will the thirsty find water in space?
>
> Playing with the bliss that dwells
> Between the vajra and the lotus,

157. The idea here seems to be that, in order to inject the vitalizing energy and evacuative energy into the central *dhūti* channel, one has to unravel the sixfold heart knot, which can only be done by deep (meaning reaching to the instincts and their physical correlates in the subtle nervous system) realization of the selflessness or intrinsic truthlessness of all things, which has a cognitive habit pattern diametrically opposed to the truth-habits.

Relying on it without having the ability,
How will the hope of the three realms ever be fulfilled?

To quote the *Reality Accomplishment*:

Finely examining the well-considered,
The wise should enter into that;
Otherwise, entering into fire,
One will not succeed even a sixteenth!

Knowing thatness by thatness
Who relies on a goddess,
He will achieve; and otherwise,
He will fall into [287b] the great hell!

Also, from the *Esoteric Accomplishment*:

Even with thatness as the pure jewel self,
One who has abandoned all faults—
Should that one abandon the divine art,
Contradict one's commitments and so on,
And come to practice in some other ways;
That one will roast in hell and so on.
Just as there the fire will burn
The heap of grass and wood
And turn it into ashes,
And from it sprouts will never grow.
Likewise lacking [the wisdom of] thatness
Even making a few great seeming wonders,
Until one can dwell [aloft] in space,
After one's death, one will go to hell.

Thus, the wise should engage [in the tantric conduct,] having well investigated things in fine detail. If you have not become wise by determining well the import of thatness and abandoning all elaborations, there are stated to be extremely heavy dangers in taking the general and distinctive passion for sense objects as your path. However, if you cultivate well the subtle paths of reasoning of Nāgārjuna and company in regard to the point of the profound definitive meaning scriptural references, [you will avoid those dangers.] By the key point of the great rarity of such a determination about this matter, those who claim to be tantrics in this land seem to be very weak in dedication to this system [wherein deep insight into the profound must empower the focus on the path of passion]. Therefore, those with keen discernment, as the *Accomplishment [Ascertaining] Wisdom and Art* says:

> Setting the mind in the reality of enlightenment,
> Enjoying the bliss of objects, one achieves in this very life.
> All these are pure in intrinsic reality,
> Ordinary objects being selfless and illusory,
> Like [288a] hallucinations and optical illusions,
> Nonlocal, delivered from thought conventions.
> When noble persons totally realize
> The magnificent ambition and the habit-free mind,
> Then the orgasmic realization prevails,
> And the power of these objects can no longer bind.

So it is stated that, from the perspective of ascertaining the two realities unerringly by the way of [experiencing both] the melting bliss arising from enjoying objects of desire and [the insight that] all dreamlike and illusory things are fittingly functional even though even their atoms lack intrinsic identifiability, if you lack the skill in the art of the bliss-void-union orgasmic intuition, you will be overwhelmed by objects that lead you to the great danger. Therefore, with open-minded intellect, subtle and acute, you should unceasingly investigate the art of producing the orgasmic intuition of the union of bliss and void.

[**VI.B.3.c.ii.** – Specific explanation of the unexcelled (yoga tantric) conduct]

Second, the specific explanation of the unexcelled [yoga tantric] conduct has three parts: [A′] How the analysis of conduct is declared; [B′] The definition of each of the three conducts; and [C′] The method of learning the conducts.

[**VI.B.3.c.ii.A′** – How the analysis of conduct is declared]

In the context of the titles of the *Root Tantra*'s chapters five and seven, respectively "Supreme All-Around Conduct" and "Supreme Mantric Conduct,"[158] [Chandrakīrti,] in the *Illuminating Lamp*, explains the meanings as, [respectively,] the superlative conduct achieving all the aims of self and other and the three conducts of the mantric reciter. The former is a general name of all three [tantric] conducts. [288b] As [Chandrakīrti] says in the *Illuminating Lamp* about the meaning of statements in the *[Root Tantra]* ninth chapter about the two conducts, [those] of bodhisattvas and of transcendent buddhas, the first is the mantrī/nī engaging to the best of one's ability in whatever will fulfill the aims of beings, whether or not it contravenes mundane conventions, and the second is the jewel-like mantrī/nī realizing the perfection stage and transforming one's own actuality in this very life by the engaged conduct that is not withdrawn in meditative equipoise. The former is the general conduct of bodhisattvas, and the latter mentions the perfection stage by way of example only, intending chiefly the jewel-like person, but includes all the distinctive unexcelled conducts of engaging with the objects of desire.

As [Chandrakīrti] says in *Illuminating Lamp* about the meaning of statements in the sixteenth chapter about truly undertaking the discipline of the science consort, they refer to engaging in activities having transformed oneself and the science consort into the likeness of deities dressed with the appropriate clothing.

As far as the supreme three conducts mentioned in the commentary on the sixth chapter, though the two old translations and Patsab's translation all take these as referring to enjoyment conducts and liberating conducts, Chag's translation is better in its "the supreme of these conducts is the conduct of eating, sleeping, and defecating [*bhusuku*]" as [this passage] does not indicate other conducts. In the *Further Tantra*, when it mentions the "all-around conduct" and the "mantrī/nī conduct," [it uses] the former as the general name for the three conducts and the latter for the seventeenth chapter's mention of maintaining the mundane and transcendental [289a] commitments and vows.

[Āryadeva,] in his *Integrated Practices*, states the division of the passion-

158. *Samantacaryāgra* and *Mantracaryāgra* chapters, respectively.

developed bodhisattva's conduct into the three, elaborated, unelaborated, and extremely unelaborated, and the *Second Stage* and the *Illuminating Lamp* also mention the three. As for the chief desire object of the conducts, it is the desire object of the science consort, among whom there are actual sciences and sciences who are contemplative wisdom-seals. [Āryadeva] argues that the first of those is engaged with in the first two conducts and the latter is engaged with in the third conduct. The mention in the *Integrated Practices* and in the *Second Stage* of the three conducts of the perfection-stage practitioner is just by way of example, since each of the two stages has its own set of three conducts. As [Chandrakīrti] says in the *Illuminating Lamp* tenth chapter:

> When the yogi/nī, while achieving the supreme and abiding in the ordinary, after experiencing her or his practice of the three conducts, the elaborated conduct and so forth, does not reach any accomplishments, then s/he must compel the essence of her or his deity.

Thereby he states that the conducts of the two stages are undertaken in order to achieve accomplishments according to one's situation, and that if one does not achieve them one should compel the essence [of one's deity] particular to whichever of the two stages. In comment on the seventh chapter, when [Chandrakīrti] equates the elaborated [conduct] with general meaning, the unelaborated with hidden meaning, and the extremely unelaborated with ultimate meaning, he intends the meditation and aspiration of engaging in the conducts, and he is not arguing that general meaning conduct did not include the other conducts; [289b] since he mentions in comment on the *[Root Tantra]* fifteenth chapter the unelaborated conduct of the five transcendent buddhas of the creation stage, and since, though the extremely unelaborated [conduct] is not assigned to the creation-stage practitioner in terms of its meditation and aspiration, it is assigned [to them] in terms of activities and so on.

In general, there are two kinds of conducts of those who make passion for desire objects into the path, conducts at the time of consecration making one a suitable vessel for meditating the two stages and conduct at the time of meditating the path, already having become a suitable vessel. In the latter case there are again two [conducts], conducts to produce the path when it has not been produced, and conducts, having already produced the path, in order to intensify the impact. The former of these occurs from the beginning of first meditating the path for as long as one has not attained the nonlearning state. As is stated in the *Condensed [Sādhana]*, you should practice in such a way once you enter the creation stage:

> Not suffering from the ascetic abandoning
> Of the five desire objects,
> Following the yoga tantra
> You should achieve enlightenment through bliss.

Regarding the second [kind of conducts, those focused to intensify the impact], Kṛshna Samayavajra states that one engages in conducts only at two times, since there are only two occasions of intensifying the impact [of realization]; intensifying impact to achieve ordinary accomplishments, after you have completed the subtle and coarse creation stages, and intensifying impact to achieve the supreme accomplishment, once you have achieved the perfection stage with the three isolations and the two realities.

Tsunmojen, relying on statements such as "knowing the different types of instinctual natures and luminances," also says there are three occasions in general [290a] for performing the conducts, and two on the perfection stage, after you attain the magic body and after you attain the learner's union.

My own interpretation is that there are four occasions of intensifying impact on both the stages, as follows. First, on the occasion of the creation stage, it is as above [in the theory of Kṛshna Samayavajra]. [Second,] I have already established the need to engage in the conducts in order to achieve the magic body, having attained the mind isolation on the perfection stage. [Third,] having attained the magic body, you must practice the conducts in order to attain the goal of the learner's union and in order to terminate the abandonable addictions. As [Chandrakīrti states] in comment on the sixteenth chapter's statement of the benefits of engaging in the unelaborated conducts of the three clans:

> The intuitive wisdom of the three vajras arises . . .

[Chandrakīrti comments:]

> There is the creation here of the vajra body and so forth by means of the body vajra [*OṀ*] and so forth. The buddha-enlightenment is the ultimate reality. To enter there is to attain. Clear light transparence causes the attainment of the pure intuition body.

Thus [in this context] he explains the benefits of causing the attainment of the intuition body purified by clear light, since there is no [need for] purifying of the magic body by clear light after you have attained communion.

[Fourth,] as for engaging in the conducts having attained the learner's communion, you can understand it from the previous quotes from the *Five Stages* and Nāgabodhi's [*Stage of Arrangement*]. You can also understand it from what [Āryadeva] explains in the *Integrated Practices* about the practitioner engaged in the conducts realizing the superficial reality; that being connected to the two embodiments of the superficial magic body of the third and the fifth stages. Furthermore, [Āryadeva] states in the *Integrated Practices*:

> You cannot [290b] terminate the instincts of beginningless addictions without the conducts of the discipline.

Therefore, all the cognitive obscurations that are the actuality of the addictive instincts cannot be terminated without the disciplinary conducts, so you cannot terminate them in this life without those conducts. Since the very swift termination of those seeds of addictions called instincts depends on that, you can understand why you need to practice the conducts for the sake of the learner's and nonlearner's communions.

If you wonder here, "If you are making desire for sense objects into the path from the time of taking consecration, the chief three conducts are no more than just that; although you can engage in conducts outside of that [overall] situation, what is the need?"

The conducts needed to intensify impact on the perfection stage are for attaining enlightenment in this life. As the *[Five Stages'] Second Stage* says:

> Knowing to distinguish luminance from the instincts,
> One relies on the fourth thatness—
> Who does not learn the three forms [of the conducts]
> Will not swiftly attain the fruit.

Just as the fire abides in the womb of wood,
But does not emerge without rubbing,
So without the practice of enlightenment,
It will not emerge here in this very life.

Also, the *Integrated Practices* and the *Illuminating Lamp* explain that the supreme is achieved in this very life by engaging in the conducts.

As for the way that is, when you can produce the three intuitions by the power of consummating the energy yoga, you cannot produce the completely qualified mind-isolation intuition without the friendship of the outer seal [consort]. Relying on her for that purpose has already been explained. Thus, even though you can withdraw the energies by the power of penetrating the vital point within the body and, burning the inner fire, consummate the ability to melt [291a] the enlightenment spirit, still beyond that to attain the greatly distinctive form of those by relying on the seal, it is clear that there is a stage of proceeding to the intensive development of the realization of thatness. Therefore, when you have completed your ability in the art of penetrating the vital point within the body, combining it with enjoyment with all components of the desire object of the seal, and then meditating on thatness—that is the meaning of "the conduct," the conduct that intensifies the impact of the perfection stage.

While not developing the special bliss from penetrating the vital points in the inner wheels, from the specifics of the actuality, enumeration, distinction of access, and intensity of power of the seal, a variety of distinct types of bliss is produced. So you should understand that at that time there are many ways of progressing to entry of the special realization from meditating on voidness with that [bliss].

If you wonder, "Well, if the common accomplishments are not attained without engaging in those conducts, that contradicts the explanation that the path taught in those tantras enables the attainment of the whole range of common accomplishments from practicing the three lower tantras; and even if you allow that those common accomplishments are there anyway by implication, what is the benefit in achieving them by engaging in those conducts?"

Though you do not need to meditate on voidness to achieve many trivial common accomplishments, it is explained that you do need to meditate on voidness to achieve many distinctive accomplishments that accrue in the lower tantras. And while some say that it is indispensable for such achievement, others say that it is easier to achieve them if that realization is there. Among the unexcelled [tantra] creation [291b] stage yogi/nīs attainments of common accomplishments, there are many not achieved by the former [lower tantras]. One does engage in the conducts as a method of achieving the ultimate among common accomplishments, and easily achieving them in a very short time, as stated in many other [texts] how "by the three [conducts], accomplishments will be achieved before seven days, a fortnight, a month, or two and a half." When the creation stage is consummated and the signs of touch and sight are found, by meditating on the PHAṬ letter in the door of the secret place and so forth, one can block the emission of the enlightenment spirit, and so uniting with the seal, generate bliss. Meditating on voidness with that bliss, distinctive accomplishment is created, and it is easy to achieve accomplishments. I already explained how just by that there is the meditation of bliss-void also in the creation stage.

If some person completes the subtle creation stage, it is also possible that the energies will be injected into the central channel; and if that person knows the vital point of using the union with the outer consort as vitalizing energy control, relying on that [practice], it is possible that s/he can generate the four joys from dissolving the energies into the *dhūti*. Those two achievements thus may arise in the creation stage, but when one defines the path, they must be taken as the perfection-stage path; as it is explained in the *Personal Instruction*, [even] before meditating the path, on the occasion of initiation, the orgasmic [wisdom] thus arising is of the perfection stage. This engaging in the conducts for the sake of common accomplishments on the occasion of the creation stage is not [the affair] of the supreme jewel-like person, but is that of the white-lotus-like person of inferior faculties, [292a] whose mind is attracted by the common accomplishments.

[VI.B.3.c.ii.B′ – The definition of each of the three conducts]

When the three kinds of passionate enlightenment conducts are declared, which tantras are their source and what is the definition of each?

The *Integrated Practices* explains that the elaborated conduct is in the *Extensive All Transcendent Buddha Ārali*, as taught in the *Consolations of the Transcendent Buddha and Vajradhara*; the unelaborated is playing somewhat on the power of intention from the *Always Pervading*; and the extremely unelaborated conduct is the practicing by abandoning all crowds, living on the food of samadhi alone, and uniting contemplatively with the intuition seal. Just as the three, wood, palm leaves, and cotton are not different when burned to ashes, so all three of the conducts will lead to attaining the exaltation of Vajradhara, even though by differentiation into small, medium, and great, you must learn the three conducts [and apply them appropriately like medicines] according to your age.

In that regard, the statement from the *[Buddha] Union* that the five clans tame beings with the five consolations is the first consolation; and the second consolation is the consolation that tames beings by means of Vajrasattva. Depending on this, the ancient [mentors] claimed that in the context of [one's being engaged] in the procedures of the conducts, chiefly there will be no more than six death-transitions. As it is taught, though in the context of the six consolations the [conduct as taught in the] *Extensive Ārali* is absent, in general they have the meaning explained in the *[Buddha] Union*; "*ārali*" having the meaning of "game" or **[292b]** "play." And that refers to what is spoken of in the *Integrated Practices* as the seal and responding to it, and so on. Some practitioners strive in the practices stated from the tantras such as *Reality Compendium*, with the gestures, the worship with song, the way of postures, theater, dance, and so on. Others engage in the conducts—stated in tantras such as the *Glorious Supreme [Prime]*—such as the cross-legged sitting posture and the nine aesthetic moods of dance and so on; and all of these are explained by the *Integrated Practices* as [pertaining to] the elaborated conducts.

Therefore, as for the unelaborated conducts, in general one must always perform those conducts, and sometimes when necessary one can leave them. However, in this concern, there still are many elaborations such as a special house along with seats, friends to perform the rites, and the Dharma equipment, and food and drink and so on. Nevertheless, as the practices are classified as extremely unelaborated, the elaborations in the activities are very little. By three examples it is shown that the goal can be attained by each of the three conducts, showing that it is not necessary to practice all three. The former among the three, wood etc., are the harder to burn, the latter easier, which explains that by the three kinds of conduct there is a range from difficult to easier. As for "small, medium, and great," some say it refers to bigger, medium, and smaller equipment, and some explain it is small, medium, and great wisdom, and others explain it as great, medium, and small passion.

However, it is mentioned in terms of bigger, medium, and smaller equipment, small, medium, and great age, and small, medium, and great inclination [293a] that enjoys elaborations. As for the mention of not having enough equipment, this is not the context of having attained the magic body, so it is in terms of engaging in the conducts prior to that.

As for the first of those conducts, it is explained in the *[Buddha] Union*, while the *Community* mentions only the last two, according to the explanation of the *Integrated Practices*. As for the seal and so on taught in the yoga tantras, s/he is [employed] for engaging in the unexcelled conduct; if you analyze it, this intends the first conduct, and is not in terms of those [unexcelled yoga] tantras. Intending that the extensive elaborations of activities previously mentioned are not stated in the *Community*, [the above] states that the last two conducts only are taught in the *Community*. As for the *Illuminating Lamp* mention that the *Community* text teaches the first conduct, it is not contradictory since it is [referring to] the teaching of behaving according to your desire while engaged in elaborations and the mere intention and contemplation of engaging in elaborated conducts by the creation-stage practitioner.

In the *Integrated Practices*, [Āryadeva] explains that, if you could never perform the elaborated conducts described in the *[Buddha] Union*, due to insufficiency of wealth, [then,] concerning the explanation to perform the two latter conducts according to that tantra's statement:

> Each day, or each month,
> Or likewise, each year,
> While being richly blessed,
> Perform the dance of Buddha Super Bliss!

—this teaches the two latter [types of] the conduct, performed in the two later times [mentioned]. As Chag's translation phrases it, "While by your achievement itself," explaining that you should perform [the conducts] as your wealth allows, [293b] which intends that this teaches the two latter conducts. One should not interpret the two latter conducts of this text [as being the same as] the two conducts of the *Community*. In this [*Buddha Union*] text, the [Teacher] asserts that the former conducts being set down as three are in fact two, from the perspective of the intentions involved; the intention of engaging in desire and the intention of learning the embodiment. The first of these is the threefold engagement by a person with intense thirst and lust, with the intention of the conduct with whatever desirable objects are desired, while experiencing only through the organs, through the organs and samadhi both, and only through samadhi; [these three] explained respectively as the intentions to engage in the three [conducts], elaborated, unelaborated, and extremely unelaborated. As the *Root Tantra* seventh chapter declares:

> In regard to all enjoyment of desires,
> Resorting to them at your pleasure,
> By that sort of union [practice],
> You will quickly attain buddhahood.
>
> All enjoyment of desires,
> You should resort to them at pleasure,
> By the union of your own deity,
> You should worship self and other.

And:

> Do not recite while eating alms-food,
> Do not take pleasure in begging—
> Enjoying all desires,
> Recite not losing the elements of mantra.

The first of these verses means that the yogi/nī should practice as s/he pleases according to his or her faculties, engaging in elaborated conducts. The second means that in terms of the unelaborated, one should satisfy by worshiping self and other by the samadhi of one's own nature with the five sense objects for tasting bliss as one desires. The third means [294a] that, with the "eating of alms-food" as an example, not to recite [mantra] by engaging in seeking and so forth like someone going begging. Not only should you not be attached to begging but your body should abide without craving even food, which is the way to engage in the extremely unelaborated conducts. This is asserted in accordance with the explanation in the *Illuminating Lamp*. Relying on the statement in the former case "to engage in accordance with one's faculties," it is interpreted as revealing the three intentions with which one engages in the conducts.

Here the main thing is to engage with sense objects aiming for the purpose of the nondual communion, great bliss wisdom, as is explained above as similar for all three conducts. You can understand by what the *Root Tantra* says—

> The passionate one who desires intuitive wisdom
> Always resorts to the [five] objects of desire . . .

—that this is not engaging only for the sake of the organs. Engaging in sense objects thus becomes the art of freshly producing enlightenment spirit where there was none before, maintaining [the already produced] without loss, and maximizing it even more, this is enjoying ceaselessly as one pleases according to one's inclinations and desires; and this is the same for all three conducts. So the two [verses' two] lines that begin with "desire" and the third that begins with "enjoying all desires" are similarly stated. Thus, in order for those teachings not to be redundant, it is said that they teach the three conducts. The passage, from "begging and so forth . . . ," rejects the obstacle to meditating the path [294b] caused by distraction from activities of seeking and getting, due to excessive craving for food. It is not rejecting always practicing from the point of view of understanding the nature of desire objects, so the statement that "you should be content just by keeping the body maintained" means you should maintain the body without harming the increase of its elements, and does not just mean keeping one's life sustained. That such a way is not a distinctive characteristic of the third conduct can be known from the section in the sixteenth chapter where you depend on the food of the unelaborated. As for not interpreting this to refer to merely sustaining your life, you can know that by analyzing the necessity in general, that you should always rely on desire objects.

As for the intention to learn the embodiment, while the former [conducts done with the intention of engaging in desires] keep the senses focused on the sense objects, here [the three are] the learning of the deity in the context of the first conduct, the learning in the context of mere mind in the second [conduct], and the intention of meditating on voidness in the third [conduct]. Here the *Illuminating Lamp* seventh chapter explains that the general, hidden, and ultimate meanings of the enjoyment of sense objects apply to [the occasions of] the three conducts.

In the context of the path, [Chandrakīrti] interprets [the enjoyment of desires in the three conducts] as respectively referring to [first,] the stages from single-mindedness up to the beginner's achievement, [second,] the stages from body isolation up to the magic [body], and third, the stages of clear light and communion. By learning the elaborated conduct, while meditating the desire objects as divine with the intention to meditate engaging with desire objects, you meditate the five objects from form to texture as from Vairochana to Akshobhya and offer [each] to [its] own clan deity. And while each object has inferior, mediocre, [295a] and superior [qualities], they are the same when meditated as divine, so still you worship with the five supreme [sense objects]. Otherwise, Chandrakīrti states in the *Illuminating Lamp* that the goddesses such as Lochanā, or the meditating on the five Vajrā [sense object goddesses, Rūpavajrā etc.], should be enjoyed while seeing all of them as the enjoyments of Vajradhara. Thus, as for the statement of the three ways, in answer to the question, "through desire for passionate wisdom, what are you going to do by that reliance on sense objects in all paths of the conducts?" it is stated:

> "Please the bodhisattva! Desire the sun of enlightenment!"

The *Illuminating Lamp* says that this means that, having pleased the bodhisattva of the eye and other sense organs you should satisfy the [female] "bodhisattvas," [the goddesses] of the four elements and the sun, the [buddhas of the] five aggregates; so it is for the purpose of expanding one's senses, elements, and five aggregates. As for offering to one's own clan deity, it is to take Vairochana and so on as the chief, and is not just that alone. It teaches that you should worship with the supreme objects, intending that, as to the aspect of whatever object meditated as divine, when you directly enjoy it, your sense organ with its support will expand if it is attractive, and will not expand if it is otherwise [unpleasant], so you should worship [both kinds] with the supreme [qualities in mind]. When you meditate the five objects as the four goddesses Lochanā and so on, you identify Māmakī as both in the vajra and jewel clans, so you meditate her as both sound and texture.

Though the three [conducts] are thus explained, the chief sense object is the sense object of the wisdom [consort], so you should meditate the latter two [sense objects, taste and texture,] as chief. As for the way of [295b] putting this into practice, the seventh chapter [of the *Community*] states:

> Constantly unite your mind
> To form, sound, taste, and so on;
> This concentrates the secret essence
> Of all the buddhas.

And the *Illuminating Lamp* explains that you should always day and night develop the mental orientation toward meditating objects as divine and this is the usually hidden art that is the means of attaining the exalted state of buddhahood, hence the "concentrated essence." Thus, in meditating the five objects as deities, by meditating continuously, specifically making [yourself] see forms and so on as deities, you must first produce a stable experience [of those objects as deities].

Furthermore, you visualize that the Rūpavajrā goddess, emerging from the transformation of all the inner and outer material sense-media, holds in her lotus-soft hand a mirror, which she beholds with a calm eye, and her pearl necklace pendant hangs on her swelling breast, her blouse slightly loosened to reveal her beautiful torso—so from looking steadily at her form, you contemplate the arisal of great bliss. Likewise sounds are created as Shabdavajrā, singing sweet songs and playing on the lute; scents are created as Gandhavajrā, dancing and holding a jeweled vessel filled with scents such as saffron, eaglewood, snake-essence sandalwood, and camphor, pervading everything with excellent scents; tastes are created as Rasavajrā, holding precious vessels of gold and silver filled with various tastes and divine elixirs; and [296a] textures are created as Sparshavajrā, adorned with all signs, with the three [brow-]creases of fierce intensity, with a slender waist and wide navel curling clockwise, with exquisite lower torso and pelvis, her movements slow and graceful, her face completely smiling and gazing [at you] with passionate eyes. In this way you contemplate the expansion of great bliss by enjoying forms, sounds, scents, and tastes and engaging with textures through mutual embrace. Those ways of meditating can also be employed with Lochanā and so on, and you should analyze whether you must meditate [her] as like Vairochana, very beautiful in form and the three middle [buddha-goddesses] as having hand signs as above, and whether the fifth [buddha-goddess] holds textures of superior clothes. One would think that for each of them one should meditate the different members of the clan in common.

When one practices like that, first of all, bliss is produced in the mind, and then gradually, indirectly, the body endowed with the supported sense faculty expands; since the Lord of Reasoning [Dharmakīrti] said:

> When this transforms, those also
> Are experienced as transforming

—that is, when the mind becomes extremely blissful, the body also is seen to gain a good glow, and so samadhi becomes the cause of expansion that expands the body's elements. Such being the case, the jasmine-like enlightenment spirit increases, and the melting-bliss samadhi increases, and by meditating voidness with it the supreme realizations of the perfection stage are completely produced, and their root of virtue is developed. Once such samadhi becomes stable, [296b] when the senses directly enjoy the five sense objects, you realize the samadhi previously meditated, and by restraining the attitude of ordinariness that is the counteragent of great bliss—that is said to be the supreme discipline of the system of this path that binds the door of the senses.

This is the intention of meditating the conduct with the sense objects, from the beginning of meditating the path for as long as one cannot develop the voids by dissolving the energies into the *dhūti* by the power of meditating the penetration of the vital points of the body. Further, when you unite bliss and void by dissolving the energies into the *dhūti* by the power of such meditation, as long as you cannot eclipse the sign-habit elaborations, it is called "the intention of the elaborated [conduct]." Though the creation-stage practitioner lacks the two latter conducts from the point of view of meditation and intention, they have all three types of conducts from the point of view of the measure of elaborations concerning objects and activities.

This instruction must be implemented from the beginning of the creation stage, as it is extremely important for the beginner. From the time when you can develop the voids as the energies dissolve by the power of meditation, for as long as you have not attained the fourth stage clear light, you develop the previously trance-induced voids, and in the aftermath context, you create yourself as Vajradhara and you seal with the three voids both conducts engaged with sense objects, and you enjoy them in the mode of offering them to Vajradhara. In comparison with the former, your elaborations of signs are slight, but you have not directly realized thatness, so your meditational intention is to learn the unelaborated conduct. Furthermore, from the point of view of meditation and intention, [297a] while you have neither the elaborated nor the extremely unelaborated conducts, you do have all three conducts from the point of view of ritual activities and so forth.

From the time of attaining the learner's communion, for as long as you have not attained the nonlearner's communion, in the aftermath occasion, you seal your engagement with sense objects with the development of the direct realization of thatness, and you are liberated from the seeds of truth insistence and sign-habit elaborations, and so have the meditation and intention of the extremely unelaborated conduct. Both this and the former [conducts] have the meditation and intention for the sense objects to dawn as deities. This [conduct], though it lacks both the two previous conducts from the point of view of meditation and intention, if you classify it from the point of view of activities and so on, it is like the previous, [more advanced practitioner's conducts].

[**VI.B.3.c.ii.c′** – The method of learning the conducts]

The third has two parts: [1′] The way of achieving the elaborated and unelaborated conducts; and [2′] The way of achieving the extremely unelaborated conduct.

[**VI.B.3.c.ii.c′1′** – The way of achieving the elaborated and unelaborated conducts]

The first has two parts: [a′] Common procedures [for both]; and [b′] Particular procedures [for each].

[**VI.B.3.c.ii.c′1′a′** – Common procedures (for both)]

As for the place where these two conducts are achieved, from the old translation of the *Integrated Practices* quote of the *[Buddha] Union*:

> Further, practice [anywhere] in the three realms,
> Or in a pleasure garden.

And from the Patsab translation:

> The three worlds are your pleasure garden.

And the Chag translation:

> Practice in a holy place,
> Or in your own pleasure garden.

Or in the separate translation of the tantra [itself]:

> Practice in your own place
> Or in a pleasure garden.

As in all these, you should practice in your own abode or in a pleasure garden, a place agreeable to your mind, free from any [297b] ill-destined persons.

As for how to get your house together, you should make it a three-storied deity house made of glazed brick, with four doors, four corners, and four porticos, adorned with various ornaments such as jewel decorations. Otherwise an earthen house with a strong fence wall adorned with ornaments. Those two are the excellent and the inferior [kinds of] houses, though they should be the same in having three stories; so the latter should not be some sort of three-level earthen cave. Therein, as for the process of adorning through worship; on the first floor are the kitchen and the gathering areas, on the second floor you should arrange the lutes and song and music equipment, and the upper floor, as above explained, you should adorn with the jewel ornaments, the bells and yak tails and canopies and so on, since it is the place of the gathering of supremely fortunate yogis and yoginīs of multifarious glories. Up to there the two [later] conducts are similar.

If there you engage in elaborated conduct, set up twenty variegated lotus seats covered with cloths with one more for the chief. If it is unelaborated, set them up according to the number of the gathering. As for the change of costumes of the yogis and yoginīs, according to the explanation of the *[Buddha] Union* and as explained in the *[Community]* sixteenth chapter:

> Of the body, speech, and mind vajras,
> Meditating the body, speech, and mind,

> Do that by one's own natural way—
> Thus you will attain accomplishments.

—and in commentary on that:

> "One's [own natural] way . . ." is doing it by the very change of costume, not just [298a] by meditating.

Thus, the yogi/nīs of three vajras when they performs the discipline of the science [consort], this is explained for them and their consort seal. As for the substance of the mask, the Great Translator's and Patsab's version of the *Integrated Practices* and the separate translation of the *[Buddha] Union* state "the nature of the element and life and arisen from a root," about the latter of which, Chag's translation "a living being, [and] arisen from a root" is better. This means you should make the mask out of precious elements such as gold or silver, or human bone, or animal products, or from the root of a tree, and so on. The *Illuminating Lamp* explains that you should make it out of wood etc. As for the form of craftsmanship, it can either be poured in a mold, carved in relief, manufactured by beating, or painted. You should make it according to the deity as far as faces and arms etc., color, and symbolic implements. As the old translation of the *Integrated Practices* and the Chag translation say:

> Surround it with the seal,
> Who practices oriented toward one's deity

—they explain that you do not need the seal who serves as the science [consort] of this [deity]. Nevertheless, as Patsab['s translation] says:

> The masks of one's deity
> Do bring forth the seal of accomplishment

—so the masks of one's deity do occasion the accomplishment that is the costumed seal, which is the meaning of "surround." Also, the separate translation of the *[Buddha] Union*:

> You should perform with the seal of achievement
> In the costume of your deity. **[298b]**

The *Integrated Practices* old translation says:

> Poured or carved,
> Manufactured or painted,
> Images of various forms,
> Thus conceive the marked seal.

The "marked seal" here is not explained as "masked," since it is clearly explained in the tantra to be the marked seal's symbolic implement. Thus, Patsab's translation [separating images and marked seal with] "images of various forms and . . ." is preferable.

The *Integrated Practices* old translation says:

> Instructing well the consorts,[159]
> Endowed with your own deity,
> The fortunate one is marked by his/her own seal.
> Thus conceive the group mandala.

The meaning of the first phrase is like what is stated in the separate translation of the tantra, "similar to your own deity." As for how it is similar, you should understand it according to Patsab's translation:

> By the masks of your own deity
> Practice well with the consorts.

However, "instruct well" is a preferable translation. This arrangement of the places of yogis and yoginīs who are costumed according to the number of deities of the mandala is called "the group mandala." In the *[Buddha] Union Root Tantra* it is stated that here the disciple is given consecration.

Further, [there is] the yogi/nī who is the agent of conduct in the center

159. Though the word is *bud med rnams*, "women," I translate "consorts," to make this applicable as instruction for a yoginī as well as a yogi, which the tradition maintains as theoretically possible if practically only rarely done. The inflected Sanskrit and Tibetan grammars rarely resort to gender-differentiated pronouns, and when they do, the male by grammatical rule stands for both male and female, as the English "man" generically includes women in the category of humankind. In what follows from the *Buddha Union*, the goddesses etc. cannot so easily be neutralized in gender.

of the mandala; and the four consorts respectively in the east, south, west, and north of the first row of that are established as the four goddesses, Saṁvaramāyā, Ahosukhā, Dīpā, and Shashī. The last of these are translated by Chag as "*ri bong can*" [Shashī, i.e., Moon]. These [299a] are consorts for accompanying the conduct.

In the clockwise direction in the quarter directions from the southeast there are four consorts who are established as the four goddesses, Buddhabodhī, Dharmachakrī, Tridhātuvijayī, and Kamānkushī.

Outside of those in the second row also clockwise in the quarter directions from the southeast there are four consorts arrayed as the four goddesses, Lingbuma, Gyumangma, Gyugcigma, and Gyutugpoma, the latter three of which can be recognized from the seal section of the *[Buddha] Union* as Piwangma, Ngadumma, and Dzangama.[160]

Outside of those in the third row also clockwise in the quarter directions from the southeast there are four consorts arrayed as the four goddesses, Vajrapushpā, Vajragandhā, Vajradīpā, Vajrāṇjalī, holding, respectively, flowers, incense, a fine lamp, and a conch vessel full of perfume.

In the third row clockwise from the east[161] in the doors are four consorts standing in the form of Āshvāsyā, Vajrashukārāsyā, Vajrālokā, and Rajaḥpranashanavetạlā, whose [name] means "zombie having died and become dust." The other sixteen are recognized by the meaning of being consorts with whom one is to engage.

The *Illuminating Lamp* fifteenth chapter states that you should make the mandala with the mandala rites of the context of the unelaborated conduct of the creation stage, and such [299b] is the position of the master Gö; [yet] it is preferable to perform [the rites] by drawing well the mandala with watercolors. If you are an unelaborated yogi/nī of the *Community*, draw the *Community* mandala with watercolors, and enter with costumes and masks that conform to the size of the group, setting each deity in its place.

160. If the *Sang rgyas mnyam sbyor* exists in Sanskrit, one would have more confidence about these names in Sanskrit—Saṁvaramāyā, Emahosukhā, Dīpā, and Shashi; Buddhabodhī, Dharmachakrī, Tridhātuvijayī, and Kamāṇkushī; Dhvaninalā, Bāhutantrī, Ekatantrī, Ghaṇatantrī (also Vīnā, Dundubhī, Mṛdaṇgī).

161. The text says "southeast," but the doors are in the cardinal, not quarter, directions, so I have emended.

[VI.B.3.c.ii.C′1′b′ – Particular procedures (for each)]

The second has two parts: [i′] The elaborated rites; and [ii′] The unelaborated rites.

[VI.B.3.c.ii.C′1′b′i′ – The elaborated rites]

Granted that the noble father and sons do not state clearly that the *Esoteric Community* practitioner should perform the elaborated and unelaborated rites in such a way, they do advocate the performance of the elaborated conduct from the point of view of the *Community*. As for performing it, [considering] how it is performed, [it is] granted that some people say you should perform it adding two goddesses in the male and female yogi/nī costumes to the twenty goddesses explained in the *[Buddha] Union*. Nevertheless, the *Integrated Practices* states that you should perform it together with the disciple included in the same clan; thus the rites of the mandalas of the *[Buddha] Union* and the *Community* are not in common. Therefore, if you perform the elaborated conduct with the system of the *Community*, you must do it adding the elaborations such as seal and seal response explained in other tantras, keeping them equal to the number of deities of the *Community*.

If you perform it according to the *[Buddha] Union*, together with the yogi/nīs of the two stages, meditating voidness objectified as ultimate reality, then you create [the mandala] with complete characteristics, beginning with the stacked elements and mount Meru, on top of which emerge the lotus and variegated vajra-cross producing the earth base, up to the [300a] measureless mansion with vajra pinnacle, containing the deity seats. Then you create Vajrasattva etc., whichever lord, by the process of self-consecration, and you sit in the manner of being lord of the mandala and then create the retinue, creating twenty consorts in the actuality of such and such a goddess, and they themselves each create themselves in such a manner. The *Integrated Practices* only expresses that much in words; it is clear that you must fill in the procedure by such things as previously meditating the defense wheel and bringing in the wisdom heroes.

Then, you engage with desire objects; first preparing by remembering that you have the nature of the pattern of true samadhi, thinking "I must satisfy the transcendent buddhas abiding within my body mandala!" First engage with visual, audial, and olfactory objects. Then, as for engaging with tastes, purify, transmute, and blaze your foods, remember your natural inner fireplace and eat with the attitude that you are offering burnt offerings to the mouth of the samadhi hero. Thereby it will be easily digested and will become an elixir practice. Thus, by food and drink you satisfy the aggregates and elements of your physical vajra body. Finally, the way of engaging with textures, within the twenty together-engaging and after-engaging goddesses, take a seal as you please who is skilled in the arts of desire, and place her on your lap. Thinking, "Relying on this one, I will achieve completely the great seal accomplishment!" [300b] create a stable determination, engage in the process from coupling with her up to stimulating the channels, and you abide in the action of union endowed with the posture of your own clan.

Here, the *Integrated Practices* states that you should use postures such as the transcendent, vajra, jewel, lotus, and action [clan postures], which is the system of the death-transition of each specific lord. Then from the friction of the vajra and the lotus, all the transcendent buddhas, who are the actuality of the aggregates and so forth, melt the vowel and consonant enlightenment spirits down from the 72,000 channels beginning from the crown, like streams of water cascading down a mountain cliff. Then, with [the mind] descending by the stages of generating dispassionate luminance, passionate radiance, and semipassionate imminence, finally each yogi/nī introspectively comes to realize the actuality of transcendent wisdom, universal void clear light. This is principally explained according to the system of the *[Buddha] Union*, as the experience of the four joys falling from the crown to the jewel-tip. However, it is not that this system does not also, as will be explained below, [teach] the generation of the four voids through the process of dissolving into the heart center. Here, as for the statement that the yogi/nī who attains the supreme performs the wondrous deeds of punishing and upholding in that very group mandala from the door of the six clans, it is mostly [referring to] the time after attaining the learner's communion; and those deeds are stated in the *[Buddha] Union*.

Thus, at the end of cultivating the creation of the orgasmic [wisdom-intuition] by relying on the consort seal, [301a] arising from that, the lord who is the actuality of great bliss, in order to teach strongly the great *ārali* play, which quickly gives rise to the Dharma of fulfilling the aims of self and other, there is the stage of performing the dance of the buddha-music.

Together with the yoginīs, the lord shows seal-gestures, the science [consort] shows a response to that seal-gesture; and so by the gesture and the gesture response, the worship and the worship response, the dance and the dance response, and the song and the song response, and by those physical and verbal signs the symbolic conventions are performed. When the *Integrated Practices* explains the latter two [conducts], except for the brief mention of seal-gesture and seal-gesture-response and worship and worship-response, it does not mention the others, so they must be known from other [sources]. As for the need for performing those, the *Integrated Practices* says that it is for the sake of not letting the mind turn elsewhere and to mutually delight each other, meaning that the mind should not deviate from great bliss, and to mutually increase the bliss.

You should totally engage in the conduct day and night, by the previously explained meditation and intention, meditating the orgasmic [wisdom] in trance relying on engagement with desire objects, and arising from that in the aftermath engaging with desire objects through many elaborations concerning the seal consort and so forth. If you perform the elaborated conducts with the system of the *Esoteric Community*, at the end of meditating according to the performances of the two stages, having established on thirty one seats in the deity places yogis and yoginīs equal in number to the thirty-two deities with thirty-two costumes, [301b] after having enjoyed the five desire objects as taught above, you should add the elaborations of performing the seal-gestures and the gesture responses. The procedure of the rites will be explained [below].

[**VI.B.3.c.ii.c′1′b′ii′** – The unelaborated rites]

The *Integrated Practices* teaches three ways of the unelaborated conduct; if you cannot completely make the condensed mandala for the unelaborated conduct due to insufficient wealth, you should perform the unelaborated conduct with the five thatnesses together with the five seal consorts; or, if you do not have that, you should perform the unelaborated conduct together with a single consort. Or if you have sufficient wealth you should perform the unelaborated conduct having completely created the condensed mandala. Then, if you cannot create the condensed mandala completely, it is a question of having or not having all the equipment such as costumes and so on for the yogis and yoginīs equal in number to the deities, it is not a matter of performing or not performing the meditative rites in the complete mandala. Since the *Illuminating Lamp* fifteenth chapter states, in the context when the Akshobhya yogi/nī performs the unelaborated conduct together with his/her seal consort, that the deities of the mandala meditated as the Akshobhya mandala should adorn the mandala, the meditation of the full deities of the mandala is the same in all three forms of the unelaborated conduct.

Thus, in the watercolor drawn mandala, the arrangement of the thirty-one variegated lotus seats covered with cloths as the deities' places and the [302a] twenty-three yogis and nine yoginīs arrayed with the deity costumes is the expansive unelaborated. As for the medium unelaborated, the conduct of the thatness of the five secrets, the *Illuminating Lamp Root Commentary* fifteenth chapter states that you should place day and night the practitioner meditated as Vajradhara on the central seat and four consorts well learned in mantra and tantra visualized as the actualities of the four goddesses Lochanā etc. on the seats of Lochanā etc. [On the other hand,] the *Integrated Practices* states that four consorts with the forms of the four goddesses Rūpavajrā etc. should be placed in the four quarters, and one consort with the form of Sparshavajrā should abide upon your lap. If you only have five consorts, then it is obvious you have to choose between those two [options]. The sixteenth chapter *[Illuminating Lamp]*'s explanation that the three-clan yogi/nīs should practice with Lochanā, Māmakī, and Pāṇḍarāvāsinī is cited by the *Integrated Practices* as a source for the unelaborated conduct with a single consort. Thus, it is not definite that the lord's consort seal should be created as only Sparshavajrā, which should also be understood with regard to the other two [forms of the] unelaborated conduct. Therefore, if you perform the medium unelaborated, you should place five variegated lotuses covered with cloths in the center of the mandala and in the inner four corners; or you should place the five seats and six costumes on the second row four corners [and in the center]. If you perform the condensed unelaborated, you should use two seats and two costumes.

Then, as for the actual stages of the rite, the *Integrated Practices* states:[162]

162. This quote closely corresponds to the extant text (CW, Tib. p. 636), as do the following passages identified as from the Patsab translation, which could either be paraphrase or quite likely alternate translation, not available to us. It is very close to the existing text in general terms.

> There create the measureless mansion with the vajra jewel pinnacle, purify the outer seal consort, [302b] and you should practice the great seal [embrace] together with the disciple included within one clan. The process of that is, first only, understanding ultimate reality, then arising by the process of self-consecration, emitting and then internalizing Akshobhya, you abide as the very lord and master of the mandala.

As for the way of creating the retinue, Patsab's translation of the *Integrated Practices* is clear:

> Then, having visualized the deities of the mandala such as Vairochana, the retinue unwaveringly free of any notions of ordinariness who serve as members of your own body mandala, you should propitiate the whole mandala circle.

[It goes on to] state that:

> Then, together with your seal consort you enter ultimate reality by the stages of holistic holding and serial dissolution [samadhis]. Then the goddesses, Lochanā etc., exhort you with the verses "You the vajra mind" and so on, you arise instantaneously by the self-consecration stage, and, in order to experience the supreme joy, with the nine aesthetic moods, you first engage with form, sound, scent, and taste, and then with texture, taking whichever consort, such as one of the butcher caste, and uniting with her.

There, it is not clear in fine detail about just how you perform the rite of prime union. The position of master Gö is that [right] from the defense wheel [visualization] you should completely meditate the prime union, claiming that to be the position of Tsunmojen and Trinshugjen,[163] and the creation-stage practitioner should follow the evocation by using the three rite creation and so on, [303a] while the perfection-stage practitioner should use the instantaneous creation. There are also explanations in other trea-

163. *sPrin shugs can*, presumably another adept with a tradition of personal instructions.

tises that you should use instantaneous creation in the self-creation context, once you have completed the creation stage.

In regard to the tendency of the *Integrated Practices* statements, they are suitable for both the Vajradhara and Akshobhya practitioners; in general, they serve for the taking [whichever] as chief from [among] the six clans, and are similar for both stages. As for creating the measureless mansion on the peak of Sumeru, it was explained previously in the context of the mother tantras, but is unnecessary here. The creation-stage practitioner in this [*Esoteric Community*] context is capable of producing the distinctive orgasmic [wisdom-intuition] by means of the four joys in all three occasions, the prime union, the entry into clear light at the end of the supreme mandala triumph, and the reliance on the actual science consort upon arising therefrom; therefore this is not the same as other [tantras'] creation-stage occasions.

As for the supreme mandala triumph, once you enter the trance-union with the actual science consort, you create the habitat and inhabitant mandala in the mother's lotus. As for emitting Akshobhya, bringing him into oneself after radiating [many emanations of] him and so on, and thus becoming Anger Vajra, it is in terms of two clans; and you should do it correspondingly in terms of whatever other clan [lord] as chief [deity]. Having emitted [the deities] from Vairochana to Sumbharāja and having dissolved them into the thirty-one male and female yogi/nīs of your retinue, you should imagine them as indivisible. By meditating your retinue with deity yoga you eliminate the pride of ordinariness, and so should not be disturbed by that concept [of ordinariness].

As for the meaning of [the deities'] becoming components of your body mandala, those members of the retinue [303b] are the members of your body, visualizing the parts as of the nature of the [five] aggregates and so forth. Both you and your retinue should meditate in that way. In regard to [practicing] with the five seal consorts and with the one seal consort, you should dissolve the [visualized deities] into whichever are actually there, and in the case of those who are not there, you should do the same dissolving each into their own place. In regard to the expression "having pleased the entire circle of the mandala," the Chag translation has "having impassioned," which means that you have already reached the supreme mandala triumph and you have pleased the deities by uniting in trance with the actual science consort, from the point of view of the deities being parts of your body. It is not only [a question of] just having united and entered into clear light, but it also means adding the meditations of yoga through the two contemplations and creating the four voids through the door of compressing the energy-mind into the heart center, as previously explained. That is to be understood as applicable to other contexts of trance-union, though [ultimately] it is connected to the perfection stage itself.

As for being exhorted by songs after immersing in clear light, you should visualize it in the extensive unelaborated [conduct], in the case where there are four consorts in the inner corner directions meditated as Lochanā and so forth, actually exhorting with song meditated as the five Vajrā [sense goddesses], and [to be visualized] in the case where there is but the single consort seal. Or else it is obvious that it is also suitable that in the former case the four goddesses in this context are held with the pride of being Lochanā and so on and so exhort [you]. Arising from that, as for the statement about enjoyment of the good, bad, and medium of the first four [desire-]objects, it obviously intends that from just this boundary of the path, the inferior objects serve as auxiliaries [304a] to your inner bliss.

When you are in the first three occasions of the perfection stage, and, having attained the beginning of the path of mind isolation, you are performing the conduct for the sake of the magic body, you can create it instantaneously without creating it from syllable and symbolic implement and so on. Above the measureless mansion, you create the intuition place, and on the occasion of compressing the visualization into clear light, it is compressed by the power of dissolving the energies. Although both magic body [adepts] and learner's communion [adepts] can practice this, there is a great difference [between them] in intensity of power.

As for resurrecting from the void in the body of the primal savior, you can arise from the energy-mind in conformity with the third-stage magic body at the time of mind isolation. If you are a magic body [adept] it actually can be done, but when you enter the void while still not having realized the clear light, it does not serve to purify the magic body. When you arise, it is an arisal of the mind from the metaphoric clear light and is not an arisal in a new body. When you attain communion [in the future], there is no interruption of the homogeneity of the magic body, so [at this stage] you should enter into and arise from the clear light basing [yourself] on the mind and not upon the magic body. Therefore, from both of those [stages], when you arise from clear light you should take up in your mind whatever [deity] body you already have [developed] through the process of visualization.

As for maintaining the emanation body, you should create your coarse body as an emanation body by bringing back together what was separated from the coarse body. Though you have attained [only a measure of] virtual conformity with the magic body, you can make it similar to the actual [magic body] in the experience of your mentality.

In those explanations, you should understand [their application to all three;] the occasion of the prime union, [304b] the creation of the orgasmic [intuition] from union with the science consort at the end of the supreme mandala triumph, and the arisal from that and so forth. In the *[Root Tantra]* seventeenth chapter commentary, as it explains that, after the arisal upon exhortation with song, you uphold the pride of the four clans such as Vairochana and you perform the unions with all four goddesses, Lochanā and so forth, it is clear that here also you must perform that, the same in both stages. And that corresponds with taking those four goddesses as the consorts who unite with the chief [deity]. Further, those uniting consorts, since they serve as the science consorts of the lord, are also clearly engaging as Rūpavajrā and so on also. By that reason, in the case of the medium and concise form of the unelaborated conduct, they are classified according to the number of the circle of science consorts and not according to the number of male [deities].

As for the *Integrated Practices* statement that you should perform relying on whichever of the five, such as low-caste consorts and so forth, it is in terms of there being no certainty about caste for the perfection-stage practitioner; the creation-stage practitioner is explained as having a consort of his own clan. Whichever of the two clans are there, as for the actual conduct, having trance-united with the consort of your own occasion, you create orgasmic joy and meditate through uniting bliss and void; you do not meditate yourself as the lord [alone], in a mantric body if a creation-stage practitioner, and in a magic body if a magic body [adept].

There is no explicit explanation as to how often in a day you practice this rite of the conduct, but since the sixteenth chapter root commentary states, in the context of the conduct, that you should make the secret offering while trance-united with the science consort in the four times, [305a] you should perform this in four sessions.

The *[Buddha] Union* states that the group circle rite, relying on the group mandala, should be performed once each year and once each month. The *Integrated Practices*, concerning its statement about the two latter conducts, as it is not referring to the conduct in the context of its explanation of the four boundaries when performing the conduct, its meaning is not an explanation of whether or not there is elaboration of time in the conduct that has arrived at the high path of the two stages relying on that scriptural reference. If you engage in the elaborated [conduct] after engaging in textures, you perform from the perspective of your own specific meditation and intention concerning the seal gesture and its response; if you are [engaging in] the unelaborated [conduct], you do not perform [in that way]. Therefore, the old translation of the *Integrated Practices* wrote "here you should completely perform the *ārali*," but the Patsab translation "cause the accomplishment of the *ārali*" is better.

As for the statement that you should eat in solitude, having cleansed and so on the five meats and the five elixirs, it is similar for all the conducts of the two stages.

As for the *Integrated Practices* statement that

> All this should be perfected by the inner self itself, without binding of the consort, neither painting a mandala nor offering [in it] the symbolic universe, not performing external hearth fire sacrifice, not making stupas for placing clay images and so forth, not reading scriptures, abandoning physical asceticism, not performing prostrations to painted or wood or stone carved icons, not taking refuge in saints or hermit buddhas, and not relying on any astrology and so forth . . .

—this refers to the context of the conduct of the perfection stage; and does not include the context of conduct [on the creation stage; since it contains such a prohibition of] the binding of the seal consort [305b] and the painting of the mandala and so forth. By mistaking statements about not doing such things in the *Community*, and in many other tantras, the *Esoteric Accomplishment*, and the *Enlightenment Songs*, and so on, it seems that many act even from the time of being a beginner in such a way that the sharp minded do not perform those practices instantaneously and the dull-minded do them more gradually.

[**VI.B.3.c.ii.C′2′** – The way of achieving the extremely unelaborated conduct]

Second, as for which embodiment should perform this extremely unelaborated conduct, Tsunmojen explains it is only the perfection-stage practitioner and Kānhapa declares it can be anyone on the two stages; of these two you should take the latter as preferable, according to the view of master Gö.

As for the place, you should use a solitary mountain, a riverbank, near a waterfall, and a charnel ground and so forth—you do not practice this in a three-storied house.

As for the companion to provide your food, you should get a creature such as a forest spirit devotee, or a superior practitioner companion, or get your food from a large [monastic] community. As for the latter, Patsab translates "by getting just your rice gruel from a minister," meaning that wealthy persons such as ministers should serve as patrons. If you can get a forest spirit devotee, since wealth comes with performing either the elaborated or unelaborated [conduct], it is not definite that this [extremely unelaborated conduct] is performed only for the reason of lack of wealth of equipment.

As for the particulars of intention, there are four. First is when as a somewhat beginning practitioner you remember the beginningless suffering of the life cycle and desire the bliss of nirvana, you should abandon all socializing, and finally you should meditate the notion of suffering even concerning the gaining of power [306a] over the entire kingdom. Second, the two new translations are good, saying "you should destroy any entertaining of even anything as much as a grain of sesamum," which should be interpreted as not holding on to any accumulation of equipment such as a mere grain of sesamum, and you should not take it as meaning you should not identify the manifestations of the truth-habits. Third, through your faith in meditating clear light as ultimate reality, you should not be concerned for your body and life. Fourth, you should not be ambitious for the minor mundane accomplishments or the eight great [mundane] accomplishments, because they can become distractions and causes for regression.

For a creation-stage practitioner to perform the conduct, since s/he has the fully qualified spirit of enlightenment, granted s/he wants to attain buddhahood in general, since s/he performs the conduct with her/his mind attracted by common accomplishments, as long as s/he has not completed the creation stage and produced the perfection stages, except for the second intention, [s/he should focus on that, since] the other three apply only to the perfection-stage practitioner.

As for the distinctions of the seal consort, the *Integrated Practices* says[164] that, thus, abandoning the outer consort, you should perceive yourself uniting rather with the wisdom consort abiding in the heart center, thinking "thereby I will more quickly attain the vajradharahood," and you should perform the conduct only being alone, [meaning obviously that you should use] a wisdom consort. As for that wisdom consort, though Lakshmī says that the creation-stage practitioner brings forth the goddess with shape from within the heart center and the perfection-stage practitioner unites with the wisdom seal just through his/her meditation on voidness, [306b] it is rather the case that the perfection-stage practitioner also unites with the wisdom seal as having the form of a goddess. The *Illuminating Lamp* fifth chapter says that if you do not obtain an actual consort, you should bring forth the mother of buddhas, Transcendent Wisdom, from within your heart and perform union with her; and proves [that statement] with reasons. The sixteenth chapter *[Root Tantra]* says:

> Contemplating with the three-syllable vajra,
> Visualize your own consort with your mind,
> Thereby the omniscient buddhas
> Will doubtless be delighted.

The *Commentary* here says that this text teaches uniting with the wisdom seal, and that "contemplating with the three-syllable vajra" means that a three-vajra yogi such as Vairochana, who has no concern for any outer consort, brings forth as his seal the Vajradhātvīshvarī who dwells in his heart.

Thus, as for the explanation that "if you cannot find an outer consort, rely on the wisdom consort," it implies that the [reliance on a] wisdom seal cannot produce the samadhi of great bliss as [well as] the reliance on an external consort, and this intends that if you do find an outer consort, you should do the opposite of the previous statement about abandoning her and

164. The following closely paraphrases the canonical Tibetan (CW, p. 647).

relying on the wisdom consort. Further, it is like the statement of the *Illuminating Lamp* seventeenth chapter—both new translations—that those whose minds are not stable in union with the wisdom consort should rely on a physical consort. Though the old translation of the *Illuminating Lamp* states that "you should rely on the physical consort when your mind is stable," the above translations are better.

Like that, [307a] there seem to be particular [choices made] according to the type of a person and the way of learning with a wisdom consort after first meditating the path. In this regard, the creation-stage practitioner may indeed give up other elaborations, but the stage of the procedure is clearly similar, so one unites with the wisdom seal when completing the mandala triumph, generating the orgasmic joy by the processes of the four joys and meditating bliss-void. Thereupon, you arise exhorted by the songs of the meditated goddesses, enjoying the food and the science consort's desire objects through your contemplative visualization. In the three occasions of the perfection stage, relying on the appropriate process of the procedure of the evocation, when you unite with the wisdom consort, by the force of your combining it with the perfection of the yoga of the inner energies, you cut off the many dualistic elaborations and realize a distinctively excellent four voids. Then again, from the process of compressing that gathers the energy-mind in the heart center and the descent of the enlightenment spirit to the tip of the vajra, you have the ability to generate whatever possible of the four voids, but the main thing is to perform the previous [compression of the energies in the heart center].

Concerning this, the *Integrated Practices*' explanation of the aggregates' etc. subtle elements entering into energy, that into mind, that into mental functions, and that entering into misknowledge and after that your meditating the clear light—all this is performed relying on the wisdom seal; in the other conducts it is similar but relying on an actual seal. Nevertheless, here the statement of cultivating the sleep clear light itself is on the occasion of the conduct of the perfection stage, and that again, by this, by intermittent [307b] meditation of clear light, it seems to mean that you meditate with a merging of the clear light with sleep. And it does not mean that you perform separate ways of meditation of the clear light as on other occasions, when not merged with sleep but in waking time, and when merged with sleep in sleeping time. This you can understand when you understand all the keys of merging.

Thus, when you practice by performing the conducts on the two stages, except for differences of degree of the four joys and the four voids, by both you entrance yourself and rely on union with the wisdom consort and cultivate the orgasmic [bliss] and clear light itself. When you cannot abide therein and so arise, again, relying on that consort and increase that meditation as before. Here, your creativity is extremely intense, you are averse to elaborations, and from the perspective of your intense faith in meditating the orgasmic [wisdom] you perform the conduct as before; and this is called "the bhusuku conduct," because it is to maintain the conduct of eating, sleeping, and evacuating. As follows, the first syllable derives etymologically by adding syllables from *bhuñjana* and gives you "eating food," *sutana* is explained as sleeping, and *kuṭisara* is explained as evacuating by expelling excrement and urine. Except for just those three ideas, you abandon socializing, you don't consider body, sensations, objects, and senses, and you perform by merging sleep and clear light. Some also analyzed the *bhu* as coming from *bhukta*, again meaning "to eat."

By such a perfection-stage conduct, you will be caused to swiftly attain the magic body where your actual being transforms, the learner's communion vajra body, and the nonlearner's communion vajra body, without requiring the other two conducts. Thus, the sixth chapter commentary states that the "*bhusuku* conduct" is the supreme conduct. The *Integrated Practices* often cites the extremely unelaborated [308a] conduct as what you should explain as being the process explained by the *Crazy Discipline Sutra*, which occurs in the sixteenth chapter of the *Vajra Essence Ornament Tantra*. Concerning this, both new translations of the *Integrated Practices* follow the way and the process stated in the tantra, and state "you should practice the extremely unelaborated conduct by the crazy discipline." The Great Translator translates very well here "the sutra that teaches the crazy discipline." In that chapter, the conduct of the discipline is taught, that is said to be the "crazy discipline," and "taught" means "teach the crazy discipline," since this is not taught in the explanatory tantras of the *Community*.

By engaging in the conduct according to both that tantra and the *Community*, the goal to be achieved by that being practiced for six months is the exaltation of buddhahood; hence that is not the conduct of the creation stage.

The *Integrated Practices* declares that by learning the three conducts in a fortnight, or one month, or six months, the eight signs of the universal seal, such as subtle form and light texture, etc., and the dream signs stated in the *[Root] Tantra* fifteenth chapter will emerge. You will achieve whenever those signs emerge, even before six months. In that regard, the eight masteries such as mastery of the body are supreme accomplishments, as the Chag translation says:

> Subtle matter and light touch,
> True attainment, true pervasiveness,
> Firm extreme illumination itself—
> Mastery [308b] itself and all fulfillment.

These eight are called the "eight excellences of mastery," and not the "eight masteries." As to their meaning being explained by the previous, it seems that you cannot find an explanation of the eight excellences of mastery, so you should apply the explanation of the eight excellences of mastery by Avalokitavrata. Regarding that, such mastery involves the subtle causing the creation and destruction of the world of beings, the light causing of the creation and destruction of the world of things, and the ownership of the creation and destruction of both of them; so here the yogi/nī has the ability to emanate and dissolve those things.

The latter is shown by "true attainment." Going wherever the mind thinks [to go] is indicated by "true pervasiveness." Being worshipped by all elemental spirits is shown by one's appearing extremely illuminating and overwhelming all others by light and majesty. "Mastery" is having the power to [both] punish and support beings. As an excellence, developing the power of fulfillment is to possess "all fulfillment." This is shown by the ability to get whatever you want to get, relying on abiding in fulfilled delight.

Attaining the supreme in less than six months refers to the attaining of the learner's union. When you perform the conducts on the four occasions previously explained, since you practice until you attain your fruition, you do not calculate whether or not there is the elaboration of time.

Although you have practiced conduct thus by the two stages, if you do not swiftly achieve the fruition of each particular occasion, as for the way of being urged along [309a] each of the two stages, you should understand it from the *Root Tantra* tenth chapter commentary and Nāropa's *Further Tantra Commentary*.

[**VI.B.4.** – How the fruition will be attained at meditation's end]

Fourth, as for the way of realizing the fruition at the end of meditating the path, the *Illuminating Lamp* declares:

> Further the need is to be explained,
> The ritual procedures of peace and so on,
> Likewise, the eight accomplishments,
> And buddhahood as the supreme.

Thus, buddhahood is best, the eight great accomplishments is medium, and the deeds of peace, growth, power, and terror is least.

As for the eight accomplishments, the *Wisdom Vajra Compendium* directly mentions six and omits two:

> Mantra, medicine, fire sacrifice, powder, eye salve, swift foot, and so on, the eight great accomplishments.

The *Four Goddess Dialogue* explains the achievement of the eight substances and the limbs:

> Pills, and eye-salve medicines,
> The underground, the sword accomplishment,
> Flying in the sky, invisibility,
> Deathlessness, and healing sicknesses.

The *Vajra Pavilion* says:

> Eye salve, speed travel,
> Sword, underground accomplishments,
> Pill, sky-walking,
> Invisibility, and fasting.

The latter two fruitions [eight accomplishments and four deeds] are collected in the common accomplishments, giving two kinds, supreme and common, as the *Further Tantra* says:

The accomplishments of invisibility and so on
Are explained as the ordinary [ones];
Buddha proclaimed the attainment of buddhahood,
To be the supreme accomplishment.

At the end of learning the creation stage and its conduct, [309b] as for the way of achieving the common accomplishments, you can understand it from reading the *Tantra Commentary*.

At the end of learning the perfection stage and its conduct, as for the way of achieving the nonlearner's communion, it is as previously explained. When you have realized the predawn clear light transparence through the two enlightenments outer and inner, at the time of the manifestation of the ultimate truth body, the learner's communion magic body becomes the nonlearner's communion magic body, and you abide without deviating from those two bodies as long as the samsaric life cycle lasts [for other beings].

As for the objective clear light transparence endowed with two such purities, it is called the "uncreated truth body," the "subjective clear light intuition truth body," and the "great bliss body."

Its support embodiment matter body is the beatific body made of energy-mind only, those two bodies being [merely] conceptually different but one in actuality, frequently referred to as the "intuition body nondual with the matter body," so you should understand that the claim that the noble father and sons' positions are that the matter body is not included in the buddha-stage but only in the continuum of the disciples, that the matter body is [coarsely] material and actually different from consciousness, and that there is no intuitive wisdom in the context of fruition, and so forth, is not a valid claim.

Such a communion body creates many emanations such as the supreme emanation body, and having taken the emanation body communion body as one, you can understand well the arrangement of the two [beatific and truth] bodies in the communion body. In other mantra treatises there certainly are explanations of emanation body matter body as embodiment of intuitive wisdom, mind as [310a] truth body, and speech as beatific body, but the position of the father and sons is as above.

As previously explained, at the end of other paths you add the distinctive mantric path and attain buddhahood in Akanishta heaven, and that is accepted as unexcelled buddhahood. However, that does not contradict the explanation of attaining buddhahood in an embodiment that desires buddhahood in one lifetime from entering the unexcelled path from the beginning; because positing buddhahood through the unexcelled system and attaining buddhahood having entered the unexcelled path from the beginning do not have the same meaning. You can understand from what was explained above the subtle differences of the systems of achieving the truth and matter bodies of these two kinds of buddhahoods.

As for attaining buddhahood in the embodiment of a magic body person who has attained the magic body in a human embodiment, it is easy to understand how that is buddhahood in a human embodiment. When a yogi/nī in a human embodiment, having given up his/her human lifespan, achieves the magic body in place of becoming a between being, that embodiment for attaining buddhahood in that embodiment, though it is not included in the six migrations of beings, is not contradicted; just as, for example, the nonreturner [saint] attains nirvana in the between and attains arhatship in that [between] embodiment.

Having meditated such a path, one abides in the buddha-beatific-body with its seven components, but there is no certainty about the emanation body. Therefore, as for the sky union component of the beatific body, it is declared that it creates the bestowal of the great bliss of play through the entrancement of union with many science companions such as the orgasmic [science consorts], [310b] and in conformity with that fruition, in the time of the path, one performs totally expansive great bliss by the way of playing with the desire objects of youth and beauty.

On the occasion of the fruition, you must settle [your insight] through objections and answers, and though there seem to be many more, here I have explained those points of the greatest difficulty. And I have not written about [all] the difficult points of formulations common to both universal vehicles, both because you can understand them from others and I fear the book will become too long.

Thus, as prophesied to teach the ultimate definitive meaning of the sutras, the ultimate of all sutras, the sole jewel of the three worlds, the *Glorious Esoteric Community*, the great king of tantras famous as the sun and moon, the savior Nāgārjuna, father and sons, having realized the meaning, elucidated it as they had seen it themselves, and fully and clearly explained all the meanings of the keys of the glorious *Five Stages*. If you do not understand well the lower paths and theories from which this is distinctive, then you will not understand the subtle and extraordinary distinctive specialties of the higher paths and theories. And especially, if you do not develop the precise intellectual discernment derived from cultivating the ultimate, definitive meaning, profound voidness and the definitive meaning sutras, and the extremely subtle reasoning processes of the savior Nāgārjuna, you will not discover the key of the general path that leads to liberation and omniscience. And in particular, you will not identify well the essence of the subjects of the two nondual [father and mother] tantras, the orgasmic intuitive wisdom from practicing the joining of bliss [311a] and void; though you will admire it, you will see it as merely a matter of faith.

Therefore, I studied well the treatises of our own and others' schools, our individual and universal vehicles, [the latter with] both its transcendence and mantra vehicles, and the four classes of vajra vehicle tantras. Further, through intensive practice I conducted far-reaching investigations concerning the way of leading the disciple through the processes of the completion of the body of each particular path, adorned by the specific appropriate personal instruction, concerning the determining of voidness and, having determined it, meditated it, and developed the way of explaining the specific systems of the *Community* as above explained. [Then, taking] the full measure of the Tibetan translations of the Indian treatises of the noble literature, and all the personal instructions [connected with these], I comparatively connected well the *Root Tantra* and the explanatory tantras. [Then,] I prayed extensively and encountered distinctively excellent signs for composing a treatise. [Thus,] with the pure motivation to restore to excellence the extremely degenerated *Community* system of the noble literature and to see it endure for a long time without degenerating [again], I wrote [this treatise].

The supreme lamp dispelling beings' mental darkness,
The sole mine of all jewels of good eloquence,
Peerless Teacher, crown of all philosophers,
The pervasive Lord, Glorious Vajradhara King,
Taught more than two million two billion
Of the unexcelled yoga tantras.

Thus, like an emperor among the kings of earth,
Surrounded by retinues of fabulous [311b] tantras,

Ruling the continent of jewel sutras,
Fulfilling the hopes of the thousand bodhisattvas.
Serving as the summit of all the sutras—
Such is the *Glorious Community, King of Tantras.*

Having consummated all stages by its path,
The supreme adept Nāgārjunapāda
Well elucidated its hidden intention,
And [that intention] was developed
By Āryadeva, Nāgabodhi,
Shākyamitra, and Chandrakīrti—
Who composed this feast of new true eloquence,
The supreme *Illuminating Lamp*, illuminating
All the key points of the five stages,
Dispelling all the darkness of nonunderstanding and
misunderstanding,
About the *Five Stages*, itself the essence of true eloquence.

The sutras in general and especially the noble tradition,
Having tremendously declined for a very long time,
To discern the hard to fathom meaning of the tantra,
The contemplation playing in bliss, is indeed difficult.

Still, by this performer of good evolutionary action,
Exceedingly blessed with a good share of discerning genius,
Schooled in critical discernment by the vast sphere
Of the intelligence of [my] many expert [teachers],
Rich with treasures of insight that restored me
And energized [my mind] beyond all doubt—
For [you, you] superior ones, here at this end of time,
This unprecedented lucid teaching cannot not be given.

Having worked hard on this way, and researched afar,
I have composed, analyzing well and in detail;
Yet my mind inadequate, the tantra's meaning hard to fathom,
Therefore, whatever errors I have committed,
As loving parents still hold as wondrous

Even the errors of speech of their little child,
So may the divine host of Akshobhyavajra
And the masterful beings please do likewise! [312a]

For someone who does not take the treatises as personal
instructions—
Unskilled in our and others' theories, content with prejudice,
Not struggling with the subtleties of the path of reason—
To take up the key points of a path so long lost [to the world]
Is like a child who climbs up on a stone stand
Struggling wildly to catch the sun—
Such a one can be said only to be well-meaning.
Thus, it is right [only] for the discerning to make the effort.

For even the slightest sliver of your deeds
To enter the heart is so rare and precious,
Yet you made the well-hidden meaning brilliantly clear—
May Your Holiness, Wisdom Treasure, please protect me!

By whatever good evolutionary force I gain,
By making effort on this treatise,
Seeing which and thinking over its meaning
Captivates the mind of the wise.
As a lover's heart is [enchanted]
By the form of a beautiful woman,
May all beings understand precisely
The key points of the tantras, so hard to discern,
And then accomplish their [profound] meaning,
And so proceed to the state of Vajradhara!

As long as the axial mountain Meru stands in the stamen
Of the eight-petalled lotus of earth's continents,
So long may this true eloquence, for fortunate beings,
Long make clear the ultimate [meaning] of the path!

And may I from now for all my lives,
Never be apart from this ultimate of paths,

And may I always please the holy spiritual friend,
The peerless root of the mass of excellence!

[COLOPHON]

Thus, as for this *Brilliantly Illuminating Lamp of* [312b] *All Key Meanings of the Profound Five Stages, the Essence of the King of Tantras, the Glorious Esoteric Community*—due to being repeatedly petitioned to write down a clear and detailed version of the keys of the path of the *Five Stages*, taking with the crown of my head the dust from the feet of the holy mentors such as His Holiness reverend Khyungpo Lhaspa and His Holiness reverend [Rendawa] Kumāramati, the *Glorious Esoteric Community* yogi and learned mendicant, the Easterner Tsong Khapa Losang Drakpay Pal, in the Ganden Triumph Monastery on Great Nomad Mountain, [composed this text], and the scribe was Rinchen Pal, an *Esoteric Community* practitioner upholding the fourfold asceticism.

Mangalam

Appendix
Topical Outline (sa bcad) of Tsong Khapa's Brilliantly Illuminating Lamp

Topical Outline of Tsong Khapa's Brilliantly Illuminating Lamp Topic [Structure: I. A. 1. a. i. A′ 1′ a′ i′ A″ 1″ a″ i″ A‴ 1‴ a‴ i‴]	Tib. (*Zh*) Where Mentioned	Tib. (*Zh*) Where Discussed
CHAPTER 1: INTRODUCTORY		
I. Arrangement of the two [kinds of] tantras	02b.5	02b.6–19b.4
A. History of the origin of the various names of the unexcelled yoga tantras	02b.6	02b.6–03a.5
B. Showing the difference of the two tantras according to the meaning of their names	02b.6	03a.5–13a.2
1. Setting forth the points of doubt	03a.5	03a.5–03b.4
2. Explaining the individual positions concerning them	03a.5	03b.4–13a.2
a. Others' systems	03b.4	03b.4–04b.5
b. Our own system	03b.4	04b.5–13a.2
i. How to establish tantras of nondual art and wisdom	04b.6	04b.6–07a.1
A′ The actual meaning	04b.6	04b.6–05b.6
B′ Refuting objections	04b.6	05b.6–07a.1
ii. Showing the meaning of tantras of separate art and wisdom	04b.6	07a.1–13a.2
A′ Explanation from such [texts] as the *Stainless Light*	07a.1	07a.1–08b.1
B′ Explanation from such [texts] as the *Vajra Pavilion*	07a.1	08b.1–13a.2
1′ Refutation of others' extreme notions	08b.1	08b.1–11b.2
a′ Others' interpretations	08b.1	08b.1–09a.4
b′ Their refutation	08b.1	09a.4–11b.2
2′ Establishing the most worthwhile position	08b.1	11b.2–13a.2

C. Explaining in particular the art tantras	02b.6	13a.3–19b.4
1. Threefold divisions of the art tantras	13a.3	13a.3–13b.6
2. Explanations of the *Esoteric Community* in particular	13a.3	13b.6–19b.4
a. Showing the meaning of "root tantra" and "further tantra," and showing the number of [their] explanatory tantras	13b.6	13b.6–15b.5
b. Showing the way in which the explanatory tantras explain	13b.6	15b.5–19b.4
i. How the *Further Tantra* and the *Revelation of the Hidden Intention* explain	15b.5	15b.6–17a.1
ii. How the [other] three, such as the *Vajra Rosary*, explain	15b.6	17a.1–19b.4
II. Expression of the greatness of the *Community*	02b.5	19b.4–21b.2
III. The process of elucidating the inner intention of that [*Esoteric Community*]	02b.5	21b.2–23b.6
IV. Enumeration of the treatises in the noble [ārya] literature	02b.5	23b.6–30a.6
A. How the treatises of the noble father and son were composed	23b.6–24a.1	24a.1–26a.5
B. How the treatises of the other three sons were composed	24a.1	26a.5–28b.2
C. How the treatises of their followers were composed	24a.1	28b.2–30a.6
V. The way the private instructions [of the *Community*] were transmitted in Tibet	02b.5	30a.6–31a.5
VI. The import of the actual precious jewel of personal instruction	02b.5–6	31a.5–312a.6
A. The way of learning the general path or that common to the two universal vehicles	31a.5	31a.5–34b.3
Chapter 2: General Learning of the Tantric Path		
B. The way of learning the special, uncommon *Community* path	31a.5	34b.3–312a.6
1. How to become a fit vessel for the path of the two stages	34b.3	34b.4–6

Topical Outline of Tsong Khapa's Brilliantly Illuminating Lamp Topic [Structure: I. A. 1. a. i. A′ 1′ a′ i′ A′′ 1′′ a′′ i′′ A′′′ 1′′′ a′′′ i′′′]	Tib. (*Zh*) Where Mentioned	Tib. (*Zh*) Where Discussed
2. Having become fit, how to purify vows and commitments	34b.3	34b.6–35a.3
3. Having purified vows and commitments, how to meditate	34b.3	35a.3–312a.6
a. Verifying the order of the two stages	35a.4	35a.4–37a.5
b. How to meditate the two stages in order	35a.4	37a.5–277b.2
i. The way to meditate the creation stage	37a.5	37a.5–39b.2
A′ The need to meditate what sort of creation stage	37a.6	37b.1–38b.1
B′ How to learn that creation stage	37a.6–37b.1	38b.1–39b.2
ii. The way to meditate the perfection stage	37a.5–6	39b.2–277b.2
A′ Summary meaning of the two [syllables] *E VAṀ*, the main subject of the perfection stage in general	39b.2	39b.3–41b.4
B′ Detailed explanation of the meaning of the two [syllables] *E VAṀ*	39b.2	41b.4–66a.3
1′ Detailed explanation of definitive meaning of both *E* and *VAṀ*	41b.4–5	41b.5–59a.3
a′ Explaining the meanings of the voidness and compassion involved in bliss-void-indivisibility	41b.6	41b.6–53a.3
i′ Explaining the import of voidness	42a.4	42a.5–46b.4
A′′ Identifying the root of the life cycle	42a.5	42a.5–43a.1
B′′ Teaching the corresponding system of investigating the view of selflessness, which terminates that [samsaric life cycle]	42a.5	43a.1–44a.3
C′′ Refuting positions that differ [from that]	42a.5	44a.3–46b.4

ii′ Explaining the import of bliss	42a.4	46b.4–49a.3
iii′ Explaining the process of union of bliss-void-indivisible	42a.4–5	49a.3–53a.3
A′′ The actual meaning	49a.3	49a.3–50b.3
B′′ Rebutting objections	49a.3	50b.3–53a.3
b′ Explaining the meanings of the voidness and compassion involved in the bliss-void-indivisibility	41b.6	53a.3–56b.5
i′ The actual meaning	53a.3	53a.3–54b.6
ii′ The reason for the need for such explanation	53a.3	54b.6–59a.3
A′′ The proof through the perspective of its being the extraordinary cause of the [buddha's] material body	55a.2	55a.3–56b.5
B′′ The proof through the perspective of its being the extraordinary key of the base of purification	55a.2	56b.5–57a.4
C′′ The proof relying on the key of the way to create the deity	55a.2–3	57a.4–57b.2
D′′ The proof relying on the key of [its being] actuality of the indivisibility and art wisdom-	55a.3	57b.2–59a.3
2′ Showing how, to produce that, one must penetrate the vital points in the body through the entry of the sign EVAṂ	41b.5	59a.3–66a.3
a′ The way one must penetrate the vital points in the body to generate the orgasmic [intuition] of bliss-void-indivisible	59a.3	59a.4–62b.2
i′ Teaching the two arts in general	59a.4	59a.4–60a.4
ii′ Explaining them separately	59a.4	60a.4–62b.2

Topical Outline of Tsong Khapa's Brilliantly Illuminating Lamp **Topic** [Structure: **I. A. 1. a. i.** A′ 1′ a′ i′ A′′ 1′′ a′′ i′′ A′′′ 1′′′ a′′′ i′′′]	**Tib. (*Zh*) Where Mentioned**	**Tib. (*Zh*) Where Discussed**
A′′ The art of the science consort	60a.4	60a.4–60b.5
B′′ The art of meditating the inner channels, energies, and so forth	60a.4	60b.5–62b.2
b′ The way one must penetrate the vital points in the body to generate the two reality indivisible communion	59a.3–4	62b.3–66a.3
i′ Explaining how the perfection-stage paths must be generated according to the processes of birth, death, and between	62b.3	62b.3–65a.3
ii′ Explaining the art of penetrating the vital points in the body relying on that	62b.3	65a.3–66a.3
Chapter 3: Explanation of the Perfection Stage of This Tantra in Particular		
C′ Explaining the perfection stage of this tantra in particular	39b.2–3	66a.3–277b.2
1′ Explanation of the way of thorough evaluation of the ultimate private instruction	66a.4	66a.4–67b.6
2′ The need to reconcile the other private instructions of the ancient mentors with this [ultimate private instruction]	66a.4	67b.6–69b.5
3′ The actual explanation of the stages of the path of the perfection stage	66a.4	69b.5–277b.2
a′ Categories of the perfection stage	69b.6	69b.6–77b.2
i′ The actual categories	69b.6	69b.6–72a.4
ii′ The way to reconcile the five stages and the six branches	69b.6	72a.4–77b.2
A′′ Setting forth the various systems	72a.4	72a.4–74b.2
1′′ Setting forth the systems of the [Indian] commentators	72a.4–5	72a.5–73b.3
2′′ Setting forth the systems of the Tibetan mentors	72a.5	73b.3–74b.2

Outline		
B´´ Analyzing their correctness and incorrectness	72a.4	74b.2–77b.2
1´´ Analyzing the accuracy of the [Indian] commentators	74b.2	74b.2–75b.3
2´´ Analyzing the accuracy of the Tibetan explanations	74b.2	75b.3–77b.2
b´ Certification of their order	69b.6	77b.2–79a.6
c´ Certification of their number	69b.6	79a.6–83b.6
i´ The actual meaning	79b.1	79b.1–82a.6
ii´ How to reconcile other paths with this path	79b.1	82a.6–83b.6
Chapter 4: Body Isolation		
d´ The import of the individual divisions [of the perfection stage]	69b.6	83b.6–277b.2
i´ How to learn the samadhis of the three isolations	83b.6	83b.6–203b.5
A´´ How to learn the body isolation body vajra samadhi	83b.6	84a.1–107b.1
1´´ Analysis of which of two stages has body isolation	84a.1	84a.1–88a.3
a´´ Setting forth individual interpretations	84a.2	84a.3–85a.5
b´´ Analysis of their correctness and incorrectness	84a.2–3	85a.5–86b.2
c´´ Setting forth our own interpretation	84a.3	86b.2–88a.3
2´´ Sequence of creation stage and distinctive body isolation	84a.1	88a.3–90a.4
3´´ Identification of body isolation	84a.1–2	90a.4–91b.2
a´´ Others' interpretations	90a.4	90a.4–90b.5
b´´ My interpretation	90a.4	90b.5–91b.2
4´´ Typology of body isolations	84a.2	91b.2–96a.2
a´´ Body isolation of the holy hundred clans	91b.2	91b.3–95a.6

Topical Outline of Tsong Khapa's Brilliantly Illuminating Lamp **Topic** [Structure: **I. A. 1. a. i.** A′ 1′ a′ i′ A″ 1″ a″ i″ A‴ 1‴ a‴ i‴]	Tib. (*Zh*) Where Mentioned	Tib. (*Zh*) Where Discussed
i″ Body isolation of the five aggregates	91b.3	91b.3–92a.3
ii″ Body isolation of the four elements	91b.3	92a.3–92b.6
iii″ Body isolation of the six faculties	91b.3	92b.6–94a.2
iv″ Body isolation of the five objects	91b.3	94a.2–95a.6
b″ Body isolation of the thatness five clans	91b.2–3	95a.6–95b.3
c″ Body isolation of the secret three clans	91b.3	95b.3–96a.1
d″ Body isolation of the great secret single clan	91b.3	96a.1–96a.2
5″ How it serves as retraction and contemplation branches [of the six yoga branches]	84a.2	96a.2–100a.3
a″ How retraction is contained within body isolation	96a.2	96a.3–97a.5
b″ How contemplation is contained within body isolation	96a.2–3	97a.5–100a.3
6″ How to put the body isolation into practice	84a.2	100a.3–107b.1
a″ How to concentrate the energies by meditating the subtle	100a.3	100a.3–102a.2
b″ How melting bliss arises from that	100a.3	102a.3–105a.4
c″ How to cultivate samadhic and aftermath [body isolations] when [bliss] arises	100a.3	105a.4–107b.1

Chapter 5: Speech Isolation in General		
B″ How to learn the speech isolation speech vajra samadhi	83b.6–84a.1	107b.1–176a.6
1″ The order of body isolation and speech isolation	107b.1	107b.2–108a.2
2″ Refuting the assertion that speech isolation is a creation-stage path	107b.1	108a.2–109a.2
3″ Teaching the reality of energy, the knowable object of speech isolation	107b.1	109a.2–130b.4
a″ The import of gradually learning energy, mantra, and vajra recitation	109a.2–3	109a.4–109b.3
b″ Advantages and disadvantages of knowing and not knowing the reality of energies	109a.3	109b.3–110a.1
c″ Analysis of energies	109a.3	110a.1–111a.1
d″ Explanation of each type	109a.3	111a.1–118b.2
i″ Explaining the meaning of the five root energies	111a.1	111a.1–116a.2
ii″ Explaining the meaning of the five branch energies	111a.1	116a.2–116b.5
iii″ Explaining the meaning common to the two energies	111a.1	116b.5–118b.2
e″ How the energies transit	109a.3	118b.2–126a.1
i″ The way [the energy] transits or does not transit from one nostril to another	118b.2–3	118b.3–122a.2
ii″ The way it transits from one petal and elemental sphere to another	118b.3	122a.2–125b.6
f″ What sort of functions the energies perform	109a.3	126a.1–128b.4
g″ Teaching how to know the vital key of practice relying on that	109a.3–4	128b.5–130b.4

Topical Outline of Tsong Khapa's Brilliantly Illuminating Lamp **Topic** [Structure: **I. A. 1. a. i. A′ 1′ a′ i′ A′′ 1′′ a′′ i′′ A′′′ 1′′′ a′′′ i′′′**]	**Tib. (*Zh*) Where Mentioned**	**Tib. (*Zh*) Where Discussed**
4′′ Teaching the ultimate reality of mantra	107b.1–2	130b.4–138b.6
a′′ Collecting the mantra	130b.4	130b.4–133a.6
b′′ The symbol of mantra	130b.4	133a.6–134a.5
c′′ The import of mantra	130b.4	134a.5–134b.4
d′′ The ultimate of mantra	130b.4	134b.4–135a.1
e′′ Short *A*, root of mantra	130b.4	135a.1–138b.6
5′′ The way that speech isolation becomes a component of breath control	107b.2	138b.6–143b.1
CHAPTER 6: SPEECH ISOLATION—HOW TO PRACTICE		
6′′ The way to put speech isolation into practice	107b.2	143b.1–176a.6
a′′ The stage of meditating the three vitalizing energy controls	143b.1	143b.2–156a.2
i′′ Meditating vitalizing energy control of the mantra drop at the heart center nose tip	143b.2	143b.2–149a.5
A′′′ The way to meditate the partial mantra drop	143b.2–3	143b.3–146b.6
B′′′ The way to meditate the mantra wheel	143b.3	146b.6–149a.5
ii′′ Meditating vitalizing energy control of the light drop at the face nose tip	143b.2	149a.5–155b.2
A′′′ In what place and with what energy does one practice the vajra recitation	149a.5	149a.6–152a.2

B′′′ The way of uniting energy and mantra, showing the way to differentiate [various types of] vajra recitation	149a.5–6	152a.2–155b.2
iii′′ Meditating vitalizing energy control of the substance drop at the secret nose tip	143b.2	155b.2–156a.2
b′′ The uncommon function of vajra recitation	143b.1	156a.2–163b.5
i′′ Showing how the vajra recitation releases the channel knot at the heart center	156a.2–3	156a.3–159a.6
ii′′ Showing how that release of the heart-center channel knot is the principal channel-knot release	156a.3	159a.6–163b.5
c′′ Having meditated vitalizing energy control, the stage of generating experience	143b.1–2	163b.5–176a.6
i′′ How to produce experience by meditating on the heart center indestructible	163b.5–6	163b.6–166b.1
ii′′ How to produce experience by meditating on the other vitalizing energy-control practices	163b.6	166b.1–176a.6
A′′′ How to generate month-by-month experience by practicing vajra recitation	166b.1	166b.2–168b.5
B′′′ How to make the energies dissolve into the central *dhūti* channel by vajra recitation	166b.1–2	168b.5–172a.2
C′′′ How to make the furor fire ignite	166b.2	172a.2–176a.6
Chapter 7: Mind Isolation		
C′′ How to learn the mind isolation mind vajra samadhi	84a.1	176a.6–203b.5
I′′ The reason you must understand the reality of the mind	176a.6–176b.1	176b.2–177a.4

Topical Outline of Tsong Khapa's Brilliantly Illuminating Lamp **Topic** [Structure: **I. A. 1. a. i.** A′ 1′ a′ i′ A″ 1″ a″ i″ A‴ 1‴ a‴ i‴]	**Tib. (*Zh*) Where Mentioned**	**Tib. (*Zh*) Where Discussed**
2″ The way the natural pattern of that mind is declared in the sutras	176b.1	177a.4–178a.4
3″ Demonstration that the especially excellent art for realizing the nature of the mind is the unexcelled [yoga] tantra	176b.1–2	178a.4–180b.3
4″ Teaching the tantra's import, the three luminances and the instinctual natures	176b.2	180b.3–203a.2
a″ Luminance	180b.3	180b.4–187a.3
i″ Synonyms of the three luminances	180b.3	180b.4–183b.5
ii″ Definitions of each of the three luminances	180b.3	183b.5–187a.3
b″ The instinctual natures	180b.3	187a.3–191b.2
c″ How to generate luminance intuition	180b.3	191b.2–203a.2
i″ Setting forth the separate systems	191b.2	191b.3–194b.2
ii″ Setting forth the correct opinions among them	191b.2–3	194b.2–203a.2
A‴ Analyzing how are those systems	194b.2	194b.3–196b.4
B‴ Setting forth the enduring opinion	194b.2–3	196b.4–203a.2
1‴ The way the wisdoms are produced from outer and inner conditions	196b.4	196b.5–201b.5
2‴ The way such bliss and void are united, and so forth	196b.5	201b.5–203a.2

5'' Showing the dangers and the advantages of not knowing and knowing that [import] correctly	176b.2	203a.2–203b.5
Chapter 8: Two Reality Perfection Stage		
ii' How to learn the samadhis of the two realities	83b.6	203b.5–277b.2
A'' The perfection stage of the two realities severally	203b.5	203b.5–263b.3
1'' The perfection stage of superficial magic	203b.6	203b.6–242b.1
a'' The actual instruction of the magic body	203b.6	203b.6–223a.2
i'' What should what sort of disciple do	203b.6–204a.1	203b.6–206b.1
ii'' The teacher's teaching process	204a.1	206b.1–223a.2
A''' How to explain the preliminaries to the actual magic body	206b.1	206b.2–208a.2
B''' Explaining the actual stage of magic body	206b.2	208a.2–223a.2
1''' How to establish the basis of the magic body precept	208a.2	208a.2–210b.1
2''' Relying on that, explanation of the way to attain the magic body	208a.2	210b.1–223a.2
a''' Explaining how it is expressed in the treatises of the father and sons	210b.1	210b.2–214b.3
b''' Explaining very clearly the way it is achieved, along with its excellences	210b.1–2	214b.3–218a.1
c''' Explaining what comes from the mentors' precepts	210b.2	218a.1–223a.2
i''' How it is given in the personal instruction tradition	218a.1	218a.1–220b.1
ii''' Explaining that import in connection with the treatise[s]	218a.1	220b.1–223a.2

Topical Outline of Tsong Khapa's Brilliantly Illuminating Lamp **Topic** [Structure: **I. A. 1. a. i.** A′ 1′ a′ i′ A′′ 1′′ a′′ i′′ A′′′ 1′′′ a′′′ i′′′]	Tib. (*Zh*) Where Mentioned	Tib. (*Zh*) Where Discussed
b′′ The associated instructions	203b.6	223a.2–242b.1
i′′ Providing the context for explaining the sources of the instructions	223a.2	223a.3–228b.6
ii′′ The actual explanation of the instructions of sleep, dream, and so forth	223a.2–3	228b.6–242b.1
A′′′ Explaining the sleep and dream mergers	228b.6	228b.6–235b.3
1′′′ The sleep merger	228b.6	228b.6–232b.5
2′′′ The dream merger	228b.6	232b.5–235b.3
B′′′ Explaining the death and between mergers	228b.6	235b.3–242b.1
1′′′ The way of merging buddhahood in the between	235b.3	235b.3–239a.6
2′′′ The way of merging buddhahood after becoming reborn	235b.3	239a.6–241a.3
3′′′ Demonstrating the analysis and the synthesis of the mergers	235b.3	241a.3–242b.1
CHAPTER 9: ULTIMATE CLEAR LIGHT TRANSPARENCE		
2′′ The perfection stage of ultimate clear light	203b.6	242b.1–263b.3
a′′ The import explained in the *Five Stages* and the *Integrated Practices*	242b.1	242b.2–260b.2
i′′ Procedure to ascertain the sequence, along with how to become eligible	242b.2	242b.2–244b.3
ii′′ Explaining the practical instruction in clear light to such a person	242b.2	244b.3–254a.2

A''' Explaining both outer and inner manifest enlightenments	244b.3–4	244b.4–248a.5
1''' The actual meaning	244b.4	244b.4–247a.5
2''' Rebutting objections	244b.4	247a.5–248a.5
B''' Explaining the two contemplations, the art of realizing them	244b.4	248a.6–253a.2
C''' Explaining their synonyms, along with their greatness	244b.4	253a.2–254a.2
iii'' The way that stage also reaches the end of other paths	242b.2	254a.2–260b.2
b'' The import explained in the endurance branch statement of the *Further Tantra*	242b.1	260b.2–263b.3
CHAPTER 10: THE PERFECTION STAGE OF COMMUNION		
B'' The perfection stage of the two realities inseparably	203b.5	263b.3–277b.2
1'' Explanation of the meaning of the *Five Stages* and *Integrated Practices* passages	263b.3–4	263b.4–275b.4
a'' Question	263b.4	263b.4–264a.3
b'' Answer	263b.4	264a.4–275b.4
i'' The answer to the second question	264a.6	264a.6–267b.6
ii'' The answer to the third and fifth questions	264a.6	267b.6–270a.3
iii'' The answer to the first question	264a.6	270a.3–274a.6
iv'' The answer to the fourth and sixth questions, along with some remaining thoughts	264a.6	274a.6–275b.4
2'' Explanation of the two branches coming from the *Further Tantra*	263b.4	275b.4–277b.2

Topical Outline of Tsong Khapa's Brilliantly Illuminating Lamp Topic [Structure: I. A. 1. a. i. A′ 1′ a′ i′ A″ 1″ a″ i″ A‴ 1‴ a‴ i‴]	Tib. (*Zh*) Where Mentioned	Tib. (*Zh*) Where Discussed
CHAPTER 11: THE CONDUCT, THE ART OF HEIGHTENING IMPACT ON THE TWO STAGES		
c. The conduct that is the method of heightening impact on the two stages	35a.4	277b.2–309a.1
i. The general arrangement of conducts	277b.2	277b.2–288a.4
A′ Explaining the divisions of conduct in general	277b.3	277b.3–280a.1
B′ Eliminating scriptural contradictions with the distinctive conduct	277b.3	280a.1–288a.4
1′ Setting forth the *Integrated Practices* statements and explaining their meaning	280a.1–2	280a.2–283b.4
2′ Rebutting others' objections to that	280a.2	283b.4–288a.4
ii. Specific explanation of unexcelled [yoga tantric] conduct	277b.2–3	288a.4–309a.1
A′ How the analysis of conduct is declared	288a.5	288a.5–292a.1
B′ The definition of each of the three conducts	288a.5	292a.1–297a.3
C′ The method of learning the conducts	288a.5	297a.3–309a.1
1′ The way of achieving the elaborated and unelaborated conducts	297a.3	297a.4–305b.2
a′ Common procedures [for both]	297a.4	297a.4–299b.2
b′ Particular procedures [for each]	297a.4	299b.2–305b.2
i′ The elaborated rites	299b.2	299b.2–301b.1
ii′ The unelaborated rites	299b.2	301b.1–305b.2
2′ The way of achieving the extremely unelaborated conduct	297a.4	305b.2–309a.1
4. How the fruition will be attained at meditation's end	34b.4	309a.1–312a.6

Glossaries

English-Tibetan-Sanskrit Glossary

This glossary combines an adaptation of the glossary I created for my *Central Philosophy of Tibet* (a study and translation of Tsong Khapa's *Essence of True Eloquence*) with the glossary of terms extracted from this present perfection-stage work. The author often refers to his centrist (*mādhyamika*) philosophical terminology since he considers the Nāgārjuna, Āryadeva, and Chandrakīrti of the centrist works and the eponymous authors of the tantric works to be the very same persons. Further, he considers the centrist and unexcelled yoga tantric studies and practices to be totally integrated as wisdom and art studies and practices.

English	Tibetan	Sanskrit
abode (place, locus)	gnas	āśraya
absolute (exclusion) negation	med dgag	prasajyapratiṣedha
absolute (ultimate)	don dam pa	paramārtha
absolute (ultimate) reality	don dam bden pa	paramārthasatya
absolutism	yod par smra ba, yod par 'dzin pa	bhāvavāda, bhāvagraha
absolutist extreme	yod mtha'	bhāvānta
absolutist extremism	yod mtha'dzin pa	bhāvāntagraha
absolutistic imagination	yod pa nyid du yongs su brtags	bhāvatvaparikalpana
accessories of enlightenment	byang chub kyi phyogs chos	bodhipakṣikadharma

English	Tibetan	Sanskrit
accomplishment (power)	dngos grub	siddhi
accumulation path	tshogs lam	saṁbhāramārga
action	bya ba	karaṇa
action (evolution)	las	karma
activity	bya ba	kriyā
actuality (reality, thatness)	de nyid, de kho na nyid	tattva
addicted	kun nas nyon mongs pa	saṁkleśika
addiction	nyon mongs	kleśa
addictive mentality	nyon yid	kliṣṭamana
addictive misknowledge	nyon mongs can gyi ma rig pa	kliṣṭāvidya
addictive obscuration	nyon sgrib	kleśāvaraṇa
aftermath intuition	rjes thob ye shes	pṛṣṭhalabdhajñāna
aggregate	phung po	skandha
alien fundamentalist	gzhan mu stegs can	paratīrthika
alienated individual	so so'i skye bo	pṛthagjana
all-accomplishing intuition	bya sgrub ye shes	kṛtyānuṣṭhāna-jñānaṁ
Analyst	bye brag smra ba	vaibhāṣīka
analytic (critical) insight	lhag mthong	vipaśyana
analytic meditation	dpyad sgom	savicārabhāvana
analytic rational cognition	dpyod pa'i rigs shes	*savicārayuktijñāna
ancestral mentor tradition	bla ma brgyud rim	guru-purva-krama
angel, ḍākinī	mkha' 'gro ma	ḍākinī
animate	rgyu ba	jaṅgama
annihilism	chad lta	ucchedadṛṣṭi
annihilistic extremism	chad mthar 'dzin pa	ucchedāntagraha
anomalous creation	ldan min 'du byed	viprayuktasaṁskāra

ENGLISH	TIBETAN	SANSKRIT
antagonist (opponent)	phyir rgol	
anxiety	'gyod pa	kaukṛtya
anxiety	dogs pa dang bcas pa	cakita
apperception (introspection)	rang rig	svasaṁvitti, svasaṁvedana
apperceptive experience	rang gis rig pa	svasaṁvedya
arisal, resurrection	ldang ba	vyutthāna
arrangement	rnam gzhag	vyavasthāna
array	rnam par dgod pa	vinyāsa
arrogance	khengs pa (nga rgyal)	māna
art intuition	thabs kyi ye shes	upāya-jñāna
art, method	thabs	upāya
articulation	mngon par brjod pa	abhilāpana
ascendance	mngon mtho	abhyudaya
ascending (energy)	gyen rgyu, steng rgyu	udāna (vāyu)
ascetical observances	dka' thub sdom pa	duṣkara-niyama
ascriptive (substantive) designation	ngo bor brtags pa	svabhāvavikalpana
aspect, form	rnam pa	ākāra
atom, subatomic particle	rdul phra rab	paramāṇu
attitude, mental function	yid la byed pa	manaskāra
attractive	yid du 'ong ba	manojña
bad migration	ngan 'gro, ngan song	apāya, durgati
base, basis	gzhi	ādhāra
base, ground	gzhi, gnas	āśraya, ādhāra
beatific body	longs sku	saṁbhogakāya
beginner	las dang po pa	ādikarmika

English	Tibetan	Sanskrit
being	sems can, 'gro ba, skye bo	sattva, jana, jagat, jantu
between	bar do	antarābhava
between-being	srid pa bar ma pa	antarābhavin
bhusuku	bu su ku	bhusuku
bile	mkhris pa	pitta
birth, life	skye ba	janman
birthless, unproduced	skye ba med pa	anutpāda
blame	smad pa	nindā
blissful lord	bde bar gshegs pa	sugata
bodhisattva	byang chub sems dpa'	bodhisattva
body	lus, sku	kāya, deha, bimba, mūrti, śarīra, vigraha, kalevara
body isolation	lus rnam par dben pa	kāya-viveka
body vajra	sku rdo rje	kāya-vajra
boldness	dka' ba la sbyor ba	sāhasa
bond	bcing ba, 'ching ba	bandhana, prabandha
brahmin	bram ze	brāhmaṇa
breath	dbugs	niḥśvāsa, śvāsa
bubble	chu'i chu bur	budbuda
buddha	sangs rgyas	buddha
buddhahood	sangs rgyas nyid	buddhatva
buddhaverse	sangs rgyas kyi zhing	buddha-kṣetra
categorical differential	rang ldog	*svavyāvṛtti
causal process	rgyu mtshan	nimitta, hetunimitta
cause	rgyu	hetu
central way	dbu ma, dbu ma'i lam	madhyamaka, madhyamapratipat

ENGLISH	TIBETAN	SANSKRIT
centrism	dbu ma'i lta ba	mādhyamika-dṛṣṭi
centrist	dbu ma pa	mādhyamika
champion	shing rta chen po	mahāratha
champions' way	shing rta'i srol	mahārathanaya
champions' way pioneer	shing rta'i srol phye ba	*mahārathanayakara
charnel ground	dur khrod	śmaśāna
choice (implicative) negation	ma yin dgag	paryudāsapratiṣedha
chosen deity	rang gi lha	svādhidaiva
circle, retinue	'khor lo, tshogs	cakra
clan	rigs	kula
class, gene, lineage	rigs	gotra
clear enlightenment	mngon par rdzogs par byang chub pa	abhisaṁbodhi
clear enlightenment stage	mngon par byang chub pa'i rim pa	abhisaṁbodhi-krama, saṁbodhikrama
clear light	'od gsal	prabhāsvara
clear light intuition	'od gsal ye shes	prabhāsvara-jñāna
coarse	rags pa	audārika, sthūla
cognition	shes pa, blo	jñāna, buddhi
cognitive status	blos grub pa	
cognitive superficial reality	shes pa'i kun rdzob bden pa	
coincidental	glo bur ba	āgantuka
collection	'dus pa	sannipāta
commoving (energy)	yang dag par rgyu ba'i (rlung)	saṁvāha (vāyu)
communion, union	zung du 'jug pa	yuganaddha
Community	'dus pa	samāja

English	Tibetan	Sanskrit
Community practitioner	'dus pa'i don la zhugs pa rnams	sāmājika
companion	lhan cig spyod pa	sahacarī
compassion, empathy	snying rje	karuṇā, kāruṇya
conceit	rlom sems	manana
concept, conceptuality	rnam par rtog pa, rnam rtog	vikalpa
conception (perception) aggregate	'du shes kyi phung po	saṁjñā-skandha
conception of the spirit (of enlightenment)	(byang chub kyi) sems bskyed pa	(bodhi)citta-utpāda
conceptual object	zhen yul	abhiniveśya
concomitance	khyab pa	vyapti
conduct, lifestyle	spyod pa	caryā
confutation through similarity of reasons	rgyu mtshan mtshungs pa'i mgo snyoms	
conscious futile view	kun btags kyi 'jig lta	parikalpita-satkāyadṛṣṭi
consciousness	rnam par shes pa	vijñāna
consecrated, blessed	byin gyis brlabs pa	adhiṣṭhita
consecration, blessing	byin gyis brlabs pa	adhiṣṭhāna
consequence	thal ba	prasaṅga
consort, seal, gesture	phyag rgya	mudrā
construct, thought	rtog pa	kalpana
constructed reality	rnam brtags kyi ngo bo nyid	vikalpitasvabhāva
consummation, ultimate	mthar thug pa	paryanta
contact	reg pa	sparśa
contemplation (branch)	bsam gtan (yan lag)	dhyāna (aṅga)
continuum, continuity	rgyun, rgyud	tantu, prabandha
convention (verbal and symbolic)	(ming dang brda'i) tha snyad	(nāmasaṁketa) vyavahāra

English	Tibetan	Sanskrit
conventional cognition	tha snyad pa'i shes pa	vyāvahārikajñāna
conventional existence	tha snyad du yod pa	vyāvahārikasat
conventional rational cognition	tha snyad pa'i rigs shes	*vyāvahārikayuktijñāna
conventional reality	tha snyad bden pa	vyāvahārikasatya
conventional status	tha snyad du grub pa	vyavahārasiddha
conventional truth	tha snyad bden pa	vyāvahārikasatya
conventional validating cognition	tha snyad pa'i tshad ma	vyāvahārikapramāṇa
conventionally ascriptive intellect	tha snyad 'dogs pa'i blo	
conviction	zhen pa	abhiniveśa
courage	sems dpa' (sems pa)	cintā
crafty	gyo	śaṭha
craving	sred pa, skom pa	tṛṣṇā
creation	bskyed pa	utpatti
creation	'du byed	saṁskāra
creation stage	bskyed rim	utpattikrama
critical wisdom	shes rab	prajñā
crown-protrusion, ushnisha	gtsug gtor	uṣṇīṣa
crucial point	don gyi dbang	artha-vaśa
cryptic expressions	sgra sbas pa	nigūḍha-śabda
cyclic life, life cycle	'khor ba	saṁsāra
ḍākinī, angel	mkha' 'gro ma	ḍākinī
dance, drama	gar	nāṭaka
deceitful	sgyu	kapaṭa
dedication	yongs su bsngo ba	pariṇāmana
deed	bya ba	kriyā

English	Tibetan	Sanskrit
defining characteristic	rang gi mtshan nyid	svalakṣaṇa (Abhidharma)
definitive meaning	nges pa'i don, nges don	nītārtha
deity body	lha'i sku	devatā-rūpa, -mūrti
deity body formation	lha nyid du bskyed pa	devatā-niṣpatti
deity embodiment	lha'i sku	devatā-vigraha
deity reality	lha'i de kho na nyid	devatā-tattva
deity vision	lha ru nye bar dmigs pa	devatopalabdhika
deity yoga	lha'i rnal 'byor	devatā-yoga
deluded	rmongs pa	mohita
dependent designation	brten nas gdags pa	upādāyaprajñāpati
dependent origination (relativity)	rten cing 'brel bar 'byung ba	pratītyasamutpāda
depression	skyo ba	kheda
descriptive (qualitative) designation	khyad par du brtags pa	viśeṣavikalpana
designation	rnam pa	ākāra
designation	gdags pa, brtags pa	prajñapti, vikalpa
designative base (referential base)	gdags gzhi, gdags don	prajñapya, prajñapyārtha
designative existence	gdags su yod pa	prajñaptisat
designative superficial reality	btags pa'i kun rdzob bden pa	
desire (lust)	'dod pa	kāma
desire objects	'dod pa'i yon tan	kāma-guṇa
desire realm	'dod pa'i khams	kāmadhātu
destruction	mngon spyod	abhicāruka
determinate (cognition)	rnam ldan (gyi shes pa)	sākāra (jñāna)
determination	gtan la 'bab pa, rnam par nges pa, yongs su gcod pa	viniścaya, nirṇaya, paricchinna

English	Tibetan	Sanskrit
determine, ascertain	nges pa	niścaya
development, maturation	rnam par smin pa	vipāka
devotee hero	dam tsig sems dpa'	samayasattva
devotion	mos	bhakti
dedication	mchog tu gzhol ba	parāyaṇa
devotional practice	brtul zhugs kyi spyod pa	vrata-caryā
Dharma (dharma)	chos	dharma
dialectical (public) reason	gshan grags kyi rtags	paraprasiddhahetu
dialectical consequence	thal ba	prasaṅga
dialecticist	thal 'gyur ba	prāsaṇgika
diamond smithereen	rdo rje gzegs ma	
diamond-like samādhi	ting nge 'dzin rdo rje'i gzugs lta bu	vajra-bimbopamaṁ-samādhi
differential	ldog pa	vyāvrtti
digits	nying lag	pratyaṅga
direct objective basis of expressions	brjod byed kyi dngos yul	
discerned	yongs su bcad pa	parichinna
discernment	rnam dpyod	
disciple	nyan thos	śrāvaka
disciple vehicle	nyan thos theg pa	śrāvaka-yāna
discipline	brtul zhugs	niyama
discipline	'dul ba	vinaya
discourse, scripture, sutra	mdo	sūtra
dispassion	'dod chags bral ba	virāga
dispassionate practice	chags bral spyod pa	virāga-caryā
dissolving contemplation	rjes gzhig bsam gtan	anubheda-dhyāna
distinctive characteristic	rang gi mtshan nyid	svalakṣaṇa (Abhidharma)

ENGLISH	TIBETAN	SANSKRIT
distinctive specialty	thun mong min pa'i khyad chos	asādharaṇaviśeṣa
divine lord	bcom ldan 'das	bhagavan
dogmaticism, privacy	rang rgyud	svātantryā
dogmaticist	rang rgyud pa	svātantrika
dogmaticist centrist	dbu ma rang rgyud pa	svātantrikamādhyamika
dogmatist	rtog ge pa	tarkika
domination, power	dbang	vaśya
doubt	som nyi	saṁśaya
dream	rmi lam	svapna
dreamlike	rmi lam lta bu	svapnopama
dual	gnyis pa	dvaya
dualism	gnyis su 'dzin pa	dvayagraha
dualism, dualistic theory	gnyis su smra ba	dvayavāda
earth	dbang chen	māhendra
education	bslab pa	śikṣa, adhiśikṣa
effort, enterprise	brtson pa, brtson 'grus	vīrya
effortless (spontaneous)	lhun gyis grub pa	anābhoga
egocentric person	mtshur mthong	arvāgdarśana
egoism, "I"-habit	ngar 'dzin	ahaṁkāra
eight great powers	grub chen brgyad	aṣṭa-mahāsiddhi
eight superhuman powers	yon tan gyi dbang phyug brgyad	aṣṭaguṇaiśvarya
eight worldly concerns	'jig rten chos brgyad	aṣṭa-loka-dharma
eighth stage god	sa brgyad dbang phyug	aṣṭamīśvāra
elaborated conduct	spros bcas spyod pa	prapañcacaryā
elaboration, fabrication, proliferation	spros pa	prapañca

English	Tibetan	Sanskrit
element, realm	khams	dhātu
elemental derivative	'byung ba las gyur pa	bhautika
elixir	bdud rtsi	amṛta
elixir of immortality	ra sa ya na	rasāyana
eloquence	legs bshad, spobs pa	subhāṣita, pratibhāna
eloquent elucidation	legs bshad	subhāṣita
emanation body	sprul sku	nirmāṇa-kāya
embracing	'khyud pa	āliṅgana
emitting, shining	spro ba, 'byung ba	spharaṇa
emptied	gang stong pa'i gzhi	śūnyatādhāra
emptied, voided	gang gis stong pa	yad śunyatā
emptiness of objective self	chos bdag gi stong pa nyid	dharmātmaśūnyata
emptiness of personal self	gang zag gi stong pa nyid	pudgalaśūnyata
emptiness of relative with respect to imagined	kun brtags kyis stong pa'i gzhan dbang	*parikalpitaśūnyaparatantra
emptiness of subject-object substantial dichotomy	gzung 'dzin rdzas tha dad kyis stong pa nyid	*grahyagrahakadravyabhedatvena
emptiness, voidness	stong pa nyid	śūnyata
endurance (branch)	'dzin pa (yan lag)	dhāraṇā (aṅga)
energy, wind	rlung	vāyu, vāta
energy reality	rlung gi de kho na nyid	vāyu-tattva
enlightenment	byang chub, sangs rgyas nyid	bodhi, buddhatvam
enthusiasm	spro ba	utsāha
entranced	snyoms par zhugs pa	samāpanna
entrancement	mnyam par gzhag pa	samāhita
envy	phrag dog	mātsarya
equality intuition	mnyam nyid ye shes	samatā-jñāna

English	Tibetan	Sanskrit
equanimity	btang snyoms	upekṣa
erotic	snyan, sgeg pa	śṛṅgāra
erotic mood	sgeg pa'i ro	śṛṅgāra rasa
erotic play, music	rol pa, rol mo	krīḍā, līla
error	'khrul pa	bhrānti
establishment, status	grub pa	siddha
eternalistic extremism	rtag mthar 'dzin pa	śāṣvatāntagraha
ethics, morality, justice	tshul khrims	śīla
etymology	nges tshig	nirukti
evacuative, evacuating	thur sel	apāna
evil, ugliness	mi dge ba	aśubha
evolution advocate	las su smra ba	karma-vādin
evolution, evolutionary action, action	las	karma
evolutionary development	las kyi rnam par smin pa	karmavipāka
exclusion	rnam bcad	vichinna
exclusion negation, absolute negation	med dgag	prasajyapratiṣedha
exclusion, differential	ldog pa	vyāvrtti
exhalation, consolation	dbugs 'byung ba	ucchvāsa, niḥśhvāsa
exhaustion	dub pa	klamatha
existence	srid pa	bhava
existence	yod pa	sat
existent, thing	dngos po	bhāva
experience	rjes su myong ba	anubhava
experiential medium, medium	skye mched	āyatana
experientialist, idealist	rnal 'byor spyod pa pa	yogācārika

English	Tibetan	Sanskrit
expert	mkhas pa	paṇḍita
explanatory tantra	bshad rgyud	vyākhyā-tantra
explicit expression	bshad pa'i sgra	uttāna-śabda
expressible, subject	brjod bya	abhidheya
expressive verbal universal	brjod byed sgra spyi	*abhidhānaśabdasāmānya
external object	phyi don	bāhyārtha
external-object-status	phyi don du grub pa	bāhyārthasiddha
extreme void	shin tu stong pa	atiśūnya
extreme, limit	mtha'	anta
extremely unelaborated	shin tu spros pa med pa	atyanta-niṣprapañcatā
extremely unelaborated conduct	shin tu spros pa med pa'i spyod pa	atyanta-niṣprapañcatā-caryā
extremely unelaborated lifestyle	shin tu spros pa med pa'i spyod pa	atyanta-niṣprapañca-caryā
extremism	mthar 'dzin	antagraha
extremist view	mthar 'dzin gyi lta ba	antagrahadṛṣṭi
fabrication, elaboration	spros pa	prapañca
face value	stobs zhugs	
facticity, reality	chos nyid	dharmatā
faith	dad pa	śraddhā
fire	me	tejas, hutabhug, agni
fire offering	sbyin bsregs	homa
fire-offering-pit	thab khung	kuṇḍa
five desire objects	'dod pa'i yon tan lnga	pañcakāmaguṇa
five elixirs	bdud rtsi lnga	pañcāmṛta
five intuitions	ye shes lnga	pañca-jñāna
five migrations	'gro ba lnga	gati-pañcaka, pañcagati
five stages	rims lnga	pañca-krama

English	Tibetan	Sanskrit
five subjectivities	shes pa lnga	pañca-jñāna
flirtation	rnam par rol pa, rnam par sgeg pa	vilāsa
fluency	shin sbyangs	praśrabdhi
form, appearance	rnam pa	ākāra
form, matter	gzugs	rūpa
formability	gzugs su rung ba nyid	rūpyatā
formable	gzugs su rung ba	rūpya
formless realm, immaterial realm	gzugs med khams	ārūpya-dhātu
formless, immaterial	gzugs med pa, rnam pa med pa	arūpin, nirākāra
foundation, base	gnas, gzhi	ālaya, āśraya
foundationless, baseless	gzhi med, gnas med	anālaya
four divine abodes	tshangs pa'i gnas pa bzhi	catur-brahma-vihāra
four noble truths	'phags pa'i bden pa bzhi	caturāryasatya
four voids	stong pa rnam pa bzhi	śūnya-catuṣṭaya
fourfold procedure	tshul rnam pa bzhi	caturvidha-nyāya
functional capacity	don byed nus pa	arthakriya
functional reasoning	bya ba byed pa'i rigs pa	kṛtyakaraṇayukti
fundamental consciousness	kun gzhi rnam shes	ālayavijñāna
fundamentalist vehicle	mu stegs can gyi gnas	tīrthāyana
further tantra	rgyud phyi ma, rgyud bla ma	uttara-tantra
futile view	'jig lta	satkāyadṛṣṭi
future life	'jig rten pha rol	paraloka
gene, spiritual gene, class, lineage	rigs	gotra
genealogical determinism	rigs nges pa, mthar thug rigs nges pa	gotraniyata, atyantagotraniyata

English	Tibetan	Sanskrit
generality, universal	spyi	sāmānya
generosity	sbyin pa	dāna
glory	dpal	śrī
goal	bsgrub par bya ba	sādhya
god, deity	lha	deva, devatā
goddess	lha mo	devī
good and evil, beauty and ugliness	dge ba dang mi dge ba	śubhāśubha
good, virtue, beauty	dge ba	kuśala, śubha
grace, kindness	bka' drin	prasāda
gradual engagement	rim gyis 'jug pas	kramaśaḥ
gradual process	rim gyis 'jug pa	krama-vṛtti
great bliss	bde ba chen po	mahāsukha
great community school	dge 'dun chen po pa	mahāsaṁghika
great compassion	snying rje chen po	mahākṛpā
great hero	dpa' bo chen po	mahāvīra
great messiah	sems dpa' chen po	mahāsattva
great person	skyes bu chen po	mahāpuruṣa
Great Sage	thub pa chen po	mahāmuni
great void	stong pa chen po	mahāśūnya
great yoga	rnal 'byor chen po	mahāyoga
great yoga tantra	rnal 'byor chen po'i rgyud	mahāyoga-tantra
gross (self-habit)	(bdag 'dzin) rags pa	audārika (ātmagraha)
ground differential	gzhi ldog	*āśrayavyāvṛtti
ground of symbolic designation	brda 'dogs pa'i gnas	
group-mandala	tshogs kyi dkyil 'khor	gaṇa-maṇḍala
habit	'dzin pa	graha

English	Tibetan	Sanskrit
habit pattern	'dzin stangs	muṣṭi
habitat	rten	ādhāra
habitual adherence	mngon par zhen pa	abhiniveśana
hallucination	mig yor	pratibhāsa
happy migration	bde 'gro	sugati
hatred, anger	zhe sdang	dveṣa
heaven	mtho ris	svarga
hell	dmyal ba	naraka
hero	dpa' bo	vīra
holistic samadhi	ril 'dzin ting nge 'dzin	piṇḍagraha samādhi
hollow	gso ba	rikta
holy bliss	bde ba dam pa	satsukha
holy teaching	dam pa'i chos	saddharma
holy word	gsung rab	prāvacanika
human	mi	nara
hundred clans	rigs brgya	śata-kula
hunger	bkres pa	kṣut
I-habit, ego-assertion	ngar 'dzin pa, bdag tu rlom pa	ahaṁkāra
idealism (*see also* mind-only)	sems tsam	vijñānavāda
identification	mtshon pa	lakṣa
identified	mtshan gzhi	lakṣya
identity (intrinsic)	rang gi mtshan nyid	lakṣaṇa
identity-unreality	mtshan nyid ngo bo nyid med pa	lakṣaṇa
identity-unreality	mtshan nyid ngo bo nyid med pa	lakṣaṇaniḥsvabhāvatā

ENGLISH	TIBETAN	SANSKRIT
identity, characteristic, definition	mtshan nyid	lakṣaṇa
identityless	mtshan nyid med pa	alakṣaṇa
identitylessness	rang mtshan med pa, rang bzhin med pa	alakṣaṇatva, niḥsvabhāva
identitylessness	mtshan nyid med pa	alakṣaṇata
ignorance, delusion	gti mug	moha
ignorance, misknowledge	ma rig pa	avidyā
imagination	yongs su brtags pa	parikalpana
imaginative yoga	rtog pa'i rnal 'byor	kalpita-yoga
imaginatively constructed reality	kun btags kyi ngo bo nyid, yongs su brtags pa'i ngo bo nyid	parikalpita
imagined nature	kun brtags kyi mtshan nyid	parikalpitalakṣaṇa
imagined reality	kun brtags kyi ngo bo nyid	parikalpitasvabhāva
immaterial, formless	gzugs med pa	arūpa
imminence	nyer thob	upalabdhi
imminence intuition	nyer thob ye shes	upalabdha-jñāna
impassioned, reddened	kun du chags pa	rakta
imperceptible	dbang po las 'das pa	atīndriya
imperishable, inexhaustible	mi zad pa, zad pa med pa	akṣaya
impermanent, impermanence	mi rtag pa	anitya
implicative (choice) negation	ma yin dgag	paryudāsapratiṣedha
implicit meaning	sgra ji bzhin ma yin pa	ayathāruṭa
inanimate	bems po, mi rgyu ba	jaḍa, sthāvara
inclination, aspiration	bsam pa	āśaya
inconceivable	bsam gyis mi khyab pa	acintya
incorporeal	rnam pa med pa	nirākāra

English	Tibetan	Sanskrit
indeterminate cognition	rnam med kyi shes pa	anākāra-jñāna
individual vehicle	theg dman	hīnayāna
Individualist	theg dman pa	hīnayānika
individuating intuition	so sor rtog pa'i ye shes	pratyavekṣaṇā-jñānaṁ
indivisible	dbyer med, mi phyed pa	abheda, abhedya
inexpressible	brjod du med pa	anabhilāpya, anākhyeya, avācya
inference	rjes su dpag pa	anumāna
inference and syllogism	rang don dang gzhan don rjes dpag	svārthaparārtha-anumāna
inferential rational cognition	rjes dpag rigs shes	*ānumānikayuktijñāna
inferential validating cognition	rjes dpag tshad ma	anumāṇapramāṇa
infinite, endless	mtha' yas pa	ananta
inhabitant	brten pa	ādheya
inhalation	dbyugs rngub pa	praśvāsa
initiation, empowerment	dbang bskur ba	abhiṣeka
innate, orgasmic, natural	lhan skyes, lhan cig skyes pa	sahaja
insider	nang pa, rang sde	ādhyātmika
insistent	mngon par zhen pa	abhiniviṣṭa
instant	thang cig	lava
instantaneously	skad cig tsam gyis	jhaṭiti
instinct, proclivity	bag chags, bag la nyal ba	vāsana, anuśaya
instinctual pattern, nature	rang bzhin	prakṛti
instinctual, unconscious futile view	lhan skyes 'jig lta	*sahaja-satkāya-dṛṣṭi
insubstantial, unreal	dngos med, rang bzhin med	niḥsvabhāva
intellectual futile view	'jig lta kun brtags	parikalpitasatkāyadṛṣṭi

English	Tibetan	Sanskrit
intellectual misknowledge	kun brtags kyi ma rig pa, kun btags kyi ma rig pa	parikalpita-avidyā, parikalpita-satkāyāvidyā
intellectual reification	sgro 'dogs kun brtags	parikalpita-samāropa
intellectual self-habit	bdag 'dzin kun brtags, kun btags kyi bdag 'dzin	parikalpita-ātmagraha
intellectual supposition	blos rloms pa	
intellectual truth-habit	bden 'dzin kun brtags	parikalpita-satyagraha
intelligence (information) only	rnam par rig pa tsam	vijñaptimātra
intelligence, intellect	blo, blo gros	buddhi (mati)
intended	dgongs gzhi	saṁdhyā
intended meaning	dgongs don	saṁdhyārtha
intention	dgongs pa	abhiprāya, abhisaṁdhi
intentional	dgongs pa can	ābhiprāyiki
intentional speech	dgongs te gsungs pa, dgongs pas bshad pa	saṁdhyāya-vacana, saṁdhyā-vacana
intentionality	zhe rtsis	
internal verbalization	yid kyis brjod pa	manojalpa
interpretable meaning	drang don	neyārtha
intimation, intention	dgongs pa	abhisaṁdhi
intimative superficial reality	brjod pa'i kun rdzob bden pa	
intrinsic identifiability	rang mtshan gyis grub pa	svalakṣaṇasiddha
intrinsic identity	rang gi mtshan nyid	svalakṣaṇa
intrinsic objectivity	rang gi ngo bos grub pa	svarūpasiddha
intrinsic reality-status	rang bzhin gyis grub pa, rang gi ngo bo nyid kyis grub pa	svabhāva-siddha, svarūpa-siddha
intrinsic reality, nature	rang bzhin, rang gi ngo bo nyid	svabhāva
intrinsic, self-	rang	sva

English	Tibetan	Sanskrit
intrinsically identifiable intrinsic objectivity	rang mtshan grub pa'i rang gi ngo bo nyid kyis grub pa	*svalakṣaṇasiddha-svarūpa-siddha
intrinsically identifiable intrinsic reality	rang mtshan grub pa'i rang bzhin	*svalakṣaṇasiddha-sval-abhāva
intrinsically identifiable intrinsic reality	rang mtshan grub pa'i rang bzhin yod pa	*svalaṣaṇasiddha-svabhāva-sat
intrinsically identifiable intrinsic reality status	rang mtshan grub pa'i rang bzhin gyis grub	*svalakṣaṇasiddha-svabhā-va-siddha
intrinsically identifiable status	rang mtshan gyis grub pa	svalakṣaṇasiddha
introspectively known	so so rang gis rig pa	pratyātmavedya
intuition (wisdom) body	ye shes kyi sku	jñāna-mūrti
intuition (wisdom) consort	ye shes kyi phyag rgya	jñāna-mudrā
intuition (wisdom) eye	ye shes kyi mig	jñāna-cakṣu
intuition (wisdom) hero	ye shes sems dpa'	jñāna-sattva
intuition, consciousness	shes pa	jñāna
intuition, intuitive wisdom	ye shes	jñāna
intuitional validating cognition	mngon sum tshad ma	pratyakṣapramāṇa
invariable concomitance	khyab pa	vyapti
investigation	yongs su tshol ba	parāmarṣa
invisible	snang ba med pa	nirābhāsa
irrational	rigs pa ma yin pa	na yuktitaḥ
irreversible	phyir mi ldog pa	avaivartika
isolation, isolated	dben pa	viveka, vivikta
jargon (nonliteral) expressions	sgra ji bzhin ma yin pa	ayathāruta-śhabda
jewel	rin po che, rin chen	ratna
joy	dga' ba	ānanda
kissing	'o byed pa	cumbana

English	Tibetan	Sanskrit
language	skad	ruta
languid	dal ba	stabdha
learning	bslabs pa	abhyāsa
learning, erudition	bslab pa, thos pa	śikṣā, śruta
letter	yi ge	vyañjana
liberation, nirvana	thar pa, grol ba, mya ngan las 'das pa	mokṣa, vimokṣa, nirvāṇa
life, life cycle	'khor ba	saṁsāra
lifestyle (conduct) of bodhisattva	byang chub sems dpa'i spyod pa	bodhi-caryā
lifetime	tshe rabs	jīvita, jāti
light	'od	prabhā
light ray	'od zer	kiraṇa, raśmi
limb, branch	yan lag	aṅga
literal	sgra ji bzhin pa	yathāruta
literal insistence	sgra ji bzhin du zhen pa	yathārutābhiniveśa
literal meaning	sgra ji bzhin pa'i don	yathārutārtha
logical range	rigs pa'i yul	yuktigocara
logical reasoning	thad pas sgrub pai rigs pa	upapattisādhanayukti
logician	rigs par smra ba, tshad ma pa	naiyāyika, prāmāṇika
Lord of Secrets	gsang ba'i bdag po	guhyakādhipati
lotus	padma	padma
lovemaking	rab tu dga' ba	surata
luminance-imminence	snang ba nyer thob	ālokopalabdha[ka]
luminance-imminence intuition	snang ba nyer thob ye shes	ālokopalabdha-jñāna
luminance-radiance	snang ba mched pa	ālokābhāsa
luminance, light	snang ba	āloka

ENGLISH	TIBETAN	SANSKRIT
lump	gong bu	piṇḍa
machine	'khrul 'khor	yantra
mad discipline	smyon pa'i brtul zhugs	unmatta-vrata
magic	rgyu ma	māyā
magic body	sgyu ma'i sku, sgyu lus	māyādeha
magic net	sgyu 'phrul dra ba	māyā-jāla
magical	sgyu ma lta bu, sgyu ma 'dra	māyopama
magical samādhi	sgyu ma lta bu'i ting nge 'dzin	māyopama-samādhi
magician	sgyu ma mkhan	māyākāra
magnificent	rgya che ba	vistara, udāra
Mahayanist, Universalist	theg pa chen po pa	mahāyānika
mandala, sphere	dkyil 'khor	maṇḍala
manifest	lung du bstan pa	vyākṛta
mantra	sngags	mantra
mantra body	sngags kyi lus	mantra-mūrti
mantra collection	sngags btu ba	mantroddhāra
mantra lord	sngags kyi bdag po	mantrādhipati
mantra reality	sngags kyi de kho na nyid	mantra-tattva
mantrin	sngags pa	mantrin
master	bdag po	svāmin
material sciences	phyi'i bstan bcos	bāhya-śāstra
materialism	dngos por 'dzin pa	bhāva-graha
materialistic construction	ril 'dzin brtags pa	piṇḍagrahakalpana
materialistic view	ril 'dzin lta ba	piṇḍagrahadṛṣṭi
matter aggregate	gzugs kyi phung po	rūpaskandha
matter body, form body	gzugs sku	rūpakāya
matter, form	gzugs	rūpa

English	Tibetan	Sanskrit
meaning, aim, referent, object, import	don	artha
measureless mansion, palace	gzhal yas khang	vimāna, kūṭāgāra,
meditation	bsgom pa, sgom pa	bhāvanā
meditative object	bsgom par bya ba	bhāvaka
medium	skye mched	āyatana
mendicant	dge slong	bhikṣu
mental factors	sems las byung ba	caitasika
mental habit	bzung ba, 'dzin pa	graha
mentality	yid	manas
mentor	bla ma	guru
merit	bsod nams	puṇya
metabolic (energy)	mnyam gnas, me dang mnyam du gnas pa	samāna
method, way	tshul	naya
migrant being	'gro ba	jagat
migration	'gro ba	gati
mind	sems	citta, cetas
mind conduct	sems kyi spyod pa	citta-carita
mind isolation	sems dben	citta-viveka
mind only (*see also* idealism)	sems tsam	citta-mātra[tā]
mind vajra	sems rdo rje	citta-vajra
mind-made body	yid kyi rang bzhin gyi lus (sku)	manomayadeha
mind-vajra samadhi	thugs rdo rje'i ting nge 'dzin	citta-vajra-samādhi
mindfulness (branch)	dran pa (yan lag)	smṛti (aṅga)
mindfulness domain	dran pa'i nyer gzhag	smṛti-upasthāna

English	Tibetan	Sanskrit
mine- (property-) habit, possessiveness	ngar sems pa, nga yir 'dzin pa	mamakāra
miracle	rdzu 'phrul	ṛddhi
mirage	smig rgyu	marīci[ka]
mirror	me long	ādarśa, darpaṇa
mirrorlike intuition	me long lta bu'i ye shes	ādarśa-jñāna
misknowledge	ma rig pa	avidya
moment, instant	skad cig	kṣana
Mount Sumeru	ri'i rgyal po ri rab	sumeru
mutual dependence, interdependence	phan tshun ltos pa	parasparāpekṣa
mutually dependent designative status	phan tshun ltos pa'i gdags grub	parasparāpekṣaprajñāpti-siddha
mutually dependent status	phan tshun ltos grub	parasparāpekṣasiddha
naïve, fool, child	byis pa	bāla
name	ming	nāma
name and form, mind-body	ming gzugs	nāmarūpa
natural clear light transparence	rang bzhin gyis 'od gsal ba	prakṛti-prabhāsvara
natural conventional validating cognition	lhan skyes tha snyad pa'i tshad ma	*sahajavyāvahārika-pramāṇa
natural radiance	rang bzhin snang ba,	prakṛty-ābhāsa
natural reasoning	chos nyid kyi rigs pa	dharmatāyukti
natural recitation	rang bzhin bzlas pa	prakṛti-jāpa
natural, unconscious, instinctual, innate, orgasmic	lhan skyes	sahaja, nija
natural instincts	rang bzhin gyi rtog pa	prakṛti
nature	chos, mtshan nyid, rang bzhin	dharma, lakṣaṇa, svabhāva
nature-possessor	chos can	dharmin

English	Tibetan	Sanskrit
nature, intrinsic reality	ngo bo nyid, rang bzhin, ngo bo	svabhāva
naturelessness, unreality, insubstantiality	dngos med	niḥsvabhāva
negate, refute	dgag pa, bkag pa	pratiṣedha, niṣedha
negatee, negandum	dgag bya	pratiṣedhavya, niṣedhya
negation-ground (base)	dgag gzhi	
negation, refutation	dgag pa	pratiṣedha
negative conditioning	gnas ngan len	dauṣṭhulya
neural channel	rtsa	nāḍī
nihilism	med par smra ba ('dzin pa)	abhāvavāda (graha)
nihilist	med pa pa	abhāvavādin
nihilistic extreme	med mtha'	abhāvānta
nihilistic extremism	med mthar 'dzin pa	abhāvāntagraha
nine aesthetic moods	nyams rnam pa dgu	nava-nāṭya-rasa
nirvana	mya ngan las 'das pa	nirvāṇa
noble	'phags pa	ārya
noble aftermath intuition, intuitive wisdom	'phags pa'i rjes thob ye shes	āryapṛṣṭhalabdhajñāna
noble aftermath rational cognition	'phags pa'i rjes thob kyi rigs shes	*āryapṛṣṭhalabdha-yukti-jñāna
noble child, noble son	rigs kyi bu	kulaputra
noble daughter	rigs kyi bu mo	kula-duhitṛ
noble entranced intuition, intuitive wisdom	'phags pa'i mnyam bzhag ye shes	āryasamāhitajñāna
nominal convention	ming gi tha snyad	*nāmavyavahāra
nominal designation	ming gis 'dogs pa	
non-analytic	dpyod med	avicāra
non-analytic conventional validating cognition	dpyod med tha snyad pa'i tshad ma	*avicāravyāvahārika-pramāṇa

English	Tibetan	Sanskrit
non-analytic natural self-habit	dpyod med bdag 'dzin lhan skyes	avicārasahajātmagraha
non-analytic presentation	dpyod med rnam gzhag	avicāravyavasthāna
nonconceptual	rnam rtog med pa	nirvikalpa
nondeceptive	mi slu ba	avisaṁvādaka
non-entranced yoga	mnyam par ma bzhag sbyor ba	asamāhita-yoga
non-mental-functioning	yid la mi byed pa	amanasikāra
nonperception of related fact reason	'brel zla ma dmigs pa'i rtags	
nondual	gnyis su med pa, gnyis med	advaya
noumenally omniscient intuition	ji lta ba mkhyen pa'i ye shes	yathāvadjñāna
noumenon, transcendent, transmundane	chos nyid, don dam, 'jig rten las 'das pa	dharmatā, paramārtha, lokottara
object	don	artha
object	gzung ba, gzung	grāhya
object of names and signs	ming dang brda'i yul	*nāmasaṁketaviṣaya
objectifying view	dmigs par lta ba	upalambha-dṛṣṭi
objective	chos kyi bdag	dharmātma
objective (external), objectivity status	phyi don, phyi don du grub pa	bāhyārtha, bāhyārthasiddha
objective condition	dmigs rkyen	ālaṁbanapratyaya
objective generality, objective universal	don spyi	arthasāmānya
objective object	dmigs pa'i yul	ālaṁbanaviṣaya
objective obscuration	shes bya'i sgrib pa	jñeyāvaraṇa
objective reality	rang gi ngo bo nyid	svarūpatva, svabhāvatva
objective self	chos kyi bdag	dharmātma
objective self-habit	chos kyi bdag 'dzin	dharmātmagraha

English	Tibetan	Sanskrit
objective selflessness	chos la bdag med	dharma-nairātmya
objective status	rang gi ngo bos grub pa	svarūpasiddha
objective-reality-status	rang gi ngo bo nyid kyi grub pa	svarūpasiddha
obscuration	sgrib pa	āvaraṇa, nivaraṇa
obsession, insistence	mngon par zhen pa	abhiniveśa
occasion of entrancement	mnyam par bzhag pa'i gnas skabs	samāhitāvasthā
occasion, context	gnas skabs	avasthā
one way	tshul gcig pa	eka-naya
one-pointedness	rtse gcig pa	ekāgratā
optical illusion	mig 'phrul	indrajāla
ordinary	tha mal pa	sāmānya, prākṛta
ordinary body	tha mal pa'i lus	prākṛta-deha
ordinary pride	tha mal pa'i nga rgyal	prākṛtāhaṁkāra
orientation, visualization	lhag par mos pa	adhimukti
original, self-created	rang byung	svayaṁbhū
other-emptiness	gzhan stong	paraśūnyata
outsider	phyi rol pa	bahirdhā
overlord, lord	bdag po	adhipati
own chosen deity	bdag nyid lha	svādhidevatā
particular, ultimate	rang gi mtshan nyid (tshad ma pa'i)	svalakṣaṇa (prāmanīka)
passion, lust	'dod chags, chags pa	rāga
path of philosophy, path of reason	rigs pa'i lam	nyāyamārga, yuktimārga
path of ten virtuous evolutionary actions	dge ba bcu'i las kyi lam	daśa-kuśala-karma-patha
peerless	gnyis med	nirdvandva

English	Tibetan	Sanskrit
perception	’du shes	saṁjñā
perception aggregate, conception aggregate	’du shes kyi phung po	saṁjñāskandha
perception of inconsistent fact reason	’gal zla dmigs pa’i rtags	
perceptual and conceptual object	snang yul dang zhen yul	
perceptual habit	’dzin stangs, ’dzin pa	muṣṭi, graha
perceptual object	snang yul	*ābhāsaviṣaya
perfect	yongs su grub pa	pariniṣpanna
perfect buddha	rdzogs pa’i sangs rgyas	sambuddha
perfect enlightenment	yang dag par rdzogs pa’i byang chub	samyak-saṁbodhi
perfect identity	yongs su grub pa’i mtshan nyid	pariniṣpannalakṣaṇa
perfect nature	yongs su grub pa mtshan nyid	pariniṣpannalakṣaṇa
perfect reality	yongs su grub pa ngo bo nyid, yongs grub kyi mtshan nyid	pariniṣpannasvabhāva
perfect, perfected	yongs su grub pa	pariniṣpanna
perfection stage	rdzogs rim	niṣpanna-krama
perfectly enlightened buddha	yang dag par rdzogs pa’i sangs rgyas	samyaksaṁbuddha
performance tantra	spyod pa’i rgyud	caryā-tantra
performance, practice	sgrub thabs	sādhana
permanent, permanence	rtag pa	śāśvata
permission	rjes su gnang ba	anujñā
permoving (energy)	rnam par rgyu ba	vivāha (vāyu)
person	mi	puruṣa
person	gang zag	pudgala

English	Tibetan	Sanskrit
personal (subjective) self	gang zag gi bdag	pudgalātma
personal inference (internal)	rang don rjes dpag	svārthānumāna
personal instruction	man ngag	upadeśa, āmnāya
personal selflessness	gang zag gi bdag med	pudgalanairātmya
personal subjective self-habit (conscious, unconscious)	gang zag gi bdag 'dzin	pudgalātmagraha
pervading (energy)	khyab byed	vyāna
phenomenally omniscient intuition	ji snyed mkhyen pa'i ye she	yāvatjñāna
phenomenon, thing	dngos po, chos	bhava, dharma
philosophy (reason, theory)	smra ba (rigs pa, grub mtha')	vāda (nyāya, siddhānta)
phlegm	bad kan	śleṣma
play	'gying bag	līlā
play	a ra li	ārali
pleasure, bliss	bde ba	sukha
pledge, commitment	dam tshig	samaya
point, meaning, etc.	don	artha
position, thesis, direction	phyogs (dam bca)	pakṣa (pratijña)
possession	thob pa	prāpti
possessiveness	bdag gir (nga yir) 'dzin pa	ātmīyagraha
potency, power	mthu	prabhāva
power, accomplishment	dngos grub	siddhi
practical instruction	gdams ngag	
practice art, performance	sgrub pa'i thabs	sādhana
practitioner	sgrub pa po	sādhaka
present, represent	rnam par gzhag pa	vyavasthāp

English	Tibetan	Sanskrit
presentation of the non-analytic conventional	ma dpyad pa'i tha snyad du 'jog pa	
presentation, arrangement	rnam par gzhag pa	vyavasthāna
pride	nga rgyal, ngar 'dzin pa, bdag tu rlom pa	ahaṁkāra
primally unborn	gzod nas ma skyes pa	ādyanutpanna
prior momentum	sngon gyi 'phen shugs	pūrvāvedha
privacy, logical	rang rgyud	svātantrya
private (dogmatic) syllogism	rang rgyud rjes dpag	svatantrānumāna
private (dogmatic) thesis	rang rgyud kyi dam bca	svatantrapratijñā
private (dogmaticist) reason	rang rgyud kyi rtags	svatantrahetu
private inference	rang rgyud rjes dpag	svatantrānumana
private reason	rang rgyud kyi rtags	svatantrahetu
private thesis	rang rgyud kyi dam bca	svatantrapraijña
probandum	sgrub bya	sādhya
probandum property	sgrub bya'i chos	sādhyadharma
proclivity, instinct	bag la nyal ba, bag chags	anuśaya, vāsana
production unreality	skye ba ngo bo nyid med pa	*utpādanaiḥsvābhavya
profound	zab mo, zab pa	gambhīra, gambhīrya
property	bdag gi ba, nga yi ba	ātmīya
prospering, increasing	rgyas pa	pauṣṭika
protagonist	sngar rgol	
prove	yid ches par bgyi ba	pratyaya
public (dialectical) inference/syllogism	gzhan grags kyi ries dpag	paraprasiddhānumāna
public (dialectical) reason	gzhan grags kyi rtags	paraprasiddhahetu
public inference/syllogism	gzhan don rjes dpag	parārthānumāna
pulsation	rnam par gyo ba	saṁspandita

English	Tibetan	Sanskrit
pure	rnam dag, dag pa	śuddha
pure information, pure intelligence	rnam par rig pa tsam	vijñaptimātra
purification	rnam par dag pa, rnam par sbyang ba	viśhuddhi, vyavadāna
purification of the radiances	snang ba rnam par dag pa	ābhāsa-viśhuddhi
purity	gtsang pa	śuciḥ
qualitative (descriptive) designation	khyad par du brtags pa	viśeṣavikalpa
quality, property, thing	chos	dharma
range, sphere, province	spyod yul, yul	gocara
rational cognition	rigs shes	*yuktijñāna
rationality, reason, philosophy	rigs pa	yukti, nyāya
real	yang dag pa	bhūta
real production	rang bzhin gyis skyes pa	svabhāvotpāda
real status	rang bzhin gyis grub pa	svabhāvasiddha
Realist	dngos por smra ba	bhāvavādin
realistic view	yang dag lta ba	samyakdṛṣṭi
reality	de nyid, de kho na nyid, bden pa, rang bzhin, rang gi ngo bo nyid	tattva, satya, svabhāva, svarūpa,
reality (truth) status	bden grub, rang bzhin grub	satyasiddha, svabhāvasiddha
reality limit	yang dag pa'i mtha'	bhūta-koṭi, bhūtānta
reality realm perfection intuition	chos kyi dbyings rnam par dag pa'i ye shes	suviśuddha-dharma-dhātu-jñānaṁ
reality source	chos 'byung ba	dharmodaya
reality, thing	dngos po	bhāva
reality, truth, fact	bden pa	satya
realitylessness, truthlessness	bden med, rang bzhin med, ngo bo nyid med pa	asatyatā, naiḥsvabhāvasiddha

ENGLISH	TIBETAN	SANSKRIT
realization	rtogs pa	adhigama
realm of reality	chos kyi dbyings	dharmadhātu
reason (rational cognition)	rtags, rigs pa (rigs shes)	hetu, yukti, nyāya
reason, validating cognition	tshad ma	pramāṇa
reasoning	tshul, rigs pa	nyāya, yukti
rebirth, future life	yang srid pa, srid pa gzhan	punarbhava
recitation	bzlas pa	japa
referent	gdags don	
referent	don, gzhi	artha, vastu
referent of designation	gdags don	prajñapyārtha
referential base	gdags gzhi	
reflection	gzugs brnyan	pratibimba
refutation	bkag pa, sun 'byin pa	pratiṣedha, nirākaraṇa
refute, negate	dgag pa	pratiṣedha
reification	sgro 'dogs pa	samāropa, adhyāropa
relational reasoning	ltos pai rigs pa	āpekṣāyukti
relative (nature, reality)	gzhan dbang	paratantra
relative reality	gzhan dbang gi mtshan nyid	paratantrasvabhāva
relative, dependent	gzhan gyi dbang	paratantra
relativistic origination	rten cing 'brel bar 'byung ba	pratītyasamutpāda
relativity, dependent origination	rten cing 'brel bar 'byung ba	pratītyasamutpāda, idaṁprayayatā
reliance	rton pa	pratiṣaraṇa
remedy, antidote	gnyen po	pratipakṣa
representation	rnam par gzhag pa	vyavasthāna
repudiation	skur ba 'debs pa	apavāda
resistance	mi mthun phyogs	vipakṣa
retention	gzungs	dhāraṇī

English	Tibetan	Sanskrit
retinue	'khor	parivāra
retraction branch	so sor sdud pa'i yan lag	pratyāhāra-aṅga
rite, evolution, action	las	karman
ritual action	bya ba	kriyā
ritual gesture	phyag rgya	mudrā
ritual manual	rtog pa	kalpa
ritual procedure	cho ga	vidhi
ritually prepared	'dus byas pa	saṁskṛta
root of virtue	dge ba'i rtsa ba	kuśala-mūla
root tantra	rtsa ba'i rgyud	mūla-tantra
rosary, garland	phreng ba	mālā
sacred tradition	man ngag yang dag par 'gro ba	saṁpradāya
saint	dgra bcom pa	arhant
salutation	phyag 'tshal ba	namaskara
samadhi	ting nge 'dzin	samādhi
samadhi conducive to the real	yang dag pa'i tshul gyi bdag nyid can gyi ting nge 'dzin	bhūta-nāyātmaka-samādhi
samadhi-hero	ting nge 'dzin sems dpa'	samādhi-sattvas
samsara, life cycle	'khor ba	saṁsāra
science	rig gnas	vidyāsthāna
science (teaching manual)	bstan bcos	śāstra
science consort discipline	rig pa'i brtul zhugs	vidyā-vrata
scriptural tradition	gsung rab	pravacana
scripturalist, traditionalist	mdo sde	sautrāntika
scripture (reference)	lung	āgama
scripture, discourse, sutra	mdo	sūtra

English	Tibetan	Sanskrit
seal	phyag rgya	mudrā
seal reality	phyag rgya'i de kho na nyid	mudrā-tattva
secret mantra way	gsang sngags kyi tshul	mantranaya
seed, seed syllable	sa bon	bīja
self	bdag	ātma
self (nature)	bdag (bdag nyid)	ātman
self-awareness	rang rig, rang gi ye shes	sva-saṁvitti
self-consciousness (apperceptive)	rang rig	svasaṁvitti
self-consecration	bdag la byin gyis brlab pa	svādhiṣṭhāna
self-consecration stage	bdag la byin gyis brlab pa['i rim pa]	svādhiṣṭhāna-krama
self-creation	bdag las skyes pa	ātmotpāda
self-habit	bdag 'dzin	ātmagraha
self-performance	bdag la bsgrub pa	ātma-sādhana
selfless	bdag med pa	anātmaka
selflessness	bdag med pa	anātmatā, nairātmya
semen	sa bon	śukra
sensation	tshor ba	vedanā
sensation aggregate	'tshor ba'i phung po	vedanāskandha
sense cognition	dbang shes	indriyajñāna
sense faculty	dbang po	indriya
sense-medium	skye mched	āyatana
sense, sense organ	dbang po	indriya
serenity, quiescence	zhi gnas	śamatha
shaking	bskyod pa	spandana
shame	ngo tsha shes pa	lajjā

English	Tibetan	Sanskrit
sign	mtshan ma, rgyu mtshan, brda	nimitta, saṁketa
sign-habit	mtshan mar 'dzin pa	*nimittagraha
signification (symbol)	brtag pa (brda)	saṁketa
signification process	mtshan mar 'gyur pa	nimittabhūta
signlessness	mtshan ma med pa	animitta
simile	dpe	dṛṣṭānta, upamā
simultaneous, sudden	cig car	yugapat
sin	sdig pa	pāpa
single-mindedness	dran pa gcig pa	eka-smṛti
six transcendences	pha rol tu phyin pa drug	ṣaṭpāramitā
sleep	gnyid log pa	svapna
sloth, stupor	le lo, gnyid	ālasya, styāna
social convention	'jig rten gyi tha snyad	lokavyavahāra
society	'du ba	saṁgaṇikā
sound, word	sgra	śabda
space	nam mkha'	ākāśa, ambara, kha
space-like	nam mkha' dang mnyam pa	khasama, khopama
speech	ngag	vāk
speech isolation	ngag dben	vag-viveka
speech vajra	gsung rdo rje	vāg-vajra
spell, formula	rig sngags	vidyā
sphere, domain, province	yul, spyod yul	viṣaya
spheres, three (of an act)	'khor gsum	trimaṇḍala
spirit of enlightenment	byang chub sems	bodhicitta
spiritual gene, genus	rigs	gotra
spiritual guide, spiritual friend	dge ba'i bshes gnyen	kalyāṇa-mitra

English	Tibetan	Sanskrit
spiritual seeker, vacationer	dge sbyong	śramaṇa
split second	yud tsam	muhūrta
stage	rim pa, sa	krama, bhūmi
stage leading to communion	zung du 'brel par 'jug pa'i rim pa	yuganaddha-vāhi-krama
state	gnas, go 'phang	pada, avasthā, bhāva
status, establishment	grub pa	siddha
store	tshogs	saṁbhāra
strength	stobs	sāmarthya, bala
subjectivity	'dzin pa, 'dzin rnam	graha, *grahakākāra
subjectivity reality	bdag gi de kho na nyid	ātma-tattva
subjectlessness	chos can ma grub pa	*asiddhadharmin
substance	rdzas	dravya
substantial existence	rdzas su yod pa	dravyasat
substantial status	rdzas su grub pa	dravyasiddha
substantial subject-object dichotomy	gzung 'dzin rdzas tha dad	*grāhyagrahakadravyabheda
substantive (ascriptive) designation	ngo bor brtags pa	svabhāvaprajñapti
subtle	phra mo, phra ba, zhib pa	sūkṣma
subtle element	khams phra ba	sūkṣma-dhātu
subtle yoga	phra mo'i rnal 'byor	sūkṣma-yoga
success, accomplishment	dngos grub	siddhi
suchness	de bzhin nyid	tathatā
sucking	rngub pa	cūṣaṇa
suffering	sdug bsngal, sdug	duḥkha
superficial	kun rdzob [kyi]	saṁvṛti
superficial reality	kun rdzob bden pa	saṁvṛti-satya
superknowledge	mngon par shes pa	abhijñā

English	Tibetan	Sanskrit
support	gzhi, rten	ādhāra
supreme joy	mchog tu dga' ba	paramānanda
surmoving (energy)	rab tu rgyu ba (rlung)	pravāha (vāyu)
sutra, discourse	mdo, mdo de	sūtra, sūtraka, sūtrānta
syllable	yi ge, yig 'bru	akṣara, lipika, varṇa
syllable, undestroyed	yi ge, mi 'gyur ba	akṣara
symbol	mtshan ma	cihna
symbol (convention)	brda	saṁketa
symbol-seal	mtshan ma'i phyag rgya	cihna-mudrā
sympathy	[thugs] brtse ba	anukampā
system	lugs, rnam gzhag	naya, vyavasthāna
systematizer, pioneer	srol phye ba	
taint	dri ma	mala
tantra, continuity	rgyud	tantra
taste, mood	ro	rasa
teacher	slob dpon, ston pa	ācārya, śāstṛ
teaching	chos	dharma
teaching	bstan pa, bstan bcos	deśanā, śāstra
ten-stage lord	sa bcu'i dbang phyug	daśabhūmīśvara
ten energies	rlung bcu	daśa vāyu
texture	reg bya	sparśa
thatness (immanent)	de nyid, de kho na nyid	tattvam
thatness, reality	de kho na nyid, de nyid	tattva
the naïve, the foolish	byis pa'i skye bo, byis pa	bāla, bāliśa
theologian, dogmatist	rtog ge pa	tārkika
theoretical (conscious, intellectual) self-habit	kun brtags bdag 'dzin	parikalpitātmagrahādi
theory, philosophy	grub mtha'	siddhānta

English	Tibetan	Sanskrit
thesis	dam bca'	pratijñā
thing	dngos po, chos	bhāva, padārtha, dharma
thorough insight	yongs su shes pa, rtogs pa	parijñāna
thorough investigation	yongs su 'tshol ba	paryeṣṭi
three conducts, three lifestyles	spyod pa rnam gsum	trividhacaryā
three consciousnesses	rnam par shes pa gsum	vijñāna-traya
three luminances	snang ba gsum	āloka-traya
three mandalas	dkyil 'khor gsum	trimaṇḍala
three radiances	snang ba gsum	ābhāsa-traya
three realities	ngo bo nyid gsum	trisvabhāvam
three realities	de nyid gsum	tri-tattva
three realms	khams gsum, sa 'og dang sa steng dang mtho ris	tridhātu, bhūrbhuvaḥsvaḥ
three syllables	yi ge gsum	akṣara-traya, tryakṣara
three times	dus gsum	try-adhva, trikāla
three vehicles	theg pa gsum	triyāna
three voids	stong pa gsum	śūnya-traya
three worlds	'jig rten gsum	triloka
tolerance	bzod pa	kṣānti
torpor	gnyid, rmugs	middha
traditionalist, scripturalist	mdo sde pa	sautrāntika
transcendence	pha rol tu phyin pa, nges legs	pāramitā, niḥśreyasa
transcendence vehicle	phar phyin theg pa	pāramitāyāna
transcendent	'jig rten las 'das pa	lokottara
transcendent lord	de bzhin gshegs pa	tathāgata
transcendent reality (suchness)	de bzhin nyid	tathata

English	Tibetan	Sanskrit
transcendent renunciation	nges par 'byung ba	apavarga, niryāṇa
transcendent wisdom	shes rab kyi pha rol tu phyin pa	prajñāpāramitā
transcendental (opposite of mundane, social)	'jig rten las 'das pa	lokottara
transformation	yongs su log, yongs su gyur pa	parāvṛtti, pariṇāmana
transparence, clear light	'od gsal ba	prabhāsvara
triple realm	srid pa gsum	tri-bhuvanaṁ
triple realm	khams gsum	traidhātuka
true existence	bden par yod pa	*satyasat
true production	bden par skyes pa	*satyotpāda
truth body	chos kyi sku	dharma-kāya
truth-habit	bden par 'dzin pa	satyadraha
truth-status	bden par grub pa	satyasiddha
truth, reality	bden pa	tathya, satya
truthlessness	bden par med pa, bden par ma grub pa	asatyasiddha
twelve ascetical practices	sbyangs pa'i yon tan bcu gnyis	dvādaśa-dhūta-guṇa
twelve links of dependent origination	rten 'brel bcu gnyis	pratītya-dvādaśāṅga
twelve similes of magic	sgyu ma'i dpe bcu gnyis	dvādaśa-māyā-dṛṣṭānta
two [sexual] organs	dbang po gnyis	dvayendriya
two realities	bden pa gnyis	satyadvaya
ultimacy analytic rational cognition	don dam dpyod pa'i rigs shes	*paramārthavicārayukti-jñāna
ultimacy status	don dam du grub pa	paramārthasiddha
ultimacy-analytic rational cognition	don dam (mthar thug) dpyod pa'i rigs shes	*paramārthavicārayukti-jñāna
ultimate (reality)	don dam (bden pa)	paramārtha (satya)

English	Tibetan	Sanskrit
ultimate production	don dam du skyes pa	paramārthotpāda
ultimate unreality	don dam ngo bo nyid med pa	paramārtha
ultramoving (energy)	nges par rgyu ba	nirvāha (vāyu)
unanalyzed existence	ma brtags par yod pa	
unanalyzed social convention	ma dpyad (brtags) pa'i 'jig rten gyi tha snyad	
unborn	skye ba med pa	anutpanna
unconquered	zil gyis mi non pa	anabhibhūta
unconscious, instinctual	lhan kyes	sahaja
unconscious, instinctual futile view	'jig lta lhan skyes	sahajasatkāyadṛṣṭi
unconscious, instinctual, misknowledge	ma rig pa lhan skyes	sahajāvidyā
unconscious, instinctual, self-habit	bdag 'dzin lhan skyes	sahajātmagraha
uncontaminated	zag pa med	anāsrava
uncontrived, unfabricated	ma bcos pa	akṛtaka
uncreated	'dus ma byas pa	anabhisaṁskṛta, asaṁskṛta
undeducible	brtag tu med pa	apratarkya
unelaborated	spros pa med pa	niṣprapañca
unelaborated conduct, unelaborated lifestyle	spros pa med pa'i spyod pa	niṣprapañca-caryā
unerring	mi 'chor ba	akṣūṇa
unerring suchness	ma nor ba de bzhin nyid	avitathatā
unexcelled	bla na med pa	anuttara
unification	gcig sbyor ba	eka-yoga
union	sbyor ba	yoga
unique vehicle	theg pa gcig pa	ekayāna
uniting liṅga and bhaga	bha ga dang liṅga'i sbyor ba	bhaga-liṅga-yoga

ENGLISH	TIBETAN	SANSKRIT
universal (great) seal	phyag rgya chen po	mahāmudrā
universal monarch	'khor los sgyur ba	cakravarti
universal vehicle	theg pa chen po	mahāyāna
universal void	thams cad stong pa	sarva-śūnya
universal, generality	spyi	sāmānya
Universalist	theg pa chen po pa	mahāyānika
unlocated nirvāṇa	mi gnas pa'i mya ngan las 'das pa	apratiṣṭhita-nirvāṇa
unmanifest	mi mngon	avyakta
unobstructed	thogs pa med pa	asaṅga
unproduced	skye ba med pa	anutpāda
unreal, unreality, non-existent	med, med pa, yod ma yin pa, dngos med	abhāva, abhūta
unreality	dngos med, ngo bo nyid med pa	niḥsvabhāva, niḥsvabhāvatā
unreflective (inquiry, usage)	rang dga ba ('i brtag pa, 'jug pa)	
unshakeable samadhi	mi gyo ba'i ting nge 'dzin	āsphānaka-samādhi
unspoken, syllableless	yi ge bral, yi ge med pa	anakṣara
unstruck [sound]	mi shigs pa	anāhata
unvirtuous, unskillful	mi dge ba	akuśala
unwavering	mi gyo [ba]	acala
upmoving (energy)	ldang zhing rgyu ba	udvāha (vāyu)
utterance	brjod pa	udāhāra
utterly peaceful	rab tu zhi ba	praśānta
vajra	rdo rje	vajra
vajra body	rdo rje lus	vajradeha
vajra intuition	rdo rje'i ye shes	vajra-jñāna
vajra mentor	rdo rje slob dpon	vajraguru

English	Tibetan	Sanskrit
vajra recitation	rdo rje bzlas pa	vajra-jāpa
vajra samadhi	rdo rje lta bu'i ting nge 'dzin	vajropama-samādhi
vajra teacher	rdo rje slob dpon	vajrācārya
vajra vehicle	rdo rje theg pa	vajrayāna
vajra word	rdo rje'i tshig	vajra-pada
Vajrayanist	rdo rje theg pa [rnams]	vajrayānika
validating cognition	tshad ma	pramāṇa
validating rational cognition	tshad ma'i rigs shes	*prāmāṇikayuktijñāna
vanity	gsog	tuccha
vase	bum pa	kalaśa
vehicle	bzhon pa	vāhana
venerable master (Nāgārjuna)	rje btsun, klu sgrub zhabs	bhaṭṭāraka-pāda
verbal designation	ming gis gdags pa	nāmaprajñapti
verbal formulation	ming gis brjod pa	nāmābhidhāna
verbal token	ngag gi brda	vāk-cchomā
verbal universal	sgra spyi	śabdasāmānya
victor	rgyal ba	jina
victor lord	rgyal dbang	jinendra
view	lta ba	dṛṣṭi
virtuous and nonvirtuous, beautiful and ugly, skillful and unskillful	dge ba dang mi dge ba	śubhāśubha
vision, perception	snang ba, nye bar dmigs pa	darśana, upalabdhi
visualized, imagined	brtags, kun brtags pa	parikalpita
vitality control, vitalizing energy control (branch)	srog dang rtsol ba (yan lag)	prāṇāyāma (aṅga)
vitality, vitality [air]	srog	prāṇa

English	Tibetan	Sanskrit
void, empty	stong pa	śūnya
voided, emptied	stongs gzhi	yena śūnyatā, śūnyādhāra
voidness, emptiness	stong pa nyid	śūnyatā
vow, prayer	smon lam	praṇidhāna
vowels	dbyangs	svara
vowels and consonants	ā li kā li	ālikāli
waking	gnyid ma log pa	jāgrat
water-moon	chu zla	udaka-candra
well-known, public	grags	prasiddha
wheel of existence, cycle	'khor ba	bhava-cakra
will to enlightenment, spirit of enlightenment	byang chub kyi sems	bodhicitta
wind, energy	rlung	vāta, vāyu
wisdom	shes rab	prajña
wisdom and art	shes rab dang thabs	prajñopāya
wisdom transcendence	shes rab kyi pha rol tu phyin pa	prajñāpāramitā
wisdom-intuition	shes rab kyi ye shes	prajñā-jñāna
wisdom-intuition initiation	shes rab dang ye shes kyi dbang bskur ba	prajñā-jñānābhiṣeka
wise expert	mkhas pa	paṇḍita
withstand analysis, ability to	dpyad bzod pa	
world	'gro ba	jagat
world (people)	'jig rten pa	loka
world-mentor	'gro ba'i bla	jagad-guru
world-realm	'jig rten gyi khams	lokadhātu
worldly	'jig rten pa	laukika
worldly concern	'jig rten pa'i chos	loka-dharma

English	Tibetan	Sanskrit
worship, offering	mchod pa	pūjā
yogi/nī (male or female)	rnal 'byor pa	yogī
yoginī	rnal 'byor ma	yoginī
zombiess	ro langs ma	vetālī

Glossary of Numerical Categories

two contemplations (*dhyāna – bsam gtan*). These are: (1) the dissolvent (*rjes gzhig*) and (2) holistic (*ril 'dzin*) contemplations used to reinforce the concentration needed to dissolve the energies into the central channel in the context of the higher stages of the perfection stage.

two obscurations (*āvaraṇadvaya*). (1) Addictive obscuration (*kleśāvaraṇa*) and (2) objective obscuration (*jñeyāvaraṇa*). The former may be eliminated by arhats and bodhisattvas of a certain stage, while the latter is eliminated only at buddhahood.

two realities (sometimes "truths") (*satyadvaya*). (1) The superficial reality (*saṁvṛtisatya*) and (2) the ultimate reality (*paramārthasatya*), or the relative truth and the absolute truth, or the conventional reality and the supreme reality.

two selflessnesses (*nairātmyādvaya*). (1) Subjective or personal selflessness (*pudgalanairātmyā*) and (2) objective selflessness (*dharmanairātmyā*), both being descriptions of the ultimate reality, which is devoid of the "two kind of selves," the realization of which is called "transcendent wisdom" (*prajñāpāramitā*).

two selves (*ātmādvaya*). (1) Subjective, or personal, self (*pudgalātmā*) and (2) objective self (*dharmātmā*), which are the ultimately non-existent assumed objects we seem to perceive as the essential cores of persons and things.

two stores (*puṇyajñānasaṁbhāra*). The stores of (1) merit and of (2) wisdom; all deeds of bodhisattvas contribute to their accumulation of these two stores, which ultimately culminate in the buddha-bodies of matter (*rūpakāya*) and of truth (*dharmakāya*).

three bad migrations (*durgati*). The migrations in: (1) hell, (2) the limbo of hungry ghosts, or (3) the animal kingdom.

three bodies of the Buddha (*trikāya*). (1) The "truth body" (*dharmakāya*), (2) the "beatific body" (*saṁbhogakāya*), and (3) the "emanation body" (*nirmāṇakāya*). A buddha is no longer an ordinary being, a self-habit-ridden individual caught inside his skin. Buddhists have developed a number of ways to express the extraordinary qualities of the experience of enlightenment. The three bodies is one of the most important of these. The ordinary mind at enlightenment expands in an experience of oneness with the infinity of beings and things, which becomes a permanent awareness, called the body of truth or reality. This is the highest fruit of wisdom, a state of virtual omniscience—nirvana—a perfect, ultimate freedom, and the uttermost fulfillment of all selfish concerns. At the same time, the ordinary speech and body do not lose their continua of life. Body and speech are seen by Buddhists as being interactive with others: body reaches out from self-centeredness to touch other persons and things; speech communicates the content of mind to others, linking mind to mind. Therefore, the continuum of speech expands as a celebration of the mind's attainment of infinite oneness, becoming a consummate and infinite joy experienced as a body of beatitude; a sort of subtle or ethereal body made of the sheer joy at being free of suffering, at having realized the absolute nature of reality. It is as infinite as reality, a subtle radiant omnipresence of a buddha's joy throughout all things. Finally, the continuum of ordinary body expands with enlightenment into an emanation body; a limitless number of individuated manifestations arises out of the background energy of the beatific body when a buddha spontaneously interacts with ordinary beings who cannot perceive their oneness with the beatific presence in and around them and persist in the misknowing individual theater of suffering and alienation. For the buddhas, infinite mind and speech magically create whatever gross embodiments are appropriate to relate to such beings, liberate them from their suffering, and ultimately inspire them to discover their own enlightenment and beatitude. These three buddha-bodies are aligned with the ordinary processes of death, between, and life, with sleep, dream, and waking, as well as with mind, speech, and body.

three concentrations (*samādhi*). (1) The heroic meditation (*śuraṁgama*), (2) the illusory meditation (*māyopama*), and (3) the adamantine meditation (*vajropama*).

three conducts (*caryā – spyod pa*). These three are: (1) the elaborated conduct, (2) the unelaborated conduct, and (3) the extremely unelaborated conduct. They are special lifestyles adopted by the tantric adept on either the creation-stage or the perfection-stage level. They were somewhat scandalous by ancient or modern codes of social and sexual behavior, but perhaps less so in the less puritanical and aesthetically sophisticated urban and court society of ancient India. They are meant to be esoteric, yet throughout tantric history definitely inspired imitation by people not at all at the level of insight and yogic self-mastery required to pursue such exercises. Thus, they gave tantric adepts a bad name in some quarters. They are part of the "crazy discipline" (*unmattavrata – myon pa'i brtul bzhug*) that aims to transform the pride of ordinariness of perception and conception into the vivid vision of purified perception of self and others and the environmental world. The elaborated is suitable only for adepts of great wealth and social position—such as kings and the like—in that it involves elaborate residences, elegant equipment and dress and musical organizations, and the assembling of a cast of actors who are all on the path and are adepts of some level in their own right. The unelaborated is simpler and easier to keep esoteric. The extremely unelaborated is very sparse, involving only a couple and a very modest, retreated lifestyle.

three defilements (*mala*). There is no conclusive evidence as to whether this refers to the taints of the three poisons or to the three contaminations (*āsrava*), by desire etc.

three doors (of evolutionary action) (*karmamukha*). (1) Body (*kāya*), (2) speech (*vāk*), and (3) mind (*citta*).

three doors of liberation (*vimokśamukha*). (1) Voidness or emptiness (*śūnyatā*), (2) signlessness (*animittā*), and (3) wishlessness (*apraṇihitā*).

three intuitions, intuitive wisdoms, or gnoses (*jñāna – ye shes*) of the subtle mind. These are: (1) luminance, (2) radiance, and (3) imminence (*āloka-ābhāsa-upalabdhi – snang mched nyer thob*) experienced as moonlit, sunlit, and darklit (or evening twilight or midnight darkened) sky spaces, when the energies have dissolved into the central channel and the eighty instinctual natures have subsided. Attainment of these three leads to conscious immersion in the clear light transparence that is the "fourth state," experienced as a diamond crystal grey predawn twilight transparence or transparency. This is called the "extremely subtle mind," normally experienced but not noticed at death, fainting, falling asleep, and orgasm. It is embodied nondually in the extremely subtle body of the indestructible drop. See "thirty-three instinctual natures," "forty instinctual natures," and "seven instinctual natures."

Three Jewels (*Triratna*). The three precious things in Buddhism: (1) the Buddha, (2) the Dharma (his teaching), and (3) the Saṁgha (the community of practitioners of that teaching).

three knowledges (*vidyā*). Three of the six superknowledges (see entry): (1) knowledge of former (and future) lives (*pūrvanivāsāna smṛtijñāna*), (2) knowledge of magical operations (*ṛddhividhijñāna*), and (3) knowledge of termination of birth and defilement (*utpādāsrava-kśayajñāna*).

three realms. See "three worlds."

three spiritual heroes (*sattva – sems dpa'*). These are: (1) the devotee hero (*samayasattva – dam tshig sems dpa*), (2) the wisdom or intuition hero (*jñānasattva – ye shes sems dpa'*), and (3) the samadhi hero (*samādhisattva – ting nge 'dzin sems dpa'*).

three worlds (*tridhātu*). (1) The desire world (*kāmadhātu*), (2) the material world, (*rūpadhātu*), and (3) the immaterial world (*ārūpyadhātu*).

four applications of mindfulness (*smṛtyupasthāna*). These are the stationing, or focusing, of mindfulness on: (1) the body, (2) sensations, (3) the mind, and (4) things. These four are the first four of the thirty-seven accessories of enlightenment (see entry).

four branches of a creation-stage performance practice (*seva*, *anusādhana*, *sādhana*, and *mahāsādhana – bsnyen pa, rjes su sgrub pa, sgrub pa, sgrub pa chen po*). These segments of a creation-stage contemplative performance may be translated as (1) service, (2) practice, (3) performance, and (4) great realization.

four contemplations (*dhyāna*). (1) The first contemplation is the attainment of the joy and bliss (*prītisukha*) arising from solitude and freedom from desires and sins. (2) The second is the attainment of the joy and bliss arising from the cessation of discursive thought. (3) The third is the attainment of equanimity, with mindfulness, awareness, and physical ease, and beyond any feeling of joy. (4) The fourth is the utter purity of awareness of equanimity, without pleasure or pain, elation or depression. These four contemplations combine with the four trances (see entry) and the final state of utter cessation to form the nine sequential states (*anupūrvavihāra*) leading to the highest liberation. These contemplations also correspond to the four divine abodes (*brahmavihāra*), which are respectively subdivided into three, three, three, and seven layers of heavens where pure matter realm deities dwell.

four immeasurables (*apramāṇa*). (1) The immeasurable of love: wishing all living beings to have happiness and the cause of happiness. (2) The immeasurable of compassion: wishing all living beings to be free of suffering and the cause of suffering. (3) The immeasurable of gladness: wishing all living beings not to be apart from supreme happiness of liberation. (4) The immeasurable of impartiality: being free of affection and aversion. These correspond to the four contemplations and the four divine abodes.

four insignia (or epitomes) of the Dharma (*dharmamudrā* or *dharmoddāna*). The four are as follows: (1) all compounded things are impermanent (*anityāḥ sarvasaṁskārāḥ*), (2) all defiled things are suffering (*duḥkhāḥ sarvasāsravāḥ*), (3) all things are selfless (*anātmanāḥ sarvadharmāḥ*), and (4) nirvana is peace (*śāntaṁ nirvāṇaṁ*).

four joys (*ānanda – dga ba*). These are attained by the yogi/nī when s/he injects the neural energies into the central *dhūti* channel, kindles the furor fire, and melts the white spirit of enlightenment from the brain wheel down the central channel from wheel to wheel. (1) When it melts from the crown wheel to the throat wheel, there is joy; (2) from the throat wheel to the heart wheel, supreme joy; (3) from the heart wheel to the navel wheel, ecstatic joy; and (4) from the navel wheel to the genital wheel, orgasmic joy. This process can be repeated with even greater intensity going back upward: in reverse order from genital to navel, joy; from navel to heart, supreme joy; from heart to throat, ecstatic joy; and from throat to crown, orgasmic joy. Or the four joys can proceed by going progressively inward in the heart wheel alone. The various tantras are full of ways of cultivating the great bliss that realizes ultimate voidness. This process of four joys parallels a set of four voids: brain to throat, void; throat to heart, great void; heart to navel, extreme void; navel to genital, universal void. They can also correspond to the three luminances and clear light.

four main elements (*mahābhūta*). These are: (1) earth (*pṛthivī*), (2) water (*ab*), (3) fire (*teja*), and (4) wind (*vāyu*).

four māras, devils. These are: (1) the addictive (*kleśamāra*), (2) aggregative (*skandhamāra*), (3) deadly (*mṛtyumāra*), and (4) heavenly devils (*devaputramāra*).

four noble truths (*āryasatya*). The noble truths of (1) suffering (*duḥkha*), (2) its origin (*samudaya*), (3) its cessation (*nirodha*), and (4) the path (*mārga*) to its cessation.

four reliances (*pratisāraṇa*). To attain higher realizations and final enlightenment, the bodhisattva should rely (1) on the teaching and not on the person (who teaches it); (2) on the meaning (of the teaching) and not on the expression; (3) on discourses of definitive meaning and not on discourses of interpretable meaning; and (4) on gnosis and not on normal consciousness.

four social graces (*saṁgrahavastu*). This is a classification of the four ways in which a bodhisattva forms a group of people united by the common aim of practicing the Dharma: (1) giving (*dāna*); (2) pleasant speech (*priyavaditā*); (3) accomplishment of the aims (of others) by teaching Dharma (*arthacaryā*); and (4) consistency of behavior with the teaching (*samānārthatā*).

four trances (*samāpatti*). (1) Nearly disembodied trance states in the spheres of infinite space (*ākāśānantyāyatana*), (2) infinite consciousness (*vijñānānantyāyatana*), (3) nothingness (*akiṁcanyāyatana*), and (4) neither consciousness nor unconsciousness (*naivasaṁjñānaivāsaṁjñāyatana*). In my opinion, these states are the exoteric Buddha's hints about the esoteric schema of the subtle and extremely subtle mind states of the three luminances and the clear light transparence.

four voids (*śūnya – stong pa*). (1) Void, (2) great void, (3) extreme void, and (4) universal void. The father tantras focus more on the four voids and the mother tantras on the four joys. See "four joys."

five addictions (*kleśa*). The number five here is somewhat arbitrary, as there are "three," "six," and even "twenty" in other texts. In the tantras, the following five correspond to the five buddha-clans: (1) pride (*abhimāna* – jewel), (2) envy (*īrśya* – karma), (3) desire (*kāma* – lotus), (4) hatred (*dveśa* – vajra), and (5) folly (*moha* – buddha).

five branch energies. They are: (1) the upmoving (*udvāha*), also called dragon, empowering vision; (2) permoving (*vivāha*), also called tortoise, empowering hearing; (3) commoving (*saṁvāha*), also called chameleon, empowering smell; (4) surmoving (*pravāha*), also called devadatta, empowering taste; and (5) ultramoving (*nirvāha*), also called Dhanujit, empowering touch (discussed above, pp. 228, 238).

five buddha-clans (*tathāgata-kula*). (1) Vajra clan of Akṣhobhya, (2) Buddha-clan of Vairochana, (3) Jewel clan of Ratnasaṁbhava, (4) Lotus clan of Amitābha, and (5) Karma clan of Amoghasiddhi.

five channels. (1) "Moon-part," (2) "Luminance," (3) "Reverence," (4) "Hidden crystal," and (5) "Liver," through which operate the five branch energies (see p. 238).

five components of the contemplation branch (of the six branches of the perfection stage). (1) Examining, (2) analyzing, (3) being joyful, (4) having great bliss of suchness, and (5) actualizing one-pointed mind.

five compulsive aggregates (*upādānaskandha*). These are the aggregates of: (1) matter (*rūpa*), (2) sensation (*vedanā*), (3) perception (*saṁjñā*), (4) creation (*saṁskāra*), and (5) consciousness (*vijñāna*), which make up the body-mind complex of most living beings.

five corruptions (*kaśāya*). The five corruptions of our "dark" age (*kāliyuga*), namely, (1) the corruptions of lifespan (*āyuḥ*), (2) view (*dṛṣṭi*), (3) addictions (*kleśa*), (4) living beings (*sattva*), and (5) cosmic era (*kalpa*).

five energies. These are: (1) the vitalizing (*prāṇa – srog 'dzin*), (2) evacuating (*apāna – thur sel*), (3) metabolic (*samāna – me mnyam*), (4) ascending (*udāna – gyen gyu*), and (5) pervading (*vyāna – khyab byed*).

five impediments (*nīvaraṇa*). These are five mental impediments that hinder meditation: (1) impediments of desire (*kāmacchanda*), (2) malice (*vyāpāda*), (3) depression and sloth (*styānamiddha*), (4) wildness and excitement (*auddhatyakaukṛtya*), and (5) doubt, or perplexity (*vicikitsa*).

five paths (*mārga - lam*). These represent the stages of development of any practitioner of Buddhism, who progresses from one to another gradually. They are the paths of: (1) accumulation (*saṁbhāramārga*), (2) application (*prayoga-*), (3) insight (*darśana-*), (4) meditation (*bhāvanā-*), and (5) mastery (*aśaikśa-*).

five perfection stages (*pañcaniṣpannakrama – rdzogs rim lnga*). These are counted variously; the most common way is: (1) body isolation, (2) speech isolation, (3) mind isolation, self-consecration, and magic body counted as one, (4) clear enlightenment or clear light, and (5) communion.

five powers (*bala*). These are the same as the five spiritual faculties, at a further stage of development.

five pure aggregates (*dharmaskandha*). The five (metaphoric) aggregates of the truth body of a buddha: (1) justice (*śīla*), (2) concentration (*samādhi*), (3) wisdom (*prajñā*), (4) liberation (*vimukti*), and (5) knowledge and vision of liberation (*vimuktijñānadarśana*).

five spiritual faculties (*indriya*). These are called "faculties" (*indriya*) by analogy, as capacities to be developed: (1) the spiritual faculties of faith (*śraddhā*), (2) effort (*vīrya*), (3) mindfulness (*smṛti*), (4) concentration (*samādhi*), and (5) wisdom (*prajñā*). These are included in the thirty-seven accessories of enlightenment.

five superknowledges (*abhijñā*). These are more often listed as six: (1) divine eye or vision (*divyacakśu*), (2) divine hearing (*divyaśrotra*), (3) telepathy (*paracittajñāna*), (4) knowledge of former (and future) lives (*pūrvāpara-nivāsānusmṛtijñāna*), (5) knowledge of magical operations (*ṛddhipāda*), and (6) knowledge of the termination of defilements (*āsravakśayajñāna*). Scholars generally agree that five are obtained by eliminating knowledge of magical operations from the classification.

five wisdoms (intuitions, gnoses – *jñāna – ye shes*). These are the transmutations of the five poisons of (1) hatred, (2) delusion, (3) avarice, (4) lust, and (5) envy into: (1) ultimate reality, (2) mirror, (3) equalizing, (4) individuating, and (5) all-accomplishing wisdoms. Tsong Khapa gives a helpful analysis (p. 197): "[Āryadeva] in the *Integrated Practices* describes them, after the purification of virtuous and nonvirtuous instincts: [respectively] as: (1) (mirrorlike), the simultaneous knowledge of all things as reflections in a mirror; (2) (equalizing), the realization of all beings of the four types—footless etc.—as being of the single aspect "merely mental"; (3) (individuating), the abiding, doubt-free individual discernment of all inner and outer things, knowing that if investigated "all have the nature of buddhas," yet distinguishing these "members of the class of all things" as separate, like the petals of a lotus; (4) (all-accomplishing), the full accomplishment of self and other's duties of body, speech, and mind; and (5) (ultimate reality perfection), the deliverance from affliction and evolution, purifying the obscurations of body, speech, and mind. These descriptions concern the fruitional stage of the intuitive wisdoms."

six parameters (*śatkoṭi – mtha drug*). This is a key set of tantric hermeneutical terms, consisting of three pairs of levels of speech: (1–2) literal meaning speech and jargon meaning speech; (3–4) direct speech and indirectly intentional speech; and (5–6) interpretable meaning speech and definitive meaning speech. A key point in tantric hermeneutics is that the same expression can have three or four levels of interpretation by analysis according to these different levels of meaning.

six sense faculties (*indriya*). These are: (1) eye, (2) ear, (3) nose, (4) tongue, (5) body, and (6) mind.

six sense-objects (*viṣaya*). These are: (1) colors/forms (*rūpa*), (2) sounds (*śabda*), (3) scents (*gandha*), (4) tastes (*rasa*), (5) textures (*spṛṣṭavya*), and (6) mental sense objects (*dharma*).

six superknowledges (*abhijñā*). See "five superknowledges."

six transcendences (*pāramitā*). These are the main categories of the bodhisattva's activities: (1) giving (*dāna*), (2) justice (*śīla*), (3) tolerance (*kśānti*), (4) effort (*vīrya*), (5) contemplation (*dhyāna*), and (6) wisdom (*prajñā*).

six wheels (*cakra – 'khor lo*). These are neural complexes with lotus-petal-shaped spokes in the subtle body neural system, their centers strung on the central channel up and down the body, called: (1) the secret wheel (genital – 32 petals); (2) the emanation (navel – 64 petals); (3) the dharma (heart – 8 petals); (4) the fire (chest – 3 petals), (5) the beatific (throat – 16 petals); (6) the wind (brow – 6 petals); and (7) the great bliss (brain – 32 petals). This list of seven becomes six by leaving out the secret wheel; sometimes five wheels are listed by leaving out the fire and wind wheels, and sometimes four wheels listed by leaving out the secret, fire, and wind wheels. Some tantras, such as the *Time Machine*, have different arrangements of neural channel wheels.

six yoga branches (*yogāṇga*). These are: (1) retraction (*prātyāhāra*), (2) contemplation (*dhyāna*), (3) vitalizing energy control (*prāṇāyāma*), (4) endurance (*dhāranā*), (5) mindfulness (*anusmṛti*), and (6) samadhi branches.

seven factors of enlightenment (*bodhyaṅga*). These are the factors of: (1) mindfulness (*smṛti*), (2) discrimination between teachings (*dharmapravicaya*), (3) effort (*vīrya*), (4) joy (*prīti*), (5) fluency (*praśrabdhi*), (6) concentration (*samādhi*), and (7) equanimity (*upekṣā*). These seven form a part of the thirty-seven accessories of enlightenment (see entry).

seven natural instincts of the imminence intuition state (*upalabdhijñānaprakṛti – nyer thob ye shes kyi rang bzhin rtog pa*). (1) Medium attachment, (2) forgetfulness, (3) mistakenness, (4) reticence, (5) fatigue, (6) laziness, and (7) doubt. See also "thirty-three instinctual natures" and "forty instinctual natures"

eight branches of the noble path (*āryamārgāṇga*). These are the well-known: (1) realistic view (*saṁyagdṛṣṭi*), (2) realistic motivation (*saṁyaksaṁkalpa*), (3) realistic speech (*saṁyag vāk*), (4) realistic terminal action (*saṁyakkarmānta*), (5) realistic livelihood (*saṁyagājīva*), (6) realistic effort (*saṁyagvyāyāma*), (7) realistic remembrance (*saṁyaksmṛti*), and (8) realistic concentration (*saṁyaksamādhi*).

nine mergings (**melana – bsre ba*). The nine mergings are: (1) merging trance with the body of truth, (2) merging waking magic body with the beatific body, (3) merging the waking coarse body with the emanation body, (4) merging sleep with the body of truth, (5) merging dream with the beatific body, (6) merging waking with the emanation body, (7) merging death with the body of truth, (8) merging the between with the beatific body, and (9) merging birth with the emanation body.

ten directions (*daśadik*). These consist of: (1–8) the eight points of the compass, (9) straight up, and (10) straight down. As a conventional formula, it is tantamount to "all directions."

ten skillful acts (virtues) (*kuśala*). These are the opposite of the ten sins, i.e., refraining from engaging in activities related to the ten sins and doing the opposite. There are: three physical virtues: (1) saving lives, (2) giving, and (3) sexual propriety. There are four verbal virtues: (4) truthfulness, (5) reconciling discussions, (6) gentle speech, and (7) religious speech. There are three mental virtues: (8) loving attitude, (9) generous attitude, and (10) realistic views.

ten stages (*bhūmi*). These are the ten stages through which the bodhisattva ascends on his way to buddhahood: (1) the joyous (*pramuditā*), (2) the immaculate (*vimalā*), (3) the brilliant (*prabhākāri*), (4) the radiant (*arciśmati*), (5) the invincible (*sudurjayā*), (6) the confronting (*abhimukhī*), (7) the far-reaching (*durāṅgama*), (8) the immovable (*acalā*), (9) the positive intelligence (*sādhumati*), and (10) the cloud of dharma (*dharmameghā*).

ten transcendences (*pāramitā*). These consist of: (1–6) the six transcendences, with the addition of (7) skill in liberative art (*upāyakauśalya*); (8) prayer, or vow (*praṇidhāna*); (9) power (*bala*); and (12) gnosis intuition (*jñāna*).

ten unskillful acts (sins) (*akuśala*). These are the opposite of the ten skillful acts (virtues), and consist of: (1) killing, (2) stealing, (3) sexual misconduct, (4) lying, (5) harsh speech, (6) backbiting, (7) frivolous speech, (8) covetousness, (9) malice, and (10) false views.

twelve ascetic practices (*dhūtaguṇa*). These consist of (1) wearing rags (*pāṁśukūlika*), (2) (in the form of only) three religious robes (*traicivarika*), (3) (coarse in texture as) garments of felt (*nāmantika*), (4) eating by alms (*paiṇḍapātika*), (5) having a single mat to sit on (*aikāsanika*), (6) not eating after noon (*khalu paścād bhaktika*), (7) living alone in the forest (*āraṇyaka*), (8) living at the base of a tree (*vṛkṣamūlika*), (9) living in the open (not under a roof) (*ābhyavakāśika*), (10) frequenting burning grounds (Indian equivalent of cemeteries) (*śmāśānika*), (11) sleeping sitting up (in meditative posture) (*naiṣadika*), and (12) accepting whatever seating position is offered (*yāthāsaṁstarika*).

twelve light rays. The following passage from the *Vajra Rosary* describes these as follows: "Reality of bliss dwelling in the heart center, light illuminating the buddha-sun, with the form of subject and object—that constitutes the twelve light rays. (1) Light increase, (2) light ray, (3) refulgent, (4) clear, (5) blaze, and (6) light blaze—depending on eye and so forth, they hold all outer [objects,] form etc., (7) light ray, (8) light full (*'od ma*), (9) luminant, (10) clear beauty, (11) clear light, (12) solar clear—the aspect of outer forms etc., these six are also proclaimed as light."

twelve sense-media (*āyatana*). They are: (1) eye-medium (*cakśurāyatana*), (2) form-medium (*rūpa-*), (3) ear-medium (*śrotra-*), (4) sound-medium (*śabda-*), (5) nose-medium (*ghrāṇa-*), (6) scent-medium (*gandha-*), (7) tongue-medium (*jihvā-*), (8) taste-medium (*rasa-*), (9) body-medium (*kāya-*), (10) texture-medium (*spraśtavya-*), (11) mental-medium (*mana-*), and (12) mental-object-medium (*dharmāyatana*). The word *āyatana* is usually translated as "base," but the Sanskrit, Tibetan, and Chinese all indicate "something through which the senses function" rather than a basis from which they function; hence "medium" is preferable.

eighteen elements (*dhātu*). These introduce the same six pairs as the twelve sense-media, as elements of experience, adding a third member to each set: the element of consciousness (*vijñāna*), or sense. Hence the first pair gives (13) the triad eye-element (*cakṣurdhātu*), (14) form-element (*rūpadhātu*), and (15) eye-consciousness-element, or eye-sense-element (*caksurvijñānadhātu*), and so on with the other five, noting the last, (16) mind-element (*manodhātu*), (17) mind-object-element (*dharmadhātu*), and (18) mental-consciousness-element (*manovijñānadhātu*).

thirty-two signs of the great being (*mahāpuruṣalakṣaṇa*). They are as follows: (1) His head has a turban-shaped protrusion on the crown; (2) his hair curls to the right; (3) his forehead is broad and even; (4) he has a white hair between his eyebrows; (5) his eyes are very dark, with lashes like a cow; (6) he has forty teeth; (7) his teeth are even, (8) without gaps, and (9) very white; (10) he has a keen sense of taste; (11) he has a lion's jaw; (12) his tongue is long and slender; (13) he has an excellent voice; (14) his shoulders are round and even; (15) the back of his body has seven round curves [buttocks, thighs, shoulders, and back]; (16) his trunk is thick; (17) his skin is smooth and golden-hued; (18) his arms reach his knees when he stands straight up; (19) his torso is like a lion's; (20) his body has the proportions of a banyan tree [height equal to arm span]; (21) his bodily hairs curl to the right; (22) they stand straight up; (23) his penis is concealed in a sheath; (24) his thighs are well-rounded; (25) his ankle-bones do not protrude; (26) the palms of his hands and feet are soft and delicate; (27) he has webbed fingers and toes; (28) he has long fingers; (29) he has wheel-signs on the palms of his hands and feet; (30) his feet are well set [upon the ground]; (31) his arches are broad and high; (32) and his calves are like an antelope's.

thirty-three instinctual natures of the luminance intuition state (*ālokajñānaprakṛti*). These are (1–3) [small], medium, and great dispassions; (4–5) mental internalizing and externalizing; (6–8) [small, medium, and intense] sorrows; (9) peace; (10) mental construction; (11–13) small, medium, and intense fears; (14–16) small, medium, and intense craving; (17) appropriation; (18) nonvirtue; (19) hunger; (20) thirst; (21–23) [small,] medium, and intense sensation moments; (24) knower; (25) knowable; (26) introspective discernment, conscience; (27) compassion; (28–30) small, medium, and great loves; (31) anxiety; (32) greed; and (33) envy. (Sanskrit from CMP has slight variations from Tsong Khapa's choices, which he mentions: *virāgo madhyamaś adhimātra*; *manogatāgataṁ*; *śokāditritayaṁ tathā*; *saumyaṁ vikalpo bhītaś madhyabhīto 'tibhītakaḥ*; *tṛṣṇā madhyatṛṣṇā atitṛṣṇā*; *upādānakaṁ niḥśubhaṁ kṣut tṛṣā*; *vedanā samavedanā ativedanākṣaṇaś*; *vettṛviddhā*; *pratyavekṣaṇa lajjā kāruṇyaṁ*; *snehatas trayam*; *cakitaṁ saṁcayaś mātsaryaṁ*.) See also "forty instinctual natures" and "seven natural instincts."

thirty-seven accessories of enlightenment (*bodhipakśikadharma*). These consist of: (1–4) the four applications of mindfulness; (5–8) the four realistic efforts; (9–12) the four bases of magical powers; (13–17) the five spiritual faculties; (18–22) the five powers; (23–29) the seven factors of enlightenment; and (30–37) the eight branches of the noble path.

forty instinctual natures of the radiance intuition state (*ābhāsajñānaprakṛti*). These are: (1) desire, (2) attachment, (3) pleasure, (4) medium pleasure, (5) intense pleasure, (6) delight, (7) indulgence, (8) amazement, (9) excitement, (10) satisfaction, (11) embracing, (12) kissing, (13) sucking, (14) stability, (15) zeal, (16) pride, (17) activity, (18) possessiveness, (19) aggressiveness, (20) enthusiasm, (21–23) small, medium, and great boldness; (24) hostility, (25) charm, (26) resentment, (27) virtue, (28) lucid truthfulness,

(29) untruthfulness, (30) certitude, (31) non-appropriation, (32) generosity, (33) initiative, (34) heroism, (35) shamelessness, (36) deceitfulness, (37) sharpness (38) wickedness, (39) ungentleness, and (40) crookedness. See also "thirty-three instinctual natures" and "seven natural instincts."

eighty instinctual natures (*prakṛti*). See "thirty-three instinctual natures," "forty instinctual natures," and "seven natural instincts."

eighty marks (of the great being) (*anuvyañjana*). These accompany the thirty-two signs and consist of: (1) fingernails the color of brass, (2) shiny and (3) long; (4) round fingers; (5) tapered fingers; (6) fingers wide-spreading; (7) veins not protruding, and (8) without tangles; (9) slender ankles; (10) feet not uneven; (11) lion's gait; (12) elephant's gait; (13) swan's gait; (14) bull's gait; (15) gait tending to the right; (16) graceful gait; (17) steady gait; (18) his body is well-covered, (19) clean, (20) well-proportioned, (21) pure, (22) soft, and (23) perfect; (24) his sex organs are fully developed; (25) his thighs are broad and knees round; (26) his steps are even; (27) his complexion is youthful; (28) his posture is not stooped; (29) his bearing is expansive, yet (30) extremely poised; (31) his limbs and fingers and toes are well-defined; (32) his vision is clear and unblurred; (33) his joints are not protruding; (34) his belly is relaxed, (35) symmetrical, and (36) not fat; (37) his navel is deep and (38) wound to the right; (39) he is completely handsome; (40) he is clean in all acts; (41) he is free of spots or discolorations of the skin; (42) his hands are soft as cotton; (43) the lines of his palms are clear, (44) deep, and (45) long; (46) his face is not overlong and is (47) bright as a mirror; (48) his tongue is soft, (49) long, and (50) red; (51) his voice is like an elephant's trumpet or like thunder, (52) yet sweet and gentle; (53) his teeth are rounded, (54) sharp, (55) white, (56) even, and (57) regularly arranged; (58) his nose is long and (59) straight; (60) his eyes are clear and wide; (61) his eyelashes are thick; (62) the pupils and whites of his eyes are clearly defined, and (63) the irises are like lotus petals; (64) his eyebrows are (65) long, soft, (66) evenly haired, and (67) gently curved; (68) his ears are long-lobed and (69) symmetrical; (70) his hearing is acute; (71) his forehead is high and (72) broad; (73) his head is very large; (74) his hair is as black as a bee, (75) thick, (76) soft, (77) untangled, not (78) unruly, and (79) fragrant; (80) and his feet and hands are marked with lucky signs.

the one hundred buddha-clans, used in body isolation meditation. These charts (on the following six pages) are adapted—with permission and some terminology changes—from those made by Christian Wedemeyer, as appendices to his study and translation of Āryadeva's *Lamp That Integrates the Practices*, a work that H. H. the Dalai Lama described as the *rtsa ba* (the "root text") of the present work of Tsong Khapa's, published in this same series. The body isolation homologizes all phenomena of physical and mental perception with specific male and female buddhas, in order to finally—at subtle as well as coarse levels of visualization—isolate one's sense of self-identity from any kind of sense of being ordinary. This state of strict body-mind self-identification as a community of buddhas provides the subtle mandalic platform upon which the yogi/nī can embark upon the speech isolation vajra recitation practice, safely and effectively.

I. The Five Aggregates (25 clans)

	Akṣhobhya	Vairochana	Ratnasambhava	Amitābha	Amoghasiddhi
Matter (Vairochana)	Matter known from personal experience	Matter – outer, inner, both shapes, long and short	Matter in the mode of self, other, or both	Exterior, interior matter of five colors	Exterior, interior matter as lights of sun and moon
Sensation (Ratnasaṁbhava)	Sensations from bile and humor conjunction	Ambivalent sensations	Sensations born from phlegm and wind	Pleasurable sensations	Painful sensations
Perception (Amitābha)	Perceptions of bipeds	Perceptions of unmoving beings	Perceptions of quadrupeds	Perceptions of the legless	Perceptions of the many-legged
Creation (Amoghasiddhi)	Mental creations	Bodily creations	Creations of the three worlds	Verbal creations	Creations for liberation
Consciousness (Akṣhobhya)	Tactile consciousness	Visual consciousness	Audial consciousness	Smell consciousness	Taste consciousness

II. The Four Elements (20 clans)

	Akṣhobhya	Vairochana	Ratnasambhava	Amitābha	Amoghasiddhi
Earth element, internal (Lochanā)	Secretions, intestinal, bile, heart	Hair, bone, feces, spleen, heart	Body hair, nails, pus, heart	Teeth, skin, flesh, heart	Tendons, flesh, ribs, heart
External earth	Pūrvavideha	Mount Meru	Jambudvīpa	Godānīya	Uttarakuru
Water element (Māmakī)	Urine	Phlegm and tears	Sweat	Blood	Saliva
External water	Ocean water	Waterfalls	River water	Spring water	Pond water
Fire element (Pāṇḍarāvāsinī)	Heart heat	Head heat	Navel heat	Limb heat	Belly heat
External fire	Perpetual fire	Stone fires	Sun-crystal fire	Wood fires	Forest fires
Wind element (Tārā)	Vitalizing	Pervading	Evacuating	Ascending	Metabolic
External winds	Eastern wind	Zenith wind	Southern wind	Western wind	Northern wind

III. The Five Media (25 clans)

	Akṣhobhya	Vairochana	Ratnasambhava	Amitābha	Amoghasiddhi
Visual media (Kṣhitigarbha)	Grape-sized visual sense organ	Perception of the three forms	Nature of the pupil of the eye	Forms seen with the peripheral vision	Movement of the eye
Hearing media (Vajrapāṇi)	Greatly convo-luted aural sense	Nature of the ear	Perception of the three sounds	Ear orifice	Root of the ear
Smell media (Khagarbha)	Śhalākā-shaped olfactory sense organ	Nature of the nose	Septum	Perception of the three scents	Nostrils
Taste media (Lokeshvara)	Half-moon shaped gustatory sense organ	Nature of the tongue	Root of the tongue	Tip of the tongue	Perception of the three tastes
Touch media (Sarvanīvaraṇaviṣhkambhin)	Perception of the three contacts	Tactile sense organ (body)	Nature of bones	Nature of flesh	Nature of skin
Mental sense media (Samantabhadra / Mañjushrī)					

IV. The Five Auxiliary Energies (25 clans)

Energy	Akṣhobhya	Vairochana	Ratnasambhava	Amitābha	Amoghasiddhi
Upmoving (visual)	Forms of play, erotic flirtation,	Visual forms	Forms to which one is attached	Forms pleasant, unpleasant, ambivalent	Forms that perform all activities
Permoving (hearing)	Calm or harsh sounds of *hūṁ*	Ear, head, or wind sounds	Singing and stringed instruments	Palatal, labial, and vocal sounds	Sounds of trees, rivers, snaps, claps, musical instruments
Commoving (smell)	Unpleasant scents	All scents	Scent of the entire body	Distinguishing three scents	Scent of vital fluid
Surmoving (taste)	Bitter flavors	Sweet flavors	Astringent flavors	Salty flavors	Distinguishing the six flavors
Ultramoving (touch)	Sensing subtle mind through sexual union	Holding still union sensation	Embracing sensation	Kissing sensation	Sucking sensation

V. The Five Intuitions (5 clans)

	Akṣhobhya	Vairochana	Ratnasambhava	Amitābha	Amoghasiddhi
Five intuitive wisdoms	Reality realm perfection	Mirrorlike	Equalizing	Individuating	All-accomplishing

Glossary of Unique Translation Terms

adamantine, diamond (see also "vajra"). The Sanskrit *vajra* means "thunderbolt," "diamond," "adamantine," and so forth, various objects connoting immutability and unbreakability. In Vedic India it was the weapon of the tribal father-god, Indra, a thunderbolt that he threw down from the heavens to break the citadels of the enemy. The Buddhists took this primal symbol of the supreme power of the universe and made it a symbol of universal love and compassion, in order to affirm their vision that love is the strong force in the universe—the clear light of the void. Thus "vajra" is used in names of buddha-deities to indicate that they are in touch through wisdom with the realm of ultimate reality and that they express the natural universal compassion.

adept, great. "Adept" is used to translate the Sanskrit *siddha*, referring to a practitioner of tantra who has attained buddhahood in his or her ordinary body, having gone beyond life, death, and the between, yet remaining in association with his or her previous gross body in order to relate liberatingly with contemporary beings.

addiction (*kleśa – nyon mongs*). This word has been translated "passion," and more recently "affliction," neither wrong. Its etymology comes from the verb root *kliś-* to "torment," "twist," so it is definitely something painful. Lust, hatred, delusion, envy, pride, fanaticism—all emotions that are painful to experience—cause painful outcomes through unskillful interactions with others. Passion is an intense emotion that can however be exalting and beautiful, or at least it has that connotation. Affliction is basically the same as suffering, not as much a cause of suffering. An addiction is a habitual behavior that seems to benefit one's state of being and so seduces the addict, but actually causes suffering to the addict and those around him or her. One can be addicted to lust, addicted to hate, addicted to confusion, to a fanatical belief, to pride or envy or avarice. Those addictions then inevitably cause suffering and affliction.

aggregate (*skandha*). The five—*rūpa*, *vedanā*, *saṁjñā*, *saṁskāra*, and *vijñāna*—have such a particular technical sense that some may wish to leave them untranslated. Nevertheless, it seems preferable to give a translation—in spite of the drawbacks of each possible term—in order to convey the same sense of a useful schema of the psychophysical complex. (1) For *rūpa*, "matter" is preferred to "form" because it more concretely connotes the physical and gross. (2) For *vedanā*, "sensation" is preferred to "feelings," as not so inclusive of emotions. (3) For *saṁjñā*, "perception" is preferable to "conception," as itself meaning conceptually determined experience. (4) For *saṁskāra*, which covers a number of mental functions as well as anomalous forces, "creation" or "function" gives the general idea. (5) And "consciousness" is so well established for *vijñāna* (although what we normally think of as consciousness is more like *saṁjñā*, i.e., conceptual and notional, and *vijñāna* is rather the "pure awareness" prior to concepts) as to be left unchallenged.

Akṣhobhya (Buddha). One of the five archetypal transcendent buddhas, lord of the vajra buddha-clan, he represents the ultimate reality perfection wisdom, the transmutation of the poison of hatred, the color blue, and the aggregate of consciousness.

alienated individual (*pṛthagjana – so sor skye bo*). Often translated "common person," this term in Buddhism refers to a person who is cognitively the opposite of a "noble" (*ārya*) person. A "noble" person is defined as one who has attained the vision path (*darśanamārga*) and thus has had an initial nonconceptual experience of selflessness, becoming "noble" by realizing the equality of others' perspective to his or her own. The opposite of this kind of noble person is one who is enclosed within a sense of exclusive and absolute self as different from and opposed to others, and who thus does not consider others' perspective from any visceral level. Such an automatically self-centered person is necessarily alienated from the "otherness" of the world as a whole and hence is very aptly described as "alienated." Etymologically both *pṛthag* and *so sor* refer to separateness.

all-accomplishing wisdom. This is one of the five wisdoms, resulting from the transmutation of envy, associated with the emerald and the color green, and with the Archetype Buddha Amoghasiddhi.

Amitābha. One of the five archetypal transcendent buddhas, lord of the lotus buddha--clan. He is associated with the western direction and the buddhaverse Sukhavatī. He represents the individuating wisdom, the transmutation of the poison of lust, the color red, and the aggregate of perception. His buddha-consort is Paṇḍāravāsinī.

Amoghasiddhi. One of the five archetypal transcendent buddhas, lord of the karma buddha-clan, associated with the northern direction. He represents the all-accomplishing wisdom, the transmutation of the poison of envy, the color green, and the aggregate of creations. His buddha-consort is Tārā, sometimes called Samayatārā.

ancestral mentor (**paramparāguru – brgyud pa'i bla ma*). Usually translated as "lineage lama," it is opposite of root lama or direct mentor, and refers to gurus or mentors who were mentors to one's direct or personal mentor. Since the Tibetan Buddhist karmic tradition has largely replaced blood lineages with Dharma lineages, "ancestral" is preferred, moving a bit further in the same direction as "lineage," which itself transvalues blood lineage to spiritual lineage.

angel (*ḍāka* or *ḍākinī – mkha 'gro* or *mkha 'gro ma*). These beings can be mundane or transmundane ("buddhine"), male or female, more concrete than the Jungian archetypes *animus* and *anima*, but serving in a similar role in tantric culture.

archetype, or chosen, deity (*iṣṭadevatā – yi dam*). A divine buddha-form used in tantric practice to visualize oneself as an embodiment of the understandings and abilities one is cultivating in order to become a buddha oneself to benefit all beings. The sustained visualization of such an embodiment in the creation-stage practice aims to develop such a stability of focus that when the perfection-stage practitioner reaches into the subtle out-of-body zones in simulation of death and dying states, he or she can arise for the subtle energy plane in the archetypal form of whatever is his or her chosen embodiment. Such a buddha-form can be approached as an independent being in some ritual and contemplative and narrative contexts, while it can also be adopted as a contemplative role-model, in practices in which the yogi/nī identifies with the deity and seeks to become the deity itself. Thus the deity's form becomes an ideal or archetypal structure of the enlightenment desired by the practitioner.

art (*upāya*). This is the expression in action of the great compassion of the Buddha and the bodhisattvas. One empathetically aware of the troubles of living beings would, for his or her very survival, devise the most potent and efficacious arts possible to remove those troubles, and the troubles of living beings are removed effectively only when they reach liberation. I prefer "art" to the usual "method" and "means" because it has a stronger connotation of subtlety and skill; also, art is identified with the extreme of power, energy, and efficacy, as symbolized in the *vajra* (adamantine scepter), and in tantra it is associated with male qualities, paired with "wisdom," associated with female qualities. This use of "art" fits with the educational usage "arts and sciences," where the arts include all the humanities, writing, architecture, engineering, medicine, law, various technologies, and so forth, along with the creative arts, disciplines seeking to understand the nature of reality from various angles, which should include wisdom as well.

avadhūti. The central channel (*madhyamanāḍī – rtsa dbu ma*) of the yogic subtle body, running from mid-brow up to crown center then down just in front of spinal column all the way to the base of the genitals then out to the tip of the male or female sexual organ, believed to be choked off in normal persons in five places at the center of the five main neural channel wheels, but opened by adept yogi/nīs through perfection stage practices. Often referred to in Tibetan simply as "the *dhūti*."

beatific. The adjective from "beatitude," used to translate Sanskrit *saṁbhoga*, the term for the bliss body of buddhahood. The evolutionary perfection of buddhahood is said to be experienced in the form of three bodies, of which this body represents the ultimate but subtle subjective enjoyment of being a buddha as a being who has realized perfect union with the infinite freedom of ultimate reality. See "three bodies of the Buddha (*trikāya*)" in the Glossary of Numerical Categories.

between (*antarābhava – bar do*). This word is used in at least three senses; its basic colloquial sense of the whole period between death and rebirth, its technical sense in the set of the six betweens—life, dream, meditation, death-point, reality, and existence betweens—and in the sense of "phase of a between," where the experience of a particular period in one of the six betweens is itself called a between.

between-being (*antarābhavī – bar do pa*). A being who has passed through death and whose mind, soul, or life-continuum has emerged from the gross body of the lost life, has embodied itself in a subtle energy, "mind-imaged" body, similar to the simulated embodiment of consciousness in a dream, and experiences the processes in the between of wandering in search of either liberation or an ordinary rebirth.

bliss, great (bliss-void-indivisible). Sanskrit *sukha* means "happiness" as the opposite of *duḥkha*, "suffering," in a range from modest relief and comfort up to physical orgasmic bliss and supreme spiritual bliss. In the tantric context, the Universalist emphasis on compassion (the will to relieve the suffering of others) transmutes into the implementation of love (the will to provide happiness to others) and so the conscious cultivation of bliss becomes a technical concern. To transmit happiness to others, one must develop one's own happiness to overflowing. Thus, the highest tantric expression of the nonduality of relative and absolute realities is the term "bliss-void-indivisible," where bliss is the relative, wisdom-generated forms of the buddhaverse and void is the ultimate freedom reality that makes such creativity possible.

bodhisattva. Sanskrit *bodhisattva* is composed of *bodhi*, meaning "enlightenment" (wisdom of selflessness/selfless compassion), and *sattva*, meaning "being" or "hero/ heroine." Most simply, it means someone who has dedicated him or herself to do whatever it takes over countless lifetimes in order to attain perfect enlightenment in order to save all beings from suffering. A being becomes a bodhisattva by conceiving the spirit of enlightenment, through (1) imagining the possibility of enlightened consciousness, (2) seeing how it alone gives the ability effectively to help others find their happiness, (3) seeing how dedicating all one's lives of efforts toward that goal is the only sensible way to live, and (4) resolving to undertake that universal responsibility oneself. This transformation from ordinary being to "enlightenment hero/heroine" is formally sealed by the solemn taking of the vow of the bodhisattva. Thus a beginner bodhisattva need not be very advanced in enlightenment, merely firmly dedicated to universal love and compassion. In the modern context, it is important to mention that the messianic bodhisattva vow only makes sense for those who feel convinced that they are going to be around in the life-process for an infinite future in any case, so they might as well undertake the saving of all beings. Such a messianic complex would be insane for those who consider their existence to last only one lifetime; there would never be time for such a universal saving of beings, and so such a pressure would be pointless.

body isolation. This refers to the first of the five perfection stages, a stage wherein the body becomes isolated from ordinariness of experience, and concretely re-envisioned as a wisdom-perfected body expressing the compassion of all buddhas, using the hundred buddha-clan, five-clan, three-clan, or one-buddha-clan art of homologizing all bodily structures and body-mind functions with divine buddha-aesthetic-activities. (See the charts of the one hundred buddha-clans, beginning p. 651 above.)

channel, neural channel (*nāḍī – rtsa ba*). These are the neural structures of the tantric yogi/nī's subtle body, which consists of channels, energies (*vāyu*), and neural drops (*bindu*). There are five, six, or seven main channel wheels, and 72,000 subtle neural channels linking them together, around a main axis consisting of the central *dhūti* channel and the right and left *rasanā* and *lalanā* channels.

clan (as in the five buddha-clans) (*kula – rigs*). This word is often translated as "family," which has the modern connotation of nuclear family, i.e., parents and children. "Clan" conveys the ancient extended family, which includes cousins, uncles, and aunts, and so forth, which is more appropriate for the *buddha-kula*, which includes a larger number of members. The five clans are the vajra, buddha, jewel, lotus, and evolution clans, respectively fathered by the five Buddhas, Akṣhobhya, Vairochana, Ratnasaṁbhava, Amitābha, and Amoghasiddhi, mothered by the female buddhas, Sparshavajrā,

Lochanā, Māmakī, Pāṇḍarāvāsinī, and Tārā, and each including a number of male and female bodhisattvas, fierce deities, and adept heroes and heroines.

clear light, transparence (*prabhāsvara – 'od gsal*). This is the level of the extremely subtle body-mind, the indestructible drop and the state of universal void. It is likened to the gray light before the dawn, when you can see your hand but not the lines in the palm; this follows with the moonlit sky of luminance, the sunlit sky of radiance, and the darklit or unlit light of imminence. Clear light is thus a pure transparency, beyond the duality of light and dark, day and night, when there are no shadows because everything is self-illuminated from within. It also connected to the vajra or diamond nature of the void, the level of reality where the infinite energy of bliss flows into and through the structures of life as universal love and compassion. This clear light can never be perceived in a dualistic way, since the perceiver is also clear light; it seems to rather be the case that the buddha-mind is overtaken by it in a realization that it has always been it and so surrenders to it without losing anything it was not already. It is of course ultimately inexpressible, though it has many names and evocations, this state of universal communion (*yuganaddha*), in which the duality realizes oneness while enjoying the play of opposites and embracing all that suffers in its potentiality of bliss.

communion, union (*yuganaddha – zung 'jug*). The fifth and highest of the five stages of the perfection stage, its final form being buddhahood itself. Used with prefix "com-" (paralleling the *yuga – zung*) for the standard "union," it indicates the nondual union of bliss and void, divine and human, absolute and relative, infinite and finite, ultimate and conventional, etc. It still preserves distinctly the pair that is united without collapsing either one into the other. The resonance with the Christian usage is not a problem, perhaps enhancing the power of this very sacred concept for tantra-oriented universal vehicle Buddhists, and its possible continued usage in English will add this usage of "communion" to dictionary lists of its meanings. See "five perfection stages" in the Glossary of Numerical Categories.

conception of the spirit of enlightenment (*bodhicittotpāda*). This can also be rendered by "initiation of . . ." because it means the mental event occurring when a living being, having been exposed to the teaching of the Buddha or of his magical emanations, realizes simultaneously his own level of conditioned ignorance. The living being's habitual stream of consciousness is like sleep compared to that of one who has awakened from ignorance; with initiation, he has the possibility of his own attainment of a higher state of consciousness; and the necessity of attaining it in order to liberate other living beings from their stupefaction. Having realized this possibility, he becomes inspired with the intense ambition to attain, and that is called the "conception of the spirit of enlightenment." "Spirit" is preferred to "mind" because the mind of enlightenment should rather be the mind of the Buddha; and it is preferred to "thought" because a "thought of enlightenment" can easily be produced without the initiation of any sort of new resolve or awareness.

conceptualization (*vikalpa*). This brings up another important group of words that has never been treated systematically in translation: *vikalpa*, *parikalpa*, *samāropa*, *adhyāropa*, *kalpanā*, *saṁjñā*, and *prapañca*. All of these refer to mental functions that tend to superimpose upon reality, either relative or ultimate, a conceptualized reality fabricated by the subjective mind. Some translators have tended to lump these together under the rubric "discursive thought," which leads to the misleading notion that all thought is bad, something to be eliminated, and that sheer "thoughtlessness" is "enlightenment," or whatever higher state is desired. According to Buddhist scholars, thought in itself is simply a function, and only thought that is attached to its own content over and above the relative object, i.e., "egoistic" thought, is bad and to be eliminated. Therefore I have chosen a set of words for the seven Sanskrit terms, respectively: "conceptualization," "imagination," "presumption," "exaggeration," "construction," "conception" or "notion," and "fabrication." This does not mean that these words are not somewhat interchangeable or that another English word might not be better in certain contexts; it only represents an attempt to achieve consistency with the original usages.

conscious awareness (*apramāda*). This denotes a type of awareness of the most seemingly insignificant aspects of practical life, an awareness derived as a consequence of the highest realization of the ultimate nature of reality. As it is stated in the *Anavataptaparipṛcchāsūtra*: "Who realizes voidness, that person becomes consciously aware." "Ultimate realization," far from obliterating the relative world, brings it into highly specific, albeit dreamlike, focus.

consort, seal (*mudrā*); evolution (*karmamudrā*), wisdom or intuition (*jñānamudrā*), and science (*vidyā*). These expressions refer to the partner, either male or female, but more usually female, in a buddha-couple, such as Vairochana and Lochanā. Sometimes the father and mother in a buddha-father-mother-couple are considered different divine beings, sometimes only the double manifestation of a single being. The Buddhist belief is that all beings, whatever the superficial sexual identity, are potentially both male and female—each has male and female aspects and energies in his or her being. The empathetic ability to transcend sexual identity-habits is cultivated by tantric archetype meditation wherein a male will meditate himself as a female archetype buddha, a female will meditate herself as a male archetype buddha, or either will meditate him- or herself as a male and female buddha-couple in union.

continuum (*tantra – rgyud, rgyun*). This is the root word for *tantra*, standing for the confluence of several continua: the basis continuum of the basis, that of the nature, and that of the fruition. Sometimes, exoterically, it is known as "life-continuum" (*saṁtāna*): the energy-continuity of a living being that proceeds from moment to moment in a life and from life to life in an individual's evolutionary progression. To quote Tsong Khapa, quoting in his great commentary the *Esoteric Community Further Tantra* and Nāropa: "Tantra is renowned as 'continuum'; that continuum is of three types: differentiated in terms of the basis (*ādhāra*), likewise, nature (*prakṛti*), and non-deprivation (*asaṁhārya*). As for their aspects, the nature one is the cause; similarly, the non-deprivation is the fruition; the basis is called the art. Those three comprise the meaning of 'tantra' (GST, xviii.34–35). The etymological definition of 'tantra' is 'continuum.' According to Nāropa's explanation of the threefold division of tantra in the verse, 'nature' means the nature of the jewel-like adept; this is the causal tantra. 'Basis' refers to the art tantra, the four branches of service and performance of the two stages. The tantra of 'fruition'—of which no one can deprive you—is the holy communion body of non-local nirvana, Vajradhara" (J.R.C. Campbell, "Vajra Hermeneutics" [Ph.D. diss., Columbia University, 2009], Appendix 1, p. 8).

creation (*saṁskāra*). See "aggregate."

creation stage (*utpannakrama – bskyed rim*). This is the preliminary part of the unexcelled yoga tantra, where the yogi/nī creates a divine environment and a divine self and embodiment, using serenity meditation to focus on the purified forms and critical insight meditation to recognize the voidness of all those visualized forms, thus planting the seed patterns and creating the templates for the subtle and extremely subtle body-mind needed to traverse the ultimate yogas of the perfection stage and actually reach real, magical buddhahood. It therefore does "develop" (*rnam par smin pa*) the practitioner, but its main function is to begin the creation of the buddha-world along with the buddha-embodiment needed to accelerate the time to buddhahood. So though some use "development stage," I prefer "creation stage." Nāgabodhi in his *Stage of Arrangement* explicitly links the creation of the mandala universe to a mythic, theistic cosmogony pattern.

death. This is the point of freedom when the subtle mind, indestructible clear light drop, or soul of a particular life loses connection with the embodiment of that life. It is perhaps beyond consciousness and unconsciousness, though ordinary people transit it unconsciously, never noticing the all-too-rapid (for them) transition from the unconscious segment of imminence into clear light and back into imminence. Thus death is understood as a pure negation, a perfect zero, a timeless moment, a widthless boundary, and is aligned with absolute reality, with the body of truth, with the ultimate clear light. A buddha, an enlightened being, is thus one whose death is an infinite body of ultimate reality, a concrete permanent resting place, which nevertheless not only never obstructs their relative experience of the interconnected realm of beings, it makes it indivisible from freedom and openness and therefore perfectly blissful. Needless to say, such a being is no longer afraid of death.

definitive meaning (*nītārtha*). This refers to those teachings of the Buddha that are in terms of ultimate reality; it is opposed to those teachings given in terms of relative reality, termed "interpretable meaning," because they require further interpretation before being relied on to indicate the ultimate. Hence definitive meaning relates to voidness etc., and no statement concerning the relative world, even by the Buddha, can be taken as definitive.

designation (*prajñapti*). This occurs in the axiomatic Mādhyamika description of all things as existent by virtue of "mere designation" (*prajñaptimātra*).

Dharma. One of the Three Jewels, the Jewel of the Buddha's teaching. It can also mean the ultimate reality itself that is taught in the teachings, the path that leads to its realization, the qualities that derive from it, and so forth. In Indian usage prior to the Buddha's time, it tended to mean "religion," "law," "duty," "custom," and so forth, patterns that hold human behavior and thought under control. These "pattern-maintaining" meanings still coexist in Sanskrit and other Buddhist languages with the Buddha's more liberating or "pattern-transcending" meanings, causing considerable confusion for translators in some contexts.

dhūti. See "avadhūti."

discourse (*sūtra – mdo*). Though *sūtra* in general means a string of aphorisms meant to be memorized in Indian oral education system, in Buddhism in particular it has come to mean a recorded discourse of the Buddha.

Divine Lord (*Bhagavān*). "Divine Lord" translates well the title *bhagavān* because it is the term of greatest respect current in our "sacred" language, as established for the Deity in the Elizabethan version of the Bible. Indeed, the Skt. *Bhagavān* was given as a title to the Buddha, although it also served the non-Buddhist Indians as an honorific title of their particular deities. As the Buddha is clearly described in the sutras as the "Supreme Teacher of Gods and Men," there seems little danger that he may be confused with any particular deity through the use of this term (as indeed in Buddhist sutras various deities, creators, protectors, etc. are shown in their respective roles). The often used "Blessed One" comes from the early translations, and conveys the subliminal suggestion to the nineteenth-century reader that the Buddha too is "blessed," i.e., found acceptable in the eyes of the Western "God"—still a looming presence over the work of introducing Buddhism—even for the atheistic philologist.

drops (*bindu – thig le*). This word refers to physical, chemical essences (something like the modern notion of neurotransmitters) that focus awareness within the subtle nervous system. In the subtle body, the channels form the structure, the energies move things and cause transformations of experience, and the drops serve as the nodes of subjectivity that focus awareness within this realm that opens up when consciousness has been withdrawn from its functions in receiving and coordinating sense-data from the gross senses. These drops are also associated with the genetic material that is the essence of the male and female sexual fluids, and the yogic mastery of their subtle potentials represents the sublimation of the creative energies that ordinarily build up the suffering life cycle into the reconstruction of the divine realm of the enlightened mandala. Thus, red drops refer to the female genetic essence, carried within the blood, and the white drops refer to the male genetic essence, carried within the semen. This is a difficult and abstruse subject, but this note can orient you to what is meant by this expression.

duality, dualism (*dvaya, dvayagraha*). "Duality" is largely self-explanatory. To be pointed out here is the connection between the mental habit of dualism and verbalization, insofar as dualism is inherent in the structure of language, in which things are presented in terms of opposites.

emanation body (*nirmāṇakāya*). This refers to the miraculous power of buddhas and bodhisattvas of a certain stage to emanate apparently living beings in order to develop and teach other beings. This power reaches its culmination in the *nirmāṇakāya*, the "emanation body," which is one of the three bodies of buddhahood and includes all physical forms of all buddhas, including Śhākyamuni, whose sole function as incarnations is the development and liberation of living beings. See "three bodies of the Buddha (*trikāya*)" in the Glossary of Numerical Categories.

emptiness (*śūnyatā*). See "voidness."

energy (*vāyu – rlung*). This term—sometimes "neural energy"—is used for the elemental function of "wind" (defined simply as "motility" or "movement" [*cala – gyo ba*]), and more importantly for the subtle inner energies that contribute the activity to the subtle body, moving the "drops" around the "channels." Their supremely subtle form constitutes the extremely subtle body of the indestructible drop that is the mount of the clear light enlightened awareness of the subtlest soul. There are five main energies and five branch energies. The five main energies are the life or vitalizing, evacuating, ascending, metabolic, and pervading energies, each associated with a particular channel wheel, with a particular archetype buddha, a particular wisdom, and so forth. The branch energies are associated with the buddha-consorts and the five elements and so forth. These energies are also extremely important in Buddhist medicine, underlying the technology of acupuncture and the understanding of most mental as well as many physical disorders. See also "wind."

enlightenment (*bodhi*). This word requires too much explanation for this glossary because, indeed, the whole of Buddhist literature tries to explain only this. The translation equivalent "awakening" is frequently used, which is perfectly alright as well, though should not be adopted due to some idea that the Buddha's enlightenment is somehow diametrically opposed to the Western "Enlightenment" of Diderot and Voltaire, et al. The dogmatic materialism and even nihilism that accrued to the Western Enlightenment is different from Buddha's transcendent realization of the exact and complete nature of reality. However, the Western movement's achievement in breaking away from irrational and unrealistic theories of reality, using reason and experience to distinguish the real from the unreal, its discoveries of many of the workings of macro and micro nature and so on, its elevation of empirical science, its appreciation of the human potential, and so on, these are all part and parcel of the Buddha's enlightenment, which preceded the Western one by more than 2,000 years. Also, Sanskrit *buddha* is glossed as *vibuddha* and *prabuddha*, i.e., not only "awakening from the sleep of ignorance," but also "expanding the knowledge of reality into omniscience"; so "awakening" may not contain both aspects quite fully.

equalizing wisdom. One of the five wisdoms, this one associated with the buddha Ratnasambhava, the color yellow, the transmutation of pride and miserliness, and the apotheosis of the sensation aggregate.

Esoteric Community. The Guhyasamāja tantric tradition, in which the subtleties and intricacies of unexcelled yoga are particularly well explained and systematically arranged for study and practice, and which is the "Lamp" that illuminates the world, brightened especially by Chandrakīrti in his *Illuminating Lamp*, and was even more brilliantly illuminated by Tsong Khapa in the present work.

evolution, evolutionary. Sanskrit *karma* and *karmika*, translated in this way because "action" may be too general and vague. Karma specifically means mental/verbal/physical action that leads to life-affecting, eventually life-constituting consequences. It is the key concept in the Buddhist theory of biology, the study of how life is constituted. The modern materialistic worldview considers the structures of our present lifetimes to have been caused by the genetic re-embodiment of the subtly encoded experiences of millions of previous representatives of our species through the processes of biological evolution. The Buddhist worldview considers the structures of our present lifetimes to be caused by the spiritually genetic re-embodiment of our own experiences from millions of previous lifetimes, subtly encoded in a spiritual gene we bring with us, combined with the physical genes we receive from our parents, in a complex process of spiritually directed and physically conditioned biological evolution.

extremely subtle body-mind. This nondual combination of the indestructible drop composed of the subtlest energies and the clear light enlightened awareness is the Buddhist "soul," that entity or continuum that can be said to progress from life to life, and to mutate out of the suffering of the life cycle into enlightenment. Note that at this super micro level, the dualities of matter and mind are transcended, and even the duality of micro and macro. See "subtle body or mind."

father tantra (*pitātantra – pha rgyud*). This is a class of unexcelled yoga tantras—all of which (in Tsong Khapa's interpretation) are nondual in terms of magic body and clear light—where the emphasis is on the creation of the magic body at the stage of mind isolation through the mind objective and the self-consecration, by the grace of the mentor. See also "mother tantra."

furor, furor fire (*caṇḍa – gtum mo*). This is the physical heat generated by mental concentration that focuses deep down upon the subatomic energies within the molecules and atoms of the yogi/nī and taps there the inexhaustible nuclear energies that can be mechanically released in fission or fusion reactions. The yogi/nī carefully channels that fire into the central nervous system to melt the "drops" that embed states of consciousness causing them to flow into the neural centers of the channel wheels and generate the subtle bliss consciousness that liberates from entrapment in the conceptually constructed world of samsara, consisting of the hopeless duality of self versus the entire universe of other beings, time, and space. The long observed, studied, and verified ability of such yogi/nīs to melt icy sheets in winter, to raise at will their whole body temperature or the temperature of specific parts of their bodies is only a relatively unimportant side-effect of this super subtle energy-tapping through concentration. "Furor" is a good translation since the heat of anger is similar to this subatomic heat energy. Anger and bile are in Buddhist medical fact connected to intelligence and the dissective power of critical analysis, which is what this concentration requires to break through the coarse levels of reality structure and penetrate the clear light energy of voidness ultimate reality.

gene (*gotra – rigs*). See spiritual gene.

gnosis (intuition, intuitive wisdom) (*jñāna, āryajñāna*). This is nondual, subject-object-dichotomy-transcending knowledge of the nonconceptual and transcendental, which is realized by those attaining higher stages.

grace (*adhiṣṭhāna*). The "supernatural power" with which the buddhas sustain the bodhisattvas in their great efforts on behalf of living beings, which is bestowed as consecration when entering the tantric mandala realm.

great, or universal, bliss (*mahāsukha – bde ba chen po*). This is the orgasmic ecstasy stabilized and not dissipated as experienced in focus on and immersion in universal voidness, felt not only in ordinary, genitally organized sexual melting in normal, quickly dissipated sexual ecstasy, but felt steadily in every fiber and cell of the body and every neural energy of the mind and leading to the full experience of the void freedom of communion with clear light reality of all buddhas' body of truth: known as bliss-void-indivisible. This bliss is the secret engine of universal compassion also, as it remains with the enlightened being in no matter what circumstance, and spontaneously overflows to lift suffering beings out of their trap of alienation into the bliss of which they also are made. The art (*upāya*) of doing that is necessary because the alienated being will only get more bound tight by simply a flood of energy, even if it is really bliss: so the blissed-out compassionate being must create an entertainment that will attract the alienated beings according to their inclinations and open their minds to understand their deeper realities.

great, or universal, compassion (*mahākaruṇā*). This refers to one of the two central qualities of a buddha or high bodhisattva (see "enlightenment" entry): his feeling born of the wish for all living beings to be free of suffering and to attain the supreme happiness. It is important to note that this great compassion has nothing to do with any sentimental emotion such as that stimulated by such a reflection as "Oh, the poor creatures! How they are suffering!" On the contrary, great compassion is accompanied by the clear awareness that ultimately there are no such things as living beings, suffering, etc. in reality. Thus it is a sensitivity that does not entertain any dualistic notion of subject and object; indeed, such an unlimited sensitivity might best be termed "empathy."

great seal. Sanskrit *mahāmudrā* indicates the same radical and direct approach to ultimate realization. It refers to the bliss-void-indivisible experience in its extreme perfection, where the adept experiences all of reality as her or his partner in inexhaustible blissful communion. It is a terminology based on the embrace of reality as a seal of experience, ultimate reality being the supreme seal of universal bliss wisdom's complete insight.

high resolve, or messianic ambition (*adhyāśaya*). This is a stage in the conception or initiation of the spirit of enlightenment. It follows upon the positive thought, or aspiration to attain it, wherein the bodhisattva becomes filled with a lofty determination that he himself should attain enlightenment, that it is the only thing to do to solve his own problems as well as those of all living beings. This high resolve reaches its most intense purity as a messianic drive when the bodhisattva simultaneously attains the path of insight and the first bodhisattva stage, the stage of joy.

identity and identitylessness (*svabhāva, niḥsvabhāvatā*). *Svabhāva* is usually rendered as "self-nature," sometimes as "own-being," both of which have a certain literal validity. However, neither artificial term has any evocative power for the reader who has no familiarity with the original, and a term must be found that the reader can immediately relate to his own world to fulfill the function the original word had in its world. In our world of identities (national, racial, religious, personal, sexual, etc.), "identity" is a part of our makeup; thus, when we are taught the ultimate absence of identity of all persons and things, it is easy to "identify" what is supposedly absent and hence to try to understand what that entails.

imagination yoga (**kalpanāyoga – rtog pa'i rnal 'byor*). This is the category of the creation stage and lower tantric practices where visualization is a primary focus.

imminence. This is the deepest state of the subtle mind, just next to the extremely subtle mind of clear light wisdom. It is divided into two halves, an initial moment when there is a consciousness of intense darkness, and a second moment of total unconsciousness. It is called "imminence" (*upalabdhi – nyer thob*) because it is the state where ultimate reality clear light is about to occur in consciousness, where it is imminent. Its synonyms are "neuter," "the perfect," "consciousness," "delusion," "equal reality" (these in common with sutra usages), and "HŪṀ," "luminance-imminence," "great void," "misknowledge," and "medium passion."

indestructible drop (*akṣarabindu – mi shigs pa'i thig le*). This is the extremely subtle body-mind of a sentient being, more or less qualifying as the "soul" (*jīva*) continuum that takes rebirth life after life and eventually becomes self-aware and expands into being the truth body-mind of all buddhas. During the life of a being, from conception to death, it resides in the central chamber of the heart-center channel wheel. "Death" is defined as the moment when the sixfold neural knot around that central chamber unravels and the indestructible drop departs into the clear light of universal void. This is not subjectively perceived by an ordinary being who, after a time of unconsciousness, arises in the subtle dreamlike body of the between state. In the case of a bodhisattva attaining buddhahood (either after three incalculable eons of bodhisattva deeds or in the context of the unexcelled yoga tantra perfection stage called mind objective, perhaps both), the unraveling of the heart knot is done consciously and carefully. The yogi/nī remains consciously aware during the descent through the three luminance gnosis intuitions into the clear light extremely subtle place where the duality of micro and macro is also transcended. Thus there is complete freedom to remain ever blissful in diamond-like clear light transparence infinite truth body communion, which free remaining in such supreme bliss does not at all preclude spontaneous and effortless emanations in magic bodies manifesting whatsoever educates whomsoever about their own reality of bliss-freedom indivisible. This indestructible drop, or Buddhist soul continuum, is part of the esoteric tradition, although hinted at in the individual vehicle refusal to state whether there is any sort of self after death or after nirvana, and more graphically in the universal vehicle buddha-nature teaching, in order to help naïve beings not project onto it their unrealistic habitual views and subliminal habits of a coarse reality personality- and identity-bearing immortal, unchanging, fixated, independent self or soul.

individual vehicle (*hīnayāna – theg dman*). This is the universal vehicle (Skt. *mahāyāna*) term for the foundation form of Buddhism, what I also call "individualist," or "monastic" Buddhism. The term was originally derogatory, referring to the narrow-minded refusal of early monastic Buddhists to accept the possibility of the Buddha also having taught a universal, messianic form of Buddhism. In recent eras of universalist civilizations, it is descriptive and not derogatory, as the foundational aspect of monastic Buddhism is respectfully accepted. Thus, when it is used in Tibet nowadays, it means a vehicle suitable for transporting the individual to freedom and enlightenment. In the modern, pluralistic context, "individual vehicle," while descriptively accurate, need not be taken as derogatory, since for all beings to be liberated from suffering, they must achieve that happy condition one individual being at a time.

individuating wisdom. One of the five wisdoms, transformation of conceptions, the transmutation of lust, associated with the Buddha Amitābha, the lotus buddha-clan, the color red, and the awareness of the distinctions between things, their particularity and individuality.

initiation (*abhiṣekha – dbang bskur ba*). Often translated by "empowerment," it means literally "anointment," as in the coronation of a king or queen, the ritual acknowledgment of a being's assumption of a special transformation, blessing, authority, and responsibility. In unexcelled yoga tantra there are four main initiations, the vase, secret, wisdom-intuition, and word initiations, that empower body, speech, mind, and the integration of all three to learn, practice, and realize all levels of the tantric path.

instinct (*vāsanā – bag chags; prakṛti – rang bzhin*). The subconscious tendencies and predilections of the psychosomatic conglomerate, the two Sanskrit and Tibetan terms in brackets reflecting usages in exoteric and esoteric contexts, respectively. This most obvious English word is seldom used in this context because of the hesitancy of Buddhist translators to employ materialist, "scientific" terminology.

interpretable meaning (*neyārtha*). See "definitive meaning."

Kālachakra Tantra – The *Time Machine Tantra*. This is one of the most important and elaborate of the unexcelled yoga tantras, with a number of distinctive features. It is one of the favorites of the Dalai Lamas, and the Namgyal Monastery of the Potala Palace in Lhasa (presently at the Thekchen Chöling in Dharamsala) is the monastery most renowned for its expertise in the arts associated with this tantra. Its vision of buddhahood and the buddhaverse is of its being an evolutionary time machine, an omnipresent force of wisdom and compassion in close contact with planetary beings throughout all the intricacies of their history. It is a unique vision of time as universal compassion, offering beings a theater in which to evolve toward freedom, rather than seeing time mainly as a destroyer and bringer of death by impermanence.

lalanā. The left channel of the subtle yogic neural system, white in color, running next to the central channel, called *iḍa* in Hindu tantra. See "avadhūti."

lama. This means guru or spiritual teacher in Tibetan, and represents a highly honored profession, since the lama is the indispensable doorway to the practice and performance of tantra. I sometimes use the Tibetan word, and translate it as "mentor" when it seems best to translate it.

liberative art (*upāya*). See "art."

life (*saṁsāra – 'khor ba*). This translation seems natural, instead of either the awkward "transmigration" or the vague "the round," because it conveys well the sense of the transformations of living things; it also connotes to all modern readers the whole span and scope of the world of living things. "Life" can translate three other Tibetan words: *tshe*, which means "lifespan" or "life-time"; *skye ba*, which literally means "birth"; and *srog*, which means "vitality" or "vital principle."

luminance (*āloka – snang ba*). The most surface state of the subtle mind, it is that which corresponds to the desire-oriented instinctual natures, and has the experiential sign of moonlit autumn sky during the death dissolutions and birth arisals. The other two states of the subtle mind, the sunlit radiance, and the darklit imminence, are also sometimes called "luminances," and sometimes "luminance wisdoms." Its synonyms are said to be "wisdom," "the relative," "mind," "anger," "the void side reality" (these in common with sutra teachings), and "*OṀ*," "luminance," "void," "mind," and "dispassion."

magic body (*māyādeha, māyākāya – sgyu lus*). A subtle body attained through the blessing of the mentor at the self-consecration stage of the perfection stage, and created, according to Tsong Khapa, "in order to bring to fruition one's former vows, to abandon the nihilistic tendency gotten from the teaching of the god Maheshvara (Shiva), to accomplish beings' aims until the end of the eon, and to abandon the cessation truth accepted as enlightenment by the disciples" (Tib. 78a). This subtle body seems to be a kind of death-birth-between embodiment, resembling a conscious dream embodiment, and holds (is made of) the extremely subtle mind of great bliss clear light. It is needed to compress eons of altruistic bodhisattva lifetimes into the single life of the perfection-stage adept, in order to realize the matter body of a buddha that manifests the merit and compassion side of the truth body of a buddha.

mandala (*maṇḍala – dkyil 'khor*). There are many types of mandala, which means "realm that protects the essence," the essence of life in the Buddha's view being the universal bliss energy of the clear light of void reality. There are habitat and inhabitant mandalas, which are, respectively, the environment of palace and gardens and death grounds around and firewalls surrounding, and the divine beings within the habitat. Then within that on a more subtle level, there are (1) the spirit of enlightenment mandala, within which one receives the secret empowerment of red and white spirits of enlightenment from the mentor father-mother; (2) the dharma-source or vagina mandala within which one receives the wisdom-intuition empowerment with the consort; and (3) the word mandala, wherein one receives the great fourth empowerment, the word empowerment.

mantra (*mantra – sngags*). Literally meaning "saving (*-tar or -tra*) the mind (*manas*)," a mantra is a creative sound considered expressive of the deepest essence of things and understandings, so that its repetition can evoke in a formulaic or even magical way a state of enlightenment or positive energy. Some mantras resemble sentences, and express some wish, vision, or affirmation, and others are just a single syllable or two, containing the germ of a deity, realm, or state of concentration.

materialism (*vastugraha, bhavagraha – dngos por 'dzin pa*). This is the grasping at things that conceives of material objects as possessing intrinsically real substantiality.

matter (*rūpa*). See "aggregate."

matter body (of a buddha) (*rūpakāya – gzugs sku*). The altruistic aspect of enlightenment, developed from the individual's continua of body and speech, subdivided into the beatific and emanation bodies. It has usually been called "form body," by confusing the two meanings of *rūpa*: "form" as specifically visible object, and "matter" as substantial entity, whether visible or not.

mental quiescence, or serenity (*śamathā*). "Mental quiescence" is a general term for all types of mind practice, meditation, contemplation, concentration, etc. that cultivate one-pointedness of mind and lead to a state of peacefulness and freedom from concern with any sort of object. It is paired with "transcendent insight," which combines the analytic faculty with this one-pointedness to reach high realizations such as selflessness (see "transcendent insight").

mentor (*guru – bla ma*). The guru figure returns to esoteric Buddhism in the context of initiation, and for the depth psychological purpose of guiding the advanced spiritual adventurer who seeks reality and the attainment of buddhahood by diving into the unconscious realm of instincts and lucidly experiencing and mastering the processes of life and death. Though the Sanskrit word means "heavy" and so connotes the weight of the patriarchal authority figure, the Tibetan word fits with the "unexcelled" idea of unexcelled yoga (see "unexcelled yoga tantra") and so connotes a relationship beyond that of father or mother, rather the all-embracing immanence of the buddha-presence that is actually indivisible from even the ignorant being, and thus infuses the disciple with the buddha-presence, rather than holding it above as something far away and unattainable. Certainly, the tantric initiation doesn't "take" unless the recipient visualizes the mentor as indivisible from Vajradhara Buddha himself (or herself as with Vajrayoginī). But the point then of the initiation is to ritually and contemplatively open the door in the recipient's imagination for his or her own identity with the Vajradhara Buddha. Thus the lama mentor serves more as an exemplar of person-buddha communion in order for the disciple practitioner to find that same communion with him- or herself. The relationship is abused when the reception of initiation becomes a justification for worship of the lama, as if the lama was more one with the buddha than the disciple; such an initiation only makes a disciple feel less empowered and more dependent on the lama, rather than empowered to discover the buddha-reality of him- or herself.

mind isolation (*cittaviveka – sems dben*). The third of the five perfection stages, consisting of mind objective, self-consecration, and magic body attainments. Mind herein is isolated from coarse and ordinary reality in the buddha and divine reality of enlightenment.

mirrorlike wisdom. One of the five wisdoms, the transformation of the matter aggregate, the transmutation of delusion, associated with the buddha Vairochana, the transcendent buddha-clan, the color white, and the awareness that even relative things reflect ultimate reality, as in a perfect mirror.

mother tantra (*mātātantra – ma rgyud*). This is a class of unexcelled yoga tantras, all of which (in Tsong Khapa's interpretation) are nondual in terms of magic body and clear light, where the emphasis is on the deepening of immersion in the clear light transparence and intensification of the four joys both before and after the creation of the magic body at the stage of mind isolation through the mind objective and the self-consecration, by the grace of the mentor, deepening it even more during the fourth stage clear enlightenment practice. See "father tantra."

nirvana (*nirvāṇa – mya ngan las 'das pa*). The opposite of samsara, the blowing away of suffering, the peace that surpasseth all understanding, the supreme good, the actual reality of the universe. In the dualistic Buddhism of the individual vehicle, it is represented as a place apart from the world of samsara, an otherworldly elsewhere where the liberated saint could go to freedom, though Buddha was careful not to present it as a state of annihilation. Its highest form was called "nirvana without remainder." In the nondualist universal vehicle teaching, nirvana and samsara were taught to be ultimately the same, though relatively still opposite, and the highest nirvana was called "unlocated," rather than "remainderless." Thus, this very world, if understood by an enlightened mind, was revealed to actually be nirvana, a place of abundant happiness, bliss, freedom, love, and compassion. The task then for the bodhisattva is to destroy the ignorance that prevents us from knowing that bliss, and then share the discovered bliss with beings still caught in suffering by ignorance.

nonapprehension (*anupalambha – dmigs med*). This refers to the mental openness cultivated by the bodhisattva who has reached a certain awareness of the nature of reality, in that he or she does not seek to apprehend any object or grasp any substance in anything; rather, he or she removes any static pretension of the mind to have grasped at any truth, conviction, or view.

nonduality (*advayatvā*). This is synonymous with reality, voidness, etc. But it must be remembered that nonduality does not necessarily mean unity, that unity is only one of the pair unity-duality; hence nonduality implies nonunity as well.

ordinariness (*prākṛta – tha mal pa*). A tantric concept, where the world as perceived by the unenlightened is considered ordinary, because of being maintained by delusion and filled with suffering. The real world, revealed through wisdom and perceived through enlightened senses, is considered "extraordinary" (*tha mal pa ma yin pa*), a purified, enlightened, mandalic, buddhaversal realm of happiness and abundance. "Ordinary" is frequently used with "pride" (*prākṛtāhaṁkāra*) "perception," "conception," "body," and other terms. The tantric yogi/nī seeks to replace these with "deity-pride," "pure perception and conception," and so forth.

outsider (**bāhyapuruṣa – phyi rol pa*). This means a person who has not entered within the refuge of the Buddha, Dharma, and Sangha, as opposed to an "insider" who has. It is often translated as "non-Buddhist" or sometimes as "heterodox," equated with the somewhat more derogatory *tīrthika* (*mu stegs pa* – "fundamentalist"). There is no standard Sanskrit or Tibetan term to translate the English "non-Buddhist," or even "Buddhist" for that matter, at least until modern times.

patron deity (*adhidaivatā – lhag pa'i lha*). A practitioner's especially important buddha-deity form.

perception (*saṁjñā*). See "aggregate."

perfection stage. This is the second stage of the unexcelled yoga tantras, which follows on the successful completion of the creation stage (see above). After the yogi/nī has developed the ability to totally transform his or her perception and conception, so that s/he stably perceives the environment as the pure mandala, her or his body as a deity body, his or her speech as mantra, and her or his mind as buddha-wisdom, all three isolated from ordinariness, imperfection, and impurity, s/he is ready and secure enough to enter the practice of the rehearsal of death, the between, and the rebirth processes with a view to accelerating the evolutionary accumulation of the stores of merit and wisdom to gain buddhahood within a single lifetime or at maximum a few lifetimes. These processes are usually numbered five, including the stages of: (1) body isolation, (2) speech isolation, (3) mind isolation/self-consecration/magic body, (4) clear light/enlightenment, and (5) communion.

performance, practice (*sādhanā – sgrub thabs*). This word is usually translated as "practice," which leads to locutions like "practicing the practice." Wayman tried "evocation" occasionally. In contemporary practitioner circles the Sanskrit *sādhana* is used as an English word. I have discovered that "performance" works quite well in some cases, in that these contemplative sequences used in the unexcelled yoga tantras and other categories of tantra involve memorization, practice, ritual forms of gesture, speech, and visualization, and thus very much turn into contemplative performances, either by a solitary individual or a group.

private, or personal, instruction (*upadeśa – man ngag*). This is an instruction that connects to the exoteric and esoteric texts and transmits the technique and art of the tradition to the person seeking to understand the texts and put them into practice. Tsong Khapa is very clear that these instructions are not ever in contradiction to the treasured teachings in the texts, simply that they are needed to fully implement them, to bring them out from their hiding places in the indirect, intentional, and cryptic encodings in the texts. They also are required to fully realize the practices; so the serious practitioners requires both the mastery of the textual traditions and the personal instructions of a qualified and exemplary teacher.

psychonaut. A "voyager into the soul," an apt term for the Buddhist adept, who voluntarily abandons the pseudosecurity of this planet of delusion, with its solid ground of ordinary, individuated suffering, to launch him- or herself through the death-dissolutions into the subtle between states to deepen his/her wisdom by exploring the unconscious and to expand her compassionate heroism by serving universes of beings on the subtle level, and then to return to be reborn in his/her old ordinary embodiment of the adept to assist his/her contemporaries.

radiance (*ābhāsa, ālokābhāsa – mched pa, snang ba mched pa*). The middle, sunlit state of the subtle mind, the luminance-radiance wisdom, corresponding to the desire-related instinctual natures, between the states of luminance and imminence. Some of its synonyms are "art," "imagined," "mentality," "lust," "sight side reality" (these in common with sutra usage), and "*ĀḤ*," "luminance-radiance," "extreme void," "mental function," and "passion."

rasanā. The right channel in the subtle yogic neural system, red in color, called *piṅgala* in the Hindu yogic systems.

Ratnasaṁbhava. One of the five archetypal transcendent buddhas, lord of the jewel buddha-clan, associated with the southern direction and the buddhaverse Ratnavyūha. He represents the equalizing wisdom, the transformation of the aggregate of sensations, the transmutation of the poison of pride or avarice, and the color yellow. His buddha-consort is Māmakī.

reality (*dharmatā, satya*, even *dharma – chos nyid, bden pa, chos*). An important word in Buddhism since enlightenment purports to be the perfect knowledge and awareness of the actual condition of things, and the possibility of liberation from suffering is based on the truth of that condition and the untruth of the ordinary condition of suffering.

reincarnation, rebirth (*punarjāti, punarbhāva*). It is well to make a distinction between "rebirth" and "reincarnation." "Rebirth" is the normal process following the death of a normal living being. "Reincarnation" is the conscious and voluntary descent into a physical body of a bodhisattva or buddha who, because of his or her transcendence of the bonds of action and addictions, is not compelled to be born, but voluntarily incarnates in order to develop and liberate other living beings.

relativity (*pratītyasamutpāda*). This Sanskrit term is usually translated as "dependent origination," which serves in certain contexts. However, in the centrist (*Mādhyamika*) context, which is an important context in this text, *pratītyasamutpāda* describes ultimate reality. It is equated to shūnyatā, voidness, the nature of birthlessness; thus "origination" is somewhat out of place, since ultimately no thing originates. "Relativity," which T. Stcherbatski used perhaps overzealously by extension for "voidness" itself, seems ideal to convey the sense that nothing exists independent of relation with something else; therefore there is no absolute, permanent, independent self-substantial thing-only things that exist conventionally, dependent on their verbal and intellectual designations.

samadhi (*samādhi – ting nge 'dzin*). An important Sanskrit word for meditational practice and meditational achievement. Usually defined as "one-pointedness of mind," it can also refer to creative mind states after enlightenment, mental concentrations that produce special light rays, liberating environments for disciples, and so forth. It has now entered the English dictionary so there is no need for a diacritical mark.

Saṁgha. The third of the Three Jewels, being the fourfold community of those who live in refuge in the Dharma and Buddha Jewels. Its inclusion is extended in universal vehicle and tantric literatures to include noble, angelic, and divine beings.

samsara (*saṁsāra – 'khor ba*). This is existence controlled by ignorance, desire, and hatred, which is always suffering for beings caught in it. It is by now an English word, and so can be written without diacritical marks. It is sometimes translated as cyclic existence, life cycle, or simply life. See "life."

savior (*nātha – mgon po*). This is usually translated "protector," but so is Dharmapala (*chos bsrungs, chos skyongs*), a name for mundane guardians of the tradition. Nātha as in Nātha Nāgārjuna, Maitreyanātha, refers to an angelic or divine, messianic buddha-being who nurtures and guards the evolutionary essence, the spiritual soul, and so saves you from lifetimes of suffering in samsaric hells and wasted migratory lives.

self (*ātmā – bdag*). It is crucial to understand what is meant by "self," before one is able to realize the all-important "selflessness." Before we can discover an absence, we have to know what we are looking for, what we have been assuming to be present. In all Buddhist teachings, there is a self of persons (subjectivities) and a self of things (objectivities), both presumed habitually by living beings and hence informative of their perceptions. Were these "selves" to exist as they appear because of our presumption, they should exist as substantial, self-subsistent entities within things, or as the intrinsic realities of things, or as the intrinsic identities of things, all permanent, unrelated, and nonrelative, etc. The nondiscovery of such "selves" within changing, relative, interdependent persons and things is the realization of ultimate reality, or selflessness.

selflessness (*anātmatā*, or *nairātmyā*). This describes actual reality, as finally there is no enduring person himself or herself or thing-in-itself, since persons and things exist only in the relative, conventional, or superficial sense, and not in any ultimate or absolute sense. To understand Buddhist teaching correctly, we must be clear about the two senses (conventional/ultimate, or relative/absolute), since mistaking denial of ultimate self as denial of conventional self leads to nihilism, and mistaking affirmation of conventional self as affirmation of ultimate self leads to absolutism. Nihilism and absolutism effectively prevent us from realizing our enlightenment, hence are very much to be avoided.

signlessness (*animittā*). In ultimate reality, there is no sign, as a sign signals or signifies something to someone and hence is inextricably involved with the relative world. We are so conditioned by signs that they seem to speak to us as if they had a voice of their own. The letter *A* seems to pronounce itself to us as we see it, and the stop-sign fairly shouts at us. However, the configuration of two slanted lines with a crossbar has in itself nothing whatsoever to do with the phenomenon made with the mouth and throat in the open position, when expulsion of breath makes the vocal cords resonate "ah." By extending such analysis to all signs, we may get an inkling of what is meant by "signlessness," which is essentially equivalent to voidness, and to wishlessness.

soul (*atisūkṡmacitta, bindu, gotra, saṁtāna, jīva – shin tu phra mo'i sems, gnyugs sems, thig le, rigs, rgyun, srog*). That which is the deepest personal essence of a living being, the super-subtle continuum that journeys from life to life and takes rebirth, and which becomes enlightened finally. The Buddha's famous teaching of selflessness has often been translated in the past as "soul-lessness," and was used to confirm the Western sense that Buddhism is nihilistic and atheistic. The Buddha rejected any absolute, unchanging, fixed, intrinsically substantial, intrinsically identifiable soul, just as he rejected the same kind of intrinsically real self or ego, and the same kind of intrinsically real rock, or tree, or entity, of any kind. But relative, changing, relational, living, conventional entities that can usefully be termed ego, self, or soul are never prohibited in Buddhist psychology.

soul-ejection (**cyuta – 'pho ba*). This is a special yogic method of, anticipating the moment of a normal death, consciously ejecting the indestructible drop soul-continuum from out of the heart center of a particular coarse embodiment up through the central channel and out the crown of the head into a buddha-realm. An adept is supposedly able to mentally line up with the soul-continuum of another person in the midst of their dying process or even soon after they have departed the physical body and boost them into ejecting from their between-state body into a buddha-realm.

speech isolation (*vāgviveka – ngag dben*). This is the second of the five perfection stages, wherein the main practice is the vajra recitation, which mainly consists of uniting inbreath, held-breath, and outbreath with the OṀ ĀḤ HŪṀ—body, speech, and mind of all buddhas—mantras, and maintaining that awareness mindfully all day for six months of meditation until the coarse energies dissolve into the central channel and the four voids and four joys are experienced on the way to first immersion into the metaphoric clear light transparence.

spiritual gene (*gotra – rigs*). Sanskrit *gotra* (in esoteric context sometimes *bīja*, or *bindu*) means the seed of one's propensities, structures, affinities, and fortune developed from the evolutionary action of previous lives. It is a gene that carries the codes of the mind and attitudes of a being, just as the genes of father and mother structure that being's body. It encodes within the extremely subtle life-continuum of an individual the instinctual residue of his or her past lives' evolutionary experiences and actions, which is carried as a subtle "drop" into the next life. If the individual is mammalian, it interacts with the physical genes from father and mother to determine the character of the being in that life. The Buddhist vision of conception is rather beautiful, a moment where the father's white drop meets the mother's red drop, and the individual's blue drop enters within their union.

spiritual teacher (*kalyāṇamitra – dge ba'i bshes gnyen*). The model of teacher in the universal vehicle tradition is that of a virtuous friend who inspires to virtue, consciously avoiding the authoritarian guru archetype prevalent in Indian culture. See "mentor."

subtle body or mind (*sūkśma-śarīra* or *-citta*). The subtle body is constituted by channels, energies, and neural drops (*nāḍivāyubindu*), a kind of neural energy and substance net that resides within the coarse body of flesh and blood and bone and the five sense organs. The coarse mind of fivefold sense-consciousnesses dissolves here into the subtle mind that manifests in this neural network body and consists of the eighty subconscious instinctual natures (*prakṛti*), distributed into three intuition zones, called luminance, radiance, and imminence (experienced as white, red, and blue-black empty spaces); these only appear when the instincts have been calmed by concentration on voidness and the injection of their mounts, the neural energies, into the central channel. One of the symbolic meanings of the three faces, black, red, and white, of the Esoteric Community Buddha form Akṣhobhyavajra may be the three layers of the subtle mind, as well as perhaps the three associated central channels. See "channel, neural channel," "drops," "energy."

sutra (*sūtra – mdo*). This is used in Tibetan as the opposite of tantra, alone or in combination with "vehicle," referring to the exoteric as opposed to esoteric teachings. See "discourse."

tantra (*tantra – rgyud*). The late master tantric abbot, Tara Tulku, in verbal communication defined tantra as follows: "after wisdom has destroyed the ignorance-driven world of samsaric suffering, tantra continues as the art of re-creating the world of the buddhas' compassion out of wisdom itself." There are root tantras, explanatory tantras, further tantras, action, performance, yoga, unexcelled yoga tantras, father tantras, mother tantras, mahāyoga, anuyoga, and atiyoga tantras. There are also medical tantras, and other traditions wherein a "tantra" is a codified technology of an art or science. See "continuum."

time (*kāla – dus*) divisions. A "session" (*thun*) is three Western hours; a "transit" (*'pho ba*) is 90 minutes; an "hour" (*chu tshod*) is 45 minutes; and a "period" (*dbyu gu*) is 22.5 minutes. Internal time of a day (21,600 breaths) is divided into 8 sessions of 2,700 breaths (connected with 8 petals of heart wheel), 16 half-sessions of 1,350 breaths (connected with 16 petals of throat wheel), 32 quarter-sessions of 675 breaths (connected with 32 petals of brain wheel), and 64 eighth sessions of 337.5 breaths (connected with 64 petals of navel wheel).

tolerance (patience) (*kśānti – bzod pa*). This is itemized under the "six transcendences" (see Glossary of Numerical Categories). Here we are concerned with the "intuitive tolerance of the birthlessness (or incomprehensibility) of all things" (*anutpattika-dharmakśānti* or *anupalabdhidharmakśānti*). To translate *kśānti* as "knowledge" or "conviction" defeats entirely the Sanskrit usage and its intended sense. In the face of birthlessness or incomprehensibility (i.e., the ultimate reality), ordinary knowledge and especially convictions are utterly lost. This is because the mind sees through the objectifiability of anything and has nothing to grasp, and its process of coming to terms may be described only as a conscious cancellation through absolute negations of any false sense of certainty about anything. Through this tolerance, the mind reaches a stage where it can bear its lack of bearings and can endure this kind of extreme openness, this lack of any conviction, etc. There are three degrees of this tolerance: verbal (*ghoṣānuga*), conformative (*anulomikī*), and complete.

trance (*samāpatti – mnyam gzhag*). "Trance" has been translated as "meditation," "contemplation," "attainment," etc., and any of these words might serve. It would be good to establish a main English word for each of the important Sanskrit words *samāpatti, dhyāna, samādhi, bhāvanā*, etc., so as to preserve a consistency with the original. Here are used for these terms, respectively, "trance," "contemplation," "concentration" and "meditation," "realization" or "cultivation," using "meditation" also for general use with any of the terms when they are used not in a specific sense but to indicate mind practice in general. See "four trances" in the Glossary of Numerical Categories.

transcendence (*pāramitā*). This has been widely translated as "perfection" following E. Conze's pioneering work with the sutras of transcendent wisdom, which is therefore fine, even standard. I prefer "transcendence," as it conveys the ambiguity in the Sanskrit and Tibetan terms of a "going beyond," for those languages have other terms for complete or perfect. Thus "transcendent wisdom" is a degree of wisdom that goes beyond wisdom, as well as being a wisdom that goes beyond all ignorance. A transcendent generosity goes beyond generosity, as it bears a selfless awareness that doesn't perceive any giver, recipient, or act of giving, and just naturally, effortlessly happens.

transcendent insight (*vipaśyanā – lhag mthong*). This is paired with "mental quiescence." In general "meditation" is too often understood as only the types of practices categorized as "quietistic"—which eschew objects, learning, analysis, discrimination, etc. and lead only to the attainment of temporary peace and one-pointedness. However, in order to reach any high realization, such as personal selflessness, phenomenal selflessness, or voidness, "transcendent insight," with its analytical penetration to the nature of ultimate reality, is indispensable. The analysis is called "transcendent" because it does not accept anything it sees as it appears. Instead, through analytic examination, it penetrates to its deeper reality, going ever deeper in infinite penetration until tolerance is reached. All apparently self-sufficient objects are seen through and their truth-status is rejected—first conceptually and finally perceptually, at buddhahood. Thus "meditation," to be efficacious, must include both mental quiescence (*śamatha*) and transcendent insight (*vipaśyanā*) in integrated combination.

truth (*satya, dharma – bden pa, chos*). For the most part a synonym of reality, though sometimes a statement that corresponds or indicates that reality. See "reality."

truth body (*dharmakāya*). See "three bodies of the Buddha (*trikāya*)" in the Glossary of Numerical Categories.

truth-habit (*satyagraha – bden 'dzin*). This refers to a type of objective self-habit, a subliminal form of misknowledge that reifies in things an unrealistic intrinsic reality that is not possibly there.

ultimate (*paramārtha – don dam*). "Ultimate" is preferable to the usual "absolute" because it carries fewer connotations than "absolute"—which, however, when understood logically, is also correct. It is contrasted with "superficial" (*samvṛtti*) or "relative" (*vyavahāra*) to give the two types, or "levels," of truth. It is synonymous with ultimate reality, the uncompounded, voidness, reality, limit of reality, absolute, nirvana, ultimate liberation, infinity, permanence, eternity, independence, etc. It also has the soteriological sense of "sacred" as opposed to "profane" as is conveyed by its literal rendering "supreme" (*parama*) "object" (*artha*).

unexcelled yoga tantra (*anuttarayogatantra – bla med rnal 'byor rgyud*). This is the highest category of tantric teachings, according to the new translation schools (Kadam-Geluk, Sakya, and Kagyu orders), perhaps corresponding to the mahā-, anu-, and ati-yoga tantras of the old translation school (Nyingma order). The word *anuttara* is often translated "highest," and they are placed highest in a hierarchy of efficacy. However, there are Sanskrit words for "highest," notably *parama*, or *uttama*, and so I prefer "unexcelled," to convey the sense that these teachings cannot be surpassed, and all other teachings end up in them. Rather than being above the other teachings, they are at their heart or core, and so reaching full realization of whatever teaching the Buddha gives brings you to the place of the unexcelled.

universal vehicle (*mahāyāna – theg chen*). The messianic form of Buddhism, that emphasizes the teaching of love and compassion, the inevitable implication of selfless wisdom, providing a social teaching and a vehicle to carry all beings to enlightenment, built upon the foundation of the individual or monastic vehicle that is designed to carry beings one by one.

vagina (*bhaga – bha ga, pad ma*). The sexual organ of a female practitioner or consort, standing also for voidness, the ultimate nature of reality. Thus, in unexcelled yoga tantras the Buddha Vajradhara is said to be dwelling in the "vaginas of the vajra women," i.e., in the ultimate reality of voidness experienced as a sensitive membrane that contains great bliss.

Vairochana. One of the five archetypal transcendent buddhas, lord of the transcendent buddha-clan, associated with the eastern direction. He represents the mirrorlike wisdom, the transmutation of the poison of delusion, the color white, and the aggregate of matter. His buddha-consort is Lochanā.

vajra (*vajra – rdo rje*) (*see also* "adamantine, diamond"). This term is translated in Tibetan with the word for "diamond" (lit. "supreme stone"), which word and object holds a simile for the unbreakability of the intuitive knowledge of the ultimate reality of all things, the infinite energy of the clear light of the void, the ground and substance of all things, known and manifested by all buddhas. The Sanskrit word had the Vedist meaning of "thunderbolt" and was the invincible weapon of Indra, king of the Vedist gods, transformed into a magical scepter, symbolizing for tantric Buddhists the invincible power of universal compassion. Along with liṅga, it refers to the phallus, paired with bhaga and padma for the vagina.

Vajradhara. The tantric buddha par excellence, manifesting as a dark blue royally attired handsome male, a metamorphosis of Shākyamuni and other humanoid buddhas in the context of teaching tantric revelations.

Vajrapāṇi. The same buddha (as Vajradhara/sattva), here as a fierce black ogre-like bodhisattva who asks the Vajradhara Buddha manifestation the tough tantric questions, receives the teachings, and remembers and preserves the tantric sutras.

Vajrasattva. The same buddha (as Vajradhara), here presented as a "diamond hero," an exemplary practitioner of the tantra.

vehicle (*yāna – theg pa*). A conveyance that carries you from one place to another. There are transcendence, sutra, mantra, tantra, vajra, and orgasmic (*sahaja*) vehicles, and also individual, universal, disciple, hermit buddha, and buddha vehicles.

voidness (*śūnyatā – stong pa nyid*). I prefer to translate this term as "voidness" because this English word is more rarely used than "emptiness" and does not refer to any sort of ultimate nothingness, as a thing-in-itself, or even as the thing-in-itself to end all things-in-themselves. It is a pure negation of the ultimate existence of anything or, in Buddhist terminology, the "voidness with respect to subjective and objective selves," or "with respect to intrinsic identity," or "with respect to intrinsic nature," or "with respect to essential substance," or "with respect to self-existence established by intrinsic identity," or "with respect to ultimate truth-status," etc. Thus voidness is a concept descriptive of the ultimate reality through its pure negation of whatever may be supposed to be ultimately real, including itself. It is an absence, hence not existent in itself. It is synonymous therefore with "infinity," "absolute," etc., themselves all negative terms, i.e., formed etymologically from a positive concept by adding a negative prefix (in + finite = not finite; ab + solute = not compounded, etc.). But, since our verbally conditioned mental functions are habituated to the connection of word and thing, we tend to hypostatize a "void," analogous to "outer space," a "vacuum," etc., which we either shrink from as a nihilistic nothingness or become attached to as a liberative nothingness; this great mistake can be cured only by realizing the meaning of the "voidness of voidness," which brings us to the tolerance of inconceivability (see "tolerance").

wind (*vāyu, vāta – rlung*). The fourth element in the scheme of five elements (earth, water, fire, wind, and space); also one of the three ills, or humors (*doṣa – nad*) in Buddhist medicine. The same term is used for the ten inner energies that move things around in the body at coarse, subtle, and supersubtle levels, including electrical, magnetic, metabolic, neural, and other circulatory forces, which I have simply translated as "energies." See also "energy," above.

wisdom (*prajñā, jñāna – shes rab, ye shes*). This word can be used for transcendent wisdom or for gnostic intuition. There is the wisdom of selflessness, the wisdom that realizes voidness, the five wisdoms, and so forth. This word also can be a name for the buddha-consort, as in the "wisdom-intuition initiation" (*prajñā-jñāna-abhiṣekha*).

wishlessness (*apraṇihitā – smon pa med pa*). Third of the three doors of liberation. Objectively, it is equivalent to voidness; subjectively, it is the outcome of the noble gnosis of voidness as the realization of the ultimate lack of anything to wish for, whether voidness itself, or even buddhahood.

yoga (*yoga – rnal 'byor*). From the verbal root *yuj-* "to yoke," yoga means uniting or connecting, the Tibetan translating "connecting with the essence," the "essence" (*rnal*) here being the bliss-void-indivisible, the ultimate or actual reality nondually united with the relative reality of life, the unlocated nirvana nonseparate from samsara, the diamond clear light transparence of the void actual reality as the infinite energy of love and compassion tapped by the wisdom of selflessness, etc. There is a set of "six yogas" employed in performance of the creation stage: yoga, continuing yoga (*anuyoga*), great (*mahā-*) yoga, extreme yoga, mandala triumph yoga and evolutionary (*karma*) triumph yoga.

The currently famous Haṭha Yoga, though traditionally connected with the Saṁkhya philosophy, rather seems to have arisen from Buddhist and Hindu tantra, as the *ha* and the *ṭha* seem to refer to the right and left channels of the tantric yogic subtle nervous system, and the Haṭha Yoga focus on the body as a vehicle of enlightened experience seems contradictory to the Saṁkhya dualism and its effort to escape the body and the differentiated world into *nirvikalpasamādhi*, rather stemming from a Vedāntic or Mādhyamika nondual vision of life.

yogi or yogi/nī (*yogī – rnal 'byor pa*). I use this gender-combined word throughout since in Sanskrit and therefore tacitly in Tibetan the masculine case in all words refers to both genders, as "man" in English is supposed to do when referring to "mankind" as "humankind." Other English words tend to assume only the masculine unless modified in this way, just as *his* does not include the feminine referent, so all bodhisattvas are represented as male, unless we write "his or her." I go to this length especially in this tantric context, in which there has been a lot of ink spilled to make it out as a male chauvinist preserve, while the tradition itself is distinguished by its special emphasis on honoring women in theory and practice (even though most of the historical authors have been men).

yoginī (*yoginī – rnal 'byor ma*). A female yogi. This word is used in certain contexts where a female yoginī deity is involved or mother tantra is intended.

Bibliographies

Modern Sources

Abé, Ryuichi. *The Weaving of Mantra: Kūkai and the Construction of Esoteric Buddhist Discourse*. New York: Columbia University Press, 1999.

Aris, Michael. *Hidden Treasures, Secret Lives: A Study of Pemalingpa (1450–1521) and the Sixth Dalai Lama (1683–1706)*. London and New York: Kegan Paul International, 1989.

Bagchi, S., ed. *Guhyasamāja Tantra or Tathāgataguhyaka*. Darbhanga: Mithila Institute, 1965.

———, ed. *Mahāyāna-sūtrālaṅkāra of Asaṅga*. Darbhanga: Mithilal Institute, 1970.

Bentor, Yael. *Consecration of Images and Stūpas in Indo-Tibetan Tantric Buddhism*. Leiden: E.J. Brill, 1996.

Bhattacharyya, Benoytosh. *An Introduction to Buddhist Esoterism*. London: Oxford University Press, 1932; Delhi: Motilal Banarsidass, 1989.

———. *Two Vajrayāna Works*. Baroda: Oriental Institute, 1929.

Bhattacharyya, Benoytosh, ed. *Guhyasamāja Tantra or Tathāgataguhyaka*. Baroda: Oriental Institute, 1931.

———, ed. *Sādhanamālā*, 2 vols. Baroda: Oriental Institute, 1925; reprint, 1968.

Chakravarti, Chintaharan, ed. *Guhyasamājatantrapradīpodyotanaṭīkā-ṣaṭkoṭīvyākhyā*. Patna: Kashi Prasad Jayaswal Research Institute, 1984.

Chandra, Lokesh. *A Tibetan-Sanskrit Dictionary*. New Delhi: Sharada Rani, 1985.

———. *Tibetan-Sanskrit Dictionary; Supplementary Volume*. 7 vols. New Delhi: International Academy of Indian Culture and Aditya Prakashan, 1992–94.

———, ed. *Sarva-tathāgata-tattva-saṅgraha: Sanskrit Text with Introduction and Illustrations of Maṇḍalas*. Delhi: Motilal Banarsidass, 1987.

Carelli, Mario E. *Sekoddeśaṭīkā of Naḍapāda (Nāropā): Being a Commentary of the Sekkodeśa Section of the Kālacakra Tantra*. Baroda: Oriental Institute, 1941.

Chakravarti, Chintaharan. *Guhyasamājatantrapradīpodyotanaṭīkā-ṣaṭkoṭīvyākhyā*. Patna: Kashi Prasad Jayaswal Research Institute, 1984.

Chimpa, Lama, and Alaka Chattopadhyaya. *Tāranātha's History of Buddhism in India*. Simla: Indian Institute of Advanced Study, 1970; Calcutta: K. P. Bagchi & Co., 1980.

Dalai Lama, Dzong-ka-ba, and Jeffrey Hopkins. *Yoga Tantra: Paths to Magical Feats*. Ithaca: Snow Lion Publications, 2005.

Das, Sarat Chandra. *A Tibetan-English Dictionary with Sanskrit Synonyms*. Calcutta: Bengal Secretariat Book Depot, 1902; Kyoto: Rinsen Book Company, 1993.

Davidson, Ronald. *Indian Esoteric Buddhism: A Social History of the Tantric Movement*. New York: Columbia University Press, 2002.

Davidson, Ronald, and Christian K. Wedemeyer, eds. *Tibetan Buddhist Literature and Praxis: Studies in its Formative Period, 900–1400. PIATS 2003: Tibetan Studies: Proceedings of the Tenth Seminar of the International Association for Tibetan Studies, Oxford, 2003*. Leiden: E.J. Brill, 2006.

Dorje, Gyurme, and Matthew Kapstein, trans. and ed. *The Nyingma School of Tibetan Buddhism: Its Fundamentals and History*. 2 vols. Boston: Wisdom Publications, 1991.

Dowman, Keith. *Masters of Mahamudra: Songs and Histories of the Eighty-four Buddhist Siddhas*. Albany: SUNY Press, 1985.

Farrow, G.W., and I. Menon. *The Concealed Essence of the Hevajra Tantra with the Commentary Yogaratnamālā*. Delhi: Motilal Banarsidass, 1992.

Fremantle, Francesca. "A Critical Study of the Guhyasamāja Tantra." Ph.D. dissertation, University of London, 1971.

George, Christopher. *The Caṇḍamahāroṣanatantra*. New Haven: American Oriental Society, 1974.

Gray, David. *The Discourse of Śri Heruka: The Cakrasaṃvara Tantra*. New York: AIBS/CBS/THUS, 2008.

Gyatso, Janet. *Apparitions of the Self: The Secret Autobiographies of a Tibetan Visionary*. Princeton: Princeton University Press, 1998.

Harrison, Paul. *The Samādhi of Direct Encounter with the Buddhas of the Present: An Annotated Translation of the Tibetan Version of the* Pratyutpanna-Buddha-Sammukhāvasthita-Samādhi-Sūtra. Tokyo: The International Institute for Buddhist Studies, 1990.

Hodge, Stephen. *The Mahā-vairocana-abhisambodhi Tantra*. London: Routledge Curzon, 2003.

Jiang, Zhongxin, and Toru Tomabechi. *The Pañcakramaṭippaṇī of Muniśrībhadra*. Berne: Peter Lang, 1996.

Kalff, Martin. "Abhidhanottara Tantra: Selected Chapters." Ph.D. dissertation, Columbia University, 1978.

Kapstein, Matthew T. *The Tibetan Assimilation of Buddhism: Conversion, Contestation, and Memory*. Oxford: Oxford University Press, 2000.

Kværne, Per. *An Anthology of Buddhist Tantric Songs*. Oslo: Universitetsforlaget, 1977; Bangkok: White Orchid Press, 1986.

Lal, Banarasi, ed. *Āryamañjuśrīnāmasaṁgīti with Amṛtakaṇikā-ṭippaṇī of Bhikṣu Raviśrījñāna and Amṛtakaṇikodyota-nibandha of Vibhūticandra*. Sarnath: Central Institute of Higher Tibetan Studies, 1994.

La Vallée-Poussin, Louis de. *Études et Textes Tantriques: Pañcakrama*. Gand: H. Engelcke, 1896.

Lessing, F. D. and Alex Wayman. *mKhas Grub rJe's Fundamentals of the Buddhist Tantras*. The Hague: Mouton, 1968; Delhi: Motilal Banarsidass, 1978. Reprint, *Introduction to the Buddhist Tantric Systems*. New York: Samuel Weiser, 1980.

Loizzo, Joseph J., et al. *Nāgārjuna's Reason Sixty with Chandrakīrti's Reason Sixty Commentary*. New York: AIBS/CBS/THUS, 2007.

Losang Tsephel, Geshe, et al. *Paths and Grounds of Guhyasamaja According to Arya Nagarjuna*. Dharamsala: Library of Tibetan Works and Archives, 1995.

Matsunaga, Yukei. *The Guhyasamājatantra: A New Critical Edition*. Osaka: Toho Shuppan, 1978.

Mimaki, Katsumi, and Tōru Tomabechi, eds. *Pañcakrama: Sanskrit and Tibetan Texts Critically Edited with Verse Index and Facsimile Edition of the Sanskrit Manuscripts*. Tokyo: The Center for East Asian Cultural Studies for Unesco, 1994.

Mullin, Glenn. *Tsongkhapa's Six Yogas of Naropa*. Ithaca: Snow Lion Publications, 1996.

Monier-Williams, Monier. *A Sanskrit-English Dictionary*. Oxford: Clarendon Press, 1899; Delhi: Motilal Banarsidass, 1990.

Negi, J. S. *Bod skad dan legs sbyar gyi tshig mdzod chen mo* [Tibetan-Sanskrit Dictionary]. 16 vols. Sarnath: Central Institute of Higher Tibetan Studies, 1993–2005.

Obermiller, E. *History of Buddhism (Chos-ḥbyung)*. 2 vols. Heidelberg: O. Harrasowitz, 1931–1932.

Pāṇḍey, Janārdan Shastri. *Caryāmelāpakapradīpam*. Sarnath, Varanasi: Central Institute of Higher Tibetan Studies, 2000

———. "Durlabh Granth Paricaya." *Dhīḥ: A Review of Rare Buddhist Texts* 10 (1990): 3–24.

———. "Durlabh Granth Paricaya." *Dhīḥ: A Review of Rare Buddhist Texts* 25 (1998): 9–18.

Pandeya, Ram Chandra. *The Pramāṇavārttikam of Ācārya Dharmakīrti*. Delhi: Motilal Banarsidass, 1989.

Roerich, George. *The Blue Annals*. Calcutta: Royal Asiatic Society of Bengal, 1949; Delhi: Motilal Banarsidass, 1988.

Ruegg, David S. *Buddha-nature, Mind and the Problem of Gradualism in a Comparative Perspective: On the Transmission and Reception of Buddhism in India and China*. London: School of Oriental and African Studies, 1989; Delhi: Heritage Publishers, 1992.

———. *The Literature of the Madhyamaka School of Philosophy in India*. Wiesbaden: Otto Harrassowitz, 1981.

Skorupski, T. *The Sarvadurgatipariśodhana Tantra*. Delhi: Motilal Banarsidass, 1983.

Snellgrove, David L. *The Hevajra Tantra: A Critical Study*. 2 vols. London: Oxford University Press, 1959.

———. *Indo-Tibetan Buddhism*. 2 vols. Boston: Shambhala, 1987.

Sonam Rinchen, Geshe, and Ruth Sonam. *Yogic Deeds of Bodhisattvas: Gyel-tsap on Āryadeva's Four Hundred*. Ithaca: Snow Lion Publications, 1994. Reprint, *Āryadeva's Four Hundred Stanzas on the Middle Way: with commentary by Gyel-tsap*. Ithaca: Snow Lion Publications, 2008.

Sparham, Gareth. *The Fulfillment of All Hopes: Guru Devotion in Tibetan Buddhism*. Boston: Wisdom Publications, 1999.

Steinkellner, Ernst. "Remarks on Tantristic Hermeneutics." In *Proceedings of the 1976 Csoma de Kőrös Symposium*, edited by L. Ligeti. Budapest: Akadémiai Kiadó, 1978.

Suzuki, Daisetz T., ed. *Chibetto Daijōkyō—The Tibetan Tripiṭaka*. Kyoto: Tripitaka Research Institute, 1955–61.

Takasaki, Jikido. *A Study on the Ratnagotravibhaga (Uttaratantra), being a treatise on the Tathagatagarbha theory of Mahayana Buddhism*. Roma: Istituto Italiano per il Medio ed Estremo Oriente, 1966.

Thurman, Robert A. F. *The Holy Teaching of Vimalakīrti: A Mahāyāna Scripture*. University Park and London: The Pennsylvania State University Press, 1976.

———. *Tsong Khapa's Speech of Gold in the* Essence of True Eloquence: *Reason and Enlightenment in the Central Philosophy of Tibet*. Princeton, NJ: Princeton University Press, 1984.

———. "Vajra Hermeneutics." In *Buddhist Hermeneutics*, edited by Donald S. Lopez, Jr. Honolulu: University of Hawai'i Press, 1988.

———. *The Tibetan Book of the Dead*. New York: Bantam, 1993.

Tomabechi, Tōru. "Étude du Pañcakrama: Introduction et Traduction Annotée." Ph.D. dissertation, Université de Lausanne, 2006.

Tsong-ka-pa, and Jeffrey Hopkins. *Tantra in Tibet: The Great Exposition of Secret Mantra Vol. 1*. London: George Allen & Unwin, 1977. Reprint, H.H. the Dalai Lama, Tsong-ka-pa, and Jeffrey Hopkins. *Tantra in Tibet*. Ithaca: Snow Lion Publications, 1987.

———. *Yoga of Tibet: The Great Exposition of Secret Mantra Vol. 2 and 3*. London: George Allen & Unwin, 1981. Reprint, H.H. the Dalai Lama, Tsong-ka-pa, and Jeffrey Hopkins. *Deity Yoga*. Ithaca: Snow Lion Publications, 1987.

Tsong-kha-pa. *The Great Treatise on the Stages of the Path to Enlightenment*. 3 vols. Ithaca: Snow Lion Publications, 2000–2004.

Tsuda, Shiníchi. *The Saṁvarodaya-tantra: Selected Chapters*. Tokyo: The Hokuseido Press, 1974.

Tucci, Giuseppe. *Tibetan Painted Scrolls*. 3 vols. Roma: Libreria della Stato, 1949.

Wallace, Vesna. *The Inner Kālacakratantra: A Buddhist Tantric View of the Individual*. New York: Oxford University Press, 2001.

———. *The Kālacakra Tantra: The Chapter on the Individual*. New York: AIBS/ CBS/ THUS, 2004.

———. *The Kālacakra Tantra: The Chapter on Sādhanā*. New York: AIBS/CBS/ THUS, 2010.

Walshe, Maurice. *Thus Have I Heard: The Long Discourses of the Buddha*. London: Wisdom Publications, 1989. Reprint, *The Long Discourses of the Buddha: A Translation of the Digha Nikāya*. Boston: Wisdom Publications, 1995.

Wayman, Alex. *The Buddhist Tantras: Light on Indo-Tibetan Esotericism*. New York: Samuel Weiser, 1973; Delhi: Motilal Banarsidass, 1993.

———. *Yoga of the Guhyasamājatantra*. New York: Samuel Weiser, 1977; Delhi: Motilal Banarsidass, 1991.

Wayman, Alex, and R. Tajima. *The Enlightenment of Vairocana*. Delhi: Motilal Banarsidass, 1992.

Wedemeyer, Christian K. "Antinomianism and Gradualism: The Contextualization of the Practices of Sensual Enjoyment (*caryā*) in the Guhyasamāja Ārya Tradition." *Indian International Journal of Buddhist Studies* n.s. 3 (2002): 181–95.

———. "Beef, Dog, and Other Mythologies: Connotative Semiotics in Mahāyoga Tantra Ritual and Scripture." *Journal of the American Academy of Religion* 75 (2): 383–417.

———. "On the Authenticity of the *Caryāmelāpakapradīpa Commentary* Attributed to Śākyamitra." Paper presented at the XIVth Conference of the International Association of Buddhist Studies, London, U.K., 2 September 2005.

———. "Sex and Death in Mainstream Eleventh-Century gSar-ma Esoterism: 'Gos Khug-pa Lhas-btsas, *caryā* (*spyod pa*), and *abhicāra* (*mngon par spyod pa*)." Paper presented at the XIIIth Conference of the International Association of Buddhist Studies, Bangkok, Thailand, December 13, 2002.

———. "Tantalising Traces of the Labours of the Lotsāwas: Alternative Translations of Sanskrit Texts in the Writings of rJe Tsong-kha-pa." In *Tibetan Buddhist Literature and Praxis*, edited by Ronald Davidson and Christian Wedemeyer. Leiden: Brill, 2006.

———. "Tropes, Typologies, and Turnarounds: A Brief Genealogy of the Historiography of Tantric Buddhism." *History of Religions* 40(3): 223–59.

———. "Vajrayāna and Its Doubles: A Critical Historiography, Exposition, and Translation of the Tantric Works of Āryadeva." Ph.D. dissertation, Columbia University, 1999.

———. *Āryadeva's Lamp That Integrates the Practices (Caryāmelāpakapradīpa): The Gradual Path of Vajrayāna Buddhism.* New York: AIBS/CBS/THUS, 2007.

White, David Gordon. *The Alchemical Body: Siddha Traditions in Medieval India.* Chicago: The University of Chicago Press, 1996.

Yarnall, Thomas F. *Great Treatise on the Stages of Mantra. Chapters XI–XII: The Creation Stage.* By Tsong Khapa Losang Drakpa. New York: AIBS/CBS/THUS, 2013.

Zhang, Yisun. *Bod rGya Tshig mDzod Chen Mo* [The Great Tibetan-Chinese Dictionary]. 3 vols. Peking: Mi Rigs dPe sKrun Khang, 1984.

Cited Texts (Sanskrit and Tibetan)

Accomplishment Ascertaining Wisdom and Art

Sanskrit: *Prajñopāyaviniścayasiddhi*
Tibetan: *thabs dang shes rab rnam par gtan la dbab pa sgrub pa*
Tibetan cited as: *thabs shes gtan la dbab pa grub pa; thabs dang shes rab grub pa*
Author: Anaṅgavajra / yan lag med pa'i rdo rje
Tōhoku no.: 2218
Derge location: rgyud wi, 28b–36b

Achala Unexcelled Tantra (uncertain identification)
Sanskrit: *Ārya-Acalakalpa-tantrarāja*
Tibetan: *'phags pa mi g-yo ba'i rtog pa'i rgyud kyi rgyal po*
Tibetan cited as: *mi g-yo ba bla med kyi rgyud*
Author: Kangyur
Tōhoku no.: 432
Derge location: rgyud, ca, 1b–12a

Always Pervading (unidentified)
Tibetan cited as: *rtag tu khyab pa*

Analysis of Tradition
Sanskrit: *Vinaya-vibhaṅga*
Tibetan: *'dul ba rnam par 'byed pa*
Tibetan cited as: *lung rnam 'byed*
Author: Kangyur
Tōhoku no.: 3
Derge location: 'dul ba, ca, 21a–nya, 26a

Angel Ocean
Sanskrit: *Śrī-ḍākārṇava-mahāyoginī-nāma-tantrarāja*
Tibetan: *dpal mkha' 'gro rgya mtsho rnal 'byor ma'i rgyud kyi rgyal po chen po zhes bya ba*
Tibetan cited as: *mkha' 'gro rgya mtsho*
Author: Kangyur
Tōhoku no.: 372
Derge location: rgyud, kha, 137a–264b

Arts of Achievement (Lūyipa's Sādhana) Commentary by Lawapa
Sanskrit: *Śrī-cakrasamvarābhisamaya-ṭīkā*
Tibetan: *dpal 'khor lo bde mchog gi mngon par rtogs pa'i 'grel pa*
Tibetan cited as: *'grel pa*
Author: Lawapa
Peking no.: P.4661

Arts of Achievement (Sādhana) Commentary Autocommentary by Tathāgatavajra
Sanskrit: *Lūyipābhisamaya-vṛtti-ṭīkā-viṣeśadyota-nāma*
Tibetan: *l'u yi pa'i mngon par rtogs pa'i 'grel pa'i T'i k'a khyad par gsal byed ces bya ba*
Tibetan cited as: *de bzhin gzhegs pa'i rdo rjes*
Author: Tathāgatavajra / de bzhin gshegs pa'i rdo rje
Tōhoku no.: 1510
Derge location: rgyud, zha, 285a–308b

Arts of Achievement Sādhana by Lūyipa
Sanskrit: *Śrī-bhagavad-abhisamaya-nāma*
Tibetan: *dpal bcom ldan 'das mngon par rtogs pa zhes bya ba*
Tibetan cited as: *sgrub thabs*
Author: Lūyipa
Tōhoku no.: 1427
Derge location: rgyud, wa, 186b–193a

Black Yamāri Tantra
Sanskrit: *Sarvatathāgata-kāyavākcitta-kṛṣṇayamāri-nāma-tantra*
Tibetan: *de bzhin gshegs pa thams cad kyi sku gsung thugs gshin rje gshed nag po zhes bya ba'i rgyud*
Tibetan cited as: *nag gi rgyud; gshin rje gshed*
Author: Kangyur
Tōhoku no.: 467
Derge location: rgyud, ja, 134b–151b

Bodhisattva Stages
Sanskrit: *Yogacāyrabhūmau-bodhisattvabhūmi*
Tibetan: *rnal 'byor spyod pa'i sa las byang chub sems dpa'i sa*
Tibetan cited as: *byang sa*
Author: Asaṅga / thogs med
Tōhoku no.: 4037
Derge location: sems tsam, wi, 1b–213a

Buddha Skull-Bowl
Sanskrit: *Śrī-Buddhakapāla-nāma-yoginītantrarāja*
Tibetan: *dpal sangs rgyas thod pa zhes bya ba rnal 'byor ma'i rgyud kyi rgyal po*
Tibetan cited as: *sangs rgyas thod pa*
Author: Kangyur
Tōhoku no.: 424
Derge location: rgyud, nga, 143a–167a

Buddha Union
Sanskrit: *Śrī-sarvabuddha-samāyoga-ḍākinījāla-sambara-nāma-uttaratantra*
Tibetan: *dpal sangs rgyas thams cad dang mnyam par sbyor ba mkha' 'gro ma sgyu ma bde ba'i mchog ces bya ba'i rgyud phyi ma*
Tibetan cited as: *mnyam sbyor; sangs rgyas mnyam sbyor*
Author: Kangyur
Tōhoku no.: 366
Derge location: rgyud, ka, 151b–193a

Captivator of Yogi/nīs
Sanskrit: *Pañcakramārtha-yogimanohara-ṭippaṇī-nāma*
Tibetan: *rim pa lnga'i don mdor bshad pa rnal 'byor pa'i yid kyi 'phrog ces bya ba*
Tibetan cited as: *rnal 'byor pa'i yid 'phrod*
Author: Muniśrībhadra / thub pa dpal bzang po
Tōhoku no.: 1813
Derge location: rgyud, ngi, 148b–195b

Centrist Treatise Wisdom, The
Sanskrit: *Prajñā-nāma-mūlamadhyamakakārikā*
Tibetan: *dbu ma rtsa ba'i tshig le'ur byas pa shes rab ces bya ba*
Tibetan cited as: *dbu ma'i gzhung*
Author: Nāgārjuna / klu sgrub
Tōhoku no.: 3824
Derge location: dbu ma, tsa, 1b–19a

Clear Meaning of the Five Stages
Sanskrit: *Pañcakrama-vṛttārthavirocana-nāma*
Tibetan: *rim pa lnga'i don gsal bar byed pa zhes bya ba*
Tibetan cited as: *rim lnga'i 'grel pa*
Author: Lakṣmī
Tōhoku no.: 1842
Derge location: rgyud, chi, 187b–277a

Clear Meaning of the Five Stages
Sanskrit: *Pañcakramārthabhāskaraṇa-nāma*
Tibetan: *rim pa lnga'i don gsal bar byed pa zhes bya ba*
Tibetan cited as: *don gsal ba; don gsal; 'grel pa don gsal*
Author: Nāgabodhi (attrib.) / klu byang
Tōhoku no.: 1833
Derge location: rgyud, ci, 207b–237a

Clear Ornament of Vows Tantra 100,000,000 (unidentified)
Tibetan cited as: *dam tshig mngon rgyan stong phrag 'bum*

Commentary Boat
Sanskrit: *Śrī-ḍākārṇava-mahāyoginī-tantrarāja-vārāhī-ṭīkā-nāma*
Tibetan: *dpal mkha' 'gro rgya mtsho rnal 'byor ma'i rgyud kyi rgyal po chen po'i 'grel pa gru gzings zhes bya ba*
Tibetan cited as: *'grel ba gru gzings*
Author: Padmavajra / pad+ma rdo rje
Tōhoku no.: 1419
Derge location: rgyud, dza, 1b–318a

Community Commentary
Sanskrit: *Aṣṭadaśapaṭala-vistaravyākhyā*
Tibetan: *le'u bco brgyad pa'i rgya cher 'grel pa*
Tibetan cited as: *'dus pa'i rgyud kyi 'grel pa*
Author: Nāgārjuna (attrib.) / klu sgrub
Tōhoku no.: 1784A
Derge location: rgyud, sa, 284a–324a

Compendium Tantra 1,000 (unidentified)
Tibetan cited as: *kun las btus pa 'bum phrag gcig*

Concentrated Personal Instructions of the Marpa tradition (unidentified)
Tibetan cited as: *man ngag bsdus pa*

Concise Five Stages Elucidation
Also cited as: *Concise Five*
Sanskrit: *Pañcakrama-saṃgraha-prakāśa*
Tibetan: *rim pa lnga bsdus pa gsal ba*
Tibetan cited as: *rim lnga bsdus pa gsal ba; rim lnga bsdus pa*
Author: Nāropa (attrib.)
Tōhoku no.: 2333
Derge location: rgyud, zhi, 276a–278a

Concise Source on the Stages
Sanskrit: *Kramāntarbhāvanopadeśa-nāma-prakaraṇa*
Tibetan: *rim pa khongs su bsdu ba'i man ngag ces bya ba'i rab tu byed pa*
Tibetan cited as: *rim pa khongs su bsdu ba*
Author: Nāgabodhi (attrib.) / klu byang (attrib.)
Tōhoku no.: 1812
Derge location: rgyud, ngi 147a–148b

Condensed Sādhana
Sanskrit: *Piṇḍīkṛta-sādhana*
Tibetan: *sgrub pa'i thabs mdor byas pa*
Tibetan cited as: *mdor byas*
Author: Nāgārjuna / klu sgrub
Tōhoku no.: 1796
Derge location: rgyud, ngi, 1b–11a

Consciousness Migrating Sutra
Also cited as: *Inquiry of Bhadrapala the Consciousness Migrating Sutra*
Sanskrit: *Vijñāna-saṁkrānti sūtra*
Tibetan: *rnam par shes pa 'pho ba'i mdo*
Tibetan cited as: *rnam shes 'pho ba'i mdo; bzang skyong gis zhus pa*
Author: Kangyur
Tōhoku no.: 83
Derge location: dkon brtsegs, cha, 71a–94b

Consolations of the Transcendent Buddha and Vajradhara (unidentified)
Tibetan cited as: *de bzhin gshegs pa dang rdo rje 'chang gi dbugs dbyung*

Crazy Discipline Sutra (unidentified)
Tibetan cited as: *smyon pa'i brtul zhugs kyi mdo*

Ḍākinī Vajra Pavilion Tantra
Also cited as: *Diamond Pavilion; Diamond Pavilion Yogini Tantra; Vajra Pavilion*
Sanskrit: *Ḍākinīvajrapañjaramahātantrarājakalpa*
Tibetan: *mkha' 'gro ma rdo rje gur zhes bya ba'i rgyud kyi gyal po chen po'i brtag pa*
Tibetan cited as: *mkha' 'gro ma rdo rje gur gi rgyud; rdo rje gur; gur; rnal 'byor ma'i rgyud gur*
Author: Kangyur
Tōhoku no.: 419
Derge location: rgyud, nga, 30a–65b

Determination of the Meaning of the Four Initiations (uncertain identification)
Sanskrit: *Sekacatuḥprakaraṇa*
Tibetan: *dbang bzhi pa'i rab tu byed pa*
Tibetan cited as: *dbang bzhi'i don gtan la 'bebs pa*
Author: Nāgārjuna / klu sgrub
Tōhoku no.: 1799
Derge location: rgyud, ngi, 35a–38a

Dharma Song (unidentified)
Tibetan cited as: *chos kyi glu*
Author: Atīśa

Dialogue on the Glorious Meaning of the Commentary (unidentified)
Tibetan cited as: *'grel pa'i don dpal gyi dris lan*

Dialogue with the Householder Ugra
Sanskrit: *Ārya-Gṛhapati-Ugraparipṛcchā-nāma-mahāyānasūtra*
Tibetan: *'phags pa khyim bdag drag shul can gyis zhus pa zhes bya ba theg pa chen po'i mdo*
Tibetan cited as: *khyim bdag drag shul can gyis zhus pa*
Author: Kangyur
Tōhoku no.: 63
Derge location: dkon brtsegs, nga, 257a–288a

Disciples' Stages
Sanskrit: *Yogacaryābhūmau śravakabhūmi*
Tibetan: *rnal 'byor spyod pa'i sa las nyan thos kyi sa*
Tibetan cited as: *nyan sa*
Author: Asaṅga / thogs med
Tōhoku no.: 4036
Derge location: sems tsam, dzi, 1b–195a

Discipline Amoghasiddhi Tantra (uncertain identification)
Sanskrit: *Śrī-Vajraḍāka-nāma-mahātantrarāja*
Tibetan: *rgyud kyi rgyal po chen po dpal rdo rje mkha' 'gro*
Tibetan cited as: *'dul ba don yod par grub pa'i rgyud*
Author: Kangyur
Tōhoku no.: 370
Derge location: rgyud, kha, 1b–125a

Disclosure of the Spirit of Enlightenment
Sanskrit: *Bodhicitta-vivaraṇa-nāma and Bodhicitta-vivaraṇa*
Tibetan: *byang chub sems kyi 'grel zhes bya ba and byang chub sems kyi 'grel*
Tibetan cited as: *byang chub sems 'grel*
Author: Nāgārjuna / klu sgrub
Tōhoku no.: 1800
Derge location: rgyud, ngi, 38a–42b

Discrimination between Interpretable and Definitive
Sanskrit: *(N/A)*
Tibetan: *drang ba dang nges pa'i don rnam par phye ba'i bstan bcos legs bshad snying po*
Tibetan cited as: *drang nges rnam par 'byed pa*
Author: (N/A) / tsong kha pa
Tōhoku no.: 5396
Tashi Hlunpo location: pha, #4

Eight Thousand
Sanskrit: *Ārya-Aṣṭasāhasrikā-prajñāpāramitā*
Tibetan: *'phags pa shes rab kyi pha rol tu phyin pa brgyad stong pa*
Tibetan cited as: *brgyad stong pa*
Author: Kangyur
Tōhoku no.: 12
Derge location: shes phyin, ka, 1b–286aa

Elixir Secret (See *Stages of the Path of Vajradhara*, by Ekādaśanirghoṣa)

Elucidation of the Esoteric Reality
Sanskrit: *Guhyatattvaprakāśa-nāma*
Tibetan: *gsang ba'i de kho na nyid rab tu gsal ba zhes bya ba*
Tibetan cited as: *de kho na nyid gsal ba; gsang ba'i de kho na nyid gsal ba*
Author: Kṛṣṇapa / spyod pa nag po pa
Tōhoku no.: 1450
Derge location: rgyud, wa, 349a–355b

Elucidation of the Root Downfalls and Gross Infractions (uncertain identification)
Sanskrit: *Sthūlāpatti*
Tibetan: *ltung ba sbom po*
Tibetan cited as: *rtsa ltung dang sbom po'i rnam bshad*
Author: Aśvaghoṣa / rta dbyangs
Tōhoku no.: 2479
Derge location: rgyud, zi, 179b–180a

Elucidation of the Seven Ornaments
Tibetan: *ye shes rdo rje kun las btus pa'i rgyud las 'byung ba'i rgyan bdun rnam par dgrol ba*
Tibetan cited as: *rgyan bdun rnam par dgrol ba*
Author: Śraddhākaravarman / dad byed go cha
Tōhoku no.: 1789
Derge location: rgyud, aa, 8b–10a

Empowerment Summary (unidentified)
Tibetan cited as: *dbang mdor bstan*

Enlightenment Song (Doha) Treasury
Sanskrit: *Dohākoṣagīti*
Tibetan: *do ha mdzod kyi glu*
Tibetan cited as: *dho ha; do ha*
Author: Saraha
Tōhoku no.: 2224
Derge location: rgyud, wi, 70b–77a

Equal to Space Tantra
Sanskrit: *Śrī-Khasama-tantrarāja-nāma*
Tibetan: *dpal nam mkha' dang mnyam pa'i rgyud kyi rgyal po*
Tibetan cited as: *nam mkha' dang mnyam pa'i rgyud*
Author: Kangyur
Tōhoku no.: 386
Derge location: rgyud 'bum, ga, 199a–202a

Equality Esoteric Tantra 5,000 (unidentified)
Tibetan cited as: *mnyam nyid gsang ba stong phrag lnga*

Equality Triumph Tantra 210 (unidentified)
Tibetan cited as: *mnyam nyid rnam rgyal nyis brgya bcu*

Equipoise Magic Illusion Instruction (unidentified)
Tibetan cited as: *mnyam gzhag sgyu ma'i gdams pa*

Esoteric Accomplishment
Sanskrit: *Sakalatantrasambhavasañcodanī-śrīguhyasiddhi-nāma*
Tibetan: *rgyud ma lus pa'i don nges par skul bar byed pa dpal gsang ba grub pa zhes bya ba*
Tibetan cited as: *gsang ba grub pa*
Author: Mahāsukhanātha (Padmavajra) / dpal mgon po bde ba chen po
Tōhoku no.: 2217
Derge location: rgyud, wi, 1b–28b

Esoteric Community Further Tantra
Also cited as: *Community Further Tantra; Further Tantra*
Sanskrit: *Uttaratantra*
Tibetan: *rgyud phyi ma*
Tibetan cited as: *gsang ba 'dus pa phyi ma'i rgyud; 'dus pa phyi ma; 'dus pa'i rgyud phyi ma; rgyud phyi ma*
Author: Kangyur
Tōhoku no.: 443
Derge location: rgyud, ca, 148a–157b

Esoteric Community Tantra
Also cited as: *Community Root Tantra; Community; Community Tantra; Esoteric Community Root Tantra; Esoteric Community; Glorious Esoteric Community Śhrī Guhyasamāja; Glorious Esoteric Community Tantra; Glorious Esoteric Community Yoga; Community; Glorious Community*
Sanskrit: *Sarvatathāgata-kāyavākcitta-rahasya-guhyasamāja-nāma-mahākalparāja*
Tibetan: *de bzhin gshegs pa thams cad kyi sku gsung thugs kyi gsang chen gsang ba 'dus pa zhes bya ba brtag pa'i rgyal po chen po*
Tibetan cited as: *gsang 'dus pa'i rgyud; 'dus pa; 'dus pa'i rtsa rgyud; 'dus pa'i rtsa ba'i rgyud; 'dus pa'i rgyud; 'dus pa'i rtsa rgyud; gsang ba 'dus pa; dpal gsang ba 'dus pa; dpal ldan gsang ba 'dus pa'u rgyud; dpal gsang ba 'dus pa rnal 'byor gyi rgyud; 'dus pa; dpal ldan 'dus*
Author: Kangyur
Tōhoku no.: 442
Derge location: rgyud, ca, 90a–148a

Esoteric Community Tantra 1,000 (unidentified)
Tibetan cited as: *gsang ba 'dus pa stong phrag gcig*

Esoteric Lamp
Sanskrit: *Sarvaguhyapradīpa-ṭīkā*
Tibetan: *gsang ba thams cad kyi sgron ma'i rgya cher 'grel pa*
Tibetan cited as: *gsang ba'i sgron me*
Author: Yaśobhadra / snyan grags bzang po
Tōhoku no.: 1787
Derge location: rgyud, ha, 203b–234a

Explanation of Vajra Recitation
Sanskrit: *Vajrajapaṭīkā*
Tibetan: *rdo rje bzlas pa'i rgya cher bshad pa*
Tibetan cited as: *dgongs pa lung ston nas gsungs pa'i rdo rje'i bzlas pa'i bshad pa*
Author: Śraddhākaravarman / dad byed go cha
Tōhoku no.: 1788
Derge location: rgyud, aa, 1b–8b

Extensive All Transcendent Buddha Ārali (unidentified)
Also cited as: *Extensive Ārali*
Tibetan cited as: *de bzhin gshegs pa thams cad kyi A ra li rgyas pa; A ra li rgyas pa*

Famous Treatise (unidentified)
Tibetan cited as: *bsgrag pa'i gzhung*

Fierce Moon Drop Tantra 500,000 (unidentified)
Tibetan cited as: *khro zla thig le 'bum phrag lnga*

Five Point Treatise
Also cited as: *Five Point Treatise on the Five Stages; Fivefold Import of the Five Stages; Five Point; Fivefold Import*
Tibetan: *don lnga ma sogs gsang 'dus nag khrid kyi skor yig sna nyer bdun tsam yod pa*
Tibetan cited as: *don lnga ma; rim lnga don lnga ma*
Author: (N/A) / gser sdings pa gzhon nu 'od
MHTL no.: 11941
TBRC work id.: W12563

Five Stages
Also cited as: *Second Stage; Third Stage; Fourth Stage; Unexcelled Intention; Vajra Recitation Stage*
Sanskrit: *Pañcakrama*
Tibetan: *rim pa lnga pa*
Tibetan cited as: *rim lnga; rim pa gnyis pa; rim pa gsum pa; rim pa bzhi pa; dgongs pa bla na med pa; rdo rje zlas pa'i rim pa*
Author: Nāgārjuna / klu sgrub
Tōhoku no.: 1802
Derge location: rgyud, ngi, 45a–57a

Five Stages by Ghaṇṭapāda
Sanskrit: *Śrī-cakrasaṁvara-pañcakrama*
Tibetan: *dpal 'khor lo bde mchog gi rim pa lnga pa*
Tibetan cited as: *rim lnga*
Author: Ghaṇṭapāda / dril bu pa
Peking no.: P.4624

Five Stages Difficult Point Commentary
Sanskrit: *Pañcakrama-pañjikā-nāma*
Tibetan: *rim pa lnga pa'i dka' 'grel zhes bya ba*
Tibetan cited as: *rim lnga'i dka' 'grel*
Author: Bhavyakīrti / skal ldan grags pa
Tōhoku no.: 1838
Derge location: rgyud, chi, 1b–7b

Five Stages Difficult Point Commentary
Sanskrit: *Pañcakrama-pañjikā-prabhāsārtha-nāma*
Tibetan: *rim pa lnga pa'i dka' 'grel don gsal ba zhes bya ba*
Tibetan cited as: *rim lnga'i dka' 'grel*
Author: Vīryabhadra / brtson 'gros bzang po
Tōhoku no.: 1830
Derge location: rgyud, ci, 142b–180b

Five Stages Simultaneous (unidentified)
Tibetan cited as: *rim lnga cig car ba*

Five Stages Single Session
Also cited as: *Father Tantra Quintessence*
Tibetan: *gsang 'dus rim lnga gdan rdzogs*
Tibetan cited as: *rim lnga gdan rdzogs; pha rgyud yang snying*
Author: (N/A) / gser sdings pa gzhon nu 'od
MHTL no.: 11938
TBRC work id.: W12560

Five Stages Single Session Vital Manual (unidentified)
Tibetan cited as: *rim lnga gdan rdzogs kyi dmar 'khrid*

Five Stages Triple Nested Spiritual Heroes (unidentified)
Tibetan cited as: *rim lnga sems dpa' sum brtsegs*

Five Stages, Personal Instruction in the Community
Sanskrit: *Śrīguhyasamājopadeśapañcakrama-nāma*
Tibetan: *dpal gsang ba 'dus pa'i man ngag rim pa lnga pa*
Tibetan cited as: *'dus pa'i man ngag rim pa lnga pa*
Author: Nāropa (attrib.)
Peking no.: P.4789

Five Vajra Community Tantra 1,000 (unidentified)
Tibetan cited as: *rdo rje lnga 'dus stong phrag gcig*

Flower Bouquet
Sanskrit: *Kusumañjali-guhyasamāja-nibandha-nāma*
Tibetan: *gsang ba 'dus pa'i bshad sbyar snyim pa'i me tog ces bya ba*
Tibetan cited as: *snyim pa'i me rtog*
Author: Śāntipa
Tōhoku no.: 1851
Derge location: rgyud, ti, 202b–thi, 120a

Four Goddess Dialogue
Sanskrit: *Catudevī-paripṛcchā*
Tibetan: *lha mo bzhis yongs su zhus pa*
Tibetan cited as: *lha mo bzhis zhus pa*
Author: Kangyur
Tōhoku no.: 446
Derge location: rgyud, ca, 277b–281b

Four Goddess Dialogue Commentary
Sanskrit: *Caturdevatāparipṛcchāvyākhyānopadeśapauṣṭika-nāma*
Tibetan: *lha mo bzhis yongs su zhus pa'i rnam par bshad pa man ngag rgyas pa*
Tibetan cited as: *lha mo bzhis zhus ni de'i 'grel pa*
Author: Smṛtijñānakīrti / ye shes grags pa
Tōhoku no.: 1915
Derge location: rgyud, phi, 217b–249b

Four Goddess Dialogue Tantra 170 (unidentified)
Tibetan cited as: *lha mo bzhis zhus brgya bdun cu*

Four Hundred Commentary (unidentified)
Tibetan cited as: *bzhi brgya pa'i 'grel pa*

Four Hundred Fifty
Sanskrit: *Śrī-Guhyasamāja-maṇḍala-vidhi-nāma*
Tibetan: *dpal gsang ba 'dus pa'i dkyil 'khor gyi cho ga zhes bya ba*
Tibetan cited as: *bzhi brgya lnga bcu pa*
Author: Dīpaṅkarabhadra / mar me mdzad bzang po
Tōhoku no.: 1865
Derge location: rgyud, di, 69a–87a

Four Point Treatise
Also cited as: *Four Point*
Sanskrit: *gsangs 'dus 'khor lo med pa don bzhi ma*
Tibetan cited as: *don bzhi ma*
Author: (N/A) / gser sdings pa gzhon nu 'od
MHTL no.: 11940
TBRC work id.: W12562

Four Procedures of Explanation, Ya Ra La Wa (unidentified)
Tibetan cited as: *ya ra la wa sogs tshul gzhir bshad pa*

Four Seats
Sanskrit: *Śrī-catuḥ-pīṭha-vikhyāta-tantrarāja-nāma*
Tibetan: *dpal gdan bzhi pa'i rnam par bshad pa'i rgyud kyi rgyal po zhes bya ba*
Tibetan cited as: *gdan bzhi*
Author: Kangyur
Tōhoku no.: 430
Derge location: rgyud, nga, 260a–304a

Further Tantra Commentary (unidentified)
Tibetan cited as: *rgyud phyi ma'i 'grel pa*
Author: Nāropa

Glorious Supreme Prime
Sanskrit: *Śrī-Paramādyamantrakalpakhaṇḍa-nāma*
Tibetan: *dpal mchog dang po'i sngags kyi rtog pa'i dum bu zhes bya ba*
Tibetan cited as: *dpal mchog dang po; dpal mchog*
Author: Kangyur
Tōhoku no.: 488
Derge location: rgyud, ta, 173a–265b

Goddess Treatise Tantra 507 (unidentified)
Tibetan cited as: *lha mo bstan bcos lnga brgya bdun*

Great Commentary on the Community
Sanskrit: *Śrī-guhyasamāja-mahātantrarāja-ṭīkā*
Tibetan: *rgyud kyi rgyal po chen po dpal gsang 'dus pa'i rgya cher 'grel pa*
Tibetan cited as: *'grel pa chen mo*
Author: Ānandagarbha (attrib.) / kun dga' snying po (attrib.)
Peking no.: P.4787

Great Commitment [Tantra] 55 (unidentified)
Tibetan cited as: *dam tshig chen po lnga bcu lnga*

Great Seal Drop
Sanskrit: *Śrī-Mahāmudrātilaka-nāma-mahāyoginī-tantrarājādhipati*
Tibetan: *dpal phyag rgya chen po'i thig le zhes bya ba rnal 'byor ma chen mo'i rgyud kyi rgyal po'i mnga' bdag*
Tibetan cited as: *phyag chen thig le*
Author: Kangyur
Tōhoku no.: 420
Derge location: rgyud, nga, 66a–90b

Great Secret Compendium Tantra 150 (unidentified)
Tibetan cited as: *gsang chen bsdus pa brgya lnga bcu*

Great Treatise on the Stages of Mantra (sngags rim chen mo)
Also cited as: *Stages of the Path of Vajradhara (sngags rim chen mo)*
Sanskrit: *(N/A)*
Tibetan: *rgyal ba khyab bdag rdo rje 'chang chen po'i lam gyi rim pa gsang ba kun gyi gnad rnam par phye ba*
Tibetan cited as: *rdo rje 'chang chen po'i lam gyi rim pa; rdo rje 'chang gi lam gyi rim pa*
Author: (N/A) / tsong kha pa
Tōhoku no.: 5281
Tashi Hlunpo location: ga, #1

Great Treatise on the Stages of the Enlightenment Path (lam rim chen mo)
Sanskrit: *(N/A)*
Tibetan: *mnyam med tsong kha pa chen pos mdzad pa'i byang chub lam rim che ba*
Tibetan cited as: *byang chub lam gyi rim pa*
Author: (N/A) / tsong kha pa
Tōhoku no.: 5392
Tashi Hlunpo location: pa, #2

Great Voidness Session
Sanskrit: *(N/A)*
Tibetan: *gsang ba 'dus pa'i stong thun*
Tibetan cited as: *stong thun chen mo; stong thun*
Author: (N/A) / 'gos khug pa lhas btsas
TBRC work id.: W15436

Headdress Vajra Tantra 705 (unidentified)
Tibetan cited as: *cod pan rdo rje bdun brgya lnga*

Heart Sutra Commentary (unidentified)
Tibetan cited as: *shes rab snying po 'grel pa*

Heroes' March Samadhi Sutra
Sanskrit: *Ārya-śūraṅgamasamādhi-nāma-mahāyāna-sūtra*
Tibetan: *'phags pa dpa' bar 'gro ba'i ting nge 'dzin zhes bya ba theg pa chen po'i mdo*
Tibetan cited as: *dpa' bar 'gro ba'i mdo*
Author: Kangyur
Tōhoku no.: 132
Derge location: mdo sde, da, 253b–316b

Heruka Sādhana Instruction Based on the Mahāmāyā Tantra
Also cited as: *Kukuripa, Following the Mahāmāyā Tantra in His Heruka Sādhana*
Sanskrit: *Mahāmāyā-tantrānusāriṇī-heruka-sādhana*
Tibetan: *sgyu 'phrul chen mo'i rgyud kyi rjes su 'brang ba'i he ru ka'i sgrub pa'i thabs*
Tibetan cited as: *ku ku ri pas maha'a ma'a ya'i rgyud la brten nas; ku ku ri pa'i maha'a ma'a ya'i man ngag*
Author: Kukuripa
Tōhoku no.: 1627
Derge location: rgyud, ya, 228b–230b

Hevajra Extensive Tantra 500,000 (unidentified)
Also cited as: *Hevajra 500,000*
Tibetan cited as: *rgyud rgyas pa 'bum lnga; 'bum lnga dgyes pa'i rdo rje*

Hevajra Sādhana
Sanskrit: *Śrī-hevajra-sādhana*
Tibetan: *dpal dgyes pa rdo rje'i sgrub thabs*
Tibetan cited as: *kye rdo rje'i sgrub thabs*
Author: Saroruha / mtsho skyes
Tōhoku no.: 1218
Derge location: rgyud, nya, 1b–7a

Hevajra Tantra
Also cited as: *Hevajra; Hevajra Root Tantra*
Sanskrit: *Hevajra-tantrarāja-nāma*
Tibetan: *kye'i rdo rje zhes bya ba rgyud kyi rgyal po*
Tibetan cited as: *kyee rdo rje rgyud; kyee rdor; kyee rdo rje; kye rdor; kye rdo rje; dgyes pa'i rdo rje; brtag gnyis; 'bum lnga dgyes pa'i rdo rje*
Author: Kangyur
Tōhoku no.: 417
Derge location: rgyud, nga, 1b–13b

Hymn of the Names of Mañjuśhrī
Sanskrit: *Mañjuśrī-jñānasattvasya paramārtha-nāmasaṁgīti*
Tibetan: *'jam dpal ye shes sems dpa'i don dam pa'i mtshan yang dag par brjod pa*
Tibetan cited as: *mtshan brjod*
Author: Kangyur
Tōhoku no.: 360
Derge location: rgyud, ka, 1b–13b

Illuminating Lamp
Also cited as: *Brilliant Lamp Root Tantra Commentary*
Sanskrit: *Pradīpoddyotana-nāma-ṭīkā*
Tibetan: *sgron ma gsal bar byed pa zhes bya ba'i rgya cher bshad pa*
Tibetan cited as: *sgron gsal; sgron gsal rtsa 'grel*
Author: Candrakīrti / zla ba grags pa
Tōhoku no.: 1785
Derge location: rgyud, ha, 1b–201b

Illuminating Lamp Subcommentary
Sanskrit: *Pradīpoddyotana-nāma-ṭīkā*
Tibetan: *sgron ma gsal ba zhes bya ba'i 'grel bshad*
Tibetan cited as: *sgron gsal gi 'grel bshad a'r+ya*
Author: Āryadeva (attrib.) / 'phags pa lha (attrib.)
Tōhoku no.: 1794
Derge location: rgyud, khi, 155a–205a

Illuminating Lamp Concise Commentary "Heart Mirror"
Also cited as: *Brilliant Lamp Concise Commentary "Heart Mirror"; Heart Mirror*
Sanskrit: *Pradīpoddīpa-ṭippaṇī-hṛdayādarśa-nāma*
Tibetan: *sgron ma gsal ba mdor bshad pa'i sa bcad snying gi me long zhes bya ba*
Tibetan cited as: *sgron gsal gyi mdor bshad snying gi me long; snying gi me long*
Author: Kumāra
Tōhoku no.: 1791
Derge location: rgyud, 'a, 170b–201b

Illuminating Lamp Concise Difficult Point Elucidation
Sanskrit: *Pradīpoddyotana-viṣama-pañjikā-nāma*
Tibetan: *sgron ma gsal bar byed pa'i dka' ba btus pa'i 'grel ba zhes bya ba*
Tibetan cited as: *sgron gsal gyi dka' ba btus pa'i bshad pa*
Author: Bhāvaviveka (attrib.) / legs ldan 'byed (attrib.)
Tōhoku no.: 1792
Derge location: rgyud, 'a, 201b–212a

Illuminating Lamp Explanation Verses (unidentified)
Tibetan cited as: *sgron gsal gyi bshad sbyar*
Author: Kuladhara (?)

Illuminating Lamp Extensive Commentary
Sanskrit: *Pradīpoddyotanoddyota-nāma-pañjikā*
Tibetan: *sgron ma gsal bar byed pa'i gsal byed ces bya ba'i dka' 'grel*
Tibetan cited as: *sgron gsal gyi 'grel bshad*
Author: Karuṇaśrīpāda / thugs rje dpal
Tōhoku no.: 1790
Derge location: rgyud, 'a, 10b–170a

Integrated Practices
Also cited as: *Lamp of Integrated Practices*
Sanskrit: *Caryāmelāpaka-pradīpa*
Tibetan: *spyod pa bsdus pa'i sgron ma*
Tibetan cited as: *spyod bsdus; spyod bsdus sgron ma*
Author: Āryadeva / 'phags pa lha
Tōhoku no.: 1803
Derge location: rgyud, ngi, 57a–106b

Integrated Practices Commentary
Sanskrit: *Caryāsamuccaya-pradīpa-nāma-ṭīkā*
Tibetan: *spyod pa bsdus pa'i sgron ma zhes bya ba'i rgya cher bshad pa*
Tibetan cited as: *spyod bsdus kyi 'grel pa; 'grel pa*
Author: Śākyamitra (attrib.) / shAkya'i bshes gnyen
Tōhoku no.: 1834
Derge location: rgyud, ci, 237b–280b

Integrated Practices old translation
Tibetan cited as: *spyod bsdus 'gyur rnying*
Tōhoku no.: 1803

Introduction to the Art of Self-Accomplishment
Sanskrit: *Ātmasādhanāvatāra-nāma*
Tibetan: *bdag sgrub pa la 'jug pa zhes bya ba*
Tibetan cited as: *bdag sgrub pa'i thabs la 'jug pa*
Author: Buddhaśrījñāna (Jñānapāda) / sangs rgyas ye shes zhabs
Tōhoku no.: 1860
Derge location: rgyud, di, 52a–62a

Introduction to the Central Way
Sanskrit: *Madhyamakāvatāra-nāma*
Tibetan: *dbu ma la 'jug pa zhes bya ba*
Tibetan cited as: *dbu ma la 'jug pa*
Author: Candrakīrti / zla ba grags pa
Tōhoku no.: 3861
Derge location: dbu ma, 'a, 201b–219a

Introduction to the Central Way Commentary
Sanskrit: *Madhyamakāvatārabhāṣya-nāma*
Tibetan: *dbu ma la 'jug pa'i bshad pa*
Tibetan cited as: *'jug 'grel*
Author: Candrakīrti / zla ba grags pa
Tōhoku no.: 3862
Derge location: dbu ma, 'a, 220b–384a

Jewel Heap Sutra
Also cited as: *Jewel Heap*
Sanskrit: *Ārya-Mahāratnakūṭadharmaparyāyaśatasāhasrika-granthe trisaṁvaranirdeśaparivarta-nāma-mahāyānasūtra*
Tibetan: *'phags pa dkon mchog brtsegs pa chen po'i chos kyi rnam grangs stong phrag brgya pa las sdom pa gsum bstan pa'i le'u zhes bya ba theg pa chen po'i mdo*
Tibetan cited as: *dkon brtsegs*
Author: Kangyur
Tōhoku no.: 45
Derge location: dkon brtsegs, ka, 1b–45a

Jewel Rosary
Sanskrit: *Pañcakrama-ṭīkā-maṇimālā-nāma*
Tibetan: *rim pa lnga pa'i bshad pa nor bu'i phreng ba zhes bya ba*
Tibetan cited as: *nor bu'i 'phreng ba; 'grel pa nor bu'i 'phreng ba*
Author: Nāgabodhi (attrib.) / Klu byang (attrib.)
Tōhoku no.: 1840
Derge location: rgyud, chi, 14a–157a

Jewel Tree Tantra 907 (unidentified)
Tibetan cited as: *rin chen sdong po dgu brgya bdun*

King of the Gods Dialogue (uncertain identification)
Sanskrit: *(N/A)*
Tibetan: *lha'i dbang po brgya byin gyis bstod pa*
Tibetan cited as: *lha'i dbang pos zhu pa*
Author: Kangyur
Tōhoku no.: 673
Derge location: rgyud, ba, 211a–211b

Lama's Speech Light Rays Teaching (unidentified)
Tibetan cited as: *bla ma'i gsung gi 'od zer bstan pa*
Author: Marpa (attrib.)

Liberation Drop
Sanskrit: *Muktitilaka-nāma*
Tibetan: *grol ba'i thig le zhes bya ba*
Tibetan cited as: *grol ba'i thig le*
Author: Buddhaśrījñāna (Jñānapāda) / sangs rgyas ye shes zhabs
Tōhoku no.: 1859
Derge location: rgyud, di, 47a–52a

Liberation Drop Commentary
Sanskrit: *Muktitilaka-nāma-vyākhyāna*
Tibetan: *grol ba'i thig le zhes bya ba'i rnam par bshad pa*
Tibetan cited as: *grol ba'i thig le'i 'grel pa*
Author: Vitapāda / sman zhabs
Tōhoku no.: 1870
Derge location: rgyud, ni, 45b–59a

Lucid Exposition
Sanskrit: *Mūlamadhyamakavṛtti-prasannapadā-nāma*
Tibetan: *dbu ma rtsa ba'i 'grel pa tshig gsal ba zhes bya ba*
Tibetan cited as: *tshig gsal*
Author: Candrakīrti / zla ba grags pa
Tōhoku no.: 3860
Derge location: dbu ma, 'a, 1b–200a

Magic Net Tantra
Sanskrit: *Māyājāla-mahātantrarāja-nāma*
Tibetan: *rgyud kyi rgyal po chen po sgyu 'phrul dra ba zhes bya ba*
Tibetan cited as: *sgyu 'phrul dra ba*
Author: Kangyur
Tōhoku no.: 466
Derge location: rgyud, ja, 94b–134a

Magic Supreme Bliss Tantra
Sanskrit: *Śri-Sarvabuddhasamāyogaḍākinījālasambara-nāma-uttaratantra*
Tibetan: *dpal sangs rgyas thams cad dang mnyam par sbyor ba mkha' 'gro ma sgyu ma bde ba'i mchog ces bya ba'i rgyud phyi ma*
Tibetan cited as: *sgyu ma bde mchog*
Author: Kangyur
Tōhoku no.: 366
Derge location: rgyud, ka, 151b–193a

Magnificent Play Sutra
Also cited as: *Magnificent Play*
Sanskrit: *Ārya-Lalitavistara-nāma-mahāyānasūtra*
Tibetan: *'phags pa rgya cher rol pa*
Tibetan cited as: *rgya cher rol pa'i mdo; rgya cher rol pa*
Author: Kangyur
Tōhoku no.: 95
Derge location: mdo sde, kha, 1b–216b

Mandala Rite 20 (uncertain identification)
Also cited as: *Mandala Rite (by the Noble Master)*
Sanskrit: *Śrīguhyasamājamaṇḍalavidhi-nāma*
Tibetan: *dpal gsang ba 'dus pa'i dkyil 'khor gyi cho ga*
Tibetan cited as: *dkyil chog cho ga nyi shu pa; dkyil chog*
Author: Nāgārjuna (attrib.) / klu sgrub (attrib.)
Tōhoku no.: 1798
Derge location: rgyud, ngi, 15b–35a

Mandala Rite 20 by Nāgabodhi
Also cited as: *Rite 20 (Nagabodhi's)*
Sanskrit: *Śriguhyasamājamaṇḍalaviṁśatovidhi-nāma*
Tibetan: *dpal gsang ba 'dus pa'i dkyil 'khor gyi cho gnyi shu pa*
Tibetan cited as: *cho ga nyi shu pa; dkyil chog co ga nyi shu pa*
Author: Nāgabodhi / klu'i byang chub
Tōhoku no.: 1810
Derge location: rgyud, ngi, 131a–145b

Mandala Rite by Rāhulaśhrīmitra (uncertain identification)
Sanskrit: *Yuganaddhaprakāśa-nāma-sekaprakriyā*
Tibetan: *zung du 'jug pa gsal ba zhes bya ba'i dbang gi bya ba*
Tibetan cited as: *dkyil chog*
Author: Rāhulaśrīmitra / sgra gcan 'dzin dpal bshes gnyen
Tōhoku no.: 1818
Derge location: rgyud, ngi, 232b–247a

Mandala Rite by Samayavajra (uncertain identification)
Sanskrit: *Pañcakrama-pañjikā*
Tibetan: *rim pa lnga'i dka' 'grel*
Tibetan cited as: *dkyil chog*
Author: Samayavajra / dam tshig rdo rje
Tōhoku no.: 1841
Derge location: rgyud, chi, 157b–187a

Manifest Enlightenment Stage
Sanskrit: *Abhibodhikramopadeśa*
Tibetan: *mngon par byang chub pa'i rim pa'i man ngag*
Tibetan cited as: *mngon par byang chub pa'i rim pa*
Author: Āryadeva / 'phags pa lha
Tōhoku no.: 1806
Derge location: rgyud, ngi, 114b–117a

Mañjuśhrī Hero Tantra 100,000 (unidentified)
Tibetan cited as: *'jam dpal dpa' bo 'bum phrag gcig*

Mentor Fifty
Sanskrit: *Gurupañcāśikā*
Tibetan: *bla ma lnga bcu pa*
Tibetan cited as: *bla ma lnga bcu pa*
Author: Aśvaghoṣa / rta dbyangs
Tōhoku no.: 3721
Derge location: rgyud, tshu, 10a–12a

Mirror of Poetry (unidentified)
Tibetan cited as: *snyan dngags me long*

Mission to Laṅka
Sanskrit: *Ārya-laṅkāvatāra-mahāyāna-sūtra*
Tibetan: *'phags pa lang kar gshegs pa'i theg pa chen po'i mdo*
Tibetan cited as: *lang kar gshegs pa; lang gshegs*
Author: Kangyur
Tōhoku no.: 107
Derge location: mdo sde, ca, 56a–191b

Moon Esoteric Drop
Sanskrit: *Śrī-Candraguhyatilaka-nāma-mahātantrarāja*
Tibetan: *dpal zla gsang thig le*
Tibetan cited as: *zla gsang thig le*
Author: Kangyur
Tōhoku no.: 477
Derge location: rgyud, ja, 247–303a

Moon Esoteric Drop Tantra 1,700 (unidentified)
Tibetan cited as: *zla gsang thig le stong bdun brga*

Moonlight Commentary; Moonlight
Sanskrit: *Pañcakrama-mati-ṭīkā-candraprabhā-nāma*
Tibetan: *rim pa lnga pa'i dgongs 'grel zla ba'i 'od zer zhes bya ba*
Tibetan cited as: *'grel pa zla 'od; zla ba'i 'od*
Author: Abhayākaragupta / 'jigs med 'byung gnas sras pa
Tōhoku no.: 1831
Derge location: rgyud, ci, 180b–203a

Nondual Triumph Tantra
Sanskrit: *Śrī-sarvatathāgata-guhyatantrayoga-mahārājādvayasamatā-vijaya-nāma-vajraśrīvara-mahākalpādi*
Tibetan: *dpal de bzhin gshegs pa thams cad kyi gsang ba rnal 'byor chen po rnam par rgyal ba zhes bya ba mnyam pa nyid gnyis su med pa'i rgyud kyi rgyal po rdo rje dpal mchog chen po brtag pa dang po*
Tibetan cited as: *gnyis med rnam; rgyal rgyud; gnyis med rnam rgyal brdzus ma*
Author: Kangyur
Tōhoku no.: 453
Derge location: rgyud, cha, 103a–331a

One Hundred Fifty Ways Commentary
Sanskrit: *Āryaprajñāpāramitānayaśatapañcāśatkā-ṭīkā*
Tibetan: *'phags pa shes rab kyi pha rol tu phyin pa tshul brgya lnga bcu pa'i 'grel pa*
Tibetan cited as: *tshul brgya lnga bcu pa'i 'grel pa*
Author: Jñānamitra / ye shes bshes gnyen
Tōhoku no.: 2647
Derge location: rgyud, ju, 272b–294a

Orgasmic Luminance
Also cited as: *Black Yamāri Tantra Commentary, Orgasmic Luminance*
Sanskrit: *Śrī-yamāritantra-pañjikā-sahajāloka-nāma*
Tibetan: *dpal gshin rje gshed kyi rgyud kyi dka' 'grel lhan cig skyes pa'i snang ba zhes bya ba*
Tibetan cited as: *dgra nag gi 'grel pa lhan cig skyes pa'i snang ba*
Author: Śrīdhara / dpal 'dzin
Tōhoku no.: 1918
Derge location: rgyud, bi, 81b–123b

Ornament of Realization of the Community
Sanskrit: *Samājābhisamayālaṁkaravṛtti*
Tibetan: *gsang ba 'dus pa'i mgnon par rtogs pa'i rgyan gyi 'grel pa*
Tibetan cited as: *'dus pa'i mngon rtogs rgyan*
Author: Candrakīrti (attrib.) / zla ba grags pa (attrib.)
Tōhoku no.: 1817
Derge location: rgyud, ngi, 210b–232b

Ornament of Realizations
Sanskrit: *Abhisamayālaṁkāra-nāma-prajñāpāramitopadeśa-śāstra-kārikā*
Tibetan: *shes rab kyi pha rol tu phyin pa'i man ngag gi bstan bcos mngon par rtogs pa'i rgyan zhes bya ba'i tshig le'ur byas pa*
Tibetan cited as: *mngon rtogs rgyan*
Author: Maitreyanātha / byams pa mgon po
Tōhoku no.: 3786
Derge location: shes phyin ka, 1b–13a

Performance Incorporating the [Community] Sutras
Sanskrit: *Śrī-guhyasamāja-mahāyogatantrotpādakrama-sādhana-sūtra-melāpaka-nāma*
Tibetan: *rnal 'byor chen po'i rgyud dpal gsang ba 'dus pa'i bskyed pa'i rim pa bsgom pa'i thabs mdo dang bsres pa zhes bya ba*
Tibetan cited as: *mdo bsre*
Author: Nāgārjuna / klu sgrub
Tōhoku no.: 1797
Derge location: rgyud, ngi, 11a–15b

Performance of Hūṁkāra (uncertain identification)
Sanskrit: *Vajrahūṁkārasādhana*
Tibetan: *rdo rje h'um mdzad kyi sgrub thabs*
Tibetan cited as: *h'um mdzad kyi sgrub thabs*
Author: Nāgārjuna (attrib.) / klu sgrub (attrib.)
Tōhoku no.: 3289 AND/OR 3359 AND/OR 3634
Derge location: rgyud, bu, 33a AND/OR mu, 38b–39a AND/OR mu, 250a–250b

Personal Instruction of Mañjuśhrī
Also cited as: *Personal Instruction; Personal Instruction of His Holiness*
Sanskrit: *Dvikramatattvabhāvanā-nāma-mukhāgama*
Tibetan: *rim pa gnyis pa'i de kho na nyid bsgom pa zhes bya ba'i zhal gyi lung*
Tibetan cited as: *'jam dpal gyi zhal gyi lung; zhal lung; rje brtsun gyi gsungs pa'i zhal lung*
Author: Buddhaśrījñāna (Jñānapāda) / sangs rgyas ye shes zhabs
Tōhoku no.: 1853
Derge location: rgyud, di, 1b–17b

Personal Instruction of Mañjuśhrī Commentary
Sanskrit: *Sukusuma-nāma-dvikrama-tattva-bhāvanā-mukhāgama-vṛti*
Tibetan: *mdzes pa'i me tog ces bya ba rim pa gnyis pa'i de kho na nyid bsgom pa zhal gyi lung gi 'grel pa*
Tibetan cited as: *zhal lung gi 'grel pa*
Author: Vitapāda
Tōhoku no.: 1866
Derge location: rgyud, di, 87a–139b

Personal Instruction of the Triple Continuum of Magical Illusion (unidentified)
Tibetan cited as: *sgyu ma sum rgyud kyi man ngag*
Author: (N/A) / gser sdings pa gzhon nu 'od

Philosophical Sixty
Sanskrit: *Yuktiṣaṣṭhikākārikā-nāma*
Tibetan: *rigs pa drug cu pa'i tshig le'ur byas pa zhes bya ba*
Tibetan cited as: *rigs pa drug cu pa*
Author: Nāgārjuna / klu sgrub
Tōhoku no.: 3825
Derge location: dbu ma, tsa, 20b–22b

Philosophical Sixty Commentary
Sanskrit: *Yuktiṣaṣṭhikākā-vṛtti*
Tibetan: *rigs pa drug cu pa'i 'grel pa*
Tibetan cited as: *'grel pa*
Author: Candrakīrti / zla ba grags pa
Tōhoku no.: 3864
Derge location: dbu ma, ya, 1b–30b

Precious Rosary
Sanskrit: *Rājaparikathā-ratnamālā*
Tibetan: *rgyal po la gtam bya ba rin po che'i phreng ba*
Tibetan cited as: *rin chen 'phreng ba*
Author: Nāgārjuna / klu sgrub
Tōhoku no.: 4158
Derge location: spring yig, ge, 107a–126a

Precious Rosary
Sanskrit: *Piṇḍīkṛta-sādhana-vṛtti-ratnāvalī-nāma*
Tibetan: *mdor bsdus pa'i sgrub thabs kyi 'grel pa rin chen phreng ba zhes bya ba*
Tibetan cited as: *rin chen 'phreng ba*
Author: Śāntipa (attrib.)
Tōhoku no.: 1826
Derge location: rgyud, ci, 1b–95a

Purification of Evolutionary Obstructions Sutra
Sanskrit: *Ārya-Karmāvaraṇaviśuddhi-nāma-mahāyānasūtra*
Tibetan: *'phags pa las kyi sgrib pa rnam par dag pa*
Tibetan cited as: *las kyi sgrib pa rnam par dag pa; las kyi sgrib pa rnam par dag pa'i mdo*
Author: Kangyur
Tōhoku no.: 218
Derge location: mdo sde, tsha, 284a–297b

Purification of the Mind's Obstructions
Sanskrit: *Cittāvaraṇaviśodha-nāma-prakaraṇa*
Tibetan: *sems kyi sgrib pa rnam par sbyong*
Tibetan cited as: *sems kyi sgrib sbyong*
Author: Āryadeva / 'phags pa lha
Tōhoku no.: 1804
Derge location: rgyud, ngi, 106b–112a

Reality Accomplishment
Sanskrit: *Tattvasiddhi-nāma-prakaraṇa*
Tibetan: *de kho na nyid grub pa zhes bya ba'i rab tu byed pa*
Tibetan cited as: *de kho na nyid grub pa*
Author: Śāntarakṣita / shi ba 'tsho
Tōhoku no.: 3708
Derge location: rgyud, tsu, 26b–89a

Reality Compendium
Sanskrit: *Sarvatathāgata-tattvasaṁgraha-nāma-mahāyāna-sūtra*
Tibetan: *de bzhin gshegs pa thams cad kyi de kho na nyid bsdus pa zhes bya ba theg pa chen po'i mdo*
Tibetan cited as: *de nyid bsdus pa; de kho na nyid bsdus pa la sogs pa'i rtsa ba'i rgyud*
Author: Kangyur
Tōhoku no.: 479
Derge location: rgyud, nya, 1b–142a

Reality Tantra 70,000,000,000 (unidentified)
Tibetan cited as: *de nyid brgya stong brgya stong bdun*

Reason in Elucidation
Sanskrit: *Vyākhyāyukti*
Tibetan: *rnam par bshad pa'i rigs pa*
Tibetan cited as: *rnam bshad rigs pa*
Author: Vasubandhu / dbyig gnyen
Tōhoku no.: 4061
Derge location: rgyud, shi, 29a–134b

Red Yamāri Tantra
Sanskrit: *Śrī-raktayamāri-tantrarāja-nāma*
Tibetan: *dpal gzhin rje'i gshed dmar po zhes bya ba'i rgyud kyi rgyal po*
Tibetan cited as: *dmar gi rgyud; gshed dmar gyi rgyud*
Author: Kangyur
Tōhoku no.: 474
Derge location: rgyud, ja, 186a–214b

Revelation of the Hidden Intention 4,000 (unidentified)
Tibetan cited as: *dgongs pa lung ston stong phrag bzhi*

Revelation of the Hidden Intention Tantra
Sanskrit: *Sandhi-vyākaraṇa-nāma-tantra*
Tibetan: *dgongs pa lung bstan pa zhes bya ba'i rgyud*
Tibetan cited as: *dgongs pa lung ston; dgongs pa lung bstan pa*
Author: Kangyur
Tōhoku no.: 444
Derge location: rgyud, ca, 158a–207b

Rite of Burning Corpses
Sanskrit: *Śmaśānavidhi*
Tibetan: *ro sreg pa'i cho ga*
Tibetan cited as: *ro bsreg gi cho ga*
Author: Āryadeva (attrib.) / 'phags pa lha (attrib.)
Tōhoku no.: 1807
Derge location: rgyud, ngi, 117a–118b

Rosary of Complete Yoga
Sanskrit: *Niṣpannayogāvali-nāma*
Tibetan: *rdzogs pa'i rnal 'byor gyi phreng ba*
Tibetan cited as: *rnal 'byor rdzogs 'phreng*
Author: Abhayākaragupta / 'jigs med 'byung gnas sbas pa
Tōhoku no.: 3141
Derge location: rgyud, phu, 94–151a

Samadhi of Direct Experience of the Present Buddhas
Sanskrit: *Ārya-Pratyutpanne Buddhasaṁmukhāvasthitasamādhi-nāma-mahāyānasūtra*
Tibetan: *'phags pa da ltar gyi sangs rgyas mngon sum du bzhugs pa'i ting nge 'dzin*
Tibetan cited as: *da ltar gyi sangs rgyas mngon sum du bzhugs pa'i ting nge 'dzin*
Author: Kangyur
Tōhoku no.: 133
Derge location: mdo sde, na, 1b–70b

Samantabhadra Sādhana (uncertain identification)
Sanskrit: *Samantabhadra-nāma-sādhana*
Tibetan: *kun tu bzang po zhes bya ba'i sgrub pa'i thabs*
Tibetan cited as: *bsgrub pa'i thabs kun tu bzang po*
Author: Buddhaśrījñāna (Jñānapāda) / sangs rgyas ye shes zhabs
Tōhoku no.: 1855 - 1856
Derge location: rgyud, di, 28b–36a, 36a–42b

Samputa Further Tantra
Sanskrit: *Mahātantrarāja-śrī-sampuṭa-tilaka-nāma*
Tibetan: *rgyud kyi rgyal po chen po dpal yang dag par sbyor ba'i thig le zhes bya ba*
Tibetan cited as: *sam bhu' Ta'i rgyud phyi ma*
Author: Kangyur
Tōhoku no.: 382
Derge location: rgyud, ga, 158b–184a

Sampuṭa Tantra
Also cited as: *Sampuṭa, Glorious*
Sanskrit: *Sampuṭa-nāma-mahātantra*
Tibetan: *yang dag par sbyor ba shes bya ba'i rgyud chen po*
Tibetan cited as: *sam bhu Ta; saM bhu Ta; dpal saM bhu Ta*
Author: Kangyur
Tōhoku no.: 381
Derge location: rgyud, ga, 73b–158b

Self-Consecration Stage
Also cited as: *Self-Consecration (by Aryadeva)*
Sanskrit: *Svādhiṣṭhānakrama-prabheda*
Tibetan: *bdag byin gyis brlab pa'i rim pa rnam par dbye ba*
Tibetan cited as: *bdag byin gyis brlab pa'i rim pa; bdag byin brlabs*
Author: Āryadeva / 'phags pa lha
Tōhoku no.: 1805
Derge location: rgyud, ngi, 112a–114b

Sheaf of Instructions
Sanskrit: *Śrī-saṁpuṭa-tantrarāja-ṭikā-amnāyamañjarī-nāma*
Tibetan: *dpal yang dag par sbyor ba'i rgyud kyi rgyal po'i rgya cher 'grel pa man ngag gi snye ma zhes bya ba*
Tibetan cited as: *man ngag snye ma; man snye*
Author: Abhayākaragupta / 'jigs med 'byung gnas sras pa
Tōhoku no.: 1198
Derge location: rgyud, cha, 1b–316a

Six-Branched Yoga
Sanskrit: *Ṣaḍaṅgayoga-nāma-ṭikā*
Tibetan: *sbyor ba yan lag drug pa zhes bya ba'i 'grel pa*
Tibetan cited as: *sbyor ba yan lag drug*
Author: Chandrakīrti (attrib.) / zla ba grags pa (attrib.)
Tōhoku no.: 1786
Derge location: rgyud, ha, 201b–203b

Spring Drop, The
Sanskrit: *Vasantatilaka-nāma*
Tibetan: *dpyid kyi thig le zhes bya ba*
Tibetan cited as: *dpyid kyi thig le; dpyid thig*
Author: Kṛṣṇācārya / nag po spyod pa ba
Tōhoku no.: 1448
Derge location: rgyud, wa, 298b–306b

Stage of Arrangement
Sanskrit: *Samājasādhana-vyavasthāli-nāma*
Tibetan: *'dus pa'i sgrub pa'i thabs rnam par gzhag pa'i rim pa zhes bya ba*
Tibetan cited as: *rnam gzhag rim pa; rnam gzhag*
Author: Nāgabuddhi / klu'i blo
Tōhoku no.: 1809
Derge location: rgyud, ngi, 121a–131a

Stage of Arrangement Commentary
Sanskrit: *(N/A)*
Tibetan: *rnam bzhag rim pa'i rnam bshad dpal gsang ba 'duz pa'i gnad kyi don gsal ba*
Tibetan cited as: *rnam gzhag rim pa'i rnam bshad*
Author: (N/A) / tsong kha pa
Tōhoku no.: 5290
Tashi Hlunpo location: cha, #1

Stages of the Path of Vajradhara (OR *Elixir Secret*)
Sanskrit: *Mahāvajradhara-patha-kramopadeśāmṛta-guhya*
Tibetan: *rdo rje 'chang chen po'i lam gyi rim pa'i man ngag bdud rtsi gsang ba*
Tibetan cited as: *rdo rje 'chang gi lam rim*; OR *bdud rtsi gsang ba*
Author: *Ekādaśanirghoṣa OR *Ekādaśasvara / sgra dbyangs bcu gcig pa
Tōhoku no.: 1823
Derge location: rgyud, ngi, 266b–278a

Stages of Yoga Practice
Sanskrit: *Yogacaryābhūmi*
Tibetan: *rnal sbyor spyod pa'i sa*
Tibetan cited as: *rnal 'byor spyod pa'i sa*
Author: Asaṇga / thogs med
Tōhoku no.: 4035
Derge location: sems tsam, tshi, 1b–283a

Stainless Light
Also cited as: *Great Commentary Stainless Light; Great Commentary (Stainless Light)*
Sanskrit: *Vimalaprabhā-nāma-mūlatantrānusāriṇī-dvādaśasāhasrikā-laghu-kālacakra-tantra-rāja-ṭīkā*
Tibetan: *bsdus pa'i rgyud kyi rgyal po dus kyi 'khor lo'i 'grel bshad, rtsa ba'i rgyud kyi rjes su 'jug pa stong phrag bcu gnyis pa dri ma med pa'i 'od ces bya ba*
Tibetan cited as: *dri med 'od; 'grel chen dri med 'od; 'grel chen*
Author: Puṇḍarīka (Avalokiteśvara) / pad+ma dkar po
Tōhoku no.: 1347
Derge location: rgyud, tha, 107b–277a AND/OR dus 'khor 'grel bshad, shr'i, 1b–469a

Summary of Initiations Commentary
Sanskrit: *Paramārthasaṁgraha-nāma-sekoddeśaṭīkā*
Tibetan: *dbang mdor bstan pa'i 'grel bshad don dam pa bsdus pa*
Tibetan cited as: *dbang mdor bstan gyi 'grel pa*
Author: Nāropa
Tōhoku no.: 1351
Derge location: rgyud, na, 220b–289a

Summary Teaching
Sanskrit: *Śrīmanvimalaprabhātantrāvatāraṇīvādācalahṛdayāloka*
Tibetan: *dpal ldan dri ma dang bral ba'i 'od kyi rgyud la 'jug pa'i bshad sbyar mi g-yo ba'i snying po snang ba*
Tibetan cited as: *mdor bstan pa*
Author: (N/A)
Tōhoku no.: 1349
Derge location: rgyud, na, 20a–72b

Summary Teaching of the Five Stages (unidentified)
Tibetan cited as: *rim lnga'i mdor bstan*
Author: Nāgārjuna

Supreme Bliss Eulogy Commentary
Sanskrit: *Lakṣābhidhānād uddhṛta-laghutantra-piṇḍārtha-vivaraṇa-nāma*
Tibetan: *mngon par brjod pa 'bum pa las phyung ba nyung ngu'i rgyud kyi bsdud pa'i don rnam par bshad pa zhes bya ba*
Tibetan cited as: *bde mchog bstod 'grel*
Author: Vajrapāṇi / phyag na rdo rje
Tōhoku no.: 1402
Derge location: rgyud, ba, 78b–141a

Supreme Bliss Five Stages (by Ghaṇṭapāda)
Sanskrit: *Śrī-cakrasaṁvara-pañcakrama*
Tibetan: *dpal 'khor lo sdom pa'i rim pa lnga pa*
Tibetan cited as: *dril bu zhabs kyi rim lnga; dril bu pa'i rim lnga; bde mchog rim lnga*
Author: Ghaṇṭapāda / dril bu pa
Tōhoku no.: 1433
Derge location: rgyud, wa, 224b–227a

Supreme Bliss Tantra
Also cited as: *Root Tantra of the Supreme Bliss Tantra; Supreme Bliss; Supreme Bliss Wheel*
Sanskrit: *Tantrarāja-śrīlaghu-saṁvara-nāma*
Tibetan: *rgyud kyi rgyal po dpal bde mchog nyung ngu zhes bya ba*
Tibetan cited as: *bde mchog gi rgyud; bde mchog gi rgyud la rtsa rgyud; bde mchog; 'khor lo bde mchog*
Author: Kangyur
Tōhoku no.: 368
Derge location: rgyud, ka, 213b–246b

Supreme of All Secrets 1,000 (uncertain identification)
Sanskrit: *Caturdevatāparipṛcchā*
Tibetan: *lha mo bzhis yongs su zhus pa*
Tibetan cited as: *thams cad gsang ba'i mchog ces bya ba stong phrag gcig*
Author: Kangyur
Tōhoku no.: 446
Derge location: rgyud, ca, 277b–281b

Ten Levels Sutra
Sanskrit: *Daśabhūmika-sūtra*
Tibetan: *mdo sde sa bcu pa*
Tibetan cited as: *mdo sde sa bcu pa; sa bcu pa*
Author: Kangyur
Tōhoku no.: 44 (ch. 31)
Derge location: phal chen, ka–aa

Terminal Action Investigation Sutra
Sanskrit: *Karmāntavibhaṅga-nāma*
Tibetan: *las kyi mtha' rnam par 'byed pa zhes bya ba*
Tibetan cited as: *las mtha' rnam 'byed kyi mdo*
Author: Nāgabuddhi / klu'i blo
Tōhoku no.: 1811
Derge location: rgyud, ngi, 145b–147a

Time Drop Tantra 180 (unidentified)
Tibetan cited as: *dus kyi thig la brgya brgyad cu*

Time Machine Tantra
Also cited as: *Prime Buddha Tantra*
Sanskrit: *Paramādibuddhoddhṛta-śrī-kālacakra-nāma-tantrarāja*
Tibetan: *mchog gi dang po'i sangs rgyas las phyung ba rgyud kyi rgyal po dpal dus kyi 'khor lo zhes bya ba*
Tibetan cited as: *dus 'khor; dang po'i sangs rgyas*
Author: Kangyur; Tengyur (Derge)
Tōhoku no.: 362; 1346
Derge location: rgyud, ka, 22b–128b; rgyud, tha, 1b–107a

Treasury of Clear Science
Also cited as: *Treasury*
Sanskrit: *Abhidharmakoṣa-kārikā*
Tibetan: *chos mngon pa'i mdzod kyi tshig le'ur byas pa*
Tibetan cited as: *mngon pa mdzod; don mdzod*
Author: Vasubandhu / dbyig gnyen
Tōhoku no.: 4089
Derge location: mngon, ku, 1b–25a

Treatise on Validating Cognition
Sanskrit: *Pramāṇavārttika-kārikā*
Tibetan: *tshad ma rnam 'grel gyi tshig leu'r byas pa*
Tibetan cited as: *rigs pa'i dbang phyug*
Author: Dharmakīrti / chos kyi grags pa
Tōhoku no.: 4210
Derge location: tshad ma, ce, 94b–151a

Triple Rite
Sanskrit: *Śrī-kṛṣṇayamāri-tantrarāja-trikalpa-nāma*
Tibetan: *dpal gshin rje'i gshed nag po'i rgyud kyi rgyal po rtog pa gsum pa zhes bya ba*
Tibetan cited as: *rtog pa gsum pa*
Author: Kangyur
Tōhoku no.: 469
Derge location: rgyud, ja, 164a–167b

Ultimate Contemplation Tantra
Sanskrit: *Dhyānottara-paṭala-krama*
Tibetan: *bsam gtan gyi phyi ma rim par phye ba*
Tibetan cited as: *bsam gtan phyi ma*
Author: Kangyur
Tōhoku no.: 808
Derge location: rgyud, wa, 223a–225b

Ultimate Continuum
Sanskrit: *Mahāyānottaratantra-śāstra*
Tibetan: *theg pa chen po rgyud bla ma'i bstan bcos*
Tibetan cited as: *rgyud bla ma*
Author: Maitreyanātha / byams pa dgon po
Tōhoku no.: 4024
Derge location: sems tsam, phi, 54b–73a

Unexcelled Clear Articulation
Sanskrit: *Abhidhāna-uttaratantra-nāma*
Tibetan: *mngon par brjod pa'i rgyud bla ma zhes bya ba*
Tibetan cited as: *mngon brjod bla ma*
Author: Kangyur
Tōhoku no.: 369
Derge location: rgyud, ka, 247a–370a

Unexcelled Clear Articulation 100,000 (unidentified)
Tibetan cited as: *mngon brjod 'bum pa*

Urad Tantra 208 (unidentified)
Tibetan cited as: *Au rad tantra nyis brgya brgyad*

Urad Tantra Extra Explanation Tantra (unidentified)
Tibetan cited as: *nye bar bshad pa'i rgyud*

Vairochana Enlightenment
Sanskrit: *Mahāvairocanābhisaṁbodhi-vikurvitādhiṣṭhāna-vaipulya-sūtreindrarāja-nāma-dharmaparyāya*
Tibetan: *rnam par snang mdzad chen po mngon par rdzogs par byang chub pa rnam par sprul pa byin gyis rlob pa shin tu rgyas pa mdo sde'i dbang po'i rgyal po zhes bya ba'i chos kyi rnam grangs*
Tibetan cited as: *rnam snang mngon byang*
Author: Kangyur
Tōhoku no.: 494
Derge location: rgyud, tha, 151b–260a

Vairochana Magic Tantra 1,100 (unidentified)
Tibetan cited as: *snang mdzad sgyu 'phrul stong dang brgya*

Vajra Angel
Sanskrit: *Śrī-vajraḍāka-nāma-mahātantra-rāja*
Tibetan: *rgyud kyi rgyal po chen po dpal rdo rje mkha' 'gro zhes bya ba*
Tibetan cited as: *rdo rje mkha' 'gro*
Author: Kangyur
Tōhoku no.: 370
Derge location: rgyud, kha, 1b–125a

Vajra Angel Further Tantra
Sanskrit: *Vajraḍāka-nāma-uttaratantra*
Tibetan: *rdo rje mkha' 'gro zhes bya ba'i rgyud phyi ma*
Tibetan cited as: *rdo rje mkha' 'gro*
Author: Kangyur
Tōhoku no.: 371
Derge location: rgyud, kha, 1b–125b–136b

Vajra Ārali
Sanskrit: *Vajrārali-mahātantrarāja-nāma*
Tibetan: *rdo rje A' ra li zhes bya ba'i rgyud kyi rgyal po chen po*
Tibetan cited as: *rdo rje A ra li*
Author: Kangyur
Tōhoku no.: 426
Derge location: rgyud, na, 171a–176a

Vajra Door Tantra (unidentified)
Tibetan cited as: *rdo rje sgo'i zhes bya ba'i rgyud*

Vajra Essence Commentary on Hevajra
Sanskrit: *Hevajra-piṇḍārtha-ṭīkā*
Tibetan: *kye'i rdo rje bsdus pa'i don gyi rgya cher 'grel pa*
Tibetan cited as: *rdo rje snying po'i 'grel pa*
Author: Vajragarbha / rdo rje snying po
Tōhoku no.: 1180
Derge location: rgyud, ka, 1b–126a

Vajra Essence Ornament Tantra
Sanskrit: *Śrī-vajrahṛdayālaṁkāra-tantra-nāma*
Tibetan: *dpal rdo rje snying po rgyan gyi rgyud ces bya ba*
Tibetan cited as: *rdo rje snying po rgyan gyi rgyud; rdo rje snying po rgyan*
Author: Kangyur
Tōhoku no.: 451
Derge location: rgyud, cha, 36a–58b

Vajra Mandala Ornament Tantra
Sanskrit: *Śrī-vajramaṇḍalālaṁkāra-nāma-mahātantrarāja*
Tibetan: *dpal rdo rje snying po rgyan zhes bya ba'i rgyud kyi rgyal po chen po*
Tibetan cited as: *rdo rje dkyil 'khor rgyan zhes bya ba'i rgyud*
Author: Kangyur
Tōhoku no.: 490
Derge location: rgyud, tha, 1b–82a

Vajra Rosary Commentary
Sanskrit: *Śrī-vajramālā-mahāyogatantra-ṭīkā-gaṁbhīrārtha-dīpikā-nāma*
Tibetan: *rnal 'byor chen po'i rgyud dpal rdo rje phreng ba'i rgya cher 'grel pa zab mo'i don gyi 'grel pa zhes bya ba*
Tibetan cited as: *rdo rje 'phreng ba'i 'grel pa*
Author: Alaṁkakalaśa
Tōhoku no.: 1795
Derge location: rgyud, gi, 1b–220a

Vajra Rosary Tantra
Also cited as: *Vajra Rosary; Vajra Rosary, Explanatory Tantra; Vajra Rosary Short Tantra; Rosary*
Sanskrit: *Śrī-vajramālā-abhidhāna-mahāyogatantra-sarvatantra-hṛdaya-rahasya-vibhaṅga-nāma*
Tibetan: *rnal 'byor chen po'i rgyud dpal rdo rje phreng ba mngon par brjod pa rgyud thams cad kyi snying po gsang ba rnam par phye ba zhes bya ba*
Tibetan cited as: *rgyud rdo rje 'phreng ba; rgyud rdor 'phreng; rdo rje 'phreng ba; rdor 'phreng; bshad kyi rgyud rdo rje 'phreng ba; rdo rje 'phreng ba nyung ngu'i rgyud; 'phreng ba*
Author: Kangyur
Tōhoku no.: 445
Derge location: rgyud, ca, 208a–277b

Vajra Rosary Tantra 300,000 (unidentified)
Tibetan cited as: *rdo rje 'phreng ba 'bum phrag gsum*

Vajra Secret Ornament Tantra 1,000 (unidentified)
Tibetan cited as: *rdo rje gsang rgyan stong phrag gcig*

Vajra Secret Ornament Tantra 5,000 (unidentified)
Tibetan cited as: *rdo rje gsang rgyan stong phrag lnga*

Vajra Secret Treasury Tantra 7,000 (unidentified)
Tibetan cited as: *rdo rje gsang mdzod stong phrag bdun*

Vajra Skull Tantra 208 (unidentified)
Tibetan cited as: *rdo rje thod pa nyis brgya brgyad*

Vajra Summit
Sanskrit: *Vajraśekhara-mahāguhya-yogatantra*
Tibetan: *gsang ba rnal 'byor chen po'i rgyud rdo rje rtse mo*
Tibetan cited as: *rdo rje rtse mo; rtse mo*
Author: Kangyur
Tōhoku no.: 480
Derge location: rgyud, nya, 142b–274a

Vajra Triumph Tantra 90,000 (unidentified)
Tibetan cited as: *rdo rje rnam rgyal brgya dgu brgya*

Vajra Underground 120 (unidentified)
Tibetan cited as: *rdo rje sa 'og brgya nyi shu*

Vajrapāṇi Initiation Tantra
Sanskrit: *Ārya-vajrapāṇyabhiṣeka-mahātantra*
Tibetan: *'phaga pa lag na rdo rje dbang bskur ba'i rgyud chen po*
Tibetan cited as: *lag na rdo rje dbang bskur ba'i rgyud*
Author: Kangyur
Tōhoku no.: 496
Derge location: rgyud, da, 1b–156b

Vajrapāṇi Praise Commentary (unidentified)
Tibetan cited as: *phyag rdor stod 'grel*

Vajrasattva Pūjā Art (uncertain identification)
Sanskrit: *Vajrasattva-pūjāviddhi*
Tibetan: *rdo rje sems dpa mchod pa'i cho ga*
Tibetan cited as: *rdo rje sems dpa'i mchod chog*
Author: Samayavajra Kṛṣṇa-pa / dam tshig rdo rje
Tōhoku no.: 1820
Derge location: rgyud, ngi, 258b–261a

Vajrasattva Sādhana by Chandrakīrti
Sanskrit: *Vajrasattva-sādhana-nāma*
Tibetan: *rdo rje sems dpa'i sgrub thabs zhes bya ba*
Tibetan cited as: *rdo rje sems dpa'i sgrub thabs*
Author: Candrakīrti / zla ba grags pa
Tōhoku no.: 1814
Derge location: rgyud, ngi, 195b–204b

Vajrasattva Sādhana by Kukuripa
Sanskrit: *Vajrasattva-sādhana*
Tibetan: *rdo rje sems dpa'i sgrub thabs*
Tibetan cited as: *rdo rje sems dpa'i sgrub thabs*
Author: Kukuripa
Tōhoku no.: 1628
Derge location: rgyud, ya, 230b–231a

Illuminating Lamp Intention Elucidation
Sanskrit: *Pradīpoddyotanābhisaṁdhi-prakāśikā-nāma-vyākhyā-ṭīkā*
Tibetan: *sgron ma gsal bar byed pa'i dgongs pa rab gsal zhes bya ba bshad pa'i Ti'i k'a*
Tibetan cited as: *sgron ma rab gsal; sgron gsal gyi bshad sgron ma rab gsal; rab tu sgron gsal*
Author: Bhavyakīrti / skal ldan grags pa
Tōhoku no.: 1793
Derge location: rgyud, ki, 1b–khi, 155a

Vow Arisal
Sanskrit: *Śrī-Mahāsaṁvarodaya-tantrarāja-nāma*
Tibetan: *dpal bde mchog 'byung ba zhes bya ba'i rgyud kyi rgyal po chen po*
Tibetan cited as: *sdom 'byung*
Author: Kangyur
Tōhoku no.: 373
Derge location: rgyud, kha, 265a–311a

Vow Arisal Commentary
Sanskrit: *Śrīsaṁvarodaya-mahātantrarāja-padminī-nāma-pañjikā*
Tibetan: *dpal sdom pa 'byung ba'i rgyud kyi rgyal po chen po'i dka' 'grel padma can shes bya ba*
Tibetan cited as: *sdom 'byung 'grel pa; sdom 'byung gi 'grel pa*
Author: Ratnarakṣita
Tōhoku no.: 1420
Derge location: rgyud, wa, 1b–101b

Vow Upholding (uncertain identification)
Sanskrit: *Bodhisattvasaṁvaragrahaṇavidhi*
Tibetan: *byang chub sems dpa'i sdom pa gzung ba'i cho ga*
Tibetan cited as: *sdom pa gzung ba*
Author: Abhayākaragupta / 'jigs med 'byung gnas sbas pa
Tōhoku no.: 3970
Derge location: rgyud, gi, 248b–250b

Wheel Endowed
Tibetan: *gsang 'dus rim lnga 'khor lo'i can*
Tibetan cited as: *'khor lo can*
Author: (N/A) / gser sdings pa gzhon nu 'od
MHTL no.: 11939
TBRC work id.: W12561

Wisdom Lamp
Sanskrit: *Prajñāpradīpamūlamadhyamakavṛtti*
Tibetan: *dbu ma'i rtsa ba'i 'grel pa shes rab sgron ma*
Tibetan cited as: *shes rab sgron me*
Author: Bhāvaviveka / legs ldan 'byed
Tōhoku no.: 3853
Derge location: dbu ma, tsha, 45b–259b

Wisdom Vajra Compendium
Sanskrit: *Vajrajñānasamuccaya-nāma-tantra*
Tibetan: *ye shes rdo rje kun las btus pa zhes bya ba'i rgyud*
Tibetan cited as: *ye shes rdo rje kun las btus*
Author: Kangyur
Tōhoku no.: 447
Derge location: rgyud, ca, 282a–286a

Wisdom Vajra Compendium Commentary
Sanskrit: *(N/A)*
Tibetan: *dpal gsang ba 'dus pa'i bshad pa'i rgyud ye shes rdo rje kun las btus pa'i Tik+ka*
Author: (N/A) / tsong kha pa
Tōhoku no.: 5286
Tashi Hlunpo location: ca, #5

Wisdom-Intuition Drop (uncertain identification)
Sanskrit: *Śri-Jñānatilakayoginītantrarājaparamamahādbhuta-nama*
Tibetan: *dpal ye shes thig le rnal 'byor ma'i rgyud kyi rgyal po chen po mchog tu rmad du byung ba*
Tibetan cited as: *ye shes thig le*
Author: Kangyur
Tōhoku no.: 422
Derge location: rgyud, nga, 96b–136b

Wishing Jewel Secret Drop Tantra 100,000 (unidentified)
Tibetan cited as: *nor bu gsang thig 'bum phrag gcig*

World-Transcending Praise
Sanskrit: *Lokātītastava*
Tibetan: *'jig rten las 'das par bstod pa*
Tibetan cited as: *'jig rten las 'das par bstod pa*
Author: Nāgārjuna / klu sgrub
Tōhoku no.: 1120
Derge location: bstod tshogs ka, 68b–69b

Index of Cited Personal Names (Sanskrit and Tibetan)

Index of Cited Texts (Sanskrit and Tibetan)

General Index

H

I

J

L

M

N